12-00   N/C

JORGE LUIS BORGES

JORGE
LUIS
BORGES

A Literary Biography

Emir Rodriguez Monegal

PARAGON HOUSE PUBLISHERS
New York

Grateful acknowledgment is given the following for permission to quote from copyrighted material: JORGE LUIS BORGES: *The Aleph and Other Stories 1933–1969.* Edited and translated by Norman Thomas di Giovanni. English translation copyright © 1968, 1969, 1970 by Emecé Editores, S.A., and Norman Thomas di Giovanni; copyright © 1970 by Jorge Luis Borges, Adolfo Bioy-Casares, and Norman Thomas di Giovanni. Autobiographical Essay and Commentaries © 1970 by Jorge Luis Borges and Norman Thomas di Giovanni./JORGE LUIS BORGES, with Margarita Guerrero: *The Book of Imaginary Beings.* Revised, enlarged, and translated by Norman Thomas di Giovanni. Copyright © 1969 by Jorge Luis Borges and Norman Thomas di Giovanni./JORGE LUIS BORGES: *The Book of Sand.* Translated by Norman Thomas di Giovanni. Copyright © 1971, 1975, 1976, 1977 by Emecé Editores, S.A., and Norman Thomas di Giovanni./JORGE LUIS BORGES: *Doctor Brodie's Report.* Translated by Norman Thomas di Giovanni. Copyright © 1970, 1971, 1972, by Emecé Editores, S.A., and Norman Thomas di Giovanni./JORGE LUIS BORGES: *The Gold of the Tigers: Selected Later Poems.* Translated by Alastair Reid. English translation Copyright © 1976, 1977 by Alastair Reid./JORGE LUIS BORGES: *A Universal History of Infamy.* Translated by Norman Thomas di Giovanni. Copyright © 1970, 1971, 1972 by Emecé Editores, S.A., and Norman Thomas di Giovanni./JORGE LUIS BORGES: *Dreamtigers.* Translated by Mildred Boyer and Harold Morland. Copyright © 1964 by the University of Texas Press. All rights reserved./JORGE LUIS BORGES: *Other Inquisitions, 1937–1952.* Translated by Ruth L. C. Simms. Copyright © 1964 by the University of Texas Press. All rights reserved./JORGE LUIS BORGES: *Ficciones.* Edited by Anthony Kerrigan. Copyright © 1962 by Grove Press, Inc./JORGE LUIS BORGES: *Labyrinths, Selected Stories and Other Writings.* Translated by James E. Irby, Donald A. Yates, and L. A. Murillo. Copyright © 1962, 1964 by New Directions Publishing Corporation. Reprinted by permission of New Directions./JORGE LUIS BORGES: *Selected Poems 1923–1967.* Edited, with an Introduction and Notes, by Norman Thomas Di Giovanni. Copyright © 1968, 1969, 1970, 1971, 1972 by Jorge Luis Borges, Emecé Editores, S.A., and Norman Thomas Di Giovanni. Reprinted by permission of Delacorte Press/Seymour Lawrence./RICHARD BURGIN: *Conversations with Jorge Luis Borges.* Copyright © 1969 by Richard Burgin. Reprinted by permission of the publishers Holt, Rinehart and Winston./RONALD CHRIST: "The Art of Fiction XXXIX," in *Paris Review.* Copyright © 1967 by Paris Review.

This book is dedicated
to all the sisters of
Clementina Villar and Beatriz Viterbo,
and especially to
the one who is
"dark, despotic, and beautiful."

Contents

Eight pages of photographs follow page 278

Part One

1.
The Family Museum

Borges once said that for years he believed he had been brought up on the outskirts of Buenos Aires in "a suburb of adventurous streets and visible sunsets." But, he added, "the truth is that I grew up in a garden, behind a speared railing, and in a library of unlimited English books" (*Carriego,* 1955, p. 9).* Years later he simplified the account of his life further by stating: "If I were asked to name the chief event in my life, I should say my father's library. In fact, sometimes I think I have never strayed outside that library" ("Essay," 1970, p. 209).

Borges' imaginary life finds its roots in this library, and, up to a point, it would be possible to write his literary biography without leaving that magic space of "unlimited English books." But the truth is more complex: Borges lived, simultaneously, inside and outside of his father's library; he was an inhabitant of an imaginary world created by books in English and of a real world, a Buenos Aires district with an Italian name, Palermo, where, in a house with a garden, he actually spent his childhood.

Borges was born in 1899 in a house at 840 Tucumán Street, close to the downtown area. It was a "small unassuming" house: "Like most of the houses of that day, it had a flat roof; a long, arched entranceway, called a *zaguán;* a cistern where we got our water; and two patios" (ibid., p. 203). This house, which years later his sister, Norah, depicted in her drawings and paintings, belonged to his mother's parents. Borges' mother had been born there in 1876.

Both maternal grandparents were still alive at the turn of the century, when Georgie—as he was called at home—was born. In his

* See the Bibliography for full data.

3

younger years the grandfather, Isidoro de Acevedo Laprida, had fought in the civil war against Rosas, the "tyrant" who ruled Argentina from 1835 to 1852. Later Don Isidoro retired to a long, secluded life at home. Borges knew very little of him. In his poem "Isidoro Acevedo," he admits he has only a few dates and place names to remember his grandfather by: "Frauds and failings of the words." But what he knew was enough. He knew that in dying, in 1905, his grandfather had relived his distant days and met the death of a hero.

> While a lung ailment ate away at him
> and hallucinatory fevers distorted the face of the day,
> he assembled the burning documents of his memory
> for the forging of his dream.
> . . . .
> In the visionary defense of his country that his faith
>   hungered for (and not that his fever imposed)
> he plundered his days
> and rounded up an army of Buenos Aires ghosts
> so as to get himself killed in the fighting.
>
> That was how, in a bedroom that looked onto the garden,
> he died out of devotion for his city.
>   (*Poems*, 1972, translated by
>   Norman Thomas di Giovanni, pp. 53–55)

The poem also documents Georgie's incredulity at the news of his grandfather's death, the first he had experienced.

> It was in the metaphor of a journey that I was told
>   of his death, and I did not believe it.   ´
> I was a boy, who knew nothing of dying; I was immortal,
> and afterward for days I searched the sunless rooms for him.
>   (Ibid., p. 55)

Many years later Borges based one of his stories, "The Other Death," on his grandfather's last dream. Since it was customary then for young couples to live with their relatives during the first years of marriage, Jorge Guillermo and Leonor were staying at her parents' home when their first child was born. Some six years before his grandfather's death, in the winter of 1899—August 24 to be precise—Jorge Luis had been born, prematurely, in the eighth month of his mother's preg-nancy. As blindness was endemic in the Borges family, Borges' father, who had very poor eyesight, made sure to examine his son's eyes. He discovered that the baby had blue eyes, like his wife. "He is saved," he told her. "He has your eyes." When Borges' mother told me this anecdote in 1971, she apparently was not aware that all babies have blue eyes. His father was also wrong in his hopeful prediction: Georgie would be affected, like him, with near blindness for the better part of his life; he is the sixth generation of the Borgeses to be so afflicted.

For a while the family had no worries. A second child, a daughter, Norah, was born in 1901. In photographs of the time both parents look splendid, thriving and fashionable.

Georgie never addressed his parents as Mummy and Daddy. He always used the formal Mother and Father, a traditional form that suggests the Victorian household. Both parents came from old families, established in South America since the time of the Spanish conquest. On her paternal side, Mother was related to Francisco Narciso de Laprida, who presided in 1816 over the Congress of Tucumán, which declared Argentine independence. He died in 1829, in an early civil war. More than a century later Borges dedicated to him his "Conjectural Poem," in which he presents Laprida evoking his own death at the hands of the rebellious gauchos and contrasts his own destiny with Laprida's savage end:

> I who longed to be someone else, to weigh
> judgments, to read books, to hand down the law,
> will lie in the open out in these swamps;
> but a secret joy somehow swells my breast.
> I see at last that I am face to face
> with my South American destiny.
> I was carried to this ruinous hour
> by the intricate labyrinth of steps
> woven by my days from a day that goes
> back to my birth. At last I've discovered
> the mysterious key to all my years,
> the fate of Francisco de Laprida,
> the missing letter, the perfect pattern
> that was known to God from the beginning.
> In this night's mirror I can comprehend
> my unsuspected true face. The circle's
> about to close. I wait to let it come.
>
> My feet tread the shadows of the lances
> that spar for the kill. The taunts of my death,
> the horses, the horsemen, the horses' manes,
> tighten the ring around me . . . Now for the first
> blow, the lance's hard steel ripping my chest,
> and across my throat the intimate knife.
>> (*Poems,* 1972, translated by
>> Norman Thomas di Giovanni, pp. 83–85)

Mother's maternal grandfather, Colonel Isidoro Suárez, had also fought in the war of independence and went into exile in Uruguay at the time of the Rosas dictatorship. He married into a Uruguayan family, the Haedos, which had been very active in political and artistic life. Borges later dedicated a poem to him. Titled "A Page to Commemorate Colonel Suárez, Victor at Junín," the poem refers, like others devoted to the family pantheon of heroes, to a single instant: the heroic deed at Junín that the old man continuously reenacts. But there is a difference. At the very end of the poem the distant past is suddenly made present, and Borges' ancestor's fight is made one with the fight against another unnamed dictator ruling Argentina in 1953:

> His great-grandson is writing these lines,
> and a silent voice comes to him out of the past,
> out of the blood:
>
> "What does my battle at Junín matter if it is only
> a glorious memory, or a date learned by rote
> for an examination, or a place in the atlas?
> The battle is everlasting and can do without
> the pomp of actual armies and of trumpets.
> Junín is two civilians cursing a tyrant
> on a street corner
> or an unknown man somewhere, dying in prison."
> (Ibid., translated by Alastair Reid, p. 91)

Borges' family piety reflects his mother's attitude toward her ancestors. Georgie was born and brought up in a house that was, up to a point, a family museum, presided over by the almost ghostly presence of grandfather Acevedo. The place of honor went to the swords that had liberated South America at Junín and Cepeda; the uniforms were carefully preserved against injury from moths; the daguerreotypes framed in black velvet memorialized a parade of dark, sad gentlemen or reserved ladies, many of them prematurely widowed. Georgie was surrounded by the sacred objects of family history and the ritual repetition of the deeds of his heroic ancestors. These stories of courage and silent dignity in defeat, of poverty and pride, were a permanent part of his heritage. Many years later he was to acknowledge: "On both sides of my family, I have military forebears; this may account for my yearning after that epic destiny which my gods denied me, no doubt wisely" ("Essay," 1970, p. 208).

Father belonged to an even older family. One of his ancestors, Jerónimo Luis de Córdoba, was the founder of Córdoba, the most traditional and Catholic of Argentine cities, the one most like Boston in the history of the United States. For the traditional Cordobeses, Buenos Aires will always be, like New York for Bostonians, the immigrant's city. It is populated mainly by poor foreigners, illiterate Spaniards and Italians not worthy of representing European culture. But Father himself had not been born in Córdoba. In the nineteenth century the family had moved closer to the Buenos Aires area. His own father had been born in Paraná, Entre Ríos, and at the time Father was born Grandfather Borges was a colonel in the Santa Fe garrison, in the pampas. Both provinces belonged to a more primitive and simple world: the frontier between the Argentine settlers and the still unruly Indians. From Entre Ríos came the caudillo (chieftain) Justo José de Urquiza, the man who in 1852 finally defeated Rosas at Pavón.

Father was not so devoted to the memory of his heroic ancestors as Mother was. But he maintained interest in the political struggle in Paraná; and in 1921, when he was retired and living in Spain, he wrote a curiously anachronistic novel, *El caudillo* (The Chieftain), which recaptures the romantic climate of violence, intrigue, and passion that surrounded so many Borges males during the civil wars.

On his mother's side, Father had a completely different tradition. Frances Haslam had been born in 1845 in Staffordshire, England, of Northumbrian stock. Borges has described her arrival in Argentina:

> A rather unlikely set of circumstances brought her to South America. Fanny Haslam's elder sister married an Italian-Jewish engineer named Jorge Suárez, who brought the first horse-drawn tramcars to Argentina, where he and his wife settled and sent for Fanny. I remember an anecdote concerning this venture. Suárez was a guest at General Urquiza's "palace" in Entre Ríos, and very improvidently won his first game of cards with the General, who was the stern dictator of that province and not above throat-cutting. When the game was over, Suárez was told by alarmed fellow guests that if he wanted the license to run his tramcars in the province, it was expected of him to lose a certain amount of gold coins each night. Urquiza was such a poor player that Suárez had a great deal of trouble losing the appointed sums.
>
> It was in Paraná, the capital city of Entre Ríos, that Fanny Haslam met Colonel Francisco Borges. This was in 1870 or 1871, during the siege of the city by the *montoneros,* or gaucho militia of Ricardo López Jordán. Borges, riding at the head of his regiment, commanded the troops defending the city. Fanny Haslam saw him from the flat roof of her house; that very night a ball was given to celebrate the arrival of the government relief forces. Fanny and the Colonel met, danced, fell in love, and eventually married. ("Essay," 1970, pp. 204–205)

Colonel Francisco Borges was twelve years older than his wife. Very little is known about the marriage except that they seemed happy

7

and had two sons. Father was the younger. In 1874 Colonel Borges was killed by a Remington rifle in one of the civil wars. He was barely forty-one. His grandson discovered an irony in his death:

> In the complicated circumstances surrounding his defeat at La Verde, he rode out slowly on horseback, wearing a white poncho and followed by ten or twelve of his men, toward the enemy lines, where he was struck by two Remington bullets. This was the first time Remington rifles were used in the Argentine, and it tickles my fancy to think that the firm that shaves me every morning bears the same name as the one that killed my grandfather. (Ibid., pp. 205–206)

The stories his grandmother told him about living on the frontier resurfaced many years later in "The Story of the Warrior and the Captive." The first half summarizes and expands on a story taken from different European sources (Croce, Gibbon, Dante); the second half is based on one of Fanny Haslam's frontier tales. An English girl, taken by the Indians in one of their raids, is forced to marry a warrior and is converted to barbarism. Grandmother had met her briefly at the army post her husband commanded and had tried to persuade her to return to civilization. She failed, and the girl went back to her man and two children. In the conclusion of the story Borges explores one of the meanings of this symbolic confrontation between the two English ex-iles: "Perhaps the two women felt for an instant as sisters; they were far from their beloved island and in an incredible country; . . . perhaps then my grandmother was able to perceive in this other woman, also held captive and transformed by the implacable continent, a monstruous mirror of her own destiny" (*Labyrinths*, 1964; p. 130). In a sense, the story is right: Fanny Haslam was also a captive. Although she had married a colonel and a gentleman, and she had been able to preserve her native tongue and even to transmit it to her sons and grandchildren, she still was a captive in a primitive and violent land, imprisoned forever in a world dominated by an alien tongue.

Her husband's death left Fanny Haslam very much on her own. She had two sons to care for and bring up. Undaunted, she opened her home to paying guests, young American women who came to Argentina to teach under an educational program conceived by President Sarmiento when he visited the United States. Borges does not tell this part of his grandmother's story in his "Autobiographical Essay"; nor has he ever mentioned it in his interviews. He prefers to emphasize the less prosaic details of her life, the frontier adventures. But although not picturesque, Fanny Haslam's solid Victorian upbringing saved the day. She managed to keep the family within the bounds of middle-class respectability and saw to it that both her sons had a position in life. The elder followed in his father's footsteps and became a naval officer; Father became a lawyer. Perhaps the fact that Father inherited the Borges blindness explains the choice of a civil career. The consequence of this decision was that he was to remain very much under his mother's influence; that is, under the British influence. This was decisive for his son's fate.

Although Father was proud of his English ancestry and especially of English culture, he was not a fanatic. Borges has pointed out that "he used to joke about it, saying with feigned perplexity, 'After all, what are the English? Just a pack of German agriculture laborers' " ("Essay," 1970, p. 206). Borges writes:

> My father, Jorge Guillermo Borges, worked as a lawyer. He was a philosophical anarchist—a disciple of Spencer's—and also a teacher of psychology at the Normal School for Modern Languages, where he gave his course in English, using as his text William James' shorter book of psychology. . . .
> My father was very intelligent and, like all intelligent men, very kind. Once, he told me that I should take a good look at soldiers, uniforms, barracks, flags, churches, priests, and butcher shops, since all these things were about to disappear, and I could tell my children that I had actually seen them. The prophecy has not yet come true, unfortunately. My father was such a modest man that he would have liked being invisible. . . . His idols were Shelley, Keats, and Swinburne. As a reader, he had two interests. First, books on metaphysics and psychology (Berkeley, Hume, Royce, and William James). Second, literature and books about the East (Lane, Burton, and Payne). It was he who revealed the power of poetry to me—the fact that words are not only a means of communication but also magic symbols and music. . . . He also, without my being aware of it, gave me my first lessons in philosophy. When I was still quite young, he showed me, with the aid of a chessboard, the paradoxes of Zeno—Achilles and the tortoise, the unmoving flight of the arrow, the impossibility of motion. Later, without mentioning Berkeley's name, he did his best to teach me the rudiments of idealism. (Ibid., pp. 204–207)

By his ancestors, by his double cultural origins, Father at once confirmed and modified Mother's familial museum. He added more colonial prototypes and more army brass to the pantheon, more vivid memories of heroic deeds. He also incorporated an element that was totally absent in Mother's piety: irony, a mind gifted with the most elegant skepticism. Georgie inherited this gift.

2.
The Personal
Myth

From his father's side, the family museum, this private *pietas,*
was seen through very ironic glasses. In a book-length interview with
Jean de Milleret, Borges has explained his peculiar interpretation of
the family tradition. While he readily admits that the Borgeses can be
traced back to the Spanish conquerors, his own pantheon does not go
back that far: "I am so much an Argentine that I can't really be interested in my distant ancestors, those who came before 1810. You know
that I never talk about them . . . I am also very ignorant of their lives.
Besides, they were people with very little intelligence, Spanish professional soldiers, and from Old Spain" (De Milleret, 1967, p. 203). In
contrast to Mother's attitude of family worship—the carefully preserved genealogical tree, the daguerreotypes, the sacred swords and
uniforms—Borges' dismissal of the family's colonial inheritance reflects
Father's sense of irony and subtle understatement. The difference was
rooted in the conflict between Spanish and English values, a conflict
that culminated in the wars between England and Spain but did not
end there: in Latin America it is alive today.

For the boy, that conflict must have been muted by affection,
buried in the deepest and darkest layers of subconscious feeling. In the
everyday experience of life at home, as in a childish charade, Georgie
was confronted by the cultural abyss that separated his father's side of
the family from his mother's. Some sixty years later, in the same long
interview, Borges gives his view of his mother's family: "The Acevedos
are incredibly ignorant. For instance, for them, descendants of the old
Spanish settlers, to be a Protestant is synonymous with being a Jew, that
is, an atheist, or a freethinker, or a heretic; in short, they put everything in the same bag. There is no real difference between these words

for them" (ibid., p. 39). It is obvious that Borges is here simplifying and exaggerating the Acevedos' prejudices, which mirrored those of many ignorant Argentine Catholics. But it is the irreverent tone that is particularly significant. It makes explicit Georgie's subconscious reaction to the two sides of his family.

Borges later defined the traditional character of the Acevedos by stating: "When I was growing up, religion belonged to women and children; most men in Buenos Aires were freethinkers—though, had they been asked, they might have called themselves Catholic" ("Essay," 1970, p. 207). Although irony is absent here, it is evident that Borges is subtly antagonistic to his mother's religious stand. In the same essay, Borges praises what he calls his mother's "hospitable mind." To illustrate that hospitality, he writes: "From the time she learned English, through my father, she has done most of her reading in that language" (ibid., p. 207). English is once more presented as a certificate of culture, of an open and hospitable mind, to be opposed implicitly to the narrow, ignorant, Catholic mind of the Acevedos. But Borges also remarks on the limitations of the cult of Englishness: "My fondness for such a Northern past has been resented by some of my countrymen, who dub me an Englishman, but I hardly need point out that many things English are utterly alien to me: tea, the Royal Family, 'manly' sports, the worship of every line written by the uncaring Shakespeare" (ibid., p. 252). Thus, in recollection at least, Borges seems equally distant to both the Spanish and the English sides of his family.

Borges' memory in the "Autobiographical Essay" is selective. He makes no mention of his Portuguese origins. His surname is undoubtedly Portuguese: Borges means a citizen of the burgos, or cities, a bourgeois. In a late poem called "The Borges" he refers to these unknown ancestors:

> My Portuguese forebears. They were a ghostly race,
> Who still play in my body their mysterious
> Disciplines, habits, and anxieties.
> Indecipherably they form a part
> Of time, of earth, and of oblivion.
> (Poems, 1972, translated by Alastair Reid, p. 137)

In a 1970 interview for the Brazilian weekly Veja Borges dwells on these shadowy Portuguese ancestors and on the possibility that through them he may be connected with the wandering tribes of Israel. He asks rhetorically:

> I, Borges Ramalho, descendant of a Portuguese sailor and, on top of that, having a mother called Acevedo: might I not be a Jew? . . . When I visited

Lisbon many years ago, I tried to do some research on my origins. I looked into the phone book and got the scare of my life: all the people there were my relatives, because those who were not Borges were Ramalho or Acevedo! I didn't know I had such a family and just in Lisbon! . . . Whatever the case, I would be very proud to belong to one of the civilized races in the world, to a branch of humanity that had already invented Job's story and *The Song of Songs* while other countries were still submerged in the original barbarism. (Ribeiro, 1970, pp. 4–5)

The question of Borges' Jewish origins, lightly and humorously touched on here, was a very sensitive one in Argentina, especially in the 1930s and 1940s, when the army was aping the Italians and Germans and the Church and the upper classes were solidly anti-Semitic. In those days a nationalistic magazine called *Crisol* (The Crucible) accused Borges of being a Jew. He thereupon wrote a piece for the journal *Megáfono* entitled "I, a Jew," which is a masterpiece of teasing. He begins by stating that he has played more than once with the idea that he had some Jewish ancestors; he admits that Acevedo is generally included in a list of surnames of Jewish origin compiled by an Argentine historian who was trying to prove that practically all the families in Rosas' time had a "Jewish-Portuguese" ancestry. On the other hand, research done by a member of his family had proved that the Acevedos came not from Portugal but from Spain—and, to be more precise, from Catalonia. He concludes then that it is a hopeless task to try to prove his Jewish ancestry. Apart from the ironic value of this "search," it is obvious that Borges did not take the question seriously. Not a word is said about the obvious Portuguese origin of his surname, which could have helped to establish the missing Jewish link. But in ambiguously denying his ancestors (which he recognizes in 1970), Borges aimed to destroy the basis of the accusation. The end of the article presents a new argument:

Statistically speaking, the Jews were very few. What would we think of someone in the year 4000 who discovers everywhere descendants of the inhabitants of the San Juan province [one of the least populated in Argentina]? Our inquisitors are seeking Hebrews, never Phoenicians, Numidians, Scythians, Babylonians, Huns, Vandals, Ostrogoths, Ethiopians, Illyrians, Paphlagonians, Sarmatians, Medes, Ottomans, Berbers, Britons, Lybians, Cyclops, and Lapiths. The nights of Alexandria, Babylon, Carthage, Memphis have never succeeded in engendering one single grandfather: only the tribes of the bituminous Black Sea had that power. (*Megáfono*, April 1934, p. 10)

In poking fun at the Fascist obsession with Jewish ancestors as proof of some obscure blemish or original sin, Borges even includes the mythological Cyclops and Lapiths among the old tribes who failed to engender one grandfather. His jokes advance the main object of the article: to demythify the subject once and for all. If to be a Jew means that somewhere in the past a Jewish ancestor looms, then who can be sure, in Spain and Portugal, in Latin America, of not having at least one great-grandfather of that origin? From that point of view, to be a Jew has no meaning. An irony revealed by Borges' "research" must not be overlooked. It is the very Catholic and traditional branch of the Acevedos that seems the most likely carrier of the Jewish blood into Borges' ancestry—they who shared, with the nationalist and the Fascist in Argentina, the cult of the universal religion of Rome and who believed that any freethinker, any Protestant, any mason, was a Jew. Such ignorance turned Borges from his mother's side of the family.

It is obvious that this aspect of the family conflict was not self-evident to Georgie, at least in his childhood. Although his father was an agnostic and his paternal grandmother a Protestant, he was probably brought up as a Catholic in a Catholic household. Religious instruction, if any, was in his mother's hands, and his father probably accepted it. But if the conflict was not evident at that stage, it was nevertheless part of the personal myth Georgie was already developing. If English was the language of culture, Spanish was to become the language associated with the deeds of arms and the gods of war. In constantly being reminded of the family past, in hearing once and again the tales of brave feats accomplished especially by the Suárezes and the Acevedos, Georgie was initiated into another religion: the worship of the family gods and of manly courage. In this religion the differences between Father's and Mother's side were erased: all ancestors were united in the family cult. In his "Autobiographical Essay" Borges indicates explicitly how Georgie reacted to this heroic ancestry: "I was always very near-sighted and wore glasses, and I was rather frail. As most of my people had been soldiers . . . and I knew I would never be, I felt ashamed, quite early, to be a bookish kind of person and not a man of action" ("Essay," 1970, p. 208).

The two sides of the Borges household represent, as in an allegorical tableau, the famous contrast between arms and letters, a topic to which Don Quixote had something to add. Although on both sides of the family Georgie had professional soldiers, it was the Acevedo branch that at the time of his birth offered vivid examples. The only grandfather still living was Isidoro de Acevedo Laprida, who had fought so bravely and died in a dream of battles long ago. On his father's side what prevailed was not the image of Colonel Francisco Borges (who died twenty-five years before Georgie was born) but that of Fanny Haslam, the English grandmother who held the key to the world of English and of English books, the world of culture. Father himself was a lawyer and a man of books, the owner of that infinite library.

The personal myth of Borges begins here: it is, at the same time, a myth of despair at not having been a man of arms and a myth of compensation. The reader and the writer found in books, in the desire and guilt aroused by books, what was lacking in his "real" life. Because Father had preceded him in this path—he too was a descendant of warriors who chose books and the law—Borges would have to find, many years later, a solution to the latent Oedipal conflict. In his case, parricide would assume a most unexpected disguise: total submission to his father's will.

3.
The Act of Reading

Borges learned to read English before he could read Spanish. He first read *Don Quixote* in English translation. From the very beginning the English language was inseparably related to the act of reading. For Georgie, it was the code that gave him access to the world of books. That world, limited only by the imagination, came to be more fabulous than the real world. Here lies the origin of his personal myth and of his well-known predilection for British—and, by extension, North American—letters. At the same time, something more important also originated here: the dual emotions of desire and guilt that haunted the child and later the writer.

Borges' familiarity with English and English letters did not make him an English writer. He never felt that English really belonged to him. Turning to the subject in his "Autobiographical Essay," with a humility that sometimes seems excessive but that is undoubtedly authentic, he mentions his conflict with a language "I am unworthy to handle, a language I often wish had been my birthright" ("Essay," 1970, p. 258). On the other side was his exasperation, and attitude of resignation, regarding the Spanish language, which did belong to him as his birthright.

The fact that he learned to read English before he could read Spanish, which now seems so strange and even artificial (he seemed to be the victim of a baroque experiment, like Prince Segismundo in *Life Is a Dream*), was not at all artificial to Georgie as a conscious experience. Linguistic duality was a basic fact of his home life. Living with his parents was his paternal grandmother, Frances Haslam, who had been born in England. Though she had come to Argentina as a young woman and had married an Argentine gentleman, Fanny continued to inhabit an English-speaking world. Like so many of her compatriots, she carried the imperial language with her. She taught English not only to her son but to her grandson as well. Even her daughter-in-law would eventually be colonized. The peculiar conditions that gave rise to the bilingualism of the Borges household explain why speaking and reading, and later even writing, in a language which was not that of his native country was not unusual to Georgie. In his home (a closed, autarchical world) English was, equally, a natural language. Not until he went to school did Georgie discover that this language belonged to him a little less than Spanish did.

Since both English and Spanish were spoken at home, Georgie was unaware for some time that they were two different languages. Years later he told one of his interviewers, Rita Guibert: "When I was talking to my paternal grandmother I had to speak in a manner that I afterward discovered was called English, and when I was talking to my mother or her parents I had to talk a language that afterward turned out to be Spanish" (Guibert, 1973, p. 81). It is obvious that in Georgie's experience, rather than being two different languages, English and Spanish more nearly resembled two systems of address, like calling someone by his surname instead of his Christian name.

The conflict approached the critical stage when Georgie started reading in English, for it was his paternal grandmother who took charge of this part of his education. Alicia Jurado, one of his biographers, who was undoubtedly relying on information confided to her by Borges or his mother, evokes this scene: "Before he learned the alphabet, Fanny Haslam used to sit him on her lap and read to him from some children's magazines in English, bound in a very heavy volume he called the 'lectionary,' a word that united the idea of both a dictionary and a lecture" (Jurado, 1964, p. 26). Perhaps this bound volume contained a collection of the popular Victorian magazine *The Boy's Own Journal* or the no less famous *Tit-Bits,* though the latter might have been too melodramatic for Fanny Haslam. The fact that the volume was bound suggests that the grandmother had used it for the father's education as well.

After a time the child passed from the stage of being read to and started reading himself. His instruction was placed in the hands of an English governess, Miss Tink, who also looked after his sister, Norah, two years younger. The reason the family gave for not sending the children to school, where instruction was naturally in Spanish, was its dread of contagious childhood diseases. That is at least what Alicia Jurado reports (ibid., p. 28). But Borges is perhaps more candid in his "Autobiographical Essay": "I did not start school until I was nine. This was because my father, as an anarchist, distrusted all enterprises run by the State" ("Essay," 1970, pp. 211–212). One must remember that when Borges says that his father was an anarchist he means it in a purely philosophical sense, since his father counted himself among the followers of Spencer, not Bakunin.

Perhaps there were religious motives as well to avoid the state schools. As religious instruction was regularly given in those schools, his father probably did not wish to have the children exposed at such an early age to dogmatic instruction. Besides, the English grandmother was a Protestant. At any rate, the immediate consequence of not attending school and of having instead an English governess was that Georgie continued to develop his knowledge of English as the language of culture. Spanish was relegated to strictly domestic concerns. On the other hand, even if Georgie had gone to the state schools at a very young age, his attitude toward the Spanish language as a literary code would probably not have been much different. English was too deeply rooted in him. Looking back, Borges has spoken of his bilingualism in these bilingual terms: "I'm used to thinking in English, and I also believe some English words are untranslatable, so I occasionally use them *for the sake of precision. I'm not showing off.* Since *I've done most of my reading in English,* it's natural that the first word that comes to mind is often an English one" (Guibert, 1973, p. 100; the italicized words are in English in the Spanish original of this interview: Guibert, 1968, p. 55).

The Borgeses' attitude toward the state schools was not unusual in Argentina at the turn of the century. The Argentine upper classes were ambivalent toward everything Hispanic, which in a subtle way also affected the language. Many cultivated Argentines preferred to call Spanish the *idioma nacional* (national tongue) so as to avoid peninsular connotations. There was also a question of status, which Borges reveals:

> In Buenos Aires, Spaniards always held menial jobs—as domestic servants, waiters, and laborers—or were small tradesmen, and we Argentines never thought of ourselves as Spanish. We had, in fact, left off being Spaniards in 1816, when we declared our independence from Spain. When, as a boy, I read Prescott's *Conquest of Peru,* it amazed me to find that he portrayed the conquistadors in a romantic way. To me, descended from certain of these officials, they were an uninteresting lot. ("Essay," 1970, pp. 218–219).

Where Georgie's father did not hold with the tradition of the Argentine upper classes was in the choice of cultural model. In Argentina, as in almost all of Latin America, that model was the French one. Well-to-do people sent their children to French schools. Many writers (especially women) preferred that language as their mode of expression. One of the most remarkable cases was that of Victoria Ocampo, who was later to be so influential in Borges' literary career. She was schooled by a French governess, was given diction lessons with Marguerite Moréno—an outstanding actress from the Comédie Française and the wife of the writer Marcel Schwob—and wrote her first books in French. Even though her native language was Spanish, French was her literary language. In time Victoria Ocampo learned to write in Spanish as well. But her case, while perhaps extreme, was not exceptional.

Argentina at that time (like the United States in the nineteenth century) was a land of immigrants still clinging to Old World traditions and languages. Of the immigrants who came to Argentina, those most firmly attached to their native language were the English (a category that in Argentina included Scots, Welsh, and even Irish). As if it were their only heritage of value, the English preserved their language against all possible contamination. The oldest among them got along with an almost total ignorance of Spanish or with the barest vocabulary. The second generation (of which Borges' father was a good example) was perforce bilingual but did not abandon its attachment to the original language; rather, it changed English into an instrument of culture, a tool of the spirit. No effort seemed excessive to them when it came to defending that umbilical cord that tied them to the center of the British empire. They lived in Argentina as their compatriots did in India. It is not surprising, then, that Borges felt such admiration for the work of Rudyard Kipling.

Though the Borgeses were not wealthy, they had a British governess to protect their children from all forms of contagion, not just from childhood diseases. In addition to these solid family reasons, there was then rampant in Argentina a sort of pro-British snobbery that would dominate Buenos Aires society as the century advanced. French fashions were gradually giving way to English ones. This change had an economic base. Even though Argentina had been within a French-influenced cultural sphere since the beginning of the nineteenth century, from an economic standpoint the independence of the River Plate area was achieved under the aegis of British diplomacy and commerce. Until World War II, Argentina belonged to the pound sterling international trading zone and was virtually part of the Commonwealth. When Perón seized power, at the end of the war, English imperialism remained one of his main targets. Sometime later, in 1955, England openly supported the military revolt that overthrew him. Owing to these circumstances, it was not unusual for Argentine families without any English members whatsoever to send their children to local British schools or, in the case of wealthy families, to have British governesses. What today seems very unusual was, at the time, merely a consequence of the colonial status of the economy and of Argentine culture. In Borges' case, that cultural colonialism was even more justified because the unwitting colonizer was already permanently set up at home.

That paradoxical situation, normal in appearance to the child though in reality profoundly anomalous, would not provoke a crisis until much later. Even though Georgie was "naturally" bilingual, his bilingualism contained the seeds of a fateful distinction between the two languages. The act of reading in English when he had still not learned to do it in Spanish established a radical and decisive difference between the two codes. English became the key to reading and writing. Imagination, dreams, and longings that were aroused or intensified by books would become known to Georgie in English. In English and only in English would they exist for him. In that language he would subsequently find a key to decipher invisible words. Spanish, by contrast, was not only the language of his mother's side of the family (less valid from a cultural point of view because the child could not read it) but the language of servants, those anonymous Galicians and Basques who kept coming to the River Plate area in search of an elusive El Dorado. Thus, until the child was well along in years, Spanish was not a language of culture and, still less, a literary code.

As Georgie grew and became even more aware of the world outside his home, the strangeness of his fate began to dawn on him. Like the Minotaur in Borges' story "The House of Asterion," Georgie had no idea of his uniqueness. But away from the confines of his home he found that things happened in a different way; people spoke a single language, and their values were different. Inside, the restricted and bilingual world of English and Spanish (in that order of cultural and even social importance) alternated smoothly. Outside the garden gate began the exclusive domain of Spanish, a powerful but undeniably common language. No wonder that for Georgie Spanish was associated with a more primitive or elemental form of life, while English gave him access to a higher level of life, to a dream and desire tantalizingly controlled by words and books. Of the two linguistic codes that the boy learned in his childhood, his mother's would be the culturally inferior one.

To this linguistic crisis which pervaded his experience he would attempt to give a paradoxical solution in works that, while written in that inferior language, Spanish, are syntactically closer to the English tongue. On the literary as well as the biographical level, Georgie would become Borges. The child who had an early access to the English code of reading and writing and who theoretically could have become an English writer (George Borges) was to transform himself into an Hispanic writer (Jorge Luis Borges), reverting to the code originally taught by his mother. But though Borges might develop an awesome mastery of Spanish and become the language's foremost writer, he would always feel that in this accomplishment he had sacrificed total mastery of the other code.

The future struggle between English and Spanish on the level of writing and literary production appeared in an already defined form (though visible only at the unconscious level) in the basic act of reading. On the conscious level the child accepted and learned the two languages, went from one to the other with complete ease, and handled all the rules without apparent effort. But on the unconscious level the linguistic conflict was implanted in the core of his experience and caused an inner split in Georgie before doing likewise to Borges. As soon as Georgie reached total awareness, through the basic act of reading, of those two languages that were his without his knowing it, a sense of dualism took root in him. The two codes appeared facing each other, as in a mirror. On learning to read, the child had had no choice but to accept his bilingualism. Now he realized that the garden gate separated something more than home and the city. It was the dividing line between two linguistic systems. It was Alice's mirror. Gradually Georgie would learn to cross at will from one side to the other. The unconscious daily experience of bilingualism would become the conscious experience, accepted without argument and accomplished without the effort of crossing "through the looking glass." It would be, in the end, trivial. But dualism, once consciously discovered, would never be abandoned.

4.
The Two Mothers:
The Two Codes

There is obviously much more in Borges' relationship with his parents than has been indicated here. Some of his autobiographical texts talk freely about Mother, but they reveal little that is relevant to his childhood years. He mentions the help he received from her after his father's death and after his own blindness made it very difficult for him to read and write. About his father, on the contrary, he is always explicit and precise. Even when he is confronted with an interviewer, like Jean de Milleret, who is determined to subject him to a bit of simplified Freudianism, Borges is adamant. Again and again he dodges a question about his mother's supposedly dominant personality and attributes everything to his father's strong will. When he is asked, rather directly, if he thinks that his was "an oppressive mother," he answers that it was his father who was a decisive influence on his life because it was through him that he learned English and had access to a vast library. When pressed again to admit that Mother was a sort of tyrannical Genitrix, he refuses to accept such a characterization and wonders aloud who could have thought of that. He denies any mother fixation and predictably concludes: "It was my father who had an influence on her and not the reverse. My mother was a young woman of a good Argentine family and my father was a liberal and cultivated man: his mother was English and a Protestant; he had a good library at home. I must say that he lived, intellectually speaking, in a more complex world than my mother" (De Milleret, 1967, p. 213). It is obvious that Borges is here denying any attempt to "psychoanalyze" him or his relationship with his parents.

Borges' resistance to any type of analysis (not only to the instant one attempted by De Milleret) is well known. In another interview he even makes a joke about it: "I've rather forgotten the time I spent in my mother's womb—although, according to the Freudians, it must have been very important to me" (*Triunfo*, November 15, 1969, p. 36). More straightforward is an exchange recorded by Richard Burgin:

BURGIN: I take it you don't think much of Freud, either.
BORGES: No, I always disliked him. But I've always been a great reader of Jung. I read Jung in the same way as, let's say, I might read Pliny or Frazer's *Golden Bough;* I read it as a kind of mythology, or as a kind of museum or encyclopedia of curious lores.
BURGIN: When you say that you dislike Freud, what do you mean?
BORGES: I think of him as a kind of madman, no? A man laboring over a sexual obsession. Well, perhaps he didn't take it to heart. Perhaps he was just doing it as a kind of game. I tried to read him, and I thought of him either as a charlatan or as a madman, in a sense. After all, the world is far too complex to be boiled down to that all-too-simple scheme. But in Jung, well, of course, Jung I have read far more widely than Freud, but in Jung you feel a wide and hospitable mind. In the case of Freud, it all boils down to a few rather unpleasant facts. But, of course, that's merely my ignorance or my bias. (Burgin, 1969, p. 109)

Borges' resistance to Freud is revealing and, in a sense, as curious as that shown by Nabokov. They even use similar words. While Nabokov calls Freud a "crank," Borges suggests he is either a "charlatan" or a "madman." Borges is obviously overreacting, and it is this overreaction that attracts attention. At the root of his bilingualism is an unconscious conflict whose symptoms and origins are clear. The fact that he was taught Spanish by his mother and English by his grandmother established from the beginning a conflict between the two codes. The immediate manifestations of this conflict are well known. He had some difficulty in learning to talk. According to Mother, "when he was very small, he had the most extraordinary way of talking: Perhaps he didn't hear well? He disfigured completely many words" (Mother, 1964, p. 10). Later on he developed a slight stammer that became more evident when he was in the company of strangers or when he had to talk in public. Not until he was forty-five did he seriously attempt to overcome his stammer. The fact that it was his English grandmother who taught him the English code and who introduced him to the world c f books added some confusion to the already confusing double language he learned to use while a child. Georgie had two "mothers" instead of one, as he had two languages. At the level of the personal myth, the fact that the second mother was his father's mother only increased Father's sphere of influence. Father became duplicated: he was represented by a virile figure who ran everything at home and by a maternal version who was (implicitly) Mother's rival in teaching the boy how to speak. In view of the complexity of that original configuration, it is easy to understand Borges' resistance to De Milleret's "Freudian" line of questioning.

At the conscious level, he always saw Mother under the influence of Father, and there was no doubt about that. It is possible to go one step further and assume that for Georgie Mother had a secondary role in her own household: she was also under Fanny Haslam's influence because Grandmother was the owner of the most powerful linguistic code—English. Mother was like the beautiful concubine in some of the tales of the *One Thousand and One Nights* that Father (and later Georgie) loved to read in Richard Burton's unexpurgated translation. She was a sort of slave who was tolerated as the Heir's mother, but the real Queen, the only legitimate wife, was Father's mother. This configuration explains the part Mother plays in Borges' personal myth: she is always there, she is always courteously referred to, but she is always kept (in a very subtle way) in a subordinate position.

A purely psychoanalytical reading of this situation is impossible here. It has been attempted more than once with various results. The best analysis so far is one done by Didier Anzieu in 1971. Although the French psychoanalyst lacked all the necessary biographical information and had less than complete bibliographical data, he was able to develop many original insights. Instead of following the traditional Freudian line, he relied both on Melanie Klein's theories about the relationship between the body and the unconscious (Klein, 1975) and also on Jacques Lacan's subtle reading and rewriting of Freud (Lacan, 1966). According to these views, the child continues to be one with the mother long after the umbilical cord has been severed and the child is being breast-fed; the unity of his and his mother's body survives even the weaning, because the mother never ceases to talk to him; that is, to teach him the linguistic code. The teaching of that code creates a link that substitutes for the umbilical cord. One may call the new bond the vocal cord. Because it is the mother who teaches the child the first sounds, and later the first words and phrases, her teachings become for him deeply associated with the other functions she performs. Feeding him, nursing him, talking to him: all become one. From this point of view, the mouth of the mother is another breast.

In Georgie's case, there was another mother who did not breast-feed him but who also took care of him and (after the weaning) helped to feed him. This second mother, being an Englishwoman, had a different linguistic code; she taught Georgie this second code. If the sharing of the linguistic code is nothing but a symbolization of the unity of the body of the mother and that of the child, to adopt a second linguistic code implies that the original unity is threatened and the body is split. Georgie accepted the double code but at the cost of becoming permanently injured. His body rebelled. It is known that he had difficulty in speaking and "disfigured completely many words." At the conscious level, the splitting of the original unity into two different codes (two mothers, two bodies) was accepted. At the unconscious level, the seeds of a tragic conflict were sown.

The rebellion of Georgie's unconscious was quenched after a while. He stopped making mistakes; he learned to speak properly and to separate the two languages. But deep inside him, at the level where the poems he was to write and the stories he was to tell were already being formed, at the truly archaic level, prior to any discovery of the differences between the sexes and the Oedipus complex, something irreversible had happened. It would take almost four decades of unconscious work for the conflict to come out into the open. In the stories Borges wrote after his father's death in 1938 the conflict at last emerges in beautiful and mysterious formulations.

Two of these stories have been singled out by Anzieu to prove his views. "The God's Script," originally included in *The Aleph* (1949), presents a Mayan priest who has been thrown into a cell by Alvarado, the Spanish conquistador. In the next cell is a beautiful jaguar. The priest spends endless nights attempting to understand the meaning of the defeat of his god. He finally decides that his god has left, somewhere, a secret message to his followers:

> The god, foreseeing that at the end of time there would be devastation and ruin, wrote on the first day of Creation a magical sentence with the power to ward off those evils. He wrote it in such a way that it would reach the most distant generations and not be subject to chance. No one knows where it was written nor with what characters, but it is certain that it exists, secretly, and that a chosen one will read it. I considered that we were now, as always, at the end of time and that my destiny as the last priest of the god would give me access to the privilege of intuiting the script. (*Labyrinths*, 1962, p. 170)

Slowly, painfully, the priest comes to the conclusion that the message is inscribed in the jaguar's skin. After more long sessions of dreaming and thinking and suffering, he has a mystical vision and is made one with the god. He is now ready to decipher the inscription.

> It is a formula of fourteen random words (they appear random) and to utter it in a loud voice would suffice to make me all-powerful. To say it would suffice to abolish this stone prison, to have daylight break into my night, to be young, to be immortal, to have the tiger's jaws crush Alvarado, to sink the

sacred knife into the breasts of Spaniards, to reconstruct the pyramid, to reconstruct the empire. Forty syllables, fourteen words, and I, Tzinacán, would rule the lands Moctezuma ruled. But I know I shall never say those words, because I no longer remember Tzinacán.

May the mystery lettered on the tigers die with me. Whoever has seen the universe, whoever has beheld the fiery designs of the universe, cannot think in terms of one man, of that man's trivial fortunes or misfortunes, though he be that very man. That man *has been he* and now matters no more to him. What is the life of that other to him, the nation of that other to him, if he, now, is no one? This is why I do not pronounce the formula, why, lying here in the darkness, I let the days obliterate me. (Ibid., p. 173)

In mastering his god's code, Tzinacán has reached his goal: the mystical union with the divine. Now that he has the secret of the divine script, he doesn't need to use it. Interpreting the story, Anzieu points out that the mystical union through language symbolizes the fusion with the mother: Tzinacán is happy in the depths of his prison because he is now one with his god; in the same way, the child is happy outside his mother's body because the possession of the linguistic code makes the two bodies one (Anzieu, 1971, pp. 185–186). One could add that even the fact that Tzinacán keeps the secret formula to himself stresses the character of a private and unique relationship that the child has with his mother.

The other story, "The Library of Babel," is according to Anzieu Borges' best. It came out originally in *The Garden of Forking Paths* (1941) and was later included in *Ficciones* (1944). To Anzieu, the infinite library is a symbol of the unconscious: "It has all the characteristics of the unconscious, not only according to Freud, but also according to Lacan; it is universal, eternal and, also, it is structured like a language" (ibid., p. 196). There is another link between the library of Babel and the unconscious: both are susceptible to infinite combinations. "To the point where the body articulates itself with the code, where the child talks then writes for his mother, whose mouth speaks and later writes for him, the unconscious proposes to the discourse many possibilities of fantastic combinations, because of their number, their form, and their content." Thus, according to Anzieu, "the mystical journey of the narrator through the library of Babel is a symbolical exploration of the mother's body—a feeding breast which is also a mouth that speaks, a mouth that teaches the entranced child the phonological code" (ibid., p. 198).

This story also contains traces of the trauma caused by the double linguistic code. The collection of books in the library is infinite and at the same time monstrous. In his report on the library the anonymous narrator recalls some axioms, the second of which is:

The orthographical symbols are twenty-five in number.[1] This finding made it possible, three hundred years ago, to formulate a general theory of the Library and solve satisfactorily the problem which no conjecture had deciphered: the formless and chaotic nature of almost all the books. One which my father saw in a hexagon on circuit fifteen ninety-four was made up of the letters MCV, perversely repeated from the first line to the last. Another (very much consulted in this area) is a mere labyrinth of letters, but the next-to-last page says *Oh time thy pyramids*. This much is already known: for every sensible line of straightforward statement, there are leagues of senseless cacophonies, verbal jumbles and incoherences.

[1] The original manuscript does not contain digits or capital letters. The punctuation has been limited to the comma and the period. These two signs, the space and the twenty-two letters of the alphabet are the twenty-five symbols considered sufficient by this unknown author. *Editor's note. (Labyrinths,* 1962, p. 53)

The body of the library that contains such books has been destroyed by chaos, quartered and made absurd by the application of an insane code. The dream of order has turned into a nightmare. In the same way, for Georgie, the institution of a second code (based more on a conscious than on an unconscious logic) will destroy the unity of Mother's body. Thus, the role of the second mother, of Grandmother Haslam, would, at the unconscious level, be that of the disruptive element of chaos. But the conflict will remain hidden in Georgie's unconscious until he first learns to read, in English and not in Spanish. Then, by a strange permutation, Grandmother's code becomes the first, and Father, who had so far remained in the background, becomes the most important person in the household. As a carrier of English (the privileged code), Father drastically displaces both Mother and Grandmother Haslam and assumes the role of teacher, the master of the new code of reading. At the conscious level, Georgie accepts the change. But at the unconscious level (at the level where all his fantastic tales had already started to be produced), he never accepts it. And only in Mother's discarded and despised code—Spanish—will he later succeed in symbolizing all that archaic repressed material: the stuff bodies (and poetry) are made of.

5.
The Playmate

For the better part of his childhood Georgie had an accomplice. It was his sister, Norah, two years his junior. Although in the "Autobiographical Essay" very little space is devoted to Norah—she is mentioned only four or five times—in Georgie's emotional experience Norah was very important. For some fifteen years they shared everything: every evening they had to leave the adult world and go upstairs to sleep in their separate bedrooms; they were taught English by the same governess; they spent their holidays together, playing endless games invented by Georgie in which Norah had the leading roles, as guide and protector. They shared love, dreams, terrors. If Georgie was older, Norah had a more determined character. She did not inherit the Borges blindness. On the contrary, her eyes were enormous, as if slightly bewildered by the world's profusion of shapes and colors. In the extant photographs of their childhood Norah's eyes are strong and inquisitive, a petulant smile on her lips, while Georgie's eyes are dreamier, more evasive. Norah was destined to become a painter and a draftswoman, and in her works she leaves testimony of the familial world she shared with her brother. Her paintings and drawings offer an almost infantile, naïve vision of that world, as if her eyes could remember the garden only before the Fall.

In her reminiscences to a French interviewer Mother commented on their close relationship: "He was shy, extremely reserved. He adored his sister, and they both invented an infinite number of extraordinary games. They never quarreled and they were always together before Georgie found in Switzerland some schoolmates" (Mother, 1964, p. 9). In a more neutral tone, Borges evokes the same period of his childhood: "I have already said that I spent a great deal of my boyhood indoors. Having no childhood friends, my sister and I invented two imaginary companions, named, for some reason or other, Quilos and the Windmill. (When they finally bored us, we told our mother that they had died.)" ("Essay," 1970, p. 208).

This short reference is tantalizing because of its reticent evocation of a period that was so important in his life. It is also revealing for the hints it gives of Georgie's precocious gift for language. The names of the imaginary characters are significant. Quilos suggests immediately the phonetic transcription of the Spanish plural *kilos* (kilograms); but it may come from another, more scholarly, source that Georgie could have picked up in a dictionary. In Spanish the digestive juices are called *quilos* (from the Greek *khylós*, according to Corominas, 1967, p. 487); this opens up the possibility of a pun. The other character's name, the Windmill, is easier to place. The garden of the Borgeses' house on the outskirts of Buenos Aires had a windmill. During a storm, the windmill's whining and screeching used to scare Georgie. In a poem he wrote when he was thirty, "Natural Fluency of Memory" (included in *San Martín Copybook*, 1929), which evokes his childhood home and neighborhood, he singles out the windmill. It was red and had a laborious wheel; it was "the honor of our home" because the neighbors did not have windmills and had to get their water from carriers who came from the river with their wooden wagons. He vividly recalls the windmill's circular basement, "its jail of subtle water" (*Poemas*, 1943, pp. 126–127).

The poem also recalls the garden and the neighborhood. In attempting to capture the magic and beauty of those days, Borges cannot help adding a few sinister touches. He remembers the beautiful tree in which a magpie had settled to devour her offspring despite the protests of the other birds. The horror of the occasion is concentrated in a single word: depredation. Addressing the garden, Borges says:

> The sleep of your trees and mine
> still blend in darkness
> and the depredation of the magpie
> left an old fear in my blood.
> (Ibid., p. 127)

Mother remembered that Georgie loved to play in the garden near the palm tree that is mentioned in the poem:

> Palm tree, the highest of that heaven
> and little bird's tenement
> (Ibid., p. 126)

"Under that palm tree," Mother recalled, "he invented with his sister games, dreams, projects; they created characters with whom they played; it was their island (Mother, 1964, p. 10).

Norah has also confided her memories of those days. In Alicia Jurado's book it is her version that prevails. She recalls the games and the terrors, the windmill and the magpie. But she adds other images to their childhood iconography. According to that source, Norah could see Georgie

> in her memory, always reading, lying on his stomach on the ground dressed in a light brown wrapper. He didn't like any manual work or any game of skill, except the diavolo [a game played with a wooden hoop], but he liked to reenact with her scenes taken from books: he was a prince and she the queen, his mother; standing on a staircase, they leaned over to hear the acclamations of an imaginary multitude; or they traveled to the moon in a missile built by folding a red silk Chinese screen, embroidered with golden birds and flowers, into which they tumbled after sliding down the banister of the staircase. Sometimes, they traveled dangerously on the flat roofs, searching for a room where they'd never been, a mysterious place that ought perforce to exist. (Jurado, 1964, p. 29)

They used to spend their summers in Uruguay, visiting Mother's relatives in a villa on the outskirts of Montevideo or on a ranch up the Uruguay River, near Fray Bentos. There they had a playmate, a cousin, Esther Haedo, who also had been educated by an English governess. According to Norah's reminiscences, at Esther's place

> there was a lookout tower, with a spiral staircase and colored windows, from which came undoubtedly the red and green lozenges of Triste-le-Roy [a villa in Borges' story "Death and the Compass"]. In that lonely place, the children founded the Society of the Three Crosses, created to defend the boy from an imaginary enemy who wanted to kill him. General headquarters was a gazebo of painted wood with a gallery whose only access was through a little bridge. They wrote messages in a code invented by the supposed victim, and they roamed around the villa with cloth masks. (Ibid., pp. 29–30)

As a child, Georgie had been fascinated and repelled by masks. At carnival time he used to peer out from the safety of the garden into the street, where the masked revelers filled the air with their drums and riotous water play. In the poem quoted above he mentions the "coarse carnival." Perhaps he had had a bad experience with masks: Mother confided to Alicia Jurado that as a child Georgie only once "consented to put on a disguise, and then he insisted—perhaps significantly—on a devil's costume" (ibid., p. 26). This childhood fear of masks prevailed in later years. One of his closest friends, Silvina

Ocampo, described Borges' astonishing reaction once "when some masked and costumed friends crashed in during carnival time" (ibid., p. 26).

In his fiction Borges has always associated masks and disguises with evil or murder. In *A Universal History of Infamy*, one of the most revealing stories is "The Masked Dyer, Hakim of Merv," about a false prophet who hides his leprosy under a mask of gold. In one episode of "Death and the Compass" (a story later included in *Ficciones*), the criminal uses masks to lure the detective into a plot that endangers his life. Masks are terrifying not only because they hide one's real features but because on them the expression of character is forever fixed. They are absolutes in a world of contingency and change. Masks are also a symbol of the duality of man: the two that fight inside each person. Perhaps Georgie was not consciously aware of the meaning of masks, but he felt that they were disgusting and rejected them, or wore them only when he wanted to play a sinister role: the devil (in Mother's reminiscences) or the persecuted victim (in Norah's recollections).

His games of pursuit with Norah and Esther came to a climax one day: "A whole summer they lived in terror of the fabrications of their own imagination, which came to be so vivid that once, at siesta time, the three saw the murderer reflected in one of the terrible mirrors of the wardrobe. It was, Norah tells, blurred and green-colored" (Jurado, 1964, pp. 29–30). The haunting, sleepless mirror is one of the recurrent images in Borges' work. But before becoming a literary image, it had been an obsession. According to Alicia Jurado:

Norah still remembers the nights of terror [when] they were left alone upstairs in their bedrooms. Georgie was afraid even of the vague reflection of his face in the polished mahogany of his bed. Many years later, we will recognize that mood in a poem in which he talks about the

> masked
> mahogany mirror which in the mist
> of red twilight erases
> that face which looks and is looked upon.
>   (Ibid., pp. 25–26)

This poem, "The Mirror," continues revealingly:

> Glasses spy on us. If between the four
> walls of my bedroom there is a mirror,
> I am no longer alone. There is another one.
> There is the reflection
> which creates a silent theater at dawn.
>   (*Obra*, 1964, pp. 183–85)

Georgie's fear and even horror of mirrors seems to go against everything that is known about children's reactions to them. According to Jacques Lacan's theory about the importance of the mirror stage in the evolution of the subconscious, the child discovers in the mirror an image of himself as a unified body, a totality; before that experience, he has only a partial image of himself. This discovery brings joy to him because he thus anticipates in his imagination his future control over his own body (Lacan, 1966, pp. 93–100). In Georgie's case, this joy did not seem to have existed. To him—as Didier Anzieu has suggested in his psychoanalytical study (Anzieu, 1971, p. 200)—the specular reflection only confirms the fact that his body has been torn apart from the body of his mother. Instead of reassuring Georgie, the discovery ratifies the pain, the intolerable awareness of being another. What he sees in the mirror is the other; that is, himself. To put it in a different way, he sees himself not as he wants to be (one with his mother) but as he is (the other). That could be the origin of an obsession that his bilingualism could only have strengthened.

A different reading of the same obsession, to which Anzieu only alludes in his study (ibid., pp. 199 and 202), could be attempted. On several occasions, but chiefly in his clinical study of the Wolf-Man, Sigmund Freud identified another, related trauma that sometimes involves mirrors: the primal scene. Often the parents' sexual activities are discovered accidentally by children through the reflection in a mirror. The fact that George was haunted by a mirror in his own bedroom, and that he was even afraid of seeing his image in the polished mahogany of his bed, seems to suggest the possibility of that reading.

There are other hints that point to the same connection in several of Borges' stories. On many occasions he establishes an unexpected link between mirrors and copulation. The first time he does it is in "The Masked Dyer, Hakim of Merv," a story mentioned earlier for its use of masks. In a section of that story called The Abominable Mirrors, Borges summarizes the protagonist's cosmogony: "The world we live in is a mistake, a clumsy parody. Mirrors and fatherhood, because they multiply and confirm the parody, are abominations. Revulsion is the cardinal virtue" (*Infamy*, 1972, p. 84). Although Borges quotes at the end of *A Universal History of Infamy* a list of historical sources for the stories in the book, it has been proved satisfactorily that no source exists for that particular "cosmogony." In a second story, "Tlön, Uqbar, Orbis Tertius," Borges attributes a similar concept to an even more exotic source. It is presented as the opinion of a heresiarch from Uqbar. According to the story, Borges was having dinner with a friend, Adolfo Bioy Casares, and at a certain point in their conversation Bioy recalled that one of the heresiarchs of Uqbar had declared that "mirrors and copulation are abominable, because they increase the number of men" (*Labyrinths,* 1964, p. 3).

This is the starting point for a long and eventually successful quest for the exact source of that quotation, which Borges calls "a memorable observation." When Bioy Casares produces the volume of the Anglo-American Encyclopedia that contains the article on Uqbar, the heresiarch's doctrine is quoted again: "The heresiarch's name was not forthcoming, but there was a note on his doctrine, formulated in words almost identical to those he [Bioy] had repeated, though perhaps literarily inferior. He had recalled: *Copulation and mirrors are abominable.* The text of the encyclopedia said: *For one of those gnostics, the visible universe was an illusion or (more precisely) a sophism. Mirrors and fatherhood are abominable because they multiply and disseminate that universe"* (ibid., p. 4).

Perhaps it would be useful to point out that in the Spanish text both Bioy Casares' rendering of the heresiarch's statement and the heresiarch's slightly different wording are given in English and then translated into Spanish, to increase perhaps the verisimilitude of the passage. But what is even more important is the confrontation of the three basic texts: the one in "The Masked Dyer" and the two in "Tlön." They seem to state the same thing, but their contexts differ considerably. In Hakim of Merv's cosmogony "mirrors and fatherhood" are compared, as they are in the heresiarch's version in "Tlön," while Bioy Casares' version makes a more explicit and general reference to "copulation and mirrors."

There are other differences between the three texts. In "The Masked Dyer" the comparison between mirrors and fatherhood is based on the fact that they both "multiply and confirm" the world we live in, which is (for Hakim) a "parody." In the first quotation from "Tlön" Bioy Casares refers explicitly to the fact that they "increase the number of men." In the heresiarch's text there is a return to Hakim's notion: there is one universe, real, and another one, reflected, multiplied, and disseminated by mirrors and fatherhood. Again, the similarity between Hakim's and the heresiarch's versions suggests a common doctrine. It is easy to recognize in them an allusion to the gnostic belief that the world was created not by God but by subaltern gods (or demons) who actually parodied God's creation.

In spite of this similarity, there are important differences between the first and the last text. Both state that mirrors and fatherhood "multiply" the universe. But they differ in the second verb: the first text talks about confirming the world; the second, about disseminating it. The change is significant and is even clearer in the Spanish original. There Borges does not use the verb *diseminar* (disseminate) but the verb *divulgar* (divulge), which etymologically implies to spread among the *vulgo,* the common people. In James E. Irby's translation the word "disseminate" carries another weight: it contains the concept of semen or seminal, which is obviously implied in Borges' text. The translation thus makes even more explicit the underlying sexual meaning of the "memorable observation."

This kind of reading of "Tlön" not only seems legitimate but is suggested by the text itself. Very significantly, the whole story evolves from a discussion in which "Borges" and "Bioy" are concerned about "the composition of a novel in the first person, whose narrator would omit or disfigure the facts and indulge in various contradictions which would permit a few readers—very few readers—to perceive an atrocious or banal reality" (*Labyrinths,* 1962, p. 3). If the word "story" is substituted for "novel," as some critics have suggested, the text would contain a reference to "Tlön" itself because the story describes an imaginary world that is actually the earth—"Orbis Tertius," as it was called in Renaissance cosmography. Behind the elaborate mask of Uqbar, an atrocious or banal reality is hidden: the reality of a world that is a parody, created by inferior gods, and that perpetuates itself through mirrors and fatherhood.

How much of this revulsion for the act of fatherhood (or copulation, as Bioy Casares remembered it) has to do with the discovery of the primal scene through the complicity of a mirror? The only evidence that exists is the one buried in Borges' texts. In another part of the poem "The Mirror" the tantalizing link is again established:

> Infinite I see them, elementary
> executors of an old pact,
> to multiply the world as the generative
> act, sleepless and fatal.
> *(Obra,* 1964, p. 184)

In his writings the impact of that primal scene proliferates in tantalizing allusions and, sometimes, in very explicit statements. There is another story, "The Sect of the Phoenix," originally published in *Sur* (Buenos Aires, September–October 1952) and later included in the 1956 edition of *Ficciones.* It is disguised as a historical reconstruction of an obscure pagan sect. Camouflaged under many observations that are not always false, Borges talks about the "Secret" which assures immortality to the worshippers of the Phoenix.

This Secret . . . is transmitted from generation to generation, but good usage prefers that mothers should not teach it to their children, nor that priests should; initiation into the mystery is the task of the lowest individuals. A slave, a leper, and a beggar serve as mystagogues. Also one child may indoctrinate another. The act in itself is trivial, momentary, and requires no description. The materials are cork, wax, or gum arabic. (In the liturgy, mud is mentioned; this is often used as well.) There are no temples especially dedicated to the celebration of this cult, but certain ruins, a cellar, or an entrance hall are considered propitious places. The Secret is sacred but is always somewhat ridiculous; its performance is furtive and even clandestine and the adept do not speak of it. There are no decent words to name it, but it is understood that all words name it or, rather, inevitably allude to it and thus, in a conversation, I say something or other and the adept smile or become uncomfortable, for they realize I have touched upon the Secret. . . . A kind of sacred horror prevents some faithful believers from performing this very simple rite; the others despise them, but they despise themselves even more.

. . . I have attained in three continents the friendship of many devotees of the Phoenix; I know that the Secret, at first, seemed to them banal, embarrassing, vulgar, and (what is even stranger) incredible. They could not bring themselves to admit their parents had stooped to such manipulations. What is odd is that the Secret was not lost long ago; in spite of the vicissitudes of the Universe, in spite of wars and exoduses, it reaches, awesomely, all the faithful. Someone has not hesitated to affirm that it is now instinctive. (*Labyrinths*, 1962, pp. 102–104)

The Secret, which Borges wishes to reveal to the reader gradually, is none other than copulation, which insures the reproduction of the species and therefore grants "eternity to a lineage of its members, generation after generation, would perform the rite" (ibid., p. 102). But not all readers decipher the Secret. At least one, Ronald Christ, dared to ask Borges about it. As he tells the story, he approached the writer in New York in 1968. Borges' reaction was to keep him guessing for another day; when they met again at a reception the following evening, he "leaned over and whispered into my ear so that no one else could hear: 'Well, the act is what Whitman says "the divine husband knows, from the work of fatherhood." When I first heard about this act, when I was a boy, I was shocked, shocked to think that my mother, my father had performed it. It is an amazing discovery, no? But then too it is an act of immortality, a rite of immortality, isn't it?' " (Christ, 1969, p. 190).

In the story itself Borges notes the astonishment of some believers when told of the act: "They could not bring themselves to admit that their parents had stooped to such manipulations." The same reaction occurs in an earlier story by Borges, one of the few that touches on a sexual subject, "Emma Zunz," first published in *Sur* (September 1948) and later included in *The Aleph* (1949). It is about a young woman whose father is forced by a business partner to commit suicide. To avenge his death, she plans to accuse the partner of having raped her and then to kill him. But one fact threatens to undermine her story: she is still a virgin. In order to lose her virginity, she sells herself to an unknown sailor. (The plot, the weakest aspect of the story, was given to Borges by a woman friend.) Borges describes Emma's reaction during coitus:

> During that time outside of time, in that perplexing disorder of disconnected and atrocious sensations, did Emma Zunz think *once* about the dead man who motivated the sacrifice? It is my belief that she did think once, and in that moment she endangered her desperate undertaking. She thought (she was unable not to think) that her father had done to her mother the hideous thing that was being done to her now. She thought of it with weak amazement and took refuge, quickly, in vertigo. (*Labyrinths,* 1962, p. 135)

The roots of Borges' evasiveness, reticence, and even self-censorship when dealing with sexual subjects—as has been illustrated by the above quotations—can be found in Georgie's discovery of the mystery of sex. It is impossible to know how much of this knowledge he shared with Norah. The differences in their adult lives indicate a radical difference in the impact these childhood games and discoveries in the secluded garden or in the mirrored bedrooms had for each of them. In her late twenties Norah married the Spanish critic and poet Guillermo de Torre; George remained a bachelor until his late sixties, and the marriage lasted only three years. While Norah had two sons, Georgie never fathered a child.

In that Palermo garden Norah and Georgie were closer than ever. She was his protector, a mother surrogate and a good alter ego, not the one that haunted mirrors. She and Esther Haedo, the Uruguayan cousin, defended Georgie from an imaginary enemy. In their eagerness to protect him, they even shared his hallucinations, and one day (Norah is our witness) they both saw the murderer's hideous image reflected in a mirror. Contagious magic, as Frazer would say? Probably, because both girls were totally submissive to Georgie's imagination and will. But they also shared his taste for dreams and art. Regarding his own visual style and Norah's, Borges has commented:

BURGIN: You love painting and architecture, don't you? I mean your stories seem to me very vivid visually.
BORGES: Are they really visual, or does the visibility come from Chesterton?
BURGIN: You seem to have that ability to make a purely imagined world, such as the city of the immortals, come to life.
BORGES: I wonder if they really come to life.
BURGIN: For me they do. I can only speak for myself.

BORGES: Yes, of course. Now my sister paints. She's a fine painter.
BURGIN: What style does she paint in?
BORGES: She's always painting, well, large gardens and old-fashioned pink houses or if not those, angels, but angels who are musicians. She's a very unobtrusive painter. For example, well, she studied perspective drawing and so on. But people who know little or nothing about painting think of her paintings as being just scrawls done by a child. (Burgin, 1969, p. 99)

Borges' subtle irony is at his best here; moving around Burgin's naïve questions, he plays a gentler Johnson to a twentieth-century Boswell. The reference to Chesterton as a source for his "visual" style is one of his critical leitmotifs. But what really matters most is his observation about how people are fooled by Norah's lack of visible skills and her apparent naïveté. That is the precise quality that helped her to maintain a child's vision in works done with the utmost sophistication. Her paintings and drawings preserve the world she shared with Georgie, but in a completely different tonality from that used by her brother. With simple lines and pastel colors, she re-creates the houses and patios, the little squares and monuments, the men and women and children (all with big, round, black eyes) of their childhood. Her work is the positive of the negative inscribed by Georgie. She shows the light of her brother's world of darkness: a world in which an enemy is always hidden in the dark reflection of mirrors. Her private mythology is not the opposite but the complement of her brother's.

One more observation about their childhood games—it is significant that, in playing Kings and Queens, Norah (who was two years younger) became the Queen Mother and not the Princess, as might have been expected at that healthy incestuous stage of their lives. The powerful repression of the Oedipal conflict seems to be at work already. In changing his sister (his equal) into his "mother" (a superior; thus an unreachable being), Georgie was exorcising a potential incestuous relationship that would have been normal at their age. The garden at Palermo was to be Eden; no serpent was allowed to weave its way into that secluded space.

6.
The Inhabitant of the Labyrinth

The garden at Palermo was a privileged place from which Georgie could watch the outside world. It was a holy place. But it was also the door that gave access to another reality: the reality of people who lived next to him in houses of only one story, people who had no water of their own and didn't know the security of possessing their own gardens. Very seldom did Georgie and Norah leave their haven. Apart from visits to relatives, especially to the two grandmothers, the only place they went to regularly was the Buenos Aires zoo, which was located not very far from home. In her recollections Mother evoked some of Georgie's reactions to these excursions: "He was passionate about animals, especially wild beasts. When we visited the zoo, it was difficult to make him leave. And I, who was small, I was afraid of him, so big and strong. I was afraid that he'd get into a rage and beat me. . . . However, he was very kind. When he did not want to give in, I took his books away. That was decisive" (Mother, 1964, p. 10).

Mother's image of a raging, bullying Georgie is unsettling. Even more disturbing are her feelings of being weak and small in front of him: a giant of a boy although generally kind. To overcome her feelings of inferiority, she had to resort to drastic measures. By taking away his books (or perhaps only threatening to do so), she regained her authority. Her method was effective, but it must have been damaging to her relationship with Georgie. From the moment he learned to read in English before he could read in Spanish, the balance tipped toward the first language. Now the punishment of taking his books away when he misbehaved came from the parent who was associated with Spanish. Mother's method might have been effective, but it only confirmed the child's prejudices.

Taking away books was not the only punishment Mother used. She confided to Alicia Jurado that one day Georgie had to be shut in his room "after a horrid tantrum he threw because he had been taken from the zoo at a time he thought was too soon. He was offered a reprieve if he would say tht he didn't mean to react in the way he did." He refused and continued to shout, " 'I did mean it,' until the punishment was over" (Jurado, 1964, p. 25). There is an untranslatable pun in Georgie's words. In Spanish "I didn't mean it" is "Lo hice *sin* querer" (literally: I did it *without* willing it). But Georgie revises the idiomatic phrase and shouts "Lo hice *con* querer" (literally: I did it *with* willing it). The episode seems significant not only in what it shows of Georgie's mettle and determination but especially in what it proves of the child's linguistic imagination. He was already coining his own phrases.

It is obvious that he took language seriously, almost as seriously as going to the zoo. Of all the animals he saw there, his favorite was the tiger. His maternal grandmother, Leonor Suárez de Acevedo, used to chide him for the preference and tried unsuccessfully to persuade him that lambs were prettier. But he insisted on "the ferocious tiger," as he used to say in English, according to Mother's reminiscences as transmitted by Alicia Jurado (ibid., p. 26). In an interview in the French publication *L'Herne,* Mother completed the picture:

> When he was very young, he would draw animals. Lying down on his stomach on the floor, he would always begin at the end, drawing the feet first. He would draw tigers, which were his favorite animals. Later, from tigers and other savage beasts, he moved to prehistoric animals, about which for two years he read all he could get hold of. Then he became enthusiastic about Egyptian things, and he read about them—read with no end in sight—until he threw himself into Chinese literature; he has a lot of books on the subject. In short, he loves everything that is mysterious. (Mother, 1964, p. 11)

When Georgie was very young his paternal grandmother, Fanny Haslam, probably read him Blake's poem "The Tiger," which develops the comparison between that beast and fire and contains the biblical opposition with the lamb that Grandmother Acevedo had presented as an alternative. But in adoring the tiger, Georgie was not only being true to these literary or religious prototypes. He was being true to one side of his family: to those ancestors who fought first for Spain during the conquest and later for Argentina during the wars of independence; men who died on the battlefield, covered with wounds, or less heroically but not less truly in their own beds, dreaming of a violence that had been finally denied them. In Borges' future work the tiger comes to symbolize many things but always of the same kind. It is darkness and fire, primeval innocence and evil, the sexual instinct and the blind violence that obliterate everything. In text after text the tiger emerges as a symbol of time, which devours men (as in the lyrical conclusion to his essay "A New Refutation of Time," collected in *Inquisitions*, 1964) or as a "string of labored tropes" the poet is trying vainly to capture in the seclusion of a library (as in the poem "The Other Tiger," written when Borges was almost sixty; *Poems*, 1972, pp. 129–131). But for Georgie there was only one tiger: the real one he used to watch at the Palermo zoo. To that tiger (and to the memories and dreams it engendered) Borges devoted one of his most eloquent pieces. It was written in the 1930s and published for the first time in the literary section of the Argentine newspaper *Crítica* (September 15, 1934), under the pseudonym of Francisco Bustos. Not until 1960 was it collected in 'a volume of Borges' writing, *El hacedor* (*Dreamtigers*, 1964). The title of the piece, "Dreamtigers," is in English in the Spanish original:

> In my childhood I was a fervent worshipper of the tiger: not the jaguar, the spotted "tiger" of the Amazonian tangles and the isles of vegetation that float down the Paraná, but that striped, Asiatic, royal tiger, that can be faced only by a man of war, on a castle atop an elephant. I used to linger endlessly before one of the cages at the zoo; I judged vast encyclopedias and books of natural history by the splendor of their tigers. (I still remember those illustrations: I who cannot rightly recall the brow or smile of a woman.) Childhood passed away, and the tigers and my passion for them grew old, but still they are in my dreams. At that submerged or chaotic level they keep prevailing. And so, as I sleep, some dream beguiles me, and suddenly I know I am dreaming. Then I think: This is a dream, a pure diversion of my will; and now that I have unlimited power, I am going to cause a tiger.
>
> Oh, incompetence: Never can my dreams engender the wild beast I long for. The tiger indeed appears, but stuffed or flimsy, or with impure variations of shape, or of an implausible size, or all too fleeting, or with a touch of the dog or the bird. (*Dreamtigers*, 1964, p. 24)

The tiger Borges was trying to dream was similar to the ones Georgie used to draw, which are preserved in his childhood notebooks. It is shapeless, ambiguous, wrong. But it is, nevertheless, a symbol of what was lacking in the child's life: adventure, passion, violence. The tiger was also, unconsciously, associated in Georgie's mythology with other incomprehensible forces. In a poem written when he was in his seventies Borges summarizes what the tiger was to him in the different periods of his long life. It is called "El oro de los tigres" (The Gold of the Tigers) and is the last poem in the book of the same name (1973). He begins by recalling the many times he saw (as a child) the powerful Bengal tiger

toing and froing on its paced-out path
behind the labyrinthine iron bars,
never suspecting them to be a prison.

Later, he would meet other tigers: Blake's blazing tiger, "the amorous gold shower disguising Zeus," the ring from the *Edda Minor* that every ninth night

gives light to nine rings more, and these, nine more,
and there is never an end.
                                                    (*Gold*, 1977, p. 47)

The poem concludes on a very personal note. His blindness has obliterated all colors but yellow: the gold of the tigers, the primeval gold, and the even more precious gold of his loved one's hair.

Moving from the first image of the tiger in the Palermo zoo to the gold of the woman he longs for, Borges establishes the link between the wild beast and the sexual appetite that engenders and perpetuates life. The allusion to a passage in the *Edda Minor* (which is elucidated in a note to the poem) makes the image of the tiger as a progenitor very clear. The insistence on the nine nights that engender the nine rings contains an allusion to the nine months of gestation and stresses the same obsession with fatherhood that he had dealt with in "The Sect of the Phoenix." Another clue is contained in a reference to one of Zeus' metamorphoses. The tiger thus becomes the symbol of terrifying parenthood. The primal scene finds its primeval symbol.

Tigers were not the only beasts in Georgie's imaginary zoo. In Mother's recollections she mentions prehistoric animals. According to Alicia Jurado, "Norah and he had a toy collection made of such animals" (Jurado, 1964, p. 27). But that was to be a passing fancy. Of all the other beasts he discovered as a child, only the Minotaur became as central to his personal myth as the tiger. Although Borges dedicated one of his most tantalizing stories to the Minotaur, and the Minoan labyrinth, the symbol that is perhaps the most obviously Borgesian of all, critics have not discussed it at length. Borges himself provides some clues in an interview with Herbert Simon, an American computer scientist. They met in Buenos Aires in 1971, and their conversation was recorded and published by the Argentine weekly *Primera Plana* (January 5, 1971, pp. 42–45). Borges confides to Simon that he remembers "having seen an engraving of the labyrinth in a French book" when he was a boy. The book must have been Lemprière's Greek mythology, to which he makes a passing reference in his autobiographical sketch ("Essay," 1970, p. 211). The conversation with Simon continues on a rather ironic note: that illustration showed the labyrinth as "a circular building without doors but with many windows."

BORGES: I used to look at the engraving and I thought that if I used a magnifying glass I would be able to see the Minotaur.
SIMON: Did you find it?
BORGES: As a matter of fact my eyesight was never very good. Later I discovered a bit about life's complexity, as if it were a game. I'm talking about chess now. (Simon, 1971, p. 43)

To illustrate his thoughts, he quotes a poem about being too old to love but not so old as not to see the immense night that surrounds us; not so old not to be still amazed by something hidden in love and passion. Once again, Borges uses a quotation to mask his thoughts; once again, he moves from the subject of the labyrinth and the Minotaur to the subject of passionate love. They are, in fact, closely related: the Minotaur was conceived by Pasiphae out of her bestial passion for a white bull; the labyrinth was the house built by Daedalus to hide (mask) the monster offspring of that union. Love is still amazing. That is, literally, love throws you into a maze. For Borges, as he tells Simon: "Such is the form in which I perceive life. A continuous amazement. A continuous bifurcation of the labyrinth" (ibid., p. 43). Further on in the same conversation he explains that he was less attracted to the idea of the Minotaur than "by another name attributed to that mythological being. I found the name, *Asterion,* in a dictionary. It had connotations of an asteroid or a star. It is an image which I always thought could please the readers" (ibid., p. 43). For Borges, the Minotaur is not just a symbol or a mythological character; it is a name, a word he has found in a dictionary. Images, words: those are the stuff Borges' (and obviously Georgie's) dreams were made on.

In using the myth of the Minotaur and the labyrinth, Borges is aware of its tradition. In a piece he wrote for *The Book of Imaginary Beings* he points out that the invention of the labyrinth is even more strange than that of its inhabitant: "The idea of a house built so that people could become lost in it is perhaps more unusual than that of a man with a bull's head; both ideas go well together and the image of the labyrinth fits with the image of the Minotaur. It is equally fitting that in the corner of a monstrous house there be a monstrous inhabitant" (*Imaginary,* 1969, p. 158).

But the labyrinth was not only built to confuse and mislead people. It was built both to protect the Minotaur and to imprison him. If it is difficult to find a way into the labyrinth, it is equally difficult to find the way out. A paradoxical place, the labyrinth fixes forever the symbolical movement from the exterior into the interior, from the form to the contemplation, from time to the absence of time. It also represents the opposite movement, from inside out, according to a well-known progression. In the center of the labyrinth there is a being, a monster or a god (because monstrosity is sometimes a divine attribute). God or monster, at the center of the labyrinth there is a mystery.

Labyrinths thus become, according to tradition, the representation of ordered chaos, a chaos submitted to human intelligence, a deliberate disorder that contains its own code. They also represent nature in its least human aspects—an immense river is a labyrinth of water; a jungle is a labyrinth of trees—and some of the proudest human achievements—a library is a labyrinth of processed trees; a city is a labyrinth of streets. The same symbol can also be used to invoke the invisible reality of human fate, of God's will, the mystery of artistic creation.

All these allusions can be found in Borges' work. Some of his favorite authors (Joyce and Kafka, for instance) have been attracted by the same image. In spite of that, the explicit symbol of the labyrinth appears very rarely in his work until 1938, when he began to write some of his strangest fiction. The symbol is even less frequent in his verse. The first mention occurs in the poem "Of Heaven and Hell," written in 1942. From then on it is almost constantly present. "Conjectural Poem" (1943), which dramatizes the fate of one of his ancestors, is really a poem on man's labyrinthine fate.

Borges tries to unravel the mystery of the labyrinth in a story called "The House of Asterion," collected for the first time in *The Aleph* (1949). A quotation from Apollodorus (*The Library*, III, 1) which briefly states that the Queen gave birth to a son called Asterion, opens the story, which is divided into two parts. The first part consists of Asterion's monologue. He says that he lives alone in an unfurnished palace whose plan (the reader slowly realizes) is that of a labyrinth. Some observations make perfectly clear that Asterion is a vain young man, very ignorant of the uses of this world. It is also clear that every nine years he kills nine men and that he is waiting with hope for his redeemer to come. The brief second part (some five lines) identifies the redeemer as Theseus and indicates obliquely the death of the Minotaur. As in stories such as "Streetcorner Man" and "The Shape of the Sword," the first-person narrative helps Borges to omit part of the tale and hide its real meaning until the very last lines of the text. In this particular case, he is trying to hide from the reader the real identity of Asterion. By avoiding the words "Minotaur" and "labyrinth," he manages to keep the mystery and enhance the suspense, as in any good detective story. Unfortunately, Di Giovanni's translation (in spite of its merit) makes a crucial error in substituting for Borges' ambiguous rendering of Apollodorus' words the more scholarly translation: "And she gave birth to Asterius, who was called the Minotaur" (*Review,* 1973, p. 63).

Borges is also concerned with defining, in an oblique manner, the true nature of the Minotaur. Only indirectly, by allusion, is its monstrous nature indicated. In order to prove that he is free to move around and even to go out in the streets, Asterion says:

> As a matter of fact, one evening I did step out into the street; if I came back before nightfall I did so out of the horror that the faces of the common people stirred in me—colorless, flattened faces like an open palm. The sun had already set, but the helpless wail of a child and the crude supplications of the mob showed that they knew me. Men uttered prayers, fled, fell before me on their knees. Some clambered up the steps of the Temple of the Axes, others gathered stones. One or two, I believe, sought refuge beneath the waves. Not for nothing was my mother a queen; I cannot mingle with the crowd, even if my modesty were to allow it. (Ibid., p. 63)

In this indirect way Borges provides the reader with important information: Asterion lives in a house next to the Temple of the Axes, which alludes to one of the possible etymologies for labyrinth (from the Greek *labrys,* the two-headed ax); his mother was a queen, that is, Pasiphae, wife of Minos, the king of Crete; even more important, his face is neither colorless nor flat. Asterion's reaction to the human face is strong—he feels horror—but the crowd's reaction to him is no less strong. People are also horrified, although Asterion is vain enough not to notice it. Later, in describing his innocent pastimes, he adds another significant detail: "Like a butting ram, I rush down these stone passages until I fall to the ground in a daze." He also describes a game he plays with his double, an imaginary Asterion who comes to visit him and to whom he shows the house: "Bowing low, I say to him: 'Now we are back at the same crossway,' or 'Now we find our way into a new courtyard,' or 'I knew you'd like this water trough,' or 'Now you're about to see a cistern that has filled with sand,' or 'Now you'll see how the cellar branches right and left.' Sometimes I make a mistake and the two of us have a good laugh" (ibid., p. 63).

In the last paragraph of the monologue, when Asterion describes how he greets the nine men whom he has "to deliver from all evil," as he euphemistically puts it, there also are some hints about his monstrous nature: "I hear their footsteps or their voices along the stone passages and, full of joy, I rush to find them. The ceremony lasts only minutes. One after the other they go down, and my hands are unsullied. Where they fall they remain; these corpses help me to tell apart one passageway from another" (ibid., pp. 63–64). The fact that he kills them without using his hands suggests that he does it with his horns; the charging of the bull is also alluded to in the words "I rush to find them." In the last phrases of the monologue, when he is pondering the coming of a redeemer prophesied by one of his victims, he asks himself: "What will my redeemer be like? I ask myself. Will he be a bull or a man? Can he possibly be a bull with a man's face? Or will he be like me?" (ibid., p. 64). In a later text, which is included in *The Book of Imaginary Beings*, Borges explains the problems raised by the representation of a monster, half bull, half man. "Ovid in a line that is meant to be clever speaks of the *semibovemque vitum, semivirumque bovem* ('the man half bull, the bull half man'). Dante, who was familiar with the writings of the ancients but not with their coins or monuments, imagined the Minotaur with a man's head and bull's body (*Inferno*, XII, 1–30)" (*Imaginary*, 1969, p. 158). In the same text Borges summarizes the legend:

> The Minotaur . . . was born of the furious passion of Pasiphae, Queen of Crete, for a white bull that Neptune brought out of the sea. Daedalus, who invented the artifice that carried the Queen's unnatural desires to gratification, built the labyrinth destined to confine and keep hidden her monstrous son. The Minotaur fed on human flesh and for its nourishment the King of Crete imposed on the City of Athens a yearly tribute of seven young men and seven maidens. Theseus resolved to deliver his country from this burden when it fell to his lot to be sacrificed to the Minotaur's hunger. Ariadne, the King's daughter, gave him a thread so that he could trace his way out of the windings of the labyrinth's corridors: the hero killed the Minotaur and was able to escape from the maze. (Ibid., p. 158)

There are very important differences between Borges' rendering of the myth and Asterion's version. Some facts are omitted in the latter's monologue. There is no indication that he feeds on the body of his victim, although this could be taken as an oversight on his part. But there are more significant differences. His monologue indicates another cycle for the tribute to be paid: nine years instead of every year; nine men instead of seven young men and seven maidens. Asterion (in Borges' story) is not concerned at all with women. The change in the figure (nine instead of seven) could be attributed to the fact, already indicated in the story, that Asterion cannot read or write, and that he does not know how to count. Also, by prolonging the period of tribute, Borges avoids the cannibalistic implication of the sacrifice and by changing it to nine reinforces the allusion to the months of gestation.

There is an interesting difference between the Spanish text of the piece on the Minotaur in *The Book of Imaginary Beings* and the English version done by Di Giovanni in collaboration with the author. The principal change concerns the words used to describe Pasiphae's attachment to the bull. In Spanish Borges twice uses the same euphemistic word, *amores,* which means "loves." In the English translation he is more explicit but still reticent: "furious passion" the first time; "unnatural desires" the second. But the main point is that the three expressions avoid using the exact word: lust. And that is what the myth is all about. At the end of the article on the Minotaur Borges writes: "The worship of the bull and of the two-headed ax . . . was typical of pre-Hellenic religions, which held sacred bullfights. Human forms with bull-heads figured, to judge by wall paintings, in the demonology of Crete. Most likely the Greek fable of the Minotaur is a late and clumsy version of far older myths, the shadow of other dreams still more full of horror" (ibid., p. 159). On this tantalizing note, the piece ends. One can only conjecture about these far older myths and dreams. But Borges gives another hint in the epilogue to the Spanish edition of *The Aleph,* where he indicates some of the sources of the story: "To a painting by Watts, done in 1896, I owe 'The House of Asterion' and the character of its sad protagonist" (*El Aleph,* 1949, p. 171). The painting shows Asterion in profile and from the back, leaning on one of the palace's parapets and looking rather longingly to the world outside. It is this feeling of sadness and loneliness which Borges has taken from Watts and subtly introduced in the story.

In a text quoted by Di Giovanni in his introduction to the English version of the story, Borges recognizes this. "It is a sad story—a story of loneliness and stupidity. . . . It stands for feeling lonesome, for feeling useless" (*Review,* 1973, p. 62). The story was originally published in the magazine *Los Anales de Buenos Aires,* which Borges edited between 1946 and 1948. According to Di Giovanni, Borges wrote it in two days in 1947. He was closing an issue of the magazine and discovered he had two pages to fill. "He commissioned a half-page drawing of the Minotaur on the spot and then sat down and wrote his tale to measure." Knowing Borges' extremely slow process of composition, especially at the time he was writing those stories, it seems hard to believe that he wrote "The House of Asterion" just like that. He probably had some notes, a sketch or a first draft somewhere, and the pressure to fill those two pages must have acted as a spur. But if he actually did complete the story in two days, it might have been because the theme of the labyrinth and its monstrous inhabitant cut very deeply into his own being. Somehow the story began to be written while Georgie was poring over Lemprière's book with the engraving of the labyrinth, believing that if he looked hard enough and with a magnifying glass, he might be able to see poor, sad Asterion.

In identifying himself with the Minotaur, Georgie was paving the way for Borges' future mythology. At the time, he probably felt, somewhat obscurely, that he was a bit like Asterion. He didn't live alone in a palace built like a labyrinth; but his garden was a labyrinth, and from its gates he could watch strange people moving around in the streets, busy with their mysterious errands, different, alien. Inside the garden life was simpler. Only at night, when the garden was closed and it was time to go to bed, did the horrors of everyday life take over. From mirrors came terror. The other self was waiting there, shapeless and green-colored. These were the really old myths, "the shadow of other dreams still more full of horror" that Borges talks about in his piece on the Minotaur in *The Book of Imaginary Beings*.

Georgie even had with him (like the imaginary double with which Asterion played) a carnal double, his sister, Norah, always ready to participate in his games and to share his dreams and obsessions. But her more important function—that of protecting him against a ruthless and invisible enemy—is also presented, in symbolic form, in the myth of the Minotaur. At the end of "The House of Asterion" Borges quietly incorporates this new element. The last paragraph of the story says:

> The morning sun glinted off the bronze sword.
> It no longer showed even a trace of blood.
> "Would you believe it, Ariadne?" said Theseus.
> "The Minotaur barely put up a fight."
> (*Review*, 1973, p. 64)

The Minotaur's reaction can be explained by the fact that he believed Theseus to be his redeemer. And up to a point he was right, because Theseus' function was to free him from his monstrosity. Death was a liberation. In shifting the narrative focus from Asterion's monologue to an impersonal narrator who follows very closely Theseus' actions and words, Borges also shifts his allegiances and those of his reader. The protagonist of the story is no longer Asterion but Theseus. And from this new point of view, Asterion is reduced to a monster that had to be slain. But that is not the real meaning of the shift. What Borges insinuates is that Asterion and Theseus are doubles: two sides of the same personality. Asterion's sacrifice or redemption is really a metamorphosis: out of the labyrinth comes Theseus, the new Asterion.

A new character is introduced obliquely at the end of the story: Ariadne, the invisible and silent presence to whom Theseus' words are addressed. She is the daughter of Minos and Pasiphae, and in giving Theseus the thread to get safely out of the labyrinth, she goes against her father's authority. She is also an ambiguous, or double, character. In helping Theseus to kill the Minotaur, she seems to be against her half-brother. But as Theseus is also the redeemer, her action is finally beneficial to the Minotaur. In her duplicity, Ariadne stands for Norah: both were linked to their brothers by blood; their function was to protect the best part of them. Both succeeded in bringing them alive out of the labyrinth.

As happens in dreams, each section of the story shifts points of view and changes the identity of the characters. The stories told by dreams play on permutation and metamorphoses. In the dreams written by authors, the same happens. Out of those dreams, and the day-dreamings of childhood, tales are written. Thus in 1947 Borges could compose in two days a story Georgie probably never told anybody but endlessly and symbolically rehearsed with the help of Norah, his playmate, his Ariadne, his guide in the labyrinth of his inner self.

7.
The Italian Quarter

Before Norah was born, the Borgeses moved to Palermo, a poor neighborhood on the outskirts of Buenos Aires. Georgie was only two. In a poem written in 1929 and explicitly dedicated to "The Mythological Foundation of Buenos Aires" (he changed the adjective later to "Mythical"), Borges tells how he discovered his native city: first, in the history books he read at school; later, through his own experience. The identification of the poet with his city is made explicit in the fourth stanza, where he disputes the history books' claim that Buenos Aires was founded in the Riachuelo district:

> but that is a story dreamed up in the Boca.
> It was really a city block in my district—Palermo.
>
> A whole square block, but set down in open country,
> attended by dawns and rains and hard southeasters.
> identical to that block which still stands in my neighborhood:
> Guatemala—Serrano—Paraguay—Gurruchaga.
> *(Poems, 1972, translated by Alastair Reid, pp. 48–49)*

The city block he mentions is where his home stood—at 2135 Serrano Street. In a 1964 conversation with Napoleon Murat he gives these recollections of Palermo:

> When I was a boy, the town ended there, fifty yards from our home. There was a rather dirty stream which was called Maldonado, then some empty lots, and the town began again at Belgrano. What was in between the Pacific bridge and Belgrano was not the countryside, that word would be too beautiful, but empty lots, and villas. The neighborhood was very poor. At Serrano Street there were only three two-story houses with patios. One had the

48

feeling of being at the edge of town. When I wrote the biography of Carriego, I looked for old folks and they told me a lot of stories of those days, stories that had to do with the tango, etc. However, and this is rather strange, I do not have personal memories of those things. . . . (Murat, 1964, p. 373)

In his 1930 biography of Carriego, a popular neighborhood poet, Borges also included a description of Palermo as it might have been in the late nineteenth century. In his description there is perhaps an echo of how the place looked to Georgie some years later. Using and perhaps abusing the rhetorical device called hypallage—in which a quality of one object is displaced to another object—Borges writes:

Toward the boundary with Balvanera in the east, there were sprawling houses with strings of patios, the sprawling yellow or ocher houses with an arched door—an arch which was mirrored by another arch in the inner door of the house, delicately cast in iron. When the impatient nights of October took chairs and people out to the sidewalks and the profound houses opened up for inspection their backyards, and there was a yellow light in the patios, the street was cozy and light and the empty houses were like lanterns in a row. (*Carriego,* 1930, p. 20)

But perhaps those recollections were purely literary, carefully made up of words drawn from Carriego's verses or writings about his life. Writing much later, when he was seventy, Borges included in his "Autobiographical Essay" memories that confirm, or elaborate on, what he had already said to Napoleon Murat:

I cannot tell whether my first memories go back to the eastern or to the western bank of the muddy, slow-moving Río de la Plata—to Montevideo, where we spent long, lazy holidays in the villa of my uncle Francisco Haedo, or to Buenos Aires. I was born there, in the very heart of that city, in 1899, on Tucumán Street, between Suipacha and Esmeralda, in a small, unassuming house belonging to my maternal grandparents. . . . We must have moved out to the suburb of Palermo quite soon, because there I have my first memories of another house with two patios, a garden with a tall windmill pump, and on the other side of the garden an empty lot. Palermo at that time—the Palermo where we lived, Serrano and Guatemala—was on the shabby northern outskirts of town, and many people, ashamed of saying they lived there, spoke in a dim way of living on the Northside. We lived in one of the few two-story homes on our street; the rest of the neighborhood was made up of low houses and vacant lots. I have often spoken of this area as a slum, but I do not quite mean that in the American sense of the word. In Palermo lived shabby, genteel people as well as more undesirable sorts. There was also a Palermo of hoodlums, called *compadritos,* famed for their knife fights, but this Palermo was only later to capture my imagination, since we did our best—our successful best—to ignore it. Unlike our neighbor Evaristo Carriego, however, who was the first Argentine poet to explore the literary possibilities that lay there at hand. As for myself, I was hardly aware of the existence of *compadritos,* since I lived essentially indoors. ("Essay," 1970, pp. 203–204)

Although Georgie's knowledge of Palermo was limited, some of the neighborhood's most colorful aspects caught the boy's attention. In the poem dedicated to his home garden, Borges gives tantalizing glimpses of what could be seen from the garden or from the second floor of their house. He talks about the horse carriages and the carnival, the sound of popular music and the hoodlums who hung around the general store: a world teeming with strange, almost exotic life. The Borgeses were doubly alienated from Palermo: they were half English and came from old Argentine stock. Palermo, on the contrary, was a town where immigrants settled, a kind of no-man's land where the "poor but respectable" working class lived next door to petty criminals whose energies were devoted to pimping, whoring, and random violence.

As its name indicates, Palermo had Italian origins. According to one source quoted by Borges in his biography of Carriego, the neighborhood took its name from an Italian called Domenico who changed his name into the more Spanish Domínguez and added the name of his native town, Palermo, as homage. This happened in the early seventeenth century. Two centuries later, the Italian immigrants who came to Argentina chose that neighborhood, perhaps because of its name, perhaps because it was cheap and not too far from the downtown area. In his reminiscences Borges never mentions the Italians or the Italian origin of the word "Palermo," possibly because he was writing for an Argentine audience that already had that information. The only proof that he was aware of the Italians in the Palermo of his childhood is one specific mention of the Calabrese in his reminiscences with Napoleon Murat, already quoted. But why the Calabrese and not the Neapolitans or the Genovese? In his book on Carriego there is a short explanation; in describing the Maldonado, a small and dirty stream close to his home, Borges writes: "Toward the Maldonado, native hoodlums were scarce, their places taken by the Calabrese, people with whom nobody wanted to get involved because of the dangerously long time they bore grudges or the long-lasting scars of their knifings" (*Carriego,* 1930, p. 22).

To understand Borges' prejudice against the Italians it is necessary to point out that in the years before Borges was born, Argentina had a predominantly Spanish population. Borges' ancestors on both sides had their roots in the colonial period: warriors who had conquered the land, settlers who had tamed it, heroes who had fought to free it from Spain and from local tyrants. They were the icons of Borges' family museum. But these pious traditions clashed brutally with Argentine reality at the turn of the century. Some eight million Italians had come to the River Plate area in the last decades of the nineteenth century. They were peasants from the poorest parts of Italy, illiterate and hungry, and they viewed Argentina as the new El Dorado. The Argentine government had opened up the country to them because it needed them to populate the vast spaces of the pampas, to till the fields, to work in the new factories. President Sarmiento had initiated this policy, which he took (with so many other things) from the United States. As happened also in the United States, the Italian immigrants began to influence the national character. By the time Borges was born and his parents had decided to move to Palermo, Buenos Aires was beginning to look like an Italian city. But Georgie knew little of this. He continued to live in his garden, protected from the world outside by his imagination and the stories his English grandmother read to him.

The house where he had been born, close to the downtown area, was still part of the traditional Buenos Aires of people of Spanish stock. But Palermo was already another country. His father's decision to move there must have been prompted by financial considerations. He probably could not afford a two-story house with a garden in any other part of Buenos Aires. Borges recalled many years later that many "shabby, genteel people" lived there. What he does not say in his "Essay" is that many of these people were Italians.

Today it is hard to understand his omission. The Italian component of Argentine culture is so strong that it seems impossible not to acknowledge it. But in a symbolic sense Georgie never left Father's library of English books or Mother's secluded Hispanic garden. Although he later learned Italian well enough to read and reread Dante, Ariosto, and Croce, he has always maintained that he cannot understand spoken Italian; he has claimed he seldom goes to see an Italian movie because he cannot follow the dialogue. (Subtitles have always been too small for him to read.) His prejudice is as strong as the one he holds against Spaniards. The roots are similar. In Borges' household the language of culture and refinement was English. Spanish was only second best, because it was the language of servants and illiterate people. Italian was not even considered. It was the language of peasants who could not speak it properly and had little to do with the great Italian poets and novelists. Georgie refused to even acknowledge its existence. He might have heard a few words of Italian slang in the conversations between servants and delivery boys, but he fails to acknowledge even this, possibly because the Italians corrupted not only their own language (the tongue of Dante and Petrarch) but also Argentine Spanish.

The slang spoken in the slums of Buenos Aires was called *lunfardo* (from *lunfa*, a petty thief). Experts agree that it was not a language but an argot: words and idioms used to hide more than reveal what the speakers were saying. It had the same origin as the famous language of Germania, spoken by Spanish soldiers who came home from the German wars of the sixteenth century and widely used in picaresque novels, even in *Don Quixote*. *Lunfardo* was metaphorical, vivid, and colorful, and it spread to all classes of Argentine society mainly through tango lyrics and the short fiction and popular theater of the day. In a 1927 lecture called "El idioma de los argentinos" (The Language of the Argentines), later collected in a book of the same title, Borges has this to say:

> There is no general dialect of our popular classes: the language spoken in the slums is not it. The old native Argentines do not use it, women seldom speak it, even the local hoodlums only parade it to look tougher. The vocabulary is extremely poor: it is formed by some twenty concepts, and a sick proliferation of synonyms complicates it. So narrow is it that the popular playwrights have to invent words and have even resorted to the very telling ingenuity of inverting the common ones. That destitution is not normal, because the language of the slums is nothing but a decantation or divulgation of *lunfardo*, which is a jargon invented to conceal what thieves had to say. *Lunfardo* is a trade vocabulary, as with so many others; it is the technology of the *furca* (half-Nelson or lock) and the skeleton key. (*Idioma*, 1928, pp. 166–167)

Once more, Borges avoids mentioning the linguistic components of *lunfardo*. It was based on Spanish but with a strong Italian influence, plus some specific words from the argot used by French pimps and whores. Those were the days when a French prostitute was highly prized and a profitable traffic was established between Marseilles and Buenos Aires. That part of *lunfardo* was as technical (to use Borges' expression) as one could desire. But if Borges omits mention of Italian or French, it is only because he is more interested in other things. In the book on Carriego written in 1930 he says very little about *lunfardo*. Carriego, who was born in the provinces, used it sparingly. Only a few of his writings are cited in José Gobello's excellent *Lunfardía* (1953). More probably exist, but for the most part Carriego used the common speech of Buenos Aires and not a limited patois. And that is what Borges was interested in proving.

In reissuing the book some twenty-five years later, Borges added a few new pieces. The most important is "History of the Tango," in which he rewrites and updates an article published in 1927 under the title "Progeny of the Tango." As the most popular music produced in the River Plate area, the tango has come to symbolize Argentina. Borges deplored this identification, primarily because the most widely known tango form is not the one he likes best (or dislikes least, to be more precise). The popular tango is either the choreographed version Valentino illustrated in the Paris sequence of *The Four Horsemen of the Apocalypse* (Metro, 1920) or the sentimental ballad forever associated with the name of Carlos Gardel, the Sinatra of that era. Borges considered the Paris version a fake. The tango was born in the brothels of Montevideo and Buenos Aires and for decades was considered too obscene to be danced in public. Only the hoodlums dared to dance it in the streets, and then both dancers were always men. For Borges, the Valentino version was despicable. His opinion of Gardel was no less critical. He believed that the sentimentality of the lyrics the singer had made so popular and his affected delivery of them ruined a music which could easily do without lyrics. Against the most popular topics of tango lyrics (unmanly lament for a lost love or a betrayal), Borges stresses in his writings that the tango originated in the rivalry among hoodlums, confronting each other in a game of power, violence, and deadly skills. The fact that the tango began in brothels had served to emphasize its heterosexual connotations. But men do not go to brothels just to meet women; they also go to meet, and compete, with other men. The men who danced the tango in the streets were engaged in a show of physical skill with sexual undertones.

In "History of the Tango" Borges reports that "as a boy I could see in Palermo, and years later in Chacarita and Boedo, that it was danced on the streetcorners by couples of men, because working-class women didn't want to have anything to do with a tramp's dance" (*Carriego*, 1955, p. 145).

This brief glimpse of Georgie, at the garden gate or in the street, watching a couple of hoodlums going through the elaborate motions of the tango is tantalizing. The boy couldn't have had a precise idea of what he was seeing, except that it was a very reprehensible activity because not even working-class women would stoop to it. At the time Georgie was living in Palermo, the tango had not yet become fashionable in Europe, and upper-class Buenos Aires society, as well as the respectable poor, rejected it completely. Both the upper and the lower classes were right to do so, because in aiming at respectability they rejected physical violence. But the hoodlums could survive only through violence. And sexual violence as it was practiced in the brothel was not too far from the violence men did to each other in their fights for supremacy. The tango, according to Borges, expressed both sides of the coin:

> The sexual character of the tango was noticed by many, but not its quarrelsome nature. It is true that both are modes or manifestations of the same impulse, and thus the word *man,* in all the languages I know, has a connotation both of sexual capacity and fighting capacity, and the word *virtus,* which in Latin means courage, comes from *vir,* which is man. Similarly, in one of *Kim*'s pages, an Afghan states: "When I was fifteen, I had shot my man and begot my man," as if the two acts were essentially the same. (Ibid., pp. 146–147)

In this interpretation the tango is not only an elaborate ritual to conceal and reveal the mating urge; it is also a test of manliness, a close fight (body against body) with a rival as skillful and powerful as oneself. The latent homosexual component of that fight, on which Borges does not comment, is thus made visible.

In criticizing the tango, Borges has some good words to say about one of the tango's ancestors, the milonga. Although it never attained the tango's international fame, the milonga is considered superior by some aficionados. Its rhythm is quicker; it avoids elaborate footwork and requires a certain agility. And its lyrics are generally free of sentimentality. In his later years Borges composed lyrics for some milongas, celebrating the courage and skill of the infamous hoodlums.

In "History of the Tango" Borges rectifies his earlier view of Italian immigrants:

> I recall that around 1926 I was fond of attributing to the Italians . . . the decline of the tango. In that myth, or fantasy, of a "native" tango ruined by the "wops," I see now a clear symptom of some nationalistic heresies which later ravaged the world—promoted by the "wops," of course. It was not the accordion, which I once called cowardly, nor the dutiful composers of the waterfront which made the tango what it is, but the whole nation. Besides, the old native folk who engendered the tango were called Bevilacqua, Greco, or de Bassi. (Ibid., p. 162)

Besides an occasional glimpse of two hoodlums dancing an elaborate dance on a streetcorner, Georgie had few contacts with the tango and its world. One of these may have been John Tink, an authentic hoodlum who was a cousin of Miss Tink, Georgie's English governess. Like so many of Borges' heroes and heroines, John Tink was a soul divided between two loyalties: to a European tradition of culture represented by his cousin, and to a native, more barbarous experience. As with the English captive in Borges' tale "The Story of the Warrior and the Captive," John Tink was ensnared by the environment and became "Juan Tink, el inglés," one of the hoodlums who hung around streetcorners (De Milleret, 1967, p. 23). It is not known how much Georgie knew about him, nor with what Victorian sternness Miss Tink reacted to her cousin's fate. What is known is that the only hoodlum Georgie saw at close quarters was an Englishman. Not until years later, upon writing his biography of Carriego, would Borges come across the real native product.

Georgie met one other representative of the tango and its strange world. One of his paternal cousins, Alvaro Melián Lafinur, was a minor writer and a bit of a bohemian. He had relatives in Uruguay and apparently had a wide experience of brothels on both sides of the River Plate. Alvaro, like Prince Danilo in Strauss' *Merry Widow*, burned his candle at both ends. In his escapades he did not confine himself to prostitutes; maidens, married women, and widows were also fair game. From Alvaro, Georgie gained some tantalizing glimpses of a life he would experience briefly during his residence in Spain. Alvaro was also very fond of tangos and, accompanied by his own guitar, used to sing them on the Sundays he came to visit the Borgeses.

Thus a whiff of the forbidden world outside the garden reached Georgie every once in a while.

8.
The Other Bank of
the River

Borges had few memories of the Palermo quarter where he lived as a child, but among his most vivid recollections were the holidays spent with his family in Uruguay, on the other bank of the River Plate. Every February, when Father was on vacation, the Borgeses crossed the muddy, wide river to spend a whole month at the villa of Mother's cousin Francisco Haedo. The villa was located on the outskirts of Montevideo in Paso Molino (literally: the pass to the mill). Once a rural village, Paso Molino, by the beginning of the twentieth century, was a small town that had been swallowed by Montevideo. In those days South Americans were just beginning to discover the beauty of a suntan and the stimulation of sea air. Beaches and all the amenities of the coastline had until then been left to fishermen and beachcombers. Since respectable grown-ups did not spend much time on the coast, the children had to amuse themselves in the garden surrounding the villa, one considerably larger than the garden at Palermo. Francisco's daughter, Esther, became a valued and trusted participant in Georgie and Norah's games. She was always willing to help Norah to come to the boy's defense against unseen but ever present enemies.

Summer days (which in that part of the world correspond exactly to winter in the Northern hemisphere) were long and lazy, made tolerable only by the children's imagination. When the heat was unbearable—and it can be unbearable in the months of January and February in the low-lying, humid River Plate basin, where the big tropical rivers of the south come finally to the sea—the children were taken to the river banks and neighboring Capurro beach. In those days Capurro still had some pretensions to gentility. There were villas and a promenade overlooking the River Plate, which at that point is so wide that it is impossible to see the Argentine bank. Nearby, as a backdrop to the beach, the volcanolike structure of Montevideo's small Cerro could be seen. This modest, conical hill, topped by a Spanish fortress, probably gave the town its name. (One of the etymologies of Montevideo is *monte vide eu,* which perhaps meant "I have seen a mountain," a statement attributed to one of Magellan's Portuguese sailors, who discovered it in 1519.) The children were probably taken to see the fortress, a sturdy building constructed by the Spaniards in 1724 to contain and control the already worrisome Portuguese expansion southward from Brazil.

Today Capurro is a slum. The whole Cerro area has become part of a working-class town, with meat-packing factories and tenements, big oil tanks, and an active traffic of small vessels. There is a busy crowd now where ladies and gentlemen of the Belle Epoque once strolled with their children, their dogs, and their servants. A French engineer, visiting Montevideo in the first decade of the twentieth century, made a quick inspection of the shoreline and recommended to President Batlle (the man who shaped modern Uruguay) that the city be developed not toward the west or the north but toward the east. There, a string of beaches with the softest white sand and invigorating breezes coming from the Atlantic Ocean made the summer bearable. President Batlle took the advice to heart, and in implementing it he created one of the sources of Uruguayan prosperity for decades to come. Summer resorts eventually extended along the entire northern bank of the River Plate toward the Atlantic and the Brazilian frontier.

But when the Borgeses went summering in Paso Molino, all this belonged to the future. Instead of the wavy coastline of Punta del Este and La Paloma, they met only the sweet and mildly polluted waters of Capurro. Many years later Borges celebrated the river with a famous line in his poem "The Mythological Founding of Buenos Aires," calling it "that torpid, muddy river" (*Poems,* 1972, p. 49). In the Spanish text the river is described not as "torpid" but as "sleepy." The River Plate must have seemed sleepy and muddy to Georgie every summer. The usual way of crossing the river in those days was on a large ferryboat with paddles which took no less than twelve hours to reach Montevideo. It had elegant drawing rooms and a good restaurant, with comfortable first-class cabins. It left Buenos Aires in the evening and reached Montevideo in the early hours of the next morning. Adults used to stay awake all night—to see dawn, they claimed, but probably to get drunk and/or do some explorations of their own in the darkest corners of the boat. But children, after having exhausted the possibilities of adventure on the many staircases and corridors, were sent to bed.

The Haedos came from the northwest and had a ranch near

Fray Bentos, on the Uruguay River. (Uruguay gets its name from that river, which separates it from Argentina and runs almost directly northward into the River Plate.) The Borgeses used to go to the ranch in the summer. Many years later, in a short story called "Funes, the Memorious," Borges evoked some memories of the San Francisco ranch and the Haedos, although placing the anecdote in a time, 1884, when he had not yet been born. Georgie learned to swim on the waters of the Uruguay River. They were swift, live waters, and only a strong swimmer could withstand the currents. Georgie became a very good swimmer. Fifteen years later, when swimming in the Rhone in Geneva or, even later, in the Mediterranean, he boasted of his early training in the swift waters of the Uruguay. (He also boasts about his swimming skills in his "Autobiographical Essay," p. 219.)

Georgie did some swimming too in a small stream close to the Paso Molino villa. The water there was not so swift and thus was less challenging, but the children welcomed the chance to escape from the heat of the summer. Either on the Uruguay or in the small stream in Paso Molino, Georgie spent part of each summer practicing the only sport he really liked. Only when forced by his poor eyesight, following an accident in which the retina of one of his eyes was separated, did he give up swimming for good. Borges' poem "Poema del cuarto elemento" ("Poem to the Fourth Element") echoes these childhood experiences:

> Water, I beg you. For this sleepy
> Chain of numbered words I am telling you,
> Remember Borges, your swimmer, your friend,
> Do not make yourself scarce at the very last moment.
> (*Obra*, 1964, p. 151)

On the Uruguayan bank life seemed easier. Georgie always considered Uruguay, and especially Montevideo, more traditional than Buenos Aires, more authentically rooted in the River Plate's history and old ways. Years later, in a poem originally published in 1924 and later collected in *Moon Across the Way* (1925), Borges expressed his feelings for the town that belonged to him through his Acevedo and Haedo ancestors:

> You are the Buenos Aires we had, the one that quietly went away,
> You are backwatery and clear in the afternoon as the memories of a
>   smooth friendship.
> Fondness grows in your stones as a humble grass.
> You belong to us, you're like a party, as the star that the waters reflect.
> False exits to time, your streets look at the lightest past.

Light from your morning comes to us, over the sweet muddiness of waters.
Before lighting up my shades your low sun brings happiness to your villas.
City that sounds like a verse.
Streets with patio light.

(Poemas, 1943, pp. 91–92)

"Montevideo" summarizes Borges' feelings for his mother's native country and the hospitality the Haedos always gave him. In the fourth line the Spanish text is even more explicit. It literally says "You are ours and holidaylike"; in the sixth verse there is a description of the slow River Plate waters he had to cross every summer.

Three years after writing that poem, Borges stated in a prologue to Ildefonso Pereda Valdés' *Anthology of Modern Uruguayan Poetry* his rights to be and feel like an Uruguayan:

What is my justification for being at the entrance-door [of this book]? None except that river of Uruguayan blood that goes through my chest; none except for the Uruguayan days there are in my days and whose memories I know I deserve. Those stories—the Montevidean grandfather who left to join the Grand Army in 1851 and lived twenty years of war; the grandmother from Mercedes who united in the same tone of rejection Oribe and Rosas—allow me to participate, in a mysterious but constant way, in Uruguay. Then, there are my memories, also. Many of them ancient, I found, belong to Montevideo; some—a siesta, the smell of wet earth, a different light—I could not tell from which river bank they come. That fusion or confusion, that community, can be beautiful. (Valdés, 1927, pp. 219–220)

The prologue ends by comparing the differing attitude of Argentines and Uruguayans toward their respective countries:

We Argentines live in the lazy conviction of belonging to a great country, a country whose excessive extension makes us visible enough because of the multiplicity of its bulls and the fertility of its plains. If the providential rain and the providential Italian immigrant do not fail us, we will become the Chicago of this side of the planet and even its bakery. But the Uruguayans do not behave like that. Thus, their heroic disposition to differentiate themselves [from us], their persistence in being themselves, their searching and early-rising soul. If on many occasions, they not only search but find, it will be mean to envy them for it. The sun, in the mornings, passes by San Felipe of Montevideo before it comes here. (Ibid., p. 221)

The last words of the prologue (which, by the way, was printed as an epilogue) repeat the image already used in the seventh verse of "Montevideo." But if Borges was then trying to stress both the differences and similarities between the two banks of the River Plate, in another piece written only three years later he erased the distinctions to show what they had in common: the tradition of their origins and development, which both countries share so intimately and which is expressed in Borges' own ancestors. The piece was published as an introduction to a book on the Uruguayan painter Pedro Figari, who lived a very important part of his life in Buenos Aires and painted subjects that belong to both countries: "Figari paints the Argentine memoir. I say *Argentine* and in using that word I am not practicing an absent-minded annexation of Uruguay, but I am making an irreproachable reference to the River Plate, which, unlike the metaphorical one of death, has two banks: the one as Argentine as the other, both selected by my hope" (*Figari*, 1930).

The feeling of these references to Uruguay and his own Montevidean experiences is also reflected in some of his more recent interviews. Here and there, a small detail surfaces from the depths of the past. In talking to Jean de Milleret about the house in which he was born, Borges evokes one of his most peculiar childhood memories: that of a cistern where the rainwater was collected.

At the bottom of the cistern there was a tortoise, to purify the water, people believed. Mother and I have drunk for years that tortoise water without ever thinking about it even though the water was rather "unpurified" by the tortoise. But that was the custom and nobody paid any attention. Nevertheless, when you rented a house you always asked if there was a tortoise in the cistern. . . . But in Montevideo things were different. Estela Canto once told me that they had toads there and not tortoises. Thus, when you were renting a house and asked the question, they answered, "Don't you worry, Madam, there is a toad," and then you drank the rain water purified by that live filter, without any qualms whatsoever. (De Milleret, 1967, pp. 18–19)

In a later interview, with Cesar Fernández Moreno, he refers to the same anecdote and concludes:

The first memories I have are the memories of a garden, a railing, a rainbow, but I don't known on which side of the river they were located. It could be in Palermo, it could be a villa in Adrogué, or it could be the villa of an uncle of mine, Francisco Haedo, in Paso Molino, Montevideo. Yes, they are like that, very vague, and I don't know on which bank of the River Plate to place them: on the east or the west bank. (Fernández Moreno, 1967, p. 8)

To the Uruguayan side of his family Georgie owes another discovery of his childhood: the pampas. Visiting the ranch of one of his Acevedo uncles, he came across a place which had till then loomed larger in his reading than in actual experience. According to the "Autobiographical Essay," he was almost ten when he went to a place near San Nicolás, northwest of Buenos Aires. His recollections are limited but precise: "I remember that the nearest house was a kind of blur on the horizon. This endless distance, I found out, was called the pampa" ("Essay," 1970, pp. 212–213). When he learned that the farmhands were gauchos, Georgie was moved: he had already met them in books, and that fact "gave them a certain glamour." Borges can recall only a few details of the gaucho life Georgie saw:

> Once, I was allowed to accompany them on horseback, taking cattle to the river early one morning. The men were small and darkish and wore *bombachas,* a kind of wide, baggy trouser. When I asked them if they knew how to swim, they replied, "Water is meant for cattle." My mother gave a doll, in a large cardboard box, to the foreman's daughter. The next year, we went back and asked after the little girl. "What a delight the doll has been to her!" they told us. And we were shown it, still in its box, nailed to the wall like an image. Of course, the girl was allowed only to look at it, not to touch it, for it might have been soiled or broken. There it was, high up, put out of harm's way, worshipped from afar. (Ibid., p. 213)

In telling these anecdotes, Borges seems intent on depriving the gauchos of the mythological trappings that a century and a half of regionalist literature had given them. To the poetic image of the gaucho and his habitat, he opposes the commonsense attitude of the real farmhands, who had very limited notions about the country they lived in (swimming doesn't come to their minds) or about the joys of life (a toy becomes an icon). But in stressing only this aspect of gaucho life and reducing the pampas to a vast emptiness, Borges deliberately omits everything that justifies the mythology. Perhaps Georgie was unable to see it at the time, and Borges is now trying to recapture his original perspective. Not until his return from Europe in 1921 could Georgie truly discover his native city and, a few years later, the entire country. The pampas and the gauchos, and all the writers who had written about them, would then be the object of several of his essays. But for Georgie in 1909, the excursion to one of the places where the River Plate nations originated was rather disappointing. He was still very much under the influence of a family who had long memories of fighting the gauchos and the gauchos' hated chieftains: Rosas, López, Jordán, Urquiza. As Borges told Leo Gilson Ribeiro, in one of his most interesting interviews, his mother never spared the gauchos. When she called somebody "a gaucho," it was not as praise: she meant he was "rough, coarse, and illiterate" (Ribeiro, 1970, p. 4).

Little by little, at the garden in Palermo or in the zoo, on the summer excursions to the other bank of the river, and even in the discovery of the pampas, Georgie was collecting the feelings and experiences that would later be essential to Borges. The roots of his rather unexpected regionalism can be found in these modest beginnings.

9.
The House of
the Body

The Borgeses spent some of their summer holidays in Argentina. To avoid humid and hot Buenos Aires, they rented a house in Adrogué, a small town some ten or fifteen miles to the south of the capital. Borges recalls that

> during all these years, we usually spent our summers out in Adrogué . . . where we had a place of our own—a large, one-story house with grounds, two summer houses, a windmill, and a shaggy brown sheepdog. Adrogué then was a lost and undisturbed maze of summer houses surrounded by iron fences with masonry planters on the gate posts, of parks, of streets that radiated out of the many plazas, and of the ubiquitous smell of eucalyptus trees. We continued to visit Adrogué for decades. ("Essay," 1970, p. 212)

The house was located in front of a square. It had a red-tiled roof and a veranda to protect the rooms from excessive heat. In his "Essay" Borges fails to mention the fact that they did not keep the house for long. Although they continued spending their summer holidays in Adrogué, they went instead to the Hotel Las Delicias (The Pleasures), whose long corridors with mirrors and "effusive honeysuckles" are mentioned in "Tlön, Uqbar, Orbis Tertius" as part of the setting for the presentation of Herbert Ashe, a fictitious Englishman modeled on Borges' father.

The real hotel was a sort of neoclassical building, done in the Belle Epoque style, which was probably modeled with due modesty on some half-forgotten Riviera prototype. An engraving done later by Norah, and reproduced in *Borgès par lui même* (Rodríguez Monegal, 1970, pp. 78–79), shows the portico with columns and the niches with half-dressed, or half-undressed nymphs, opening on a patio with black and white diamond-shaped tiles. Alicia Jurado recalls a visit with Borges to the hotel: "I went with him to say good-by to the Adrogué Hotel before it was demolished; we walked in darkness through ravaged floors, glimpsing patios and windows which brought memories to him, sitting on the broken bench of a ruined garden he loved and in a square full of trees and covered with fallen leaves from which he pointed out to me the house they had had for many a summer" (Jurado, 1964, p. 20). This melancholy excursion may have occurred during the 1950s. But long before that Borges had transformed his memories of the hotel into the villa owned by General Berkeley in "The Shape of the Sword": "The house was less than a century old, but it was decayed and shadowy and flourished in puzzling corridors and in pointless antechambers" (*Labyrinths*, 1964, p. 69).

Those few words condense more than the memories of the story's protagonist. Georgie's own astonishment in walking along the seemingly endless and mazelike corridors and antechambers of the Adrogué Hotel is preserved there as well. In another story, "Death and the Compass," Borges creates a nightmarish vision of the hotel to which he probably added a few touches from the Haedo villa at Paso Molino. In the first paragraph of the story he warns the reader that the "intermittent stories of murders which constitute the plot will come to a culmination amid the incessant odor of eucalyptus trees at the villa Triste-le-Roy" (*The Aleph*, 1970, p. 65). In a note to the story he wrote for the American edition he acknowledges that

> Triste-le-Roy, a beautiful name invented by Amanda Molina Vedia, stands for the now demolished Hotel Las Delicias in Adrogué. (Amanda had painted a map of an imaginary island on the wall of her bedroom; on her map I discovered the name Triste-le-Roy.)
> . . . I have embedded many memories of Buenos Aires and its southern outskirts in this wild story. Triste-le-Roy itself is a heightened and distorted version of the roomy and pleasant Hotel Las Delicias, which still survives in so many memories. (Ibid., pp. 268–269)

Perhaps Borges was struck by the name not only because it was beautiful but also because, in its association with the Adrogué Hotel and his childhood games, he could invest it with the terrors of his early years, when he was a prince who had to be protected from some powerful unseen enemy by his sister (the queen mother) and his cousin Esther. In the story's last episode the protagonist, Eric Lönnrot, finally reaches the villa where the fourth murder is going to be committed and discovers that he has fallen into the trap of his archenemy, Red Scharlach; that he is the last victim. Critics have pointed out that Lönnrot and Scharlach are really doubles, a sort of Dr. Jekyll and Mr. Hyde: the detective and the criminal share the same symbolic color, red, which is evident in Scharlach's nickname and barely hidden in Lönnrot's. (*Rot* means red in German and Scandinavian.) Borges relies on his memories of the Adrogué Hotel to describe the villa:

> Night was falling when he saw the rectangular mirador of the villa Triste-le-Roy, almost as tall as the surrounding black eucalyptus trees. . . .
> A rusted iron fence bounded the villa's irregular perimeter. The main gate was shut. Lönnrot, without much hope of getting in, walked completely around the place. Before the barred gate once again, he stuck a hand through the palings—almost mechanically—and found the bolt. The squeal of rusted iron surprised him. With clumsy obedience, the whole gate swung open.
> Lönnrot moved forward among the eucalyptus trees, stepping on the layered generations of fallen leaves. Seen from up close, the house was a clutter of meaningless symmetries and almost insane repetitions: one icy Diana in a gloomy niche matched another Diana in a second niche; one balcony appeared to reflect another; double outer staircases crossed at each landing. A two-faced Hermes cast a monstrous shadow. Lönnrot made his way around the house as he had made his way around the grounds. He went over every detail; below the level of the terrace he noticed a narrow shutter.
> He pushed it open. A few marble steps went down into a cellar. Lönnrot, who by now anticipated the architect's whims, guessed that in the opposite wall he would find a similar set of steps. He did. Climbing them, he lifted his hands and raised a trapdoor.
> A strain of light led him to a window. He opened it. A round yellow moon outlined two clogged fountains in the unkempt garden. Lönnrot explored the house. Through serving pantries and along corridors he came to identical courtyards and several times to the same courtyard. He climbed dusty stairways to circular anterooms, where he was multiplied to infinity in facing mirrors. He grew weary of opening or peeping through windows that revealed, outside, the same desolate garden seen from various heights and various angles; and indoors he grew weary of the rooms of furniture, each draped in yellowing slipcovers, and the crystal chandeliers wrapped in tarlatan. A bedroom caught his attention—in it, a single flower in a porcelain vase. At a touch, the ancient petals crumbled to dust. On the third floor, the last floor, the house seemed endless and growing. The house is not so large, he thought. This dim light, the sameness, the mirrors, the many years, my unfamiliarity, the loneliness are what make it large.
> By a winding staircase he reached the mirador. That evening's moon streamed in through the diamond-shaped panes; they were red, green, and yellow. He was stopped by an awesome, dizzying recollection. (Ibid., pp. 73–75)

The recollection is of the diamond-shaped objects that had been used as emblems in previous murders. Too late, Lönnrot realizes he has fallen into a trap. The rather banal and summery reality of the Adrogué Hotel and (perhaps) the Paso Molino villa has been transformed by Borges' nightmarish imagination into these decayed corridors, these haunted mirrors, these sinister staircases and menacing windowpanes. Perhaps the transformation did not happen in 1942, when Borges published "Death and the Compass" in *Sur,* but much earlier when Georgie was roaming the endless corridors, the symmetrical staircases, the labyrinthine construction that the sedate Adrogué Hotel became in his childhood imagination.

Borges never stopped writing variations on the labyrinthine corridors of the Adrogué Hotel. In two other stories it is possible to see how that playground of his childhood is metamorphosed by the dreams of the adult. In describing the hideous and ruined City of the Immortals in the story "The Immortals," Borges manages to produce a space that is the perversion of all architecture. Before reaching the city, the narrator has a nightmarish experience among some very primitive tribes. He longs to get into the city he can see from afar: "At the foot of the mountain, an impure stream spread noiselessly, clogged with débris and sand; on the opposite bank (beneath the last sun or beneath the first) shone the evident City of the Immortals. I saw walls, arches, façades and fora: the base was a stone plateau" (*Labyrinths,* 1964, p. 108). But soon the protagonist discovers the difficulties of reaching the city.

I had to skirt several irregular ravines which seemed to me like quarries; obfuscated by the City's grandeur, I had thought it nearby. Toward midnight, I set foot upon the black shadow of its walls, bristling out in idolatrous forms on the yellow sand. I was halted by a kind of sacred horror. Novelty and the desert are so abhorred by man that I was glad one of the troglodytes had followed me to the last. I closed my eyes and awaited (without sleeping) the light of day.

I have said that the City was founded on a stone plateau. This plateau, comparable to a high cliff, was no less arduous than the walls. In vain I fatigued myself: the black base did not disclose a single door. The force of the sun obliged me to seek refuge in a cave; in the rear was a pit, in the pit a stairway which sank down abysmally into the darkness below. I went down; through a chaos of sordid galleries I reached a vast circular chamber, scarcely visible. There were nine doors in this cellar; eight led to a labyrinth that treacherously returned to the same chamber; the ninth (though another labyrinth) led to a second circular chamber equal to the first. I do not know the total number of these chambers; my misfortune and anxiety multiplied them. The silence was hostile and almost perfect; there was no sound in this deep stone network save that of a subterranean wind, whose cause I did not discover; noiselessly, tiny streams of rusty water disappeared between the crevices. Horribly, I became habituated to this doubtful world; I found it incredible that there could be anything but cellars with nine doors and long branched-out cellars; I do not know how long I must have walked beneath the ground; I know that I once confused, in the same nostalgia, the atrocious village of the barbarians and my native city, amid the clusters.

In the depths of a corridor, an unforeseen wall halted me; a remote light fell from above. I raised my confused eyes; in the vertiginous, extreme heights I saw a circle of sky so blue that it seemed purple. Some metal rungs scaled the wall. I was limp with fatigue, but I climbed up, stopping only at times to sob clumsily with joy. I began to glimpse capitals and astragals, triangular pediments and vaults, confused pageants of granite and marble. Thus I was afforded this ascension from the blind region of dark interwoven labyrinths into the resplendent city.

I emerged into a kind of little square or, rather, a kind of courtyard. It was surrounded by a single building of irregular form and variable height; to this heterogenous building belonged the different cupolas and columns. Rather than by any other trait of this incredible monument, I was held by the extreme age of its fabrication. I felt that it was older than mankind, than the earth. This manifest antiquity (though in some way terrible to the eyes) seemed to me in keeping with the work of immortal builders. At first cautiously, later indifferently, at last desperately, I wandered up the stairs and along the pavements of the inextricable palace. (Afterwards I learned that the width and height of the steps were not constant, a fact which made me understand the singular fatigue they produced.) "This palace is a fabrication of the gods," I thought at the beginning. I explored the uninhabited interiors and corrected myself: "The gods who built it were mad!" I said it, I know, with an incomprehensible reprobation which was almost remorse, with more intellectual horror than palpable fear. To the impression of enormous antiquity others were added: that of the interminable, that of the atrocious, that of the complexly senseless. I had crossed a labyrinth, but the nitid City of the Immortals filled me with fright and repugnance. A labyrinth is a structure compounded to confuse men; its architecture, rich in symmetries, is subordinated to that end. In the palace I imperfectly explored, the architecture lacked any such finality. It abounded in dead-end corridors, high unattainable windows, portentous doors which led to a cell or a pit, incredible inverted stairways whose steps and balustrades hung downward. Other stairways, clinging airily to the side of a monumental wall, would die without leading anywhere, after making two or three turns in the lofty darkness of the cupolas. I do not know if all the examples I have enumerated are literal; I know that for many years they infested my nightmares; I am no longer able to know if such and such a detail is a transcription of reality or of the forms which unhinged my nights. "This City" (I thought) "is so horrible that its mere existence and perdurance, though in the midst of a secret desert, contaminates the past and the future and in some ways even jeopardizes the stars. As long as it lasts, no one in the world can be strong or happy." I do not want to describe it; a chaos of heterogenous words, the body of a tiger or a bull in which teeth, organs, and heads monstrously pullulate in mutual conjunction and hatred can (perhaps) be approximate images.

I do not remember the stages of my return, amid the dusty and damp hypoges. I only know I was not abandoned by the fear that, when I left the last labyrinth, I would again be surrounded by the nefarious City of the Immortals. I can remember nothing else. This oblivion, now insuperable, was perhaps voluntary; perhaps the circumstances of my escape were so unpleasant that, on some day no less forgotten as well, I swore to forget them. (Ibid., pp. 109–111)

The literary sources of this story are so obvious—Poe's "The Pit and the Pendulum" as well as Richard Burton's books of his journeys in the Near East and Franz Kafka's *The Castle*—that the reader may overlook how much of the story is based on Borges' insomnia, which he suffered from for years. It is the "atrocious lucidity of insomnia" (as he once called it) that the story tries to capture on its surface. But underneath that experience is Borges' nightmarish view of reality. The City of the Immortals is another version of the haunted, abandoned villa he calls Triste-le-Roy in "Death and the Compass," as well as the house where Asterion lives in the story of that name. That is, it is a labyrinth, a hideous place. These stories have at their root a recurring nightmare: the house that protects is also a prison.

Many centuries before Borges was born, an Italian artist engraved a series of nightmarish palaces very much in the style of the City of the Immortals. In calling them *carceri* (prisons), Gianbattista Piranesi revealed their hidden meaning. These monumental ruins of nonexistent palaces, this horrid fabric of brick and stone and stucco, could have been built only in the dreams and terrors of man. Borges has always been very fond of Piranesi and obviously conceived his City of the Immortals along the lines of the etchings. But he was also following another model, one that (for him) was even older: Georgie's unconscious obsessions.

Both "Death and the Compass" and, in a more revealing way, "The Immortals" allude to the experience of being trapped in a labyrinth. In both stories the search for a center becomes the search for a solution. In "Death and the Compass" the answer, when found, is death. In "The Immortals" it is the reverse, immortality, but at the price of total forgetfulness; that is, at the price of the death of memory. Coming out of the labyrinth into the "real" world, the solution is simpler, as "The House of Asterion" shows: there is no way out but through death, and the fact that the story is told from the naïve (and thus comic) point of view of the Minotaur only helps to disguise its horror. Death or forgetfulness is the only way out of the labyrinth. Why? Anzieu has pointed out in his psychoanalytical study that the house is the mother's body, the womb where the child finds his first abode. In Borges' "The Immortals" (as in Poe's "The Pit and the Pendulum") some details of the journey inside the labyrinth have very revealing connotations. When talking about the vast circular chamber through which he would eventually find access to the City of the Immortals, the narrator indicates that it had "nine doors" that led to nine labyrinths, only one of which, "the ninth," did not return to the same chamber. The choice of the number nine and the emphasis put on the ninth indicate the importance of that figure, which corresponds to the nine months of gestation, of life inside the labyrinth of the mother's womb, from which the child is bound to emerge in the ninth month. The other connotations of that secret chamber are also indicative. It is silent except for the sound of wind and water; the way out, when found, is through a remote hole in the ceiling through which the blue, almost purple sky can be seen.

Even the rejection that the City of the Immortals inspires in the narrator corresponds to the rejection of the brutality and violence of the external world that is so common in infants. The loss of memory that follows the experience of discovering the City of the Immortals (that is, of getting into the world) is equally characteristic of the birth trauma. Even in the sinisterly comic version of the same myth in "The House of Asterion" Borges could not refrain from including an allusion to the nine months of gestation. The subconscious identity between the space of these stories, the space of Georgie's and Borges' nightmares, and the mother's womb is clear.

10.
The Infinite
Library

"I have always been a greater reader than a writer," Borges once told Richard Burgin, and he has never tired of recalling the adventure of reading, the inexhaustible source of pleasure and horror books represented to him (Burgin, 1969, p. 4). It all began at home. Father was not only an avid reader but also an aspiring author. He had collected a large library of English books that Georgie's imagination would make as limitless as the universe. Without setting a foot outside, Georgie had the world of fable and romance at hand. He spent the better part of his childhood in the library, and in retrospect, as he grew old, the memories of that library assumed epic proportions. He remembered having spent more time reading Father's books than playing with his sister in the garden or exploring the neighborhood. The library became his habitat.

One of the first occasions on which Borges talks publicly about this library is in the prologue to the second edition of his biography of Evaristo Carriego; there he contrasts the world of books with the real world he had so much trouble in mastering.

For years I believed I had grown up in one of the suburbs of Buenos Aires, a suburb of adventurous streets and visible sunsets. The truth is that I grew up in a garden, behind a speared railing, and in a library of unlimited English books. In every corner of Palermo (I have been told) knives and guitars were teeming, but those who filled my mornings and gave a horrid pleasure to my nights were Stevenson's blind buccaneer, dying under the horses' hoofs, and the traitor who abandoned his friend on the moon, and the time traveler who brought from the future a faded flower, and the spirit incarcerated for centuries in Solomon's jar, and the veiled prophet of Khorassan who hid behind precious stones and silk, his face ravaged by leprosy. (*Carriego*, 1955, p. 9)

This list of his readings does not attempt to be complete. Borges alludes not to the central subjects of the books but to episodes that caught his childhood fancy. Thus Stevenson's *Treasure Island* is identified not by any reference to the protagonist, Jim Hawkins, or his even more famous antagonist, Long John Silver, but through a minor character, the sinister, blind Pew, whose brutal death must have haunted Georgie's nightmares. In Wells' science-fiction masterpiece *The First Men on the Moon* Borges' memory selects not the success of the space journey but the betrayal and fearful destiny of the man left behind; again, in Wells' *The Time Machine,* it is not the conception of a flight through time that he recalls but the inexplicable flower of the future that the time traveler brings back to earth. In an article published in 1945 and later included in *Other Inquisitions* (1952) Borges develops the haunting notion of a flower made of time. It is called "The Flower of Coleridge" and links Wells' invention to James' *The Sense of the Past* and to Coleridge's note on the same subject. The image had sunk deep into Georgie's mind.

The other two books mentioned are older and reflect a different type of literature. To the *One Thousand and One Nights* belongs the story of the genie imprisoned in the bottle; to Thomas Moore's *Lalla Rookh, an Eastern Romance* belongs the story of the veiled prophet of Khorassan. Georgie must have read the first in Father's copy of the unexpurgated Richard Burton translation. Many years later Borges wrote an article, "The Translators of the *One Thousand and One Nights,*" collected in *History of Eternity* (1936), which discusses the merits of the different translations of that book. Moore's silly romance became one of the sources of "The Masked Dyer, Hakim of Merv," a tale written by Borges in 1933 and later included in *A Universal History of Infamy* (1935). Again, what matters is not the sources but what Borges' (and Georgie's) memory selected from them. In the vast, sprawling, and occasionally obscene *One Thousand and One Nights* his memory selected the imprisoned spirit; in *Lalla Rookh* (a book teeming with cloying sentimentality and tepid eroticism), the horrifying face of the leper behind the bejeweled and silky mask. Those were Georgie's images, the ones that haunted him as a child and were more real than the house, the garden, and the slightly dilapidated suburb of Buenos Aires in which he lived.

In recalling those same childhood years for his "Autobiographical Essay," Borges emphasizes the importance of that first contact with English books:

> If I were asked to name the chief event in my life, I should say my father's library. In fact, I sometimes think I have never strayed outside that library. I

can still picture it. It was in a room of its own, with glass-fronted shelves, and must have contained several thousand volumes. Being so nearsighted, I have forgotten most of the faces of that time (perhaps even when I think of my grandfather Acevedo I am thinking of his photograph), and yet I vividly remember so many of the steel engravings in *Chambers' Encyclopaedia* and in the *Britannica.* ("Essay," 1970, p. 209)

A private library of several thousand volumes was not unusual then in the River Plate countries. Public libraries were generally poor and out of date, and carried very few books in languages other than Spanish or French. English was then too exotic, and only a small segment of the population—generally, wealthy people—read it. So readers of English used to collect their own books. A few bookstores catered to them; the most famous was Mitchell's, in the downtown area. Father had a very good excuse to become a book collector. The fact that he acquired the Burton translation of the *Arabian Nights* (a very expensive edition limited to subscribers) proves that for him books were not only to be read. The actual title of that famous translation is *The Book of the Thousand Nights and a Night,* and it was published in seventeen volumes in London around 1885. The volumes contain suggestive illustrations and long, explicit notes about the sexual mores of the Arab world, which explains why its sale was limited to wealthy subscribers. Pornography (or what Mrs. Grundy believed to be pornography) was tolerated in Victorian England only if it was expensive.

In his "Autobiographical Essay" Borges recalls: "The Burton, filled with what was then considered obscenity, was forbidden, and I had to read it hiding up on the roof. But at the time, I was so carried away with the magic that I took no notice whatever of the objectionable parts, reading the tales unaware of any other significance" (ibid., p. 209).

Borges' selective memory omits any mention of the illustrations, which stressed the erotic significance of the book. These illustrations, in a coy academic style, would be considered rather mild today; nevertheless, they were there, opening up a tantalizing perspective for the young child. Nor does he mention Burton's explicit notes, which never tired of discussing some of the most fashionable perversions of the Near East. Mrs. Burton, as is well known, was not amused. Nor, apparently, was Father, because the Burton translation was out of bounds for Georgie. That did not prevent the child from finding a time and place to enjoy the magical erotic tales in private.

There is nothing in the "Autobiographical Essay" about *Lalla Rookh,* which played such an important part in the second prologue to *Evaristo Carriego* and is mentioned by Borges in a note to *A Universal*

History of Infamy. In talking about the sources of "The Masked Dyer, Hakim of Merv," he says: "The Prophet's fame in the West is owed to a long-winded poem by Thomas Moore, laden with all the sentimentality of an Irish patriot" (*Infamy,* 1972, p. 79).

The story of the veiled prophet is only one of the four tales told by Moore in *Lalla Rookh;* instead of concentrating his narrative on the prophet, Moore prefers the point of view of one of his captives, Zelica, who had to face a destiny worse than death at the hands of the prophet. Forty lines are devoted to the seduction of poor Zelica by the sadistic fiend. After a short introduction in which he stresses the links that tie Zelica to him and makes mockery of their wedding—

> Yes, my sworn bride, let others seek in bow'rs
> Their bridal place—the charnel vault was ours!

—before taking her to the harem, he unveils his face:

> And now thou seest my *soul*'s angelic hue,
> 'Tis time these *features* were uncurtain'd too—
> This brow, whose light—o rare celestial light!
> Hath been reserv'd to bless thy favour'd sight;
> These dazzling eyes, before whose shrouded might
> Thou'st seen immortal Man kneel down and quake—
> Would that they *were* heaven's lightnings for his sake!
> But turn and look—then wonder, if thou wilt,
> That I should hate, should take revenge, by guilt,
> Upon the hand, whose mischief or whose mirth
> Sent me thus maim'd and monstrous upon earth;
> And on that race who, though more vile they be
> Than mowing apes, are demigods to me!
> Here—judge if hell, with all its power to damn,
> Can add one curse to the foul thing I am!—
> He rais'd his veil—the Maid turn'd slowly round,
> Look'd round at him—shriek'd—and sank upon the ground!
> (Moore, 1929, pp. 359–360)

The image of the lepered prophet remained in Georgie's imagination long enough to become the source of a tale written some twenty-five years later; but instead of developing the sado-masochistic destiny of the prophet along the romantic lines indicated by Moore, Borges develops the almost metaphysical problem of appearance and reality expressed by the gold mask over the leprous face. Again, what attracts him is the monster that lurks inside, like the Minotaur in his labyrinth. In Borges' story, "The Masked Dyer Hakim of Merv," only a few references to the prophet's excesses of the flesh remain. One has already been discussed here: his belief that mirrors and fatherhood are abominable. The other is equally terse but more ironic: "The petty tasks of government were delegated to six or seven devotees. Ever mindful of serenity and meditation, the Prophet kept a harem of a hundred and fourteen blind women, who did their best to satisfy the needs of his divine body" (*Infamy*, 1972, p. 83).

Another book may have added to Georgie's horror of masks and mirrors. In talking to Jean de Milleret, he recalls:

> There was a book which also made me afraid, especially its illustrations. I believe its title is *The Viscount of Bragelonne*, in which there is the Iron Mask. There was an engraving which represented a nobleman with the Iron Mask who was promenading very sadly on a terrace over the sea, I believe; and all that frightened me. That got mixed up with a Moore poem on the veiled prophet of Khorassan, who was a leper. Those two images—the idea of the Persian veiled prophet and the idea of the Iron Mask—all that went together and frightened me. (De Milleret, 1967, pp. 24–25)

Although this is the only time Borges has ever mentioned reading Alexandre Dumas' crowded novel, it is singular that he chose that particular episode. *Le vicomte de Bragelonne* is the third and last book in the Musketeers saga. It is an episodic novel, full of incidents. One of the episodes concerns the Iron Mask, a famous political prisoner during Louis XIV's time who was condemned to wear a mask over his face to avoid identification. For reasons of his own, and against historical evidence, Dumas made him into the king's twin brother. But what Borges remembers is not the plot but the vivid image of the Iron Mask's loneliness, an image that can be linked to Watts' painting of the Minotaur, which spawned "The House of Asterion." A masked Persian prophet, the Iron Mask, the Minotaur: Georgie's heroes have two traits in common—monstrosity and loneliness.

In the "Autobiographical Essay" Borges gives a list of childhood reading: "The first novel I ever read through was *Huckleberry Finn*. Next came *Roughing It* and *Flush Days in California*. I also read books by Captain Marryat, Wells' *First Men on the Moon*, Poe, a one-volume edition of Longfellow, *Treasure Island*, Dickens, *Don Quixote*, *Tom Brown's School Days*, Grimm's *Fairy Tales*, Lewis Carroll, *The Adventures of Mr. Verdant Green* (a now forgotten book), Burton's *A Thousand Nights and a Night*" ("Essay," 1970, p. 209). The list is singular not only for the books not mentioned in previous listings but also for the ones it omits. In the *Evaristo Carriego* prologue he alludes to only five books, all English, even if one (the Burton) is only a translation. Sixteen years later, in mentioning his childhood readings, he omits two of the books alluded to in 1955: Wells' *The Time Machine* and Moore's *Lalla Rookh*. If these omissions are puzzling, no less intriguing is the inclusion of a title such as *The Adventures of Mr. Verdant Green, an Oxford Freshman,* written by Edward Bradley and originally published in 1853–1857. It is the only mention in the vast Borgesian corpus of such a forgotten novel. Other titles are more predictable: Grimm's *Fairy Tales* and Captain Marryat's works were the usual fare for children of those days, along with Dickens' novels, *Tom Brown's School Days,* Lewis Carroll's Alice books, and the already mentioned Wells' *Time Machine* and Stevenson's *Treasure Island.*

What is really new in the 1970 list is the place taken by North American authors. In an interview with Rita Guibert, Borges stresses the importance of his North American readings: "From those days of my childhood in which I read Mark Twain, Bret Harte, Hawthorne, Jack London, Edgar Allan Poe, I have been very fond of the United States and I am still fond of it" (Guibert, 1973, p. 49).

In both lists the first author mentioned is Mark Twain. In an earlier interview with Ronald Christ, Borges says:

> Look here, I'm talking to an American: there's a book I *must* speak about— nothing unexpected about it—that book is *Huckleberry Finn.* I thoroughly dislike *Tom Sawyer.* I think that Tom Sawyer spoils the last chapters of *Huckleberry Finn.* All those silly jokes. They are all pointless jokes; but I suppose Mark Twain thought it was his duty to be funny, even when he wasn't in the mood. The jokes had to be worked in somehow. According to what George Moore said, the English always thought: "Better a bad joke than no joke." I think that Mark Twain was one of the really great writers but I think he was rather unaware of the fact. But perhaps in order to write a really great book, you *must* be rather unaware of the fact. (Christ, 1967, p. 132)

The same year, in a manual written with the help of Esther Zemborain de Torres, Borges dedicated a few lines to *Huckleberry Finn:* "From this great book, which abounds in admirable evocations of mornings and evenings and of the dismal banks of the river, there have arisen in time two others whose outline is the same—*Kim* (1901) by Kipling and *Don Segundo Sombra* (1926) by Ricardo Güiraldes" (*American Literature,* 1971, p. 37).

Georgie obviously found much to his liking in *Huckleberry Finn.* His experience of both banks of the wide River Plate, the lazy summers spent at Paso Molino or at Fray Bentos, on the banks of the Uruguay River, must have provided the necessary elements for an identification. And the fact that Borges would comment on his hatred for the good Tom Sawyer and would reject Mark Twain's feeble attempts at developing a plot at the end of the book indicates very clearly that what

Georgie loved was the free flow of the narrative, its dreamy pastoral quality.

Of the other North American authors mentioned, Borges singles out Bret Harte. As evidence of his interest, he wrote a preface to a Spanish version of Harte's California tales. In it he defends Harte against DeVoto's accusation that he was "a literary charlatan." He argues that the critic was trying to debunk Harte to exalt Mark Twain. At the end of his preface Borges stresses a faculty that Bret Harte shared with Chesterton and Stevenson: "the invention (and the bold design) of memorable visual traits. Perhaps the most strange is one that I read when I was twelve and that will follow me, I know, to the end of the road: the white and black card nailed by a firm blade to the trunk of the monumental tree, over the body of John Oakhurst, gambler" (*Prólogos*, 1975, p. 83).

But the best proof of how much Harte and Mark Twain impressed Georgie can be found in one of the tales included in *A Universal History of Infamy*, "The Dread Redeemer Lazarus Morell." Although he was probably much older when he read the two books listed as sources at the end of the volume—Mark Twain's *Life on the Mississippi* and Bernard DeVoto's *Mark Twain's America*—the melodramatic, almost Gothic vision and the terse, epigrammatic imagery of Borges' story are rooted in Georgie's readings of Harte and Twain. The other two North American authors he mentions—Hawthorne and Jack London—left different traces. About the first he wrote one of his most elaborate essays, published in *Other Inquisitions* (1952); to the second he devoted exactly one page of his *Introduction to American Literature*, filled with biographical data but also containing a very personal selection of works:

> He died at forty, leaving behind some fifty volumes. Of these we shall mention *The People of the Abyss*, for which he personally explored the low quarters of London; *The Sea Wolf*, whose leading character is a sea captain who preaches and practices violence; and *Before Adam*, a novel on a prehistoric theme, whose narrator recovers in fragmentary dreams the troubled days through which he had lived during a previous incarnation. Jack London also wrote admirable adventure stories and some fantastic tales, among which is "The Shadow and the Flash," which tells of the rivalry and the final duel of two invisible men. His style is realistic, but he re-creates and exalts a reality of his own. The vitality which permeated his life also permeates his work, which will continue to attract young readers. (*American Literature*, 1971, pp. 38–39)

It is possible that Borges' selection did not coincide with Georgie's, to whom *White Fang* and *The Call of the Wild* may have been more appealing. In his reevaluation of London's works, he devotes half the space he gives Mark Twain but twice what he dedicates to Bret Harte. The inclusion of Longfellow's poetry in the "Autobiographical Essay" list may have more to do with Father's love for his poetry than with Georgie's own taste. Longfellow rates only half a page in the *Introduction to American Literature*. One sentence summarizes Borges' opinion: "Many of the compositions of his book *Voices of the Night* [1839] won him the affection and admiration of his contemporaries, and they still endure in the anthologies. Reread now, they leave us the impression that all they lack is a final touch (ibid., p. 29).

Perhaps the place of honor given by Borges to North American writers in his "Autobiographical Essay" owes something to the fact that the piece was written especially for the North American edition of *The Aleph* (1970). In an interview with Ronald Christ, Borges explicitly indicates how aware he always is of the background of the person to whom he is talking. In spite of that, it is obvious that for Georgie North American and British authors were not basically different: they all shared the language which had become for the child *the* code of reading, the key to the world of desire and imagination. In his daydreaming he may have moved with ease from Stevenson's blind buccaneer to Poe's haunted protagonists, from Huckleberry Finn's madcap adventures to Oliver Twist's more Gothic ones. Myths and nightmares, dreams and romance, all came to him in the language that was Father's and Grandmother's and that, as a reader, he would possess forever.

The only book in the 1970 list that does not belong to the Anglo-Saxon tradition (which could also include Grimm's *Fairy Tales*) was *Don Quixote,* but even that book reached Georgie in an English version. Apparently Father's library lacked the Spanish text:

> When later I read *Don Quixote* in the original, it sounded like a bad translation to me. I still remember those red volumes with the gold lettering of the Garnier edition. At some point, my father's library was broken up, and when I read the *Quixote* in another edition I had the feeling that it wasn't the real *Quixote.* Later, a friend got me the Garnier, with the same steel engravings, the same footnotes, and also the same errata. All those things form part of the book for me; this I consider the real *Quixote.* ("Essay," 1970, pp. 209–210)

It would be easy to dismiss this statement as an exercise in paradox. It is better to recognize in it one of the basic tenets of Borges' poetics: that the reading (not the writing) creates the work. This concept is developed in a famous story written in 1939, "Pierre Menard, Author of the *Quixote,*" later included in *Ficciones* (1944). In imagining a French author who attempts to rewrite Cervantes' masterpiece in its literal entirety, Borges is not only poking fun at the notion of originality but also proving how much to write is to rewrite (that is, to write once more what has already been written) and to what extent to rewrite is simply to read. But for the child, *Don Quixote* was the source of adventure and dreams. One of his earliest attempts at writing preempted Menard's quest. He confides in his "Autobiographical Essay": "My first story was a rather nonsensical piece after the manner of Cervantes, an old-fashioned romance called 'La visera fatal'—The Fatal Helmet" (ibid., p. 211). Many years later, while living in Spain, Borges returned to *Don Quixote* and read it in the original. The book eventually became one of the most influential in developing his concept of narrative.

How much of these readings were under the guidance of Father, or done with his approval? Some books were obviously out of bounds, but it seems reasonable to assume that the majority were suggested by Father and that some books were bought especially for him. Georgie was encouraged to read by Father's example. In *Les mots* (his partial autobiography) Jean-Paul Sartre dwells on the notion that one becomes a writer by sheer imitation. It is even truer that one becomes a reader for the same reason. Georgie had a formidable model at home. But to be the kind of reader he became, more than the impulse to imitate is needed. Because Georgie became an addict. Reading was so much his passion that Mother soon discovered that for punishment when he misbehaved she had only to take away his books. Reading was for him what Valery Larbaud once called "ce vice impuni" (that unpunished vice). But Mother knew best and used books as other parents used candies.

The addiction was made even more dangerous by the fact that the child had weak eyesight. He had inherited the Borges blindness and eventually became the sixth generation to be totally blind. While he was beginning his fantastic explorations in the library of unlimited English books, he could see his own father growing blind. He himself would soon have to resort to glasses. Reading (the unpunished vice) carries its own punishment. To read is to race against blindness; that is, against time. In his ever weakening eyes, Georgie could measure his own time.

11.
The Son

When he was six, Georgie told Father he wanted to be a writer. This statement—reported by Mother (De Milleret, 1967, p. 24)—places exactly the time the child discovered his vocation. It was not unexpected: Georgie had been brought up in a library and spent most of his childhood reading. Borges later told De Milleret that when reading as a child "I tended to identify with the author, or one of his characters; for instance, when I was eleven, I was Lesage or Cervantes" (ibid., p. 21). This precocious identification, not just with the characters (which is rather common) but with the author, reveals his vocation and anticipates those poetic dramatizations in which Borges assumes the persona of Milton or Averroes, Shakespeare or Spinoza. But if the anecdote is eloquent, it tends to simplify a process which, in a sense, was even more dramatic.

Any child models himself on the person he adores. The person Georgie adored was Father, and Father was always a literary man, with a frustrated poetic vocation. Literature was in Father's blood. In his "Autobiographical Essay" Borges recalls:

> A tradition of literature ran through my father's family. His great-uncle Juan Crisóstomo Lafinur was one of the first Argentine poets, and he wrote an ode on the death of his friend General Manuel Belgrano, in 1820. One of my father's cousins, Alvaro Melián Lafinur, whom I knew from childhood, was a leading minor poet and later found his way into the Argentine Academy of Letters. My father's maternal grandfather, Edward Young Haslam, edited one of the first English papers in Argentina, the *Southern Cross,* and was a Doctor of Philosophy or Letters, I'm not sure which, of the University of Heidelberg. Haslam could not afford Oxford or Cambridge, so he made his way to Germany, where he got his degree, going through the whole course in Latin. Eventually, he died in Paraná. ("Essay," 1970, p. 210)

Father himself had tried his hand at several genres. According to Borges, he published "some fine sonnets" after the style of the Argentine poet Enrique Banchs, who was a postsymbolist. He also published a historical novel, *El caudillo* (The Chieftain), while he was living in Majorca in 1921. But the major part of his work remained unpublished and was eventually destroyed by its author; it included a book of essays, a book of Oriental stories ("in the manner of the *Arabian Nights*," according to Borges), and a drama, *Hacia la nada* (Toward Nothingness), "about a man's disappointment in his son" (ibid., p. 211).

Father never considered himself a professional writer. To find time to write, he had to fight against many odds. He was practically an orphan. His own father, Colonel Borges, had been killed in action the same year he was born; his mother, Fanny Haslam, was left with two small children in a foreign country still ravaged by civil war. In reaching adolescence, Father had to choose a more lucrative profession than writing. He read law and eventually devoted himself to this profession. He also taught psychology in the English department of a school of modern languages. But he never really gave up his literary ambitions.

He had another handicap: he belonged to the fifth recorded generation of Borgeses to have very poor eyesight. In the "Autobiographical Essay" his son observes that "blindness ran in my family; a description of the operation performed on the eyes of my great-grandfather, Edward Young Haslam, appeared in the pages of the London medical journal, the *Lancet*" (ibid., p. 250). Grandmother Haslam also became totally blind before dying. Father, in turn, became partially blind in his late thirties. At forty he was forced to retire; and in spite of several operations, he was completely blind for the remaining years of his life. The little he wrote was done in his spare time or dictated when blindness had overcome him. Borges explains the link between Father's frustrated literary ambitions and his: "From the time I was a boy, when blindness came to him, it was tacitly understood that I had to fulfill the literary destiny that circumstances had denied my father. This was something that was taken for granted (and such things are far more important than things that are merely said). I was expected to be a writer" (ibid., p. 211).

This version subtly contradicts what Mother reported to Jean de Milleret, not only because it lacks drama (the child at six declaring to Father he wanted to be a writer) but especially because it changes the accent. In the "Autobiographical Essay" it is not Georgie's decision that matters any longer but Father's. The position of both characters has changed radically: now Father occupies center stage while Georgie becomes his echo. The dramatic situation is different: instead of Siegfried, going out to kill dragons, one has Hamlet, burdened by the task of fulfilling another man's destiny.

Which of the two versions is closer to reality? It is difficult to know. Perhaps one day, when he was six, Georgie stated solemnly to Father: "I want to be a writer." This statement (transformed by Mother's recollection into an "anecedote") does not exclude the other version: a flat statement about what Father took for granted about Georgie's future. The emphasis is on his duty: fate as something inherited. By accepting the destiny of writer as a kind of paternal bequest, Georgie accepts the fact that he is a son. It will be seen later in what a curious and even paradoxical way he fulfills his mandate.

It is difficult to know if Father was *really* a writer or only a man who wanted to be a writer. He may have used circumstances to justify the lack of true literary ambitions; he may have been the kind of person who has the aptitude for a certain esthetic activity but lacks the talent and drive to produce anything valuable. In her reminiscences Mother states bluntly that he "was a very intelligent man, as intelligent as Georgie, but he lacked the genius his son has" (De Milleret, 1967, p. 67).

In a more indirect way Borges also comes to a negative conclusion about Father's work. His conversations with Richard Burgin begin with that subject:

BURGIN: Was there ever a time when you didn't love literature?
BORGES: No, I always knew, I always thought of myself as a writer, even before I wrote a book. Let me say that even when I had written nothing, I knew that I would. I do not think of myself as a good writer but I knew that my destiny or my fate was a literary one, no? I never thought of myself as being anything else.
BURGIN: You never thought about taking up any career? I mean, your father was a lawyer.
BORGES: Yes. But, after all, he had tried to be a literary man and failed. He wrote some very nice sonnets. But he thought that I should fulfill that destiny, no? (Burgin, 1969, p. 1)

Although Borges' attempts to soften the harsh judgment (Father had failed as a writer) by remembering his "nice" sonnets, it is obvious that on that matter he shares Mother's opinion. It is also obvious that his own literary destiny was molded by that failure. Somehow, he had to fulfill Father's project; he had to vindicate him. That was his main task in life.

It is difficult to assess the quality of Father's work. With a single exception—(the novel *El caudillo*)—his writings are inaccessible or have been destroyed. The novel was written around 1919, at the time the family was living in Majorca, and it was published there at his own expense in 1921. Borges recalls that Father "had some five hundred copies of the book printed and brought them back to Buenos Aires, where he gave them away to friends" ("Essay," 1970, p. 219).

Today the novel is a bibliographical rarity, even harder to get than some of Borges' early books. Father must have been forty-six when he wrote it. But it is obvious that it had been planned long before. It has all the defects of a first novel, and one written probably very quickly. Although it is amateurish, it does not lack interest. It centers on an imaginary episode during the civil war of the 1860s in Entre Ríos, Father's native province. The protagonist is Carlos DuBois, son of a landowner who emigrated to Argentina after the French revolution of 1848. Because his father is sick and has to live in Buenos Aires, Carlos goes back to the ranch, after getting a law degree. There he plans to develop a meat-packing plant. His principal neighbor is Andrés Tavares, the local caudillo, a violent and despotic man, who in the forthcoming civil war would throw his weight in favor of the province's strongman, López Jordán. Tavares has a daughter, María Isabel, also strong-willed and determined to seduce Carlos in spite of the young man's decision to be faithful to the word given to the fiancée he left in Buenos Aires. Carlos' final resistance is overcome when a flood forces Marisabel (as she is called at home) to spend the night at his ranch. The caudillo believes Carlos has deliberately abducted his daughter and sends a henchman to kill him under the pretext that the young man doesn't want to join the López Jordán forces. The ending is truly tragic. After Carlos' death, the caudillo comes to his ranch and walks by his daughter without making a sign of recognition. She is also dead to him.

The novel is perhaps better than the above résumé suggests. It begins with an Indian legend in which a young warrior attempts to hunt and destroy a big crocodile, the representative of the god of the tribe, to gain the favors of his fiancée. Although he succeeds, the god's revenge is terrible: a flood destroys the whole tribe. The legend functions as both introduction and symbolic statement. The Indian couple defy and violate the religious principles of their community as much as the novel's protagonists defy and violate those of their community. The terrifying reptile is the equivalent of the caudillo. In both stories, the flood is a symbol of God's wrath; in both, it is the woman who behaves as seductress and leads to damnation.

The novel has many clumsily told episodes; the chronology is erratic, the romantic couple too conventional. The only character who is really alive is the caudillo. From a purely literary point of view, the novel is an anachronism. Although it was written in the late 1910s, its models belong to nineteenth-century literature. A mixture of romance and the realistic novel, El caudillo mishandles both. The conflict between Carlos and Marisabel is trite; more fascinating is the one that opposes Carlos to the caudillo, and even more interesting is the one (revealed only at the end) between Marisabel and her father. But the author does not explore these conflicts thoroughly enough.

To what extent did Father's novel anticipate some of Borges' own stories? The central subject of El caudillo (a strong man who destroys a younger rival) can be seen in one of Borges' best gaucho stories, "The Dead Man," originally published in 1946 and later included in The Aleph. The caudillo Otálora is really a more sinister version of Tavares, with some sado-masochistic elements added. He pretends to be overwhelmed by the young man and even humiliated by him, because from the very beginning he has planned a deadly revenge. Like Tavares, he is deaf to compassion. Another theme anticipated by Father's novel and recurrent in Borges' fiction is that of the man brought up in the city who has to face a rural destiny. In "The South" (originally published in 1953), the protagonist—a clerk in a municipal library—ends up fighting a knife duel in the pampas, a fate anticipated by Carlos' final confrontation with the caudillo's henchman. It is true that Carlos does not accept the challenge and prefers to be murdered, whereas Borges' Juan Dahlmann meekly accepts his fate. But that difference does not alter the basic similarity of both situations.

More than a coincidence of subjects and themes is implicit here. There is in both writers a preoccupation, almost an obsession, with a certain kind of confrontation: between powerful, primitive men and weak, educated men. Father was (like his son) an intellectual who learned to make his living through the practice of law and the teaching of psychology. But his own father had been a colonel, a man of action. In Father's situation one can already recognize the conflict between arms and letters that Georgie would have to face later. It is easy to recognize in the protagonist of El caudillo, in that half-European Carlos, an alter ego of the author. In many respects, they were similar. But what is really important is that in trying to portray his own predicament Father was also concerned with understanding the caudillo's psychology. In confronting Carlos with the caudillo, Father was exploring one of his private obsessions: the feeling of inadequacy he felt in contrasting his fate with that of his own father. One of the works he had projected and apparently even wrote, according to Borges, was the drama Toward Nothingness, "about a man's disappointment in his son" ("Essay," 1970, p. 211). In the plot of that drama it is possible to read a recognition of his shortcomings as a man, when measured against the

heroic proportions of his father, Colonel Borges. The feeling was inherited by Georgie.

In spite of its literary clumsiness, *El caudillo* deserves serious
reading. Borges even believes that it ought to be reissued—in a new
version, of course. He mentions in his "Autobiographical Essay" that he
had in mind revising "and perhaps rewriting my father's novel *El caudillo*, as he asked me to years ago. We had gone as far as discussing
many of the problems; I like to think of the undertaking as a continued
dialogue and a very real collaboration" (ibid., p. 259). So far, he doesn't
seem to have attempted it.

The most ambitious poetical work produced by Father was a
Spanish version of Edward FitzGerald's English translation of Omar
Khayyam's *Rubaiyat*. It was done in the same meter as the original and
was first published in a little magazine, *Proa* (Prow), edited by Borges
and some friends in the mid-1920s. In an introductory note Georgie
not only talks about the translation's author and praises his work but
also finds words of praise for *El caudillo*. (The note was later included
in *Inquisiciones*, 1925, pp. 127–130.) In spite of the explicit introduction,
the translation was later attributed to Borges in a learned bibliography
published in Buenos Aires (Lucio and Revello, 1961, p. 75). Bibliographers, it is a well-known fact, do not read the items they record.

Many years later Borges wrote an essay on the English translation of Omar Khayyam; it is called "The Enigma of Edward
FitzGerald" and is included in *Other Inquisitions* (1952). It starts with
short, parallel biographies of the Persian poet and his Victorian translator and comes to the conclusion that, since Omar Khayyam believed in
the doctrine of the transmigration of souls, his soul must have migrated
into FitzGerald's. But immediately Borges suggests that the same effect
could have been caused by "a beneficent change":

> Sometimes clouds form the shapes of mountains or lions; Edward
> FitzGerald's unhappiness and a manuscript of yellow paper with purple let-
> ters, forgotten on a shelf of the Bodleian at Oxford, formed the poem for
> our benefit. All collaboration is mysterious. That by the Englishman and the
> Persian was more mysterious than any because the two were very different
> and perhaps in life they would not have become friends; death and vicissi-
> tudes and time caused one to know of the other and made them into a single
> poet. (*Inquisitions*, 1964, p. 78)

There is not one word in the article about the fact that Father
had translated FitzGerald's English translation into Spanish. But it is
obvious that the critic's theory could be extended to include him too, as
a third reincarnation of the Persian poet: a reincarnation that is closer
to the Victorian prototype than to the remote original. One passage in

the article may well be taken as a disguised portrait of Father. According to Borges, FitzGerald

> is less intellectual than Omar, but perhaps more sensitive and more sad. FitzGerald knows that his true destiny is literature, and he practices it with indolence and tenacity. He reads and rereads the *Quixote,* which seems to him almost the best of all books (but he does not wish to be unjust with Shakespeare and with "dear old Virgil"), and his love extends to the dictionary in which he seeks words. He knows that every man who has any music in his soul can write verses ten or twelve times in the natural course of his life, if the stars are propitious, but he does not propose to abuse that modest privilege. He is a friend of famous persons (Tennyson, Carlyle, Dickens, Thackeray), to whom he does not feel inferior in spite of the fact that he is both modest and courteous. (Ibid., pp. 76–77)

With a few alterations of names and dates, those words could have been written about Father. Borges has told us how much he loved poetry, and if one substitutes Swinburne, Shelley, or Keats for Shakespeare, Cervantes, or Virgil, one would have Father's roll of poets. By changing FitzGerald's friends into Macedonio Fernández, Marcelo del Mazo, Evaristo Carriego, and Enrique Larreta, the same function would be performed. Father had never felt inferior to his more successful friends. Other details of FitzGerald's biography seem applicable to Father. In spite of having a home, a wife, and children, Father was essentially a solitary man, sensitive and sad. He was, after all, a Victorian gentleman, with some music in his soul: a man destined to literature but indolent in spite of his lucidity. Like FitzGerald, he even took advantage of some propitious stars to versify ten or twelve times in his life.

The article also presents a kind of paradigm of the man of letters. Many of the comments can be applied to Borges himself. It is not by chance that Borges quotes FitzGerald's concept of poetry as an occasional activity for any man who had some music in his soul, in an epigraph to his *San Martín Copybook* (*Poemas,* 1943, p. 119). But if he shared some of FitzGerald's traits, Borges obviously was not a Victorian gentleman. On the contrary, he had always taken literature seriously and was closer to Samuel Johnson than to FitzGerald in his professionalism.

There is another aspect of Borges' article that is worth underlining. In writing about the metamorphoses of Omar Khayyam's poems into FitzGerald's, he suggests a concept of literature as palimpsest: for him, a literary text is always based on another text, which in turn is based on a previous text, and so on and so forth. But Borges goes even further: poets are also palimpsests. The poet who was Omar

Khayyam can be seen through the mask of the poet who was Edward FitzGerald in the same way FitzGerald can be seen through the mask that was Father. When Georgie came to his father at six to state that he wanted to be a writer, was he consciously assuming for the first time a mask that had been inherited, or bequeathed to him?

12.
The Act of
Writing

Georgie inherited Father's literary vocation. He also inherited his literary habits. Because Father loved to read English poetry aloud, Georgie continued that custom, carrying his imitation to the point of perfection. In his "Autobiographical Essay" Borges observes: "When I recite poetry in English now, my mother tells me I take on his very voice" ("Essay," 1970, p. 207). On many occasions I have heard Borges recite English poems. His voice has a deeper, warmer, almost a longing tone. The accent seems older than the one he normally uses when speaking English. A sort of rough North Country sound is superimposed on the clipped precision of the Oxonian prototype learned by Borges as a child. More than once I have thought, "He sounds like a nineteenth-century gentleman." Not until I read that passage from his autobiography did I discover why: the voice that endlessly quotes from the treasures of English poetry is Father's. Perhaps in that voice there are also echos of the grandmother who was born in Staffordshire, of Northumbrian stock.

Another of Father's literary habits inherited by Georgie was the fruitful consultation of dictionaries and encyclopedias. It is not an Argentine or Hispanic habit. As a distinguished Spanish philologist once put it: "Spaniards consult the dictionary to see if it is right." But Georgie soon learned to trust the dictionary and always look in it first. In her interview with *L'Herne* Mother stressed the importance of Father's example in shaping Georgie's mind: "As his father did, every time a word or a theme attracts his attention . . . he searches for information in a dictionary" (Mother, 1964, p. 9). In recalling his first readings, Borges never forgets to mention the two reference works he consulted most: the *Encylopaedia Britannica* and *Chambers' Encyclopaedia*.

Those books not only contain the key to knowledge; they also give access to other books. They are really a library condensed into a few volumes.

That seed (like the seed of reading) was planted by Fanny Haslam. She used to sit Georgie on her lap and read from the bound copies of an English magazine for children. Alicia Jurado mentions that Georgie called the volume a "leccionario"—a portmanteau word that combines the concepts of "diccionario" (dictionary) and "lección" (lesson) (Jurado, 1964, p. 26). From the English "leccionario" Grandmother Haslam read to him, Georgie moved to the "diccionario." There he learned the meaning of words, their origins, their curious, fascinating life; he also learned to decipher the world of objects these words refer to.

Soon the encyclopedias became Georgie's chief source of information, and a model of prose writing. Consulting encyclopedias and dictionaries became a habit of Georgie's literary life. Some anecdotes preserved by his family and retold by his biographers show how deeply embedded that habit was. When Georgie was nineteen, he asked for a German encyclopedia as a birthday present. The family was then living in Lugano, Switzerland. Georgie had just completed his secondary schooling in Geneva. The German encyclopedia became his third important instrument in the search for knowledge. A few years later, when the Borgeses returned to Argentina to settle for good, Georgie visited the National Library regularly to consult the *Encyclopaedia Britannica*. By then Father's library had been dismantled. Many years later, after Borges had been appointed director of the National Library, he answered a query from Ronald Christ about his predilection for encyclopedias:

BORGES: Ah, yes, I'm very fond of that, I remember a time when I used to come here to read. I was a very young man, and I was far too timid to ask for a book. Then, I was rather, I won't say poor, but I wasn't too wealthy in those days—so I used to come every night here and pick out a volume of the *Encyclopaedia Britannica,* the old edition.
CHRIST: The eleventh?
BORGES: The eleventh or twelfth because those editions are far above the new ones. They were meant to be *read.* Now they are merely reference books. While in the eleventh or twelfth edition of the *Encyclopaedia Britannica,* you had long articles by Macaulay, by Coleridge; no, not by Coleridge, by—
CHRIST: By De Quincey?
BORGES: Yes, by De Quincey and so on. So that I used to take any volume from the shelves—there was no need to ask for them; they were reference books—and then I opened the book till I found an article that interested me, for example about the Mormons or about any particular writer. I sat down and

read it because those articles were really monographs, really books or short books. The same goes for the German encyclopedias—Brockhaus or Meyers. (Christ, 1967, p. 154)

Eventually, Georgie owned a set of the *Encyclopaedia Britannica.* When awarded the second prize in the 1929 Municipal Literary Competition, he spent the money on a secondhand *Britannica.* The eleventh edition, of course. Because of his taste for encyclopedias and dictionaries, he has been accused of faulty scholarship. In his conversations with Jean de Milleret, Borges freely admits his debt to the *Britannica.* His only regret is not having been able to read more of it:

> If I had read it entirely, I believe I would know a lot. Really, I believe that no one in the world knows as much as any encyclopedia. The majority of the contributors do not know what the others have written; thus, as a whole, encyclopedias know more than anybody. And I am sure about their worth because to begin the study of any subject, it is necessary to read the corresponding article in a good encyclopedia. That would permit you to sketch an idea, to trace a plan of work; in short, to trim the question. (De Milleret, 1967, pp. 197–198)

Borges is the reverse of a scholar: a man whose intellectual landscape is narrowed to a precise field and whose scope is voluntarily limited. Borges is a generalist: a man who approaches books and culture with an immense appetite but without any illusions about the possibility of mastering them. Because he admits his limitations, he can move freely in the world of culture. And because he does not have any pretense to specialization, he can (very humbly) start his quest by consulting an encyclopedia. He knows, of course, that the all-embracing view given by such a tool is incomplete. He knows it is the result of a convention: a game of scholarship. In two of his most celebrated stories he offers a hallucinatory image of encyclopedias and libraries. In "Tlön, Uqbar, Orbis Tertius," written in 1940 and collected in *Ficciones* (1944), he tells of the search for a missing article in a somewhat dubious if not totally piratical encyclopedia; in "The Library of Babel" (of the same book), he satirizes the concept of a total library. More recently, in *The Book of Sand* (1975), he conceives a book of infinite pages that contains all books: the total library concentrated in a single, monstrous object.

Even more interesting than the use Borges makes of encyclopedias as a literary subject, or motif, is the fact that encyclopedias, as literary structures and as prototypes of a certain style of writing, serve as models not only for Borges' essays but for many of his most celebrated stories. Thus he generally begins an article or a story by summarizing the subject; he then moves to an analysis of the chief theme; finally, he offers conclusions that usually contradict (totally or partially) the starting point. The technique is like a reduction, by way of his skill at minimal art, of the structure of articles in the *Encyclopaedia Britannica*. Even the technique of including at the end a note with a basic bibliography corresponds to the model. The only difference (*the* difference) is that Borges' texts are not just a reduction of the model but also a parody. In parading his scholarship, Borges undermines it by introducing not only false leads but false sources, apocryphal books, misquoted texts. Long before the concept of "misreading" became a useful if popular tool in critical analysis, Borges had exhausted its parodic possibilities.

Another habit of Father's that Borges inherited was the now forgotten art of conversation. Father was not a great talker or an indiscriminate conversationalist. But he had a few friends with whom it was worth breaking the code of silence. One of his most intimate was his cousin Alvaro Melián Lafinur. Born in 1889, he was some fifteen years younger than Father. Although he had literary ambitions, his life was primarily spent in teaching and journalism. Nevertheless, he became a member of Argentina's Academy of Letters in 1936. He used to visit the Borgeses in the evenings. According to one of Borges' biographers, he always came with his guitar and used to make Georgie cry by singing "The Pirate's Song" (Jurado, 1964, p. 31).

Alvaro had an important role in Georgie's education. Being Father's young cousin and only ten years older than Georgie, he was less an uncle than an older brother, a model for a different kind of life than the one the child had at home. Apparently, Alvaro was familiar with the low life of brothels, easy women, and the tango. Once Borges told an interviewer that he learned from him how much prostitutes charged in those days. In an interview with Rita Guibert he alludes to Alvaro while discussing the origins of the tango. It began in brothels around 1880, according to what "was told to me by an uncle who was a bit of a rogue. I believe that the proof can be found in the fact that if the tango had been popular, the basic instrument would have been the guitar, as it was in the case of the milonga. Instead, the tango was always played on piano, flute, and violin, all instruments which belong to a higher economic level" (Guibert, 1968, p. 53). In Georgie's imagination, Alvaro, with his guitar and his aura of being a ladies' man, must have been a tantalizing figure. To the child who lived in a house with a garden from which evil was excluded, Alvaro's visits introduced a bit of the sounds and shapes of the sinful outside world.

Another visitor was to leave a deeper mark on Georgie's imagination. Evaristo Carriego, a popular poet and a friend of Father, came from Father's province of Entre Ríos and had been living for some time in the same Palermo neighborhood. Born in 1883, Carriego was nine years younger than Father but shared with him similar political experiences. Their families had fought against the local caudillo, Urquiza, and had finally emigrated to Buenos Aires. He also shared Father's love of poetry. But while the latter wrote only occasionally, and generally preferred to read and reread his favorite authors, Carriego was a professional poet, and a very successful one. He wrote about the lives and sentimental experiences of the poor: their joys and disappointments, their miseries and celebrations. His muse was humble and bathetic. Many of his poems were easily transformed into tango lyrics.

There was another difference: Carriego lived in the Palermo of the poor people; Father lived in the only two-storied house in sight. He was Carriego; Father was Dr. Borges. But they were friends, and Carriego used to call every Sunday upon returning from the horse races. In a literary biography of Carriego published in 1930 Borges evokes some of these visits. For him, Carriego's image is inseparable from Palermo: this poet and the neighborhood are one. In discussing one of Carriego's poems, "The Neighborhood Dogs," he interpolates his own memories of those mongrels who actually owned Palermo's streets and were perpetually rounded up by the police in a contraption called *la perrera* (the dog warden). To Borges, the wagon is a symbol of dark forces. Quoting some of Carriego's lines, he writes:

> I want to repeat this verse
>   when they drink moon-water in the pools
> and the other one about
>   howling exorcisms against the dog wagon,
> which brings back one of my stronger memories: the
> absurd visit of that little hell, anticipated by
> painful barks, and preceded—very closely—by a
> cloud of dust made of poor children who, shouting
> and throwing stones, scared another cloud of dust
> made of dogs, to save them from the noose.
>   (*Carriego*, 1930, p. 63)

There is little more about Carriego's contacts with the Borgeses in that book. But in his "Autobiographical Essay," written some forty years later, Borges tells us that Carriego's career

> followed the same evolution as the tango—rollicking, daring, courageous at first, then turning sentimental. In 1912, at the age of twenty-nine, he died of tuberculosis, leaving behind a single volume of his work. I remember that a copy of it, inscribed to my father, was one of several Argentine books we

had taken to Geneva and that I read and reread there. Around 1909, Carriego had dedicated a poem to my mother. Actually, he had written it in her album. In it, he spoke of me: "And may your son . . . go forth, led by the trusting wing of inspiration, to carry out the vintage of a new annunciation, which from lofty grapes will yield the wine of Song." ("Essay," 1970, pp. 233–234)

The lines do not seem memorable except for one thing: they bear witness that as early as 1909, when Georgie was ten, it was obvious at home that he was destined to be a poet, so obvious that the most popular Argentine poet of his time was ready to assume the prophetic mode to celebrate his verses to come.

How much of Carriego's conversation with Father was available to Georgie? In his biography Borges mentions many occasions on which Carriego talked about the books he liked, the poets he admired or hated, the people he despised (Italians and Spanish immigrants, in that order). But it is hard to say if these opinions were based on actual recollections or on Father's later reminiscences of Carriego. Because it can be assumed that talking about Carriego's visits was a normal occupation at the Borgeses'. Georgie's early reaction to Carriego may be found in Mother's reminiscences. Talking to a French interviewer, she once said: "At the beginning, Georgie did not like the visits of my husband's friends; later, he got used to it. And then, when for instance Carriego called on us, he loved to remain downstairs with the grownups, listening to the poet read his own poems, or Almafuerte's 'The Missionary'; then, he used to stay there, with his eyes wide open" (Mother, 1964, p. 10).

These two contrasted images of Georgie are worth considering. Proust has already described in minute detail the exquisite tortures of childhood when one was forced to go upstairs to sleep when a brilliant visitor was entertaining the grown-ups. Osbert Sitwell has devoted a whole volume of his five-part autobiography to the feelings of being excluded from real life when in the evening laughter pours in from the next room. But a moment came for Georgie when he was allowed to stay downstairs and hear Carriego read from his own poetry, or from the poets he admired. Then Georgie not only shared the excitement of the evening but probably got more out of it than the adults. His eyes wide open, he had the chance to see and hear a prodigy: a man who not only wrote occasional poems (as Father did) but actually devoted his entire life to writing. Carriego was to become Georgie's first literary prototype. That single volume of verses which the poet had dedicated to Father was to become Georgie's favorite reading in his long Geneva exile.

There is a third Argentine writer Father knew. Although he is now out of fashion, at the beginning of this century he was *the* most famous Latin American novelist. Born in 1873, only one year before Father, Enrique Rodríguez Larreta read law at Buenos Aires University with Macedonio Fernández and Father. They all graduated in 1898 and probably attended the same banquets to celebrate their newly minted degrees. But there is no record of any friendship after that date. Ten years later, after dropping the name Rodríguez as being too common (it is the equivalent of a name such as Smith in English), Enrique Larreta published his most successful book, *The Glory of Don Ramiro,* a historical novel of the age of Philip II, when the sun never set on the Spanish empire. A cold, precise, decorative reconstruction, the novel was written in a pastiche of Spanish Golden Age prose and became immensely popular—as popular as *One Hundred Years of Solitude* is now. Today it is hardly read; its pastry-shop style is no longer accepted. Father probably didn't think much of Dr. Larreta. In a 1945 interview Borges recalls a conversation with Father in which Dr. Larreta's name was mentioned. They were discussing one of the most famous utterances of General San Martín, Argentina's national hero: "You will be what you have to be, or you will be nothing." According to Father, it meant that "you will be a gentleman, a Catholic, an Argentine, a member of the Jockey Club, an admirer of Uriburu [the general who in 1930 deposed President Irigoyen], an admirer of Quirós' vast rustic characters—*or you will be nothing*—you will be a Jew, an anarchist, a bum, a lowly clerk; the National Commission of Culture will ignore your books and Dr. Rodríguez Larreta will not send you copies of his, enhanced by his autograph" (*Latitud,* February 1945, p. 4).

Calling the successful Larreta by his full surname and with the addition of "Dr." is one of the oldest tricks in the art of abuse, about which Borges wrote a devastatingly comic article in 1932. But there is more than abuse in the text just quoted. A whole view of Argentine life in this century is condensed here. To Father, Argentine society was deeply rooted in privilege, in social inequality, in racism and snobbery. To be somebody there one had to assume the mask of the Catholic gentleman, a supporter of army intervention in the affairs of state and an admirer of native subjects in painting. To be somebody meant to get prizes in the official literary competitions and autographed copies of Larreta's books. In short, to be somebody was to belong to the establishment. And Father was very determined not to belong to it, in spite of the fact that he came from an old family, was a lawyer, and had married a woman who belonged to an old Catholic family.

Compared with Macedonio Fernández or Evaristo Carriego, Father was part of the establishment. But compared with Dr. Rodríguez Larreta, he did not pass the test. There was too much in him of the anarchist, the freethinker, and the foreigner. The fact that he had chosen to live in Palermo, a rundown neighborhood, did not attend the Jockey Club (except for the annual banquets of the class of 1898), and had not supported Uriburu or ever admired Quirós helped to alienate him from the establishment. Furthermore (and this is the most important point) he was never graced with an autographed copy of Larreta's novels. In talking to Georgie about San Martín's dictum and in expanding and decoding it, Father was pursuing his main task of indoctrination. He wanted Georgie to become a poet and fulfill his frustrated literary vocation, but he wanted him to be different: a philosophical anarchist; not a tamed writer but a truly independent one. Father taught Georgie to shun prizes and despise honors. With his example and the corrosive wit of his conversation, he offered the best example of a man who chose to be marginal in a society in which every poet attempted to reach the center of the ring.

Georgie learned the lesson of marginality so well that he ended up making his peripheral activities the center of another (but purely literary) establishment. Many years later, when answering one of his interviewer's questions, Borges recalled an anecdote of his childhood days. Once he had told Father that he wanted to be a *raté;* that is, a failure (Arias, 1971, pp. 2–3). The French expression was rather commonly used in Argentina in those days; there was even a popular play by Henri Lenormand (*Les ratés*) on the subject. Georgie probably had heard the expression and, not knowing French well, mistook it for something desirable. But if he was wrong about the exact meaning of the word, he was right about its symbolic meaning. For the Argentine establishment of those days, what Father and Georgie really wanted to be was exactly that: *ratés,* and not the success that Dr. Rodríguez Larreta so ponderously represented.

On several occasions Borges has evoked his literary beginnings under the invisible but firm hand of Father. The versions differ only in detail. This is what he has to say in the "Autobiographical Essay":

I first started writing when I was six or seven. I tried to imitate classic writers of Spanish—Miguel de Cervantes, for example. I had set down in quite bad English a kind of handbook on Greek mythology, no doubt cribbed from Lemprière. This may have been my first literary venture. My first story was a rather nonsensical piece after the manner of Cervantes, an old-fashioned romance called "La visera fatal" (The Fatal Helmet). I very neatly wrote these things into copybooks. My father never interfered. He wanted me to commit all my own mistakes, and once said, "Children educate their parents, not the other way around." When I was nine or so, I translated Oscar Wilde's "The Happy Prince" into Spanish, and it was published in one of the Buenos Aires dailies, *El País*. Since it was signed merely "Jorge Borges," people naturally assumed the translation was my father's. ("Essay," 1970, p. 211)

In talking to Richard Burgin he stresses other details:

BORGES: I began [writing] when I was a little boy. I wrote an English handbook ten pages long on Greek mythology, in very clumsy English. That was the first thing I ever wrote.

BURGIN: You mean "original mythology" or a translation?

BORGES: No, no, no, no. It was just saying, for example, well, "Hercules attempted twelve labors" or "Hercules killed the Nemean Lion."

BURGIN: So you must have been reading those books when you were very young.

BORGES: Yes, of course, I'm very fond of mythology. Well, it was nothing, it was just a, it must have been fifteen pages long . . . with the story of the Golden Fleece and the Labyrinth and Hercules, he was my favorite, and then something about the loves of the gods, and the tale of Troy. That was the first thing I ever wrote. I remember it was written in a very short and crabbed handwriting because I was very short-sighted. That's all I can tell you about it. In fact, I think my mother kept a copy for some time, but as we've travelled all over the world, the copy got lost, which is as it should be, of course, because we thought nothing whatever about it, except for the fact that it was written by a small boy. (Burgin, 1969, pp. 2–3)

The choice of a handbook on Greek mythology for a first attempt at literary composition may seem odd in any six-year-old writer, but not in Georgie. Georgie was anticipating some of Borges' most famous works (*The Book of Imaginary Beings,* for instance), and he was already creating a literary space of his own: the space of myth. But not all the Greek myths would survive childhood. Hercules never made the grade. Or perhaps only degraded versions of Hercules did, versions in which the hero is fatally flawed and weak. But the labyrinth, on the contrary, became one of Borges' most personal symbols: the very image of life's absurdity and man's puzzling predicament. In evoking many years later, in *The Book of Imaginary Beings,* the image of the monster who sits at the center of the labyrinth, Borges writes: "Most likely the Greek fable of the Minotaur is a late and clumsy version of older myths, the shadow of other dreams still more full of horror" (*Imaginary,* 1969, p. 159). It is obvious that for Borges (and perhaps for Georgie) what was really attractive in Greek mythology in general and in the myth of the Minotaur in particular was its deep roots in the unconscious, where nightmares are produced.

In his conversation with Burgin, Borges returns to the subject of his first piece of fiction, the old-fashioned romance "La visera fatal."

He recalls that after reading a chapter or two of *Don Quixote*, he tried to write archaic Spanish: "And that saved me from trying to do the same thing some fifteen years afterward, no? Because I had already attempted that game and failed at it" (Burgin, 1969, p. 3). According to Mother, this first fictional attempt was a short tale, in "old Spanish," some "four or five pages long" (Mother, 1964, p. 10). Quoting Mother as a source, Victoria Ocampo reports that it was a story written "in a style similar to *The Glory of Don Ramiro*" and adds: "In that story, people did not die; they departed" (Ocampo, 1964, p. 21).

If Victoria Ocampo's recollections are correct, the story must have been written when Georgie was older, because *The Glory of Don Ramiro* did not come out until 1908, when the boy was nine. The point is a minor one, but what is ironic about a possible connection between Georgie's first fiction and Larreta's novel is the fact that its author was to become for him the epitome of the literary fake. More significant still is the fact that in starting his literary career Georgie had chosen as a model the exact book one of his characters would attempt to rewrite so earnestly in the 1939 short story called "Pierre Menard, Author of the *Quixote*."

There is a little anecote attached to Georgie's literary beginnings. When his translation of Wilde's "The Happy Prince" was published, a friend of Father's, Ricardo Blemey Lafont, a teacher at the Institute of Living Languages, where Father taught psychology, not only congratulated Father for the translation but adopted it as a text in one of his classes (Jurado, 1964, p. 31). The mistake is significant. Georgie's first published work would be attributed to Father. Many years later, in one of the first full-length bibliographies of his work, included among Borges' translations was Father's version of Omar Khayyam (Lucio and Revello, 1961, p. 75). The circle of false attribution was by then completed: Georgie, who became Father's specular image, had finally reached the stage in his career where Father would become his specular image.

Another of his childhood productions of which very little is known is a gaucho poem mentioned in the "Autobiographical Essay": "I think I began writing a poem about gauchos, probably under the influence of the poet Ascasubi, before I went to Geneva. I recall trying to work in as many gaucho words as I could, but the technical difficulties were beyond me. I never got past a few stanzas" ("Essay," 1970, p. 213). Borges never attempted such a task again. It was already hopelessly anachronistic by the time he tried his hand at it. Ascasubi, one of the most prolific of the gaucho poets, had died in 1875, exactly one year after Father's birth. The tradition of gaucho poetry was practically dead in Argentina, and only a few such poets remained in

Uruguay (Elías Regules, "El Viejo Pancho," Fernán Silva Valdés) to practice a genre that used to be the most popular in the River Plate area. In discussing why Uruguay kept the gaucho tradition longer than Argentina, Borges has pointed out that it is a more primitive country, a country in which gauchos still participated actively in national life. In Argentina, the fast industrialization which took place in the second half of the nineteenth century made the gaucho, and gaucho poetry, obsolete.

Not much is known about Georgie's early works, but in them we can find a key to his interests and even his obsessions. The fact that we have only titles or short descriptions to go on should not be a great obstacle. Borges has already shown how to deal with writers (Pierre Menard, Herbert Quain, Jaromir Hládik, Ts'ui Pên, Nils Runenberg, Carlos Argentino Daneri, Joseph Cartaphilus, Julio Platero Haedo, Suárez Miranda, Gasper Camerarius) of whose works there remain only a title, a fragment, an incomplete quotation, a plot summary. That much has been saved so far of Georgie Borges' works. Perhaps in the near future some devoted scholar will unearth the "lost" notebooks and will publish them with all the critical paraphernalia these crumbs will undoubtedly merit. Then it will be forever impossible to continue to speculate about Georgie's lost works.

13.
The Eton Boy

The only formal schooling Georgie had before he was nine was given him by his English grandmother or by an English governess, Miss Tink, who took care of him and his sister, Norah. Father was always there, but his teachings were of a different kind.

In 1908, when Georgie was almost nine, a momentous decision was made: to send him to the state school. As he had already learned many odd things, including English, he was placed directly in fourth grade.

The school was a day school for boys. Georgie had been used to learning in the quiet of his home, helped by people who loved him and who shared his cultural code: English. At the state school English was worse than useless; it was positively exotic and, as he soon learned, dangerous. For the first time in his life he found himself in a totally hostile world. Not until 1937, when he began working at a municipal library, would he experience similar alienation and terror. In the descriptions of his early schooldays in the "Autobiographical Essay" Borges' generally ironical narrative takes on a slightly sinister tone: "I take no pleasure whatever in recalling my early schooldays. . . . As I wore spectacles and dressed in an Eton collar and tie, I was jeered at and bullied by most of my schoolmates, who were amateur hooligans. I cannot remember the name of the school but recall that it was on Thames Street" ("Essay," 1970, p. 212).

The decision to send Georgie to a state school, disguised as an Eton boy, proved how alien the Borgeses were to the world around them. Georgie's dress, his nearsightedness, his stammering, made him the favorite target of the bullies. The thought that in an English public school he would have probably received even more brutal treatment could not have provided much consolation. Another mention of his schooldays can be found in his conversations with Richard Burgin; to a question about childhood fights, Borges replies:

> Well, my eyesight was bad; it was very weak and I was generally defeated. But it had to be done. Because there was a code and, in fact, when I was a boy, there was even a code of dueling. But I think dueling is a very stupid custom, no? After all, it's quite irrelevant. If you quarrel with me and I quarrel with you, what has our swordsmanship or our marksmanship to do with it? Nothing—unless you have the mystical idea that God will punish the wrong. I don't think anybody has that kind of idea, no? Well, suppose we get back to more . . . because, I don't know why, I seem to be rambling on. (Burgin, 1969, p. 29)

What is striking in this testimony about his schooldays is Borges' emotional tone of voice. It is possible to detect even in the written transcript the revulsion that such a "code of honor" still arouses in him. The violence and terror of those early fights were never erased.

There is an irony here. The same Georgie who suffered the humiliation of being made a scapegoat will become (much later and as a writer) a champion of physical courage, of the old skills of gun and knife play and the mythology of violence. The conflict between his military forebears and his literary vocation, between the sword and the library, here takes on a more squalid form. It comes as no surprise that Borges calls his schoolmates "amateur hooligans," but the code of honor so deeply imbedded in the Borgeses forced Georgie to conquer his revulsion and face the hooligans, participating in fights he knew he could never win.

There is an interesting lapse in Borges' school recollections: he has forgotten the name of the school, although he remembers that it was located, of all places, on Thames Street. Mother had a better memory. In a conversation with me in 1971 she remembered one of Georgie's classmates, Roberto Godel, from French stock, who used to see Georgie after school. According to her, they continued to be friends. They probably went together to the National School for their secondary studies. He is the only name that survives from those schooldays.

In discussing oblivion with Burgin, Borges observes that it is "the highest form of revenge" and adds: "If I were insulted by a stranger in the street, I don't think I would give the matter a second thought. I would just pretend I hadn't heard him and go on, because, after all, I don't exist for him, so why should he exist for me?" (Burgin, 1969, p. 28). Years later, in one of his most famous short stories, "The South," Borges dramatizes this observation. When the protagonist,

Juan Dahlmann (of mixed Scandinavian and Argentine stock), is challenged by some drunks in a tavern set in the middle of nowhere, he decides not to pay any attention to them until he is recognized by the owner and called by his name. Then he has to fight. There is an echo here of that old chivalric code which forces one to accept the challenge of another knight but never the challenge of a villain. In the same way, Georgie at school accepted his classmates' challenge and fought hopeless fights. Sixty years later, in recalling those days for Richard Burgin, his voice betrayed him: he still was fighting those nightmarish duels.

The scars that his days at school left on Georgie are still visible in the writing of Borges. One of the scars was left by his schoolmates' coarse descriptions of the mysteries of sex. In some of the stories Borges later wrote—"The Sect of the Phoenix" and "Emma Zunz" are the most revealing—it is still possible to see how shocked Georgie was.

Little is known about what Georgie actually learned at school. According to Mother, he was a good student but had some trouble with mathematics. He preferred history and ("naturally") literature, as well as grammar and philosophy (Mother, 1964, p. 11). Borges recalls that his father

> used to say that Argentine history had taken the place of the catechism, so we were expected to worship all things Argentine. We were taught Argentine history, for example, before we were allowed any knowledge of the many lands and many centuries that went into its making. As far as Spanish composition goes, I was taught to write in a flowery way: *Aquellos que lucharon por una patria libre, independiente, gloriosa* . . . (Those who struggled for a free, independent, and glorious nation . . .). Later on, in Geneva, I was to be told that such writing was meaningless and that I must see things through my own eyes. ("Essay," 1970, p. 212)

Georgie's experience helped to confirm everything that Father had been saying about the low level of the state schools. It was a further proof (if any were needed) of the backwardness and general inferiority of Argentine culture. The gap that Georgie's bilingualism had already created at home began to widen at school. Nothing that he could have learned there would erase the prejudices against everything Hispanic that he inherited from Father's side. A long residence in Spain, which led to the discovery of the poetical possibilities of Spanish and later the rediscovery of his native Buenos Aires, was needed to alter Georgie's prejudices.

But if the level of teaching and learning at the state school was rather low, Georgie continued to have the best of mentors at home. Father began to guide him firmly into the labyrinths of philosophy. According to Mother, "he read a lot and he talked to his father. . . . They began to talk about philosophy when Georgie was ten" (Mother, 1964, p. 11). In his "Autobiographical Essay" Borges mentions how Father taught him Zeno's paradoxes with the aid of a chessboard; and in Father's only novel, *El caudillo,* the protagonist, Carlos DuBois, uses a similar method to teach one of the foreman's sons the rudiments of the alphabet. Talking to Burgin, Borges indicates the importance of such a training:

BURGIN: Of course most people live and die without ever, it seems, really thinking about the problems of time or space or infinity.
BORGES: Well, because they take the universe for granted. They take things for granted. They take themselves for granted. That's true. They never wonder at anything, no? They don't think it's strange that they should be living. I remember the first time I felt that was when my father said to me, "What a queer thing," he said, "that I should be living, as they say, behind my eyes, inside my head. I wonder if that makes sense?" And then, it was the first time I felt that, and then instantly I pounced upon that because I knew what he was saying. But many people can hardly understand that. And they say, "Well, but where else could you live?" (Burgin, 1969, p. 6)

A few pages later, after a digression on women, Borges returns to the subject:

BURGIN: So you think that remark of your father's heralded the beginning of your own metaphysics?
BORGES: Yes, it did.
BURGIN: How old were you then?
BORGES: I don't know. I must have been a very young child. Because I remember he said to me, "Now, look here; this is something that may amuse you," and then, he was very fond of chess, he was a very good chess player, and then he took me to the chessboard, and he explained to me the paradoxes of Zeno, Achilles and the Tortoise, you remember, the arrows, the fact that movement was impossible because there was always a point in between, and so on. And I remember him speaking of these things to me and I was very puzzled by them. And he explained them with the help of a chessboard. (Ibid., p. 9)

Many years later Borges would make the game that Father played with Georgie into his own literary game, a game he plays endlessly in poems, short stories, and essays. In talking to Herbert Simon, Borges adds a few anecdotes about his early training:

BORGES: I inherited from Father the taste for this type of reasoning. He used to take me apart to talk or to ask me questions about my beliefs. Once he took an orange and asked me: According to you, the taste is in the orange? I told him it was. Then he asked me: Well, then you think that the orange is constantly tasting itself?

SIMON: It can be assumed that the solution to this type of questioning would take one deeply into the field of solipsism.

BORGES: Actually, Father did not lead me to the philosophical sources. He only asked concrete problems. Only after quite a long time he showed me a history of philosophy in which I found the origin of all these questions. In the same way he taught me to play chess. Although I have always been a poor player and he was very good. (Simon, 1971, p. 43)

After discussing some basic ideas about combinatory analysis, the infinite, and the labyrinth, Borges predictably concludes: "I got many of my ideas from books on logic and mathematics which I have read, but to be honest, every time I have attempted reading these books, they have defeated me; I haven't been able to interpret them thoroughly. Now, the majority of these ideas I got from Father's observations" (ibid., p. 45).

As a teacher of psychology and a follower of William James, Father also used his experiences in the classroom to introduce Georgie gradually to the complexities of thinking. In his conversations with Burgin, Borges recalls one lesson:

BORGES: I remember my father said to me something about memory, a very saddening thing. He said, "I thought I could recall my childhood when we first came to Buenos Aires, but now I know that I can't." I said, "Why?" He said, "Because I think that memory"—I don't know if this was his own theory; I was so impressed by it that I didn't ask him whether he found it or whether he evolved it—but he said, "I think that if I recall something, for example, if today I look back on this morning, then I get an image of what I saw this morning. But if tonight, I'm thinking back on this morning, then what I'm really recalling is not the first image in morning. So that every time I recall something, I'm not recalling it really. I'm recalling the last time I recalled it, I'm recalling my last memory of it. So that really," he said, "I have no memories whatever, I have no images whatever, about my childhood, about my youth." And then he illustrated that, with a pile of coins. He piled one coin on top of the other and said, "Well, now this first coin, the bottom coin, this would be the first image, for example, of the house of my childhood. Now this second would be a memory I had of that house when I went to Buenos Aires. Then the third one another memory and so on. And as in every memory there's a slight distortion, I don't suppose that my memory of today ties in with the first image I had. So that," he said, "I try not to think of things in the past because if I do I'll be thinking back on those memories and not on the actual images themselves." And then that saddened me. To think maybe we have no true memories of youth.

BURGIN: That the past was invented, fictitious.

BORGES: That it can be distorted by successive repetition. Because if in every repetition you get a slight distortion, then in the end you will be a long way off from the issue. It's a saddening thought. I wonder if it's true, I wonder what other psychologists would have to say about that. (Burgin, 1969, pp. 10–11)

The strangest thing about this anecdote is not what it says about Father's theory of memory. It is the fact that Borges did not realize that it was another version of Zeno's second paradox about the impossibility of Achilles ever reaching the tortoise. By parceling space, Zeno proved the race could never be won by the fastest Greek warrior. In Father's theory the imaginary space of memory is equally divided into infinite segments, until memory (that is, the actual and new recollection of something that once happened to us) becomes impossible. After this exercise, Father and Georgie are left with only a sad feeling. Memory also becomes part of the fictional world Father's idealist philosophy had created for Georgie to live in. The mentor had reached a point at which he could rest. The pupil is forever programmed to believe reality and fiction are one and the same.

Part Two

1.
Trapped in Switzerland

Perhaps the most momentous decision ever made by Father was his sudden determination to visit Europe in the summer of 1914. As he was becoming totally blind, he felt he could no longer pursue his career as a lawyer. He was approaching forty at the time and decided on early retirement. In his "Autobiographical Essay" Borges has this to say:

> In 1914, we moved to Europe. My father's eyesight had begun to fail and I remember him saying, "How on earth can I sign my name to legal papers when I am unable to read them?" Forced into early retirement, he planned our trip in exactly ten days. The world was unsuspicious then; there were no passports or other red tape. . . . The idea of the trip was for my sister and me to go to school in Geneva; we were to live with my maternal grandmother, who traveled with us and eventually died there, while my parents toured the Continent. At the same time, my father was to be treated by a famous Genevan eye doctor. ("Essay," 1970, pp. 213–214)

Implicit in Borges' account is the fact that the journey was to be long enough to justify the children's going to school in Geneva and to allow the parents to do some sightseeing. The trip to Europe was then, as it still is, considered essential in the education of an Argentine gentleman. It was the equivalent of the Grand Tour that eighteenth-century English gentlemen used to take after they had graduated from Oxford or Cambridge: a chance to gain a firsthand acquaintance with Western culture. Purely for economic reasons, Father had postponed the trip since his own graduation. But now he hesitated no longer. In ten days he had everybody packed, and they sailed for the Old World.

The moment seemed auspicious. The Pax Victoriana, pro-
longed by the Entente Cordiale between England and France, seemed
eternal. Europe had not had a major upheaval since the Franco-Prus-
sian war of 1870. Wars (civil or international) seemed cozily confined to
the marginal areas of Asia, Africa, and Latin America. The Borgeses
sailed off to meet a war that was to be called *The* World War before it
became World War I. Borges underscores the irony of the situation in
a 1967 interview with César Fernández Moreno: "When my father had
to retire because of his blindness, the family decided to travel in
Europe. We were so ignorant about universal history, and especially
about the immediate future, that we traveled in 1914 and got stuck in
Switzerland" (Fernández Moreno, 1967, pp. 8–9).

The decision to move to Europe for a few months to live under
the care of their maternal grandmother, Leonor Suárez Acevedo probably did not appeal to Georgie and Norah. To understand their strong
feelings of abandonment, one has to remember how closely united the
family had been till then, how inbred their affective life was, how little
the children had seen of the outside world. They must have been miserable.

From Father's point of view, the plan was simple and feasible.
His pension was small, but in those days the Argentine peso was strong.
Those were the years when landowners in Argentina, made rich by the
meat and dairy products of their ranches, used to spend a great part of
their fortune in Europe; when European elegance was carefully copied
on both banks of the River Plate; and when the wealthy journeyed to
Europe with their servants and sometimes even with their favorite
cows. Apparently they did not trust the quality of the European product. Vicente Blasco Ibáñez described them in his best-seller *The Four
Horsemen of the Apocalypse,* later immortalized in a 1920 movie directed
by Fred Niblo. In that film Rudolph Valentino epitomized the Argentine male of those years: a suave, beautiful, vaselinized Latin lover,
teaching the French ladies how to tango in and out of bed.

The Borgeses had little to do with those people. Father's pension was not large and he was no Latin lover, although he had a
fondness for easy young women. (Borges once told me that his father
was "a bit of a rogue" in these matters.) If Father failed to conform to
the tango prototype, he represented very effectively another less publi-
cized Argentine prototype: the cultivated gentleman for whom Europe
is a string of museum cities. The family's itinerary seems to support this
view. Skipping Spain for the time being, they went directly to England,
where Georgie had a glimpse of London's "red labyrinth" and of Cambridge; then they crossed the Channel to Paris. In his "Autobiographical Essay" Borges is not kind to the great city: "We first spent

some weeks in Paris, a city that neither then nor since has particularly charmed me, as it does every other good Argentine. Perhaps, without knowing it, I was always a bit of a Britisher; in fact, I always think of Waterloo as a victory" ("Essay," 1970, p. 213). From Paris the Borgeses went to Geneva. With the children safely tucked away at school, Father and Mother continued their tour alone. They were in Germany when war broke out and had some difficulty in returning to Switzerland. But as Latin Americans they were luckier than many other stranded tourists. In due time they managed to reach Geneva, where they remained until the end of the war.

In Switzerland the Borgeses re-created the family cell they had formed while living in Palermo. The family found shelter in the beautiful and melancholy city by the lake. There Georgie invented another secluded, holy space in which to continue his reading, his daydreaming with Norah, his permanent conversation with Father.

Father and Mother were still young and extremely handsome; the children had dark, sensitive features. In two studio photographs, taken in Geneva, in 1914 and 1915, they look well and prosperous, although their faces are sad.

Georgie was unhappy in Switzerland. In a short autobiographical piece he wrote for a 1927 anthology of Argentine poetry, he summarizes his experience there: "I spent the war years in Geneva; [it was] a no-exit time, tight, made of drizzle, which I'll always remember with some hatred" (Vignale, 1927, p. 93). For a boy used to the bright sun and the hot summers of Buenos Aires, Geneva's misty, damp, and cold weather must have been painful enough. What justified the hatred was probably the feeling of being trapped there. But his attitude changed with time. In a 1967 interview with Fernández Moreno, Borges recalls only the brighter of those days in Geneva:

BORGES: I came to know Switzerland very thoroughly, and to love it very much.
FERNÁNDEZ MORENO: You had remembered those days as "gray, and tight with drizzle," in a 1927 statement.
BORGES: Yes, but that was then; not now. Now, when I returned to Switzerland after forty years, I was greatly moved and had the feeling of returning home also. Because the experiences of adolescence, all that, happened there. . . . Geneva is a city I know better than Buenos Aires. Besides, Geneva can be learned because it is a normal-size city, shall we say, while Buenos Aires is such an outrageous city that nobody can ever learn it. (Fernández Moreno, 1967, p. 9)

He returns to the subject in his "Autobiographical Essay," describing the everyday routine of his life in Geneva: "We lived in a flat on the southern, or old, side of town. I still know Geneva far better than I

know Buenos Aires, which is easily explained by the fact that in Geneva
no two streetcorners are alike and one quickly learns the differences.
Every day, I walked along that green and icy river, the Rhone, which
runs through the very heart of the city, spanned by seven quite dif-
ferent-looking bridges" ("Essay," 1970, p. 215).

The apartment house where the Borgeses lived is still there, in
the old quarter, not too far from the Collège Calvin, which Georgie attended for four years. It belongs to a whole block of nineteenth-century
townhouses in the style that Baron Haussmann's reforms made so popular in Paris: solid, dignified, a bit dull. The only change brought about
by this century is in the name of the street, then called Rue Malagnou
and now called Rue Ferdinand Hodler to celebrate the twentieth-century Swiss painter. The whole quarter, built on a hill, still has winding
roads and a few medieval landmarks. In a 1975 story called "The
Other" there is a fleeting evocation of those cold days by the river in an
imaginary encounter between two Borgeses (the 1914 one, the 1969
one) on a bench on the banks of the Charles River in Cambridge, Massachusetts, which is also a bench on the Rhone in Geneva.

Although the Grand Tour plans had to be shelved because of
the war, the Borgeses still wanted to see Europe. From Geneva, the
safest summer tour seemed to be to the south, crossing the slopes to
visit northern Italy. In his "Autobiographical Essay" Borges recalls: "I
have vivid memories of Verona and Venice. In the vast and empty am-
phitheater of Verona I recited, loud and bold, several gaucho verses
from Ascasubi" (ibid., p. 214). The selection of Ascasubi may seem less
a homage to one of the masters of Argentine gaucho verse than a sort
of challenge to the Old World. To have quoted Shakespeare in Verona
would have seemed trite to Georgie. Ascasubi had the advantage of
being untainted by sophistication. He provided a way for Georgie to
espress his longing for his native land and speech. Borges gives no further details of his "vivid" memories of Venice.

The other important family event of those European years was
the arrival in Switzerland of Fanny Haslam, the English grandmother.
She may have decided to join the Borgeses because, with their pro-
longed absence, she was lonely in Buenos Aires. The "Autobiographical
Essay" makes only a short reference to her visit: "As a result of the
war—apart from the Italian trip and journeys inside Switzerland—we
did no traveling. Later on, braving German submarines and in the
company of only four or five passengers, my English grandmother
joined us" (ibid., p. 215).

Fanny Haslam's courage is a subject that Borges loves to discuss. She had proved it in her early years in Argentina when she
shared frontier life with her husband, Colonel Borges. Now, in facing

the German submarines, Grandmother showed her truly British spirit. With her arrival in Geneva, the original Borges clan was restored. Life in Geneva began to take on features of life in Palermo.

Before his grandmother's arrival, Georgie had sent her postcards which revealed his homesickness.

DE MILLERET: It's true, some of the postcards you sent your grandmother at the time show regrets which are not specifically addressed to her.
BORGES: It was a lack of tact on my part, no? When one is twelve or thirteen one is not a man of the world. (De Milleret, 1967, p. 20)

Borges uses irony here to disguise his feelings. He had attached to Buenos Aires the longing he felt for the close-knit world of Palermo. Too proud to tell his grandmother he missed her, he talked of his native city. There is another revelation in these reminiscences. By slightly reducing his real age (he was nearly fifteen when he went to Europe), Borges tries to make more acceptable the fact that he was still so attached to his grandmother's apron strings.

Grandmother was not the only relative to visit the Borgeses in Switzerland. Around 1916 some of Mother's Uruguayan cousins came to Europe. They belonged to the Haedo branch of the family. To celebrate the visit, Father took some photographs which show at least three generations of Haedo women surrounding Donā Leonor, the maternal grandmother. Among these women (eight in all), Georgie cuts a strange figure. Even with his closest relatives he seems the odd man out, the stranger. The difference is visible in the expression of the face, the sadness of the eyes behind the thick glasses, and the terribly unhappy mouth. It is also evident in the way he sits or stands, always so clumsily, as if his body, growing too quickly and with a will of its own, bothered him too much.

In those difficult days Georgie could not forget he had a body. Infrequent but tantalizing references in his poems or short stories make quite clear that Georgie did not weather the sexual problems of adolescence easily. In the story called "The Other," in which he describes a meeting between himself as an old man and as a very young man in Geneva, to convince the young Georgie that he really is his future self, Borges adduces some evidence only he could have:

I can prove I'm not lying. . . . I'm going to tell you things a stranger couldn't possibly know. At home [in Geneva] we have a silver maté cup with a base in the form of entwined serpents. Our great-grandfather brought it from Peru. There's also a silver washbasin that hung from his saddle. In the wardrobe of your room are two rows of books: the three volumes of Lane's *One Thousand and One Nights,* with steel engravings and with notes in small type at the end of each chapter; Quicherat's Latin dictionary; Tacitus' *Germania* in Latin and also in Grodon's English translation; a *Don Quixote* published by Garnier; Rivera Indarte's *Tablas de sangre,* inscribed by the author; Carlyle's *Sartor Resartus;* a biography of Amiel; and, hidden behind the other volumes, a book in paper covers about sexual customs in the Balkans. Nor have I forgotten one evening on a certain second floor of the Place Dubourg."

"Dufour," he corrected.

"Very well—Dufour." (*Sand,* 1977, pp. 11–12)

The context in which that mysterious evening on the second floor of Dufour Square is mentioned may seem purely literary. But some of the books mentioned—Lane's translation, Amiel's biography, and the hidden volume on Balkan erotic habits—are specifically associated with a forbidden subject: sex. Lane's version of the *One Thousand and One Nights* (published in 1839) bowdlerized the famous original. In an article devoted to different European translations of the book Borges discusses at some length the virtues and omissions of that version. Lane lived in Cairo for five years and learned the language and mores thoroughly, but he never relinquished (according to Borges) "his British sense of decorum." Instead of having the elegant reticence of Antoine Galland, the French translator who omitted all controversial references, Lane did not "pact with silence." He did not translate the more pornographic passages but he mentioned each omission. In his article Borges quotes expressions such as "I overlooked a most reprehensible episode," "I eliminate a disgusting explanation," "Here a line too gross to translate," "Here the story of Bujait, the slave, totally inadequate to be translated." What Borges criticizes is Lane's tendency to evade some of the original's specifics. He quotes an example: "In night 217 there is a king who slept with two women, one night with one, the following night with the other, and in that way they were all happy. Lane explains the monarch's venture by saying he treated his women 'with impartiality.' " Borges concludes that "one of the reasons [for such an evasion] is that Lane had oriented his work to the 'parlor table,' the center of alarmless reading and reticent conversation" (*Eternidad,* 1936, pp. 76–77).

In calling Lane's version of the *Arabian Nights* "a mere encyclopedia of evasion" (ibid., p. 76), Borges offers a clue to his own reticence. Like Lane, he generally avoids saying things explicitly, but at the same time, very conscientiously, he leaves tantalizing clues here and there. In a subtler way he points obliquely to the places where something has been left unsaid. In the fragment from "The Other" quoted above, the signs are clear. Not only Lane's version but also the brief reference to a biography of Amiel work as indexes: they point to what is missing. Amiel, a well-known Swiss essayist whose *Diary* was widely read, had a troubled sexual life. In not identifying which biography of Amiel Georgie possessed, Borges is playing again with the reader. But is is fair to assume that Amiel's sexual problems were not omitted in that biography. Less reticent is the reference to a book on Balkan sexual mores. The fact that the book was hidden from a casual viewer's eyes is very telling. It might have been one of those books which, according to Rousseau's famous mot, are read with one hand only. If Georgie used it for that purpose, he would have been doing only what any normal adolescent would do. But even now, writing a story that evokes that younger self, he cannot bring himself to abandon his reticence. And then there is the tantalizing reference to Dufour Square.

Only gossip is available to elucidate the reference, but it is gossip that has been around long enough to acquire a certain respectability. According to Borges' confidences to several friends, he was once taken by Father to one of those complaisant Geneva girls who catered to foreigners, loners, and young men in distress. He performed his task so quickly that he was overcome by the power of orgasm. The "little death," as the French call it, was too close to real death for him. From then on Georgie viewed sex with fear. There is another side to the story which may have more complex implications. In being initiated into sex through the offices of his father, Georgie may have assumed that the girl had performed the same services for Father; having to share the same woman with Father disturbed deep-seated taboos.

It will never be known exactly what happened at Dufour Square, if that was the place. What is known is that Borges cared enough about the episode to repeat it to friends in confidence and to include a tantalizing reference to it in one of his stories.

In his conversation with Fernández Moreno, quoted above, Borges mentions that he was greatly moved upon returning to Switzerland after forty years: he "had the feeling of returning home also. Because the experiences of adolescence, all that, happened there." Again, reticence; but if one connects this statement with the allusion in the story, things begin to fall into place. Geneva was where adolescence came to Georgie.

2.
The French Circulating Library

To be admitted to the Collège Calvin, Georgie had first to learn French. He began by taking lessons with a private teacher, then spent some time at an academy. He finally passed the admission test, although his French was still shaky. It was the third linguistic code he had had to master, but at fifteen the situation was less traumatic than when, as a child, he had had to learn Spanish and English almost simultaneously. The fact that French was a totally alien language to him, even though most educated Argentines of that era had some rudiments of French, emphasizes the paradoxical nature of his cultural upbringing. But if Georgie had to learn French the hard way, he also had to learn it thoroughly—something few of his countrymen bother to do.

Although Georgie had a rough time with the new language, his sister, Norah, mastered it very quickly. In his "Autobiographical Essay" he notes that her "French soon became so good she even dreamed in it. I remember my mother's coming home one day and finding Norah hidden behind a red plush curtain, crying out in fear, '*Une mouche, une mouche!*' It seems she had adopted the French notion that flies are dangerous. 'You come out of there,' my mother told her, somewhat unpatriotically. 'You were born and bred among flies!' " ("Essay," 1970, p. 215).

Borges also recalls some of the difficulties he had in adjusting to the Collège Calvin: "That first fall—1914—I started school at the College of Geneva, founded by John Calvin. It was a day school. In my class there were some forty of us; a good half were foreigners. The chief subject was Latin, and I soon found out that one could let other studies slide a bit as long as one's Latin was good" (ibid., p. 214).

Latin became his fourth code. Although it was never to be one of his major languages (later, in Majorca he improved his mastery of it), it gave Georgie a firm syntactic structure and an awareness of etymology that were later reflected in Borges' prose style. Combined with French, Latin erased the rhetorical vagueness inherent in Spanish and the untidiness of nineteenth-century English. Learning Latin and French simultaneously gave Georgie the linguistic discipline Borges later put to such good use.

In spite of hard work, Georgie had trouble keeping pace. Besides studying French as a separate language, he had to study all his other courses—"algebra, chemistry, physics, mineralogy, botany, zoology," he recalls (ibid., p. 214)—in that language. At the end of the year he passed all his exams except French. His schoolmates were so aware of his efforts that they decided to speak on his behalf:

> Without a word to me, my fellow schoolmates sent a petition around to the headmaster, which they had all signed. They pointed out that I had to study all of the different subjects in French, a language I also had to learn. They asked the headmaster to take this into account, and he very kindly did so. At first, I had not even understood when a teacher was calling on me, because my name was pronounced in the French manner, in a single syllable (rhyming roughly with "forge"), while we pronounce it with two syllables, the "g" sounding like a strong Scottish "h." Every time I had to answer, my schoolmates would nudge me. (Ibid., pp. 214–215)

Georgie must have responded to the warmth and concern of his schoolmates, especially in contrast to his experiences at school in Buenos Aires. Here in Geneva his singularity, even his foreignness, was not so strange. Many of the students in his class were also foreigners. To be "different" here was normal. Very soon Georgie had found among his schoolmates two of his closest friends, both two years younger. "My two friends were of Polish-Jewish origin—Simon Jichlinski and Maurice Abramowicz. One became a lawyer and the other a physician. I taught them to play *truco,* and they learned so well and fast that at the end of our first game they left me without a cent" ("Essay," p. 215).

I had the chance to visit Geneva in May 1975 and called on Dr. Jichlinski and Maître Abramowicz. They are both prosperous. Dr. Jichlinski had seen Borges again in the mid-1960s and had had the chance to refresh his memories. He told me that Borges exaggerated their ease in learning to play *truco.* He believed that Borges' account was part of his tendency to put himself in an ironic situation. Dr. Jichlinski recalled long conversations about literature while walking along the streets of the old quarter, bouts of drinking in the evening, endless meetings to discuss everything and nothing.

If Dr. Jichlinski shared more of Georgie's everyday life, it was Maître Abramowicz who shared more of his literary life. A lawyer by profession but a writer and a poet by avocation, he seemed to have total recall in talking about Georgie, whom he met at Geneva's municipal library, and read to me some of the letters Georgie wrote him from Spain in the late 1910s and early 1920s, checking on dates, names, figures.

More than once Borges has included Maître Abramowicz in a short list of his lifelong friends or has mentioned some of the writers Abramowicz taught him to love. In his conversations with Jean de Milleret, Borges acknowledges his debt to Abramowicz:

> Yes, he initiated me in the reading of Rimbaud. I remember one evening we were by the Rhone and he kept repeating:
>
> > J'ai vu des archipels sidéraux! et des îles
> > Dont les ciels délirants sont ouverts au voyageur:
> > —Est-ce en ces nuits sans fonds que tu dors et t'exiles,
> > Million d'oiseaux d'or, ô future Vigueur?
> > J'ai rêvé la nuit verte aux neiges éblouies,
> > Baisers montant aux yeux des mers avec lenteurs,
> > La circulation des sèves inouïes,
> > Et l'éveil jaune et bleu des phosphores chanteurs!
> > Mais, vrai, j'ai trop pleuré! les Aubes sont navrantes,
> > Toute lune est atroce et tout soleil amer.
>
> > (De Milleret, 1967, p. 25)

In quoting Rimbaud's *Le bateau ivre* (strophes 10, 20, 23), Borges makes a few mistakes which De Milleret corrects in a footnote. The mistakes are not important if one remembers that Borges was quoting in 1966 verses he must have learned some fifty years earlier. But what really matters is that he learned them not from a book but from Abramowicz's memory.

In a theological fantasy called "Three Versions of Judas," included in *Ficciones* (1944), Borges pays an oblique homage to their friendship. In a footnote he quotes a disparaging comment on Nils Runeberg, the protagonist of the story, and attributes that comment to none other than Maurice Abramowicz. It is doubtful that Abramowicz himself ever discussed the imaginary works of Nils Runeberg, but Borges loves to insert the names of his friends in his stories, as a form of private homage and public mystification. He did it with Bioy Casares and other literary friends in "Tlön, Uqbar, Orbis Tertius"; he included Patricio Gannon and myself in the story "The Other Death" (collected in *The Aleph*, 1949). To have Maurice Abramowicz discuss Runeberg's heresies is part of a private joke.

One of the things Georgie did as soon as he was settled in Geneva was to subscribe to a French circulating library. Thus he got the key to a literature he hardly knew. Soon French literature became the second most important of his youth. Critics have followed Borges' lead in underplaying the importance of French literature in shaping his writings; but the truth is that in spite of his preference for England and English letters, and without ever publicly admitting it, Borges was influenced by the concept of logical discourse and the subtle reasoning of French essayists. He also learned from France's poets and short-story writers.

In his conversations with Jean de Milleret, Borges recalls the names of some French writers he read while in Geneva. It is a rambling list which mentions, in the same breath, Daudet's comic masterpiece *Tartarin de Tarascon* and Gyp's rather naughty high-society novels. To justify his mentioning Gyp (who was considered extremely conservative and even anti-Semitic), Borges notes in another interview that Nietzsche also admired Gyp (*L'Herne*, 1964, p. 373). But Georgie's response to Gyp was hardly literary. Upon reaching the passage in her novel *The Passionate Woman* in which the baroness commits suicide because her lover deserts her, Georgie cried. To justify his youthful reaction, Borges ironically comments: "When one is a child, one is very snobbish, and then Gyp (the Comtesse de Martel) introduces you to a world of barons, marquises, dukes, eh!" (De Milleret, 1967, p. 26).

Gyp and Daudet were only two of his discoveries. He also read Zola very thoroughly (the whole of the Rougon-Macquart novels), many of Maupassant's books, and Victor Hugo's *Les misérables*. In reviewing with De Milleret those early readings, Borges comments: "Some ten years ago I tried to reread *L'assommoir* [The Drunkard]; I couldn't do it. In the same way, I've tried to read *Les misérables* and failed. While I can always read Hugo's poetry, that novel is so terribly emphatic" (ibid., p. 26). There is an invisible thread that links all the books mentioned by Borges: they all embody more or less the realist and naturalist style of narrative developed in the second half of the nineteenth century. This style had an enormous influence in Europe and the United States, but especially in Latin America. Even today (after the Borgesian revolution in writing) one can still find novelists and critics who praise the virtues of that long-forgotten school or attempt to refloat it under some fashionable new name. The fact that Borges, the man most responsible for having undermined its acceptance among younger writers, was exposed in his youth to the French classics of realism and naturalism is seldom mentioned by the critics. But such reading made Georgie aware of the conventions of story-telling (narrative continuity, character description, landscape) in a way that would prove useful to the future writer of *Ficciones*.

Another important aspect of reading the French realist and naturalist writers lies in their handling of the relationship between the sexes. Zola, Maupassant, and even Gyp displayed a candor (or brutality) that was new in nineteenth-century literature. In the case of Zola, well known for his socialist views, this preoccupation with a subject the romantics treated only from the point of view of feeling was reinforced by an acute perception of class conflict and an active interest in the coming struggle for power between the workers and the bourgeoisie. Because Father had been (and still was) a philosophical anarchist, Georgie accepted the view of political and social forces that Zola exposed in his novels. They paved the way for his later spontaneous, even joyful embrace of the 1917 Russian revolution.

A writer he first read then, and continued to read throughout his life, was Flaubert. In his mature years Borges devoted two essays to him (both published originally in 1954): the first, to discuss and defend *Bouvard and Pécuchet;* the second, to underline Flaubert's creation of a poetic persona, a literary mask that took the place of the writer's own personality and even obliterated it. It is obvious that Georgie could not have read Flaubert that way. He probably perused *Madame Bovary* and the celebrated *Three Stories.* (Gertrude Stein had already published her own rewriting of one of those stories in *Three Lives* in 1909.) His view of Flaubert as a sort of precursor of Valéry, or perhaps of Pierre Menard, came to fruition later.

Another French writer he read while in Geneva was the now almost forgotten but then extremely popular Henri Barbusse. During the war years Barbusse became one of the most influential French writers. His novel *The Fire* (1916) described the horrors of war in the trenches, the endless carnage that the stalemate between Germany and the Allied forces had created. Later, the German writer Erich Maria Remarque wrote *All Quiet on the Western Front* (1929), a novel that achieved even greater popularity. According to Borges in a 1937 article, Barbusse's novel was superior. But the Barbusse novel he preferred was an earlier one, *Hell* (1908), in which a man lives in a hotel and through a hole in the wall spies on his next-door neighbors. Borges has this to say about the book:

In the mixed pages of *Hell,* Barbusse attempted the writing of a classic, a timeless work. He wanted to fix the essential activities of man, free from the varied colors of space and time. He wanted to reveal the general book that lies beneath all books. Neither the plot—the poetical prose dialogues and the salacious or lethal episodes which a hole in the wall affords the narrator— nor the style, more or less derived from Hugo, allowed a good execution of that Platonic concept, which is totally inaccessible in any case. Since 1919 I had no chance to reread that book; I still remember the deep passion of its prose. Also, its more or less adequate statement about man's central loneliness. (*El Hogar*, March 19, 1937, p. 28)

In stressing the novel's basic preoccupations with man's loneliness (or alienation, as it would be called later), Borges calls attention to its major subject, one prominent in French fiction of the twentieth century, as Céline's *Voyage au bout de la nuit* (1932), Sartre's *La nausée* (1938), Camus' *L'étranger* (1942), and Alain Robbe-Grillet's *Le voyeur* (1950) bear witness. In spite of the differences in style and writing, all these novels share a preoccupation with the central loneliness in their main characters' view of life: a loneliness that makes them desperate witnesses to other people's lives. Barbusse's protagonist is a voyeur; that is, a true child of this century.

The reading of *Hell* must have had a great influence on Georgie's view of the adult world. With the exception of the book on Balkan sex life, *Hell* was probably the first book he came across that dealt explicitly with sex. He had already read Burton's and Lane's translations of the *One Thousand and One Nights*. Lane's explicit omissions and Burton's detailed footnotes on sexual mores and perversions in the Islamic world must have alerted Georgie. But the Arabian stories lacked prurience in their handling of sex. They were explicit and even salacious but never titillating. In Zola or Maupassant, Georgie may have found a more complex and even suggestive treatment of sex, although both writers had to conform to a nineteenth-century concept of decorum that was absent in the Oriental classic. But in *Hell* Georgie found something else: a vivid description of the sexual encounter as seen from the passive (and perhaps also active) point of view of the voyeur: sex is something that happens to you while you are watching what is happening to others. The voyeur is like a reader of novels; he is participating through his imagination more than through his senses in a vicarious experience.

Another popular French book that Georgie read was *Jean Christophe*, the ten-volume novel by Romain Rolland about the life and loves of a German composer. Rolland was a musicologist who in 1903 had published a celebrated biography of Beethoven. The long novel was, in a sense, an outcome of his interests both in Beethoven and in the mystique of the artist's life. Like Barbusse, Rolland was also famous for his socialist views. A firm believer in peace, he preferred exile in Switzerland to participation in the nationalistic hysteria that the war brought about. Georgie must have read *Jean Christophe* around 1917. In a short piece on Rolland written twenty years later, he points out that the protagonist is a "fusion of Beethoven and Rolland," and that even more admirable than the work is its success: "I remember that around 1917 people still repeated '*Jean Christophe* is the password of the new generation' " (*El Hogar*, July 25, 1937, p. 30). Borges' words are colored with irony. In the same article, to indicate the scope and quality of Rolland's followers, he adds: "Rolland's glory seems very firm. In Argentina, he is admired by the admirers of Joaquin V. González; in the Caribbean Sea, by those of Martí; in the United States, by those of Hendrik Willem van Loon. In the French-speaking world, he would never lack the support of Belgium and Switzerland. His virtues, by the way, are less literary than moral, less syntactic than 'panhumanist,' to use a word that makes him happy" (ibid., p. 30).

In poking fun at Rolland's admirers, Borges also pokes fun at Georgie. The irony with which he describes the kinds of admirers Rolland has (readers of best-sellers like those written by van Loon, of sentimental poets like González and Martí) or the places where he is celebrated (marginal to Paris), or even the reason for his fame (his "panhumanism") indicates very clearly the bitterness with which Borges has turned against what he once probably loved. On the other hand, it gives a glimpse of what he thought in 1937 about Switzerland in 1917: it was a place where Rolland had followers.

But in those days Georgie probably read *Jean Christophe* with passion; he must have discussed it with Maurice Abramowicz and Simon Jichlinski and discovered in it the password for his generation. In describing the book's appeal, Borges uses three adjectives: "intimate, silent, and heartfelt." While the war was still going on and people had no time to reflect on their feelings, Rolland's "panhumanism" may have seemed uplifting to all those provincial souls. The Russian revolution of 1917 and the 1918 Wilsonian peace first kindled, then drastically dissipated, the aura of that "panhumanism."

Rimbaud was not the only French poet Georgie favored. In his conversations with De Milleret, he quotes a whole list: "It was especially Rimbaud whom I loved to recite, and a forgotten poet, Ephraim Michael. I read them all in a yellow-covered book published by the *Mercure de France,* an anthology of French modern poetry where you could find Stuart Merrill, obviously Mallarmé, Rimbaud, Verlaine of course, and several minor poets of the symbolist movement. I read, I reread all that. . . . I knew many poems by heart" (De Milleret, 1967, pp. 20–21).

There is very little trace in Borges' work of those readings of his adolescence. But the few references here and there prove his familiarity with those books. In a short piece written in 1937 to review two new books on Rimbaud (one by a Catholic writer, the other by two Marxists), he not only praises Rimbaud highly but defends French literature against the accusation that instead of producing geniuses it has the talent only to "organize and polish foreign importations"; Borges also quotes a long passage from Rimbaud's *Season in Hell*. The quotation is truncated and the words are out of order; but that only proves again that Borges was quoting by heart.

A poet he forgets to mention in his conversations with De Milleret is Baudelaire, although he was naturally included in the *Mercure de France* anthology and is mentioned by Borges in Murat's interview, where he acknowledges that there "was a time I knew *Les fleurs du mal* by heart. But now I find myself far from Baudelaire. I believe that if I had to name one French poet, it would be Verlaine" (Murat, 1964, p. 383).

His resistance to Baudelaire comes across rather strongly in another piece written in 1937. In telling an anecdote about the Indian poet Rabindranath Tagore (who had recently visited Buenos Aires), Borges introduces a reference to Baudelaire:

> Three years ago I had the slightly terrible honor of talking with the venerated and honey-tongued Rabindranath Tagore. We talked about Baudelaire's poetry and somebody repeated "La mort des amants," that sonnet so cluttered with beds, divans, flowers, fireplaces, shelves, mirrors, and angels. Tagore listened to it attentively but said at the end: "I don't like your furniture poet!" I deeply sympathized with him. Now, rereading his works, I suspect that he was moved less by any horror of romantic bric-à-brac than by his invincible love of vagueness. (*El Hogar,* June 11, 1937, p. 30)

Once more, Borges' memory is playing a trick on him. There is no mention of actual fireplaces or mirrors in Baudelaire's poems. The fires and mirrors are metaphors for the lovers' hearts, burning with the ardor that is reflected in their souls:

> Nos deux cœurs seront deux vastes flambeaux,
> Qui réflechiront leurs doubles lumières
> Dans nos deux esprits, ces miroirs jumeaux.
> (Baudelaire, 1951, p. 193)

But the beauty of Borges' recollection of how Tagore reacted to Baudelaire's poem is that it allows him to disparage both poets simultaneously.

What is missing in Borges' recollections of the French poets Georgie read is a more detailed account of his reactions to Mallarmé.

In later years Borges quoted Mallarmé occasionally and always in an important context. His persona (the poet who is totally dedicated to writing and to whom the world makes sense only in a book) influenced Borges' own concept of literature and of the literary mind. Traces of Mallarmé can be detected in the invention of Pierre Menard. But if Borges has been reticent in making explicit his adolescent reaction to Mallarmé, he has been more forthright in talking about Rémy de Gourmont, another important French symbolist writer he read in Geneva. He readily admits that he read "a lot of De Gourmont in those days" (De Milleret, 1967, p. 382). De Gourmont (who died in 1915) was a dedicated critic and one of the founders, in 1889, of the *Mercure de France,* the same journal that published the symbolist anthology Georgie learned by heart. De Gourmont was then vastly read: he was quoted with respect by Eliot, had an enormous following among the Latin American poets of the turn of the century, and in a sense played the part Jean Paulhan would play in the period between the two world wars.

De Gourmont was also a novelist of a refined and slightly perverse turn of mind, and the author of a celebrated erotic treatise, *La physique de l'amour* (1903), written in the spirit of the Greek materialists Epicure and Democritus and their famous disciple, Lucretius. How much of these works Georgie read is not known. But there is one aspect of De Gourmont that he probably knew very well: his appetite for philosophical discussion, the encyclopedic criticism that knew how to balance contrary theories or find the right word to deflect them. One of his critics once pointed out that De Gourmont "is always ready to untie what he had just tied, he proclaims that the 'death of some truth is of a great benefit to men' because it has become nothing but a commonplace . . . worn-out, outdated, and bothersome" (Clouard, 1947, p. 392).

It was probably this cultivated and paradoxical side of De Gourmont that most attracted Georgie. In his essays (collected under the titles of *Promenades littéraires* and *Promenades philosophiques*), Georgie may have found the model for a certain type of writing he later developed and perfected. There are other more obvious links between De Gourmont and the future writer. De Gourmont had translated into French Enrique Larreta's *The Glory of Don Ramiro,* a book that Georgie knew from childhood. In an essay De Gourmont collected in the fourth series of his *Literary Walks* (1912), he explains his method: "I have translated his book as literally as was compatible with the elegance our language demands; one can be sure that there is nothing of the Spanish redundance. It is a clear and logical spirit" (De Gourmont, 1912, p. 121). Georgie probably laughed at De Gourmont's French prejudice against Spanish when he came across this book; he probably shared his laugh with Father.

There is another article in the same series that Georgie may have read. It is dedicated to "Louis Ménard, a Mystical Pagan." Ménard was an inventor (he discovered collodium, so useful in photography), a painter of the Barbizon school, and a poet. His more lasting work was in the domain of parody. In his youth he attempted to rewrite some of the lost plays of the Greek tragic poets and even attempted a version of Aeschylus' lost *Prometheus Unbound* which for the convenience of his readers he wrote in French, in spite of having preferred (according to De Gourmont) to write it in Aeschylus' own Greek (ibid., p. 163). His second major parody was a piece called "The Devil at the Café," which he attributed to Diderot and almost managed to smuggle into a collection of that writer's work then in progress. (Unfortunately, Anatole France exposed the hoax in time.) According to De Gourmont, Ménard liked to practice a sort of anachronistic reading of the classics: "When he read Homer, he thought about Shakespeare, placed Helen under the absent-minded eyes of Hamlet, and imagined the plaintive Desdemona at Achilles' feet" (ibid., p. 163).

Louis Ménard's literary habits (the rewriting of lost or nonexistent works, his anachronistic reading of literature) anticipate those of his namesake Pierre Menard (without any accent on the *e*), the strange postsymbolist French poet Borges invented in 1939 to poke fun at the conventions of literary criticism.

How much of what one reads into De Gourmont's article on Louis Ménard is determined by one's previous reading of Borges' short story? Is this a case of that anachronistic influence that he talks about in "Kafka and His Precursors," where the reading of a contemporary writer influences the reading of the classics? It is difficult to say. Georgie probably read De Gourmont's article on Ménard, and somewhere in his vast memory a trace was left. Twenty years later his own Menard would come into being, transforming a delightful little piece about an odd character into one of the comic masterpieces of this century. De Gourmont's Ménard was probably the small seed which, with the help of many other writers (Mallarmé, Valéry, Unamuno, perhaps Larreta, and of course Carlyle and De Quincey), finally became Borges' Menard.

A footnote to Louis Ménard. In De Gourmont's article, in talking about the invention of collodium, the author indicates that an American inventor "rediscovered" collodium and took the precaution of taking out an international patent under his own name, which was (confusion compounded) Maynard: a name that in French sounds almost the same as Ménard. The whole story is already too Borgesian.

Although Borges in years to come tried to forget how much he owed to French culture, at a time when his mind and memory were impressionable he spent the better part of five years reading Zola and Maupassant, Barbusse and Romain Rolland, Hugo and Rimbaud, Verlaine and Rémy de Gourmont. In Geneva he learned to understand and love a culture that left its traces, ineffaceable as a watermark, on his writing.

3.
The Ambassadors

Georgie's discovery of French literature in Geneva did not dull his appetite for English literature. On the contrary, he was able to continue his readings in that field thanks to a German publisher who had reprinted some of the best English and American writers in cheap, paperback editions. All books published by Bernhard Tauchnitz in Leipzig carried this sentence on the cover: "Not to be introduced into the British empire." They thus preserved the original British or American copyrights and were meant only for circulation among foreign students of Anglo-American literature or English-speaking tourists who strayed onto the Continent. They were also sold in the colonies and, naturally, in South America. In Buenos Aires Georgie was probably already familiar with their plain covers and their small, neat print.

Three of the English authors he discovered while living in Geneva had a lasting influence. These were Thomas De Quincey, Thomas Carlyle, and Gilbert Keith Chesterton. Of the three, De Quincey is the most widely read today; both Carlyle and Chesterton have gone out of fashion, although Chesterton's Father Brown mystery stories are still popular.

Borges has singled out De Quincey as the most important influence. In writing about the *Biathanatos,* the long, obscure text on suicide by John Donne, he says that his own debt to De Quincey "is so vast that to specify a part of it seems to repudiate or to silence the rest" (*Inquisitions,* 1964, p. 89). Yet it would be useless to search among Borges' essays for one explicitly dedicated to De Quincey. The omission (deliberate, of course) makes it more difficult to document his readings. Fortunately, some specifics are mentioned in a 1962 interview with James E. Irby:

I read De Quincey when I was sixteen; since then I have read and reread him innumerable times. He is a very suggestive writer, with an almost inexhaustible curiosity and erudition. As an explorer of dream life, he is unique in literature. His style is excellent, except when he attempts to be humoristic. I remember a long essay . . . which is one of his best, "The Last Days of Immanuel Kant," the description of how a powerful intelligence is put out: something intense, very sad. (Irby, 1962, p. 10)

When Borges says that De Quincey's style is excellent (with the proviso that he fails when attempting to be comic), he is stressing something that separates his model's writings from his own: where Borges is short and precise, De Quincey (in the best tradition of romantic prose) is digressive, prolix, highly emotional. In the vast collection of De Quincey's *Writings* (Borges generally quotes from the 1897 David Masson edition) Georgie discovered a model of discourse. By a process that can be compared to the miniaturization achieved in electronic circuits, Borges learned to pack into his short, fragmentary pieces the substance of De Quincey's sprawling articles. The model's digressiveness is condensed into one parenthesis; the tension of one of De Quincey's emotional paragraphs is reduced to one unexpected adjective; the serpentine footnotes of the original, which wind their way from page to page, are replaced by spare notes at the end of a piece or by pointed, reticent prologues. Where De Quincey expands, Borges contracts; where De Quincey lets passion flow, Borges becomes reticent or argumentative; where De Quincey muses, Borges is painfully lucid. But in spite of all the differences in their writings, the effect of their texts is similar.

The rather chaotic erudition of De Quincey (a journalist, after all) is equally chaotic in Borges, in spite of the latter's more professional system of quotes. Passion runs as deeply under Borges' writing as it runs on the sentimental surface of De Quincey's. Although Borges' digressions are cleverly disguised by the French method of composition he learned so well in Geneva, they are no less capricious than those of his model. If one reads De Quincey after having read Borges (the kind of reverse operation "Pierre Menard" suggests), it is impossible not to recognize the kinship.

Other forms of kinship are perhaps more obvious. Both De Quincey and Borges had well-developed memories and the rare ability to perceive analogical relationships. In his *Confessions of an English Opium Eater,* De Quincey boasts about both gifts: "Having the advantage of a prodigious memory, and the far greater advantage of a logical instinct for feeling in a moment the secret analogies or parallelisms that connected things else apparently remote, I enjoyed these two peculiar gifts for conversation" (De Quincey, 1897, p. 332). Borges could have subscribed to these words.

Another characteristic that unites them is insomnia. For many long years Borges suffered from it to the point that he even attempts to recapture in "Funes, the Memorious" what he calls its "atrocious lucidity." De Quincey, on the other hand, attributed to insomnia his craving for opium.

They also share an interest in certain subjects: strange heresies, secret societies, philosophical or religious problems (suicide is one of the most noticeable), odd linguistic theories, murder and violent death. But it is De Quincey's literary persona that chiefly influenced Borges. In him, Georgie found his prototype of the literary man, not under the guise of the successful and rather terrifying Dr. Johnson, but in the strange, slightly marginal, but intensely attractive one of De Quincey. Georgie must have been highly impressed by a writer who, from the etymological study of a word, could move quickly to a philosophical doctrine and even to a coherent view of the world. His conversations with Father, and the reading of Herbert Spencer and William James, had prepared Georgie for De Quincey's hospitable and penetrating mind, one of whose tasks would be to facilitate Georgie's entry into German philosophy. From that point of view, his piece on "The Last Days of Immanuel Kant" had a lasting impact.

In that article Georgie probably discovered another very important aspect of De Quincey's method of writing. In telling of Kant's last days, the English writer created a single text out of different narratives written by several witnesses (Wasianski, Jachman, Rink, and Borowski, among others); but instead of indicating the source in each case, he preferred to present this collage of texts as a single narrative attributed to Wasianski for the sake of unity. Borges followed De Quincey's method in composing his biographies of infamous men for *A Universal History of Infamy*. Here again, the unity of the text masks the subtle collage of sources, which are partially indicated in a note at the end of the biographical section of that book.

Another aspect of De Quincey's works which Borges underlines in his conversations with Irby is his value as an "explorer of dream life." Besides the two versions of *Confessions of an English Opium Eater* (1821, 1856) and the *Suspiria de Profundis* (1845), in which De Quincey develops his hallucinations and explores his dreams of opium, there are other, less well-known pieces—such as the description of one of Piranesi's engravings which he never saw but which (he claims) Coleridge once described to him—in which De Quincey reveals a visionary quality that must have impressed Georgie deeply. In all these essays, visions are presented not as opposed to reality but as part of it: hallucinations are not fictions but a natural dimension of the real.

On many occasions De Quincey achieves an almost surreal dimension. One of his most famous passages is the description of his life in London when, as a teenager, he was totally lost in that "red labyrinth." There he met a fifteen-year-old prostitute who befriended him and for several months was his constant companion. In the 1821 version of the *Confessions* De Quincey manages to convey the almost hallucinatory experiences of those two children in a style that preserves their innocence. Isolated from the rest of his writings as it is generally read now, this episode seems merely an anticipation of what years later both Dickens and Wilkie Collins would attempt to capture in their more robust melodramas. But if the episode is inserted in the autobiographical sequence provided by other De Quincey texts, it is easy to see its real significance. What is known of his life (mainly through his *Autobiographical Sketches*) confirms his deep affection for young girls. De Quincey's father had died when he was only seven, and his mother had always been absent, taking care of the family's business. He had been brought up in a house dominated by his older sisters and by female servants. He even congratulates himself for having spent most of his childhood under "the gentlest of sisters." In the same memoirs he remembers among the most intense experiences of his life the deaths of two of his sisters: one died at three when he was only one year and a half; the other died at nine when he was just six. Visiting the room where she was being mourned, the child had a vision in which death was contrasted with the beauty of the summer day.

When De Quincey reaches London at age sixteen, it is not as a boy who has just lost his mother, but as someone who has lost his whole family of little mothers: his sisters. In finding the fifteen-year-old prostitute and an even younger girl who shared his empty lodgings, he succeeds somehow in rebuilding, in the middle of corrupted Soho, the paradise of his childhood.

It is possible to recognize in De Quincey's emotional attachment to his real and surrogate sisters the same kind of affection that linked Georgie to his only sister, Norah. Like De Quincey, he grew up under his sister's active devotion. Although she was two years younger, she had a more outgoing personality, and in their childhood games she always played the part of the mother, protecting him from invisible and hideous enemies. In Switzerland, where he was isolated from his familiar surroundings, Norah must have continued to be his Electra, in the sense De Quincey used the word in describing the woman he eventually married and the daughter who cared for him in his last invalid years.

The parallel must not be pursued further. There is nothing in Georgie's family setup equal to the hardships that beset De Quincey. Mother was not absent. Father was very much present and cast a powerful shadow over the boy. Another decisive element was missing: the necrophiliac feelings that the death of his two older sisters aroused in De Quincey. But in spite of obvious differences, at the level of a dream (a fiction half lived, half imagined), Georgie must have found in De Quincey's autobiographical writings a key to some of the most obscure experiences of his adolescence.

Borges' debt to Carlyle is of a very different sort. At the time Georgie discovered his work, he came to think that Carlyle summarized literature. To quote from the concluding statement of one of his most important articles, "The Flower of Coleridge": "Those who carefully copy a writer do it impersonally, do it because they confuse that writer with literature, do it because they suspect that to leave him at any point is to deviate from reason and orthodoxy. For many years I thought that the almost infinite world of literature was in one man. That man was Carlyle, he was Johannes Becher, he was Walt Whitman, he was Rafael Cansinos-Asséns, he was De Quincey" (*Inquisitions,* 1964, p. 13).

As Borges generally lists writers in chronological order (that is, in the order of their birthdates), the disorder of the above list can only mean that he is citing them in the order he read them. Carlyle thus comes first not only in the text but in Borges' experience as a reader. He must have been the one to open up for Georgie a new literary perspective. The list shows something else that is relevant. If Carlyle once represented literature, he was soon displaced by other writers, and rather quickly too: Becher, Whitman, and Cansinos-Asséns were all discovered by Georgie before he was twenty-one.

Carlyle's ascent and sudden dismissal can be attributed to an inner resistance Borges later experienced to the views Carlyle commonly expressed. If at the time he discovered his works Georgie paid little attention to Carlyle's ideology, fifty years later Borges chose to discuss that aspect of his work almost exclusively. In an interview with Ronald Christ he says rather bluntly: "I rather dislike him: I think he invented Nazism and so on—one of the fathers or forefathers of such things" (Christ, 1967, p. 130). The same year, he discussed Carlyle's politics with De Milleret. Concentrating his objections on the subject of slavery, Borges accused Carlyle of being a racist and believing the fate of the blacks was to be slaves. Similar views of Carlyle have been advanced in other Borges works.

In a 1956 prologue Borges wrote for a Spanish translation of Carlyle's *On Heroes and Hero Worship,* he discusses Herbert Spencer's criticism of Carlyle's religion and summarizes the latter's political theory in one word: Nazism. The authors he quotes to substantiate his arguments are Bertrand Russell (*The Ancestry of Fascism,* 1935) and

G. K. Chesterton (*The End of the Armistice*, 1940). Using both critics and quoting Carlyle's own writings, Borges proves his relationship with totalitarianism.

This political view of Caryle was not current in Geneva. It is obvious that it was formed later, in the period between the two world wars, as the dates of Russell's and Chesterton's books indicate. The war with Germany put Carlyle's authoritarian texts in a purely political perspective. In spite of that, Borges is able to recognize other aspects of his literary personality. In the same prologue Borges adds:

> Such affirmations do not invalidate Carlyle's sincerity. Nobody has felt like him that this world is unreal (unreal like a nightmare, and atrocious). Of this general ghostliness, he saves one thing only, work: not its outcome, let's make clear, which is mere vanity, mere image, but its performance. He writes (*Reminiscences: James Carlyle*): "All human work is transitory, small, in itself contemptible; only the worker, and the spirit that dwells in him, is significant." (Prólogos, 1975, pp. 36–37)

This was probably the Carlyle Georgie read so avidly: the stoic, undefeatable, slightly mad Carlyle, not the apologist of slavery and totalitarianism. From his book on heroes and from his historical essays and biographies, Georgie must have taken the impulse to see life as a dream, a nightmare, made real only by an effort of the will. From this point of view, Carlyle must have served for Georgie as an ambassador to more complex writers: Schopenhauer and Nietzsche, whom he avidly read while in Geneva.

Among Carlyle's writings is a fictional biography that contains long excerpts from an apocryphal book. *Sartor Resartus* was, at the time it was published in three volumes (1831), merely an oddity, an elaborate joke on the same art of biography that Carlyle had practiced with some persistence (his life of Frederick the Great takes up seven volumes in the collected edition of his works; his Cromwell, three). The book can be read as a tedious parody of German romantic philosophy, very much in fashion then. But there is more in *Sartor Resartus* than meets the eye. In pretending to review and summarize a nonexistent book, Carlyle developed a format that Borges would take to its most delicate consequences: the fake review of an imaginary work by a nonexistent writer. As early as 1936 Borges included in one of his books of essays, *History of Eternity*, under the general title of "Two Notes," the "review" of a detective story called "The Approach to al-Mu'tasim," supposedly written by Mir Bahadur Ali. Although Borges even quotes some previous reviews of the book, the article is a hoax: everything, from the name of the author and the title of the novel to the English quotations in the review, was invented by Borges. Five years later, collecting "The Approach to al-Mu'tasim" in a book of short stories (*The Garden of Forking Paths*, 1941), Borges acknowledged the hoax and even justified it in a prologue:

> The composition of vast books is a laborious and impoverishing extravagance. To go on for five hundred pages developing an idea whose perfect oral exposition is possible in a few minutes! A better course of procedure is to pretend that these books already exist, and then to offer a résumé, a commentary. Thus proceeded Carlyle in *Sartor Resartus*. Thus Butler in *The Fair Haven*. These are works which suffer the imperfection of being themselves books, and of being no less tautological than the others. (*Ficciones*, 1962, p. 15)

To avoid tautology, Borges preferred to write "notes upon imaginary books." Those "notes" are "Tlön, Uqbar, Orbis Tertius," "An Examination of the Work of Herbert Quain," and "The Approach to al-Mu'tasim": all texts collected in *The Garden*.

If Borges' 1941 criticism of Carlyle reflects the viewpoint of the mature writer he had by then become, Georgie's view in 1916 must have been different. He probably was fascinated as much by Carlyle's paradoxical mind as by his flamboyant and even turgid style. At that time, he was about to enter a phase of his reading that would lead to his first published writings: a series of poems written in a rather passionate and exalted style. In this, as in his anticipation of Schopenhauer and Nietzsche, Carlyle also functioned as an ambassador.

The third English writer Georgie discovered in Geneva was one of Carlyle's most active opponents. In his prologue to the Argentine edition of *On Heroes* Borges quotes from one of Chesterton's outbursts against Carlyle. It can be found in *The End of the Armistice* and was written when Chesterton was sixty-six: "A man who has reveled in Carlyle as a boy, reacted against him as a man, re-reacted with saner appreciation as an older man, and ended, he will hope, by seeing Carlyle more or less where he really stands, can only be amazed at this sudden reappearance of all that was bad and barbarous and stupid and ignorant in Carlyle, without a touch of what was really quaint and humorous in him" (Chesterton, 1940, p. 66).

But it was not this pamphleteering side of Chesterton that Georgie discovered in Geneva; it was the master of the short story. Borges told James E. Irby that Chesterton belonged with Stevenson and Kipling to a trilogy of writers whose stories he had read so much that "I can almost re-create them in their entirety in my memory" (Irby, 1962, p. 10). In the prologue to his first collection of stories, *A Universal History of Infamy*, Borges publicly acknowledges his debt to Chesterton and Stevenson. Two years before, in one of his most important essays, "Narrative Art and Magic" (included in *Discusión*, 1932), Borges used some of Chesterton's stories to illustrate some points of his argument. According to him, magical narratives have a tightly knit structure:

> Every episode in a painstaking piece of fiction prefigures something still to come. Thus, in one of Chesterton's phantasmagorias ["The Honest Quack," from *Four Faultless Felons*, 1930], a man suddenly shoves a stranger out of the road to save him from an oncoming motorcar, and this necessary but alarming violence foreshadows the first man's later act of declaring the other man insane so that he may not be hanged for a murder. In another Chesterton story ["The Loyal Traitor," from the same collection], a vast and dangerous conspiracy consisting of a single man (aided by false beards, masks, and aliases) is darkly heralded by the lines:
>
> > As all stars shrivel in the single sun,
> > The words are many, but the Word is one.
>
> This comes to be unraveled at the end through a shift of capital letters:
>
> > The words are many, but the word is One.
>
> In a third story ["The Arrow of Heaven," from *The Incredulity of Father Brown*, 1926], the initial prototype—the passing mention of an Indian who throws his knife at another man and kills him—is the complete reverse of the plot: a man stabbed to death by his friend with an arrow beside the open window of a tower. A knife turned into an arrow, an arrow turned into a knife. Between the two there is a long repercussion. (*Prose*, 1972, pp. 214–215)

Borges remembered these Chestertonian inventions at the time he began to write his own stories. Unexplained behavior, the use of masks and disguises, emblematic situations that anticipate (in reverse) the solution of the mystery: all these tricks can be found in his stories as well as in Chesterton's.

In a note about one of his most successful stories, "The Dead Man," Borges acknowledges Chesterton's influence on the delineation of the protagonist: "Azevedo Bandeira, in that story, is a man from Rivera or Cerro Largo [two provinces in the north of Uruguay] and he is also a rough god, a mulatto, an uncouth version of Chesterton's incomparable Sunday" (*El Aleph*, 1949, p. 145). In the American edition of the book this note is replaced by one in which Borges omits all allusion to *The Man Who Was Thursday* (1908) and comments on the real sources of the story. But at the time the story was first published in book form, Chesterton was foremost in his thoughts. From the very beginning of his discovery of Chesterton, Georgie fell under his spell. He not only read and reread his stories; he came to know them by heart. And from the storehouse of concrete details he found in his narratives, Borges would continue to pick up words, sentences, tricks. His conversations with Richard Burgin include the following exchange:

BURGIN: You love painting and architecture, don't you? I mean, your stories seem to me very vivid visually.
BORGES: Are they really visual, or does the visibility come from Chesterton? (Burgin, 1969, p. 99)

His debt to Chesterton goes even further. In his concept of the detective story, as well as in his sense of evil, Borges later borrowed heavily from Chesterton. He dedicated several essays and a warm article to him on his death. Although in a 1968 interview with Rita Guibert he has admitted that many of Chesterton's surprises and tricks do not stand the wear and tear of time, while his old rival Shaw has the chance of a longer posthumous life, Borges feels that it would be a pity if Chesterton's "flavor" were ever lost.

4.
The Philosopher's Code

If the Borgeses were ignorant of the imminent outbreak of World War I when they decided to travel to Europe, they were also unwise about predicting its end. The war seemed to have reached a stalemate in the trenches of France; neither side was strong enough to make the last, decisive push. But two events of 1917 ought to have alerted the Borgeses. The entrance of the United States into the war and the October revolution in Russia were portents of the conflict's end, and also of the end of Europe as it had been viewed in the last four hundred years. At that precise moment two marginal countries were making decisions that would affect the destiny of all Europeans.

The Borgeses did not possess that kind of vision. Very few people in Europe did. Therefore, Georgie continued his studies and completed his fourth year at the Collège Calvin, avidly reading anything that was available in the French circulating library, in Tauchnitz's convenient reprints, or in the libraries of Geneva. He also continued to develop his friendship with Abramowicz and Jichlinski.

His stay in Geneva came to an abrupt end in 1918, when his maternal grandmother died. The family decided to leave Geneva and move farther up Lake Leman to Lugano. They settled at the Hotel du Lac. Georgie spent long hours there, endlessly reading, or rowing in the lake with Norah. The move to Lugano brought him close to his sister once again. Isolated from his Geneva friends and classmates, Georgie went back to her. While rowing, he used to recite to her poems from Baudelaire and the symbolists. Verlaine was probably one of his favorites, as was Rimbaud's *Le bateau ivre,* so appropriate to the occasion. He probably knew by heart Baudelaire's "Invitation au voyage," which echoes *The Song of Songs* in the way the lover addresses his mistress:

Mon enfant, ma sœur,
Songe à la douceur
D'aller là-bas vivre ensemble!

Perhaps Georgie and Norah found in the poet's longing for a paradise in the tropics a metaphor for their own longings to return to the lost paradise of the garden in Palermo. In his own recollections in the "Autobiographical Essay," Borges omits all reference to those days spent on the lake with Norah and concentrates almost exclusively on his linguistic and poetic pursuits:

> We remained in Switzerland until 1919. After three or four years in Geneva, we spent a year in Lugano. I had my bachelor's degree by then, and it was now understood that I should devote myself to writing. I wanted to show my manuscripts to my father, but he told me he didn't believe in advice and that I must work my way all by myself through trial and error. I had been writing sonnets in English and in French. The English sonnets were poor imitations of Wordsworth, and the French, in their own watery way, were imitative of symbolist poetry. I still recall one line of my French experiments: *"Petite boîte noire pour le violon cassé."* The whole piece was titled "Poème pour être récité avec un accent russe." As I knew I wrote a foreigner's French, I thought a Russian accent better than an Argentine one. In my English experiments, I affected some eighteenth-century mannerisms, such as "o'er" instead of "over" and, for the sake of metrical ease, "doth sing" instead of "sings." I knew, however, that Spanish would be my unavoidable destiny. ("Essay," 1970, p. 218)

The year spent at Lugano was a hard one. Although Switzerland had been spared the horrors of war, it suffered, like the rest of Europe, from an acute shortage of food. Recalling those days in an interview with Gloria Alcorta, Borges says: "I had never experienced hunger except in the last year of World War I. . . . I remember that we thought [then] that the only thing we wanted was a little more bread, or one extra grain of rice" (Alcorta, 1964, p. 412). Not far from Lugano, in Prague, Kafka was experiencing hunger, and his body was being further undermined by it. But in 1918 Georgie hadn't yet heard of Kafka. He kept hunger away by reading the symbolists and by writing his first poems. Soon he was to discover a new linguistic world. German was the third language he acquired while in Switzerland. He did it on his own, with the help of a German-English dictionary. Borges recalls that it was Carlyle's *Sartor Resartus* which sent him on "this adventure":

> [The book] dazzled and also bewildered me. The hero, Diogenes Devil's-dung, is a German professor of idealism. In German literature, I was look-

ing for something Germanic, akin to Tacitus, but I was only later to find this in Old English and Old Norse. German literature turned out to be romantic and sickly. At first, I tried Kant's *Critique of Pure Reason* but was defeated by it, as most people—including most Germans—are. Then I thought verse would be easier, because of its brevity. So I got hold of a copy of Heine's early poems the *Lyrisches Intermezzo*, and a German-English dictionary. Little by little, owing to Heine's simple vocabulary, I found I could do without the dictionary. Soon I had worked my way into the loveliness of the language. ("Essay," 1970, p. 216).

On two previous occasions Borges had told his interviewers how he learned German. In 1967 he said to Ronald Christ that it took him "two or three months" to get "fairly good" at reading Heine's poetry "without the aid of a dictionary" (Christ, 1967, p. 130). To De Milleret he confided his feeling that it was better to read Kant's *Critique of Pure Reason* in any language but German: "Mauthner says that in that book Kant writes with a dazzling dryness, but I found more of the dryness than of the dazzlingness; the phrases are too long" (De Milleret, 1967, p. 27).

If Spanish and English had come to Georgie naturally, and Latin and French had to be taken as part of the Collège Calvin curriculum, German was the first language he chose to learn. By that time, with four languages at his command, Georgie must have realized that he was, as he put it in an ironic autobiographical piece, "a polyglot" (Vignale, 1927). But Georgie was always selective: he chose languages for their value as keys to segments of the literary world he wanted to possess. German was for him, mainly, the language of the philosophers. He was attracted to it by Carlyle's outrageous parody of German idealism; but the fact that he attempted to begin with Kant's *Critique* shows how deadly serious he was. His defeat, and the shortcut that reading Heine's *Lyrical Intermezzo* implied, did not change his plan. He would master the language first by reading poets and novelists in order to be able to return to the philosophers.

The first book in German he managed to read in its entirety was a novel by the Viennese writer Gustav Meyrink. *The Golem* (1915) is loosely based on a cabalistic legend about a Prague rabbi who creates a creature out of mud and makes him his servant. The legend is a vehicle for Meyrink to indulge in his love for the occult and the vague Indian philosophy of redemption and even for Madame Blavatsky's theosophy, as has been pointed out by his critics. Only one paragraph in the "Autobiographical Essay" refers to this book, which influenced Borges in a very curious way: "I also managed to read Meyrink's novel *Der Golem*. (In 1969, when I was in Israel, I talked over the Bohemian legend of the Golem with Gershom Scholem, a leading scholar of Jewish mysticism, whose name I had twice used as the only possible rhyming word in a poem of my own on the Golem.)" ("Essay," 1970, p. 216). The mention cannot be more oblique. Instead of discussing the Meyrink book, he recalls a conversation he had years later with Gershom Scholem. Even the Scholem book he alludes to—*Major Trends in Jewish Mysticism* (1941)—devotes only half a page to the legend and doesn't even mention Meyrink's novel. Probably Borges had also read another Scholem book, *On the Cabala and Its Symbolism* (1960), which devotes two pages to Meyrink in the last chapter, "The Idea of the Golem." If Borges ever read this last text, he must have been surprised at the disdain with which Scholem treats the novel.

Borges discusses *The Golem* in another piece, written in 1936. In reviewing Meyrink's *Der Engel von westlich Fenster,* he says: "This novel, more or less theosophic—*The Angel of the Western Window*—is less beautiful than its title. Its author, Gustav Meyrink, was made famous by the fantastic novel *The Golem,* an extraordinarily visual book which graciously put together mythology, eroticism, tourism, Prague's local color, premonitory dreams, dreams of alien or previous lives, and even reality. That happy book was followed by other less agreeable ones" (*El Hogar,* October 16, 1936).

In this short evaluation it is possible to get closer to what Georgie must have discovered in the rambling, atmospheric, and suggestive novel. More than likely, it was not only the Golem legend that attracted his interest but also the fact that Meyrink proved that the legend was another version of the theme of the double. In his novel the protagonist and the Golem are, in a sense, doubles. At the end, in a swift change of point of view, the narrator of the story and the protagonist (who had seemed up to that point to be the same) are revealed to be two distinct characters. The narrator had, in a trance, become the protagonist.

Twenty-five years later Borges wrote a story about an Indian mystic who worships fire and creates a disciple to propagate his faith. "The Circular Ruins," collected in *Ficciones* (1944), can be seen as an anticipation of the poem on the Golem that Borges mentions in his "Autobiographical Essay." In the story an abyssal perspective is opened when the reader realizes that the mystic has also been created by another, the god Fire, while in the poem the rabbi who has created the Golem is shown to be the creation of his god. Both the story and the poem suggest that all these characters are creations of the writer, the real god of his creatures. That perspective was already implicit in Meyrink's novel.

One reason for Borges' silence in his "Autobiographical Essay" on these aspects of Meyrink's novel may be the fact that the novel is written in a highly emotional style and lacks a coherent structure. In the 1930s Georgie reacted against this aspect of fantastic writing and successfully began to develop his own brand of short, concise narratives, in which baroque rhetoric is tightly controlled by a corrosive irony. The stories, collected in *A Universal History of Infamy* (1935), have very little kinship with Meyrink's style, but in more than one sense they belong to the same world of nightmarish reality.

Georgie soon discovered two other German writers. One was the romantic Jean-Paul Richter. Borges recalls that around 1917 he tried to get interested in him "for Carlyle's and De Quincey's sake . . . but I soon discovered that I was very bored by the reading. Richter, in spite of his two English champions, seemed to me very long-winded and perhaps a passionless writer" ("Essay," 1970, p. 216). More successful was his experience with Fritz Mauthner. He does not mention him in the "Autobiographical Essay," but in his interview with Irby he talks extensively about him:

> He was a Jew, of Czech origin, who lived at the end of the last century. He published some very bad novels, but his philosophical papers are excellent. He is a wonderful writer, very ironic, whose style recalls that of the eighteenth century. He believed language only serves either to hide reality or for esthetic expression. His dictionary of philosophy, one of the books I have consulted with great pleasure, is really a collection of essays on different subjects, such as the soul, the world, the spirit, the conscience, etc. The historical part is also good; Mauthner was a scholar. He wanted his dictionary to be read in a skeptical mood. He makes some very good jokes. He talks, for instance, of the German verb *stehen* (*to stand*, in English), which has no equivalent in French or Spanish, where you have to say *être debout* or *estar de pie*, which is not the same thing. But he observes that in both French and Spanish they had to know the concept of *stehen;* otherwise they would fall to the ground. (Irby, 1962, p. 9)

Some forty years after his first encounter with Mauthner's book, Borges was still able to recall a scholarly joke he once had found amusing. More significantly, in many of his essays on philosophical subjects he takes advantage of Mauthner's scholarship and wit to help him to present a problem or find a new argument or an illustration. In discussing Korzybski's theories in a 1928 article, he quotes Mauthner to prove that the theories presented by the former in his *Manhood of Humanity* are not really new; in 1934 he uses Mauthner to discuss Nietzsche's theory of the eternal return; in 1942 Mauthner is one of the sources for his discussion of John Wilkins' analytical language. Time and again, Borges is indebted to Georgie's discovery of Mauthner.

Another German writer he read in Switzerland was the now almost forgotten Max Stirner. A sort of precursor of Nietzsche, Stirner died in 1856, but his main work, *The Ego and His Own,* had a short revival at the turn of the century. Borges has never devoted an article to Stirner or really acknowledged his influence. But there is an independent source for his knowledge of Stirner. In a brief description of how Georgie looked at the time of his first visit to Spain in 1919, Guillermo de Torre presents him in this colorful language: "He arrived [from Switzerland] drunk with Whitman, equipped by Stirner, following Romain Rolland" (De Torre, 1925, p. 62). Both Whitman and Rolland have been duly acknowledged by Borges, but the silence about Stirner is total. That makes it more tantalizing. Probably it was only a phase; soon Georgie was to discover two German philosophers whose work was to be decisive for his intellectual development: Arthur Schopenhauer and Friedrich Nietzsche. Borges does not mention the latter in his "Autobiographical Essay," but he singles out the former for an extraordinary tribute: "At some point while in Switzerland, I began reading Schopenhauer. Today, were I to choose a single philosopher, I would choose him. If the riddle of the universe can be stated in words, I think these words would be in his writings. I have read him many times over, both in German and, with my father and his close friend Macedonio Fernández, in translation" ("Essay," 1970, pp. 216–217).

From Schopenhauer, Georgie got the philosophical guidance he had looked for in vain in his attempt to decode Kant's *Critique of Pure Reason.* Implicit in that earlier failure was more than a question of language or philosophical training. While Kant wrote in the most impenetrable manner, Schopenhauer was elegant and witty. But *The World as Will and Representation* was more than an entertaining piece of writing. It was conceived by Schopenhauer to carry Kant's theories to their radical ends. If Kant had shown that the world is a product of our mind, and that the supernatural is unreachable, Schopenhauer went one step further to prove that even what we call nature is only a disguise assumed by the will, and that to escape from insanity it is necessary to elevate and transfigure the will into representation. In Kant's *Critique of Judgment* the artist is presented as free to create according to his intentions a totally arbitrary work. From the point of view of art, to attempt to be faithful to nature, to have a moral purpose, to stick to empirical truth or to a religion is totally irrelevant. Art is an end in itself. Kant also revealed the gulf between logical discourse and artistic discourse, between art and empirical experience. As some critics have pointed out, Kant completed Rousseau, while Schopenhauer completed (from this point of view) Kant. In Schopenhauer, Georgie may have found the notion that art is the only way to meaning, that art (as much as science) creates a meaningful natural cosmos out of the crumbling social order. It is possible to conjecture that Schopenhauer's paradoxical combination of idealism and nihilism (or pessimism) was extremely attractive to Georgie, who was then passing through the normal crisis of adolescence.

But Georgie may have been attracted to another side of Schopenhauer's philosophy: its denial of the existence of time and its erosion of the concepts of external reality and individual personality. Georgie had been trained by Father to understand Berkeleyan solipsism, and in reading Schopenhauer at Geneva he must have availed himself of the opportunity to discuss with Father the German philosopher's theories about reality. As he indicates in his "Autobiographical Essay," he continued to discuss Schopenhauer with his father and his father's friend Macedonio Fernández upon his return to Buenos Aires in 1921. In his first attempts at philosophical speculation—two articles printed in his first collection of essays, *Inquisiciones* (1925)—Schopenhauer is invariably quoted to forward the argument. In the more important of the two, "The Nothingness of Personality," after stressing some contradictions he finds in the German philosopher's theories, Borges quotes a dazzling sentence in which Schopenhauer maintains that "everyone who said I during all that time before I was born, was truly I." From that Borges concludes that the ego is not "individual" but a "mere logical urgency" (*Inquisiciones,* 1925, p. 95). To put it in more contemporary terms, the "I" is a *shifter:* everyone who uses it is "I" and nobody is exclusively "I." Borges was already looking in Schopenhauer for arguments to build his theory of the nonexistence of time and space, and consequently of the individual personality. In his most ambitious "metaphysical" piece, "A New Refutation of Time" (1947), he returns to Schopenhauer for arguments.

Georgie was probably very impressed (and perhaps even influenced) by Schopenhauer's pessimism. The latter's essays against women and marriage were extremely popular then, both in Spain and in Latin America. Cheap collections of some of his essays, generally translated from inexpensive French versions, flooded the market. They were generally printed in atrocious editions, on a brownish paper, and were plagued by misprints. It was probably that misogynistic side of Schopenhauer which attracted the attention of Georgie and his schoolmates.

Soon he moved on to an even more radical philosopher, Friedrich Nietzsche. If he fails to mention him in his "Autobiographical Essay," he has the following to say to Richard Burgin about his thinking:

BURGIN: Well, speaking about the will, I have the feeling that you aren't too fond of Nietzsche as a thinker.

THE PHILOSOPHER'S CODE

BORGES: No. Well, I think that I am unfair to Nietzsche, because though I have read and reread many of his books, well, I think that if you omit *Thus Spoke Zarathustra,* if you omit that book—a kind of sham Bible, no?—I mean, a sham biblical style—but if you omit that book you get very interesting books.

BURGIN: *Beyond Good and Evil?*

BORGES: Yes, I've read them in German. And I greatly enjoyed them. But yet, somehow, I have never felt any sympathy for him as a man, no? I mean, I feel a great sympathy for Schopenhauer, or for ever so many writers, but in the case of Nietzsche I feel there is something hard and I won't say priggish—I mean, as a person he has no modesty about him. The same thing happens to me with Blake. I don't like writers who are making sweeping statements all the time. Of course, you might argue that what I'm saying is a sweeping statement also, no? Well, one has to say things with a certain emphasis.

BURGIN: Don't you feel, though, in the case of Nietzsche, he might be somewhat akin to Whitman? In that the personae of their works are quite different from the actual men behind them?

BORGES: Yes, but in the case of Whitman he gives you a very attractive persona. In the case of Nietzsche he gives you a very disagreeable one; at least to me. I feel I can sympathize with Whitman, but I can hardly sympathize with Nietzsche. In fact, I don't suppose he wanted people to sympathize with him. (Burgin, 1969, pp. 102–103)

It is obvious that this view of the German philosopher is not the one Georgie had in Geneva. The fact that Borges admits having read and reread him is proof enough of his early interest. Nietzsche's name and theories are generally present in Borges' philosophical essays, especially in those dedicated to refuting the existence of time. One of his most important pieces, "The Doctrine of the Cycles," written in 1934 and collected in *History of Eternity* (1936), discusses Nietzsche's theory of the eternal return. It is true that he quotes Nietzsche to disagree with him, but the essay shows a great familiarity with his work and advances a subtle interpretation of the basic conflict between Nietzsche's personality and his philosophy. Borges points out that although Nietzsche knew that the theory of the eternal return was not his, he preferred to ignore this fact and maintain with pride: "Immortal the instant in which I engendered the eternal return. For that instant I can stand the return" (*Unschuld des Werdens,* II, 1308). According to Borges, that instant is one of Nietzsche's honors. His explanation (as he indicates) is "grammatical, I almost say, syntactical":

> Nietzsche knew that the eternal return is one of the fables or fears or entertainments which return eternally, but he also knew that the most effective of the grammatical persons is the first. For a prophet, it is possible to say that it is the only one. To derive his revelation from a treatise, or from the *Historia*

Philosophiae Greco-Romans written by the Assistant Professors Ritter and Prel-
ler, was impossible for Zarathustra, for reasons of voice and anachronism—
when not for typographical reasons. The prophetic style does not allow
quotes or the scholarly presentation of books and authors. . . .

If my human flesh assimilates brutal flesh of mutton, who will prevent the
human mind from assimilating human mental states? Because he thought
about it and he suffered it so much, the eternal return of things now
belongs to Nietzsche and not to somebody who is dead and is just a Greek
name. (*Eternidad*, 1936, pp. 63–64)

In the rest of the essay Borges quotes from other Nietzschean texts
(especially the *Nachlass,* his private notebooks) and comments on his
physical sufferings and the curse of insomnia, which the German philosopher tried to alleviate with chloral. The end of the second part of
the essay includes a memorable paragraph:

Nietzsche wanted to be Walt Whitman, he wanted to fall thoroughly in love
with his destiny. He followed a heroic method: he unearthed the intolerable Greek hypothesis of the eternal repetition and tried to educe from this
mental nightmare an occasion for joy. He searched for the most horrible
idea in the world and he proposed it to men's delectation. Weak optimists
try to imagine they are Nietzschean; Nietzsche faces them with the circles
of his eternal return and thus he spits them out of his mouth. (Ibid.,
pp. 64–65)

A doomed Nietzsche, a desperate Nietzsche, caught in the atrocious lucidity of insomnia as in one of Dante's circles: that is the
Nietzsche which Borges reveals here. This tortured Nietzsche had very
little to do with the one Borges would soon denounce as one of the
precursors of Nazism, the Nietzsche he dislikes so intensely and unfairly in his conversations with Richard Burgin. The change in perspective can be attributed to the politics that led to World War II. Today we
know that Nietzsche's sister not only edited his unpublished manuscripts but altered them to suit her Nazi husband's beliefs.

Borges' real readings of Nietzsche are to be found in his adolescent admiration for *Zarathustra* and in the brilliant 1934 essay. The
Nietzsche Georgie read was the follower of Schopenhauer who dared
to carry some of his teacher's lessons perhaps too far. If Schopenhauer
was too "bourgeois" to deplore the blind destructiveness of the will,
Nietzsche was wild enough to rejoice in it and even foresee the possibility of an ecstatic union with the will. Nietzsche also carried forward
Schopenhauer's view of the artist as one who gives meaning to the
world, to the extreme of maintaining the artist's right to be amoral and
become a law unto himself. Georgie and his schoolmates must have
been very impressed by this Dionysian vitalism and these dreams of a

Superman. The old Borges may now reject *Zarathustra* because of its "sham biblical style" and forget how much Georgie was carried away by it. But at the time Georgie read Nietzsche, it was not only himself and the small group of alienated young poets of the Collège Calvin who were spellbound by his apocalyptic texts; a whole generation of young poets and playwrights, painters, and musicians was seduced by his spirit. Georgie was a child of his times. In reading Nietzsche as well as Schopenhauer, he learned not only the philosopher's code but a code for the poetry that was being written in Europe at the time, the poetry he himself would be writing very soon.

The summer of 1918 marks the moment when Georgie's involvement with German literature and philosophy began. On his nineteenth birthday (August 24) he asked for and got as a present a German encyclopedia. Now he possessed a key to a whole new cultural world.

5.
A Brotherhood
of Poets

Heine was not the only German poet Georgie knew by heart. While in Switzerland, he discovered the works of Rilke and the expressionists. Borges speaks of Rilke only in passing references. In his article "Apollinaire's Paradox," written in 1946, he compares him favorably with the French poet and concludes that Rilke is "closer to us" (*Los Anales,* August 1946, p. 49). Some twenty years later he returns to the subject in an interview but no longer seems to appreciate Rilke's closeness: "I have the feeling he's been greatly overrated. I think of him as a very pleasant poet. I know some of his pieces by heart, or at least I did. But I could never be very interested in him" (Marx and Simon, 1968, p. 109).

Yet it is obvious that Georgie was extremely susceptible to German poetry. In his readings he had come across a group of young poets who wrote violently about love and war, about despair and hope, about a world brotherhood. They were called "expressionists" and were related to the avant-garde poets, called cubists or futurists, dadaists or imagists, who since the beginning of the century had one thing in common: the need to radically change the literary and artistic establishment's concept of art and of the world. The expressionists were the first truly mòdern poets Georgie read, the ones who introduced him to the new poetics. They achieved what neither Father with his nineteenth-century taste nor his closest Swiss friends with their fondness for symbolism could do: they made him truly conversant with what was revolutionary in contemporary letters.

In evoking those days of his adolescence in his "Autobiographical Essay," Borges states firmly that expressionism was "beyond other contemporary schools, such as imagism, cubism, futurism, surrealism, and so on" ("Essay," 1970, p. 216). In his interview with Irby he summarizes in more detailed terms the impact expressionism had on modern letters and on his own reading. Although at the time Georgie was living in Geneva he did not participate in the scholarly and literary life of the city and knew nothing about the quiet revolution in linguistics that Ferdinand de Saussure's posthumous *Course in General Linguistics* (1916) was producing, he did make good use of the French circulating library and also availed himself of the city's municipal libraries. Furthermore, he was in constant communication with aspiring young poets, such as Maurice Abramowicz. At Lugano he was more isolated. He resorted to German to fill the emptiness of his literary life. The discovery of expressionism made a lasting impact on him. As he told Irby, expressionism already contained "everything which is essential in later literature. I like it better than surrealism or dadaism, which seem frivolous to me. Expressionism is more serious and reflects a whole series of deep preoccupations: magic, dreams, Eastern religions and philosophies, the aspiration toward a world brotherhood. . . . Besides, German, with its almost infinite verbal possibilities, lends itself more easily to strange metaphors" (Irby, 1962, p. 6).

Some of the first critical pieces Georgie wrote a few years later, while in Spain, reflect the first impact of that movement on his literary imagination. For Georgie, it was to be associated with the impact produced by the seemingly endless war. Although he was a foreigner and was living in a neutral country, the war only made more evident his double exile: from faraway Argentina, its language, its people, and from the continent on which he was then living. A foreigner to Switzerland, he was also a foreigner to the war that was decimating the generation to which he belonged. In an article published in Spain in 1921—a review of *Die Aktion-Lyrik, 1914–1916,* an anthology of expressionist poetry—he points out that the majority of these self-conscious, hard, painful poems were written in the trenches of Poland, Russia, and France, where the young poets had been stationed to defend the fatherland. In another article on the same subject, written in Buenos Aires in 1923 and later collected in his first book of essays, *Inquisiciones* (1925), he comments on the note of discord expressionism brought to German literature. Expressionism aimed at intensity and the "effectiveness of details: the unusual assurance of adjectives, the brusque thrusting of verbs" (*Inquisiciones,* 1925, p. 147). Borges attributes this intensity to the experience of war. By placing everything in danger, war made the poets realize the value of life and taught them to question established notions about the world and the arts:

If for the mind, the war had been insignificant, because it only intensified Europe's diminished status, there is no doubt that for participants in the tragic farce, it was a very intense experience. How many hard visions crowded their views! To have known in the soldier's immediate experience the lands of Russia and Austria and France and Poland; to have participated in the first victories, as terrible as defeats, when the infantry in pursuit of skies and armies crossed dull fields where death looked satiated and the injury caused by arms was universal, is a desirable but certain suffering. Add to this succession of `witches' Sabbaths the innermost feeling that life, your own warm and swift life, is contingent and not certain. It is no wonder that many [poets] in that perfection of pain had resorted to immortal words to make pain recede. . . . Thus, in trenches, in hospitals, in desperate and reasonable hate, expressionism grew. War did not make it but it justified it. (Ibid., pp. 147–148)

Borges readily admits that the expressionists did not achieve "perfect works." On the other hand, he points out that three of the poets who preceded them—Karl Gustav Moeller, Rainer Maria Rilke, and Hugo von Hofmannsthal—did. But the expressionists excelled in something different: the intensity of their feelings and of the poetry through which they communicate those feelings. "Vehemence in the attitudes, and in the depth of their poetry, abundance of images and the postulation of universal brotherhood: that was expressionism" (ibid., p. 148). It was this intensity that Georgie tried to capture in his first poetical attempts.

In both articles, as well in others published during the same period in Spain, Georgie includes translations of expressionist poets. They all belong to the group closely associated with war. Of the dozen chosen by him, only four are still considered important: Johannes Beecher, Wilhelm Klemm, Ernst Stadler, and August Stramm. The first is probably the most widely known today because of his postexpressionist career, which included an activist phase as a communist poet in Hitler's Germany, a long exile in the Soviet Union, and a triumphal return as the head of cultural activities for the German Democratic Republic. Georgie was particularly interested in his poetry and believed him to be the best German poet of the time (*Cervantes*, October 1920, p. 103). In those early days Becher believed in assaulting the reader's sensitivity with aggressive and erotic metaphors. Aggressive also was the poetry of Wilhelm Klemm. (He is included in all four of the selections of expressionist poetry made by Georgie.) Klemm's violence and humanitarianism later found an outlet in Nazism: a path as alien to Borges as the one Becher took. Georgie admired him for having declared that his heart was "as wide as Germany and France reunited" and was being pierced "by the bullets of the whole world" (*Inquisiciones*, 1925, p. 152).

The other poets, Ernst Stadler and August Stramm, shared a

common fate. Both were killed on the battlefield: the first on the Western front; the second on the Russian front. But they were very different. Stadler was an Alsatian who never fully became an expressionist. He had a Whitmanesque love for mankind that owed something also to one of Whitman's French followers, the Belgian Emile Verhaeren. Stramm, on the other hand, was one of the leaders of a loosely connected group of poets who began publishing their verses in *Sturm* magazine before the war and quickly attracted attention. In his use of the possibilities of German for coining words, Stramm was second to none and has often been compared with Joyce. After his death on the Eastern front, a volume of his war poems was published in 1919. He also left a volume, *Liebesgedichte* (Love Poetry) (1919), which inspired Georgie's own erotic poems.

The other expressionist poets to whom Georgie called attention in his articles and translations were less impressive, but at the time he read them their cruel, erotic, dazzling images represented the new poetry. There was more in their poetry than challenging images or the feeling that war was hell. They all expressed, in different ways and according to different ideologies and credos, a belief in a brotherhood of man. The experience of war had made them pacifists. They had come to realize that war was always fought by those who did not start it; that its price was always paid by the sons and not the fathers. Patricide, as the Oedipus myth reveals, is only the second most evident stage of a conflict that usually begins with a filicide. It was Laius who first attempted to take his son's life. The expressionist poets had to fight a war that was one of the most tragic filicides in human history. Suddenly, under the very eyes of a society that was considered civilized, a whole generation was butchered.

Georgie had been protected from the carnage because he was an Argentine who lived in a neutral country. Nevertheless, he could not help feeling the impact of those poems that violently attacked war and proclaimed the need for all men to unite in a universal brotherhood. He discovered another link with the expressionist poets: they also had been taught by Schopenhauer and Nietzsche to believe that will, and will only, gave meaning to a chaotic world; they had discovered in *Zarathustra* the vitalism they needed to face the horrors of war and destruction. They sided with Nietzsche in preferring "the Dionysian *afflatus* over Apollonian intellectual balance," as one art critic has put it (Zigrosser, 1957, p. 11). In those days Georgie was obviously closer to Dionysius than to Apollo.

But the greatest debt Georgie incurred to the expressionists was that they led him to a poet who was to become for him *the* poet.

One day, reading an expressionist annual, he found a translation of some of Walt Whitman's verses. He tells the story in his "Autobiographical Essay":

> I first met Walt Whitman through a German translation by Johannes Schlaf ("*Als ich in Alabama meinen Morgengang machte*"—"As I have walk'd in Alabama my morning walk"). Of course, I was struck by the absurdity of reading an American poet in German, so I ordered a copy of *Leaves of Grass* from London. I remember it still—bound in green. For a time, I thought of Whitman not only as a great poet but as the *only* poet. In fact, I thought all poets the world over had been merely leading up to Whitman until 1855, and that not to imitate him was a proof of ignorance. This feeling had already come over me with Carlyle's prose, which is now unbearable to me, and with the poetry of Swinburne. These were phases I went through. ("Essay," 1970, p. 217)

Later Georgie learned to overcome his infatuation with Carlyle's prose and Swinburne's poetry, but he never really got over Whitman. Remembering those Geneva days, he told Irby in 1962 that for many years he used Whitman as a canon to judge all poetry; he then believed Whitman *was* poetry. In some of the first critical articles he wrote (later collected in *Inquisiciones*) Whitman's name is mentioned not only with reverence but with insight. In "The Nothingness of Personality," an elaborate essay which attempts to deny the existence of the individual "I," Borges discusses Whitman; he sees him as the first to express in his verses not only his own personality but the entire world's soul. As Borges puts it:

> To attempt to express yourself and to want to express life in its totality is one and the same thing. . . . Whitman was the first Atlante to attempt to perform this fierce task and put the world on his shoulders. He believed that it was enough to enumerate things to immediately taste how unique and astonishing they are. Thus, in his poems, next to many beautiful [products of] rhetoric, can be found a string of gaudy words, sometimes copied from geography or history textbooks, burning with admiration marks which imitate lofty enthusiasm. (*Inquisiciones*, 1925, p. 91)

It is possible to detect here a certain detachment that becomes even more noticeable in another piece in which Borges compares Whitman with a very fine Spanish writer, Ramón Gómez de la Serna. He stresses that both had the same appetite for things. For Ramón (as he is usually called), "things are not corridors that lead to God."

> He loves them, he pets them and caresses them, but the satisfaction he gets from them is unbinding and without any taint of oneness. In that indepen-

dence of his love we find the essential distinction which separates him from Walt Whitman. We can also see in Whitman the whole business of living; in Whitman also breathes the miraculous gratitude for the concrete and tactile and many-colored ways things are. But Walt's gratitude was satisfied with the enumeration of objects whose accumulation is the world, while the Spaniard has written comic and passionate commentaries on the individuality of each object. (Ibid., p. 125)

In spite of these reservations, Georgie continued to admire Whitman and to follow him in his discoveries of a universal brotherhood and the secrets of poetry. His reading of Whitman completed the task the expressionists had begun. Now he was ready to begin writing a new kind of poetry. The lessons of the symbolists were forgotten; Whitman and the expressionists were to dominate his imagery and feelings. One of the first poems of the new cycle he wrote is dedicated to the war. It is called "Trenches":

> Anguish.
> At the highest point a mountain walks
> Earth-colored men drown in the lowest crevice
> Fate yokes the souls of those
> who bathed their little hope in the pools of night.
> The bayonets dream of the nuptial mess.
> The world has been lost and the eyes of the dead
> look for it
> Silence howls in the sunken horizons.
> (Videla, 1963, pp. 100–101)

Living in the seclusion of Geneva or Lugano, protected by the love of his family, and doubly exiled from the war, Georgie turned to Whitmanesque verse and to the expressionists' obsession with war to find the proper outlet for his feelings. The phallic allusion in the sixth line puts the whole poem in perspective. Lost in the violent experiences of his adolescence, fighting against the anguish of a world that was being torn to pieces while he remained intact, in anguished impotence, Georgie finds in the imaginary experience of war, in the naked, brutal butchery of war, a metaphor for his own desperate feelings.

6.
Back to the
Old Country

The Borgeses' European experience did not end with the close of the war. They were in no special rush to return home, since Georgie's poor eyesight exempted him from military service. Thus, before returning to Argentina, they decided to spend a year or so vacationing in Spain. As Borges tells the story in his "Autobiographical Essay," the idea seemed very reasonable:

> Spain at that time was slowly being discovered by Argentines. Until then, even eminent writers like Leopoldo Lugones and Ricardo Güiraldes deliberately left Spain out of their European travels. This was no whim. In Buenos Aires, Spaniards always held menial jobs—as domestic servants, waiters, and laborers—or were small tradesmen, and we Argentines never thought of ourselves as Spanish. . . . Through French eyes, however, Latin Americans saw the Spaniards as picturesque, thinking of them in terms of the stock in trade of García Lorca—gypsies, bullfights, and Moorish architecture. But though Spanish was our language and we came mostly of Spanish and Portuguese blood, my own family never thought of our trip in terms of going back to Spain after an absence of some three centuries. ("Essay," 1970, pp. 218–219)

Borges' reaction reflects his anti-Spanish bias, but it is also based on fact. There was very little admiration for the grandeur of the Spanish conquest in the River Plate area. Historically, it was the last outpost of the Spanish empire and was not competely settled and organized under Spanish rule until the eighteenth century. Therefore, it was spared the worst abuses of a corrupt Spanish administration and was in effect left free to follow its own path. The descendents of the conquistadors soon developed an appetite for freedom. The notion of a federation of South American states, closely based on the North American model, began to be formed. While the Argentine San Martín succeeded in making his dreams of freedom true and went as far as Peru in his liberation campaign, the Uruguayan José Artigas failed in implementing the ideal of federation and had to leave Montevideo to seek refuge in Paraguay.

The independence achieved by Argentina and Uruguay was only independence from Spanish authority, which was quickly replaced by North American and French authority as cultural models. Latin America throughout the nineteenth century was solidly anti-Spain, and when in the second half of that century the Spaniards returned to the newly independent republics they came as poor immigrants, much as the Irish came to the United States. They were generally illiterate, and the Spanish they spoke was not elegant. They settled at the lower levels of society. Argentines and Uruguayans never thought of them as the master race.

Thus the Borgeses' trip to Spain did not imply a return to the old country in search of valid roots, although Georgie had in fact descended from the conquistadors. His genealogical tree goes back, on both sides of the family, to people who came to America at the beginning of the sixteenth century. On the Borges side there is Don Alonso de la Puente, who participated in the conquest of Peru in 1532, and Don Gonzalo Martel de la Puente, who also came to Peru at that time. There was Juan de Sanabria, one of the first settlers of Argentina, and among his ancestors were two important historical figures: Don Juan de Garay, the founder of Buenos Aires in 1591, and Don Hernando Arias de Saavedra (better known as Hernandarias), who was instrumental in settling the River Plate area and who introduced cattle with the success later centuries would prove. No less important were Don Gerónimo Luis de Cabrera y Toledo, founder of Córdoba del Tucumán in 1571, and Don Jerónimo Luis de Cabrera y Garay, who was governor of the province of the River Plate in 1641. On his mother's side Borges' ancestors lacked such resplendent titles, but they were distinguished enough.

Although once Georgie corrected a Spaniard who was boasting about the exploits of his ancestors in America with a curt "We are the descendants of the conquistadors; you descend only from the cousins who stayed at home," he never took his genealogical tree too seriously. He was chiefly attracted to the ancestors who fought the Spaniards in 1810 and freed the River Plate area. Besides, the influence of a British and Swiss education had made him less susceptible to the grandeur of Spain. In cultural matters, Spain and Spanish did not rank too high.

Not all Argentines shared the Borgeses' prejudices against

Spain. In spite of what Borges says in his "Autobiographical Essay," the River Plate area had a contingent of educated people who loved and respected the Spanish culture. Some writers, such as Enrique Larreta (who had been Father's classmate at law school) and the Uruguayan Carlos Reyles, not only lived in Spain for long periods but produced some of their most important work on Spanish subjects. At the turn of the century the Spanish-American war turned the emotional tide in favor of Spain. Now that the old country was defeated by a new empire, it was time to bury the independence hatchets and revise the purely negative attitude toward all things Spanish. In doing so, both Larreta and Reyles (and many others with them) rediscovered a culture that was a decisive part of Latin America's heritage. Before them, and in a momentous 1900 essay, *Ariel,* the Uruguayan José Enrique Rodó had pointed the way to recovery of a lost or mislaid tradition.

Georgie was not at all interested in that recovery. He was living a most contemporary life. Having discovered Whitman and the expressionists, he was concerned only with being modern, and that emphatically did not include Spain. Although it was his fate to discover in that neglected if not despised Spain a first hint of his literary gifts, in retelling the story in his "Autobiographical Essay," Borges prefers to return to the ironical view he probably had in 1919.

The Borgeses traveled by train to Barcelona and from there by boat to Majorca, in the Balearic Islands. They first settled in Palma, at the Hotel Continental, facing St. Michael's Church. In the "Autobiographical Essay" (which does not have a word to say about Barcelona) Borges writes:

> We went to Majorca because it was cheap, beautiful, and had hardly any tourists but ourselves. We lived there nearly a whole year, in Palma and Valldemosa, a village high up in the hills. I went on studying Latin, this time under the tutelage of a priest, who told me that since the innate was sufficient to his needs, he had never attempted reading a novel. We went over Virgil, of whom I still think highly. I remember I astonished the natives by my fine swimming, for I had learned in different swift rivers, such as the Uruguay and the Rhone, while Majorcans were used only to a quiet, tideless sea. ("Essay," 1970, p. 219)

The study of Latin, under the Valldemosa vicar, was the major literary event Borges now remembers of those Majorcan days. It completed and perfected the possession of a linguistic code that was to be decisive for his writings. Borges' extraordinary command of syntax, his almost uncanny feeling for words (especially for their etymological meaning), and his awareness of the infinite possibilities of the Spanish language were all enhanced by his study of Latin and of French.

The only personal note about his life in Majorca is his proud remark about his abilities as a swimmer. By the time he went to Spain he was probably as good as he claimed to be. Swimming was not yet as popular in Europe as it later came to be. People used to go to the beaches more for the sun and the fresh air than for the sea. They entered the water covered by an excess of clothes, caps, and rubber shoes. The most they attempted was a few hysterical strokes, never losing a foothold on firm ground. Children jumped and frolicked on the shoreline. A swimmer such as Georgie must have caused quite a sensation in the Majorca of those days.

The island is especially remembered in the "Autobiographical Essay" as the place where Father finally came to grips with his literary avocation and produced his first and only novel, *The Chieftain.*

> My father was writing his novel, which harked back to old times during the civil war of the 1870s in his native Entre Ríos. I recall giving him some quite bad metaphors, borrowed from the German expressionists, which he accepted out of resignation. He had some five hundred copies of the book printed, and brought them back to Buenos Aires, where he gave them away to friends. Every time the word "Paraná"—his home town—had come up in the manuscript, the printers changed it to "Panamá," thinking they were correcting a mistake. Not to give them trouble, and also seeing it was funnier that way, my father let this pass. (Ibid., p. 219)

Borges' memory plays a trick on him here. Only once in the book (which was published in 1921) does the word "Paraná" appear altered. On page 126 it is spelled "Paramá," which is a sort of Joycean hybrid of "Paraná" and "Panamá." Borges' faulty recollection makes the story sound better. But if his memory fails him, he is right about the intrusion of some expressionist images in a rather old-fashioned text.

Not all the bad images in the book come from the expressionists. Many are taken straight from nineteenth-century romantic and postromantic literature; some reflect more recent readings: the decadents and the Spanish modernists, for instance. Father was an avid reader who had very little literary training; so he borrowed right and left. But a close reading of the novel permits the identification of some of those expressionist (or para-expressionist) images that Borges talks about in his "Autobiographical Essay." Thus, on page 7, the text describes a bridge which "scars the brook"; on page 86 the same bridge crosses the brook "from side to side with the easiness of a tense muscle." The inundation, which is the protagonist's moment of truth, is described as follows on page 141: "Water in the ravine's groove jumped to the conquest of space the way a god in the fullness of hate could do it." After the storm, the sky, "terse and resplendent, was a majolica bowl with metallic reflections." In describing a pastoral scene on page 24, the text says: "The very clear sky kept a watch over its blues."

In recalling his interference with Father's prose, Borges adds in the "Autobiographical Essay": "Now I repent of my youthful intrusions into his book. Seventeen years later, before he died, he told me that he would very much like me to rewrite the novel in a straightforward way, with all the fine writing and purple patches left out" (ibid., pp. 219–220).

If Father had misgivings about the expressionist images, why did he accept them? Borges' explanation in his "Autobiographical Essay"—that he did it "out of resignation"—does not seem good enough. It was probably Father's diffidence and skepticism about all human endeavors that let him accept Georgie's corrections. Besides, he always believed that sons educated their fathers and not the other way around. And in accepting Georgie's expressionist images he was following his own convictions.

While Father was writing his novel, Georgie was busy with his own projects. In the "Autobiographical Essay" he mentions one: "I myself in those days wrote a story about a werewolf and sent it to a popular magazine in Madrid, *La Esfera*, whose editors very wisely turned it down" (ibid., p. 220). This is all he has to say about that first story, but he gives more details about its origins in an interview with Jean de Milleret. It was obviously based on a River Plate version of the lycanthrope myth. Borges begins by pointing out that there are two local names for the werewolf in that area: (1) *lobisón* (from *lobo*, wolf), used both in Uruguay, where some of Mother's relatives came from, and in Entre Ríos, Father's native province; and (2) *capiango*, a name of African origin, used in the province of Córdoba, where there was a great slave market and where the Spanish ancestors of the Borgeses came from. According to the legend, as he recalls it, "it is on Saturday evenings that in some quarters of town men change into pigs or dogs; while in Córdoba they change into *tigers*" (De Milleret, 1967, p. 29). He adds that the famous gaucho chieftain Facundo Quiroga spread the notion that "he had a regiment of *capiangos*, men who at the time of fighting became tigers; well . . . jaguars" (ibid., p. 30). In describing the legend to a foreigner, Borges makes the necessary linguistic clarifications, but he forgets to mention one important aspect of the legend, at least as it is commonly told in Uruguay: that the *lobisón* is the seventh male son in a family and that he turns into a werewolf not every Saturday evening (which would make him look more like a weekend reveler) but on nights when the moon is full. The story Georgie wrote seems lost, or at least that was what Borges wanted to suggest to De Milleret, who chided him: "You have destroyed it. You are an iconoclast" (ibid., p. 29).

In mentioning his first serious attempts at publication, Borges fails to record in his "Autobiographical Essay" an article he succeeded in having published at the time. It was a book review he wrote in French and sent to Maurice Abramowicz in Geneva. After correcting the text, Abramowicz submitted it to *La Feuille,* which published it on August 20, 1919. Titled "Chronique des lettres espagnoles" and more modestly subtitled "Trois nouveaux livres," the article was devoted mainly to reviewing two new books of essays by leading Spanish writers: Pío Baroja, best known as a prolific novelist, and Azorín, one of the most influential essayists of the time. The writing foreshadows the kind of irony which Borges later made famous. It begins with the observation that Spanish writers, when they are sincere, are always either skeptical or sad. In defining Baroja, Borges underlines his achievements as the author of "a long and remarkable series of realistic novels" and calls him "a biting, skeptical, and vigorous writer." Baroja's pessimism is not unique. According to Georgie, "all the intelligent Spaniards will tell you that their country is not worth anything now." That feeling was in part a consequence of the defeat suffered by Spain in the Spanish-American war: the Disaster, as it was called. Both Baroja and Azorín belonged to what was then baptized the Generation of 1898, to mark forever the date of the defeat. That generation had helped to eliminate the decaying traditions of the empire and had updated Spanish culture. Among his contemporaries, Baroja was considered the wildest. He was an anarchist and, as such, a loner and a permanent cause of scandal. Although the Nobel Prize was never his, when Hemingway received it he went to see Baroja to tell him that he considered himself his disciple. Being a Basque, Baroja was also an oddity in not conforming to the clericalism of his countrymen. Georgie sums up his portrait of the rebel with these words: "He is perhaps the most hated man among his [literary] confrères and especially among the clericals on whom he makes furious war."

In analyzing Baroja's latest book, *Momentum catastrophicum* (the title is in mock Latin), Georgie underlines the irony and vigor of its pages but finds it difficult to summarize its arguments. Among other targets, Baroja turns his fire on the Spanish traditionalists and praises Woodrow Wilson ambiguously for his peace crusade; he calls him a "Marcus Aurelius of the great republic of trusts and sewing machines, the one and only, the apostle and arbiter of international affairs, the flower of the arrivistes." In his commentary Georgie adds that he "had welcomed with joy the allusion to Wilson." Although Baroja's praise was not sung without some irony, Georgie favored him as long as the

Basque supported the peace movement. Those were the days when, inspired by Whitman's panhumanism and the expressionists' credo of a universal brotherhood, Georgie truly believed in mankind. In selecting Baroja's book for review, he was obviously using it to make a political statement. The same applies to Azorín's book. Titled *Between Spain and France*, it is described by Georgie as "the calmest book to have been inspired by the war." Azorín's dialectic, according to Georgie, consists in attempting to make his points by quoting extensively from the classics and being gentle with everybody. It is obvious that Georgie prefers Baroja's quick temper to Azorín's politeness.

A third book is briefly mentioned in the article: *An Apology for Christianity*, written by the Jesuit Ruiz Amado. Georgie dismisses it in a few ironic paragraphs. The author seems to believe that the first chapter of Genesis is in perfect accord with the most recent scientific discoveries; he praises the benefits of the Inquisition and fiercely attacks Voltaire (whom Georgie identifies by his real name, Arouet). The reviewer concludes: "It is curious that in a country where only scholars know the *Philosophical Dictionary* poor Arouet continues to be the scarecrow, the bête noire of the pious."

The importance of this article, a minor piece in itself, is in what it reveals about Georgie's state of mind at the time he was living in Majorca. Like many of his contemporaries, he was an aspiring poet who sided with the antitraditionalists and seriously believed in a universal brotherhood of man. Father's philosophical anarchism had helped him to develop a deep sympathy for any system or credo that attacked the establishment and offered a utopian vision of society. On the eve of his entrance into literary life, Georgie appeared to be a bonafide member of the avant-garde.

7.
A New Master

In 1919, when winter came, the Borgeses moved to the Continent. They settled for a while in Seville, the most lively of the three principal Andalusian cities. While Córdoba and Granada continued to live off the splendors of the Moorish and imperial past, Seville aimed to be modern. It had an intense literary life. Its poets and novelists were always launching little magazines, holding noisy gatherings to read their own verse or endlessly criticize their rivals; they loved to produce manifestos and in general call attention to their existence.

Seville was the center of the tourist trade, especially during Holy Week, with its carnivallike atmosphere and its numerous processions of different, rival images of the Virgin Mary, to whom the Sevillans never failed to address reverent and sometimes obscene songs. But Seville was also a city large enough to have a life of its own the rest of the year, and at the same time to preserve, in the old quarter, the feel and immediacy of a medieval town. Today the Santa Cruz (Holy Cross) neighborhood is still a labyrinth of winding streets that lead to small squares that lead to winding streets. Several imposing monuments break the monotony of its small, beautiful houses with their enclosed gardens permanently perfumed by flowers. Some of these streets—such as the one named after a famous inn, The Moor's—were favored by the young poets in their endless walks under Seville's bright, starry, overwhelming sky. In that ideal setting, which winter could not totally dull, Georgie found for the first time in his life a group of poets to whom he immediately felt close. To James E. Irby he confided: "I didn't discover anything special [in Spain] except a generous style of oral life; that atmosphere, so lively and genuine, of literary gatherings and cafés, in which literature was alive in a very striking way: an atmosphere which . . . had never existed in Argentina. In Geneva . . .

157

there was no literary life, although I had there many literary friends of different nationalities, and there were excellent bookstores where one could find the best of the current literature" (Irby, 1962, p. 6).

Seville was at the time deeply affected by the discovery of the avant-garde. The cultural establishment was still very powerful and totally committed to maintaining the tourist's image of the city, living off its glorious past as the commercial and administrative center of the New World during the Spanish conquest. But the youth of Seville cared little about that tradition. Through a local master, Rafael Cansinos-Asséns—who had already moved to Madrid—they discovered the modern movement that in only two decades had profoundly changed European literature. In little magazines published in Madrid and Seville they had come across some of the key names of the period: Mallarmé and Apollinaire, Marinetti and Tzara, Cendrars and Max Jacob. They knew little French and no English or German. Georgie was shocked by the carelessness with which they tossed around names and works they had barely read.

Recalling Seville's literary scene in his "Autobiographical Essay," he does not spare them:

> In Seville, I fell in with the literary group formed around *Grecia*. This group, who called themselves ultraists, had set out to renew literature, a branch of the arts of which they knew nothing whatever. One of them once told me his whole reading had been the Bible, Cervantes, Darío, and one or two of the books of the Master, Rafael Cansinos-Asséns. It baffled my Argentine mind to learn that they had no French and no inkling at all that such a thing as English literature existed. I was even introduced to a local worthy popularly known as "the Humanist" and was not long in discovering that his Latin was far smaller than mine. As for *Grecia* itself, the editor, Isaac del Vando Villar, had the whole corpus of his poetry written for him by one or another of his assistants. I remember one of them telling me one day, "I'm very busy—Isaac is writing a poem." ("Essay," 1970, pp. 220–221)

Borges' memory has reduced to a few ironies and a couple of anecdotes what was for Georgie a decisive if brief experience. It is true that compared with the other avant-garde movements, which Georgie already knew through books and magazines, the Seville branch must have seemed hopelessly provincial. But it was Georgie's first real contact with literary life. In the second-rate and misled poets of Seville, Georgie found his first fellow writers.

As limited as Seville was, it afforded Georgie the possibility of somehow controlling his shyness and learning to participate in literary life. Seville also was the place of another first: one of his poems was printed in *Grecia* on December 31, 1919. The magazine had been founded a little more than a year earlier (on October 12, 1918, the anniversary of Columbus' arrival in America), by a group of poets led by Isaac del Vando Villar.

At the beginning, as its name implied, *Grecia* was still under the influence of the modernists, who were the Hispanic equivalents of the French symbolists. But on April 30, 1919, Cansinos-Asséns' name appears on its editorial board. From then on, the magazine became open to the young. According to Borges, the poem he published there, "Hymn to the Sea," was very derivative.

> In the poem, I tried my hardest to be Walt Whitman:
>
>> O sea! O myth! O wide resting place!
>> I know why I love you. I know that we are both very old,
>> that we have known each other for centuries . . .
>> O Protean, I have been born of you—
>> both of us chained and wandering,
>> both of us hungering for stars,
>> both of us with hopes and disappointments . . .
>
> Today, I hardly think of the sea, or even of myself, as hungering for stars. Years after, when I came across Arnold Bennett's phrase "the third-rate grandiose," I understood at once what he meant. And yet when I arrived in Madrid a few months later, as this was the only poem I had ever printed, people there thought of me as a singer of the sea. (Ibid., p. 220)

If Seville was (at least retrospectively) somewhat disappointing, Madrid brought a personal revelation. There Georgie met the wise polyglot Rafael Cansinos-Asséns. Born in Seville in 1883, Cansinos (as he was generally called) had led a curious if not eccentric life. He did not conform at all to the conventional image of the Spanish man of letters. In the first place, instead of underlining his *casticismo*, or native origins, as all did, he stressed his Jewish background. According to Borges, he studied for the priesthood in Seville "but, having found the name Cansinos in the archives of the Inquisition, he decided he was a Jew. This led him to the study of Hebrew, and later on he even had himself circumcised" (ibid., p. 221). At the time, this insistence on his real or imaginary Jewish roots was extremely unwelcome in Spain. Years later a distinguished essayist and historian, Américo Castro, began to openly explore in depth the Jewish influence on Spanish culture. But for his time Cansinos was unique. He was also unique in having an inexhaustible appetite for languages: eventually he mastered eleven. A third aspect of his personality was equally extraordinary: he was extremely tolerant of other writers' failings, and instead of praising only the powerful and influential he loved to devote long articles and reviews to unknown and even second-rate young writers. The combination of these qualities made him an ideal master for young poets. Cansinos had an enormous impact on Georgie. Borges calls his meeting him "the great event" of his life in Madrid.

> I still like to think of myself as his disciple. Literary friends from Andalusia took me to meet him. I timidly congratulated him on a poem *he* had written about the sea. "Yes," he said, "and how I'd like to see it before I die." He was a tall man with the Andalusian contempt for all things Castilian. The most remarkable fact about Cansinos was that he lived completely for literature, without regard for money or fame. He was a fine poet and wrote a book of psalms—chiefly erotic—called *El candelabro de los siete brazos* [The Menorah, or The Seven-branched Candelabrum], which was published in 1915. He also wrote novels, stories, and essays, and, when I knew him, presided over a literary circle.
>
> Every Saturday, I would go to the Café Colonial, where we met at midnight, and the conversation lasted until daybreak. Sometimes there were as many as twenty or thirty of us. The group despised all Spanish local color— *cante jondo* [gypsy folk songs] and bullfights. They admired American jazz, and were more interested in being Europeans than Spaniards. Cansinos would propose a subject—The Metaphor, Free Verse, The Traditional Forms of Poetry, Narrative Poetry, The Adjective, The Verb. In his own quiet way, he was a dictator, allowing no unfriendly allusions to contemporary writers and trying to keep the talk on a high plane. (Ibid., pp. 221–222)

What Borges forgets to mention here is that the level of discussion was not always very high. To De Milleret he confides that one evening at the Café Colonial they had argued about the most memorable verse in all literature. They had come to the conclusion that it was one of Apollinaire's which Borges could not recall very well but in Spanish was something like "Tu lengua pez rojo en el acuario de tu voz." ("Your tongue red fish in the aquarium of your voice.") "I believe it was the worst verse Apollinaire ever wrote. . . . And that was quoted as a flower of literature. That astonished me" (De Milleret, 1967, p. 33).

In criticizing the Spanish admirers of Apollinarie, Borges nevertheless attempts to excuse the poet. "He has written very good poems, for instance his war poems," he tells De Milleret, and to prove it he quotes by heart some lines from two of Apollinaire's most famous pieces: "Désir" and "Tristesse d'une étoile." In the first poem Borges makes a couple of minor mistakes, but it is obvious that he had at one time read Apollinaire carefully.

In the "Autobiographical Essay" Borges completes his portrait of Cansinos by discussing his vast reading and his translations (De

Quincey's *Opium Eater,* the *Meditations of Marcus Aurelius,* Barbusse's novels, the complete works of Goethe and Dostoevski, the *Arabian Nights,* among others) and by describing a visit to his home: "Once, I went to see him and he took me into his library. Or, rather, I should say his whole house was a library. It was like making your way through a wood. He was too poor to have shelves, and the books were piled one on top of the other from floor to ceiling, forcing you to thread your way among the vertical columns" ("Essay," 1970, p. 222).

In praising Cansinos, he is not blind to his shortcomings:

> But he had a perversity that made him fail to get on with his leading contemporaries. It lay in writing books that lavishly praised second- or third-rate writers. At the time, Ortega y Gasset was at the height of his fame, but Cansinos thought of him as a bad philosopher and a bad writer. What I got from him, chiefly, was the pleasure of literary conversation. Also, I was stimulated by him to far-flung reading. In writing, I began aping him. He wrote long and flowing sentences with an un-Spanish and strongly Hebrew flavor to them. (Ibid., p. 222)

For the first time in his life Georgie had met a well-rounded man of letters. The impact was so great that he not only began to imitate Cansinos but acknowledged him as his master—a view that now seems hard to share.

There is a small error in Borges' reminiscences of Cansinos in the "Autobiographical Essay." He attributes to him the invention of the term "ultraism," the name of the movement led by the group of poets Georgie had first met in Seville. It is still a matter of controversy whether Cansinos really coined the word. The matter would be of secondary importance if the name were not (according to Ortega y Gasset's tart remark) the only good thing about the movement. But if Cansinos did not invent it, he helped to promote it and even contributed to the movement with some "short, laconic ultraist pieces" under the pen name of Juan Las. (The adjectives are from Borges' "Essay.") In private, Cansinos probably voiced some misgivings about the general quality of what was then being written by the young. Or at least that is the impression that Borges conveys in his "Essay": "The whole thing—I see now—was done in a spirit of mockery. But we youngsters took it very seriously" (ibid., p. 222).

Borges also fails to mention that ultraism did not originate in Spain. Before Cansinos had dreamed of supporting any avant-garde movement there, two Hispanic writers had gone to France and had returned to Spain with the new gospel. Borges mentions only one in his "Essay," and in a slightly derogatory context:

In Madrid at this time, there was another group gathered around [Ramón] Gómez de la Serna. I went there once and didn't like the way they behaved. They had a buffoon who wore a bracelet with a rattle attached. He would be made to shake hands with people and the rattle would rattle and Gómez de la Serna would invariably say, "Where's the snake?" That was supposed to be funny. Once, he turned to me proudly and remarked, "You've never seen this kind of thing in Buenos Aires, have you?" I owned, thank God, that I hadn't. (Ibid., p. 223)

Georgie's memories of Ramón Gómez de la Serna are kinder. He devoted at least two articles to him in his first book of essays, *Inquisiciones* (1925). In one he chronicles the two rival groups that dominated the literary scene: Cansinos' and Ramón's. Although Georgie openly admits he preferred the first, he has some good words for the second. In describing the differences between the two masters, he points out that whereas Ramón, a Castilian from Madrid, is thick, dense, and fleshy, Cansinos, an Andalusian, is tall like a flame and clumsy like a tree. He also opposes the first's appetite for reality to the second's sad and slow delivery, in which an old sorrow can be detected. Ramón presided over the Saturday gathering of his followers in the tight, almost jaillike bar of Pombo; Cansinos preferred the mirrored expanses of the Café Colonial for his Saturday meetings. In reviewing their rivalry, Georgie admits that Ramón finally won the day. In spite of his bias for Cansinos, he recognizes in Ramón not only the successful clown but also the tragic spirit that lies beneath layers of frivolity.

Ramón was instrumental in introducing the avant-garde to Spain. He was eight years younger than Cansinos-Asséns. In 1909 he had begun to write about futurism in *Prometeo,* a Madrid magazine he edited, and had translated for the same journal the founding manifesto published by Marinetti in *Le Figaro* (Paris, February 20, 1909). One year later *Prometeo* included a futurist proclamation to the Spaniards, written by Marinetti and translated by Ramón. In his own work Ramón had proclaimed similar ideas and had even invented a new epigrammatic form, the *greguería,* which was based on a mathematical formula: "humor + metaphor = *greguería.*" His aim was (as he once said) to "fumigate nature with new images" (Videla, 1963, p. 129). There was a lot of mystification in his attitude, and because of that many young poets did not take him too seriously. Perhaps it was this characteristic that put off Georgie. He obviously preferred Cansinos' subtle irony to the robust and slightly coarse Castilian humor of Ramón.

Cansinos himself, in an article written in 1919, praised Ramón for having introduced futurism to Spain. Cansinos also called attention in 1919 to a second champion of the new poetry, the Chilean Vicente Huidobro. Huidobro had spent two decisive years in Paris, working in close contact with Apollinaire, Max Jacob, and Pierre Reverdy and having his portrait done by Picasso, Juan Gris, and Hans Arp. He had written some graphic poems in French and had achieved a certain notoriety as a cubist and dadaist poet. His stay in Madrid in the summer of 1919 was instrumental in introducing the avant-garde into Spanish literature. After he left for Chile, ultraism was founded.

Georgie probably never met Huidobro personally, but through Cansinos he may have become acquainted with his poetry and theories. A mocking reference in one of his essays to a metaphor coined by Huidobro (*Inquisiciones,* 1925, p. 29) makes clear that he was not greatly amused by the kind of innocent playfulness found in the Chilean's poetry.

The greatest omission in Borges' chronicle of ultraist days in Spain is the part he himself played in the movement. Georgie not only sat at the feet of Cansinos, briefly visited Ramón's literary group at Pombo, and published three or four poems in little magazines, as the "Essay" indicates; he also contributed decisively to the organization and diffusion of the movement. It was his task to bring to it an original critical mind, a firsthand knowledge of contemporary literature, and a daring poetic imagination. His contribution went beyond participating in some of the movement's noisier events, such as the one that took place in Madrid on the evening of January 28, 1921. According to a colorful chronicle (Videla, 1963, p. 230), the ultraists attempted to shock the audience with tactics that had been perfected by the futurists. Georgie is included among those who then read their "beautiful poems, which had the incomparable virtue of arousing the morons"—to quote the chronicle's exalted style.

Georgie also struck up a friendship with one of the young leaders of the movement. In the "Autobiographical Essay" Borges devotes three terse lines to him: "Another of the earnest followers was Guillermo de Torre, whom I met in Madrid that spring [1920] and who married my sister Norah nine years later" ("Essay," 1970, pp. 222–223). De Torre was one year younger than Georgie, and when they met he had already been converted to the avant-garde. He had one of the largest collections of little magazines, pamphlets, and manifestos in Europe, traveled regularly to Paris, and corresponded actively with every promising young writer. He eventually chronicled the movement in a polemical book, *Avant-Garde European Literature* (1925; reissued in 1965 in a longer, more sedate and scholarly version as *History of the Avant-Garde Literatures*). What marred De Torre's efforts was his egocentrism: he was not a very good poet, and as a leader he lacked charisma. He knew more and worked harder than his colleagues, but he never commanded the attention Huidobro, Cansinos, or Ramón did. In spite of his devotion to literature, he lacked true critical insight. To stress in his book the importance of ultraism, he inverted chronology, relegating futurism to the last chapter, and started by studying the newer movement. (In 1965 he restored the normal order of things.)

De Torre seemed to have liked Georgie. In his 1925 book he quotes from him extensively and with unlimited praise. In his enthusiasm he even reproduces some of Georgie's worst poems. Norah must have been another link between the two. She used to contribute some of her graphic art to the ultraists' little magazines. Although Georgie seems to have returned the friendship, he showed an amused detachment toward De Torre's naïve promotion of ultraism, especially toward a "vertical" manifesto published as a poster by De Torre with some woodcuts by Norah. According to Enrique Díez-Canedo, a sober chronicler of ultraism, Borges, "who has talent, laughs at the cuteness of 'vertical' " (Videla, 1963, p. 58). In spite of his detachment, he continued to be friends with De Torre, and from Buenos Aires he eventually sent an ultraist manifesto of his own making to be signed and published by the vertical poet.

Georgie's main contribution to the movement at this stage of his career was the constant flow of articles and poems he published in little magazines. He dedicated no less than three articles to discussing and translating the German expressionist poets. He also wrote an article called "On the Margins of Modern Lyrics" (*Grecia,* January 31, 1920) which stressed the importance in ultraist poetry of a new spirit, a new point of view, and linked it with a "dynamic conception of the world." For him, "the fertile premise which considers words not as bridges to ideas but as ends in themselves finds in ultraism its culmination" (Videla, 1963, pp. 201–204). He also wrote an important piece, "Anatomy of My Ultra," which was published in *Grecia* on May 20, 1921. In defining his poetical intentions, he affirms his interest in the *sensation in itself* and not in the description of the spatial or temporal premises that constitute its setting; he longs for an art that can translate the naked emotion, free from the additional data which surround it; an art that avoids the superficial, the metaphysical, the egocentric, and the ironic. To achieve it, he stresses the importance of rhythm and metaphor, or as he puts it, "the acoustic element and the luminous element. Rhythm: not imprisoned in the metrical pentagrams, but in winding, loose, liberated, suddenly truncated Metaphor: that verbal curve which generally traces between two—spiritual—points the shortest way" (Fernández, 1967, p. 493).

In spite of the arch language and heavy imagery of its prose, the piece shows how clearly Georgie viewed what was essential in the new poetry. In insisting on rhythm and metaphor—he wrote another article on metaphor for *Cosmópolis* (Madrid, November 1921, pp. 395–402)—he was preaching what his new poems were practicing. No less than eleven have been identified in several little magazines of the time. In the "Autobiographical Essay," Borges admits that "three or four" found "their way into magazines." What he has to say there about his ultraist writing in Spain is pitifully brief. He mentions two books he wrote while there—one of essays and one of some twenty poems—then adds that he destroyed both books: the latter in Spain, "on the eve of departure"; the former in Buenos Aires because he failed to find a publisher for it ("Essay," 1970, p. 223).

Perhaps Borges is right in dismissing his early work, but he shows an excess of pleasure in talking about the destruction of both manuscripts. What he remembers about the book of essays does not seem too promising: "[The book] was called, I now wonder why, *Los naipes del tahur* (The Sharper's Cards). They were literary and political essays (I was still an anarchist and a freethinker and in favor of pacifism), written under the influence of Pío Baroja. Their aim was to be bitter and relentless, but they were, as a matter of fact, quite tame. I went in for using such words as 'fools,' 'harlots,' 'liars' " (ibid., p. 223). The article on Baroja, Azorín, and the Jesuit priest in *La Feuille* could probably be viewed as an example of the kind of essay Georgie had included in the first book. He may have also included other pieces on Spanish brothels, ultraist poetry, and German expressionism. The second book is easier to evaluate. According to Borges, it "was titled either *The Red Psalms* or *The Red Rhythms*. It was a collection of poems—perhaps some twenty in all—in free verse and in praise of the Russian revolution, the brotherhood of man, and pacifism." He then quotes the titles of three: "Bolshevik Epic," "Trenches," and "Russia" (ibid., p. 223).

The poems that have survived in magazines, or in scholarly works about the period, do not seem memorable. They are interesting for what they reveal about Georgie's apprenticeship. He was obsessed with a war he had seen from a distance ("Trenches"), with a revolution that for a while filled the youth of Europe with hope for social and political justice ("Bolshevik Epic," "Russia"). But in the majority of the verses he was chiefly concerned with expressing his view of reality through rare metaphors and striking similes. He had learned his poetics from Whitman and the German expressionists; he favored free verse and long-lined poems that he called (following Cansinos' example) psalms. What is still memorable today is the violence of many of his images. Thus in "Morning," published in *Ultra* (Madrid, January 1921), the sun, with its spears, claws the mirrors; in "Russia" the bayonets "carry the morning on their tips"; and in "Bolshevik Epic" the Red army is seen as a fresh forest of masts made of bayonet spouts, a candelabrum of one thousand and one phalluses (all these quotes are from De Torre, 1965, pp. 556–558).

That Georgie was obviously passing through an erotic phase is confirmed by one of the articles, "Maison Elena (Toward an Esthetic of the Whorehouses in Spain)," also published in *Ultra* (October 1921). In praising the "easy curves of a girl," Georgie cannot avoid a literary simile: he finds them "sculpted like a phrase by Quevedo" (Fernández Moreno, 1967, p. 141). Perhaps for Georgie (who had been so innocent of what was going on in Palermo's brothels until his cousin Alvaro Melián Lafinur gave him some information), literary life in Madrid was not limited to meetings to discuss poetry, manifestos, and poems. It is well known that an important part of the night life in Spain is traditionally spent in whorehouses, which are a mixture of brothel, social club, and even political caucus.

The reference to Quevedo above stresses another great discovery of Georgie's Spanish sojourn. For the first time in his life he became truly acquainted with the classics of his native language. At the same time that they were getting acquainted with the avant-garde, young Spanish poets disinterred a neglected period of Spanish letters, the baroque. They came to recognize, in Góngora's experiments with a Latinate syntax and elaborate imagery, in Quevedo's play with conceit, and in Cervantes' labyrinthine use of fiction within fiction, preoccupations similar to their own. Some of the older masters (Baroja, Unamuno, Jiménez, the Machado brothers, Valle Inclán) had also been preoccupied with these poetic problems. Georgie read them all and chose a few among them—Quevedo and Cervantes, Unamuno and Baroja—to be his guides for a while. In later essays, written and published in Buenos Aires, he discussed them, imitated them, and (finally) overcame them. If there is very little in the "Autobiographical Essay" about his reading or about all the writing he did in Spain at that time, the fault is in Borges' memory. For Georgie, the ultraist experience was decisive. Only after reaching Buenos Aires in 1921 would he be in a position to evaluate its importance.

8.
The Mythological Foundation of Buenos Aires

Georgie was barely fifteen when he left Buenos Aires, or rather Palermo, the only neighborhood of his native city he really knew. Until that time the child had seldom ventured outside the two-story house and the garden. He was familiar only with certain places: when visiting relatives, he would have a glimpse of the city; during the summer he would go to Adrogué, a small town some fifteen miles to the south of Buenos Aires, or would cross the River Plate to swim on the Uruguayan side or go north to bathe in the swift waters of the Uruguay River. Monotonous, reassuring, foreseeable, his life in Buenos Aires before 1914 made Georgie into an introverted, quiet adolescent. When he returned home in 1921, almost seven years had passed. He was a young man and had lived in Switzerland and Spain; had learned Latin, French, and German; had participated vicariously in some avant-garde movements and become an active member of a new group, the ultraists; had published reviews, articles, and a few poems; had even written two books. At twenty-one he was still shy but he was no longer unseasoned.

Buenos Aires was different too. In his "Autobiographical Essay" Borges concentrates his narrative mainly on the changes he noticed in his native city:

> We returned to Buenos Aires on the *Reina Victoria Eugenia* toward the end of March 1921. It came to me as a surprise, after living in so many European cities—after so many memories of Geneva, Zurich, Nimes, Córdoba, and Lisbon—to find that my native town had grown, and that it was now a very large, sprawling, and almost endless city of low buildings with flat roofs, stretching west toward what geographers and literary hands call the pampas.

167

It was more than a homecoming; it was a rediscovery. I was able to see Buenos Aires keenly and eagerly because I had been away from it for a long time. Had I never gone abroad, I wonder whether I would ever have seen it with the peculiar shock and glow that it now gave me. The city—not the whole city, of course, but a few places in it that became emotionally signifi-cant to me—inspired the poems of my first published book, *Fervor de Buenos Aires*. ("Essay," 1970, pp. 223–224)

The Borgeses had settled in a house on Bulnes Street, not far from their old Palermo neighborhood, and lived there for the next two years. Georgie there began a habit that he kept well into his fifties: walking endlessly along Buenos Aires streets, covering enormous dis-tances, alone or with friends, musing and perhaps sketching poems or articles in his mind, talking about anything that took his fancy. Thus he *learned* Buenos Aires, or at least *his* Buenos Aires; it was an inch-by-inch, repetitive covering of a territory that his writings would cover just as closely. Buenos Aires had existed before Georgie discovered it, but very few of its writers had taken the trouble of reinventing it so thoroughly and with such success. From 1921 onward Buenos Aires became his as much as Manhattan was Whitman's.

In recalling those days in his "Autobiographical Essay," Borges subtly downplays his literary activities. He prefers to stress the first im-pact of the city on his poetic imagination. The only thing he has to say about his literary life is, "I am still known to literary historians as the 'father of Argentine ultraism' " (ibid., p. 225), but he fails to explain why he has earned such a title. The truth is that as soon as he settled in Buenos Aires he became the leader of a group of young poets—among them his cousin Guillermo Juan Borges, Eduardo González Lanuza, Norah Lange, and Francisco Piñero—who were also interested in avant-garde literature and with whom he published a literary maga-zine, *Prisma* (Prism). Only two issues came out: December 1921 and March 1922. Borges recalls the more picturesque aspects of the en-terprise: "Our small ultraist group was eager to have a magazine of its own, but a real magazine was beyond our means. I had noticed bill-board ads, and the thought came to me that we might similarly print a 'mural magazine' and paste it up ourselves on the walls of the buildings in different parts of town" (ibid., p. 234). The idea of having a mural magazine was very much in line with all that the European avant-garde had been practicing since the cubist painters started to paste bits and pieces of journals on their canvases, Apollinaire began drawing his *Calligrammes,* and Marinetti used posters to advance the cause of fu-turism. Perhaps Norah also had something to do with the idea. She had contributed her woodcuts to several ultraist publications in Spain, and now in Argentina she became one of Georgie's most constant collaborators. A cursory examination of the little magazines of the 1920s in Argentina shows how much she was also part of the movement.

In his "Essay" Borges gives a few more picturesque details about *Prisma:* "Each issue was a large single sheet and contained a manifesto and some six or eight short, laconic poems, printed with plenty of white space around them, and a woodcut by my sister. We sallied forth at night—González Lanuza, Piñero, my cousin, and I— armed with pastepots and brushes provided by my mother, and, walking miles on end, slapped them up along Santa Fe, Callao, Entre Ríos, and Mexico streets" (ibid., p. 234). This itinerary required Georgie and his friends to work their way down Santa Fe to the downtown section; there, crossing Rivadavia Street (which divides Buenos Aires in two), they entered the Southside, where the National Library is located on Mexico Street. The journey must have taken most of the night.

The first ultraist manifesto ever signed by Georgie came out in the December issue of *Prisma.* In exalted language it begins by criticizing traditional poets who continued to use the worn-out approaches of symbolism or indulged in autobiography. It also concentrates its fire on the waste of time and energy long novels or prolix poems represent. The manifesto complains that to achieve one good, valid verse the traditionalists write a whole sonnet or take two hundred pages to say what could be said in two lines. In a parenthesis it prophesies that the psychological novel is doomed. Against all these errors, the ultraists proclaim the need to free art from its decrepit state. Poetry must concentrate on its basic element: metaphor. "Each verse of one of our poems has an individual life and represents a new vision" (Videla, 1963, pp. 199–210). The manifesto ends by stating that the task of *Prisma* is to make the new poetry available to all.

As Georgie's signature is the first on the manifesto, we can assume he was chiefly responsible for its wording. A few of its ideas (the rejection of autobiography, the attack on the novel) were very much in line with his poetical and philosophical convictions, and in spite of a radical change in his style of writing, Borges still subscribes to them.

In his recollections Borges does not mention the manifesto or the fact that *Prisma* had some impact in Madrid. On the contrary, he takes a rather dim view of the mural magazine's effect on Buenos Aires citizens: "Most of our handiwork was torn down by baffled readers, almost at once, but luckily for us Alfredo Bianchi, of *Nosotros,* saw one of them and invited us to publish an ultraist anthology among the pages of his solid magazine" ("Essay," 1970, pp. 234–235). Once more, Borges fails to mention that Bianchi did more than just ask the group to contribute its poems; he also asked Georgie to write an article explaining to the sedate readers of *Nosotros* what ultraism was about.

Georgie accepted, and his contribution (the first of many to that magazine) was published in the December 1921 issue. Because he was writing for a middle-aged audience and in a magazine that was part of the establishment (it was already in its thirty-ninth year of publication), he made an effort to write in a less baroque style, so that while the article presents the same views aired in the *Prisma* manifesto, the style is more subdued and the arguments tighter. After dismissing the symbolists and the autobiographers, he offers ultraism as "one of the answers" to the crisis of modern poetry. The most important part of the article is a four-point résumé of ultraist principles:

1. Reduction of lyric poetry to its basic element: metaphor.
2. Elimination of links, connecting phrases, and superfluous adjectives.
3. Abolition of ornamental implements, confessionalism, circumstantial evidence, preaching, and deliberate vagueness.
4. Synthesis of two or more images in one, which thus enlarges its capacity for suggestion. (Fernández Moreno, 1967, p. 495)

The article includes quotations from ultraist poetry, written by Spanish and Argentine poets. From that point of view, it was a preface to the anthology that Borges mentions in his "Autobiographical Essay" and that came out in *Nosotros* in September 1922. It includes poems by Georgie ("Saturdays," later collected in his first book of poems) and by the other *Prisma* poets. The selection is, to say the least, eclectic.

The article Georgie wrote for *Nosotros* also mentions a long list of established writers who contributed to ultraism, including Ramón, Ortega y Gasset, Jiménez, Valle Inclán, and the Chilean Vicente Huidobro. Obviously, he was trying to impress the *Nosotros* reader with this list of prominent personalities and thus find a way to legitimize the movement. In his conclusion he repeats one of his chief psychological observations: the mistake of believing in the existence of an individual ego. "Every new state which can be added to those already existing becomes an essential part of the ego and expresses it: this is true not only of that which was already part of *each individual* but also of what was *alien* to it. Any event, any perception, any idea, expresses us with identical efficacy; that is, it can be added to our *us*." For Georgie, the concept of the impersonality of the ego found its best expression in ultraist poetry, whose aim was "the transmutation of the world's concrete reality into an inner emotional reality" (ibid., p. 495).

Perhaps these metaphysical views were not shared by all Argentine ultraist poets; perhaps they represent only Georgie's views, for they appear time and again in Georgie's poems and articles. They are the result of endless discussions with Father on the subject of philosophical idealism and on Georgie's own readings of Hume, Berkeley, and Schopenhauer. Also, on his return to Buenos Aires, he had become friends with one of Father's schoolmates, Macedonio Fernández, who was also a lawyer and had a truly philosophical turn of mind. In his "Autobiographical Essay" Borges writes: "Perhaps the major event of my return was Macedonio Fernández. Of all the people I have met in my life—and I have met some quite remarkable men—no one has ever made so deep and so lasting an impression on me as Macedonio. A tiny figure in a black bowler hat, he was waiting for us on the Dársena Norte when we landed, and I came to inherit his friendship with my father" ("Essay," 1970, p. 227).

Soon Georgie began to meet Macedonio every Saturday at the Perla Café, in the busy Plaza del Once. The new ritual took the place of Cansinos' Saturdays in Spain.

> As in Madrid Cansinos had stood for all learning, Macedonio now stood for pure thinking. At the time, I was a great reader and went out very seldom (almost every night after dinner, I used to go to bed and read), but my whole week was lit up with the expectation that on Saturday I'd be seeing and hearing Macedonio. He lived quite near us and I could have seen him whenever I wanted, but I somehow felt that I had no right to that privilege and that in order to give Macedonio's Saturday its full value I had to forgo him throughout the week. (Ibid., p. 227)

Macedonio was not a great talker like Cansinos. On the contrary, on those Saturdays he would speak "perhaps only three or four times, risking only a few quiet observations," which he generally pretended had been drawn from something his listeners had said or thought. He had a great fondness for philosophical speculation and once had even exchanged some letters with William James. But if he had a mind of his own, he was no inventor of systems:

> Readers of Hume and Schopenhauer may find little that is new in Macedonio, but the remarkable thing about him is that he arrived at his conclusions by himself. Later on, he actually read Hume, Schopenhauer, Berkeley, and William James, but I suspect he had not done much other reading, and he always quoted the same authors. . . . I think of Macedonio as reading a page or so and then being spurred into thought. He not only argued that we are such stuff as dreams are made on, but he really believed that we are all living in a dream world. (Ibid., p. 229)

The impact Macedonio had on Georgie was immense. This is how Borges describes it:

> Before Macedonio, I had always been a credulous reader. His chief gift to me was to make me read skeptically. At the outset, I plagiarized him de-

votedly, picking up certain stylistic mannerisms of his that later I came to regret. I look back on him now, however, as an Adam bewildered by the Garden of Eden. His genius survives in but a few of his pages; his influence was of a Socratic nature. I truly loved the man, on this side idolatry, as much as any. (Ibid., p. 230)

If Macedonio was Socrates, Georgie would eventually become Plato. Unknown to anyone but his most intimate friends, Macedonio had been writing (and sometimes quietly publishing) since 1896. He lacked, nevertheless, the necessary impulse to complete some of his most ambitious projects—a book of metaphysical essays, a novel—and continued to accumulate manuscripts that were stuck in boxes and drawers and sometimes even got lost in one of Macedonio's constant changes of boardinghouses. Georgie was instrumental in helping him save and organize some of his works. He even persuaded Macedonio to join him and a few friends in the launching of a new magazine, *Proa* (Prow), which published three issues between August 1922 and July 1923. Each issue had only six pages; it was actually "a single sheet printed on both sides and folded twice," according to Borges' description (ibid., p. 235). On the editorial board Georgie and Macedonio were joined by other young poets. Norah again contributed her woodcuts. A note to the reader in the first issue warned that "Ultraism is not a sect designed as a prison." On the contrary, it can be seen as an open field, "an insatiable longing for faraway lands," or as an "exaltation of the metaphor." Of these two views ("intuitive the first and intellectual the second"), the reader may choose whichever he prefers.

Macedonio contributed at least three pieces to the magazine, while Georgie carried the main responsibility for its editing. In the meantime, he continued to contribute to other publications such as *Nosotros*—an article on Berkeley's metaphysics, another on Unamuno as a poet—and to *Inicial* (Initial), an avant-garde little magazine for which he wrote an article on German expressionist poets and published a few derogatory remarks on a new book by Argentina's leading poet, Leopoldo Lugones. Georgie had discovered in Seville and Madrid the pleasures of literary life; now in Buenos Aires he discovered the exhilaration of having a tribune to air his ideas. His career as editor and reviewer had begun.

Very little of his frantic activity in this period is registered in the "Autobiographical Essay." The whole period is soberly described as follows:

When I talked things over at the time with fellow poets Eduardo González Lanuza, Norah Lange, Francisco Piñero, my cousin Guillermo Juan (Borges), and Roberto Ortelli, we came to the conclusion that Spanish ultraism was overburdened—after the manner of futurism—with modernity and gadgets. We were unimpressed by railway trains, by propellers, by airplanes, and by electric fans. While in our manifestos we still upheld the primacy of the metaphor and the elimination of transitions and decorative adjectives, what we wanted to write was essential poetry—poems beyond the here and now, free of local color and contemporary circumstances. (Ibid., pp. 225–226)

The ironic summary is basically right. In articles published at the time, and later collected in *Inquisiciones,* Georgie offers a similar perspective but in a less ironic mode. Reviewing *Prisma,* a book of poems by González Lanuza, he stresses the differences between Spanish and Argentine ultraism:

Ultraism in Seville and Madrid was a desire for renewal; it was a desire to define a new cycle in the arts; it was a poetry written as if with big red letters on the leaves of a calendar and whose proudest emblems—airplanes, antennae, and propellers—plainly state a chronological nowness. Ultraism in Buenos Aires was the ambition to obtain an absolute art which did not depend on the uncertain prestige of words and which lasted in the eternity of language as a conviction of beauty. Under the powerful brightness of the lamps, the names of Huidobro and Apollinaire were usually mentioned in the Spanish gatherings. We, in the meantime, tested lines from Garcilaso [a Renaissance poet], wandering ponderously under the stars on the outskirts of town, asking for an art which was as atemporal as the eternal stars. We abhorred the blurred shades of rubenism [the Spanish American brand of symbolism] and were inflamed by metaphors because of the precision they have, because of their algebraical quality of relating remote things. (*Inquisiciones,* 1925, pp. 96–97)

In analyzing his friend's book, Georgie verifies a fact which astonishes him: without meaning to, the ultraist "had fallen into another type of rhetoric, as linked as the old ones to verbal deception. . . . I have seen that our poetry, whose flight we considered free and careless, has been drawing a geometrical figure in the air of time. What a beautiful and sad surprise to discover that our gesture, so spontaneous and easy then, was nothing but the clumsy beginning of a rite" (ibid., pp. 97–98).

In a similar vein, Georgie recalls the origins of Argentine ultraism in a prologue to a book of poems by another friend, Norah Lange. He again stresses the differences between the Spanish and the local brand:

Its desire for renewal, which was prankish and bouncing in Seville, sounded loyally and passionately among us. . . . For us, contemporary poetry was as

useless as worn-out incantations, and we felt an urgency to make a new poetry. We were fed up with the insolence of words and the musical vagueness
the turn-of-the-century poets loved, and we asked for a unique and effective
art in which beauty would be undeniable. . . . We practiced the image, the
sentence, and the epithet, swiftly compendious. (Ibid., pp. 76–77)

A third article, "After the Images," recalls the ultraists' infatuation with images, metaphors, tropes—all the rhetorical paraphernalia
that had also seduced English and North American imagists. Georgie
evokes the time when they discovered in metaphors the power to undermine the rigidity of the world: "For the believer, things are the ac-
tualization of the word of God—first the light was named and then it
shined over the world; for the positivist, they are necessities in an in-
terlocking system. Metaphor, by relating separate objects, breaks this
double rigidity" (ibid., p. 27).

With the perspective afforded by three years, Georgie is ready
to admit that "now" anyone can and does indulge in metaphors. In
praising the power the image has to transform the world ("it is witch-
craft," he writes), he also raises a voice of warning:

It is not enough to say, as all poets do, that mirrors are like water. Nor is it
enough to take this hypothesis as absolute and pretend, like any Huidobro,
that coolness comes out of mirrors or that thirsty birds drink out of them
and the frame becomes empty. We have to move beyond these games. We
have to express this whim made into a reality of one mind: we have to show
a man who gets into the glass and who persists in his imaginary country
(where there are figures and colors but they are ruled by still silence) and
who feels the shame of being nothing but a simulacrum which nights obliterate and which the twilight admits. (Ibid., p. 29)

Apart from documenting Georgie's attitude toward the use and abuse
of metaphors in ultraist poetry, the last sentence anticipates a subject
that Borges later develops in one of his most famous short stories, "The
Circular Ruins," collected in *Ficciones* (1944).

Although Borges never admitted it, the best poetry produced
by Argentine ultraism (and perhaps by Hispanic ultraism as a whole)
can be found in his own *Fervor de Buenos Aires*—a title that may be
translated as "Adoration of Buenos Aires." It is the first of three volumes in which Georgie collected his early poetry. In his "Autobiographical Essay" Borges tells the story of the book in a rather colorful
way:

I wrote these poems in 1921 and 1922, and the volume came out early in
1923. . . . I had bargained for sixty-four pages, but the manuscript ran too
long and at the last minute five poems had to be left out—mercifully. I can't

remember a single thing about them. The book was produced in a some-what boyish spirit. No proofreading was done, no table of contents was provided, and the pages were unnumbered. My sister made a woodcut for the cover, and three hundred copies were printed. ("Essay," 1970, p. 224)

Today the book is one of the most sought-after of his early works. It is a nicely printed, unassuming little white volume, with a woodcut in which Norah offered her own version of Georgie's Buenos Aires: the one-storied, balconied, palm-treed town the poems described in words. Borges' own evaluation in his "Autobiographical Essay" is predictably understated: "The book was essentially romantic, though it was written in a rather lean style and abounded in laconic metaphors. It celebrated sunsets, solitary places, and unfamiliar corners; it ventured into Berkeleyan metaphysics and family history; it recorded early loves" (ibid., p. 225). The style was, according to him, a mimicry of the Spanish baroque poets with some touches of Sir Thomas Browne's rhetoric. (It had a quotation from *Religio Medici* in the preface.) This is Borges' final summation: "I'm afraid the book was a plum pudding—there was just too much in it. And yet, looking back on it now, I think I have never strayed beyond that book. I feel that all my subsequent writing has only developed themes first taken up there; I feel that all during my lifetime I have been rewriting that one book" (ibid., p. 225).

In the "Essay" Borges wonders if the poems in *Fervor de Buenos Aires* are truly "ultraist poetry." After reviewing the origins of ultraism in Argentina and the role he played in that movement, and quoting one of its most representative poems, he comes to the conclusion that the poems are "a far cry from the timid extravagances of my earlier Spanish ultraist exercises, when I saw a trolley car as a man shouldering a gun, the sunrise as a shout, or the setting sun as being crucified in the west. A sane friend to whom I later recited such absurdities remarked, 'Ah, I see you held the view that poetry's chief aim is to startle.' " He also recalls that another friend, his French translator Néstor Ibarra, once said that he "left off being an ultraist poet with the first ultraist poem he wrote." Borges' conclusion is mockingly humble: "I can now only regret my early ultraist excesses. After nearly a half-century, I find myself still striving to live down that awkward period of my life" (ibid., pp. 226–227).

Memory deserts Borges once more. Some of the images he credits to the (discarded) Spanish period of his poetry found their way into *Fervor*. In "Prismas," a poem originally published in *Ultra* (Madrid, March 1, 1921), one line—"The new moon is a small voice up there in heaven"—is later used in a poem of the same period, "Montaña" (Mountain), published in *Tableros* (Madrid, no. 2, 1921), and also in

"Campos atardecidos" (Fields in the Evening), one of the last poems in *Fervor*. In other poems, when describing the sunsets of Buenos Aires, Georgie tends to lapse into expressionist rhetoric: hyperbole takes over, simile suggests the Apocalypse, and a Christian imagery pervades every line. In "Villa Urquiza" he talks about "the Final Judgment of every evening" (*Poemas*, 1943, p. 27); in "Arrabal" (Slums) he sees a Via Crucis in the quiet, suffering streets on the outskirts of Buenos Aires (p. 34); in "La noche de San Juan" sunset is presented as cutting distances with the edge of its sword (p. 61); in "Atardeceres" (Sunsets) a poor sunset mutilates the evening (p. 70). In "Campos atardecidos" Georgie uses this expressionist image:

> Sunset standing like an Archangel
> tyrannized the path.
>
> (Ibid., p. 71)

In spite of these purple passages, the general tone of the book is less violent than the expressionist exercises Georgie had published in Spain. The dominant mood conveyed is his rediscovery of Buenos Aires. In the very first poem "Calles" (Streets) Georgie explains which part of his native city he prefers:

> The streets of Buenos Aires
> are already the entrails of my soul.
> Not the lively streets
> bothered with haste and agitation,
> but the sweet streets of the outskirts
> softened by trees and sunsets
>
> (Ibid., p. 11)

The young poet prefers roaming around at sunset, when the bustling modern city begins to be more human. In poem after poem he talks about the square and the trees, the houses and the patios, the fields to which the last streets open up. He wanders and meditates, he feels and dreams, he is overcome by longings and hallucinations. A constant metaphysical quest runs under his wanderings. He finds refuge only in the stillness of cemeteries or in the house where his fiancée lives. Because he is in love. The joys and pains of love pervade the book. The discovery of her beauty, the longing for her, the realization that he is bound to return to Europe for another year: these permeate the book and make it a sort of diary of a young poet in love. It is a moving book, still awkward but already showing promise of the poet Georgie was to become in time.

A few of the poems in the collection deal with metaphysical

speculation. One of them, "El truco" (pp. 21–22), is fully achieved. In describing the popular card game he taught to his Geneva schoolmates, Georgie avoids the pitfalls of local color and concentrates on what makes the game eternal. The permutations of the cards, although innumerable in limited human experience, are not infinite: given enough time, they will come back again and again. Thus the cardplayers not only are repeating hands that have already come up in the past. In a sense, they are repeating the former players as well; they are the former players. In a note Borges added to the 1943 collected edition of his poems (ibid., p. 173), he explains that the intention behind the poem was to apply the Leibnitzian principle of the indiscernible to the problems of individuality and time. He also quotes from a footnote to a 1940 story, "Tlön, Uqbar, Orbis Tertius," in which he postulates that all men who perform the same basic activity (coitus, reciting a line from Shakespeare) *are* the same man. The identity of the activity assures the identity of the performers.

Another group of poems is devoted to family piety. In "Recoleta" Georgie again visits the cemetery where his ancestors are buried and where he will eventually be buried too (*Poemas*, 1943, p. 13); in "Sepulchral Inscription" he evokes the shadow of Isidoro Suárez, one of Argentina's founding fathers, who fought for independence at Junín and died in bitter exile (*Poems*, 1972, p. 5), and in "Rosas," he describes the most famous of all Argentina's dictators and a personal enemy of his family (ibid., p. 11). Georgie had already discovered the elegiac mode, which he would return to in many later pieces.

A few poems seem misplaced in this basically Argentine collection. One is dedicated to Benares, an Indian city that Georgie never visited but that haunted him from early readings of Kipling (*Poemas*, 1943, p. 51). Another, redolent of the expressionist poets, is called "Judería," a title changed to "Judengasse" in 1943 to underline the German connotations of the poem (ibid., p. 53). Although they are out of place in this collection, they anticipate the poems Borges wrote in his maturity: poems about places or men he never knew who still occupy his imagination.

The original edition of *Fervor de Buenos Aires* is a collector's item. In reissuing the book, Borges took enormous liberties with its contents. The first time he reprinted it, as part of the 1943 collection of his verses, he eliminated eight pieces and considerably altered many of the remaining poems, deleting lines, changing words, and altering some of the most explicit references to his fiancée—including her name, Concepción Guerrero, which was reduced to the initials "C.G." in the poem "Sábados" (Saturdays, ibid., p. 62). In the most recent reprint of the book, made in 1969, he eliminated another seven poems but to compensate included three new ones. He also added a preface in which he compared the poet of 1923 with the poet of the present. In stressing the similarities—"We are the same; the two of us do not believe in failure or success, in literary schools and their dogmas; the two of us are devoted to Schopenhauer, Stevenson, and Whitman"—he nevertheless comes to the conclusion that they had different tastes: "In those days, I was after sunsets, outskirts, and unhappiness; now, mornings, downtown, and serenity" (*Fervor,* 1969, p. 9).

9.
A Small Poetic Reputation

Father's eyesight was getting worse, so he decided in 1923 to return to Geneva to consult his doctor. The moment was not well chosen from Georgie's point of view. He was deeply in love with a young woman whose beautiful hair had inspired some of his verses, and his first book of poems, *Fervor de Buenos Aires,* was just off the press. But as he depended entirely on Father for his living, and was determined not to compromise his poetic pursuits by getting a job, he accepted Father's decision. He wrote a sad poem to his fiancée and did his best to speed the distribution of *Fervor* among the happy few. To this end, he devised an original method:

> Having noticed that many people who went to the offices of *Nosotros* . . . left their overcoats hanging in the cloak room, I brought fifty or a hundred copies to Alfredo Bianchi, one of the editors. Bianchi stared at me in amazement and said, "Do you expect me to sell these books for you?" "No," I answered. "Although I've written them, I'm not altogether a lunatic. I thought I might ask you to slip some of these books into the pockets of those coats hanging out there." He generously did so. ("Essay," 1970, pp. 224–225)

Upon his return to Argentina, Georgie found that some of the people had read the book and had even written about it.

The new journey to Europe may, in fact, have appealed to him as providing an opportunity to return to Spain with a small poetic reputation, or so it seems in retrospect. After visiting London and Paris, and consulting Father's doctor in Geneva, the Borgeses finally reached Madrid. They remained in Spain for almost a year, visiting Andalusia and Majorca to renew their impressions and memories, and also exploring neighboring Portugal. The Spanish literary scene was rapidly changing. By 1924 the ultraist movement had disintegrated. All the little magazines had died, and the more sedate journals accepted only what was safer in ultraism. The sense of adventure was already gone. The avant-garde was no longer necessary because Spain had finally updated its culture. Perhaps the surest sign of the change was the launching, in July 1923, of a new journal, *Revista de Occidente* (The Western Review), which was published until the outbreak of the civil war. Its founder was José Ortega y Gasset, then the leading intellectual figure of Spain. Born in 1883 and educated in Germany, Ortega was slightly younger than the men (Baroja, Unamuno, Azorín, the Machados, Jiménez) who represented the generation of 1898—the one that had had to face Spain's defeat in Cuba that same year. He was also more conversant with the latest philosophical theories in Germany and the new avant-garde writing in France. The journal launched became *the* cultural organ of the new Spain—as decisive as T. S. Eliot's *Criterion* in London or the *Nouvelle Revue Française* in Paris. Ortega also started a publishing house under the journal's imprint that was devoted mainly to the translation of important new German books.

The name of the journal had obvious links to Oswald Spengler's monumental *Decline of the West*, which was published in Germany between 1918 and 1922. Ortega had, in fact, recommended the translation of that book to one of the publishing houses he had helped to found and even wrote a prologue for it. But in the Spanish context "Western" had a different meaning. It meant that the journal's purpose was to go against the grain of all that was traditional and thus strictly peninsular in Spanish culture: the excessive nationalism, the endless exaltation of regionalism and local color, the indifference to what was happening on the other side of the Pyrenees. The 1898 Spanish-American war and the isolationism created by World War I, in which Spain fiercely kept its neutrality, had strengthened both nationalism and provincialism. Against them Ortega raised his *Revista de Occidente*.

Georgie's poems found a welcome in the journal. None other than Ramón Gómez de la Serna was to review *Fervor de Buenos Aires*. His article in the April 24 issue begins by recalling Georgie's visits to his Saturday meetings at Pombo and contrasts his presence in Madrid with the half-imagined, half-real vision of a younger Georgie, a "pale boy of great sensitivity" hidden among the thick curtains of a traditional household. The article also makes affectionate references to Norah. "Jorge Luis always seems to me close to Norah, the disturbing girl with the same pale skin of her brother's and, like him, lost among the curtains." Ramón recalls a conversation in which Norah described their home in Buenos Aires, where the "very united and patriarchal Borges family" kept themselves tightly indoors. While Norah talked, Georgie remained silent. Ramón calls him "unsociable, remote, unruly"—which for him means he is destined to become a poet. In commenting on his book, Ramón makes some perceptive observations. He discovers in Georgie's affectionate poem about the streets of Buenos Aires an echo of the equally "silent and moving" streets of Granada. He defines him as "a Góngora more conversant in things than in rhetoric" and quotes several of the poem's more striking images. Ramón's article was not only the first really important piece of criticism devoted to Georgie; it was decisive to his reputation because of the magazine in which it appeared. A second important review came out in the leading newspaper, *España;* it was signed by Enrique Díez-Canedo, one of the most perceptive critics of the new literature. All in all, Georgie's return to Spain was a success. His reputation as a young poet was certainly not small, as Borges unfairly suggests in the "Autobiographical Essay."

Georgie himself contributed two important pieces to Spanish periodicals. The first was a two-part article on metaphor published in *Alfar* (May and June–July 1924), a magazine sponsored by the Casa América de Galicia, an institute created in the north of Spain to better the relations between Latin America and the mother country. *Alfar* was at the time edited by a Uruguayan poet, Julio J. Casal, who doubled as consul of his native country. Georgie must have believed the article was worthy, because he reprinted it in his first book of essays, *Inquisiciones* (1925). It contains an elaborate defense of the role of metaphor in poetry, very much in line with ultraist theories; but what distinguishes it from others he wrote then is its approach. He begins by quoting the Spanish Luis de Granada and the French Bernard Lamy (now very much in fashion among structuralist critics) to argue that metaphors were invented to compensate for the limitations of normal language. He then proceeds to show that metaphors are scarce if nonexistent in popular poetry. Finally, he gives a general classification of metaphors. The quotations range from popular lyrics to the most unexpected learned sources (Virgil and Browning are placed next to Johannes Becher and Guillermo de Torre). Georgie's impressive range of reading and his talent for extracting the most quotable lines from a text are already evident. In future articles he repeats his basic ideas about metaphor but never again attempts such an ambitious classification.

The most important article he published in Spain at the time was one on "Quevedo's Grandeur and Defamation" in *Revista de Occidente* (October–December 1924). The great baroque poet was perhaps the most important discovery he had made during his previous visit to Spain. Other baroque writers (Cervantes, Gracián, Góngora, Villarroel) also attracted his attention, but Quevedo was the one he singled out to represent his concept of literature. In this article he is interested mainly in viewing Quevedo's work as a whole, in its excellences and limitations, as the title of the article rather elaborately indicates. Georgie stresses Quevedo's eroticism, his "fierce intellectualism," the perfection of his metaphors, antitheses, and adjectives. For Georgie, Quevedo's main virtue is to be able to "feel" the world, to be not just a part of reality but an "extra reality." The article compares Góngora's and Quevedo's schools of poetry and favors the latter: "Gongorism was an attempt urged by grammarians to alter the Castilian phrase according to the disorder of Latin; an attempt made without realizing that in Latin such a disorder is only apparent while in Spanish it would be real because of the lack of declensions. Quevedoism is psychological; it aims at restoring to all ideas the risky and abrupt character which made them astonishing the first time they came to mind."

In 1924 Georgie saw Góngora and Góngora's followers as poets exclusively interested in the formal aspect of verse; he saw Quevedo and his disciples as writers more concerned with intelligence and ideas. For him, Quevedo was chiefly interested in language as a tool of thought. Years later Borges admitted that he was wrong in believing Góngora was inferior to Quevedo (*Carriego*, 1955, p. 55). But at the time that Georgie was determined to be a poet, he saw in Quevedo a model for the kind of verse he wanted to write: a verse in which the act of thinking is itself part of the poetic subject matter. In the same article he makes an allusion that links Góngora's formal quest to the symbolists, who had greatly influenced Spanish and Spanish American poetry. In putting these two movements into the same category, Georgie also establishes a parallel link between Quevedo and the kind of ultraist poetry he was interested in.

Georgie's reading of Góngora was not popular in Spain at the time. In 1924 there were already signs of a renewal of interest in Góngora's poetry. The third centenary of his death would be celebrated in 1927 by new studies and a scholarly edition of his *Soledades,* done by a young poet, Dámaso Alonso, who was also interested in avant-garde poetry and had translated Joyce's *Portrait of the Artist as a Young Man* into Spanish.

Georgie's article on Quevedo was his first and only original contribution to *Revista de Occidente.* Perhaps he was too busy participating in Buenos Aires' hectic literary life to have time to send articles or poems to the journal. There may be another explanation. If we remember Cansinos-Asséns' rather lukewarm attitude toward Ortega and Georgie's allegiance to the Andalusian master, it is not too difficult to conjecture why he was not keen on contributing to *Revista.* Besides, he probably did not care much for Ortega's ideas about the avant-garde. In 1925 the Spanish essayist had already published his celebrated *The Dehumanization of Art,* which contained some "Ideas on the Novel" that Borges later demolished in a 1940 prologue to Adolfo Bioy Casares' *The Invention of Morel.* Perhaps already in 1924 Georgie was not terribly impressed with Ortega, and not being impressed with the Spanish master was the worst possible way to insure a permanent flow of contributions to the journal. Like any autocratic editor, Ortega was not only brilliant; he was also vain. Years later, when the Spanish essayist moved to Argentina for the duration of the Spanish civil war, Georgie avoided meeting him, although they had many friends in common.

It was during his visit to Spain in 1923–1924 that Georgie discovered Oswald Spengler's *Decline of the West.* He began to read it in the Spanish translation Ortega had sponsored, of which only two volumes had been published; eager to read it through, Georgie got the German original. Spengler's obvious debt to Nietzsche must have eased Georgie's acceptance of his apocalyptic ideas. In 1962 Borges told James E. Irby:

> Now [Spengler] is condemned for being too pessimistic, for having become a Nazi in his last years. He is being forgotten in favor of Toynbee. This may be right but I prefer Spengler. Look here: it is all right to read books for the truth they hold, but is also nice to read them for the marvelous things they contain. . . . In this way, I read Freud or Jung, for instance. Spengler was very German but he was not confined to his own country; his point of view embraced all cultures. And he was an admirable stylist, which Toynbee is not. You have to notice the poetry of German language. Observe the title of Spengler's work: *Der Untergang des Abendlandes,* which is generally translated as *The Decline of the West.* But literally it means *the going down of the evening land.* How beautiful, no? Perhaps a German-speaking person would not notice it, but those metaphors are there, in the words. (Irby, 1962, pp. 9–10)

Borges' recollection tends to minimize the impact Spengler's ideas probably had on Georgie.

By mid-1924 the Borgeses were back in Buenos Aires. For a while they stayed at the Garden Hotel. Later they moved to a two-story house closer to the downtown area than the one they had rented in 1921. It was located at 222 Avenida Quintana and had a small garden, decorated with a fountain and a nymph. A charming woodcut by Norah (reproduced in Jurado,' 1964, p. 89) preserves a view of the house, which no longer exists. (It was torn down to make way for an apartment building.) The fiancée to whom Georgie had written so many sad and charming poems had suffered a metamorphosis during his absence. Her celebrated tresses had been cut, and when Georgie met her again he realized he had lost interest in her. At least that is what Mother told Alicia Jurado (ibid., p. 37). But Mother had always taken a skeptical view of Georgie's endless fiancées. In spite of his reputation as an intellectual and a bookworm, Georgie was terribly susceptible to beautiful young women. He was constantly though briefly falling madly in love.

Borges' own view of passion is ambiguous. In a 1964 interview a very old friend, Gloria Alcorta, tried to get him to speak of it:

ALCORTA: Tell me, why in your work is there so little, or nothing, about love? *(Borges stiffens, turns his face away, astonished by the question and apparently not ready to answer it.)*
BORGES: Perhaps *(he answered after a few seconds of reflection)* I was too concerned about love in my private life to talk about it in my books. Or perhaps because what really moves me in literature is the epic. For instance, I have never cried at the movies except at pirate or gangster movies, never at a sentimental one. . . .
ALCORTA: I have seen you surrounded by women.
BORGES: Then if I do not write about that subject it is out of modesty. . . . I have experienced passion like everybody else.
ALCORTA: Not like everybody. There are people incapable of passion.
BORGES: [They must be] very egotistic people, or very vain . . . or very reasonable. . . . (Alcorta, 1964, p. 404)

To another interviewer, Carlos Peralta, Borges confided that same year: "With a certain sadness, I have discovered that I've spent all my life thinking about one woman or another. I thought I was seeing countries, cities, but always there was a woman as a screen between the object and myself. Perhaps it's possible to be in love and not behave like that. I would have preferred to be able to devote myself entirely to the enjoyment of metaphysics, or linguistics, or other subjects" (Peralta, 1964, p. 410). Two years later, when María Angélica Correa asked him to comment on the fact that there were so few love poems in his works, he observed that if she looked carefully she would see that he had written many. He is right, but the poems he alludes to are not explicitly erotic, and some are cleverly disguised as translations. The best example is a two-line poem attributed in *Dreamtigers* to a certain Gasper Camerarius:

> I, who have been so many men, have never been
> The one in whose embrace Matilde Urbach swooned.
> *(Dreamtigers*, 1964, p. 92)

By placing this poem at the end of the book and, at the same time, attributing it to a nonexistent poet, Borges both affirms and denies (or tries to deny) the importance of these lines, in which the longings of carnal love are so subtly put into words. In the same interview with María Angélica Correa, he indicates that his reticence in talking openly about love is due to the fact that he is afraid of being sentimental, that he prefers to hide his emotions because he is shy. Two years later Borges was confronted again with the same question, this time worded more bluntly. The interviewers were North American journalists:

Mr. Borges, one subject very rarely, if at all, shows up in your work, and that is sex. What would you say was the reason for that?
BORGES: I suppose the reason is that I think too much about it. When I write, I try to get away from personal feelings. I suppose that's the reason. But there has to be another reason. The other reason may be that it's been worked to death, and I know that I can't say anything new or very interesting about it. Of course, you may say that the other subjects I treat have also been worked to death. For example, loneliness, identity. And yet somehow I feel that I can do more with the problems of time and identity than with what was treated by Blake when he spoke of "weaving through dreams a sexual strife, and weeping o'er the web of life." Well, I wonder if I have woven through dreams the sexual strife. I don't think so. But after all, my business is to weave dreams. I suppose I may be allowed to choose the material. (Marx and Simon, 1968, pp. 109–110)

Borges sidesteps the subject, and once more he fails to correct the statement that the subject of sex "very rarely, if at all, shows up in your work." At the time the interview was held, Borges had already published not only many erotic poems but a few stories ("The Sect of the Phoenix," "The Intruder," "Emma Zunz," "The Dead Man," "Streetcorner Man," "The Masked Dyer, Hakim of Merv," to mention only the most important) in which sex plays a decisive role. With Adolfo Bioy Casares he had written in 1946 a parody of the detective novel, "A Model for Death," in which explicit sexual slang is used. But Borges, in answering his interviewers, preserved their ignorance and preferred to discuss his own view of the subject. As usual, it involves a paradox: one writes not to describe what one thinks of obsessively but to get away from personal feelings. Borges' answer coincides almost literally with Marcel Proust's opinion on the same subject. In *Against Sainte-Beuve* Proust objected to the French critic's biographical method of analyzing a literary work, arguing that such a work does not reflect life literally. The second part of Borges' answer is less evasive and contains a clue missed by his interviewers. In quoting Blake, Borges is suggesting an answer to the riddle: sex is not explicitly presented in most of his work because it is presented in a different manner: "weaving through dreams a sexual strife." Once again, as in his conversation with Ronald Christ about "The Sect of the Phoenix," Borges approaches the repressed subject through the web of a quotation: Whitman then, now Blake. This attitude reveals the method of his writing. Just as sex is woven in the texture of his dreams, so it is woven in the texture of the quotations he uses to mask his private voice.

But if he was shy or reticent in his writings, in his private life Georgie did not hide his feelings. Two or three years after his return to Argentina he met a woman who was destined to have, forty years later, a decisive influence on him. Around 1927 Georgie regularly visited Professor Pedro Henríquez Ureña, who taught at the University of La Plata, a small town located some sixty miles to the south of Buenos Aires. Henríquez Ureña had been born in Santo Domingo but was forced into exile because dictator Trujillo was too fond of his beautiful wife. He was the most distinguished Spanish American critic and scholar of his time and a very good friend of Georgie. Among the young women who visited Henríquez Ureña's house was a seventeen-year-old girl, Elsa Astete Millán, to whom Georgie took a fancy. Apparently she did not encourage him at all and eventually married another man. But Georgie never forgot her. When she was a widow, and he a sixty-seven-year-old bachelor, they met again and married.

10.
The Battle of the Magazines

While ultraism was almost dead (if not already buried) in Spain, the avant-garde movements were just beginning to gather strength in the River Plate area. In February 1924 the first issue of *Martín Fierro* came out in Buenos Aires. This journal was to become the most popular of the little magazines. Five years earlier a periodical called *Martín Fierro* had been founded and died. The new one, in spite of using the same name and pretending to continue its approach, was a completely different publication. The first was a political review; thus it amply justified using the name of Hernández's epic hero as its title. The second *Martín Fierro* could be called political only in the first four issues, which attacked the Pope and the Argentine Catholics, the czarist Russian ambassador (still active in Argentina in spite of the October revolution), the Liga Patriótica (equivalent to the American Legion), the mayor of Buenos Aires, the Spanish immigrants from Galicia, and a few of the most famous poets of the old generation. These attacks were generally brutal and sometimes almost obscene. There was no coherent ideology behind them except for total rejection of the establishment, the Church, the army, and cultural traditions. The tone was more dadaist than ultraist, and the editors seemed interested more in destroying than in defending a new way of thinking and writing. The editor-in-chief, Evar Méndez, was a rather mild and generous provincial poet who belonged to an older group; but the real intellectual force behind the magazine was Oliverio Girondo, a young futurist poet with a wit that later verged on the macabre. After the fifth issue (May 15–June 15, 1924), the magazine concerned itself almost exclusively with cultural matters.

As soon as he had finished unpacking, Georgie began to participate in Buenos Aires' literary life. He contributed to *Martín Fierro* one of his best poems, "Montevideo" (August–September 1924), and two articles, one on Cansinos-Asséns (October–November 1924) and a second on Ramón (January 24, 1925). The poem was later included in his second book of poems; the articles were collected in *Inquisiciones*. But by August Georgie had launched his own journal, a new *Proa*. The first had been published with the help of some young poets, under the intellectual patronage of Macedonio Fernández. For the second, Georgie had the help of Ricardo Güiraldes, the most contemporary writer of the previous generation. He was thirty-eight when he met Georgie. A postsymbolist poet and short-story writer, Güiraldes had been attracted early to the avant-garde movements he had learned of on his regular visits to France. He was a wealthy man, son of a ranchowner, and knew how to combine his enthusiasm for contemporary French and German literature with an authentic if slightly exalted love for his native country. At the time he met Georgie he was known only to a few, but he was already planning the book that was to make him the most famous Argentine novelist of the first half of the century.

In his "Autobiographical Essay" Borges tells how the second *Proa* was founded:

> One afternoon, Brandán Caraffa, a young poet from Córdoba, came to see me at the Garden Hotel. He told me that Ricardo Güiraldes and Pablo Rojas Paz had decided to found a magazine that would represent the new literary generation, and that everyone had said that if that were its goal I could not possibly be left out. Naturally, I was flattered. That night, I went around to the Phoenix Hotel, where Güiraldes was staying. He greeted me with these words: "Brandán told me that the night before last all of you got together to found a magazine of young writers, and everyone said I couldn't be left out." At that moment, Rojas Paz came in and told us excitedly, "I'm quite flattered." I broke in and said, "The night before last, the three of us got together and decided that in a magazine of new writers you couldn't be left out." Thanks to this innocent stratagem, *Proa* was born. Each of us put in fifty pesos, which paid for an edition of three to five hundred copies with no misprints and on fine paper. But a year and a half and fifteen issues later, for lack of subscriptions and ads, we had to give it up. ("Essay," 1970, p. 235)

In spite of Brandán Caraffa's innocent mystification, the group worked together nicely, and *Proa* became the best little magazine of the period. Although it did not have the impact of *Martín Fierro* (its distribution was almost clandestine), from the point of view of literary coherence and quality it was superior. In a sense, there was a lot of collaboration between the two magazines. Not only did the writers who contributed to *Proa* also contribute to *Martín Fierro*, but the latter's editor-in-chief became a member of the board of directors of a new publishing house under the *Proa* imprint, founded by Güiraldes and his group. If *Martín Fierro* was too eclectic and lacked a firm purpose, *Proa* had its goals perfectly set. In his "Autobiographical Essay," discussing the friends with whom he launched all these enterprises, Borges recalls: "Behind our work was a sincerity; we felt we were renewing both prose and poetry. Of course, like all young men, I tried to be as unhappy as I could—a kind of Hamlet and Raskolnikov rolled into one. What we achieved was quite bad, but our comradeships endured" (ibid., pp. 235–236).

Among the new friends, the one who immediately gained an important place in Georgie's affection was Ricardo Güiraldes. Borges recalls his literary generosity: "I would give him a quite clumsy poem and he would read between the lines and divine what I had been trying to say but what my literary incapacity had prevented me from saying. He would then speak of the poem to other people, who were baffled not to find these things in the text" (ibid., p. 236). In spite of Borges' ironic attempt to laugh at the poetry he was then writing, his recollection shows how kind and considerate Güiraldes really was.

In his conversations with De Milleret Borges recalls other instances of Güiraldes' generosity. According to Borges, he had a very peculiar view of contemporary French literature; Güiraldes sincerely believed Valery Larbaud and Léon-Paul Fargue to be outstanding, and once he stated that "the only Valéry I knew is Valery Larbaud." Borges, obviously, did not share his opinion and believed both Fargue and Larbaud to be writers of secondary importance. But he attributed Güiraldes' devotion to them to the fact that they were his friends. Borges also recalls that Güiraldes was very loyal to the gauchos and resented Macedonio Fernández's usual jokes about them. In the same conversation with De Milleret, Borges recalls one occasion when he told Güiraldes what one of his Uruguayan relatives, Luis Melián Lafinur, had once said about the gauchos: "Our peasants lack any remarkable traits except, of course, incest." Güiraldes' reaction was patriotic: "Perhaps that was true on the Uruguayan bank but here the gaucho was a hero." Borges, of course, refused to see any heroic difference between Argentine and Uruguayan gauchos (De Milleret, 1967, pp. 43–45).

In spite of Güiraldes' naïveté, Borges respected and loved him. In his conversations with Rita Guibert he says: "I must say I have an excellent memory of Güiraldes, of his generous friendship, of his singular fate." Then he comments on the paradoxical nature of his destiny: "Güiraldes had written many books which had been taken as gentlemen's entertainments, and then, suddenly, when he published *Don Segundo Sombra,* people saw in him a great writer. . . . Thus fame, perhaps glory, came late to Güiraldes. He published *Don Segundo Sombra* in 1926 and he enjoyed the light that was projected then on him. Later he began to feel the first symptoms of illness, went to Paris, and in 1927 died of cancer" (Guibert, 1968, p. 60). Borges once told me that the first time they met, Güiraldes admitted to him that he did not know English and added: "How lucky you are that you can read *Kim* in the original." Rudyard Kipling's novel and *Huckleberry Finn* were the two models Güiraldes used for his tale of a boy who grew up to be a gaucho under the affectionate care of an older man.

A completely different version of Borges' attitude toward Güiraldes can be seen in an interview with Estela Canto published in 1949. According to her, Borges maintained toward Güiraldes

> what could be called "gentle animosity." That is, although he respects Güiraldes—everything makes us believe that he respects him in an almost objective way—he doesn't admire *Don Segundo Sombra*.
> *Don Segundo Sombra* is a good book but undoubtedly inferior to *El paisano Aguilar*. With this observation, Borges means to say that Amorim knows much more, has been much more in contact with rural life than Güiraldes. Güiraldes had a distorted view of Don Segundo. The view not of the real gaucho but of the ranchowner. The view of one who is able to see all the tragedy and the courage of being a cattle driver. Not of one who, because he is a cattle driver, sees that heroism is something natural; somebody for whom landscape exists only as something menacing or benign, not for its esthetic value. (Canto, 1949, p. 5)

Estela Canto understood why Borges took exception to the general wave of admiration that greeted Güiraldes' *Don Segundo Sombra* in Argentina and why he found Enrique Amorim's *El paisano Aguilar* a better and more accurate description of gaucho life. She also detected the subtle mixture of attraction and rejection that was at the heart of their friendship.

Being seriously ill and too absorbed in writing his novel, Güiraldes could not devote his time to *Proa;* but as he was a wealthy man, he continued to help the magazine financially and partially supported the publishing house that had the same imprint. (It was that house which later published *Don Segundo Sombra* in book form.) In August 1925 he sent a letter to his younger friends announcing his departure. The ultraist poet Francisco Luis Bernárdez (another contributor to *Martín Fierro*) replaced him after the twelfth issue. The magazine's last issue was its fifteenth (January 1926). In it, an ironical letter signed by Georgie announced its death. The letter was later included in his second book of essays, *El tamaño de mi esperanza* (The Dimension of My Hope, 1926). The best part of the letter is its description of an editorial meeting. According to Georgie, Güiraldes played the guitar while Brandán Caraffa (who was very small) made a paper airplane out of one of his long verses and let it fly and Macedonio Fernández hid behind a cigarette his power of inventing and destroying a whole world in the time it takes to sip through two matés. Georgie also recalled other fellow poets: Pablo Rojas Paz, Francisco Luis Bernárdez, and Leopoldo Marechal, among the Argentine ultraists; Pedro Leandro Ipuche, among the Uruguayans. In spite of the affectionate tone, the letter ends on a chilly note of defiant acceptance of defeat. Georgie, admitting that each one of them would probably go his own way, says that "one hundred streets on the outskirts are waiting for me, with their moon, their loneliness, and some strong liquor." The last words are addressed to Güiraldes' wife, Adelina del Carril: Georgie asks for the hat and the cane he is sure she will deliver with her usual grace.

If at the beginning *Proa* had been the work of many, in the last issues it was mainly the work of Georgie. It was proper then that he sign the magazine's "certificate of death." For a while rumors of the revival of *Proa* under Georgie's sole editorship appeared in Buenos Aires' literary magazines. But it never happened. By the time the second *Proa* had come to an end, Georgie was too involved in his own work.

To the second *Proa* Georgie contributed three sets of poems, three reviews, and seventeen articles. The majority of these items were later collected in his second volume of poetry, *Luna de enfrente* (Moon Across the Way, 1925), and his first two volumes of essays, *Inquisiciones* (1925) and *El tamaño de mi esperanza* (1926). The range of the articles is wide: Georgie comments on his fellow ultraists' poetry, on the new gaucho verses being written in Uruguay, on some neglected baroque writers (Torres Villarroel, a disciple of Quevedo, and Sir Thomas Browne, a writer totally unknown in Latin America); he reviews some new works such as James Joyce's *Ulysses*, whose last page he translates for the magazine. In all he wrote then, a preoccupation with the new and an original reading of the old are blended. Georgie was already more concerned with discovering what was still alive in Argentine tradition than with being totally up to date. Both in his poetry and in his more important articles he attempted to capture the essence of a certain Argentine tone of voice, a form of the national identity that had been ignored by those who wanted the country to be progressive and modern. On the contrary, he found the real Argentina in gaucho poetry and in the humble outskirts of Buenos Aires. But he also rejected the folklorists' reactionary attempt to re-create a dead past. His recovery of the past was done by intuition and feeling, by an imaginative projection into an extra dimension of time.

If in his "Autobiographical Essay" Borges recalls his comrades with affection, he does not display the same warmth in remembering the group that edited *Martín Fierro:* "I disliked what *Martín Fierro* stood for, which was the French idea that literature is being continually renewed—that Adam is reborn every morning—and also for the idea that, since Paris had literary cliques that wallowed in publicity and bickering, we should be up to date and do the same. One result of this was that a sham literary feud was cooked up in Buenos Aires—that between Florida and Boedo" ("Essay," 1970, p. 236). Florida is still today a busy commercial street in downtown Buenos Aires, next to the theater and movie district, filled with cafés and bars, foreign bookshops, and art galleries. To find an equivalent of what Florida represented in the 1920s it would be necessary to imagine a street that combined Fifth Avenue with Broadway and 42nd Street (minus the porno shops). Boedo, on the other hand, was in a working-class neighborhood and stood for a kind of proletarian literature. In the same recollections Borges readily admits:

> I'd have preferred to be in the Boedo group, since I was writing about the old Northside and slums, sadness, and sunsets. But I was informed by one of the two conspirators—they were Ernesto Palacio, of Florida, and Roberto Mariani, of Boedo—that I was already one of the Florida warriors and that it was too late for me to change. The whole thing was just a put-up job. Some writers belonged to both groups—Roberto Arlt and Nicolás Olivari, for example. This sham is now taken into serious consideration by "credulous universities." But it was partly publicity, partly a boyish prank. (Ibid., p. 236)

There was more than a sophomoric prank in the artificial division of young Argentine writers into two rival groups. The publicity stunt was part of a determined effort by some writers more or less connected with the emerging Argentine Communist Party to gain control of or destroy the avant-grade movement. By dividing the new literature along party lines, Roberto Mariani, a novelist and short-story writer, was trying to call attention to his own brand of proletarian realism. In open letters sent to *Martín Fierro* and in their promotion of the mock rivalry, Mariani and his friends encouraged confrontation.

Borges, who preferred a simple, elemental view of Argentine reality, felt closer to the so-called proletarian writers of Boedo. But they rejected him for his patrician origins, for his European sophistication, and for his concept of literature as nonpolitical. On the other hand, the Boedo group attempted to enroll the novelist and playwright Roberto Arlt because of his proletarian origins and in spite of the fact that he had been Güiraldes' secretary and contributed regularly to the establishment's literary pages. The lines were thus drawn by Mariani and the Boedo group not according to literary affiliation but according to a purely political evaluation of a writer's class origins.

At the time, in a famous 1928 manifesto, the Russian formalists Jurii Tynianov and Roman Jakobsen had criticized this view; but Argentine leftists were not at all interested in a serious discussion of the problem such as was then taking place in the Soviet Union between the formalists on one side and Stalin's commissars on the other. They also ignored the polemics that currently divided the French surrealists. Their only concern was to stir up a bogus feud between Florida and Boedo. The dispute was unimportant and even ridiculous from a purely literary point of view, but its effect on Argentine literary history has been lasting. Even today the dispute is presented as an authentic confrontation between equal champions and not as a purely strategical gambit invented by leftist writers to gain notoriety and take control of the avant-garde.

Although *Martín Fierro* sidestepped the political side of the feud, it could not ignore some of the leftists' attacks and retaliated with vigor and humor against the old-fashioned realism the Boedo group was hailing as future proletarian literature. Another dispute that occupied the *Martín Fierro* contributors was even more grotesque. *La Gaceta Literaria,* a new magazine launched in Spain in 1927 with Guillermo de Torre, the champion of ultraism, as assistant editor, published an article which claimed that the "literary meridian" of Spanish America passed through Madrid. The metaphor and the article belonged to De Torre. *Martín Fierro*'s contributors reacted swiftly (June 10–July 10, 1927, pp. 6–7). Unanimously they claimed that from the Argentine point of view Paris and London were then more important than Madrid, and that as early as the turn of the century Spanish American poetry had begun to influence Spanish poetry, not the other way around. They could have also claimed that it was through the offices of Huidobro and Borges, as much as through Ramón Gómez de la Serna and Cansinos-Asséns, that avant-garde literature was finally being accepted in Spain. The discussion continued through articles in *La Gaceta* and *Martín Fierro.* De Torre apologized for his mistake. The only reasonable voice came from Miguel de Unamuno, who observed in a private letter—published in *Carátula* (Mask, October 1, 1927) and immediately reproduced in *Martín Fierro* (November 15, 1927, p. 10)—that the dispute was based on a mistake: if De Torre had said that the "publishing" meridian of Spanish America passed through Madrid, nobody would have objected because it was a fact that Spanish publishers dominated the book market. But to talk about a "literary" meridian smacked of imperialism. Georgie's contribution to the polemics was a short but barbed article in *Martín Fierro* (June 10–July 10, 1927,

p. 9) in which he enumerates chaotically and with comic effect the many instances that prove how badly Madrid understands Spanish America: the Castilians cannot play a tango without first removing its soul; they are unable to distinguish a Mexican from a Uruguayan accent; they believe that the adjective "invidious" can be used as a word of praise. After a parting shot about the Spanish obsession with "gallicisms" (words taken from the French, which Spanish academicians abhor), Georgie stresses his decision to keep intact his good memories of Madrid, although the time is not for sweet words but for truths.

Borges tends today to dismiss the *Martín Fierro* group and to emphasize his dislike for their concept of literature, fashioned on Paris and its literary coteries. But Georgie contributed actively and generously to the magazine. At least twenty-two pieces have been recorded by bibliographers. They include poems (three), articles (twelve), and reviews (seven). In addition, he participated anonymously in a popular section called the "Satirical Parnassus," in which the editors aired their prejudices in comic and sometimes outrageous epitaphs in verse. He also contributed to a translation by "B.M." of a Rudyard Kipling poem dedicated to Argentina (March 28, 1927, p. 4). It was a hoax perpetrated by Georgie and a friend (Leopoldo Marechal or Evar Méndez) to poke fun at Argentine nationalism. Kipling's well-known jingoism was the basis of the parody.

Like all avant-garde groups, the contributors to *Martín Fierro* loved to attract attention by organizing literary gatherings and banquets to celebrate the launching of a book or the arrival of some transatlantic guest. No less than eight banquets are registered in the pages of *Martín Fierro:* there were banquets in honor of the Uruguayan painter Pedro Figari, who used a distinctly fauvist technique (August–September, 1924); Jules Supervielle, the Franco-Uruguayan poet (January 24, 1925); *Martín Fierro*'s own editor, Evar Méndez (May 5, 1925); the futurist poet Oliverio Girondo (May 17, 1925); F. T. Marinetti, the futurist leader who was visiting Argentina (July 8, 1926); Ernest Ansermet, the Swiss composer and conductor (October 5, 1926); and Alfonso Reyes, the Mexican humanist who had been appointed ambassador to Buenos Aires (August 31–November 15, 1927). There was even a banquet to celebrate simultaneously the launching of Georgie's second book of poems, *Luna de enfrente*, and Sergio Piñero's book of travel chronicles, *El puñal de Orión* (Orion's Knife). On this last occasion Georgie contributed a comic poem called "The Aura with Lunch and Other Misprints," which he has mercifully left out of his collections of poems.

In these celebrations, dutifully recorded by chronicles and photographs in *Martín Fierro*'s pages, the dark, round, and rather sad face of Georgie almost always appears. At the banquet for Evar Méndez he is seen seated in the first row while the supposedly Boedo novelist Roberto Arlt is among those standing in the back; at the Girondo banquet Georgie shares the same back row with Roberto Mariani, the inventor of the Florida–Boedo feud and one of the so-called proletarian novelists.

If *Martín Fierro* was successful as propaganda, from a purely literary point of view it was too eclectic to have a lasting influence. Georgie generally selected his most ephemeral or journalistic pieces for the magazine, keeping the more thoughtful or poetic ones for publication in his own *Proa* or in other journals. By the mid-1920s he had developed into a full-fledged professional writer. Apart from the magazines already mentioned, he contributed regularly to the literary pages of *La Prensa,* one of the largest Latin American newspapers, and to a new journal, *Síntesis* (Synthesis), which was launched in June 1927 by a group of writers of diverse tendencies. Georgie's name was included last on the masthead. To it he contributed mainly literary articles and reviews. But the initial avant-garde enthusiasm was beginning to wane. The so-called revolution of 1930, in which the army took over the Argentine government, put an end to *Síntesis* and also to the period. Ultraism was dead, and the sordid realities of Argentina's political life were becoming too obvious to be ignored. The partying was over.

11.
The Return of the Native

"For many years," Borges told Rita Guibert, "I was the most secret writer in Buenos Aires" (Guibert, 1968, p. 55). But on his return from Europe in 1924 he became the acknowledged leader of the young and one of the most public writers in Argentina's literary history. As a founder of magazines (the two *Proa*s) and as a frequent contributor to some of the most important little reviews (*Martín Fierro, Inicial, Valoraciones*) as well as to established periodicals (*Nosotros, La Prensa, Criterio*), Georgie became the most ubiquitous writer of that time and place.

That was only one part of his incredible activity. Before the decade was over he had published two more volumes of poetry (*Luna de enfrente*, 1925; *Cuaderno San Martín* [San Martín Copybook], 1929), three volumes of essays (*Inquisiciones*, 1925; *El tamaño de mi esperanza*, 1926; *El idioma de los argentinos* [The Language of the Argentines], 1928) and had already begun writing a literary biography of Evaristo Carriego, which he published in 1930. His poems were included in three anthologies of the period: Julio Noé's academic *Antología de la poesía argentina moderna: 1900–1925*, published by the conservative magazine *Nosotros* (1926); the avant-garde but chaotic *Indice de la nueva poesía americana*, edited by the Peruvian Alberto Hidalgo (1926), and the youthful *Exposición de la actual poesía argentina: 1922–1927*, compiled by Pedro-Juan Vignale and César Tiempo (1927).

In all three anthologies Georgie's poems have an important place. The least conspicuous is, of course, the one assigned to him in Noé's compilation. The book was aimed at reinforcing the establishment's view of contemporary Argentine poetry. The place of honor was given to Leopoldo Lugones, a major Latin American symbolist who was still active in the 1920s. He favored standard metrical patterns and rhyme, used a vast, bookish vocabulary, and in spite of having very little Greek had "translated" Homer and written about the classics. The young poets attacked him without mercy and, generally, without taste. He replied with disdain or with poetical decrees.

At the time, Georgie sided with his young friends, although he used to take his books to Lugones, who always thanked him and never said a word about them. Lugones also sent his books to Georgie. But there was no dialogue. In his 1967 interview with César Fernández Moreno, Borges recalls some of the occasions on which he met Lugones. He was

> a solitary and dogmatic man, a man who did not open up easily. . . . Conversation was difficult with him because he used to bring everything to a close with a phrase which was literally a period. . . . Then you had to begin again, to find another subject. . . . And that subject was also dissolved with a period. . . . His kind of conversation was brilliant but tiresome. And many times his assertions had nothing to do with what he really believed; he just had to say something extraordinary. . . . What he wanted was to control the conversation. Everything he said was final. And . . . we had a great respect for him. (Fernández Moreno, 1967, pp. 10–11)

In a photograph (reproduced in Jurado, 1964, p. 97) of a meeting of the Sociedad Argentina de Escritores (Argentine Society of Writers), which was chaired by Lugones, Georgie can be seen standing respectfully in the rear and looking down. Was he ashamed of participating in the activities of the literary establishment? Perhaps. But he was not always so respectful. Barely one year after that photograph was taken Georgie contributed to a parody on one of Lugones' celebrated "Romances"; it was published in *Martín Fierro* (July 8, 1926) under the pseudonym Mar-Bor-Vall-Men, which barely hid the names of *Mare*chal, *Bor*ges, *Vall*ejo, and *Mén*dez. Today, the parody seems sophomoric. The quartet plays with Lugones' name and produces a ridiculous variant, "Leogoldo Lupones," with the stress on "goldo" (a childish pronunciation of *gordo,* fat) and "lupones" (*lupo,* wolf). Lugones was not fat or particularly wolfish.

Lugones also became the recipient of another type of attack. In 1925 in a speech in Lima he had stated bluntly his mistrust of politicians and his preference for military regimes. He had coined the phrase "It is the hour of the sword," which became a rallying cry for all the rightest elements in Argentina. Although the ultraists abstained from attacking him on political grounds, his reactionary ideology further alienated him from a group that was more sympathetic to anarchism than to authoritarianism. But the real disagreement with Lugones was based on a different conception of what poetry ought to be. From that point of view, Georgie must have hated Noé's anthology. In spite of having used some of his best poems, the editor was obviously an established man and devoted sixty-six pages to Lugones, while thirty young poets were packed into 121 pages (Georgie got six and a half).

The Hidalgo anthology, on the contrary, excluded all established poets. It meant to be an index of new Spanish American poetry and at the outset featured three polemical prologues. The first was signed by the editor and attacked "Hispano-Americanism" as a foolish political notion; Hidalgo paraded his anarchism and in general made a fool of himself. In the second prologue the Chilean Vicente Huidobro used aphorisms to defend the new poetry and the need to be constantly creative. The third prologue was written by Georgie and summarized his views of ultraism, the metaphor, and the new kind of Spanish written in Argentina. He made a rather unkind reference to Lugones, describing him as a foreigner with a tendency to make everything Greek, fond of vague landscapes built exclusively out of rhymes. Georgie's poems were allotted the same space as in Noé's anthology, but nobody else got much more. Today the Hidalgo anthology is a bibliographical rarity and also a curiosity. For the first time the important young poets of Spanish America were gathered under one roof: the Chileans Huidobro, Pablo de Rokha, and Neruda; the Peruvians César Vallejo and Juan Parra del Riego; the Mexican Salvador Novo; the Uruguayan Fernán Silva Valdés; the Argentines Borges and Ricardo Molinari. A few older poets were also included—the Mexican José Juan Tablada and the Argentines Macedonio Fernández and Ricardo Güiraldes—but they were closer to the young than to the writers of their own generation.

The third anthology was almost exclusively a young poets' book; in it Georgie had six pages. The short autobiographical note that introduces his poems is written with humor and contains at least two inaccuracies: he claimed to have been born in 1900 and to have visited Spain for the first time in 1918. He had said the same in Noé's anthology. Probably Georgie was trying to use round figures. It is hard to believe that at twenty-eight he was trying to pass for twenty-seven. But the small mystification is typical of his disdain for precision. At the back of the book a list of the poets' professions and addresses informs the reader: "Jorge Luis Borges, Polyglot. Av. Quintana 222, B.A."

By the late 1920s it was obvious in Buenos Aires that Georgie was the most important young poet there and a leader of the avant-garde writers. He was respected by the establishment, loved by the ultraists, attacked by the Boedo group. *Martín Fierro*'s "Satirical Parnassus" includes some comic epitaphs about him. The best is the one that, in alluding to the two magazines he edited under the same name, *Proa* (Prow), calls him "the man with two *Prows*" (September–October 1924, p. 12). Georgie's reputation for being finicky in matters of grammar is reflected in another epitaph which claims that he was killed by the Inquisition because he omitted one comma (August 5, 1925, p. 8). Still another epitaph (September 25, 1925, p. 8) pokes fun at his peculiar spelling, especially his tendency to omit the final *d* in any word. (It is seldom pronounced in Andalusia and the River Plate area, although it is dutifully used in writing.) The epitaph is signed "D." Sometimes Georgie's friends were less than kind; in a section called "Tall Tales" there is a line that begins "Borges saw . . .," in which his near blindness is unmercifully stressed. The final issue of *Martín Fierro* carried on its last page a parting epitaph by Leopoldo Marechal that alludes to Georgie's interest in baroque poetry (Argote is Góngora's second surname):

> Here lies, professor of dreams,
> Jorge Luis Quevedo y Argote.
> Rhetoric lost her master.
> To galvanize him is a vain task:
> He died for the lack of a mustache.
> (*Martin Fierro*,
> August 31–November 15, 1927, p. 14)

The Boedo group was less sprightly. In a magazine ponderously called *Los Pensadores* (The Thinkers) they celebrated the termination of the second *Proa:*

> The contributors to that magazine—if one can give that name to a catalogue of jokes—belong to a fortunately small number of Sarrasani-type writers [Sarrasani was the owner of a famous circus of the time]. They all try to make you laugh, and those who are serious really succeed. Superior to that magazine was the one published by the sane inmates of the state insane asylum. At least there was nobody there who claimed to have discovered the hole in the maté gourd, as did the popular troubador J. L. Borges, because that is what that type wants to prove by writing "espaciosidá" ["espaciosidad"] and "falsiada" ["falseada"] to sound native; and, who knows, with all that jingle and all that silliness, perhaps he doesn't even know how to ride a horse. (*Los Pensadores,* February 1926)

Georgie's discovery of his native town was beginning to annoy a group that pretended to be the sole arbiter of what was and was not truly national. Georgie did not bother to reply.

At the time, he was seriously interested in recovering some lost elements of the Argentine past. He went about this in a rather excessive way perhaps, but there is no doubt about his sincerity. In a sense, what he was trying to do was to integrate his personality, to claim the other side of his inheritance, which had been neglected by his English education and his French and Latin studies in Geneva, his knowledge of several languages, and his avid reading of foreign literature. Returning to Argentina, he felt like a prodigal son. He plunged into the space of Buenos Aires and into the past of those River Plate provinces with the enthusiasm of a convert. He began to spend evenings in pursuit of the remnants of an old Buenos Aires he could find only in the southern district or on the old Northside. He cultivated acquaintanceship with some hoodlums who talked, nostalgically, about the days when everybody admitted to at least one death. He learned to dance the tango and to drink the hard local liquor known as *caña*. Perhaps there was a touch of snobbery in all of it: slumming was then, as now, an activity practiced by the middle and upper classes as part of the exacting business of killing time. But it was more than that for Georgie. It was also a way out of the confined and sweetly repressive atmosphere at home. Father and Mother corresponded too closely to the prototypes of bourgeois respectability, and Georgie, in his late twenties, was experiencing a sort of delayed adolescent rebellion. Father was less strict, of course, and the episode with the young prostitute in Geneva may have established a tacit masculine complicity between the two of them. But if visiting prostitutes or even having an affair was tolerated in polite society, as long as it was done with tact and no visible consequences, to go regularly to the slums and write enthusiastically about them was not admissible. The times were still very hypocritical, and bourgeois morality wanted things done in a certain discreet way.

How far did Georgie go in his explorations of the slums? Although he has given many hints in his writings of the period, he is as usual reticent about the details. To find out more it is necessary to refer to a *roman à clef* written by a friend of the ultraist period, the poet Leopoldo Marechal, who produced in his novel *Adán Buenosayres* (1948) a portrait of the times. Marechal had been Georgie's accomplice in some of the most dadaist happenings sponsored by *Martín Fierro*. Once, to celebrate the bearded Ernest Ansermet, they and a group of friends wore false beards for the occasion (October 5, 1926, pp. 7 and 12). Marechal also wrote some of the best epitaphs for Georgie's *Inquisiciones* and reviewed *Luna de enfrente* (December 29, 1925, p. 4) in the most flattering terms. He claimed that the book was "the best argument against the old-fashioned theories of Lugones" and praised "the virile affirmation of its verses." Ten issues later (December 12, 1926, p. 8) Georgie, in turn, praised Marechal's *Días como flechas* (Days Like Arrows) and maintained that such a book "adds days and nights to reality." They also contributed to two merciless parodies: the one of Lugones already mentioned, and one of Enrique Larreta, the author of *La gloria de Don Ramiro*, who had published a new novel, *Zogoibi*, about an unhappy gaucho.

When Marechal began writing his novel in the late 1920s, his aim was to recapture in a vast book, loosely inspired by *Ulysses*, the flavor of those days. He was then living in Paris, and the self-imposed exile stimulated his recollections. But the book was put aside on his return to Argentina and was not completed until twenty years later. By then the ultraist movement had been forgotten, Georgie was Borges, and Marechal had developed into an important figure in both the Catholic and Peronist establishment. The novel suffered from the delay. Instead of a celebration of friendship, of adventure, of a collective madness, it became a subconscious retaliation against a time and a place Marechal believed he had loved but had in truth hated. Under thinly disguised names and features, the ultraists are pictured as incompetent, crass, and stupid loafers whose only merit is to provide a chorus for the protagonist, a romantic projection of Marechal as a Young Catholic Artist of unrecognized genius. Georgie is reduced to a caricature under the name of "Luis Pereda." The character is introduced as one of a small group of revelers, young poets obsessed with folklore and especially with the tango. He is described as rather stout and walking like a blind wild boar, searching rather ineffectively through a stack of records for one on which the authentic nasal voice of a primitive tango singer could be heard (Marechal, 1948, pp. 152–153). His friends are not too impressed with his act. One of them, Frank Admundsen (perhaps Francisco Luis Bernárdez in real life), makes an unkind remark: "They've sent him to Oxford to read Greek, to the Sorbonne to read literature, to Zurich to read philosophy, and he comes back to Buenos Aires to get up to his ears in a sort of phonographic nativism! Psh! The guy's crazy!" (ibid., p. 154). (Marechal knew, of course, that Georgie had never studied at Oxford, the Sorbonne, or Zurich, but he was trying to disguise the facts a bit.) Later Frank insists: "A pitiful madman! . . . If he is not a terminal case of intellectual masturbation, I'll eat my hat!" The presentation is unkind, although it does not bother "Pereda," who continues to listen to the scratchy record and laugh. Throughout the 741-page novel "Luis Pereda" is presented in the same sophomoric vein. His protuberant mouth is described as a "nobly aggressive mug" (p. 155). His walks through the poorer quarters of the city, whistling some old tango while meditating on the future avatars of Buenos Aires hoodlums, are recalled (p. 193). He is seen reciting some mildly erotic country song (pp. 203–204), attending a wake with his friends (pp. 266–286), or getting drunk with them and visiting a brothel from which they are expelled before they can perform any practical function except to talk their heads off (pp. 326–348). The only descriptions of "Luis Pereda" are scornful: "philosopher of nativism" (p. 291); "grammarian" (p. 291); "pocket agnostic," spoiled by his Calvinist education in Geneva (p. 306). (This time Marechal forgot he had "Pereda" studying philosophy at Zurich.) The culmination of the novel is a long dream sequence in which the protagonist visits an allegorical version of Buenos Aires. It is a hell divided (like Dante's) into circles according to the seven deadly sins. In the seventh, which is devoted to those who have been ravaged by wrath, and among the "pseudogogs" or false teachers, "Luis Pereda" is accused by the False Euterpe (the muse of music and lyrical poetry) of acting like a hoodlum: walking the slums of Buenos Aires with a killer's slanted stare, spitting out of the corner of his mouth, and mumbling with clenched teeth the imperfectly learned lyrics of a tango (p. 665). The False Euterpe adds that "Pereda" attempted to bring to literature "his mystico-slummy effusions, to the point of inventing a false mythology in which Buenos Aires hoodlums reach not only heroic proportions but even vague metaphysical outlines" (p. 665).

Perhaps Marechal was only trying to evoke the sophomoric atmosphere of *Martín Fierro* and the "Satirical Parnassus"—as he has pleaded in his article "Keys to *Adán Buenosayres*" (Marechal, 1966, p. 133)—but the jokes had become stale. Besides, in 1948 the circumstances were different. In 1924–1927 everybody was young and more or less shared the same ideas. When *Adán Buenosayres* was published some twenty years later, both Borges and Marechal were closer to fifty than to twenty-five and were radically opposed politically. As a Catholic and a Peronist, Marechal had been on the side of the Fascists and the Nazis during World War II, while Borges had defended the Allied cause and attacked Hitler and Mussolini long before 1939. The fact that Marechal was part of the establishment and Borges had been abruptly dismissed in 1946 by the Peronists from his modest position in a municipal library only helped to stress the differences. Marechal's cold jokes had a sinister meaning in the Buenos Aires of 1948; they smack of the jokes benevolent executioners tend to make. At least that was the way they were read then. The image of "Luis Pereda" as a fake regionalist, a bad poet, and a sissy was precisely the image of Borges that the Boedo group and its descendants, the Peronist literati, were promoting. But the real Georgie was far more complex and elusive than the inane "Luis Pereda" Marechal had sketched. His regionalism had other roots. The native had returned, but not just to the Argentina of the 1920s.

12.
A Theory of Regionalism

Looking back on this period of his literary life in his "Autobiographical Essay," Borges asserts that it

> was one of great activity, but much of it was perhaps reckless and even pointless. . . . . This productivity now amazes me as much as the fact that I feel only the remotest kinship with the work of these years. Three of the four essay collections—whose names are best forgotten—I have never allowed to be reprinted. In fact, when in 1953 my present publisher—Emecé—proposed to bring out my "complete writings," the only reason I accepted was that it would allow me to keep those preposterous volumes suppressed. ("Essay," 1970, p. 230)

About one of those collections, *El tamaño de mi esperanza* (The Dimension of My Hope, 1926), he has this to say: "I tried to be as Argentine as I could. I got hold of Segovia's dictionary of Argentinisms and worked in so many local words that many of my countrymen could hardly understand it. Since I have mislaid the dictionary, I'm not sure I would any longer understand the book myself, and so have given it up as utterly hopeless" (ibid., p. 231). In spite of his warnings, we must turn to these books to find out what his regionalism was about.

The first collection contains many pieces on ultraism, expressionism, and metaphor, and on the young and old masters of the avant-garde. The title Georgie chose for it, *Inquisiciones* (Inquisitions), plays on the etymological sense of the word, which is even more evident in another word of the same family: inquiry. But the title also reveals one of Georgie's interests at the time: the search for the Latin roots of Spanish words. In the "Autobiographical Essay" he condemns the book by stating:

JORGE LUIS BORGES

When I wrote these pieces [on Sir Thomas Browne, the metaphor, the nonexistence of the ego], I was trying to play the sedulous age to two Spanish baroque seventeenth-century writers, Quevedo and Saavedra Fajardo, who stood in their own stiff, arid, Spanish way for the same kind of writing as Sir Thomas Browne in "Urne-Buriall." I was doing my best to write Latin in Spanish, and the book collapses under the sheer weight of its involutions and sententious judgments. (Ibid., p. 231)

Borges is right about the style, but he is too negative in his evaluation of *Inquisiciones*. There is more in it than what he recalls. In the first place, a note at the end of the volume suggests that Georgie was already convinced that current rhetoric was not adequate to discuss modern literature, and that a new rhetoric was necessary: "What has always been the aim of my writing is a rhetoric that would have its point of departure not in adjusting today's literature to forms already fixed by classical doctrine but in the direct examination of it, and that would categorize the *greguería* [Ramón's own brand of dadaist aphorisms], the confessional novel, and the contemporary use of traditional figures. 'Examination of Metaphors' is a chapter of that possible rhetoric" (*Inquisiciones*, 1925, p. 160). Today Borges may ridicule that article, recalling that it "set out to classify metaphors as though other poetic elements, such as rhythm and music, could be safely ignored" ("Essay," 1970, p. 231). Lugones raised the same objections at the time. But what Borges misses is the other aspect of that article: the attempt to create a new rhetoric. From that point of view, the article is the forerunner of pieces written by Borges in the 1930s and 1940s to categorize the new type of fiction he was already writing. In attempting to explore new rhetorical paths, Georgie was doing exactly what Pound and Eliot had done in the previous decade: developing a critical theory to suit his poetical experiments.

There is another article in *Inquisiciones* which Borges now passes over in silence but which at the time had some relevance. It is devoted to Joyce's *Ulysses*, a book then known to Hispanic readers largely by reputation. (The Spanish translation did not appear until 1948.) Georgie claims to be the "first Hispanic traveler to have reached Joyce's book," which he presents under the metaphor of "a tangled and uncouth country." At the same time, he has no qualms about admitting he has not read the entire book. To justify himself he says: "I confess not having cleared away the seven hundred pages which constitute it, I confess having experienced it only in bits; nevertheless, I know what it is, with the adventurous and legitimate certitude that one has when stating one's knowledge of a city without pretending to know intimately all its streets" (*Inquisiciones*, 1925, pp. 20–21). He then gives a short biographical sketch of Joyce and a brief evaluation of the book, whose perfect amalgam of dream and reality he seems to admire; he also praises the lack of distinction between what is important and what is ephemeral in everyday life. He quotes Kant and Schopenhauer and concludes that "Minerva's olive tree projects a longer shadow on its pages than [Apollo's] laurel," which is an elaborate way of saying that it is more an intellectual than a poetic book. For Georgie, total reality is alive in *Ulysses:* both the reality of the flesh and the reality of the soul. He praises Joyce for his success in achieving the concrete presence of things and can find a parallel only in Ramón's own concrete books. He singles out Chapter 15 (the brothel scene) for its hallucinating felicity and comments enthusiastically on the wealth of words and styles the book possesses. To conclude his review, he quotes Lope de Vega's comment about Góngora as a way of indicating the baroque affiliation of *Ulysses.* (In summarizing Joyce's biography, Georgie points out that Joyce had been taught by Jesuits, masters of the baroque style.)

Among the pieces collected in *Inquisiciones* are four that reveal Georgie's early preoccupation with native reality. The first is devoted to one of the most prolific of nineteenth-century Argentine poets, Hilario Ascasubi, who fought against Rosas' dictatorship and wrote a long, rambling poem, *Santos Vega,* about a gaucho troubador. One essay is dedicated to Pedro Leandro Ipuche and one to Fernán Silva Valdés, both of whom have continued and updated the tradition of gaucho poetry in Uruguay. The last piece attempts to define a native Argentine. What Georgie praises in Ascasubi and finds still very much alive in Ipuche and Silva Valdés is a certain leisurely attitude toward life and literature, a striving not for perfection or intensity but for the reader's friendship. Ascasubi (who wrote the better part of his work in his old age while living in Paris) seems to Georgie to be an old gentleman who, in talking, takes care to pronounce every syllable distinctly and likes to evoke the past with a few grave, scornful undertones. His fate was to inspire some of the best pages of his disciple, Estanislao del Campo, and of the real master of gaucho poetry, José Hernández, the author of *Martín Fierro.* But in his imperfect verses Georgie detects a tone of voice he likes and a true, deep knowledge of the countryside and the gauchos. In the last page of his article on Ipuche, Georgie acknowledges his own limitations: "I have felt the shame of my blurred condition as inhabitant of a city" (ibid., p. 60). He also confirms what his poems state: his sadness on hearing a guitar, his love for the deep patios of old houses.

In these limitations and that nostalgia for a past that belongs to his forefathers can be found the roots of Georgie's regionalism. The last article on the subject makes it explicit. In the same way he had rejected in his poems the bustling, modern Buenos Aires of the downtown area in favor of the humble outskirts or the proletarian districts, he now rejects the conventional image of the native Argentine (a noisy patriot with an aggressive concept of progress) in favor of the real image. According to Georgie, the native Argentine prefers silence to verbal excess, is reticent and ironic. That attitude springs from a certain determinism which encourages a lack of illusion. The same traits can be recognized in Argentina's native poetry. The Spaniard's original vehemence seems there subdued; the language is softer, the images more austere. As in the best tradition of Spanish literature (*Don Quixote* is proof), failure is exalted, and suffering and nostalgia become the permanent themes of Argentine popular poetry. In quoting examples of the kind of verses he prefers, Georgie goes back to Estanislao del Campo and José Hernández, and even praises one aspect of Lugones: his reticence. He also includes William Henry Hudson (who wrote in English but was very Argentine) in his list of favorite writers. At the time Georgie wrote these essays, nativism did not imply the necessity to accept a showy nationalism. Also, it had not been contaminated by the excesses of the folklorists. What he saw in the old Argentina were the values and virtues of his own forefathers, the men who had fought for independence and were too proud and gentlemanly to boast about it. Georgie's nativism really implied a return to his own family roots. Even in praising some minor Uruguayan poets he was reclaiming one part of his heritage, the part Mother had brought to the family.

In the second book of essays Georgie further defines his nativism. The first article, "The Dimension of My Hope," gives its title to the whole volume and constitutes a sort of manifesto. In examining what is really native in Argentina, Georgie addresses himself to those readers who believe they are going to live and die in that land, not to "those who believe that the sun and the moon are in Europe" (*Tamaño*, 1926, p. 5). A summary of what the Argentines had achieved historically and literally follows. Once more he mentions Estanislao del Campo and José Hernández, and he now adds Sarmiento, Lucio V. Mansilla, and Eduardo Wilde to the honors list. The tango gets special mention because it summarizes that whole world of hoodlums and easy women, Saturday nights in the slums, and a certain way of walking that is almost dancing. In this century he finds only Evaristo Carriego, Macedonio Fernández, and Ricardo Güiraldes worth praising. He believes rather modestly that Argentina is poor in creativity: "Not one single mystic or metaphysician . . . has been engendered in this land! Our greatest man is still Juan Manuel [de Rosas]: a great example of the individual's strength, with a great confidence in his own capacity for life, but unable to build anything spiritual, and dominated by his own tyrannical power and his bureaucratic instincts" (ibid., pp. 7–8). He goes on to emphasize the difference between the greatness of true Argentine life and the barrenness of its intellectual reality. After quoting Emerson (an 1844 speech on the literary future of America), he comes to the conclusion that "Buenos Aires is already more than a city; it is a country and it is necessary to find the poetry and the music and the painting and the religion and the metaphysics which are suited to its greatness. That is the dimension of my hope, which invites every one of us to become like gods and to work to make possible its reality" (ibid., p. 9). In a last paragraph he rejects the usual Argentine view of progress (an attempt to be "almost" North American or European; that is, to be somebody else) and the usual concept of nativism, or regionalism, which to him is a concept similar to that used to define the reaction of men on horseback to those who do not know how to ride. Now it expresses only nostalgia for a pastoral life that is no longer possible. Georgie feels the need to enlarge the concept to make nativism a return not just to a lost golden age but to a reality that includes the whole external world and the ego, God, and death.

The book itself illustrates this program. Although it includes some pieces on subjects that have little to do with regionalism—"A History of the Angels," a review of a novel by Cansinos-Asséns, a review of Shaw's *Saint Joan,* an essay on Wilde's "The Ballad of Reading Gaol," a discussion of one line by Apollinaire, a commentary on Milton's condemnation of rhyme, an examination of a sonnet by Góngora, a discussion of the infinitude of language and the function of adjectives—the majority of its twenty-three pieces are devoted to nativism. There is an enthusiastic rereading of Estanislao del Campo's poem *Fausto,* in which a gaucho attends a performance of Gounod's opera and later tells a friend what he has made of it. Georgie believes that poem to be "the best thing said by our America" (ibid., p. 13). In another article he maintains that "the pampas and the slums are gods" and lists those writers who dealt with both myths, including his own name—"as long as I live there will be someone to praise me" (ibid., p. 22)—and also the name of Roberto Arlt. The favorable mention of Arlt (one of the writers promoted by the Boedo group) proves once more how false the dispute between Florida and Boedo was.

A third article is devoted to Evaristo Carriego and is a sort of dry run for the book he wrote on the same subject in 1930. He calls Carriego a "great scorpion," meaning he had a tongue that stung like the scorpion's tail; he also recalls that Carriego used to visit Father on Sundays. A fourth article is devoted to *The Purple Land,* a novel about the Uruguayan civil wars written in English by William Henry Hudson (a friend of Joseph Conrad), who was born in Argentina of North American parents. That novel is for Georgie one of the masterpieces of

Argentine regional literature; he hopes that one day it will be returned to the Spanish language, in which it was originally conceived. There is a fifth article on the Uruguayan poets' reverence for trees which repeats the now familiar notion that the poetry is (for Georgie at least) more rooted in native reality than in contemporary Argentine literature. A long article on popular Argentine songs, whose origins can be traced back to Spain, allows him to demonstrate that the real nativism is a certain humor and a certain capacity for skepticism. A section of book reviews gives him the chance to update some of his opinions on Silva Valdés' nativism (he seems to like it less and less in spite of some praise), to hail his fellow poet Oliverio Girondo's *Calcomanías* (Decals), and to criticize rather severely Leopoldo Lugones' new book of poems, *Romancero,* a collection of ballads that follow the old medieval lyric form but are loaded with sentimental contemporary subjects.

There is a last article on *lunfardo,* the pseudo-slang of the slums. While the real slang of hoodlums is purely functional (its aim is to avoid being understood by anybody outside the group), the slang of those who go slumming is only an imitation of the real thing: "Bullies who want to pretend they are outlaws and toughs, and whose bad deeds are limited to getting drunk with friends in a dive" imitate the vocabulary of jails and brothels. In its place, Georgie praises the "decent native language of our forebears" (ibid., pp. 136–137). He finds that some writers know how to use slang; but the majority do not: they only point up the limitations of a dialect that is poor in words and even poorer in meanings. The only way out of this dilemma is to find a poet who will write not the epic of the gaucho (as Hernández attempted in *Martín Fierro*) but the epic of the slums, or at least a novel of the slums. The article ends on a note of caution: it would be very difficult to write such a novel entirely in the native language. There is an emotional barrier to cross: when really moved, Argentines speak a language that goes back to their Castilian roots. Even Martín Fierro's nostalgia is expressed not in the gaucho dialect but in the purest Castilian.

Throughout the book (which contains many autobiographical allusions and includes personal anecdotes) an almost inaudible note can be heard. Georgie talks explicitly about his hopes for a new form of regionalism, for a language that will truly express the soul and the essence of his native land, its humor, and its sense of destiny; he also tacitly expresses his ambition to be the poet or the novelist who will capture that soul and that essence. He probably was then planning to write a book that would convey his feelings for the slums, a prose epic on the real hoodlums and their mythology. Georgie also offers a "Profession of Literary Faith." Near the end, he comments on the fact that each word has to be lived by the writer before it is used. He warns his colleagues: "Let nobody dare to write *slums* without having first walked endlessly along their high pavements; without having longed and suffered for them as one does for a girl; without having felt the high adobe walls, empty lots, the moon shining over humble stores, as a gift" (ibid., p. 153).

In two short pieces he includes in his next book of essays, *El idioma de los argentinos* (The Language of the Argentines), he attempts to capture the soul and essence of the slums. They can be read as fragments of the long prose poem, or novel, Georgie had outlined in his second book of essays. The shorter of the two pieces is called "Men Fought" and had previously been published in *Martín Fierro* (February 26, 1927) under the title "Police Legend." It is a narrative about the knife duel between two famous hoodlums: El Chileno (The Chilean), who came from the Southside, on the banks of the river; and El Mentao (The Famous One), whose turf was the Northside, in Palermo. Some six years later Georgie developed the same situation in a longer and more famous version, "Streetcorner Man." But in 1927 it was only a sketch.

More important is the second piece, which Georgie later included in his "A New Refutation of Time" in *Other Inquisitions* (1952). It is called "Feeling in Death" and has German metaphysical undertones. It describes an experience Georgie had one evening while walking the streets of Buenos Aires in the late 1920s. He had been roaming along the outskirts of Palermo, the neighborhood of his childhood. He arrived at an unfamiliar part of Barracas, a district that he knew more through words than in reality and that was "familiar and mythological at the same time." Suddenly he found himself on a streetcorner.

On the muddy and chaotic ground a rose-colored adobe wall seemed not to harbor moonglow but to shed a light of its own. I suspect that there can be no better way of denoting tenderness than by means of that rose color. I stood there looking at that simplicity. I thought, no doubt aloud, "This is the same as it was thirty years ago." I guessed at the date: a recent time in other countries, but already remote in this changing part of the world. Perhaps a bird was singing and I felt for him a small, bird-sized affection. What stands out most clearly: in the already vertiginous silence the only noise was the intemporal sound of the crickets. The easy thought, "I am in the eighteen hundreds," ceased to be a few careless words and deepened into reality. I felt dead—that I was an abstract perceiver of the world; I felt an undefined fear imbued with knowledge, the supreme clarity of metaphysics. No, I did not believe I had traveled across the presumptive waters of Time; rather I suspected I was the possessor of the reticent or absent meaning of the inconceivable word *eternity*. Only later was I able to define that imagining.

And now I shall write it like this: that pure representation of homogeneous facts—clear night, limpid wall, rural scent of honeysuckle, elemental clay—is not merely identical to the scene on that corner so many years ago; it is, without similarities or repetitions, the same. If we can perceive that identity, time is a delusion; the indifference and inseparability of one moment of time's apparent yesterday and another of its apparent today are enough to disintegrate it. (*Inquisitions*, 1964, pp. 179–180)

One of the literary sources of this passage is another night in another suburb, more than one hundred years before, when a romantic poet heard a nightingale sing in Hampstead. In interpretating this incident, which Borges does in a later article, "The Nightingale of Keats," also collected in *Other Inquisitions*, he suggests that the English poet discovered that the bird which was singing for him was the same bird which had sung for kings and buffoons, and for Ruth

> when, sick for home,
> She stood in tears amid the alien corn.

Each nightingale is every nightingale; its immortality and the immortality of its song are guaranteed by the immortality of the species.

In Georgie's piece the allusion to the famous ode is found in a single phrase, "Perhaps a bird was singing," a phrase that immediately leads to an observation, both prosaic and ironic: "What stands out most clearly: in the already vertiginous silence the only noise was the intemporal sound of the crickets." (Georgie knew that there are no nightingales in Argentina, but there *are* crickets.) If Keats discovers his own mortality by listening to the song of the immortal bird, Georgie, on the contrary, feels annihilated in the face of mortal time; he feels transformed into an "abstract perceiver of the world" and finds, not the personal identity that the romantic poet seeks and that Proust manages to escape only through art, but the impersonal identity of the perceiver and the object perceived: "that pure representation of homogeneous facts—clear night, limpid wall, rural scent of honeysuckle, elemental clay." Time is thus abolished, not because he feels eternal or because his art is capable of preserving him forever in the eternity of his work, but because he isn't anybody. Or, better said, he *is* nobody.

At this level of reading, Georgie's regionalism has very little to do with what the Boedo group, or even some of his fellow poets of the *Martín Fierro* crusade, had in mind. Georgie was really attempting to find a tone of voice and viewpoint that would capture not just the colorful images of the slums and the hoodlums but the essence and the soul of a part of Argentine reality which, for him, was closely linked with his family roots. He did not achieve all he wanted, but he was on the right path. The next decade would be spent exploring, in a different genre, the possibilities of a nativism that was determined not to renounce the hidden essences of reality.

Looking back on those attempts in his "Autobiographical Essay," Borges singles out the short narrative "Men Fought" for commentary:

> I was creeping out of the second book's style and slowly going back to sanity, to writing with some attempt at logic and at making things easy for the reader rather than dazzling him with purple passages. One such experiment, of dubious value, was "Hombres pelearon" (Men Fought), my first venture into the mythology of the old Northside of Buenos Aires. In it, I was trying to tell a purely Argentine story in an Argentine way. This story is one I have been retelling, with small variations, ever since. It is the tale of the motiveless, or disinterested, duel—of courage for its own sake. I insisted when I wrote it that in our sense of the language we Argentines were different from the Spaniards. Now, instead, I think we should try to stress our linguistic affinities. I was still writing, but in a milder way, so that Spaniards would not understand me—writing, it might be said, to be un-understood. ("Essay," 1970, pp. 231–232)

The most important piece in his third volume of essays, and the one that gives it its title, is a lecture called "The Language of the Argentines," which a friend read for Georgie at the Popular Institute of Lectures in Buenos Aires in 1927. In it, Georgie claims not that there is an "Argentine language" but that the Argentines use the Spanish language with a different intonation and a different feeling. What matters to him are precisely those differences: "We have not changed the intrinsic meaning of words but their connotations. That difference, unnoticeable in argumentative or didactic speech, is enormous in the matter of feeling. Our arguments may be Spanish but our poetry and our humor are already from this side of the Atlantic" (*Idioma*, 1928, p. 179). To reinforce his arguments, he quotes a few examples: the word "subject," which was normally used in monarchical Spain, has negative connotations in democratic South America; the expression "worthy of envy" implies praise in Spain, while in Argentina it seems base; two words that express two important realities—"slums" and "pampas"— have no emotional content for a Spaniard. In short, what Georgie wanted was a language that reflected a certain unique reality, the reality of his native country.

The other seventeen pieces in *The Language of the Argentines* are an assortment of articles, notes, and book reviews similar to those in Georgie's first two collections. The short prologue to the book insists on its origin in laziness. The book was made by the accumulation of prologues, that is (etymologically), "of inaugurations and commencements." Commenting on both the encyclopedic and chaotic aspects of the book, Georgie indicates the three basic preoccupations that give it its bearings: language, eternity, and Buenos Aires. To the first belongs an article on how a sentence is understood, illustrated by a word-by-word analysis of the famous beginning of *Don Quixote:* "In a certain village of La Mancha, whose name I do not wish to recall. . . ." The examination leads Georgie to the conclusion that one does not *understand* separately each articulation of the phrase but rather grasps the phrase as a totality. Then, with the help of quotations from Croce and Spiller, among others, he proceeds to analyze the mechanisms of understanding. The article is a forerunner of his more original and witty writings on the subject. To the same group of articles on rhetorical subjects belongs a new note on metaphor along with discussions of a school of Spanish baroque poetry called culteranism and of a Quevedo sonnet; of Góngora's images and Góngora's critics (he pokes fun *en passant* at some literal readings of Dámaso Alonso); of Cervantes' narrative habits; of Jorge Manrique's elegiac couplets; of the pleasure derived from poetry. The last article contains an anticipation of some of Borges' key critical concepts. Georgie discusses the metaphor "Fire, with ferocious jaws, devours the fields," without revealing its true source, as if it had been written in a different period of literary history.

Let us suppose that in a café on Corrientes or the Avenida de Mayo a writer presents the metaphor as his own. I would think: Making metaphors is now a very common task; to substitute "devour" for "burn" is not a very profitable exchange; the mention of "jaws" perhaps will astonish someone, but it shows the poet's weakness, a mere sequel to the expression "devouring fire," an automatism; in short, nothing. . . . Let us suppose now that it is presented to me as the work of a Chinese or Siamese poet. I would think: Everything becomes a dragon to the Chinese and I'll imagine a fire, lighted like a party and serpentine-shaped, and I'll like it. Let us suppose that it is used by the witness to a fire or, even better, by someone who was menaced by the flames. I would think: The concept of a fire with jaws comes really from a nightmare, from horror, and adds a human odious malignity to an unconscious fact. That phrase is almost mythological and powerful. Let us suppose that somebody tells me that the father of the image is Aeschylus and that it was in Prometheus' tongue (which is true) and that the arrested Titan, bound to a rock cliff by Force and Violence, two very severe ministers, told it to the Ocean, an aging gentleman who came to visit his calamity in a winged chariot. Then the sentence will seem appropriate and even perfect to me, considering the extravagant nature of the characters and the (already poetical) distance of its origin. I'll do what the reader did: suspend judgment until I can be sure to whom the phrase belongs. (Ibid., pp. 105–106)

The essay drifts, later, to other related subjects, but Georgie has already made his point: all judgment is relative; criticism is an activity as imaginary as that of fiction or poetry. It is possible to recognize here the critical seed of the story "Pierre Menard, Author of the *Quixote.*" The conclusion that Georgie implicitly reaches is very different from the lessons Dr. I. A. Richards derives, for example, from similar exercises in *Practical Criticism* (1929). Both start from the same experience: the discussion of a text whose author is unknown to the reader and which, therefore, can only be deciphered by itself. Yet, contrary to Dr. Richards, Georgie postulates the utter impossibility of scientific criticism. To put it differently, for him every critic (every reader) places himself, willingly or not, in a conditioned perspective; before judging, every reader prejudges. Criticism, or reading, creates the text anew.

The book also includes essays on Argentine writers (the apocalyptic poet Almafuerte, the ultraist Ricardo E. Molinari, the ironic turn-of-the-century narrator Eduardo Wilde) and on some Argentine subjects (the origins of the tango, the three lives of the milonga, the *truco*) that by now constitute permanent features of any book by Georgie. There is also an affectionate review of one of Alfonso Reyes' books, *Reloj de Sol* (Sun Dial), to which Georgie reserves the highest word of praise: it is a spoken book. The article is an anticipation of his later comments on the Mexican humanist, whom he considers his master in matters of style. Subtly, ironically, through his example, Reyes would lead Georgie away from the baroque and teach him how to write the best Spanish prose of the century.

13.
The Gift of
Friendship

In the late 1920s the Borgeses moved to a sixth-floor apartment in a new and imposing building on the corner of Las Heras and Pueyrredón; it had seven balconies overlooking a busy midtown district, with the Recoleta cemetery in the background. The building is still there, and the neighborhood has changed very little. For eleven years that was the Borgeses' residence. In spite of its monotony, which he liked to stress, Georgie's life was being subtly modified by age and literary success. In fact, the whole family was experiencing change. Father was becoming totally blind and Mother's role had turned into nurse and reader. Her English had always been very poor, but now she felt compelled to improve it, to become, as she later put it, her husband's eyes. Her education and outlook broadened. Speaking about her in his "Autobiographical Essay," Borges comments on the change: "My mother has always had a hospitable mind. From the time she learned English, through my father, she has done most of her reading in that language" ("Essay," 1970, p. 207). Unaware of it, she was preparing for the role she would assume some twenty years later: being her son's eyes. Georgie's eyesight was getting worse. In 1927 he had to be operated on for cataracts by Dr. Amadeo Natale. Mother told me in 1971 that while the operation went on, she stood next to him, holding his hand as if he were a baby. The operation was successful, and for the time being Georgie was allowed to continue reading and writing. That was the first of eight eye operations he had to go through before near blindness set in for good.

Those were the years in which Georgie formed lasting friendships. He thought he had inherited the gift of friendship from Mother (ibid., p. 207), but it is an old Argentine trait. In the desolate vastness of the pampas a friend is the most important person in the world.

In the "Autobiographical Essay" Borges recalls the 1920s as quite happy years because "they stood for many friendships" (ibid., p. 235). Among those friends, he mentions Father, Father's classmate Macedonio Fernández, and some young poets with whom he launched ultraism in Argentina: Norah Lange and Francisco Piñero. The first was a beautiful blonde, of Norwegian stock, five years younger than Georgie. He wrote a generous prologue to her first book of poems, *La calle de la tarde* (The Afternoon Street, 1925). In her short autobiographical sketch for the *Exposición de la actual poesía argentina* (1927) she calls him her "sole teacher" and remembers their Saturday meetings at her family's villa on Tronador Street, where they shared friends and some favorite tangos. She also published in *Martín Fierro* (April 28, 1927, p. 6) a short commentary on Georgie's poems in which she praises him highly with only one reservation: in his books Buenos Aires looks too quiet and Sundaylike. A few years later, Norah married a member of the ultraist movement, the poet Oliverio Girondo. In the 1930s she stopped writing poetry and devoted herself entirely to prose. Francisco Piñero was a young lawyer who had helped Georgie to launch his first literary magazine, *Prisma,* and the first *Proa.* He also contributed regularly to *Martín Fierro* and shared with Georgie the banquet held by the magazine (December 29, 1925, p. 7) to celebrate the simultaneous publication of his own book of travels, *El puñal de Orión,* and Georgie's *Luna de enfrente.* In the thirty-fifth issue of *Martín Fierro* (November 5, 1926) a short note informs its readers that Piñero had left the magazine because he was too busy to continue contributing regularly to it. And when Georgie founded the second *Proa,* Piñero was no longer on its masthead.

Borges mentions other friends in the same section of his "Autobiographical Essay": Ricardo Güiraldes, one of the editors of the second *Proa,* who died in 1927; Silvina and Victoria Ocampo, with whom Georgie collaborated in the 1930s and 1940s; the poet Carlos Mastronardi and the novelist Eduardo Mallea, both of whom Borges continues to see regularly even now; and especially Alejandro Schultz, whom he calls by his pseudonym, Xul-Solar:

> In a rough and ready way, it may be said that Xul, who was a mystic, a poet, and a painter, is our William Blake. I remember asking him on one particularly sultry afternoon about what he had done that stifling day. His answer was "Nothing whatever, except for founding twelve religions after lunch." Xul was also a philologist and the inventor of two languages. One was a philosophical language after the manner of John Wilkins and the other a reformation of Spanish with many English, German, and Greek words. He came of Baltic and Italian stock. Xul was his version of Schultz and Solar of Solari. ("Essay," 1970, p. 237)

Xul-Solar was slightly older than his ultraist friends. He was born in 1887, and while in his middle twenties he had started on a journey in a cargo boat to the Far East that was cut short at a Mediterranean port. For ten years he lived in Europe (France, England, Germany, and Italy). World War I caught him in Paris. In 1920 he shared the first exhibit of his paintings with the Italian sculptor Martini. In July 1924 he returned to Argentina and became one of the *Martín Fierro* group. Although they were both in Europe at the same time, Xul and Georgie did not meet then. *Martín Fierro* brought them together. Norah was also a link: both in 1926 and in 1940 she showed her paintings alongside those of Xul in a collective exhibition. The first show was honored by a lecture on avant-garde art given by Marinetti, who was then visiting Argentina. *Martín Fierro* duly chronicled the event (July 8, 1926, p. 1). Reproductions of Xul's strange paintings are on the front page and page 3 of that issue; in a review of the show, the architect and critic Alberto Presbich singled out Xul's "mysterious and symbolical art." Xul's paintings at that time could be easily related to Paul Klee's and (in a way) to Kafka's drawings. They have the same angularity, the phallic agressiveness, the slightly sinister humor. That fall *Martín Fierro* published a few satirical rhymes written by Georgie with the help of his cousin Guillermo Juan. One plays with the *x* in their friend's name:

> With Xul, on the street called Mexico
> We did reform the lexicon.
> (*Martín Fierro*, September 3, 1926, p. 12)

Three of Georgie's books are illustrated by Xul. The first two belong to the 1920s. Five drawings are reproduced as endpapers in *El tamaño de mi esperanza* (1926); six in *El idioma de los argentinos* (1928). They all concern the subject of war and suggest primitive warriors engaged in blurred melees or advancing behind colorful shields while flying the Argentine banner. A commentary on Georgie's nativism, a subtle parody of patriotism, an anticipation of the army's future intervention in Argentina's political affairs? Who knows. Those drawings still haunt the pages of Georgie's early books. The third and last book illustrated by Xul-Solar is the pseudonymous *Un modelo para la muerte* (A Model for Death), a parody of the detective novel, signed "B. Suárez Lynch" and actually written by Borges and Adolfo Bioy Casares. To the first, private 1946 edition of that book Xul-Solar contributed seven unsigned vignettes that look Chinese. On page 27 a four-winged, headless pig is shown. On page 83 a fat man is being carried, very erect and alive, on a stick by two porters; the stick holding him goes through a hole in his chest.

The influence of Xul-Solar on Borges' work has never been studied, although it is considerable. Up to a point, some of the strangest aspects of the literary career of "Pierre Menard" can be traced to Xul. At least five of the nineteen items in Menard's bibliography are related to some of Xul's preoccupations with language (items *b* and *c*), with the game of chess (items *e* and *g*) and with the occult (item *f*). In one of Borges' most intricate stories, "Tlön, Uqbar, Orbis Tertius," some aspects of the invented language of Tlön are similar to one of the two languages invented by Xul, the "neocriollo," or "new native." In the story Borges explains that in that language there are no words corresponding to the noun "moon," but that there is a verb, "to moon" or "to moondle." He gives the following example: *The moon rose over the sea* could be written *hlör u fang axaxaxas mlö*, or, to put it in order: *upward beyond the constant flow there was moondling*. (Xul-Solar translates it succinctly: *upward beyond the onstreaming it mooned*.) (*Ficciones*, 1962, p. 23).

Xul-Solar's unique personality is the model for one of Adán Buenosayres' friends in Marechal's novel of that name. He is thinly disguised as the astrologer and some examples of his "new nativism" are quoted in the book. But by the time the novel was published in 1948, Xul-Solar had parted company with Borges. He had become attracted to Peronism. Borges still admired him to the point of calling him, in a piece written then, "one of the most singular things that had happened in our time." In describing Xul, he also said: "A man familiar with all fields of study, curious about all mysteries, father of languages, of utopias, of mythologies, author of the 'universal chess' ['panchess' in his language], an astrologer, perfect in his indulgent irony and in his generous friendship" (quoted in Xul-Solar's obituary, *La Nación*, Buenos Aires, April 11, 1963, p. 4). In mentioning Xul in his "Autobiographical Essay," Borges chooses to remember the friendship and forget the political disagreement.

He also recalls with affection the Mexican humanist Alfonso Reyes, who was appointed ambassador to Argentina in 1927. Reyes used to invite Georgie to dinner every Sunday at the embassy. A long-lasting friendship began there. Reyes had been very precocious. His first book of essays, *Problems of Esthetics*, was published in 1911, when he was barely twenty-two. After a long sojourn in Spain, where he worked at the Center for Historical Studies and produced the first authoritative edition of Góngora's *Polifemo*, he entered the diplomatic service. He had been a close friend of Pedro Henríquez Ureña while the latter was living in Mexico. Through Don Pedro, Georgie heard of Reyes. A chronicle written by Ricardo Molinari and published in *Martín Fierro* (April 28, 1927, p. 5) refers to an occasion, "during one of our usual visits to La Plata last fall," when Henríquez Ureña read some new poems by Reyes to Molinari, Georgie, and other friends. Even before his arrival in Buenos Aires, the *Martín Fierro* group had begun to direct the attention of its readers to the Mexican humanist's work. In the issue of September 3, 1926, a note on page 8 announces his appointment as ambassador and the banquet that was being organized by Georgie and Don Pedro. Reyes' arrival was delayed and the celebration did not take place until the fall of 1927. A photograph of the banquet is reproduced in *Martín Fierro* (August 31–November 15, 1927, p. 8). A note makes reference to a "dadaist speech" read by Georgie and Marechal; unfortunately, the speech is not printed. On many occasions Borges has mentioned his friendship with Alfonso Reyes and his admiration for his prose style. In the "Autobiographical Essay" he says of him: "I think of Reyes as the finest Spanish prose stylist of this century, and in my writing I learned a great deal about simplicity and directness from him" ("Essay," 1970, p. 237).

Reyes had mastered the art of being succinct and direct without being thin or prosaic. At the time Georgie met him, Reyes already had perfected a subtle, poetic, and extremely condensed prose. Georgie was still very much under the influence of Cansinos-Asséns, who tended to be long-winded and elliptical, and Macedonio Fernández, whose stylistic mannerisms Georgie followed very closely. In the "Autobiographical Essay," while praising Macedonio and proclaiming his devotion to him, he admits that he was a bad influence on his writing (ibid., p. 230). Reyes, on the contrary, was a liberating influence. He anticipated the new writing Georgie developed so brilliantly in the 1930s.

In listing the friends of that period, Borges omits his sister, Norah. She had been very active both in *Prisma* and the two *Proas*, had illustrated Georgie's first two books of poetry, and had attended the meetings at Norah Lange's villa and other literary and artistic gatherings. Her drawings and paintings were regularly featured in *Martín Fierro*. Throughout this period, Norah's career had moved parallel to Georgie's. But if they continued to be associated in their artistic pursuits, in their private lives they were beginning to part. Georgie was more absorbed every day in his explorations of the slums, a world totally inaccessible to Norah, while she had become more and more emotionally involved with Guillermo de Torre, the Spanish poet and critic whom they had met in Spain. In his book on the avant-garde, *Literaturas europeas de vanguardia* (1925), Guillermo comments on the importance of Norah's woodcuts and in a very exalted style describes her as having a "delicate temperament, extraradial[*sic*], unique." To explain what he means, he adds: "The fibers of her marvelous sensitivity are chisels that mark the diagram of her sensitive and intellectual undulations" (De Torre, 1925, p. 55). He also compares her with more famous women artists: the French painters Marie Laurencin and Maria Blanchard.

In the same book he devotes three and a half pages to Georgie's poetry. He notes his importance as a theoretician of the ultraist movement and quotes him extensively, generally with warm approval. But he has reservations about certain characteristics of Georgie's poetry after his return to Buenos Aires: the metaphysical concepts and the baroque style. His appraisal concludes on a very positive note. Georgie, on the other hand, reviewing Guillermo's book for *Martín Fierro* (August 5, 1925, p. 4), adopts a slightly patronizing tone. Although he praises it, he calls it a "rebellious directory of literature" and points out that Guillermo is a man of the world who knows things that are out of Georgie's reach: for instance, how to choose a tie or play tennis. In a more serious vein, he warns Guillermo that in wanting to be so up to date he runs the risk of being old-fashioned. After all, progress was invented not by Spengler but by Spencer. Then, after pointing out the North American influence on European literature (he mentions Poe, Emerson, and Whitman but not Pound and Eliot), he accurately predicts that the Spanish Americans' turn is coming.

From Spain, Guillermo had contributed regularly to Argentina's little magazines. He also wrote on Spanish and Spanish American authors for *Martín Fierro*. But in 1927 he made the fateful mistake of publishing an article in Madrid's *La Gaceta Literaria* in which he maintained that Spanish America's "literary meridian" passed through Madrid. I have already told of the cries of outrage that greeted this statement. Guillermo was visiting Argentina at the time and was probably making plans to marry Norah. He was quick to apologize for his faux pas and his apologies were accepted. But his lack of tact did not endear him to Georgie, who had always been slightly scornful of Guillermo's enthusiasm for the avant-garde and his zeal as a crusader for ultraism. Now Guillermo was plainly making a fool of himself. On a still deeper level, Norah's understanding with Guillermo must have alienated both of them from Georgie's affections. He probably thought his sister had made the wrong choice. In 1928 Norah and Guillermo married and went to live in Spain. Perhaps Georgie unconsciously felt that his Ariadne had deserted the family labyrinth to join forces with an unworthy carrier of the sword. From that moment on, Norah was no longer a part of his daydreaming life. Her role as mother surrogate had come to an end.

In "Singladura" (The Day's Run), a poem he included in his second book of verses, *Luna de enfrente,* there is a revealing reference to Norah. The poem, which may have been written on board a ship when the Borgeses crossed the Atlantic, describes the sea at night with lofty ultraist images; Georgie sees it as a "numerous sword," a "plenitude of poverty," "alone like a blindman," and "impenetrable as carved stone." From the contemplation of the sea, his eyes are raised to the sky to watch the moon "twisted around one of the masts." The poem ends with this long line:

> On deck, quietly, I share the evening with my sister, as if it were a piece of bread.

(Poemas, 1943, p. 100)

Part Three

1.
The End of a
Mythology

More than a dissatisfaction and impatience with ultraism can be detected in the articles written by Georgie in the late 1920s. In questioning the movement, he was also questioning his own attempts to create something different. He still practiced nativism but was already beginning to realize that his poetic powers of invention were not unlimited. He felt a bit stale. His youthful ambition to be a Walt Whitman or a Johannes Becher—that is, an all-embracing, cosmic poet—seemed more and more unattainable. On the first page of his *San Martín Copybook* (1929) he includes a quotation from Edward FitzGerald that indicates his vanishing hope: "As to an occasional copy of verses, there are few men who have leisure to read and are possessed of any music in their souls, who are not capable of versifying on some ten or twelve occasions during their natural lives: at a proper conjunction of the stars. There is no harm in taking advantage of such occasions" (*Poemas,* 1943, p. 121). Those words are perhaps more suited to Father's practice of poetry than to a young poet who had published three books of poems in seven years.

In retrospect, Borges is even more negative about the poems of that period. In the "Autobiographical Essay" he laments not having completely suppressed *Luna de enfrente* (1925) and calls it

a riot of sham local color. Among its tomfooleries were the spelling of my first name in the nineteenth-century Chilean fashion as "Jorje" (it was a half-hearted attempt at phonetic spelling); the spelling of the Spanish for "and" as *i* instead of *y* (our greatest writer, Sarmiento, had done the same, trying to be as un-Spanish as he could); and the omission of the final *d* in words like *autoridá* and *ciudá*. In later editions, I dropped the worst poems, pruned the eccentricities, and successively—through several reprintings—revised and toned down the verses. ("Essay," 1970, p. 232)

As a matter of fact, Borges eliminated eight poems in the first collective reprint (1943) and to compensate added two. In spite of his strictures, there are some good poems in that book. One of the most famous is "General Quiroga Rides to His Death in a Carriage," in which he brilliantly relates the brutal murder of one of the most notorious caudillos of Argentina. Georgie based his dramatic reduction of that episode on Sarmiento's masterful biography of Facundo Quiroga, but what makes the poem unique is the vigor of its images. The last quatrain is an epic evocation of Quiroga entering hell:

> Now dead, now on his feet, now immortal, now a ghost,
> he reported to the Hell marked out for him by God,
> and under his command there marched, broken and bloodless,
> the souls in purgatory of his soldiers and his horses.
> (*Poems*, 1972, translated by Alastair Reid, p. 35)

Another poem is dedicated to the pampas. Its Latin title, "Dulcia Linquimus Arua," comes from Virgil's first *Eclogue*, line 3—*nos patriae finis et dulcia linquimus arua*—which has been rendered by Dudley Fitts as "We depart from our own country, from the sweet fields [of home]," according to information provided by the editor (ibid., p. 293). Contrasting his own urban destiny with that of his ancestors, who made the pampas their home, Georgie says:

> As a town dweller I no longer know these things.
> I come from a city, a neighborhood, a street:
> distant streetcars enforce my nostalgia
> with the wail they let loose in the night.
> (Ibid., translated by Norman Thomas di Giovanni, p. 39)

San Martín Copybook fares slightly better in Borges' "Autobiographical Essay." After explaining that the title has nothing to do with Argentina's national hero General José de San Martín, and that it is "merely the brand name of the out-of-fashion copybook into which I wrote the poems," he admits that it contains some "quite legitimate pieces." He mentions "La noche que en el Sur lo velaron," whose title (according to him) has been "strikingly translated" by Robert Fitzgerald as "Deathwatch on the Southside," and "Muertes de Buenos Aires" (Deaths of Buenos Aires), a poem "about the two chief graveyards of the Argentine capital." But in spite of the more favorable evaluation, he cannot refrain from adding: "One poem in the book (no favorite of mine) has somehow become a minor Argentine classic: 'The Mythical Founding of Buenos Aires.' This book too has been improved, or purified, by cuts and revisions down through the years" ("Essay," 1970, p. 233). Actually, it lost one poem in the collected edition of 1943, and a second in the 1969 reprint.

"The Mythical Founding of Buenos Aires," which was incorrectly called "The Mythological Founding" in the first edition, is colorful and showy; at the same time, it beautifully expresses Georgie's discovery of his native city upon his return from Europe. The last two lines condense his feelings:

> Hard to believe Buenos Aires had any beginning.
> I feel it to be as eternal as air and water.
> (*Poems*, 1972, translated by Alastair Reid, p. 51)

The main tone of the book is of mourning. The section on "Deaths of Buenos Aires" shows Georgie's liking for the imagery of graveyards and tombs. Nevertheless, there was very little in him of the romantic agony. His elegiac poetry goes further back, to Latin models through the hard verses of Quevedo, the great Spanish baroque poet. In recalling the ancestors who fought and died bravely, such as his maternal grandfather, Isidoro Acevedo, or the sudden death of a poet friend, Francisco López Merino, who took his own life at twenty-four, Georgie was exploring a new territory.

Although these two books were not badly received, Georgie practically stopped writing poetry after the second was published. In the next decade he wrote exactly six poems, only four of which were published. In his 1966 conversations with De Milleret, Borges could find no reason to justify that silence except to speculate that he was not too happy with his poetry (De Milleret, 1967, p. 48). In spite of that, in 1929 *San Martín Copybook* won second prize at the annual literary competition held by the city of Buenos Aires. The prize money was three thousand pesos (one thousand dollars approximately), "which in those days was a lordly sum of money," according to Borges' recollections ("Essay," 1970, p. 233). Georgie's first decision was to spend part of the money on a secondhand set of the *Encyclopaedia Britannica,* eleventh edition. But the more important consequence of the prize was that it somehow legitimized his dedication to literature. Although Father had always supported (if not thoroughly invented) his vocation and had regularly answered inquiries from his friends about his son's occupation with a now famous phrase, "He is very busy: he is writing," Georgie probably felt that he was taking advantage of his father. The prize money freed him temporarily from that feeling and allowed him to attempt a major literary enterprise. He had always wanted to write a "longish book on a wholly Argentine subject." In the "Essay" he recalls a conversation with his parents on this topic: "My mother wanted me to write about any of three worthwhile poets—Ascasubi, Almafuerte, or Lugones. I now wish I had. Instead, I chose to write about a nearly invisible popular poet, Evaristo Carriego. My mother and father pointed out that his poems were not good. 'But he was a friend and a neighbor of ours,' I said. 'Well, if you think that qualifies him as the subject for a book, go ahead,' they said" (ibid., p. 233).

His choice was not so capricious after all. As Borges himself points out:

> Carriego was the man who discovered the literary possibilities of the run-down and ragged outskirts of the city—the Palermo of my boyhood. His career followed the same evolution as the tango—rollicking, daring, courageous at first, then turning sentimental. In 1912, at the age of twenty-nine, he died of tuberculosis, leaving behind a single volume of his work. I remember that a copy of it, inscribed to my father, was one of several Argentine books we had taken to Geneva and that I read and reread there. (Ibid., pp. 233–234)

In a sense, writing about Carriego was a roundabout way of writing about himself and his old neighborhood. But there was more to it, although Borges seems not to remember. Choosing Carriego as a fit subject for a major work, Georgie was quietly stressing his rebellion against family values. To discard major Argentine poets such as those he mentions in the "Essay" in favor of this truly minor one indicated a decision to challenge established literary values. It was another way of confirming to his parents his perverse preference for the slums, the tango, and the hoodlums: all the images that Georgie was then trying so hard to metamorphose into a new poetic mythology of Buenos Aires.

In preparing Carriego's biography, Georgie researched the scarce printed matter thoroughly, but his best sources were his family's memories of the poet, some close friends' recollections, and his own exploration of the slums. He interviewed Marcelo del Mazo, a classmate of Father and the person who was probably Carriego's closest friend. But perhaps the person who helped Georgie most to imagine what life was like in the slums at the time Carriego was alive was a famous hoodlum, Don Nicolás Paredes. He was the boss of Palermo when the poet was only fourteen and needed someone to admire. In those days hoodlums were instrumental in deciding elections: they were responsible for controlling the ballots and used to terrorize those who protested against the authority of the local caudillo. In his portrait of Paredes (more colorful and attractive than Carriego's), Georgie stresses the man's native dignity, "the entire possession of his part of reality," and describes him as he might have been on that evening in 1897 when the adolescent Carriego sought his friendship: "the chest bulging with virility, the authoritarian presence, the insolent black mane of hair, the flaming mustache, the usually grave voice which becomes effeminate and crawls with mockery when he is challenging someone, the ponderous walk, the handling of some possibly historical anecdote, of some slangy expression, of the skillful card game, of a knife and a guitar, the infinite certainty" (*Carriego*, 1930, p. 41). In Georgie's portrait, the Paredes of 1897 and the man Georgie visited thirty years later are subtly combined to project a larger-than-life character. In evoking him, Georgie also conveys the aura of a man who really didn't have to use his knife to impose discipline among his followers: the short gaucho whip he always carried, or the hard palm of his hand, was enough. Nearly forty years after Georgie's first meeting with Paredes, Borges told me a few more anecdotes about him. In 1927 Paredes was already retired and lived very frugally in a small room in the slums. He was always neat and courteous. Once he challenged Georgie to a game of *truco*, the native poker. They played for very modest stakes. Georgie won the first round, but then his "luck" turned, and in no time he lost quite a bit to his more skillful rival. When they stopped playing, Paredes refused to take his money and told him that they had been playing for fun. To perfect that object lesson, he gave Georgie an orange for the road, because (he said) he did not want anyone to leave his house empty-handed.

Georgie never forgot the man. Another anecdote about Paredes comes up in his interview with Ronald Christ, although this time he does not mention his name:

I remember I once saw a man challenging another to fight and the other caved in. But he caved in, I think, because of a trick. One was an old hand, he was seventy, and the other was a young and vigorous man, he must have been between twenty-five and thirty. Then the old man came back with two daggers, and one was a span longer than the other. He said: "Here, choose your weapon." So he gave the other the chance of choosing the longer weapon and having an advantage over him; but that also meant that he felt so sure of himself that he could afford that handicap. The other apologized and caved in, of course. I remember that when I was a young man in the slums, a brave man was always supposed to carry a short dagger, and it was worn here. Like this (*pointing to his armpit*), so it could be taken out at a moment's notice. And the slum word for the knife, or one of the slum words— well, and that has been quite lost; it's a pity—was *el vaivén*, the "come-and-go." In the word *come-and-go* (*making a gesture*) you see the flash of the knife, the sudden flash. (Christ, 1967, p. 140)

Borges had a change of heart while writing *Evaristo Carriego:*

When I began writing my book the same thing happened to me that happened to Carlyle as he wrote his *Frederick the Great.* The more I wrote, the less I cared about my hero. I had started out to do a straight biography, but on the way I became more and more interested in oldtime Buenos Aires. Readers, of course, were not slow in finding out that the book hardly lived up to its title, *Evaristo Carriego,* and so it fell flat. When the second edition appeared twenty-five years later, in 1955, . . . I enlarged the book with several new chapters, one a "History of the Tango." As a consequence of these additions, I feel *Evaristo Carriego* has been rounded out for the better. ("Essay," 1970, p. 234)

In more than one sense, Georgie's book on Carriego was a failure. It was not a good biography of the man, and as criticism of his verses it was too ironical to be of much use. But if it failed as a well-rounded literary study, it contained some fascinating glimpses of Palermo and the atmosphere that made the tango possible. It was also important as Georgie's first attempt to come to terms with the narrative problems of presenting a man's destiny. The portrait of Carriego was the first of a series of character studies Georgie created in the next decade.

Evaristo Carriego was printed on September 30, 1930, exactly twenty-four days after the army coup that deposed President Hipólito Irigoyen. That episode ended a fourteen-year period of democratic rule in Argentina, during which universal suffrage had been established, elections had been untainted by vote tampering or by terrorizing the voters, and the country's economy had been put on a solid basis by increasing its main exports (meat, wool, wheat) and by partially nationalizing oil. The army takeover began a ten-year period that Argentine historians later baptized the "infamous decade." President Irigoyen belonged to one of the established families, but he had always had a populist vision of a new Argentina: a country in which the capital and the provinces, the descendants of the old settlers and the new immigrants, the bourgeois and the workers, could find social justice and happiness. He was also a Latin Americanist in the sense that he understood perfectly that political freedom without economic independence was an illusion. He fought hard to free Argentina from the rule of local landowners and businessmen, but he fought even harder against the powerful British and North American oil and meat-packing interests. He had already served one term as president in 1916–1922. The man who followed him, Marcelo T. Alvear, had been hand-picked by him. Although Alvear proved to be easy prey to the conservative forces,

Irigoyen pretty much ran the show from behind the scenes. He engineered a triumphant comeback in 1928, when he was overwhelmingly elected to a second presidency.

Irigoyen was a strange sort of man for a politician. Instead of parading his power and seducing the masses with his eloquence, he preferred solitude and silence. He was nicknamed "El Peludo," not because he was hairy but because, like the mole, he loved to hide in his hole. In spite of his modern ideology, he was a born caudillo, a leader; he understood the masses intuitively. There was something in him of the witchdoctor, and that made him even more irresistible to the people. In his first presidency he had built an immense following which remained emotionally faithful to him until the last day of his second presidency.

For Georgie, Irigoyen's downfall was an ominous sign. He had always admired the Mole, and in one of the first essays in which he attempted to define the essence of Argentine nativism he had compared him with Juan Manuel de Rosas, the infamous nineteenth-century dictator:

> Silence combined with fatalism is effectively embodied in the major caudillos who have captured Buenos Aires' soul: Rosas and Irigoyen. Don Juan Manuel, in spite of his misdeeds and all the blood he uselessly spilled, was much loved by the people. Irigoyen, in spite of the official masquerades, governs us still. What the people loved in Rosas, understood in Roca, and now admire in Irigoyen is the scorn of theatricals, or the fact that if they use some, they do it with a comic sense. (*Inquisiciones*, 1925, p. 132)

Georgie published this article in 1925, after Irigoyen's first term was over, but he knew perfectly well that the Mole continued to pull the strings. The comparison with Rosas was meant to be favorable. It may seem paradoxical that Georgie, who came from people who had been Don Juan Manuel's mortal enemies and had fought bravely against him, could express such feelings. But he was then passing through a quiet but rebellious phase, and his return to Argentina meant (among other things) a total revision of the family museum. In Irigoyen he saw another Don Juan Manuel, a charismatic leader who in spite of his failings knew what was good for the country in a way the more articulate and perhaps more cautious leaders did not. At the time, many of Irigoyen's enemies also compared him with Rosas, stressing their arbitrariness, authoritarianism, and lack of respect for political niceties. They called them cruel tyrants and dictators. To Georgie, the parallel only stressed the favorable traits they had in common.

When Irigoyen began his campaign for a second presidency, Georgie was prominent among his supporters. A now forgotten chronicle written in 1944 by one member of that group, Ulyses Petit de Murat, offers an unexpected view of him as a political activist. Probably under the influence of a mutual friend, the young poet Francisco López Merino, Georgie and Ulyses decided to join Irigoyen's forces. According to Ulyses, they believed that the Mole had no chance of being reelected, that his enemies were going to tamper with the votes; and because his seemed a lost cause, they devoted all their enthusiasm to it. They came up with the idea of forming a Committee of Young Intellectuals, and soon Francisco Luis Bernárdez, Leopoldo Marechal, Enrique and Raúl González Tuñon, and Sixto Pondal Ríos joined them. The day they went to visit Buenos Aires' Central Committee they were received by the chairman, whose speeches bored them to tears. Suddenly, using a hoodlum's accent, Georgie turned to Ulyses and said: "Eh . . . when are they going to hand out the meat pies wrapped up in commissions?" (Petit de Murat, 1944, p. 6). Georgie's reaction was typical. Those committees were crude offices of patronage, and to attract voters they used to offer, along with the traditional wine and meat pies, the irresistible promise of an official job.

Not all the young intellectuals were attracted to Irigoyen as a lost cause. Many abstained from politics altogether. *Martín Fierro* published an editorial (August 31–November 15, 1927, p. 6) disclaiming any connection with the Committee of Young Intellectuals, many of whose members were regular contributors to the magazine. Georgie and Ulyses did not like the disclaimer and from then on ceased to participate in *Martín Fierro*'s activities. A different type of reaction came from the Boedo group. In their journal *Claridad* (April 1928) they published a poem, supposedly written by members of the committee, that included the following prayer to Irigoyen:

> Destroyer of old and obsolete regimes,
> When at last you cross the much desired threshold
> of the great presidential room,
> listen to our prayers, understand our gestures
> and give us consulates, university chairs and other commissions,
> Unequalled and extraordinary man!
>
> (Alén, 1975, p. 245)

Once more, the Boedo group and the ultraist poets were in confrontation, but this time there was an apparent change in their respective positions. While the supposedly bourgeois and even alienated intellectuals of Florida were in favor of the caudillo, the Boedo group opposed him for the same reasons the Communists would later oppose another charismatic leader, Perón: out of political alienation. The fact that Georgie was not seeking any commission (Father was his patron), and that he himself had laughed at the patronage dispensed by the chairman of the Buenos Aires Central Committee, must have been completely lost on the Boedo group. They continued to weave their neat abstractions while Argentine politics pursued its own course.

It is obvious that Georgie's enthusiasm for Irigoyen as a lost cause did not survive the Mole's triumphant return as president. Instead of claiming the meat pies and the commission, he became highly critical of the new government. And he had some justification. When the Mole was elected for a second term, he was already seventy-seven and was too tired and confused to be able to run the country efficiently. In his first presidency he had Argentina's economic prosperity, enhanced by the World War I boom in its meat and wool exports, to back his reformist political and financial measures. At that time, he not only changed the institutions but consolidated his country's wealth. Six years later, in his second term, he inherited a weaker economy, undermined by his successor's complacency with big business and the international trusts. No sooner was he in power than he had to face the 1929 crash, which damaged the national economy. His enemies accused him of mismanagement and even of stealing. Irigoyen was no longer strong enough to face them, but he did not know it. His own party was divided and he had to fight a rebellious and corrupted Congress. Surrounded by a mediocre staff, he trusted no one. His ingrained tendency to silence and secrecy became worse with age; he took too long to make decisions and, at the same time, insisted on his authority in every single piece of official business. In the last days of his regime he had alienated the best of his friends and was ruling ineffectively through people who awaited his sudden departure in the hope of sharing in the spoils. A severe flu gave them the opportunity to force his temporary resignation. Immediately the army took over. Georgie's reaction to the coup can be seen in some letters he wrote to Alfonso Reyes, who had been transferred to Rio de Janeiro. At the time that Reyes had been Mexican ambassador to Argentina, he had been an admirer of Irigoyen. To his anxious questions about what had happened to the president, Georgie made a measured if subjective reply. He called Irigoyen "el *Doctor*," which was a way of distancing him ironically:

> About the suppression of the *Doctor*, I can assure you that, in spite of the fact that it was needed, it was necessary, it was just, it has created a very disagreeable atmosphere. The revolution (or army coup supported by the people) is a victory of common sense against incompetence, against the usual dishonesty and the arbitrariness, but all these bad things corresponded to a mythology, to a tenderness, to a happiness, to the extravagant image of the *Doctor* conspiring from the presidential palace itself. Buenos Aires had to repudiate his domestic mythology and build very quickly some enthusiasm for

acts of heroism in which nobody really believes, on the basis (insignificant for the spirit) that these soldiers are not thieves. To sacrifice Myth to Lucidity, what do you think? Bernard Shaw, undoubtedly, would approve. I don't know if I make myself clear: before (I repeat) we had stupidity but with it the noisy opposition newspapers, the "Long Live" and "Death To" which flourished on the walls, in tangos and milongas; now we have *Independence Under Martial Law*, a fawning press, . . . and the established myth that the former regime was cruel and tyrannical. (*L'Herne*, 1964, p. 56)

In closing, Georgie includes a few vignettes of the "revolution"—a nonlethal shooting in the Plaza del Once; a machine gun positioned at Junín Street, two steps from home; two gunsmith shops sacked in Rivadavia Street by a gang not too sure of itself—and also promises to send the *Carriego* "in ten days." The letter shows that Georgie had finally come to believe all that a corrupted press had said about Irigoyen and his friends. But Georgie was right about the Irigoyen myth, and that was what really mattered.

Less than one year after the publication of the book, in an article Georgie wrote for a new literary review, *Sur* (South), he has a few disillusioned and ironical words to say about the government. In stressing one of Argentina's most negative traits, resentment, he gives as an example "the incomparable spectacle of a conservative government that is pushing the whole Republic to become socialist, only to annoy and sadden a middle-of-the-road party" (*Discusión*, 1932, p. 17). Georgie's political skepticism had reached its lowest point.

2.
The Invention of an Audience

At the beginning of the "infamous decade" Borges could look around him and see that he had been left with very little. Gone was the enthusiasm that made him the apostle of ultraism, the untiring founder of small magazines, the brightest new poet in Argentina. *Evaristo Carriego,* published in the wake of the army coup against Irigoyen, went practically unnoticed. Borges was quickly dissatisfied with it. He had gambled on a popular poet, and his small, sophisticated audience had not responded well. "The happy few" were ready to listen to his poetry or to his brief, ironic essays, but a rather long book on a facile and sentimental poet did not interest them. Borges himself was a bit unsure about what to do next. He had come to realize that poetry would never be his chief concern or his lasting claim to fame. He still was interested in exploring the dimensions of Argentina's reality but didn't know exactly how to go about it. By then he must have realized that to succeed in inventing a new writing, he had to invent a new kind of reader. At that precise point in his literary career he began contributing to *Sur,* the journal founded by Victoria Ocampo; it was to become for the next three decades the most influential literary publication in Latin America.

Borges had already met Victoria (as everybody has always called her) in 1925, at the time he was editing *Proa* with Ricardo Güiraldes. Ricardo and his wife, Adelina, had taken Victoria to meet the Borgeses. Borges was twenty-five at the time, and Victoria, nine years older, found him to be "a young man . . . with a certain shyness apparent in the way he walked, in his voice, in his handshake and his eyes of 'voyant' (seer) or medium, similar to those of his ravishingly beautiful sister Norah" (Ocampo, 1964, pp. 21–22). In an earlier mention, written when Borges received the 1961 Formentor Prize, Victoria gives more details:

Adelina and Ricardo used to sing praises of Georgie: "You're going to see how charming the Borgeses are!" Soon I had the chance to verify it. I went into that house, which was presided over by the smiling Leonor, and where her two *enfants terribles* were growing (no longer materially but spiritually)— they were magically terrible because of their uniqueness, let's make it clear. They both, in their different ways, seemed to walk a few inches above the earth we all tread on. . . .

One of the first times I spoke to that child with the angelic face who was called Norah, she asked me: "What do you like better, a rose or a lemon?" Immediately I saw the rose of the rose and the yellow of the lemon because Norah herself was probably seeing them. . . . Everything was happening in the world of the invisible, only visible for moments, and visible in a way that even today man hasn't been able to capture or science to name. In the same way that Norah transmitted to me (with questions which may seem childish because they are exactly the contrary of a cliché) the rose and yellow colors . . . , her brother too transmitted to me . . . everything that his words touched. Everything that belongs to us and that is supposed to be ours and that I, like he, feel as ours, as the most ours of all. (Ocampo, 1961, p. 76)

Many years later, in a 1975 conversation with me, Victoria summarized her final impression of the family group: "They were all so beautiful and gifted."

That encounter marked the beginning of a long friendship, but it was to be a friendship characterized by shyness on both sides, by reticence and reserve, by curiously comic misunderstandings that persist until today. From the very beginning, Victoria's imposing physical presence (she was one of the most handsome and regal of Argentine women), her fastidious and expensive taste in clothing, and her dominant character marked even more deeply than her seniority in age the tone of their friendship. She had a way of ordering people around— terribly well-bred but inarguable—that Borges once described to me as follows: "When Victoria invited you to visit her at San Isidro, she didn't ask you; she summoned you." Like her British namesake, Victoria had something despotic about her.

At the time they met, Victoria had already published three volumes of essays at the influential *Revista de Occidente* press. She was a friend of Ortega y Gasset, who owned the journal and the publishing house that published her first book. It came out in 1924, with an epilogue by Ortega that was half as long as her text. The book was a study of Dante's treatment of the medieval theme of sacred and profane love and started Victoria in her career as a feminist. Ortega's epilogue was respectful, warm, and patronizing: in those days even intelligent men were slightly surprised (as Dr. Johnson once suggested) that women could write at all. In Argentina, Victoria was generally viewed as an amateur, a society lady who enjoyed writing and lecturing with her beautiful, grave, educated voice. Everybody knew that she belonged to one of the oldest families, and that she was wealthy and fiercely independent. Although married very young to a distinguished member of the upper class, she lived on her own and was (at a time women in Argentina hardly ventured outside without a chaperone) what was then called, in the wake of a famous Norma Shearer movie, a free soul. Her writings were idiosyncratic and totally personal.

In fact, she didn't even write in Spanish. Educated by a French governess, she found literary French easier to cope with and had her books translated into Spanish before publication in her native language. In a sense, Victoria looked much like the caricature of the bluestocking ladies Molière and Sheridan had poked fun at. But she was closer to George Eliot and George Sand in her single-minded devotion to writing and her intellectual toughness. Only Argentina's literary machismo prevented the literary world from understanding exactly what she wanted. The sophisticated readers of the time found her style too private, her wealth and tendency to sit at the feet of great writers (Ortega, Tagore, Huxley, Valéry, Virginia Woolf) too snobbish, her feminism too militant. They were used to intelligent women who kept their places or wrote (if they ever wrote) like subdued men. Victoria's attitude was to upset and challenge these assumptions. Without breaking the rules of the upper class in which she was born and brought up, she started to change them, as quietly and effectively as she had done with the marriage conventions. The founding of *Sur* was her first step in leaving a lasting mark on Argentine culture.

The journal that began in 1931 was the result of the joint efforts at persuasion of a young Argentine novelist, Eduardo Mallea (who was Victoria's protégé), and Waldo Frank, an American novelist and essayist who was then visiting South America for the first time. They pleaded and pestered her until she agreed to launch and finance *Sur*. The title was provided by Ortega, who was hastily consulted over the phone. (The call itself has become a legend; in those days only Victoria could afford a long-distance call of that sort.) *Sur*'s logo (an arrow pointing south) made explicit the intentions of the journal. In Victoria's mind it was to serve both as a showplace for Argentine, and eventually Latin American, culture—a permanent exhibition of what it had to offer the West—and as a place where distinguished representatives of European and North American culture could mingle with local talents. In a sense, Victoria was as deeply interested in revealing the new native writing to the Argentines as in introducing the latest fashions in letters into Argentina. As one of the voices in Marcos Victoria's *Colloquium on Victoria Ocampo* (1934) said, she paid as much attention to choosing her gloves or her hats as she did to choosing "the British novelist to be worn this spring or the German philosopher to be worn next winter." The mere fact that in 1934 a pamphlet was published to discuss Victoria shows the impact she had already made.

In her recollections of Borges, Victoria stresses his role in launching *Sur*. Along with Frank and Mallea, she "counted on Borges as the chief contributor to the journal and adviser to the whole enterprise" (Ocampo, 1964, p. 22). Borges had more experience than her Argentine colleagues in editing a literary magazine. In the 1920s he had founded and edited three little reviews and had contributed to a score of others, writing regularly for several of them. Although he had not yet started to make a living from literary journalism, he was a professional in a sense that neither Victoria nor Mallea would ever be. And his contributions to *Sur* would be an asset to that journal. It was a labor of love.

Because Victoria had to finance the journal out of her own pocket, for the first ten years she could not afford to pay its contributors. At the beginning it was an elegant quarterly that came out in a rather square format, with wide, white margins and large typography, obviously inspired by Paul Valéry's *Commerce*. In the first issue Victoria insisted on including some photographs that documented the range of Argentina's topography: the pampas, the Iguazú waterfalls, the Andes, and Patagonia. Many years later Borges told Napoleon Murat that he was amazed when he saw the illustrations, and that he assumed Victoria had published the photographs to show her friends in Europe what Argentina looked like. For him it was "a real geography manual . . . but a bit funny in Buenos Aires" (Murat, 1964, p. 377). In a quick rebuttal Victoria observed that her purpose had been to show Argentina to the Argentines, who were then rather ignorant about their native land and more interested in Europe (Ocampo, 1964b, p. 41).

The disagreement over those illustrations was symptomatic of a larger one between Victoria and Borges. In spite of their friendship, they had vastly different views about literature and life, about culture, and mainly about what a journal should look like. These differences never prevented Borges from being one of *Sur*'s most faithful contributors or prevented Victoria from thinking very highly of this brilliant but unorthodox young man. In his conversations with De Milleret, Borges recalls his misgivings about some aspects of *Sur:*

> The magazine was run in a strange way. At the beginning it was a bit exclusive, had a small circulation; it was a quarterly, and after three months the previous issue was as good as forgotten. Besides, Victoria had strange ideas about what a literary journal was: she wanted to publish only pieces by famous writers and didn't want notes on plays, films, concerts, books . . . all

that is the life of a journal, no? That is, what the reader wants: if he finds a forty-page article signed Homer and a fifty-page one signed Victor Hugo, that bores him and he doesn't think that it is a journal. . . . Besides, I think that the only way to have a journal is to have a group of people who have the same convictions, the same hatreds; a collection of pieces by famous authors does not make a journal . . . in spite of that, *Sur* has been and still is a decisive element in Argentine culture and that is, essentially, Victoria Ocampo's value. (De Milleret, 1967, pp. 60–61)

There are some photographs which document the launching of *Sur.* They were taken at Victoria's Bauhaus-style house in San Isidro. Apart from her, Mallea, and Borges, the group included Pedro Henríquez Ureña, then the foremost Latin American literary historian; Francisco Romero, a leading historian of philosophy; two former ultraist poets, Oliverio Girondo and Guillermo de Torre; Eduardo Bullrich, an architect and art critic who had contributed regularly to *Martín Fierro;* Ernest Ansermet, the French composer and music critic; and Ramón Gómez de la Serna, the dadaist Spanish writer who had finally made good his often announced and regularly postponed visit to Argentina. Not present at the time the photographs were taken were two of *Sur*'s guardian angels: Ortega y Gasset and Alfonso Reyes. Reyes' son was to be the first managing editor of the journal. The cast was very impressive and showed Victoria's success in attracting the stars of the Hispanic world. Photographs taken at the launching of *Sur* also reveal the unobtrusive presence of Raimundo Lida, an unassuming philologist who for a while held the position of managing editor before leaving Argentina for a more scholarly career as editor of the *New Review of Hispanic Philology* at El Colegio de México and later as professor of Spanish literature at Harvard.

But in spite of the credentials of all those writers, thinkers, and critics, the three people who were to make a lasting impact on *Sur* were Victoria, Mallea, and Borges. *Sur* would become Victoria's tribune, the place where she could influence and change Argentine culture. By introducing new subjects or authors, by reassessing old ones, she waged a persistent and effective campaign to update Argentine (and Latin American) culture. Bitterly discussed, even mocked and vilified, she published *Sur* well into the 1960s, changing the staff, discovering bright young talents, always busy with her cultural enterprises. Today *Sur* is no longer a journal, but it continues to publish under its imprint books and volumes of essays generally organized around a common subject.

If Victoria's task was usually challenged by those who could not accept a beautiful, wealthy woman as their cultural leader, the work produced by both Mallea and Borges had a different reception. They would dominate Argentina's literary life for the next thirty years. Mallea was four years younger than Borges. Although he started his career as a short-story writer—his first book had the fanciful title *Cuentos para una inglesa desesperada* (Stories for a Desperate Englishwoman, 1928)—he very shortly began to publish novels and book-length essays. The most important of his early works was *Historia de una pasión argentina* (History of an Argentine Passion, 1937), which was a "confession" of his hopes and anguish as a true Argentine. His theory of the "invisible Argentines" who would eventually come to the fore to redirect their country toward lofty moral goals was in a sense an answer to the depressing mediocrity of the army-ruled government. But it was too optimistic and vague about the recuperative powers of a nation already seriously damaged. In spite of its weaknesses, *Sur*'s readers were led to believe, by several reviewers, that the answer to all of Argentina's problems could be found in those elegant, uplifting pages. The appointment of Mallea as literary editor of the powerful Sunday supplement of *La Nación* consolidated his fame and influence.

Because Borges wrote only very short essays, and later short stories, it was taken for granted that Mallea, who published rather bulky novels, was the more important of the two. Readers then (as now) believed that the thickness of a book guaranteed the writer's soundness. Besides, Borges' pieces always seemed frivolous or ironic. Mallea's novels, on the other hand, were determined to prove that hard thinking and solemn, unsmiling prose were what was needed in South America. His books appealed mainly to the kind of audience that liked its Pascal and Kierkegaard in quotable doses and that was also fond of the Catholic novels of François Mauriac and Graham Greene (not the latter's entertainments, of course, which were more in Borges' province). Mallea was soon translated into English, French, and Italian, hailed by specialists in Latin American literature, and included in the required reading lists of Latin American seminars.

The fare Borges offered to *Sur*'s readers was totally different. Instead of ponderous essays on Argentine life and culture, he published short, oblique pieces on isolated, sometimes banal aspects of his country's reality: one article on a forgotten, second-rate gaucho poet; another on the funny inscription horse wagons then had; a series of very short reviews of current European and American movies. Borges' irony and wit were too dazzling, his deliberate selection of minor subjects too pointed. The majority of the readers (and probably Victoria herself) were not terribly amused. But slowly and firmly he began to form a group of followers, an almost secret society whose members looked like those secret provincial young men Valéry once told Mallarmé were ready to die for him.

One of the first, if not *the* first, of those faithful young men was

Néstor Ibarra. Born in France of an Argentine father who was the son of a French Basque émigré, Néstor Ibarra went to the University of Buenos Aires around 1925 to complete his graduate education. While attending the Faculty of Philosophy and Letters he discovered Borges' poems and fell under their spell. He attempted to persuade his teachers to let him write a thesis on Borges' ultraist poetry. As the poet was not yet thirty, his teachers rejected Ibarra's plan and told him to choose a safer subject. (He eventually wrote a thesis on the late Spanish baroque writer Villarroel, whom Borges had rediscovered in the early 1920s.) The failure to convince the academic world that Borges was worth a thesis did not deter Ibarra. In 1930 he published a book called *La nueva poesía argentina: ensayo crítico sobre el ultraísmo, 1921–1929* (The New Argentine Poetry: A Critical Essay on Ultraism).

Ibarra was barely twenty when he met Borges in 1928 or 1929. For fifteen years he lived in Buenos Aires, becoming so closely acquainted with the man and his writings that Borges once paid him the tribute of acknowledging: "Ibarra knows me more intimately than anybody else" (De Milleret, 1967, p. 132). By reading and rereading Borges, by talking and arguing endlessly with him (Ibarra is no sycophant), the young Basque managed to know Borges from the *inside,* as it were. That is, he was able to decode all the shades of irony, the elaborate system of deceptions and false confessions that form the fabric of Borges' texts. Ibarra's mature view of Borges can be found in his study *Borges et Borges,* which came out in 1969. It is an elaboration of a long piece he had previously published in *L'Herne*'s special issue on Borges (1964).

Many of his memories of Borges go back to those days in the late 1920s and early 1930s when he followed the slightly older master around Buenos Aires, walking endlessly until the small hours of the morning, stopping only to rest for a while in a café or to carefully watch some rose-colored streetcorner. They had first met at one of those literary dinners so common in Argentina's banquet years. According to Ibarra's recollections: "Chance had placed us next to each other in some dinner I cannot now recall; we walked out together and he made me do fifteen kilometers in two hours. A similar adventure happened to Paul Morand later, but he did not pass the test. *After the third block, the globetrotter gave up,* Borges told me" (Ibarra, 1969, p. 16). Morand was then famous for his slightly erotic travel books, but he was a lazy traveler, fond of big hotels, slow transatlantic steamships, and luxury trains. Borges was a born walker, and allied to Johnson in his passion for roaming around the streets of his city.

Soon conversations between Borges and Ibarra took the form of a ritual. They invented a new language, coined out of the etymological meaning of words, with some surrealist (or ultraist) touches added. Ibarra recalls:

We had a small, warm slang (in the elaboration of which I had a very secondary place) . . . but totally decodable. . . . *Hypogeous* [in Latin: subterranean] meant the subway; *aquarium*, the bathroom. *Phanerogamic* was meant to designate male and female swimmers who were a shade too naked. A *seminar* was something you bought at the drugstore. [*Seminar* comes from *semen;* hence a prophylactic.] Sometimes we suddenly crossed the street to avoid being approached by an *anthropomorphous* Italian [an Italian in the form of a man]. (Ibid., pp. 16–17)

Ibarra also recalls Borges' dislike of Italians and quotes a saying by Carriego he liked to repeat: "Others are happy to hate the Italians. I hate to defame them." He also recalls Borges' dislike of Spaniards, which was almost equally irrational. Ibarra describes the Borges he then knew:

He is big enough, comfortably wide. . . . His hard and prominent eyebrows give his eyes sometimes a withdrawn expression, even a melancholic one. But as soon as his eyes look at you, you realize your mistake. Lastly, everything is alive and clear in him. In all the meanings of the word. Clear, smooth, subtle. The skin is very white. . . . The hair is very dark. Pushed back, always a bit too long. From indifference, of course, not to look like an artist. He combs it with two fingers when it tickles his temples. (Ibarra, 1964, p. 420)

Of their endless conversations Ibarra recalls mostly the joy, the intelligence, the freshness, the healthiness, and especially the inexhaustible sense of humor: "I believe that he is literally the best-humored man I ever met" (ibid., p. 21). Some of the anecdotes of those days—Borges' refusal to answer negatively a self-serving inquiry made by a hat manufacturer because he was afraid of "being accused of being at the service of the manufacturers of nonhats"; his invention of a new French school, identism, in which objects were always compared to themselves; or the suggestion that an avant-garde review should be called *Papers for the Suppression of Reality*—give some of the flavor of the iconoclastic, untiring joker Borges then was. That he was more than that is proved by Ibarra's unceasing devotion. The faithful young man Valéry talked to Mallarmé about had found a witty reincarnation in Ibarra.

3.
Discussing the Discussant

Néstor Ibarra may have been Borges' first secret young man (in the sense Valéry used the expression), but Adolfo Bioy Casares became his first, very public disciple. Born in 1914, he was barely seventeen when he met Borges, but he had already authored two books.

The exact date of their meeting is hard to pinpoint. In his recollections Borges states flatly: "We met in 1930 or 1931, when he was about seventeen and I was just thirty" ("Essay," 1970, p. 245). In a recent chronology of his life Bioy seems to prefer 1932 (Bioy, 1975, p. 36). If the exact date is irretrievable, the place and the occasion are well known: they met at Victoria Ocampo's house in San Isidro. When the visit was over, Bioy took Borges back to Buenos Aires in his car, and they had the first of their many conversations. Bioy recalls that first meeting:

> Borges was then one of our best-known young writers and I was a young man with a book published privately and another under a pseudonym. When he asked me about my favorite authors, I took the floor and, braving my shyness, which prevented me from keeping the syntax straight for a whole sentence, I launched into praise of the dull prose of a poetaster who edited the literary section of a Buenos Aires newspaper. Perhaps to clear the air, Borges widened the question.
>
> "Of course," he admitted, "but apart from So-and-So, whom else do you admire, in this or any other century?"
>
> "Gabriel Miró, Azorín, James Joyce," I answered.
>
> What do you do with such an answer? I couldn't explain what I found in Miró's vast biblical or even ecclesiastical frescoes, in Azorín's small rural pictures, or in Joyce's garrulous and half-understood cascades from which rose, like rainbowed vapor, all the prestige of what was hermetic, strange, and

modern. Borges said something to the effect that only in writers devoted to the charm of words can young men find literature in quantities enough to satisfy them. Then, talking about my admiration for Joyce: "Of course. It is an intention, an act of faith, a promise. The promise that they"—he was talking about young men—"are going to like him when they read him." (Bioy, 1968, pp. 139–140)

Borges' polite irony can be seen here at its deadliest. But Bioy didn't mind. On the contrary, he sensed that he had finally found the mentor he was looking for. In her reminiscences of Borges, Victoria Ocampo acknowledges the part she played in bringing them together:

When Adolfo Bioy Casares was only Adolfito, his mother came to see me one day and talked at length about her unique and admired son's adolescent literary inclinations. She was concerned and proud. She asked me who would be able to guide the object of her worries, which Argentine writer could take him under his wing. Without any vacillation, I said Borges. "Are you sure?" she asked me. "Absolutely," I answered. And I was not mistaken. Between the two, and in spite of the difference in age, a great friendship was about to begin. I anticipated it but could not imagine it was going to be so strong . . . . (Ocampo, 1964, p. 23)

Borges and Bioy began to see each other regularly. In a few years' time (around 1936) they began to collaborate on some very unorthodox literary ventures. Victoria was right about Borges being the mentor Adolfito needed, but she was even shrewder in foreseeing Borges' future influence on Argentine literature. By 1932, with the publication of *Discusión* (his fifth book of prose and fourth of assorted essays), Borges became finally visible.

The fifteen pieces collected in that book were written in the late 1920s and early 1930s and reveal a few basic preoccupations. Some show Borges still very much concerned with the "essence" and "true nature" of Argentina, a subject that had occupied his writings during the 1920s. In two articles devoted to the study of two gaucho poets—Ascasubi and José Hernández, the author of *Martín Fierro*—Borges uses their texts to attempt to define a certain tone of voice, a style of conversation typical of the old "criollos." In selecting their most characteristic verses, he proves to have an ear subtly attuned to the native speech. It seems obvious that he thinks highly of both men, although he points out their limitations and defects and is very harsh with the critics who have attempted to canonize one of them (*Martín Fierro* is a sort of Argentine national epic) or to prove that Ascasubi was nothing but a "precursor" of Hernández. On the contrary, Borges rejects the concept of "precursor" and believes very strongly that Ascasubi is at his best when he doesn't sound at all like Hernández; he also believes that *Martín Fierro*'s most solid claim to fame is the fact that it is *not* an epic poem but a novel in verse. In reading both authors from a new critical perspective, Borges is performing a necessary task: going back to the canonical texts of Argentine culture to discover what they still have to say. In the same critical spirit, he wrote a piece called "Nuestras imposibilidades" (the literal translation "Our Inadequacies" misses the pun in the title), in which he heaps scorn on the average citizen of Buenos Aires: the "porteño." Written in a sort of direct, colloquial Argentine, it is a strong example of the kind of satire generally associated with Juvenal.

Borges is terribly upset about the habits of the porteño. Using the well-known device of "chaotic enumeration," he quickly sketches a portrait of that "mysterious everyday specimen" who venerates the low professions of public auctioneer and meat packer, who travels in buses but believes them to be lethal, who despises the United States and is happy that Buenos Aires can almost compete with Chicago in its number of murders, who rejects the possibility of an uncircumcized and beardless Jew, who intuits a secret relation between perverse or nonexistent virility and American cigarettes (true porteños prefer the Gauloise type of dark tobacco), who in nights of joyous celebration ingests pieces of the digestive, evacuative, or genital tracts of cows, who is proud of his Latin idealism but cherishes his native trickery and naïvely believes only in trickery.

The portrait brings out the worst aspects of the type: the contradictions between what the porteño believes and what he practices show how stupid, how gross, he is. The rest of the article is devoted to commenting on his most characteristic traits. The first is a lack of imagination. Everything that is unusual is, for the porteño, monstrous. To be a foreigner is to be inexcusable, wrong, slightly unreal. Borges does not spare the upper classes and pokes fun at those illustrated magazines devoted entirely to recording the elegance of such summer resorts as Mar del Plata. (The fact that he himself occasionally visited Mar del Plata to see Victoria Ocampo or Adolfito Bioy does not stop him from being nasty.) The second trait he wants to stress is the pleasure the porteño gets out of seeing somebody fail. It is the humiliation of the defeated that he is interested in watching. In the porteño's vocabulary, "to bear up" does not mean to endure with dignity; it is an exhortation addressed to the victim in order not to spoil the pleasure of watching pain. In the same way, if an Argentine woman wants to extol the pleasures of her summer holiday, she will say to her listener, "Take that," meaning "I had all this while you had nothing."

To properly enjoy what they have, the porteños need to be sure that others are deprived of it. Further, it is always a consolation to be able to hurt somebody. Borges closes that part of his article with a reference to the tolerance with which active sodomites are regarded, while the passives are viewed only with scorn. A parting shot is addressed to the military regime that had recently deposed President Irigoyen only to prove itself unable to run the country. According to Borges, in trying to ruin the moderates, whom Irigoyen represented, the army succeeded in leading people to socialism as the only alternative. Borges believes that the army's mistake was based on a grudge against Irigoyen. The article ends with these sad words: "I have been an Argentine for several generations; it is without any joy that I formulate these complaints" (Discusión, 1932, p. 17).

The article was originally published in Sur (no. 4, 1931) and reflects Borges' immediate disenchantment with the new Argentina that the army was trying to build. It also reflects a more general uneasiness with its culture, its lack of discrimination, its chaotic integration of different ethnic traits, its cult of trickery, and its primitive machismo. Borges' concern with the double standard in matters of sodomy shows how aware he already was of one of the most appalling contradictions of Argentine machismo. While pretending to abhor sodomy in all its forms and proclaiming openly his normal heterosexual appetites, the Argentine reveals in his conversation an obsession with anal intercourse that is slightly embarrassing. Borges avoids tackling that specific situation, but in pointing out the double standard he anticipates a correct reading of native sexual mores.

Borges' article was abrasive, and by placing it at the very beginning of Discusión he obviously wanted the reader not to miss the point made by the title. The rest of the book can be easily divided into two groups of articles: those that reveal his permanent preoccupation with philosophical matters and those that discuss rhetorical points. To the first belong "The Penultimate Version of Reality," in which he discusses Korzybski's theories as they had been condensed in an article by Francisco Luis Bernárdez; "A Vindication of the Cabala," which summarizes his knowledge of that esoteric doctrine; "A Vindication of the False Basilides," in which he develops an interpretation of gnosticism; "The Duration of Hell," in which he attempts to cope with the problems of eternity and evil; and "The Perpetual Race Between Achilles and the Tortoise," in which he discusses Zeno's paradox about the impossibility of movement.

In all these articles unexpected erudition, wit, and arbitrariness abound. Borges does not pretend to know everything about a given subject, and he repeatedly stresses the limitations of his scholarship. The fact that he did not take the trouble to read Korzybski directly is telling. What matters is not his scholarship but what the articles reveal about his main metaphysical preoccupations. The negation of space (seen as an attribute of time), the questioning of the reality of time, the doubts about our capacity to perceive reality—these are the real subjects that underlie the topics he discusses. At a very early age he was trained by Father to discuss them. In his first book of essays, *Inquisiciones* (1925) he had a go at them. Now he returns to the attack, this time with a more sophisticated technique, a better, more varied bibliography, and a subtler sense of humor. But he is still far from his goal. Not until 1947 would he be able to communicate coherently his preoccupations with the nonexistence of time and space.

More substantial are the articles that discuss rhetorical questions. If the Borges who seems so preoccupied with metaphysics can be compared to De Quincey (and the comparison has already been made), the Borges who is so concerned with rhetoric is closer to T. S. Eliot. In a sense, he is doing exactly what Eliot did in the articles he put together in his *Collected Essays,* published that same year: 1932. In reevaluating Shakespeare and the Jacobean dramatists, Dante and Baudelaire, and the English metaphysical poets, Eliot was paving the way for his experiments in writing dramatic verse and philosophical poems. Both *Murder in the Cathedral* and *The Four Quartets* are implicit in the *Collected Essays.* In the same way, Borges, in his discussions of Zeno and Korzybski, Bergson and Bertrand Russell, Nietzsche and Mauthner, was developing (very quietly) a new vision that would enable him to write his metaphysical poems and stories; and in his analyses of important aspects of the rhetoric of narrative, he anticipated his own experiments in short-story writing. He had always been a critic, but not of the disinterested sort. His criticism belongs to the category Eliot had named criticism of the practicants; that is, the criticism practiced by those who are paving the way for their own creative writing. From that point of view, the essays on rhetorical matters collected in *Discusión* are of extreme importance.

Two essays, "The Other Walt Whitman" and "Paul Groussac," appear to avoid large rhetorical questions, but even these are primarily concerned with placing a particular writer in a context of ideas; they do not confine their observations to the writer's work or personality. Whitman is seen not only in his texts (Borges translates three of his poems elegantly) but as a model of a certain type of writer. In a footnote Borges appends to the article, as if it were an afterthought, he points out that in discussing Whitman's work critics tend to fall prey to two different types of errors: first, they identify the writer with the larger-than-life poetic character about whom *Leaves of Grass* has so much to say; second, they write about Whitman aping his own extraordinary style and vocabulary. The footnote is not so casual as it seems. It helps to clarify the title of the article: the "other" Whitman Borges is talking about is the writer himself, not the poetic character. The distinction is essential for Borges' theory of literature. Avoiding the biographical trap, he points directly to what really matters in criticism: the study of the texts as texts, not as expressions of a certain writer's life or dreams or as documents of a given society. His attitude is antiholistic. The article does not develop this theory any further. In 1947 Borges returned to the subject in another article, "Note on Walt Whitman," later collected in *Other Inquisitions* (1952).

The article on Paul Groussac seems even less promising. In the prologue Borges calls it "dispensable." It is a harsh sentence, not only because the article contains a witty evaluation of a man who had a decisive influence on Argentine culture (he was a French émigré who became director of the National Library and the foremost literary critic of his time) but also because it places Groussac very firmly among the writers who had a major influence on Borges' style. He begins the article by admitting that he is a hedonistic reader: "I've never let a sense of duty interfere with so personal a habit as buying books; nor have I given a second chance to an unruly author." Thus he finds very significant that in his select library he has no fewer than ten books by Paul Groussac. He concludes that Groussac's readableness (a word Borges uses in English in his text) is due to the easiness of his style. "In Spanish it is a very rare virtue: all conscientious style communicates to the reader part of the trouble that went into producing it. Apart from Groussac, I have found only in Alfonso Reyes a similar concealment or invisibility of effort" (*Discusión*, 1932, p. 125).

The statement may seem merely witty but it is more than that. It is a recognition of the two masters who taught Borges how to overcome the excesses of both baroque and ultraist prose. Borges learned from Groussac and Reyes how to avoid parading the kind of style he was going to become famous for. In the last paragraph of the article he admits that if Groussac had lived and worked in Europe or the United States he would perhaps have been only a second-rate writer. But in this "forsaken republic" he is undoubtedly a master. In writing about Groussac, Borges is not only trying to give him his due. He is also using him as a symbol and prototype of the kind of writer he prefers.

Of the three articles that deal exclusively with rhetorical questions, the clearest is "La supersticiosa ética del lector" (The Superstitious Ethics of the Reader), a piece that can be seen as a complement of the one on Groussac. Borges attacks the Argentine reader's habit of paying more attention to the details of style than to the conviction or emotion the text conveys. For him, Argentines "pay attention not to the effectiveness of the mechanism [of style] but to the way the parts are distributed. They subordinate emotion to ethics, or better, to an un-challenged etiquette" (ibid., p. 44). The rest of the article debunks the notion of a "perfect" style and defends colloquial speech. In attacking the concept of perfection, Borges is also paving the way for the view of reality—as transitory, changing, unreliable—he would present in his forthcoming fiction. The article attacked some ingrained notions Argentines had about literature and was very popular.

Less popular but more important are the other two articles: "La postulación de la realidad" (The Postulation of Reality) and "El arte narrativo y la magia" (Narrative Art and Magic). They are closely connected. The first is devoted primarily to discussing the problem of verisimilitude; that is, the problem of how to present reality in literature and make it believable. To explain his point of view, Borges uses Croce's identification between the esthetic and the expressive. More than a hint of that theory can be recognized in the previous article on style: in censuring the reading habits of the Argentines, Borges was actually complaining that they were not able to recognize the need for expressiveness in style. In this new article, Borges uses Croce's theory to point out the difference between the classicists, who seem to shun expression, and the romantics, who emphasize expression. Borges empties these categories of any historical sense; they represent for him two different ways of handling literature. The classical writer has no need to express reality; he is content with mentioning it. To put it differently, he attempts to present reality not in its immediacy but only in its final elaboration as concepts. Thus the classical writer does not try to reproduce every state of mind, every feeling, every thought of his characters; he accepts the fact that literature (like real life) is not always precise and believes that vagueness is more tolerable or believable in literature than the romantic pretension of transcribing reality in all its peculiarities. It is obvious that for Borges (although he does not put it that way) realism is, from this point of view, also "romantic."

A paradox can be detected here. Because classical writers shun a total expression of reality, they get closer to it than the romantics (or realists), who by including all the unnecessary details tend to destroy reality. In selecting his examples, Borges does not pay too much attention to conventional literary periods. Cervantes and Gibbon are presented as classicists, although from the point of view of literary history one is really a baroque writer and the other a neoclassicist. But, for Borges, both have one trait in common: they do not attempt to portray reality in its entirety; they do not make precision their goal. In the same way, the Victorian William Morris and the Argentine modernist Enrique Larreta are quoted, along with H. G. Wells, Daniel Defoe, and the films of Josef von Sternberg, to illustrate a point about the invention of circumstantial details. Borges is not really trying to do away with the usual literary labels. He is more concerned with defining a certain concept of verisimilitude. For him, verisimilitude is not what conforms to the real, or what a certain literary period or a certain genre claims to be the real. It is what gives more feeling or expresses more reality in a certain text. Verisimilitude has less to do with reality than with the conventions of a certain culture about how to portray reality.

Unfortunately, the article is not at all clear, and to be properly understood it not only needs a very careful reading but must be read along with Borges' complementary piece on narrative art and magic. Here Borges expands his point of view and defines it with greater accuracy. In attempting to study narrative techniques, he begins by admitting that the subject is relatively new and that the study of narrative has not yet reached the sophisticated stage of the study of poetry or of the art of speechmaking. With these provisos, he attempts to define a certain type of narrative: one that follows the procedures of magic. Opposing the realistic type of narrative to that one, Borges contends that writers who deal in extraordinary subjects always attempt to present the extraordinary as normal. He cites two rather unexpected examples: *The Life and Death of Jason*, a novel in verse by William Morris, and Edgar Allan Poe's only novel, *The Narrative of A. Gordon Pym*. He underlines how carefully Morris introduces centaurs and mermaids in his narrative; how cleverly Poe avoids any reference to white in describing an imaginary tribe's horror of whiteness. From his analysis he concludes that there are two types of narratives: the realistic type, which pretends to present chaotic reality in all its details and follows the arbitrary (that is, conventional) descriptions of science; and the magical type, which follows magic in its lucid and beautifully organized way of presenting reality. He concludes that because magic is more rigorous than science and does not leave anything to chance, magic works within a very formal framework. In magical narratives everything is relevant; there are no loose ends. A perfect structure forces every part to correspond to the whole. From the point of view of narrative, it means that texts are built according to a rigorous plot. All episodes have an ulterior consequence. Borges' view of narrative is based on causality. At the end of his article, he postulates a teleology of narrative, illustrating his thesis with examples from Chesterton's short fictions, Joyce's *Ulysses*, and the films of von Sternberg.

Read in connection with the previous article, "Narrative Art and Magic" becomes clearer. But with a perversity that his readers know very well, Borges separates the two articles by a series of short pieces on film. This little trick, and the fact that many early readers found it extremely difficult to follow his arguments, has perpetuated the separation between the two pieces. Even today, when criticism of Borges' texts has reached a high level of accuracy, critics tend to ignore the first article or to overlook the fact that both are based on a similar concept of verisimilitude. Today it is obvious that in those articles Borges laid the foundation for a theory of fantastic literature that he would later develop in important articles and, especially, in his fiction.

The short pieces on film show another aspect of Borges' versatile criticism. In commenting on some films by Fedor Ozep (*The Brothers Karamazov*), Charles Chaplin (*City Lights*), Josef von Sternberg (*Morocco*) and King Vidor (Elmer Rice's *Street Scene*), Borges demonstrates his familiarity with the main cinematographic trends of the 1920s and early 1930s. He also reveals a marked preference for the American cinema, especially for von Sternberg, whose visual images and use of discontinuous montage would have a great influence on his own narrative style. In "Narrative Art and Magic" and in the prologue to his first book of short stories (*A Universal History of Infamy*, 1935), he does in fact pay tribute to von Sternberg's style. Film criticism was an intermittent occupation for him. On and off, he followed the development of cinematic art, from Chaplin's *The Gold Rush* (which he reviewed in the newspaper *La Nación*) to Orson Welles' *Citizen Kane* (reviewed in *Sur*). Even today, when he is no longer able to see a movie, he loves to go to the cinema to listen to the dialogue, while an occasional companion gives him some hint of what is happening on screen.

Borges' previous books of essays had been read only by his closest friends and were, in a sense, almost underground books. With *Evaristo Carriego*, he began to find a larger audience for his prose, but it was *Discusión* that made him truly visible. The book was published as the first volume in a collection of new Argentine writers. It immediately caught the attention of the critics. In 1933 the magazine *Megáfono* devoted the second half of its August issue to a "Discussion on Jorge Luis Borges." It was the first of many attempts to evaluate his work. In its efforts to be polemical, it used a device that could be called the one-way writers' roundtable. The first writer passed his text to the next, who could refute or complement it; the second writer passed the two texts to a third; and so on. The contributors were mainly aspiring young writers. Some were enthusiastic about Borges, some tepid, some totally hostile and even rude. The result, from an intellectual point of view, was rather thin. The best pieces were written by slightly older men—the French writer Pierre Drieu la Rochelle, the Spanish linguist and critic Amado Alonso—who had a broader perspective. Drieu, a very influential novelist and essayist, had met Borges while visiting Argentina as a guest of Victoria Ocampo. In a short piece written on his way back to France, he coined a phrase that is still remembered:

"Borges vaut le voyage"—"Borges is worth the trip" (*Megáfono*, August 1933, p. 14). He was one of the first to recognize not only the extraordinary intelligence but also the sense of humor and the passion with which Borges grasped reality. For Amado Alonso, Borges was maturing into a writer totally responsible for the meaning of words. He praises him for having changed from a baroque writer whose effort to achieve an effect was too visible into a stylist whose writing seems almost effortless. He concurs with Borges' own evaluation of style in the piece, already quoted, about Paul Groussac.

The younger contributors either praised Borges too much or failed to recognize any value in his poems or essays. While Alonso had applauded his literary behavior, which he summarized in the words "responsibility, sincerity, and [a desire for] precision" (ibid., p. 19), several contributors deplored the lack of coherence in his arguments—Ignacio B. Anzoátegui claimed that the article on hell was "unworthy of a chicken's brain" (ibid., p. 17)—or lamented the fragmentary nature of his pieces. Even a faithful admirer such as Enrique Mallea (brother of Eduardo) insisted that his fragmentary approach was a negative quality, without realizing that it was a form of composition and not a defect. In a similar fashion he could have lamented that sonnets are short. Some attacked Borges for not being aware of Argentina's social and political reality. Among these, Enrique Anderson Imbert cut a striking figure: he seemed to be emphatically committed to the socialist cause and claimed to be "living a profound social enthusiasm," an attitude that was quickly satirized by another participant. Anderson Imbert was then only twenty-three; today, after living and teaching in the United States for the last thirty years, his social enthusiasm has not waned, but his judgment about Borges' place in Argentine literature has obviously changed.

If the critical level of the discussion on *Discusión* was not totally satisfactory, the importance of that special issue of *Megáfono,* as an indicator of how Borges was then evaluated, cannot be overlooked. For the first time, a member of the new generation of Argentine writers was taken seriously enough by his colleagues to be the object of a collective evaluation. The fact that the discussion even took place is what really matters. It confirmed Borges' status as the most important young writer in Argentina. Those secret young men who had been gathering around him, and of whom both Néstor Ibarra and Adolfo Bioy Casares were already so representative, were no longer the only ones to be attracted to his writings. A larger audience was slowly being formed. Borges was on the verge of an important breakthrough in his literary career.

4.
The Yellow Literary Press

The month of August 1933, when *Megáfono* published its "Discussion on Jorge Luis Borges," saw a new literary magazine in Buenos Aires. It was called *Revista Multicolor de los Sábados* (Saturday Multicolored Review) and was distributed free to the buyers of *Crítica,* the most popular Argentine newspaper of the time. *Crítica* was the best of many publications that appealed to a mass audience. It was a good example of how to produce a sensational and, at the same time, literate paper. The editor, Natalio Botana, had introduced the style and method of United States' tabloids into Argentina. If the news wasn't striking or scandalous enough, *Crítica* invented it. Once the paper went so far as to report an imaginary uprising among the Chaco Indians in northern Argentina which culminated, when the news value of the hoax was exhausted, with a bold headline: CRÍTICA MAKES PEACE AT CHACO.

Botana had always wanted to have a cultural magazine attached to *Crítica.* After several trials, he launched the *Saturday Multicolored Review.* It was designed to compete with the long-established and high-brow Sunday literary supplement published by *La Nación,* which had been edited by Eduardo Mallea since 1931. Botana decided to hire Borges as literary editor of the *Saturday Multicolored Review.* Thus, for a while, two of Victoria Ocampo's brightest young men were able to shape the taste of the Argentine audience.

Borges had more experience in literary journalism than Mallea. His contributions to *Martín Fierro* and to *Síntesis* in the late 1920s had shown his skill at writing short pieces on books and authors. Writing for *Sur* and other literary publications did not consume all his time. Thus, when Botana came up with the offer to edit the *Saturday Multicolored Review,* Borges was ready to accept. The pay was small, Botana

251

very demanding, and the pace killing. But he took to the job with enthusiasm. Ulyses Petit de Murat, one of his friends from the *Martín
Fierro* days, was there to help him; he was an ultraist poet, eight years
younger. He and Borges had been active in the committee of young
writers who supported Irigoyen's second term. Petit de Murat worked
as film critic for *Crítica,* and it was perhaps through him that Botana
approached Borges.

Apart from contributing at least twenty-nine original pieces to
the magazine, Borges also selected and translated pieces from his favorite authors for *Crítica.* Chesterton, Kipling, Wells, and the German-
Czech author Gustav Meyrink shared with Swift, Novalis, and James
Frazer the gaudy pages of the supplement. He also introduced some of
his closest friends' works. Articles by Néstor Ibarra (on Ernst Lubitsch),
Xul-Solar, his cousin Guillermo Juan Borges, and the Uruguayan nov-
elist Enrique Amorim all found in Borges a generous promoter. His
own contributions were varied and, in some cases, extraordinary.
There were a few reviews of new books by Argentine, Uruguayan, and
Brazilian writers, the best of which is a short evaluation of Ezequiel
Martínez Estrada's *Radiografía de la pampa,* published in the issue of
September 16, 1933. The book (translated into English as *X-Ray of the
Pampas*) was a metaphysical and lyrical attempt to reveal the mystery of
Argentina's vast emptiness. In his short review Borges begins by linking
Martínez Estrada with a lineage of intense German writers. According
to him, they

> have invented a new literary genre: the pathetic interpretation of the pa-
> thetic history of history and even of geography. Oswald Spengler is the most
> distinguished practitioner of that way of writing history, which excludes the
> novelesque charm of biography and anecdotes, but also the skully digres-
> sions of Lombroso, the sordid shopkeeper's arguments of the economic
> school, and the intermittent heroes, always indignant and moral, which Car-
> lyle prefers. The circumstantial does not interest the new interpreters of his-
> tory, nor individual destinies, in a mutual play of activities and passions. Its
> theme is not succession but the eternity of each man or each type of man:
> the peculiar style of intuiting death, time, the I, the others, the circum-
> stances, and the world. (Rivera, 1976, p. 23)

In pointing out Martínez Estrada's models, Borges does not fail
to mention Keyserling and Waldo Frank. Both writers had visited
South America recently and had described vividly their impressions of
Argentina. Borges finds Martínez Estrada not inferior to his models,
and he praises his prose without reservation. In commenting on his
strictures against Argentina, he has this to say: "He is a writer of splendid bitterness. I'll say more: of the most burning and difficult bitter-

ness, that goes well with passion and even with love" (Rivera, 1976, p. 23). Borges' appraisal of Martínez Estrada's book was prophetic. At the time, very few people in Argentina recognized the author's distinction. Borges never doubted it. In his criticism he anticipated the judgment of the next thirty years.

The other reviews were of less interest and in a sense were an example of the kind of supportive criticism the French call *critique de soutien*. Old friends and accomplices from the *Martín Fierro* days— Norah Lange, Ricardo Güiraldes, the Uruguayan poet Ildefonso Pereda Valdés—predominate. But if the reviews are disappointing in general, some pieces Borges wrote under the pseudonym of F[rancisco] Bustos (a family surname) were outstanding. Three of them, when collected in 1960 in *El hacedor* (called *Dreamtigers* in the English translation), show how far Borges had already gone in developing his own style. The best-known piece is "Dreamtigers," a sort of Kafkaesque parable about the tigers that he was so fond of as a child and that continued to visit his adult dreams. A second piece, "The Draped Mirrors," reveals another well-known obsession. With the utmost economy, he tells the story of a woman friend haunted by Borges' image: when looking at herself in a mirror, she sees him. The third, an even shorter piece called "Toenails," celebrates the blind obstinacy of those parts of his body that would continue to grow long after he was dead.

The major piece that Borges published under a pseudonym was a short story called "Hombre de la esquina rosada" ("Streetcorner Man" in Di Giovanni's translation). It is an expansion of an anecdote told in "Hombres pelearon" (Men Fought), which was collected in *El idioma de los argentinos* (1928). But what had been there just the bare outline of a knife duel between two hoodlums is now an elaborate narrative, written in the first person and purporting to be the oral report given to Borges by a witness to the encounter. The fight has some dramatic qualities: the challenger, Francisco Real, arrives from the north deliberately to engage Rosendo Juárez, one of Nicolás Paredes' hoodlums. Juárez does not react to the challenge and instead flees, leaving Francisco Real not only victorious but also in possession of Juárez's woman, La Lujanera (The Woman from Luján). The narrator, a young man who belongs to Juárez's gang, tells of his humiliation at his boss's cowardice, his longing for revenge, and the sudden and brutal ending: Francisco Real (after having taken La Lujanera outside with him for a quickie) comes back to the party to die from wounds inflicted in a duel. Who killed him? Juárez, the woman, somebody else? The narrator does not say. But there are two clues which hint that the narrator himself did it, to avenge the gang's honor.

The story was Borges' first, but he didn't dare acknowledge his paternity. The pseudonym helped him to face the challenge of a new genre. In a sense, the fact that the story is also about a man who hides behind the name of a narrator to avoid boasting is very relevant. "Streetcorner Man" became one of Borges' more popular stories, but he soon grew tired of it. In recalling the period of his contributions to *Crítica,* he attempts to dismiss it:

> It took me six years, from 1927 to 1933, to go from that all too self-conscious sketch "Hombres pelearon" to my first outright short story, "Hombre de la esquina rosada" (Streetcorner Man). A friend of mine, Don Nicolás Paredes, a former political boss and professional gambler of the Northside, had died, and I wanted to record something of his voice, his anecdotes, and his particular way of telling them. I slaved over my every page, sounding out each sentence and striving to phrase it in his exact tones. . . . Originally titled "Hombres de las orillas" (Men from the Edge of Town), the story appeared in the Saturday supplement, which I was editing, of a yellow-press daily called *Crítica.* But out of shyness, and perhaps a feeling that the story was a bit beneath me, I signed it with a pen name—the name of one of my great-great-grandfathers, Francisco Bustos. Although the story became popular to the point of embarrassment (today I only find it stagy and mannered and the characters bogus), I never regarded it as a starting point. It simply stands there as a kind of freak. ("Essay," 1970, p. 238)

Borges is too severe with the story. Although it is a bit stagy and mannered and the characters are probably bogus, it reveals an extraordinary sense of narrative for someone who had, so far, written only poems and essays. He has followed some obvious models: Agatha Christie's *The Murder of Roger Ackroyd* (1926), for the surprise ending (in that novel, it is again the killer who tells the story without describing the murder itself); Chesterton and Kipling for the invention of circumstantial details and vivid visual images; and von Sternberg's movies for the cutting and editing, which is sharp, lean, taut.

There is more to Borges' use of a pseudonym than shyness and a fear of criticism. In the "Autobiographical Essay," after telling how he tried to reproduce Nicolás Paredes' exact tone of voice, he adds: "We were living out in Adrogué at the time and, because I knew my mother would heartily disapprove of the subject matter, I composed it in secret over a period of several months" (ibid., p. 238). The information is revealing. In 1930 Borges had already had trouble convincing Father and Mother that the popular poet Evaristo Carriego was a suitable subject for a biography. Although they were friends of the man, they did not think highly of his poetry or of the subject he handled in his works: the slums of Buenos Aires. Borges' friendship with Nicolás Paredes (who helped him in his search for authenticity while writing the Carriego book) must have also seemed wrong to them. In this context, it is not surprising that Borges used a pseudonym. But always contradictory, by choosing the name of one of Father's ancestors, he was flaunting the pseudonym. The selection of the pen name was the kind of subtle practical joke Mother's snobbery deserved.

The most important contributions Borges made to *Crítica* were six stories he later collected (with "Streetcorner Man" and some other pieces) in his next book, *A Universal History of Infamy* (1935). In the preface to the second Spanish edition of that book (1954) he explains, rather apologetically, that the pieces "are the irresponsible game of a shy young man who dared not write stories and so amused himself by falsifying and distorting (without any esthetic justification whatsoever) the tales of others" (*Infamy*, 1972, pp. 11–12). In his "Autobiographical Essay" Borges returns to the subject to add a few more details. After discussing "Streetcorner Man," he says:

> The real beginning of my career as a story writer starts with the series of sketches entitled *Historia universal de la infamia* (A Universal History of Infamy), which I contributed to the columns of *Crítica* in 1933 and 1934. The irony of it is that "Streetcorner Man" really was a story, but these sketches and several of the fictional pieces which followed them, and which very slowly led me to legitimate stories, were in the nature of hoaxes and pseudo-essays. In my *Universal History*, I did not want to repeat what Marcel Schwob had done in his *Imaginary Lives*. He had invented biographies of real men about whom little or nothing is recorded. I, instead, read up on the lives of known persons and then deliberately varied and distorted them according to my own whims. For example, after reading Herbert Ashbury's *The Gangs of New York*, I set down my free version of Monk Eastman, the Jewish gunman, in flagrant contradiction of my chosen authority. I did the same for Billy the Kid, for John Murrel (whom I rechristened Lazarus Morell), for the Veiled Prophet of Khorassan, for the Tichborne Claimant, and for several others. I never thought of book publication. The pieces were meant for popular consumption in *Crítica* and were pointedly picturesque. I suppose now the secret value of those sketches—apart from the sheer pleasure the writing gave me—lay in the fact that they were narrative exercises. Since the general plots or circumstances were all given me, I had only to embroider sets of vivid variations. ("Essay," 1970, pp. 238–239)

Once more, in recalling the past and summarizing his intentions, Borges telescopes too much. A careful comparison between the stories and the sources reveals that he did more than "vivid variations." In some cases ("The Dread Redeemer Lazarus Morell" and "Tom Castro, the Implausible Impostor") he radically changed the axis of the story; in at least one case, "The Masked Dyer, Hakim of Merv," he added so many new things (including a whole fictional cosmogony) that the original sources were totally forgotten. Besides, many of the sources he acknowledges in the list at the end of the volume were also invented—as was the case with *Die Vernichtung der Rose* (*The Annhilation of the Rose*), Leipzig, 1927, attributed to an unknown Alexander Schulz, a name that thinly disguises Xul-Solar's real name. Borges was using the list of sources as an extra mask.

Even in the case of a story that had its roots in a real, identifiable source—such as "Tom Castro, the Implausible Impostor," based on an article by Thomas Secombe in the *Encyclopaedia Britannica* (eleventh ed.; XXVI, 932–933)—Borges altered the story substantially. The original anecdote is rather simple. A man called Arthur Orton attempts to pass himself off as Roger Charles Tichborne, the heir of one of England's wealthiest Catholic families, who had disappeared in a shipwreck off the coast of Brazil fourteen years ago. In the *Britannica* Orton is the one who conceives the impersonation scheme. He secures the help of Bogle, a black servant (who worked for the Tichbornes), only to get some information about the family. In Borges' version Bogle is the mastermind. He not only coaches Orton but guides and supports him throughout the dangerous enterprise, stage-manages the climactic encounter with Lady Tichborne, and finally defends him until his very last gasp. The *Britannica* is silent about Bogle's prominence and devotes exactly one sentence to him. In developing this incidental character into the most decisive one from the point of view of plot, Borges changes what was a rather banal narrative about a failed case of swindling into a drama. Orton and Bogle are presented as parodies of Faust and Mephistopheles. The fact that the intellectual leader is black and the protagonist is white makes it more telling.

A detailed study of the source and Borges' version reveals not only changes in emphasis but also important alterations in the actual circumstances of the story. The first encounter between Orton and Lady Tichborne is managed by Bogle with the brilliance of a stage director. In the *Britannica* the encounter, which takes place on a dark January afternoon in a Paris hotel, proves Orton's cowardice: he hides in bed, his face turned to the wall, to avoid as much as possible Lady Tichborne's questioning eyes. In Borges' version Bogle accompanies Orton to Paris and, instead of hiding him, takes him to Lady Tichborne's hotel. The January afternoon is (in the story) sunny. Upon entering, Bogle goes to the window and throws open the blinds: "The light created a mask, and the mother, recognizing her prodigal son, drew him into her eager embrace" (*Infamy*, 1972, p. 35). The dramatic boldness of Bogle's action is characteristic of Borges' boldness with his sources.

One of the general sources Borges never mentioned in print

prior to writing the "Autobiographical Essay" is Marcel Schwob's *Imaginary Lives*. Although he did not use any of the French symbolist's stories, it is obvious to any reader of both writers that the model for the Borges stories could be found in Schwob's book, especially in the best story, "MM. Burke and Hare, Murderers." According to Suzanne Jill Levine, Borges once remarked that the "concept" of *Imaginary Lives* "was superior to the book itself, and added that the last story, 'Burke and Hare,' was the best and the only one in which Schwob achieved his concept" (Levine, 1972, p. 25). "The key to this emphatic style is precisely the selection of relevant details," comments Levine. In the preface to the first edition of *A Universal History of Infamy* Borges had already acknowledged the style without identifying the general source:

> The exercises in narrative prose that make up this book were written in 1933 and 1934. They stem, I believe, from my rereadings of Stevenson and Chesterton, and also from Sternberg's early films, and perhaps from a certain biography of Evaristo Carriego. They overly exploit certain tricks: random enumerations, sudden shifts of continuity, and the paring down of a man's whole life to two or three scenes. . . . They are not, they do not try to be, psychological. (*Infamy*, 1972, p. 13)

In spite of not mentioning Schwob in the preface to that book, Borges had acknowledged at the time his interest in Schwob. One story from *Imaginary Lives* was included among the pieces he had recommended for publication in *Crítica*. "Burke and Hare" was the one he chose.

5.
The Irresponsible
Games

Although Borges had written poems about the pampas and essays on the gaucho poets, his actual knowledge of gaucho life was limited. His first real experience of that region of Argentina came around 1909, when he was ten, and produced the memory of an empty space in which the "nearest house was a kind of blur on the horizon" ("Essay," 1970, p. 212). It was not until he was thirty-five that he had the chance to visit an area where gaucho life was still commonplace. In the summer of 1934 he went to visit the Amorims, wealthy relatives who lived in Salto Oriental, overlooking the Uruguay River. Enrique Amorim was a Uruguayan novelist, a year younger than Borges, and had married Esther Haedo, Borges' cousin and companion in his childhood games. Enrique had studied in Buenos Aires and used to live part of each year in Argentina and part in his native town of Salto, in Uruguay's northwest. The Amorims had land and cattle. Although the business side was left to one of his brothers, Enrique loved to visit the countryside and even wrote some fine novels about the present-day gauchos.

Enrique's home was a beautiful, white Bauhaus-style house he himself had designed. It was called "Las Nubes" (The Clouds), because it was built on a hill which dominated the old town, closer to the sky than to the active river port. Enrique was a convivial host and loved to take home movies of his guests. Borges' visit was duly recorded in a sequence that has extremely funny moments. Like so many vacationers, Borges had let his mustache and beard grow, had completely forgotten to comb his hair, and sported a rather uncouth look. On his visit he was accompanied by his sister, Norah, and his brother-in-law, Guillermo de Torre. Borges constantly poked fun at Guillermo's truly Spanish ignorance of native things. In one of the shots Borges is seen poking Guillermo with a long pole that cattlemen use to prod cattle. The scene was symbolic in more than one sense. In assuming the gaucho side, Borges was underlining not only his hostility to Spaniards but also his undisguised lack of sympathy for Guillermo. Some other photographic documents of the visit show Borges, freshly shaved and conventionally dressed in a dark suit, at the helm of the ferry that took them up the Uruguay River.

At least five of the stories Borges wrote in the next fifteen years were influenced by that rather short visit. During his stay Borges came face to face with a type of violence he had found so far only in books and films. In those days the frontier between Uruguay and Brazil was still very rough country. Except in two places where a wide river marked the boundary (the Cuareim in the west, the Yaguarón in the east), the line that divided the two countries existed only on maps. At one point, where the Uruguayan city of Rivera met the Brazilian city of Santa Anna do Livramento, the frontier was a long, open boulevard with no customhouse whatsoever. Landowners had ranches on both sides of the frontier, an arrangement highly conducive to smuggling cattle. It was the River Plate equivalent of the Far West. Life was cheap there, and the ranchowners' hired hands were as careless with their own and other people's blood as the legendary gauchos. It was in Santa Anna do Livramento that Borges was witness to a casual killing.

In some notes he dictated for the American translation of *The Aleph and Other Stories* (1970), Borges summarizes the episode:

> A ten days' stay on the Uruguay-Brazil border seems to have impressed me far more than all the kingdoms of the world and the glory of them, since in my imagination I keep going back to that one not very notable experience. (At the time, I thought of it as boring, though on one of those days I did see a man shot down before my very eyes.) A likely explanation for this is that everything I then witnessed—the stone fences, the longhorn cattle, the horses' silver trappings, the bearded gauchos, the hitching posts, the ostriches—was so primitive, and even barbarous, as to make it more a journey into the past than a journey through space. (*The Aleph*, 1970, p. 271)

In 1964 he reconstructed the episode in more vivid terms for one of his interviewers, Carlos Peralta. Talking about his limited knowledge of Latin America at the time, Borges indicated that he spent a few days in Santa Anna do Livramento,

> where I had the chance to see a man killed. We were in a bar with Amorim, and at the next table sat the bodyguard of a very important person, a *capanga*. A drunkard came too close to him and the *capanga* shot him twice.

Next morning, the said *capanga* was in the same bar, having a drink. All that had happened at the table next to us, but I'm telling you what I was told later, and that memory is clearer than reality. I only saw a man who stopped, and the noise of the shots. (Peralta, 1964, p. 413)

With that very limited material, which somehow kept coming back to him, Borges built a few dramatic episodes that he distributed among several stories to lend them verisimilitude. One of the first uses of the visit was a sequence in "Tlön, Uqbar, Orbis Tertius," a story he originally published in 1940. In the second part of the story, when the narrator is trying to solve the riddle of that mysterious land, interpolated into reality by an apocryphal volume of a second-rate encyclopedia, he introduces a new character, Herbert Ashe, a British engineer from the Argentine Southern Railway. Recalling a conversation with Ashe about the sexagesimal system of numbering (in which 60 is written as 10), he points out that the engineer made a reference to Río Grande do Sul. "We talked of country life, of the *capanga*, of the Brazilian etymology of the word *gaucho* (which some old Uruguayans still pronounce *gaúcho*) and nothing more was said—may God forgive me—of duodecimal functions" (*Labyrinths*, 1962, p. 6).

Later, in the same story, Borges puts his experiences on the frontier to even better use. Displacing the time of the episode to suit the fantastic chronology of the story, he dates in 1942 (in a story published in 1940) the visit to the north of Uruguay. The place he now evokes is a country store owned by a Brazilian in Cuchilla Negra, on the Uruguayan side of the frontier. "Amorim and I were returning from Sant'Anna. The river Tacuarembó had flooded and we were obliged to sample (and endure) the proprietor's rudimentary hospitality. He provided us with some creaking cots in a large room cluttered with barrels and hides" (ibid., p. 16). The rest of the episode belongs to Borges' fantasy.

The same frontier setting is used in another story, "The Shape of the Sword," which he included in his second book of "legitimate" short stories, *Ficciones* (1944). The protagonist accidentally meets a man called by his neighbors the "Englishman from La Colorada" (from the name of the ranch he rented); the action takes place in Tacuarembó.

The Englishman came from the border, from Rio Grande del Sur; there are many who say that in Brazil he had been a smuggler. The fields were overgrown with grass, the waterholes brackish; the Englishman, in order to correct those deficiencies, worked fully as hard as his laborers. . . . The last time I passed through the northern provinces, a sudden overflowing of the Caraguatá stream compelled me to spend the night at La Colorada. . . . After dinner we went outside to look at the sky. It had cleared up, but beyond the low hills the southern sky, streaked and gashed by lightning, was conceiving another storm. (Ibid., pp. 67–68)

A comparison between the two episodes reveals a common element: the sudden overflowing of a stream in a desolate country, which forces the narrator to seek refuge among strangers. But in "Tlön" the place is the river Tacuarembó; in "The Shape of the Sword" it is the Caraguatá stream. Borges was obviously displacing an actual incident, which happened somewhere among the wilds of Tacuarembó, to suit the needs of each story.

Two more stories he wrote in the next few years are also located in Uruguay. One is called "The Dead Man" and was included by Borges in his third collection of stories, El Aleph (1949). Although the main setting is basically the same (Tacuarembó), the story has been set in the 1890s, a displacement that allows Borges to include tales told perhaps by members of his family who had a Uruguayan background. At only one point in the story does the experience of the author coincide with that of the main character (an Argentine hoodlum who becomes the *capanga* of a Uruguayan chieftain of smugglers): when the young thug visits the north for the first time.

> For Otálora a new kind of life opens up, a life of far-flung sunrises and long days in the saddle, reeking of horses. It is an untried and at times unbearable life, but it's already in his blood, for just as the men of certain countries worship and feel the call of the sea, we Argentines in turn (including the man who weaves these symbols) yearn for the boundless plains that ring under a horse's hooves. (*The Aleph,* 1970, p. 95)

By using Otálora as a mask, Borges is able to convey something of his experience in the wilds of Uruguay's north. There is a subtle hint that in weaving the symbols of that story he was trying to leave some indication of his personal involvement. The names of the two main characters are family names. In a note he dictated for the American edition of *The Aleph,* Borges elucidates the allusion: "Otálora is an old family name of mine; so is Azevedo, but with a Spanish *c* instead of the Portuguese *z*. Bandeira was the name of Enrique Amorim's head gardener, and the word *bandera* (flag) also suggests the Portuguese *bandeirantes,* or conquistadors" (ibid., p. 272). What Borges fails to say is that both names come from Mother's side of the family, and that the real Otálora was a slave trader in eighteenth-century Argentina. Even such a small detail as the name of the ranch where the story's plot unravels, "El Suspiro" (The Sigh), is taken from that visit to the north. "During that 1934 trip, we actually spent one night at a ranch called El Suspiro," Borges says in his note to the story (ibid., p. 272).

In the second story, called "The Other Death," the displacement is both chronological and spatial. The story basically takes place in the years 1904 and 1946, which do not coincide at all with Borges' visit to Tacuarembó, and the main Uruguayan setting is Cerro Largo, Tacuarembó's eastern neighbor. The setting is a part of Uruguay Borges never visited. It is the birthplace of the last of the great gaucho chieftains, Aparicio Saravia. In choosing that particular place, Borges was trying to recapture not just the past (as the plot of the story suggests) but a style of life, the style he discovered in his 1934 trip. One sentence in the story alludes to Uruguay's national hero, a chieftain who had also been, like Azevedo Bandeira, a smuggler. The story itself is based on the "assumption (perhaps undeniable) that Uruguay is more primitive than Argentina and therefore physically braver" (ibid., p. 106). An echo of Georgie's conflicts with the heroic traditions of his family, and his own experience while attending the state school in Buenos Aires, can be detected here. All his life Borges had lamented not having been a man of action; all his life he had felt that to be a writer was to be a coward. Now, in writing about these primitive men and about the land of Mother's ancestors, he is still trying to exorcise these feelings.

In another story, "The South," which is set exclusively in Argentina, the conflict is brought into the open. It is one of Borges' most famous stories, and was included in the second edition of *Ficciones* (1956). Under the mask of Juan Dahlmann, Borges dramatizes the conflict of a man who has both Argentine and European ancestors. In the last scene of the story, when Dahlmann is challenged to a knife duel in the pampas, there are some echoes of the day in 1934 when Borges saw a man killed. The setting is again a general store, badly lighted, with a pervasive "odor and sound of the earth" that "penetrated the iron bars of the window." Dahlmann is served a typical meal: canned sardines, some roast meat, and red wine. He relishes "the tart savor of the wine" and lets his gaze wander over the shop, noticing the kerosene lamps that hang from a beam and a group of noisy drunkards, farm workers with mestizo-type features (*Ficciones*, 1962, p. 172). The challenge made by one of these drunkards is probably based on memories of the episode of the *capanga* and the drunkard, except that in the story, for dramatic reasons, everything seems to happen in slow motion and the duel is fought with knives. But it is not the plot (a dream or nightmare Borges once had that now is Dahlmann's) but the general atmosphere which is rooted in the 1934 experience.

But perhaps it was rooted more in Borges' memory of the experience than in its actuality. In the notes to "The Dead Man" he indicates his puzzlement at the persistence in his memory of the things he then saw. The fact that he was able to use them in no less than five stories is significant. Nevertheless, he realized at the time that the experience in itself was commonplace. According to what Amorim once told me, Borges was more than ready to see wonders on that trip. On one occasion, he pointed out a group of men to his guide and with a childish relish said: "Look at those gauchos." Amorim, who was very familiar with the land and its inhabitants, corrected him with a laugh: "They are only farmhands." But in spite of his gentle warning, in Borges' imagination those farmhands were to become epic heroes, brothers to the gauchos whom he had read about in Ascasubi and Del Campo and Hernández and whom he had finally met (or believed he met) in primitive Uruguay.

That ten-day visit did not produce immediate results. Borges went back to Buenos Aires and resumed his task as literary editor of *Crítica*'s *Saturday Multicolored Review*. In 1935 he collected in *A Universal History of Infamy* the six imaginary biographies published between 1933 and 1934 in the magazine, plus "Streetcorner Man" and a few pieces (translations, adaptations, imitations) he had first published there. He added a seventh biography, that of "The Disinterested Killer Bill Harrigan," a name under which he disguised the notorious Billy the Kid. A prologue indicates some of the models for the stories and has this to say about the pieces that were appended to the book in a section called "Etcetera":

> As for the examples of magic that close the volume, I have no other rights to them than those of translator and reader. Sometimes I suspect that good readers are even blacker and rarer swans than good writers. Will anyone deny that the pieces attributed by Valéry to his pluperfect Edmond Teste are, on the whole, less admirable than those of Teste's wife and friends? Reading, obviously, is an activity which comes after that of writing; it is more modest, more unobtrusive, more intellectual. (*Infamy*, 1972, p. 13)

A few years later Borges would develop in his short story "Pierre Menard, Author of the *Quixote*" a whole poetics of reading as opposed to the poetics of writing. Here he is only trying to put into some perspective the "examples of magic" he had anticipated in *Crítica*. The perspective is that of a translator and reader. But he was more than a translator of some. As Norman Thomas di Giovanni has proved with Borges' amused collaboration, at least one of the five pieces was not a translation. It is called "The Mirror of Ink," and was then wrongly attributed to Richard Burton's *The Lake Regions of Central Equatorial Africa,* a volume Borges "has never laid eyes on," according to Di Giovanni (ibid., p. 11). The real source is another text: Edward William

Lane's *Manners and Customs of the Modern Egyptians*, "one of Borges' favorite books." The false attributions and the distortion of the sources are typical of his method of using sources as masks. Burton, like Lane, had translated the *Arabian Nights;* thus Borges attributes to him a story he picked up in Lane. That helps to confuse the traces and allows him more freedom. Because the story was included in the last section of *A Universal History* it has never been considered a legitimate Borges story. It is worth studying because it contains not only the seed of many stories to come—a man haunted by his own destiny as seen in a mirror of ink—but because the mirror itself is an Aleph, as Di Giovanni points out: a place that contains all places and all times. In "El Aleph," the title story of his third book of fictions (1949) Borges perfects the vision that makes it a symbol of his own world of writing. But already in the masked story the link between the vision and the act of writing is established. The mirror is, after all, made of ink.

The stories in *A Universal History of Infamy* were designed and written for a popular audience. In collecting them, Borges attempted to preserve their nature by keeping the melodramatic title under which they were printed in *Crítica*'s *Saturday Multicolored Review.* Furthermore, the book came out as one volume in a series of paperbacks edited by the magazine *Megáfono* (which had organized the 1933 colloquium on *Discusión*) and published by a mass publisher, Editorial Tor. But Borges, being Borges, could not avoid giving the volume some very sophisticated touches. The original 1935 prologue calls the stories "exercises in narrative prose," and in indicating some of its models Borges goes so far as to point out their limitations; he also disclaims any rights over the "examples of magic" that close the book. After these less than encouraging words, a dedication *in English* confronts the untutored Spanish reader: "I inscribe this book to I.J.: English, innumerable, and an Angel. Also: I offer her that kernel of myself that I have saved, somehow—the central heart that deals not in words, traffics not with dreams, and is untouched by time, by joy, by adversity" (*Infamia*, 1935, p. 7).

The dedication is memorable because it is the first published example of Borges' English prose. But for the mass reader the English dedication was probably as forbidding as the "Index of Sources" at the end of the book. With all these handicaps, *A Universal History of Infamy* did not attract a large audience. Borges had to return to his core of faithful readers, those secret young men in the provinces and some not so secret in the capital.

The same year the book came out, Borges was already practicing another form of deception. He had written a story that was to be published as a book review in a book of essays. In his "Autobiographical Essay" he tells the story behind the story:

My next story, "The Approach to al-Mu'tasim," written in 1935, is both a hoax *and* a pseudo-essay. It purported to be a review of a book published originally in Bombay three years earlier. I endowed its fake second edition with a real publisher, Victor Gollancz, and a preface by a real writer, Dorothy L. Sayers. But the author and the book are entirely my own invention. I gave the plot and details of some chapters—borrowing from Kipling and working in the twelfth-century Persian mystic Farid ud-Din Attar—and then carefully pointed out its shortcomings. The story appeared the next year in a volume of my essays, *Historia de la eternidad* (A History of Eternity), buried at the back of the book together with an article on the "Art of Insult." Those who read "The Approach to al-Mu'tasim" took it at face value, and one of my friends even ordered a copy from London. It was not until 1942 that I openly published it as a short story in my first story collection, *El jardín de senderos que se bifurcan* (The Garden of Forking Paths). Perhaps I have been unfair to this story; it now seems to me to foreshadow and even to set the pattern for those tales that were somehow awaiting me, and upon which my reputation as a storyteller was to be based. ("Essay," 1970, pp. 239–240)

The Garden of Forking Paths came out in 1941, not in 1942. But that is not the relevant point. In recalling the episode, Borges finally admits the importance of a hoax that was so successful that it fooled even Adolfo Bioy Casares, the anonymous friend who ordered the book from Gollancz. He was not the only one: I also believed in the existence of that novel and dutifully made an entry in my notebooks under the name of the imagined author.

More important than the success of the hoax is the fact that Borges had finally discovered a format for his future fiction which was unmistakably original. It was a combination of fiction and essay—two literary genres that convention had generally kept apart but that in Borges' peculiar view of reality were bound to mesh. By pretending that a story has already been told in a published book, Borges could offer, instead of a retelling of the story, a critique of it. The narrative discourse was submerged, masked under the critical discourse. Fiction became truth because what was invented was not the fact that the story may have happened (a commonplace task in discussing fiction) but that the story preexisted its telling. By pretending that the story had already been invented, Borges again claimed the rights of a reader, not of an author.

In including "The Approach to al-Mu'tasim" in the 1941 volume of short stories—later reissued as the first part of *Ficciones* (1944)—Borges had to finally acknowledge his paternity. In a prologue he defends his method of composition, which is "to pretend that these books already exist, and then to offer a résumé, a commentary. Thus proceeded Carlyle in *Sartor Resartus*. Thus Butler in *The Fair Haven*.

These are works which suffer the imperfection of being themselves books, and of being no less tautological than the others. More reasonable, more inept, more indolent, I have preferred to write notes upon imaginary books" (*Ficciones,* 1962, pp. 15–16). He goes on to identify the three stories based on that method: "Tlön, Uqbar, Orbis Tertius," "An Examination of the Work of Herbert Quain," and "The Approach to al-Mu'tasim." He omits the most dazzling of all his fictions, "Pierre Menard, Author of the *Quixote,*" in which he invents not only a book but the entire production of an imaginary writer.

The next book Borges published was a collection of essays called *Historia de la eternidad* (History of Eternity). It came out in 1936 under the imprint of Viau y Zona, a bookseller that specialized in bibliophile editions and occasionally published some books. Apart from the hoax played on the reader by the inclusion of "The Approach to al-Mu'tasim" as a book review, *History of Eternity* is a totally legitimate collection of essays. Its five pieces can easily be divided into two large categories: metaphysical and rhetorical. To the first belong two essays, the one that gives the volume its title and a companion piece called "La doctrina de los ciclos" (The Doctrine of Cycles). In attempting to define eternity, Borges had to go back first to the metaphysical problem of time, which had haunted him since his childhood, when Father taught him, as part of the games they shared, Zeno's paradox and the principles of Berkeleyan idealism. From those games, through some pieces already collected in *Inquisiciones* and *El idioma de los argentinos,* to the present text, Borges had traveled far and wide. In denying the notion of eternity and playing with the concept of infinity, he was paving the way for the total negation he would attempt in his most important piece on the matter, "A New Refutation of Time" (1947).

The essay on eternity is attractive but not terribly convincing. In a 1953 essay Maurice Blanchot discusses Borges' notion of infinity and proves it can be linked to what Hegel called "the bad infinite," a notion that is strictly literary. Blanchot does not criticize Borges for being a writer rather than a philosopher. On the contrary, he praises his honesty in dealing with these problems at the only level he is entitled to. Borges himself would agree with that reading of his essays. His interest in metaphysics is permeated by esthetics. In the essay on eternity, for instance, he rejects the concept of the Trinity not only for its logical difficulties (who was first, etc.) but also because it is ugly: "Conceived as a whole, the conception of a father, a son, and a ghost, articulated into a single organism, seems a case of intellectual teratology, a deformation which only the horror of a nightmare could have brought forth" (*Eternidad,* 1936, p. 20). In discussing Albertus Magnus' concept of the *universalia ante res,* he observes that scholasticism does not even suspect that God's categories may not be those of the Latin language that the theologians generally used. The other sign that Borges is not really terribly interested in discovering truth is that in indicating the bibliographical sources he has used, he points out that he has been relying too much on his own small library. The admission amounts to an exhibition of his unscholarly and hedonistic methods. In the title of the essay there is a contradiction in terms: to write the "history" of eternity implies using a method (historical discourse) for a subject that precisely denies the substance (time) on which the method is based. In the final notes Borges calls the essay a "biography" of eternity, reducing even more the scope of his attempt.

The second piece in the collection is no less personal. In reviewing the story of the concept of cyclical time, Borges actually composes a dramatic essay on Nietzsche's discovery of the concept. The core of the essay evokes that day in August 1881, in the woods near Silvaplana, when the German philosopher had the revelation of the eternal return. For his presentation of the dramatic episode, Borges uses the posthumously published *Die Unschuld des Werdens* (The Innocence of the Future, 1931) and also some passages from the *Nachlass* (Personal Notebooks). He wants to show that Nietzsche had chosen to forget that he was acquainted with the Greek philosophers who had already anticipated the concept, in order to believe that the revelation of cyclical time had come to him out of the blue. Thus dramatized, Nietzsche becomes Zarathustra; that is (in Borges' view), a sort of Walt Whitman. By bringing together these two prophets, Borges underlines the poetic vision of his own essay. In the second edition of *History of Eternity* (1953) he adds another essay on the same subject, "El tiempo circular" (Circular Time), less dramatic and more concerned with summarizing the different doctrines. The essay was originally written in 1943; by that time, it was obvious that Borges had taken the trouble to consult books other than those in his library.

An underlying rhetorical preoccupation can also be detected in his metaphysical essays. It is no wonder, then, that the three other pieces collected in the first edition of *History of Eternity* continue his rhetorical quest. One, "Las Kenningar," is a study of the system of metaphors used by the old Icelandic poets. Originally published in *Sur* in 1932, it was reprinted in pamphlet form in 1933 to correct a mistake Borges had made in translating the title into Spanish (he had originally written "Los Kenningar," making the metaphors masculine). In the corrected version the essay is basically a compilation of and a commentary on those very elaborate rhetorical figures and their code. Quoting extensively from the Eddas, Borges relates that long-forgotten poetry to the efforts made in the baroque age by Spanish poets such as Quevedo,

Góngora, and Gracián, and to the experiments of the ultraists. As a matter of fact, the essay ends with these lines: "The dead ultraist, whose ghost still inhabits me, enjoys these games. I dedicate them to a luminous companion of those heroic days, to Norah Lange, whose blood may by chance recognize them" (*Eternidad,* 1936, p. 56). There is an allusion there to Norah's Norwegian origin. In the second edition Borges added a less rambling and more important piece called "La metáfora" (The Metaphor), written in 1952, in which he quotes extensively from all kinds of literature to conclude that the basic number of analogies poets can unveil is not infinite, although the ways of indicating these basic analogies is unlimited.

The longest piece in the volume is a three-part essay, "The Translators of the *One Thousand and One Nights.*" If one remembers that in Greek the word "metaphor" meant translation, it is easy to see that Borges is still on safe rhetorical ground. To write about translations is to write about one of writing's most conscious operations: the one that perhaps lays open the function of writing as a manipulation of words and not of realities. In translating (as in parodying), the referent is not some elusive external or internal reality but the reality of words already fixed in a literary form. In this long essay Borges follows his usual method of commenting on selected texts, bringing in, at the same time, other texts to clarify or illustrate a point. It is a method of criticism that is closer to the English tradition than to the French. Only once in the essay does he attempt to indulge in a bit of theorizing. In discussing Richard Burton's translation and its relationship to Galland's and Lane's, Borges refers briefly to the famous dispute between Cardinal Newman and Matthew Arnold in 1861–1862. While Newman defended the literal approach, "the maintaining of all the verbal singularities," Arnold proposed the elimination of all the details that distract or stop the reading. Borges ironically comments: "To translate the spirit is such an enormous and ghostly intention that it may be taken as harmless; to translate the letter, such an extravagant precision that there is no risk anybody would attempt it" (ibid., p. 78).

The last piece in the book is a short exercise called the "Art of Insult." Apart from quoting some brilliant examples, Borges puts together some reflections and observations on the rhetorical aspects of insult that complete his work on metaphor, translation, and narrative techniques in this and the previous volume of essays.

The importance of *History of Eternity* in Borges' work became evident when Borges decided to have his books collected in a multivolume edition incorrectly called *Obras completas* (The Complete Works). They are far from complete and, in a sense, they are closer to being the official or canonical edition; that is, the edition by which

Borges wants to be judged. For the first volume of that collection he chose *History of Eternity*. It was a wise selection, because the book shows his maturity as an essayist at the same time that it points toward his future work. The rhetorical and metaphysical problems it raises are developed later in his best book of essays, *Other Inquisitions* (1952); the experiments in narrative anticipated in "The Approach to al-Mu'tasim" are enlarged in *Ficciones*. All things considered, *History of Eternity* is a seminal book, the first to offer in one volume all aspects of the mature writer Borges would soon become. It is a pity that the book came out under the imprint of a bookseller too small and exclusive to give it proper distribution. From that point of view, the book was a failure.

In his 1966 interview with Ronald Christ, Borges attempts to dismiss the whole enterprise as a joke:

> I remember I published a book . . . and at the end of the year I found out that no less than thirty-seven copies had been sold! . . . At first I wanted to find every single one of the buyers to apologize because of the book and also to thank them for what they had done. There is an explanation for that. If you think of thirty-seven people—those people are real, I mean, every one of them has a face of his own, a family, he lives in his own particular street. Why, if you sell, say two thousand copies, it is the same thing as if you sold nothing at all, because two thousand is too vast—I mean, for the imagination to grasp. While thirty-seven people—perhaps thirty-seven are too many, perhaps seventeen would have been better or even seven—but still thirty-seven are still within the scope of one's imagination. (Christ, 1967, p. 126)

Masking his disappointment in self-mockery is another way of avoiding coming to terms with it. In a sense, to have accepted the publication of the book under such conditions amounted to keeping it unpublished. It meant continuing to play the game of masks, deceptions, and hoaxes, this time not with the reader but with himself. Borges' shyness did more than just prevent him from acknowledging his short stories as such; it went so far as to prevent the production and distribution of the books themselves.

6.
The Dread Lucidity of Insomnia

The same year Borges visited Enrique Amorim and observed the last remaining gaucho frontier in the River Plate area, he met a young poetess who was to become one of his best and most durable friends. Silvina Ocampo was Victoria's younger sister and a close friend of Norah Borges, with whom she shared a passion for painting. It was amazing that Silvina and Borges hadn't met earlier, but the fact that she was seven years younger and extremely shy may account for it. Her interest in Borges' work preceded their friendship. In 1927 *Martín Fierro* had published a few of her sketches based on Borges' poems (see the June 10–July 10 issue). They were naïve drawings that featured a patio lighted by the moon and a rose-colored streetcorner. The drawings, which probably reached him through Norah, were published in the magazine with Borges' approval.

It took Silvina seven years to get to know him personally. In a portrait of Borges she wrote in 1964 for *L'Herne,* she remarks that she doesn't seem to remember where and when she first met Borges: "It seems to me that I have always known him, as it happens with everything one loves. He had a mustache and big, astonished eyes." That observation helps to date their meeting, because the first and last time Borges sported a mustache was after his return from visiting the Amorims. "I have detested him sometimes," Silvina adds with her usual frankness. "I have detested him because of a dog, and he has detested me, I suppose, because of a masked costume" (Silvina Ocampo, 1964, p. 26). She then describes the episode of the dog with all the minute details only a dog lover could appreciate. Apparently, once Borges had been visiting the Ocampos at the summer resort of Mar del Plata and Silvina's dog got lost. She searched the neighborhood, knocking at

270

every door and giving a very precise description of her dog. Borges was amazed at her thoroughness:

> "Are you sure you will be able to recognize your dog?" he asked, perhaps to console me.
> I was angry with him, thinking he lacked compassion.
> To hate Borges is very difficult because he doesn't realize it. I hated him; I thought: "He is mean, he is stupid, he annoys me; my dog is more intelligent than he, because he knows every person is different, while Borges thinks every dog is the same."
> Borges could not understand my pain. However, it was I who did not understand a thing, I found out later. Borges believes animals are gods or great magicians; he also thinks, whimsically, that any member of the species represents all of it. When he [now] opens the door to his office at the National Library, I know he asks the cat who belongs to that institution, "May I go in?" Perplexed, he thinks: "But the neighbor's cat I will meet on leaving is perhaps the same cat I met when I got here!" If he finds the cat sitting on his chair, he sits in another chair, not to upset him. He loves animals in his fashion. (Ibid., pp. 26–27)

The other anecdote has to do with Borges' fear of disguises. It was at carnival time. One evening after dinner Silvina and a girl friend, already disguised for a party, were walking in the garden when they met Borges. They did not pretend to hide their identity:

> Without changing our voices, we talked to him, but he didn't answer.
> "It's me, Borges. Don't you recognize me?"
> Only after I had taken off my disguise and my mask did he answer. He leaned against a leafy tree whose branches scratched his face and muttered: "Is this one also wearing a costume?" (Ibid., p. 27)

Borges' fear of masks was as old as his memory. As a child, he had been frightened by the masks he saw through the garden rails at Palermo, and he had once written a poem about the "coarse carnival." Many years later, in a detective story called "Death and the Compass," he used carnival time as the occasion for one of the story's most elaborate murders.

In her portrait, Silvina also mentions Borges' well-known susceptibility to women:

> Borges has an artichoke heart. He loves beautiful women. Especially if they are ugly, because then he can invent their faces more freely. He falls in love with them. One woman who was jealous of another woman he admired, once told him:
> "I do not find her so beautiful. She's totally bald. She has to wear a wig

even in bed when she is sleeping, because she's afraid of finding people she loves, or even a mirror, in dreams."

"Nobody would dare to be so bald," he observed with admiration. "Of course, she doesn't need a wig because she is beautiful all the same." And he added with a sincere curiosity: "Has she become bald naturally? Is it really natural?"

To my mind the lady in question became beautiful two or three years ago, when the wig fashion started. (Ibid., p. 27)

At the time Silvina met Borges she also met Adolfo Bioy Casares, whom she married six years later. She joined the two men on many summer trips and endless walks in the most destitute districts of Buenos Aires, as well as in unusual literary projects and a few original anthologies. In Silvina, Borges found a companion who was too independent to be his disciple but congenial enough to be a long-lasting friend.

Those were years when friends counted a lot, because at the core of his artichoke heart Borges was very lonely and unhappy. The unhappiness can be detected in his writings, especially in two poems he wrote then. They were written in English to help him conceal, under the mask of a langage that he knew well but did not normally use for poetry, how deeply miserable he was. They were addressed to a certain "I.J.," to whom he also dedicated *A Universal History of Infamy*. Her identity is less important now than the function she is assigned in the poems. She is the unreachable object of desire, the muse and the Beatrice of this lonely poet. In the first poem Borges is seen at dawn, after a night described with an ultraist metaphor as a "proud wave":

> The surge, the night, left me the customary shreds and odds and ends: some hated friends to chat with, music for dreams, and the smoking of bitter ashes. The things my hungry heart has no use for.
> The big wave brought you.
> Words, any words, your laughter; and you so lazily and incessantly beautiful. We talked and you have forgotten the words.

Dawn, the "useless dawn," finds him standing alone in a deserted street, with only the "toys" she has left behind:

> Your profile turned away, the sounds that go to make your name, the lilt of your laughter
> . . . .
> Your dark rich life.

Those toys are not enough. The poet really wants to get at her, "somehow."

> I want your hidden look, your real smile—that lonely
> mocking smile your cool mirrors know.
>
> (*Poemas*, 1943, pp. 157–158)

This is precisely what is denied to him. Like Dante, he would be able to have only those "toys."

The second poem is even more desperate. It begins with the eternal question:"What can I hold you with?" In summarizing the catalogue of things that make him what he is—lean streets, desperate sunsets, the moon of the ragged suburbs, the bitterness of a lonely man, his heroic ancestors, the personal insights, what "my books may hold," the manliness or humor of his life, the loyalty of an unloyal man, his central heart "that deals not in words, traffics not with dreams, and is untouched by time, by joy, by adversities"—he is terribly aware of the unworthiness of all these "toys." The last three phrases are humorous and pathetic at the same time:

> I offer you the memory of a yellow rose seen at sunset, years before
> you were born.
> I offer you explanations of yourself, theories about yourself,
> authentic and surprising news of yourself.
> I can give you my loneliness, my darkness, the hunger of my heart; I am
> trying to bribe you with uncertainty, with danger, with defeat.
>
> (Ibid., p. 160)

Part of the second poem he later used for the dedication to *A Universal History of Infamy* (1935), adding to the book's literary hoaxes the fact that it is inscribed in English to a rather tantalizingly unidentified woman. But this is only the beginning of a series of hoaxes Borges would play with her identity. In the second Spanish edition of the book, published in 1953, the initials are changed to "S.D." (*Infamía*, 1953, p. 13); and in the second edition of his collected verses, published one year later, he further identifies the recipient of the first poem (but not of the second) as Beatriz Bibiloni Webster de Bullrich (*Poemas*, 1954, p. 143). If both poems had been inscribed first to "I.J." and then to "S.D.," how on earth can only one be later inscribed to a third lady? Or is there any lady? It is well known that Alexander Pope, in publishing letters he had written, used to change not only the text but the addressee. What mattered for him was the addresser. Borges, who sincerely believed all cats and dogs were the same, must have also believed all Beatrices were one. The initials, or the complete name, really mattered little. What counted was that he had been torn by desire, that he had been lonely and miserable.

The pangs of desire were also visible in the allusions and even the topics of the literary essays collected in *Historia de la eternidad*. He may have had a literary interest in the *One Thousand and One Nights* to the point of carefully comparing several translations of it to English, French, and German. But his interest was not exclusively poetic. The book, and some of its translators and annotators, proved to be an inexhaustible mine of sexual folklore. In an article Borges repeatedly points out the different attitudes toward the book's eroticism one finds in Galland or Mardrus, Burton or Lane. In discussing Burton's translation (the most explicit about sexual matters), he comments on the translator's original contribution to the subject, which takes the form of notes to the text. Of the ones Borges singles out in his article, some are very telling: one is devoted to discussing the hairs on Queen Belkis' legs; another to the secret Night of Power or Night of Nights, which deals explicitly with one of man's oldest obsessions: the size and vigor of the penis; a third to the precise area covered by the pudenda in males and females; a fourth to the project of breeding monkeys with women to obtain a suitable race of workers. Borges' comments on Burton's comments show him at his ironical best: "At fifty, any man has accumulated tenderness, ironies, obscenities, and many anecdotes; Burton unloaded them in his notes" (*Eternidad,* 1936, p. 87). Borges, at thirty-five, was already unloading his.

The article on the translators of the *One Thousand and One Nights* was not unique in that respect. In the article that gives the volume its title, and while discussing very seriously the concept of eternity, he quotes Lucretius' elegant and precise lines about the fallacy of desire and the impossibility of attaining satisfaction in sexual embrace (ibid., p. 28). In another essay, while discussing some metaphors of the ancient Icelandic poets, he appends a note about the fights among breeding horses for the possession of "urgent mares," adding: "Of a captain who fought bravely in front of his lady, the historian observes how that stallion would not fight if he were watched by the mare" (ibid., p. 53n). In the same article, when commenting on the roots of the concept of eternity, he says epigrammatically: "The style of desire is eternity" (ibid., p. 30). Having reached the threshold of maturity, this still young man knew too well how tantalizing desire was. He also knew how destructive it was.

At the time, and for a number of years, Borges had been the victim of insomnia. In one of his articles he talks about its "atrocious lucidity." The Latinate word "atrocious" does not convey in English the colloquial undertone of the Spanish *atroz*. Perhaps it ought to be translated "fiendlike," because insomnia is generally experienced as a sort of possession by another's will—except that in this case the master and the slave are one and the same. In a poem he wrote around 1936 Borges comes to terms with it. Entitled "Insomnia," it was published for the first time in *Sur* (December 1936, pp. 71–72) and was later included in the 1943 edition of *Poemas*. Borges sees himself as the "hateful watcher" of Buenos Aires nights, unable to obliterate from memory all the things he has seen, felt, and done, all the places he has visited, his friends and enemies, his own body, the circulation of his blood and the advance of dental cavities, the inescapable universal history. Written in Adrogué while Borges was on a summer vacation, the poem has some striking lines:

> The universe of this night has the vastness
> of forgetfulness and the precision of fever.
>
> In vain I want to divert my attention from my body
> and from the wakefulness of an incessant mirror
> which multiplies and haunts it
> and from the house which repeats its patios
> and from the world which goes on as far as the broken outskirts
> of paths of clumsy mud where the wind grows tired.
>
> In vain I wait
> for the distintegration and symbols which precede sleep.
>
> (*Poemas*, 1943, p. 162)

It ends with a sort of desperate metaphysical consolation. The poet has come to believe in a "terrible immortality," that of "horrid wakefulness." Dawn, crapulous dawn ("Coarse, lye-colored clouds would dishonor the sky"), will find him still awake, with his eyelids tightly closed.

Many years later, after insomnia had somehow abated, Borges wrote a short story about a man who had a fantastic memory, "Funes, the Memorious." Originally published in *La Nación* (June 7, 1942), it was later included in *Ficciones* (1944). The protagonist, a young man from the eastern side of Uruguay, "had been thrown by a wild horse" and is "hopelessly crippled." Funes does not move from his cot and spends his days with his eyes madly "fixed on the backyard fig tree, or on a cobweb." The narrator goes to visit him and finds out what the fall had done to him.

> He told me that previous to the rainy afternoon when the blue-tinted horse threw him, he had been—like any man—blind, deaf-mute, somnambulistic, memoryless. . . . For nineteen years, he said, he had lived like a person in a dream: he looked without seeing, heard without hearing, forgot everything—almost everything. On falling from the horse, he lost consciousness; when he recovered it, the present was almost intolerable [because] it was so rich and bright; the same was true of the most ancient and most trivial memories. A little later he realized he was crippled. This fact scarcely interested

him. He reasoned (or felt) that immobility was a minimum price to pay. And now, his perception and his memory were infallible. (*Ficciones*, 1962, p. 112)

As a character in a story, Funes belongs to the race of Bartleby and Joseph K., characters afflicted, like him, with some mysterious psychological disease more than with any specific monstrosity. What is really fantastic in them is their behavior: the way Bartleby refuses to budge, or Joseph to react to his fate, or Funes to be astonished by his own pathological memory. But as a mask or persona, Funes is closer to the unhappy Borges of the 1930s. In attempting to explain how his memory worked, Funes comes to these conclusions: *"I have more memories in myself alone than all men have had since the world was a world.* And again: *My dreams are like your vigils.* And again, toward dawn: *My memory, sir, is like a garbage disposal"* (ibid., p. 112).

Haunted by his own memory, unable to forget, Funes spends his days and nights reconstructing his days and his dreams. "Two or three times he had reconstructed an entire day." To illustrate some of Funes' memory exploits, Borges uses images similar to the ones he had already used in his poem "Insomnia": "Swift writes that the emperor of Lilliput could discern the movement of the minute hand; Funes could continuously make out the tranquil advance of corruption, of caries, of fatigue. He noted the progress of death, of moisture. He was the solitary and lucid spectator of a multiform world which was instantaneously and almost intolerably exact" (ibid., p. 114). It is almost impossible for Funes to go to sleep because to sleep "is to be abstracted from the world; Funes, on his back in his cot, in the shadows, imagined every crevice and every molding of the various houses which surrounded him." In order to sleep, he had to turn his face toward the part of town that he hadn't visited and that for him was only "black, compact, made of a single obscurity" (ibid., p. 115).

In a note to the second part of *Ficciones* Borges indicates that the story is "a long metaphor of insomnia," because not being able to sleep amounts to not being able to forget. The daily rite of forgetfulness we call sleep is what the insomniac Borges (as his fictional counterpart, Funes) could hardly perform. His nights, like those of Funes, were spent in the obsessive rehearsing of everything he once did or saw or read. Funes' total recall was a metaphor of insomnia's total lucidity. On that painful and endless torture were grounded the scholarly essays and the masked stories Borges was then writing. Both "The Approach to al-Mu'tasim" and "The Translators of the *One Thousand and One Nights"* sprang from that experience: those days and nights in which Borges (as Funes) believed himself to be "the solitary and lucid spectator of a multiform world." And if Funes was crippled after the accident, Borges had also been symbolically crippled by insomnia: riveted to his bed by a pitiless disease of the mind.

At thirty-five, Borges had achieved a unique position in Argentine letters. He was considered one of the most original poets and essayists of his time. But he was really known only to a small minority of readers made up of young writers, many even younger than himself. In spite of his contributions to the most exclusive as well as the most popular literary magazines, his books were generally overlooked. *History of Eternity* had sold only thirty-seven copies in one year—a figure that is difficult to take. The paradox is that, at the same time, Borges was almost secretly engaged in fictional and critical experiments that not only would change the main course of Argentine and Latin American literature but deeply influence contemporary culture (the movies included) in France and England, Spain and Italy, the United States and Germany. Although Borges at thirty-five continued to be the exclusive object of an underground cult of young writers, he was on the verge of producing the kind of literature that would be truly revolutionary.

He was undoubtedly aware of the paradox of his position, and in some of his essays, under the mask of irony, he faced the problem. As early as the article on Paul Groussac, written in 1929, one can find his view of what it was to be a distinguished writer in Argentina. The case of Groussac was, of course, extreme. Born in France in 1848, he arrived in Buenos Aires at eighteen without any knowledge of Spanish. After a few years of hard work, he became one of the major Argentine writers of the second half of the nineteenth century, the head of the National Library, a respected and even dreaded critic, a master of style. But Groussac always felt and once even wrote that to be a master of Argentine prose was to be a nobody. In discussing Groussac, Borges points out that to see him as a mere traveling salesman of French culture among the mulattoes ("a missionary of Voltaire") was to devalue Argentine culture and Groussac's role in it. He was, Borges concluded, the Dr. Johnson of Argentina. At the same time, Borges observes that Groussac's immortality is "merely South American" (*Discusión*, 1932, p. 128); but he claims, or pretends to claim, that that immortality is enough. Nevertheless, the use of the adverb "merely" is significant. It returns with some obsessive regularity in several texts of the period. In discussing Enno Littmann's German version of the *One Thousand and One Nights,* and after comparing it with those of Burton, Lane, Galland, Mardrus, and others, Borges disagrees with the *Encyclopaedia Britannica*'s opinion that Littmann's is the best: "I hear that the Arabists agree; it is of no importance that a mere writer—and of the merely

Argentine Republic—prefers to dissent" (*Eternidad*, 1936, p. 101). The defensive attitude, the self-criticism, the paradoxical irony: those are the masks Borges had to wear to disguise his hypersensitive realization that he was engaged in a hopeless cultural enterprise.

A mere South American writer, a readership of (exactly) thirty-seven buyers: on these shaky premises Borges was to base the revolutionary work of his maturity. But to produce that incredible breakthrough (he was to be the first Latin American writer to influence Western culture), he had to go through the most elaborate and deadly ritual of initiation: the death and rebirth of the hero.

ABOVE, LEFT: *Colonel Isidoro Suárez (1799 −1846), Borges' maternal great-grandfather.*
ABOVE, RIGHT: *Colonel Francisco Borges (1833 −1874), Borges' paternal grandfather.*
BELOW: *Fanny Haslam de Borges, the English grandmother, in Paris, 1869.*

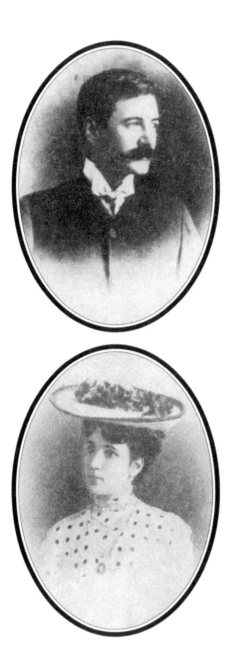

ABOVE: *Jorge Borges and Leonor Acevedo de Borges, his parents.*

OPPOSITE, ABOVE: *Norah Borges,* ca. *1918.*

OPPOSITE, BELOW: *His sister Norah (left, rear) with Borges (right, front) in Geneva, 1916.*

LEFT: *Borges in his teens.*
BELOW: *Borges as a young man.*

Norah Borges

LEFT: *A drawing of her brother by Norah, ca. 1926.*

BELOW: *Silvina Ocampo and Borges.*

BOTTOM: *Bioy Casares and Borges.*

ABOVE: *Borges with C. M. Moreno and E. R. Monegal in Montevideo,* ca. *1948.*

BELOW: *Borges being interviewed for the BBC, London, 1963.*

OPPOSITE, ABOVE: *Borges with his mother in London, 1963.*

OPPOSITE, BELOW: *Borges at Harvard, 1967. (Charles Phillips, © Time Inc.)*

Borges at the University of Wisconsin, 1976. (Penny A. Wallace)

7.
A Guide to His
Literary Mind

In spite of Borges' pessimistic attitude toward Argentine culture, Buenos Aires was then a busy literary center and attracted writers from all parts of the world. Two of the most famous young poets of the Hispanic world visited Buenos Aires in 1934. Federico García Lorca (already thirty-five and at the peak of his fame as a poet and playwright) spent several months in South America, mainly in Buenos Aires, where he gave lectures and recitals and attended the premières of several of his plays. Pablo Neruda (only thirty and still largely unknown outside his native Chile) was for a short time the Chilean consul in Buenos Aires. Neruda and Lorca met at the house of an Argentine friend and immediately struck up a friendship that became as intimate as the common pursuit of poetry and pleasure could make it. They recited verses together, made poems and drawings together, spoke publicly together to celebrate Rubén Darío, the great modernist poet. Once they disguised themselves as bearded sailors for a party, got gloriously drunk, and let their double masked images be recorded for posterity. The only thing they did not have together was sex. Federico was a homosexual, while Pablo was notoriously heterosexual. Federico and Pablo were feted by the Argentine intellectuals and got to know practically everybody, Borges included.

In his conversations with Richard Burgin, Borges could not bring himself to agree with his interviewer on the excellence of Lorca's plays:

BORGES: I don't like them. I never could enjoy Lorca.
BURGIN: Or his poetry either?
BORGES: No. I saw *Yerma* and found it so silly that I walked away. I couldn't stand it. Yet I suppose that's a blind spot because . . .

BURGIN: Lorca, for some reason, is idealized in this country.
BORGES: I suppose he had the good luck to be executed, no? I had an hour's chat with him in Buenos Aires. He struck me as a kind of play actor, no? Living up to a certain role. I mean being a professional Andalusian.
BURGIN: The way Cocteau was supposed to be, as I understand it.
BORGES: Yes, I suppose he was. But in the case of Lorca, it was very strange because I lived in Andalusia and the Andalusians aren't a bit like that. His were stage Andalusians. Maybe he thought that in Buenos Aires he had to live up to that character, but in Andalusia, people are not like that. In fact, if you are in Andalusia, if you are talking to a man of letters and you speak to him about bullfights, he'll say, "Oh, well, that sort of thing pleases people, I suppose, but really the *torero* works in no danger whatsoever." Because they are bored by those things, because every writer is bored by the local color in his own country, no? Well, when I met Lorca he was being a professional Andalusian. (Burgin, 1969, pp. 93–94)

Borges' reaction is typical of the intellectual who is fed up with local color, in Spain or in Argentina. Like another great Andalusian poet, Juan Ramón Jiménez, he preferred to pursue less trivial subjects and aimed at some sort of essential poetry. In doing this, he was bound to miss some of what makes Lorca unique, especially his sense of the theatrical, which he (like Cocteau or Noel Coward) carried into everyday life.

BORGES: . . . Lorca wanted to astonish us. He said to me that he was very much troubled about a very important character in the contemporary world—a character in whom you could see all the tragedy of American life. And then he went on in this way until I asked him who the character was, and it turned out the character was Mickey Mouse. I suppose he was trying to be clever. And I thought, that's the kind of thing you might say when you are very young and you want to astonish somebody. But after all, he was a grown man, he had no need, he could have talked in a different way. But when he started about Mickey Mouse being a symbol of America, there was a friend of mine there and he looked at me and I looked at him and we both walked away because we were both too old for that kind of game, no? Even at the time. . . . Even then we felt that that was what you call sophomoric. (Ibid., p. 94)

Faced with Lorca's mischievous sense of humor and of comic impersonation, Borges reacts with disdain. To Burgin's comment that Lorca was perhaps not a thinker but had a "gift for words," he replies:

BORGES: But I think there is very little behind the words.
BURGIN: He had a gift for hearing words.
BORGES: Well, a gift for gab. For example, he makes striking metaphors, but I wonder if he makes striking metaphors for *him,* because I think that his

280

world was mostly verbal. I think that he was fond of playing words against each other, the contrast of words, but I wonder if he knew what he was doing. (Ibid., p. 95)

At the time they met, Borges had left ultraism behind and no longer believed in the power of striking metaphors; he was moving toward a greater simplicity, toward classicism, as he once said. Lorca, on the contrary, had been seduced by surrealism and had become famous for his unexpected, brilliant metaphors. Dialogue between these two poets was impossible.

With Neruda, things went better. Borges probably met him for the first time in 1927, when Neruda visited Buenos Aires briefly. In his conversations with Burgin he is not very specific about the exact occasion:

BORGES: I met him once. And we were both quite young at the time. And then we fell to speaking of the Spanish language. And we came to the conclusion that nothing could be done with it, because it was such a clumsy language, and I said that was the reason that nothing whatever had ever been done with it, and he said, "Well, of course, there's no Spanish literature, no?" and I said, "Well, of course not." And then we went on in that way. The whole thing was a kind of joke. (Ibid., p. 95)

To Burgin's direct question about whether he admired Neruda's poetry, he answers:

BORGES: I think of him as a very fine poet, a very fine poet. I don't admire him as a man. I think of him as a very mean man.
BURGIN: Why do you say that?
BORGES: Well, he wrote a book—well, maybe here I'm being political—he wrote a book about the tyrants of South America, and then he had several stanzas against the United States. Now he knows that that's rubbish. And he had not a word against Perón. Because he had a lawsuit in Buenos Aires, that was explained to me afterward, and he didn't care to risk anything. And so, when he was supposed to be writing at the top of his voice, full of noble indignation, he had not a word to say against Perón. And he was married to an Argentine lady; he knew that many of his friends had been sent to jail. He knew all about the state of our country, but not a word against him [Perón]. At the same time, he was speaking against the United States, knowing that the whole thing was a lie, no? But, of course, that doesn't mean anything against his poetry. Neruda is a very fine poet, a great poet in fact. And when that man [Miguel Angel Asturias] got the Nobel Prize I said that it should have been given to Neruda. (Ibid., pp. 95–96)

Although it is doubtful that Neruda spared Perón just because he had a lawsuit pending in Buenos Aires, it is true that Neruda in his

Canto general blames the United States for all the evils of imperialism but has nothing to say against Perón. It was not his decision to spare Perón. The Argentine Communists, in spite of being regularly tortured and even sent to jail in freezing Patagonia, had and still have an ambivalent attitude toward Peronism. Because Perón was a populist and had helped the working class to get some overdue privileges, the Communists were afraid of alienating the workers if they opposed him too openly. They preferred to fight underground and to keep the door open for a reconciliation. Neruda, being a loyal party member, did not want to disturb that policy.

There is no record about a possible meeting between Borges and Neruda at the time he and Lorca met in Buenos Aires. Lorca went back to Spain, and to his tragic death in Granada, without ever realizing that he had briefly met the man who was to make his style of writing obsolete, both in the Hispanic and in the Western world. But Neruda left a record of his first reactions to Borges. After his brief visit to Buenos Aires in 1927, he went on a long journey which took him first to Europe and Japan and then to Burma, Ceylon, and Indonesia. From Ceylon, he wrote to Héctor Eandi, one of his Argentine friends; in a letter (dated April 24, 1929) he had this to say about Borges:

> He seems to me more worried about problems of culture and society, which do not seduce me at all, which are not at all human. I like good wines, love, suffering, and books as consolation for the inevitable solitude. I even have a certain disdain for culture; as an interpretation of things, a type of knowledge without antecedents, a physical absorption of the world, seems to me better, in spite of and against ourselves. History, the problems "of knowledge," as they call them, seems to be lacking some dimension. How many of them would fill up the vacuum? Every day I see fewer and fewer ideas around and more and more bodies, sun, and sweat. I am tired. (Neruda, 1974, p. 12)

Neruda's letter has to be placed in the context of his traumatic experiences in the Far East. The journey to that faraway land, which he had probably expected to be one of continuous discovery of the marvelous, had actually been a descent into a private inferno, out of which he derived the burning poems of his *Residence on Earth*.

Some years later, in a 1970 interview with Rita Guibert, Neruda answered some questions about Borges:

> He's a great writer and thank heavens for that! All Spanish-speaking races are very proud that Borges exists. And Latin Americans in particular, because before Borges we had very few writers to compare with European authors. We have had great writers, but a universal one, such as Borges, is a

rarity in our countries. He was one of the first. I can't say that he is the *greatest,* and I only hope there may be a hundred others to surpass him, but at all events he made the breakthrough and attracted the attention and intellectual curiosity of Europe toward our countries. That's all I can say. But to quarrel with Borges, just because everyone wants to make me quarrel with Borges—that I'll never do. If he thinks like a dinosaur, that has nothing to do with my thinking. He doesn't understand a thing about what's happening in the modern world, and he thinks that I don't either. Therefore, we are in agreement. (Guibert, 1973, p. 30)

In his conversations with Burgin, Borges tells an anecdote which shows how these two so-called enemies had come to terms with each other late in life. After attacking the winner of the 1967 Nobel Prize, the Guatemalan novelist Miguel Angel Asturias, Borges tells his interviewer what Neruda did at the time Borges visited Chile.

He went on a holiday during the three or four days I was there, so there was no occasion for our meeting. But I think he was acting politely, no? Because he knew that people would be playing him up against me, no? I mean I was an Argentine poet, he a Chilean poet; he's on the side of the Communists, I'm against them. So I felt that he was behaving very wisely in avoiding a meeting that would be quite uncomfortable for both of us. (Burgin, 1969, p. 96)

But that politeness was a late development. At the time they first met, Borges and Neruda had no political quarrel: Borges was then an intellectual anarchist. Neruda tended to sympathize with the political anarchists; he did not become a Communist until the outbreak of the Spanish civil war, in 1936. But their different attitudes toward life and letters were already settled.

In 1935 Borges met a writer who would be his friend for life. His name was José Bianco and he was ten years younger. In an article written for *L'Herne*'s special issue on Borges, Bianco evokes their first meeting. It took place near the end of April at a literary party at Victoria Ocampo's home in Buenos Aires. Borges was then engaged in translating Virginia Woolf's *Orlando* for Victoria's publishing house, and he was very busy teasing Angélica Ocampo by comparing her with one of the supposed portraits of the protagonist included in that book. Angélica was, like her sister Victoria, tall and majestic. Both loved to defy Argentina's conventions by standing, like gentlemen, erect against the fireplace with cigarettes in their hands. Bianco was then only twenty-five and was duly impressed by Victoria's prestige as well as by Angélica's striking features. But he was even more impressed by Borges. Neither Adolfo Bioy Casares nor Silvina Ocampo were present that evening; thus Borges, left to himself, "moved from group to group, introducing chaos." He was discussing *Sur,* which had already reached its tenth issue, and was pleading with Victoria to make it less "anthological," which for Bianco meant, perhaps, to make it less boring. Borges also insisted on the need to have "a punctual, devoted, modest, and intelligent contributor," who for obvious reasons had to be an imaginary being, like the sickly Mr. Banbury in *The Importance of Being Earnest.* The best way to produce such a virtuous character was by collective action. "In the forthcoming issues, and under a common pseudonym, everybody ought to write without any reservations what they really thought. [Borges] advanced several pseudonyms; and each name invented by him, a composite one, very Argentine, absurd, strangely believable, made us laugh and lightened the meeting's atmosphere" (Bianco, 1964, p. 13). Unfortunately, *Sur* was too serious-minded to perpetrate that kind of hoax.

The idea of creating a totally fictitious *homme de lettres* was not new. Pope, Swift, and some friends had attempted to introduce into eighteenth-century English literature the works of a certain Martin Scribblerus. The project didn't get very far, although it produced one masterpiece, Swift's *Gulliver's Travels.* Borges had to wait until 1946, when he became editor of a literary magazine, to practice a similar innocent deception on the Argentine public.

Bianco has this to say about Borges' style of conversation:

> . . . He enunciates rather shyly, doubtfully, not his ideas but his opinions, as if he were hoping somebody would contradict him with an interesting opinion which he was ready to acknowledge and to reconcile with his own in the most logical and, generally, in the most unpredictable way. Those who now attend his lectures and classes cannot help but admit the superiority of this distant and enigmatic man who has the gift to associate everything with everything. . . . Nevertheless, it is different to hear him talk behind a desk than privately with you or with a few friends. Another of Borges' characteristics is that he never raises his voice. Once he wrote, in a review of an Américo Castro book which caused a lot of angry reactions: "I have never observed that Spaniards spoke better than we (they speak louder, it is true, with the confidence of those who ignore doubt)." Let us add that he is interested in other people. He has also written, in a page on Bernard Shaw: "In any dialogue, one of the speakers is not the sum or average of what he says: he may be quiet and show he is intelligent, he may say intelligent things and suggest stupidity." However, as Borges is so intelligent, when talking to him, he gives us the feeling we are also intelligent. (Bianco, 1964, p. 13)

In recalling the first evening he met Borges, Bianco admits that he was too impressed to talk to him:

I just observed that young man, already famous among those of us who were much younger than he, unkempt, cheerful, aware of the world around him and at the same time distant from it, free of all solemnity and totally unconcerned about the impression he was making on others. Although courteous, Borges resembled Professor Higgins in *Pygmalion* in believing that "the great secret is not having bad manners or good manners or any particular sort of manners, but having the same manners for all human souls: in short, behaving as if you were in heaven, where there are no third-class carriages, and one soul is as good as another." Trained in the stimulating exercise of paradox, he tended to deliberately demolish tedious conversations with a joke. . . . He hasn't lost this good habit. (Ibid., p. 14)

Bianco also describes another meeting, in the summer of either 1935 or 1936, when he first went to visit the Borgeses at the Hotel Las Delicias in Adrogué. When introducing Mother, Borges asked very proudly: "How old do you think Mother is?" Bianco recalls: "Women then used very heavy makeup. . . . Mrs. Borges didn't even condescend to paint her lips. She didn't seem to be her son's eldest sister but his sister merely. Borges added, proud of his mother's youth: 'She's going to be sixty' " (ibid., p. 15).

For Bianco, Borges' mother was like the rope that keeps the kite firmly moored to the ground. Without her, "this man, so alien to life's realities," would have been lost in the clouds. Bianco also offers a snapshot of Father, "a good-looking man, reticent, with black, extinguished eyes." Bianco returned to the hotel more than once to have dinner with the Borgeses. He recalls that Father hardly ever said a word, except to bother about their guest: "Perhaps Bianco would like to have wine. Why don't you offer Bianco more of this dessert, which seems not too bad?" (ibid., p. 15). Years later, when reading Borges' story "Tlön, Uqbar, Orbis Tertius," Bianco recognized in the faded English engineer Herbert Ashe a portrait of Father.

Father's silence, his reticence, was more than justified at the time. He had never been an optimist, and now his health was declining rapidly. Totally blind and suffering from a heart condition, Father was attended with the utmost care by Mother. His will to live had been further undermined by his own mother's recent death. Fanny Haslam had lived with the Borgeses since 1901. Georgie had been very close to her; it was through her influence that an English governess was hired to teach him to read English before he learned to read Spanish. In his "Autobiographical Essay" Borges evokes his grandmother in her eighties:

Fanny Haslam was a great reader. When she was over eighty, people used to say, in order to be nice to her, that nowadays there were no writers who could vie with Dickens and Thackeray. My grandmother would answer, "On the whole, I rather prefer Arnold Bennett, Galsworthy, and Wells." When she died at the age of ninety, in 1935, she called us to her side and said, in English (her Spanish was fluent but poor), in her thin voice, "I am only an old woman dying very, very slowly. There is nothing remarkable or interesting about this." She could see no reason whatever why the whole household should be upset, and she apologized for taking so long to die. ("Essay," 1970, p. 206)

With Father declining rapidly, Borges felt the need to secure a permanent income of his own. Although he contributed regularly to *Sur* and other magazines, he earned very little. Through friends he got a commission to write for *El Hogar* (The Home), an illustrated magazine that was tailored to the interests of Argentina's upper and middle classes and that also had some literary and cultural aspirations. Some of the more established Argentine and Spanish writers contributed regularly to it. The magazine had two sections which alternated every week. One was devoted to "Books and Authors of the Spanish Language"; the other, to "Foreign Books and Authors." It was this latter page that was offered to Borges. He was also asked to write occasional critical articles for the magazine. The format of the book page had already been established when Borges began editing it on October 16, 1936. At one side, or at the top, a section called "Biografías sintéticas" (Short Biographies) summarized the life and career of an important modern writer. The rest of the page was devoted to book reviews of current titles (one long, several short) and news of the "literary life." In the last issue done by Anne Keen, Borges' predecessor, there was a biography of François Mauriac, one long review of Dos Passos' *The Big Money,* and short reviews of books by Grazia Deledda, Compton Mackenzie, and Joseph Kessel, plus some assorted news about Phillip Guedalla, Jacques Maritain, and Sigrid Undset.

Although Borges accepted the magazine's layout and format, he soon introduced some changes. In the first place, he chose less obvious writers, both for the biographies and for the reviews. Instead of writing about best-sellers or Nobel prizewinners, Borges in the first three months discussed Carl Sandburg, Virginia Woolf, Lion Feuchtwanger, T. E. Lawrence, Benedetto Croce, Victoria Sackville-West, Edgar Lee Masters, Louis Golding, and Oswald Spengler. He also gave samples, in his own translations, of the writers reviewed—a poem by Sandburg or a fragment of Mrs. Woolf's *Orlando.* And he shunned the impersonality of criticism, always writing in the first person, making statements that were very idiosyncratic. As a matter of fact, the section so thoroughly reflects his own likes and dislikes that it offers perhaps the best introduction to his critical mind. It is a hospita-

ble and curious mind but it is also a mind that knows, and even pa-
rades, its limitations. Borges is very frank about his habits as a reader,
admitting that he hadn't succeeded in getting to the last page of some
very famous books (Dostoevski's *The Brothers Karamazov* and Flaubert's
Madame Bovary are prominent among the unreadable ones) and that he
has a weakness for second-rate books with interesting plots (detective
novels, science-fiction stories). Sometimes he even indicates the exact
amount of time he spent reading a certain book: two successive nights,
from nine o'clock on; or a whole afternoon and an evening. But what
makes his handling of the section so peculiar is his inexhaustible and
perfect timing. Even the less promising subjects (a biography of Joan of
Arc, Spengler's biography) are made irresistible by his irony and gift
for paradox.

The scope of the section was truly encyclopedic; as sources,
Borges used some biographical dictionaries, the *Columbia Encyclopedia*
of 1935 (edited by Clarke F. Ansley), some reputable journals (the
Nouvelle Revue Française, the *Times Literary Supplement*), and press re-
leases from American and European publishers. He also had a passion
for book browsing, which can be detected in allusions to the best English bookstore in Buenos Aires at the time (Mitchell's). Under Borges,
the section lived up to its subtitle, "A Guide to Reading." The question
that probably arose in many literary circles then was: How many of *El
Hogar*'s readers could avail themselves of such a cicerone, one who
guided them unflinchingly through French, English, Italian, and German books, one who would not hesitate to recommend a philosophical
interpretation of history (Spengler's) on the same page that he praised
a murder story (Golding's *The Pursuer*) or a biography of an imaginary
poet (Mrs. Woolf's *Orlando*)? Borges wrote as if every reader of *El
Hogar* was as polyglot as he was. It was a large assumption. The fact
that the section survived for almost three years, until mid-1939, proves
that if few of the readers of *El Hogar* read, or even attempted to
peruse, the books Borges mentioned or reviewed, at least they loved to
read about them and probably used his witty remarks as suitable (not
attributed) quotations at the cocktail parties they attended.

It was at that time that I first came across Borges' name. I was
reading *El Hogar* (October 30, 1936) and found in the "Foreign Books
and Authors" section a short biography of Virginia Woolf which included a page from *Orlando,* some odd reviews—a book of songs from
the Mississippi, an Ellery Queen detective novel, a novel by Henry de
Montherlant, a reissue of a study of neurotic writers by Arvede
Barine—and a note headed "Literary Life" that was devoted to Joyce
and included an anecdote of his meeting with Yeats. (Joyce was quoted
as saying to Yeats that it was a pity they hadn't met before because

"now you are said to be influenced by me.") I was barely fifteen then and was promptly seduced by Borges' wit and impeccable style and the vast range of his reading. From *El Hogar* I graduated to *Sur* and in no time began to comb Montevideo's bookshops for Borges' own books. I found one of the many unsold copies of *A Universal History of Infamy* (1935) and a secondhand copy of *Inquisiciones* (1925). In 1936 or 1937 those books were not the collector's items they are today.

If I was unaware at the time of the momentous decision I was making in allowing myself to become a Borges addict, I was totally conscious of the unique value of Borges' criticism and of the rare quality of his style. My case was not so singular as it seems, and that is why I mention it. For many young readers, Borges was already beginning to perform the task of mentor: the wittiest, the most irreverent mentor that ever was. In a sense, the page he published every two weeks in *El Hogar* was, and still is, the best possible introduction to his mind and work.

8.
The Start of a Lifelong Collaboration

Although Borges had several literary outlets—the fortnightly book page in *El Hogar,* his almost monthly contributions to *Sur,* some occasional articles for *La Prensa*'s literary supplement—in 1936 he helped Bioy Casares to start a new literary magazine, *Destiempo* (Untime). The journal was as odd as its title. It consisted of exactly six pages in tabloid format, published monthly. Only three issues came out, of which the third seems irretrievably lost. Both Bioy Casares and Borges claim to have mislaid their copies, and in Sergio Provenzano's noted collection of Argentine literary magazines only the first two issues (October and November 1936) survive. Another oddity: neither Bioy Casares' nor Borges' name is on the masthead, which carries only the name of Ernesto Pissavini as "secretario," or editor. Recently Bioy Casares admitted that Pissavini was the janitor of his apartment house, on 174 Avenida Quintana.

The two extant issues show that the magazine was a rather private affair. All the well-known contributors (the Mexican writer Alfonso Reyes, the critic Pedro Henríquez Ureña, the Argentine poet Fernández Moreno, the local metaphysician Macedonio Fernández) were mentors or friends of Borges. Among the not so well known—the poet Carlos Mastronardi, the linguist and painter Xul-Solar, the short-story writer Manuel Peyrou—Borges' friends predominated. Even the translations—one of a story by Kafka, a second from Erskine Caldwell—indicate his preferences at the time. Another Borgesian contribution was the section called "Museum," which featured fragments of curious and unknown works. Some of these fragments were perhaps invented. Borges' signed contributions were few: a collection of four short pieces, under the general title of "Inscriptions," three of which had already been published in *Crítica* (September 15, 1934). The only one that was new was, characteristically, a "Dialogue About a Dialogue," in which A and Z discuss a conversation A had once with Macedonio Fernández about suicide, in which they had come to the conclusion that they ought to try it. Z's only contribution to the dialogue is this observation:

z (teasingly): But I suspect you decided against it.
A (lost in a mystical trance): Frankly, I do not remember if we tried it that evening. (*Destiempo*, October 1936, p. 3)

Bioy Casares' contributions were less polished. He was then only twenty-two and was still trying to tame an undisciplined surrealist imagination.

Silvina Ocampo also contributed regularly to *Destiempo*. The journal was underwritten by Bioy Casares' family. They owned a large dairy ranch plus some 130 milk bars in Buenos Aires alone; the chain was called "La Martona" in honor of Bioy's mother, Marta Casares. If the advertisement for the Bioys' dairy products published in *Destiempo*'s first issue was rather sober, the one in the second was less so; it began:

Yoghurt "La Martona"
Disintoxicating food recommended
to those who lead a sedentary life
(*Destiempo*, November 1936, p. 6)

It is possible to detect Borges' voice in that sound piece of advice.

About this time Bioy and Borges spent a week on the family ranch in Pardo in order to write a "commercial pamphlet, apparently scientific, about the merits of some more or less Bulgarian food," as Bioy recalls. The unnamed "Bulgarian food" is, of course, yoghurt. "It was cold, the house was in ruins, we didn't leave the dining room, where some eucalyptus logs crackled in the fireplace. That pamphlet was a valuable lesson to me; after writing it, I was a different writer, more experienced and skillful. Any collaboration with Borges is the equivalent of years of work" (Bioy Casares, 1968, p. 140).

Bioy also recalls some of the other things they did that week. They attempted to write an enumerative sonnet, of which one line read: "The mills, the angels, the *l*'s" (ibid., p. 141). They discussed a detective story, based on Borges' ideas, about a Dr. Pretorius, a "vast and smooth" German headmaster who, using games and pleasant music, tortured children to death. This story, never written, was the germ of their collaboration much later under the pseudonyms of Bustos Domecq and Suárez Lynch. In his recollections Bioy also mentions *Destiempo:*

> The title indicated our desire to escape the superstitions of the time. We objected especially to the tendency of some critics to overlook the intrinsic qualities of some works and to waste time on their folkloric, telluric aspects, or on those that had to do with literary history or the statistical and sociological disciplines. We believed that the notable antecedents of a literary school were sometimes as worthy of oblivion as the inevitable trilogies on the gauchos, middle-class seamstresses, etc. (Ibid., p. 143)

About the publication of the first issue of *Destiempo,* he offers this anecdote: "On the September morning we came out of the Colombo print shop with the journal's first issue, Borges suggested, half jokingly, half seriously, that we ought to have a picture taken for posterity. We did it at a modest neighborhood photographer. The photograph got lost so quickly that I can't even remember it" (ibid., p. 143).

For Bioy, *Destiempo* must have been a valuable first experience as editor. For Borges, it meant a diversion from more important literary projects. In those years his contributions to *El Hogar* and *Sur* took up most of his time. His output was extraordinary, both in quantity and quality. Apart from writing his twice-a-month section for *El Hogar,* he contributed to the magazine page-long articles on assorted literary subjects. In 1936 he commented on Eugene O'Neill's Nobel Prize (November 13) and celebrated the twenty-five years of poetic silence of one of Argentina's leading poets, Enrique Banchs (December 25), a writer who had influenced, with his meticulous, reticent sonnets, both Father and Borges. In 1937 he published seven special articles on subjects as diverse as the Huxleys' intellectual dynasty (January 15); the death of Unamuno (January 29); Buenos Aires as a city hospitable to provincial Argentine writers (February 26); Kipling's autobiography (March 26); a reevaluation of Jorge Isaacs' *María,* the most famous of Latin America's romantic novels (May 7); and a commentary on Raymond Lull's thinking machine (October 15). Some of these articles could be seen as an extension of his "Foreign Books and Authors" section, but the rest were on Hispanic subjects and showed how much *El Hogar* had taken to Borges. The article on Lugones (February 26, 1937)—in which he recanted his ultraist past and praised the old poet—was the object of a rejoinder from a former ultraist poet and colleague, Eduardo González Lanuza (March 12). Borges did not reply to Lanuza's well-reasoned arguments; he had already made up his mind about the subject, and nothing was going to change it.

During that same period, he also contributed regularly to *Sur.* In the magazine's first seven years (1931–1937) his name appears in eleven of its thirty-nine issues, and in some issues he had collaborations (see especially Summer 1932, September 1936, and December 1936). He wrote articles on philosophical, literary, and social subjects, book and film reviews; and, after years of poetical silence, he published a poem, "Insomnia" (December 1936). Some of the work he did for *Sur* overlapped with his writing for *El Hogar*. A note about Chesterton in *Sur* (July 1936) preceded two reviews of his books in *El Hogar* (*The Paradoxes of Mr. Pond*, May 14, 1936; *Autobiography*, October 1, 1937). An article on T. E. Lawrence's translation of the *Odyssey* in *Sur* (October 1936) anticipated by a month a review of a new biography of Lawrence of Arabia in *El Hogar* (November 13). Reviews of two novels by H. G. Wells in *El Hogar* (*Star Begotten*, July 25, 1937; *Brynhild*, October 29, 1937) followed a long review of William Cameron Menzies' movie version of Wells' *Things to Come* in *Sur* (November 1936). On the occasion of Unamuno's death, he wrote two quite different articles with subtly different titles: "Unamuno's Immortality" for *Sur* (January 1937) and "Miguel de Unamuno's Presence" for *El Hogar* (January 29, 1937). In a sense, his book reviewing in *Sur* can be seen as an extension of the work he was doing for *El Hogar*.

What was new in his contributions to *Sur* in that period was his film criticism. Borges had been a film buff since his childhood, but not until the late 1920s did he start writing regularly about movies. An article in *La Prensa*, "El cinematógrafo, el biógrafo" (April 28, 1929), played in its title with the two terms most generally used in the River Plate area to designate the "seventh art." While the upper middle classes preferred "cinematógrafo" as a more fashionable word, the lower middle classes and the workers used the old-fashioned "biógrafo," a relic from the heyday of the Biograph Company. But Borges did more than just play with words in that article; he also wrote perceptively about Chaplin's *The Gold Rush*. He started to review films in *Sur* by the third issue (Winter 1931). It took some effort to persuade Victoria Ocampo that the journal ought to include regular reviews. In his conversations with Jean de Milleret, Borges mentions Victoria's reluctance to include in her journal (which she saw as an anthology of the best possible writing) such ephemeral items as reviews of plays, movies, concerts, and books. Borges, on the other hand, believed them to be "the life of the magazine . . . all that the reader wants to find" (De Milleret, 1967, p. 60).

The first article Borges wrote, under the modest title "Films," comments on Fedor Ozep's *Der Mörder Dimitri Karamasov* (a 1931 German adaptation of Dostoevski's novel), Chaplin's *City Lights*, and von Sternberg's *Morocco*. While informing the reader about his opinions, Borges sketches briefly but firmly the basic differences between the

German, French, and North American cinemas of the time. Short, tantalizing references to other movies, and even to Garbo's "zenithal shoulders," indicate his familiarity with the medium. That article was the first of eleven that appeared up to the end of 1937. In them, he reviewed films by King Vidor, John Ford, von Sternberg, William Cameron Menzies, Alfred Hitchcock, and James Whale, as well as lesser-known directors. He also reviewed two Argentine films: Luis Saslavsky's *La fuga* (Escape), which he praised with some qualifications, and Manuel Romero's *Los muchachos de antes no usaban gomina* (The Boys of Yesteryear Did Not Use Hair Tonic), an apologia for old-fashioned machismo which Borges killed with one joke: "It is one of the best Argentine movies I've seen; that is, one of the world's worst" (Cozarinsky, 1974, p. 52).

If Victoria needed persuasion to let Borges review films in *Sur,* she was determined to have him translate some of her favorite authors. She commissioned three translations: André Gide's *Persephone* (first published in *Sur* and later issued in pamphlet form by the same magazine, 1936); Virginia Woolf's *A Room of One's Own* (in pamphlet form, 1937) and *Orlando* (1937). Borges had already attracted *El Hogar's* readers to the last in a capsule biography of Virginia Woolf which he illustrated with a fragment from *Orlando* (October 30, 1936). In judging the novel, he stressed its originality: "undoubtedly Virginia Woolf's most intense and one of the most singular and hopeless books of our time." He added: "Magic, bitterness, and joy collaborate in this book. It is, also, a musical book, not only in the euphonic virtues of its prose but in the structure of its composition, made of a limited number of themes which return and intertwine." The translation was soon to become a model. Borges had succeeded in keeping in Spanish the musical quality of Mrs. Woolf's prose.

Borges later attempted to disclaim responsibility for the translation. Writing about Mother's translations from the English, he claims in the "Autobiographical Essay" that she was the real author of those that had been attributed to him, and he mentions specifically the translations of Melville, Virginia Woolf, and William Faulkner ("Essay," 1970, p. 207). But in talking about his work of the period, he says explicitly: "On holidays, I translated Faulkner and Virginia Woolf" (ibid., p. 242). A lapse of memory, a friendly hoax, a filial accolade? It is hard to say. Probably Mother helped him with those translations. She may have even done the first draft. But the Spanish style is so unmistakably Borgesian that it would have taken Mother years of hard labor to be able to imitate it. The most one can safely assume is that, in helping him, she became another of his already distinguished corps of collaborators.

The same year, 1937, another collaboration came to light. It was the *Classical Anthology of Argentine Literature,* which Borges edited with Pedro Henríquez Ureña. Borges' friendship with the Dominican critic and scholar dated from the 1920s. He had always admired Ureña's vast knowledge and his reticent style. In a review of Ureña's collection of essays, *Seis ensayos en busca de nuestra expresión* (Six Essays in Search of Our Expression), in *La Palabra* (September 30, 1928, p. 11), Borges praised both the style and the careful research each of the six pieces reveals. In joining forces with Henríquez Ureña for this anthology, Borges accepted a secondary role. Henríquez Ureña was fifteen years his senior, and his knowledge of Latin American literature was vaster and more balanced than Borges'. As usual, Borges disclaimed any responsibility for the book. He once told me that it was done entirely by Henríquez Ureña. Perhaps, but it is possible that Borges suggested at least some less obvious authors such as William Henry Hudson, who was born in Argentina and wrote in English about River Plate subjects. In the anthology Hudson is rightfully considered one of Argentina's classic authors. Borges had already written about one of his masterpieces, *The Purple Land,* in the second *Proa* (November 1925). Some years later he wrote a definitive piece on that same book for an anthology of Hudson's prose, published in Buenos Aires in 1947. Later he included the piece in *Other Inquisitions* (1952), thus certifying his constant interest in a novel that for him was "perhaps unexcelled by any work of gaucho literature" (*Inquisitions,* 1964, p. 142). There is no record that Henríquez Ureña had ever praised Hudson so much.

9.
The Pen and the Sword

World War II was approaching. In Europe, Mussolini started his imperial expansion by attacking Abyssinia in 1935 and challenging British naval supremacy in the Mediterranean. After occupying the Rhineland, Hitler was putting pressure on Austria in the second stage of his plan to recover the lost pieces of the mystical Fatherland. In the Soviet Union, Stalin had successfully crushed the last remnants of an alternative socialism (Trotsky had found temporary refuge in Mexico) and was getting ready for the inevitable confrontation with Germany. In the Far East, Japan was methodically carving an empire out of a divided and weak China. England and France were major powers, but they were overwhelmed by national unrest, economic crises, and social demands. The United States was coming out of the Depression with a president who was both an aristocrat and a populist. In that scheme of things, Latin America had no say. It was a formerly colonized continent that was still economically dependent on the major European powers.

The example of fascism in two of the most important European countries helped to promote it in Latin America. In Brazil, Getulio Vargas designed his own version of the corporate state, while Plinio Salgado paraded his Green Shirts to match Mussolini's Black and Hitler's Brown Shirts. In Chile, General Ibáñez was a harsh ruler. Even in democratic and small Uruguay, a mild coup d'état secured President Terra's power for a long while.

Argentina was ruled by General Justo with the complicity of the army and all the trappings of democracy. Economically and financially, Argentina still belonged to the sterling area: its meat and wheat were marketed chiefly in England. But politically it was closer to the fascism of Mussolini and, by association, to Hitler's Nazism. Some of the leading army officers were of Italian descent and went back to the mother country to study the regime and pay homage to Il Duce. One of the brightest was Juan Domingo Perón, who was ready to believe that the Italian model could be easily imported into Argentina to prevent economic chaos and fight creeping communism. He was not the only one with this belief.

When, following the outbreak of the Spanish civil war in July 1936, Franco asked for and got help from Italy and Germany, the Argentines found another powerful motive to sympathize with fascism. Many were of Spanish extraction and saw Franco as the savior of Spain's tradition and culture. For the upper and middle classes of Argentina, it was fashionable to be very Catholic and fascist. The government shared both ideologies. On the other hand, the liberal tradition of French culture and the appeal of the British style of life were powerful among the smaller journals like *Sur* and colored the selection of topics and authors in the larger journals *La Nación* and *La Prensa*. Even in *El Hogar* that tradition was accepted, although the magazine catered to the conservative taste of a middle-class, Catholic, feminine audience. Another group, the left-wing intelligentsia, gathered together—under an uneasy alliance—Socialists, Communists, and even anarchists.

As if to show how few political differences existed between these groups, the reaction of both *Sur* and the left-wing intellectuals toward the Spanish civil war was similar. They shared a liberal attitude in spite of so-called ideological differences. It was the time of the popular fronts in France and Spain, the time of ironing out differences in the face of fascism, the common enemy; and although *Sur* did not participate in this movement under its banner, many of its contributors did. In the opposite camp, the Catholic and fascist establishment closed ranks around Franco and his allies. If the inane dispute between "Florida" and "Boedo" had divided the *Martín Fierro* contributors into opposite bands, now the fight for Spain, and the coming fight for Europe, would divide the Argentine intelligentsia even more drastically—although along different lines. Writers such as Leopoldo Marechal and Francisco Luis Bernárdez were to come to the defense of the Catholic establishment, while Victoria Ocampo, Eduardo Mallea, and Borges would be in the opposite camp. It was in that context that the Fourteenth International Congress of the PEN Club met in Buenos Aires on September 5–15, 1936.

The proceedings of the meeting—published in Buenos Aires in 1937—do not make for amusing reading. Some of the stars of the international PEN Club were unable to be present. André Gide was off visiting the USSR, a fateful journey that was to mark the end of his short affair with Stalinism. H. G. Wells, the PEN Club's president, was too busy with his own work to attend and sent, like Gide, a warm message. Most of the members who came to Buenos Aires either were unknown then (one, Halldor Laxness, from Iceland, eventually won a Nobel Prize in 1955) or would never show any other title to fame but their membership in the club. Still, enough truly important writers arrived to make the occasion an elaborate production. The Spanish philosopher José Ortega y Gasset and the Mexican humanist Alfonso Reyes were among the guests of honor; but if they attended the sessions, they did not participate in any of the debates. The Colombian Baldomero Sanin Cano's only function was to preside over one session. The Argentine delegation included Carlos Ibarguren, who was also the president of the congress; Victoria Ocampo, who served as vice-president; Manuel Gálvez, a naturalist novelist of large popular appeal; and Eduardo Mallea, Victoria's protégé and one of the most distinguished young writers of the time.

The fact that both the president of the congress and Gálvez were notoriously sympathetic to fascism gave a certain Alice in Wonderland flavor to the proceedings. The PEN Club had been created in the 1920s to defend culture and literature from every variety of censorship and oppression. As Wells had put it in his message: "Our club . . . is . . . small but it carries an immense and splendid banner: that of free thinking and open discussion" (PEN, 1936, p. 33). At the time the PEN Club was meeting in Buenos Aires, that freedom had already been destroyed in Italy and Germany, had been severely limited in the Soviet Union by the official association of writers, and was being attacked successfully in Spain. But not only were the citizens of these countries persecuted for their ideas. A whole group of intellectuals, among the most important in the Western world, were being deprived of physical freedom and even of their lives for belonging to the Jewish community. Racism in Germany had openly killed or exiled some of the most distinguished writers in the German language. Among the guests of the PEN Club congress were two representatives of that group: the Austrian Stefan Zweig and the German Emil Ludwig.

Also among the guests were two prominent Fascists: the one-time futurist Filippo Tommaso Marinetti and the poet Giuseppe Ungaretti. There was an almost epic clash between Marinetti and some of the liberal participants, particularly two members of the French delegation, the novelist Jules Romains (who was then completing his monumental saga *Les hommes de bonne volonté*) and Benjamin Crémieux, of Jewish extraction and a specialist in Italian literature. The exchange gave the PEN Club debates—generally bland to the point of being soporific—an unusual tone. Emil Ludwig contributed an acerbic speech in which he denounced the Hitler regime. Members of the audience came vocally to the defense of intellectual freedom; they were not reticent in demonstrating their disgust for Marinetti's histrionics and fascist rhetoric. In the end, concord prevailed, especially because the avowed policy of the PEN Club was to bring writers together in a peace movement that would help to avoid war.

The paradox was that the regime that hosted the congress and even the president of the congress were more sympathetic to Franco and Mussolini than to the democratic regimes to which they paid lip service. If the general tone of the debates was political, the papers read at the conference oscillated between the obvious and the tedious. With a few exceptions—the Belgian poet Henri Michaux, the Franco-Uruguayan Jules Supervielle, the Catholic philosopher Jacques Maritain (who was a Jew)—the participants were neither original nor brilliant. Comic relief was provided by Marinetti's gross misinterpretation of a reference made in a speech by Victoria Ocampo. Attempting to define her literary position as that of a "common reader" and acknowledging her debt to both Virginia Woolf and Samuel Johnson for that expression, Victoria had to suffer the humiliation of having Marinetti distort her words. He seemed to take them as a defense of the common man and as a not too subtle exhortation to write for the lowest possible readership. Victoria attempted lamely to explain that her "common reader" was a cultivated and almost specialized type. Marinetti's ignorance of both Dr. Johnson and Mrs. Woolf made him unresponsive. Victoria had to ask for extra time to restore her words to their original meaning.

As usual in this type of meeting, many words were produced, many egos were exhibited, and very little was accomplished. The importance of the congress resided exclusively in its place and time. Argentina in 1936 was hardly the locale where a liberal organization such as the PEN Club could speak its mind—but then how many places were still left in the world? The fact that the Fascist delegation succeeded in having Italy appointed as the meeting place for the next congress, with Japan chosen as host for 1940, indicates very clearly that the PEN Club was hopelessly confused about the future.

Although Victoria Ocampo and Eduardo Mallea participated rather actively in the congress, Borges seems not to have attended. He was not listed among the guests of honor or participants, although he was already better known, nationally and internationally, than both Victoria and Mallea. There was a very good reason. At the time, Borges hated to speak in public. Even in small gatherings, he was uncomfortable and quickly developed an audible stammer. He had always refused to lecture, and on the rare occasions when he accepted, he had his paper read by a friend while he sat in the back mouthing every word of a text he knew by heart. But he probably had other motives in avoiding the PEN Club congress. He did not suffer fools easily, and literary congresses are generally the province of fools. But he was well informed about what was going on in the congress. In *El Hogar* (September 17, 1937, p. 24), reviewing Jules Romains' long poem *L'homme blanc,* Borges identifies Romains as the one who "demolished" Marinetti at the PEN Club congress. That is the only allusion to the congress in his writings, but it is not the only political dig against Marinetti that Borges made during those years.

In another short notice written for *El Hogar* (March 4, 1938, p. 24) he laughed at one of Marinetti's new "inventions." According to a telegram from Rome, he had recommended that Italian women add to the red of their lips and nails a "light touch of the green of the Lombard plains and the white of the Alpine snows." In Borges' witty retort, those "attractive tricolor lips will utter perfect words of love and kindle the desire for a kiss in those rude soldiers who return undefeated from the wars." He also ridiculed another of Marinetti's "inventions": the substitution of sound native words for all foreign expressions which are contaminating the Italian language. Instead of the French "chic," Italians ought to use "elettrizzante" (electrifying); instead of "bar," they ought to indicate "qui si beve" (here one drinks). After pointing out that each Italian expression is longer than the foreign one, Borges stresses the similarity between Marinetti's puritanism and the preoccupations of conservative bodies such as the Spanish Royal Academy of Language. The conclusion to the short piece is that the one-time futurist impresario is not up to this kind of joke. Even more damaging is the beginning of the article: "F. T. Marinetti is perhaps the most famous example of the kind of writer who lives by his inventions and who hardly ever invents anything."

People who have come lately to Borges' work, with little knowledge of his intellectual and ideological development, tend to think that he was and is totally apolitical. The truth is that Borges always had political opinions, but as he was brought up by Father to be an intellectual anarchist (not a political one), his opinions depended less on the ephemeral strategy of newspaper headlines or the compulsion to get a place in the sun than on the deep conviction that the less government of any kind the better. He thus favored, in general, democracy, because it allowed a sort of balance of power and rejected all one-party regimes because they made dissent almost impossible. True, while a teenager in Geneva, Georgie had admired bloody revolutions and had even sung to the Red Dawn of Moscow. But soon he came to the conclusion that revolutions only change the staff while perpetuating the bureaucracy of power. In Argentine politics he only once made a feeble attempt to participate in political life, at the time of Irigoyen's second bid for the presidency. After Irigoyen proved to be inept and was deposed by the army, Borges' political skepticism grew and hardened. He stopped having anything to do with local politics; only World War II would make him react strongly.

In the meantime, he took advantage of *El Hogar* to load his "Guide to Reading" with political digs and plainly stated ideological arguments. A few references to the Spanish civil war can be gleaned here and there. One is a review (March 18, 1938, p. 14) of H. G. Wells' novel *The Brothers,* which was set in Spain at the time of the civil war. Borges stressed the rather obvious parable about the twins who command the two sides of the war, and the pedagogical solution put forth by Wells: men had to be better educated to avoid wars. About the war, which was coming to a tragic conclusion with the victory of the Fascists, Borges said nothing, but it is obvious which side he was on, by the mere fact that he liked the novel and liked the author even more. Several of Wells' new books were reviewed in *El Hogar* over a two-year period: *The Croquet Player* (February 3, 1937, p. 36); *Star Begotten* (July 23, 1937, p. 30); *Brynhild* (October 29, 1937, p. 28); *A Propos of Dolores* (December 2, 1938, p. 89), which he reviewed a second time, in *Sur* (November 1938); and *The Holy Terror* (March 24, 1939, p. 89). Borges' interest in Wells was not exclusively political, of course. He had been reading his works since he was a child and discovered *The First Men on the Moon* and *The Invisible Man.* But the writer Georgie had once read was no longer the writer Borges reviewed. Now the preoccupation with the future of mankind had taken over. Of the six novels reviewed in *El Hogar,* only two (*Brynhild, A Propos of Dolores*) were concerned more with the individual than with the species, and with private problems rather than public destinies.

Not all the reviews Borges wrote of Wells' novels were favorable. On more than one occasion he pointed out obvious faults and observed that although Wells' books were never boring they were not always good. In his review of *The Holy Terror* he observes that it is easy to prove a priori that the novel is unreadable because it is badly shaped. But he also observes that such a course is useless. To convince his reader, he declares: "I—who had been unable to read *Madame Bovary,* or *The Brothers Karamazov,* or *Marius, the Epicurean,* or *Vanity Fair*—have read in a day and a night this formless novel. The fact is telling." It is, of course, in more than one sense. It tells about Borges' impatience with some "classics of the novel"; it also reveals his interest in the literature that was then being written. The Wells of that period had for Borges the prestige of being a modern writer.

In reviewing *The Brothers,* Borges singles out one sentence: "Marx stinks of Herbert Spencer and Herbert Spencer stinks of Marx." He does not expand on Wells' utterance, but it is obvious that he was pleased with the link thus established between the holy text of socialism and the representative of old-fashioned positivism. In Wells, Borges found ammunition to fight the pomposities and fallacies of the totalitarians.

Discussing Kipling in an article published in *El Hogar* (March 26, 1937, p. 9), Borges observes that while Kipling's works are more complex than the ideas they are supposed to illustrate, the reverse is true about Marxist art: "The thesis is complex, because it comes out of Hegel, but the art that illustrates it is rudimentary." On another occasion, while discussing Isaac Babel's life, he comments ironically on the fact that Babel had to fight the czarist bureaucracy only to have to face the Soviet bureaucracy. At the time Borges wrote that article for *El Hogar* (February 4, 1938), he obviously did not know that Babel was already in disgrace and that he would become one of the most prominent victims of Stalinism.

In another article (December 2, 1938) he discusses the Marxist point of view in literature. The pretext is a manifesto called "For an Independent Revolutionary Art," signed by André Breton and the Mexican painter Diego Rivera. In the title of his article, "Copious Manifesto by Breton," Borges calls his reader's attention to the French poet's authorship. In a short introductory paragraph Borges laughs at the avant-garde mania for manifestos and ironically stresses the fact that they generally serve to attack the basis of the art they are talking about. If signed by writers, they attack rhyme and metaphor; if by painters, they vindicate (or insult) the basic colors; if by musicians, they praise cacophony; if by architects, they prefer a gas station to Milan's "excessive cathedral." Borges quickly reaches the conclusion that every one of these silly pamphlets has been surpassed by the one "emitted" by Breton and Rivera. After quoting the pamphlet's full title (a subtitle also claims to be in favor of the "final liberation of art"), Borges observes that the text is even more emotional and stuttering than the title:

It consisted of some three thousand words that say exactly two things (that are incompatible). The first is . . . that art should be free and it isn't in Russia. Rivera-Breton observe: "Under the influence of the USSR's totalitarian regime, a deep dusk has fallen over the entire world, hostile to all kinds of spiritual values. A dusk of mud and blood in which, disguised as intellectuals and artists, men who have made a resource of servilism, a game of the denial of their principles, a habit of venal false testimony, and a pleasure of the apology of crime, practice their deceptions. The official art of the Stalinist era reflects their ridiculous efforts to cheat and disguise their mercenary role. . . . To those who urge us, be it today or tomorrow, to admit that art can be submitted to a discipline we consider radically incompatible with its means, we oppose a refusal without any appellation, and our deliberate decision to stick to the formula "All sorts of license in art."

What conclusion can we draw from those words? I believe this, and only this: Marxism (like Lutheranism, the moon, a horse, a line from Shakespeare) may be an incitement to art, but it is absurd to postulate that it is the only one. It is absurd to believe that art is a department of politics. However, that is what this incredible manifesto claims. As soon as Breton has printed the formula "All sorts of license in art," he repents his daring and dedicates two furtive pages to denying that reckless statement. He rejects "political indifference," attacks pure art, "which generally serves the most impure aims of reaction," and proclaims "that the supreme task of contemporary art is to participate consciously and actively in the preparation of revolution." Immediately he proposes "the organization of modest local and international congresses." Urged to exhaust the excesses of rhymed prose, he announces that "in the next stage [of the plan] there will be world congresses which officially will celebrate the foundation of the International Federation of Independent Revolutionary Art (IFIRA)."

Poor independent art they are concocting, subordinated to pedantic committees and five capital letters! (*El Hogar,* December 2, 1938, p. 89)

In attacking Breton, Borges once more stood at a distance to judge the avant-garde. In the same way he had already rejected ultraism and futurism, he was now implicitly rejecting surrealism, which he mistakenly took to be a mere offshoot of dadaism and, especially, of German expressionism.

He had other points of disagreement. Borges' rejection of Freud and his theories could also explain his distaste for a movement that relied so much on Freud.

The article appeared at a time when surrealism was fighting to avoid being engulfed by Stalinism. But Borges was unaware of that dramatic situation. He cared little about French, or Latin American, literary strategy. He was also unaware of the fact—revealed only much later—that the real co-author of the pamphlet was not Rivera but Trotsky. The manifesto was written as a consequence of a visit to Mexico made by Breton in 1938.

If Borges was disdainful of Marinetti and futurism, attacked fascism and Stalinism, and laughed at Breton's attempts to find a way out of "revolutionary" art, he reserved his harsher political criticism for Nazism. The most damaging references contained in the articles he published in *El Hogar* are addressed to Nazism's destruction of German culture, to anti-Semitism and the cult of war. In a short review of a

German school primer on racism, *Trau keinem Jud bei seinem Eid* (literally: *Trust No Jew by His Oath*), Borges describes without any comments some of the book's illustrations:

> The first . . . is based on the thesis that the "Devil is the Jew's father."
> The second represents a Jewish creditor who confiscates the pigs and the cow of his debtor.
> The third [shows] the perplexity of a German miss, overwhelmed by a lecherous Jew who offers her a necklace.
> The fourth [shows] a Jewish millionaire (with a cigar and a Turkish cap) driving out two beggars of the Nordic race.
> The fifth [is] a Jewish butcher who tramples on meat.
> The sixth celebrates the decision of a German girl who refuses to buy a puppet at a Jewish toy shop.
> The seventh accuses Jewish lawyers; the eighth, doctors.
> The ninth comments on Jesus' words "The Jew is an assassin."
> The tenth, unexpectedly Zionist, shows a pitiful line of expelled Jews, set for Jerusalem.
> There are twelve more, no less ingenious and indisputable. Of the text itself, it would be enough to translate these verses: "The German Führer is loved by German children; God in heaven is loved by them; the Jew is despised." And then: "Germans walk, Jews crawl." (*El Hogar*, May 20, 1937, p. 26)

Two more references to the anti-Semitic campaign that was then at its shrillest in Germany can be found in *El Hogar*. One is a review (June 11, 1937) of a catalogue produced by Insel-Verlag, one of Germany's biggest publishing houses. In going over it, Borges stresses the fact that it contains only twenty-four new titles and observes that that is a very small number for such a house. Examining the books more closely, he discovers that the protagonist of one of six novels devoted to "proclaiming the merits of fishermen, woodsmen, and peasants is an unforgettable blond giant." Another book praises the founders of the British empire; a third admires the military ethic of the samurai. There is also an illustrated volume of anecdotes on the life of Frederick the Great. Another volume, *Form and Soul*, contains sixty-four reproductions of Leo von Köning's paintings, which "reflect mankind today in its most unmistakable representatives: the soldier (Hindenburg), the politician (Goebbels), the sportsman (von Cramm)." Borges also mentions *Goethe and the Olympic Idea*, a book that naturally won a prize given by the Committee on Olympic Games in Germany and that pretended to demonstrate "the importance of gymnastics in Goethe's life and thought." After this cursory examination, he reaches a terse conclusion: "Germany, literarily, is poor."

A very short item in *El Hogar* (September 3, 1937) informs the reader: "Ludendorff's magazine, *From the Sacred Source of German Strength*, continues from Munich its inexorable and fortnightly campaign against Jews, the Pope, the Buddhists, the masons, the theosophists, the Society of Jesus, communism, Dr. Martin Luther, England, and Goethe's memory." Ludendorff was one of the heroes of World War I. In another article Borges reviews a new edition of one of his most popular works, *Der Totale Krieg* (Total War). In rejecting Ludendorff's prophecies, Borges observes:

> In fifteenth-century Italy, war reached a perfection many people would call ridiculous. When two armies came face to face, generals compared the number, courage, and readiness of the opposing force and thus decided which one had to accept defeat. Chance had been eliminated, and the spilling of blood. That way of making war would not merit perhaps the lovable expression "totalitarian," but I found it wiser and more lucid than the vast sacrifice of millions of men which Ludendorff prophesies. (*El Hogar,* January 21, 1938, p. 26)

Borges' irony is at its best here. The trouble is that the joke is on him. Ludendorff was right in his prophecies. In less than two years' time Germany would begin to move its catastrophic war machine. But if Borges was wrong about the nearness of war, or about its "totalitarian" character, he knew perfectly well what war was about. While in Europe, he had shared the horror of the young for the World War I holocaust. In reviewing *The Men I Killed,* a book by the British general F. P. Crozier, Borges points out the irony in the title: the general is alluding less to the enemies he has ordered killed than to his own soldiers— cowardly men who are killed by their own officers or comrades to prevent panic in battles. They die for their country, but not in the way they are expected to. With a candor unusual in a man of his rank, Crozier admits that he always had in his battalion a man ready to execute the fainthearted ones. And he concludes: "People do not suspect these things: people imagine that battles are won with courage and not with murder" (*El Hogar,* February 18, 1938, p. 28). Borges observes that the book is dedicated both to those soldiers who "stuck it to the end" in the battlefield and to those pacifists who did it in jail. It is because he knows that war, any war, is genocide that he can find words of praise for this very unusual general.

    El Hogar's women readers were probably not quite ready for these articles. Perhaps for them, Stalinism and anti-Semitism, the Nazis and the Fascists, surrealists and Trotskyites, were too remote. It is to Borges' honor that he never once asked himself if it was wise or profitable to voice such opinions in the Argentina of the time. He went on writing and commenting on books, unaffected by questions of opportunity or convenience, leaving in the pages of the magazine a sort of ironic journal of his reactions to the coming war.

10.
Life in the
Library

In spite of being quite famous in Buenos Aires, Borges was nearing forty without having established his position in Argentine society. The many literary activities in which he was engaged—his regular contributions to *El Hogar, Sur,* and other journals—failed to assure him a regular income. He was still dependent on Father's limited pension, further eroded by inflation, and was in the awkward position of being a mature man living with his parents as if he were still an adolescent. Since Father's health was declining rapidly, Borges realized that he had to secure a permanent job. In 1937, through friends, he found a job at the Miguel Cané municipal library, named after the author of one of the most popular nineteenth-century Argentine books, *Juvenilia,* a humorous account of life in a high school. The library was located on Avenida La Plata and Carlos Calvo, and its director was the poet Francisco Luis Bernárdez, one of Borges' colleagues from the ultraist days.

Reminiscing about his work at the library in the "Autobiographical Essay," Borges begins by summarizing the "small editing tasks" which had up till then been his sole remunerative occupation: the *Crítica* supplement, the book section at *El Hogar,* and some even more obscure work his biographers have failed to identify precisely: "I had also written newsreel texts and had been editor of a pseudo-scientific magazine called *Urbe,* which was really a promotional organ of a privately owned Buenos Aires subway system" ("Essay," 1970, p. 240). Although it seems unfair to lump together his creative contributions to *Crítica* and *El Hogar* with the hack work he also did, the general conclusion he reaches is correct: "These had all been small-paying jobs, and I was long past the age when I should have begun contributing to our household upkeep." He took his first regular full-time job as a first assistant in the Miguel Cané library, which was located, according to him, in "a drab and dreary part of town to the southwest." His position on the library's staff was low: "While there were Second and Third Assistants below me, there were also a Director and First, Second, and Third Officials above me. I was paid two hundred and ten pesos a month and later went up to two hundred and forty. These were sums roughly equivalent to seventy or eighty American dollars" (*ibid.*, pp. 240–241).

The position was also dreary. There was very little work to do, and even that had to be evenly divided among some fifty people. Borges does not conceal his sarcasm in describing his reponsibilities at that patronage-ridden institution:

> At the library, we did very little work. There were some fifty of us producing what fifteen could easily have done. My particular job, shared with fifteen or twenty colleagues, was classifying and cataloguing the library's holdings, which until that time were uncatalogued. The collection, however, was so small that we knew where to find the books without the system, so the system, though laboriously carried out, was never needed or used. The first day, I worked honestly. On the next, some of my fellows took me aside to say that I couldn't do this sort of thing because it showed them up. "Besides," they argued, "as this cataloguing has been planned to give us some semblance of work, you'll put us out of our jobs." I told them I had classified four hundred titles instead of their one hundred. "Well, if you keep that up," they said, "the boss will be angry and won't know what to do with us." For the sake of realism, I was told that from then on I should do eighty-three books one day, ninety another, and one hundred and four the third. (Ibid., p. 241)

In a 1962 interview with James E. Irby, Borges gives a minute description of life at the library. In a sense, that oral report is less reticent and even more personal than the one included in the "Autobiographical Essay." In talking, Borges generally reveals more and even lets his feelings come to the surface more easily. He admits to Irby, for instance, that it was through the influence of some friends that he got a small raise in his salary, under the condition that the friends wouldn't press for another raise for him in the future.

Borges recommended a small collection of English books to improve the library's holdings (Irby, 1962, p. 8). But reading, and the accessibility of books, did not blunt the pain of having to work in such a low position. In the "Essay" Borges is not at all reticent about it: "I stuck to the library for about nine years. They were nine years of solid unhappiness. At work, the other men were interested in nothing but horse racing, soccer matches, and smutty stories. Once, a woman, one of the readers, was raped on her way to the ladies' room. Everybody said such things were bound to happen, since the men's and ladies' rooms were adjoining" ("Essay," 1970, p. 241).

To Irby, Borges confides another anecdote about the hoodlums he had for colleagues: "One day, in the men's room, one of my colleagues took off his shirt to show me the scars he had on his chest, from knife fights he had had." Understandably, Borges concludes: "That whole atmosphere depressed me" (Irby, 1962, p. 8). The irony of the situation is that for many years Georgie had roamed the outskirts of Buenos Aires, slumming for hours, getting acquainted with hoodlums, prostitutes, and pimps and talking endlessly about knife fights, courage, and sex. A great part of Georgie's writings in the late 1920s and early 1930s showed his preoccupation with violence, brutality, and death. But faced with the chance to be on almost intimate terms with such violence, he recoiled with disgust.

The paradox of his predicament was emphasized by the fact that outside of the library Borges' fame continued to grow. If Eliot had been depressed by a clerical job at a bank in London, Borges found his ordeal at the library even more sordid, in violent contrast to the kind of experiences he had outside the library. In the "Autobiographical Essay" he tells a comic anecdote about the difference between these two worlds: "One day, two rather posh and well-meaning friends—society ladies—came to see me at work. They phoned me a day or two later to say, 'You may think it amusing to work in a place like that, but promise us you will find at least a nine-hundred-peso job before the month is out.' I gave them my word that I would" ("Essay," 1970, pp. 241–242). There is a double irony in the situation. The ladies didn't seem to realize that Borges had no way of landing a better job, and he was too proud to tell them the truth. They probably wouldn't have believed it; they thought perhaps that Borges' love for slumming and his rather perverse sense of humor accounted for his choosing such a sordid place to spend his working hours.

If his position was difficult to explain to his friends, it was even more difficult to explain to his colleagues at the library. Borges recalls the humor of the situation: "Ironically, at the time I was a quite well-known writer—except at the library. I remember a fellow employee's once noting in an encyclopedia the name of a certain Jorge Luis Borges—a fact that set him wondering at the coincidence of our identical names and birthdates" (ibid., p. 242). To Irby, he tells a similar anecdote. Some of his colleagues were young lower-middle-class women who always treated him with indifference until one day they found out that he had those posh friends. They were terribly impressed the day Elvira de Alvear, one of the most dazzling of these ladies, phoned Borges to have him for tea. From that day on, the women began to pay attention to him and to ask questions about his friends, whom they tried to emulate. The questions, instead of soothing Borges' pain, must have added to his feeling of being ridiculous. While their male counterparts cared only about races or rape, those young women cared only about what was fashionable to wear that year at Palermo's horse race course.

For Borges, the situation must have been impossible. Although he was at ease with his society friends, he never shared their snobbery or their taste for expensive things. There was nothing in him of the Scott Fitzgeralds of this world. On the contrary, as a member of an old, traditional family with no money or power left, he despised worldly possessions and always had an authentic disinterest in clothes, furniture, houses, cars, and all the other material things that encumber life. If he was a friend of Elvira de Alvear, it was because he was in love with her—hopelessly in love, of course, because Elvira did not love him. But what Borges loved was her eccentricity, not her surname or her fortune. Glimpses of Elvira de Alvear can be seen (conveniently altered to suit the literary needs of the story) in some aspects of Beatriz Viterbo in his story "The Aleph." But it is not a flattering portrait.

And now Borges had the added humiliation of being respected at the library not because he was Borges—that is, one of the best Argentine writers of the time—but because he was Elvira de Alvear's friend. In his interview with Irby he summarizes his predicament: "I found myself in a very awkward position. Many people believed I was a good writer. I contributed to *Sur* and other journals, foreign writers came to Buenos Aires to see me as if I were a famous person. But my everyday life did not agree with that assumed fame: it was a curiously anonymous, annoying life" (Irby, 1962, p. 11). In the "Autobiographical Essay" he adds a few touches that communicate the grimness and pain of his position: "Now and then during these years, we municipal workers were rewarded with gifts of a two-pound package of maté to take home. Sometimes in the evening, as I walked the ten blocks to the tramline, my eyes would be filled with tears. These small gifts from above always underlined my menial and dismal existence" ("Essay," 1970, p. 242). For Borges, and Borges' family, to become a proletarian was the last stage in the journey back to the Haslams' humble rural origins.

If his personal experiences at the Miguel Cané library were humiliating, Borges succeeded, as all good writers do, in transforming them into the most unexpected literary material. He recalls the way he managed to survive the depressing atmosphere of that library: "Though my colleagues thought of me as a traitor for not sharing their boisterous fun, I went on with work of my own in the basement, or, when the weather was warm, up on the flat roof" (ibid., p. 243). Borges is obviously referring to the articles and reviews he wrote for several journals, particularly for *El Hogar* and *Sur*. But he is also alluding to other writing more specifically related to his personal experiences at the library. The most famous of these is his short story "The Library of Babel," which

> was meant as a nightmare version or magnification of that municipal library, and certain details in the text have no particular meaning. The number of books and shelves that I recorded in the story were literally what I had at my elbow. Clever critics have worried over those ciphers, and generously endowed them with mystic significance. "The Lottery in Babylon," "Death and the Compass," and "The Circular Ruins" were written, in whole or part, while I played truant. (Ibid., pp. 243–244)

Originally published in *The Garden of Forking Paths* (1941), "The Library of Babel" seemed so remote from Argentine reality that very few of his readers could have recognized then the subtle hints Borges gives of an "atrocious but commonplace reality," as he once said in another context. The story is full of allusions to the number or shape of the real shelves; there are less obvious references to the small closets where one can sleep standing up or satisfy "fecal necessities" and to the rather mysterious letters that the books have on their spines. They "do not indicate or prefigure what the pages will say," observes Borges in a disguised reference to the signs which indicate the classification of each volume. But what perhaps reflects more poignantly the atmosphere of the Miguel Cané library is the general feeling of despair, of boredom and horror, that the story conveys so effectively. In describing the insane and infinite library, Borges is describing what he felt at the time. He was stuck in an inferior, degrading activity, surrounded by hoodlums or by people who were totally indifferent to the meaning of the function they were supposed to be performing. The library of Babel was infinite and stultifying because Borges was then experiencing the horror of an absurd, pointless job.

A sort of essay version of the same experience was published in *Sur* in August 1939. Called "The Total Library," it was explicitly dedicated to discussing the origin of the concept of a library that included all books. Very formally, Borges traces the utopia of the total library back to Aristotle and Cicero; the latter coined the idea of arbitrarily juggling all the letters of the alphabet to eventually produce, or reproduce, a poetic masterpiece. In the nineteenth century Huxley perfected (or mechanized) the notion by suggesting that half a dozen monkeys, armed with typewriters, could produce, with the help of eternity, all the books contained in the British Museum library. In a note Borges observes that a single immortal monkey would do. Other writers (Lewis

Carroll, Kurd Lasswitz) added interesting details. But what really matters for Borges is not the concept of the infinite that a total library implies but its emotional consequences. In describing the infinite library he produces a chaotic enumeration that includes not only some lost masterpieces (Aeschylus' *The Egyptians*) and Novalis' conjectural encyclopedia, the never written chapters of *Edwin Drood* or Berkeley's unpublished paradoxes on time, but even some very private personal experiences ("my dreams and half-dreams on the morning of August the 14th, 1934"). The final experience conveyed by reading the essay is of chaos, absurdity, and horror. The library's shelves (which were modeled on the Miguel Cané's shelves) create vertigo; they "obliterate the day and in them chaos resides." The conviction that even the horror is "subaltern" (that is, mediocre) adds a touch of commonplace evil to the essay. Before Hannah Arendt, Borges had discovered in his own experience "the banality of evil."

In those years Borges had begun reading Franz Kafka, and it is obvious that both the essay and the story on the total library were under his influence. There are some articles on Kafka in the book page he wrote regularly for *El Hogar*. On August 6, 1937, he reviewed the English translation of *The Trial*, done by Edwin and Willa Muir. Although the review is more informative than critical (Kafka was then totally unknown in Argentina), Borges shows a familiarity with his works, quotes several of his stories, and discusses some of the critical reactions his works had already produced: they are nightmares, they are intense, they can be interpreted from a theological point of view. Borges objects to the last of these interpretations because "they are not inadequate—we know that Kafka was devoted to Pascal and Kierkegaard—but they are not necessary." He also mentions an observation, advanced by "a friend," on the connections between Kafka's fiction and Zeno's paradoxes. The friend might have been Bioy Casares, but perhaps it was only Borges' modest way of masking his own ideas. Many years later he developed this point of view in a now famous essay, "Kafka and His Precursors" (collected in *Other Inquisitions*, 1952).

In a capsule biography of Kafka published in *El Hogar* (October 29, 1937) Borges repeats the observation about Zeno's paradoxes, without quoting any friend. Among the pieces he singles out for praise are several short stories and parables. Many of these he later translated for the first collection of Kafka's stories ever published in Spanish: *La metamorfosis* (The Metamorphosis, Buenos Aires, 1938). It was not his first attempt at translating Kafka. He translated the story "Ante la ley" (Before the Law) for *El Hogar* on May 27, 1938. It comes from an early collection of stories, *A Country Doctor* (Leipzig, 1919) and was later used by Kafka as a parable in *The Trial,* a fact which Borges seems to have overlooked. He did not include it in his collection of Kafka stories.

In the preface to *La metamorfosis* Borges expands and deepens his view of Kafka's life and work. About Kafka's relationship with his father Borges writes, in parentheses: "From that conflict and his stubborn meditations on the strange mercies and unlimited demands of paternal power, he himself has declared, comes his entire work." There is a personal note here. Although Kafka felt, correctly, that he was despised by his father while Borges knew Father loved and even doted on him, there is a curious similarity between the two fathers and the two sons. The expressions Borges uses to define that similarity—"strange mercies" and "unlimited demands"—were applicable in both cases. Borges may have believed that a kind father could be more tyrannical than a harsh one. Talking about World War I and what it meant to Kafka, he observes: "The war's depression is in those works: that oppression whose most atrocious trait is the pretense of happiness and of courageous enthusiasm which forces people into. . . ." Obviously he had come a long way from his youthful enthusiasm for the war poetry of the expressionists.

In evaluating Kafka's work, Borges stresses two ideas, or obsessions, which shape it—subordination and the infinite—and comments briefly on passages in Kafka's novels and tales that illustrate both. He points out that Kafka's critics generally lament that his novels are unfinished, then argues (repeating arguments already advanced in *El Hogar*) that they are "unfinished" deliberately because Kafka wanted to emphasize the infinite number of obstacles their protagonists had to face. Their vicissitudes are as unending as those in hell. He again warns against a theological interpretation of Kafka's work, concluding: "The full enjoyment of Kafka's work . . . may precede any interpretation and does not depend on it." In the last paragraph of the preface he underlines Kafka's most unquestionable virtue: his ability to invent intolerable situations, and observes that Kafka's development of the situation is less admirable than its invention. There is only one character: the *homo domesticus,* so Jewish and German, who only wants a place, no matter how humble, in the order of things, "any Order: the universe, a ministry, an insane asylum, a prison." Plot and atmosphere are, according to Borges, essential in Kafka, "not the evolution of the fable or psychological insight." Thus he believes that his stories are superior to his novels and that a collection of them offers "in its totality the range of this singular writer" (*La metamorfosis,* 1938, p. 11).

The preface takes up only five pages of the small volume, but it contains a complete view of Kafka, and also of Borges. The importance of this volume—which preceded by some months the writing of Borges' first revolutionary story, "Pierre Menard, Author of the *Quixote*," and by three years the publication of his first volume of fantastic stories, *The Garden of Forking Paths*—lies in the fact that it was translated and published at the time Borges was getting ready to take the plunge and devote himself completely to writing fiction. The reading and translating of Kafka helped him to make this decision. In the same way that Eliot began reading and commenting on the English metaphysical poets or the Greek and Elizabethan playwrights at the time he was experimenting with a new form of verse play, Borges studied and discussed Kafka when he was about to begin a new career as a storyteller.

Perhaps his unhappiness at the Miguel Cané library also influenced that decision, for it obviously helped him to understand Kafka's predicament. The library was his ghetto, his penal colony; it was the bureaucratic hell (both horrifying and commonplace) that Kafka presented so well. Out of his misery Borges derived the strength to present not just an ironic, urbane view of the world but a view that showed its real nature. But he had still to go through an experience of symbolical death and rebirth before being able to create his own brand of hell. In the meantime, his daily life replayed the Cinderella myth: hard, unpleasant, degrading conditions of work at the library during the afternoons, and the return to a warm, friendly, affluent world in the evenings. To survive, Borges read incessantly. In his "Autobiographical Essay" he tells about the reading of that period:

A couple of hours each day, riding back and forth on the tram, I made my way though the *Divine Comedy*, helped as far as "Purgatory" by John Aitken Carlyle's prose translation and then ascending the rest of the way on my own. I would do all my library work in the first hour and then steal away to the basement and pass the other five hours in reading or writing. I remember in this way rereading the six volumes of Gibbon's *Decline and Fall* and the many volumes of Vicente Fidel López's *History of the Argentine Republic*. I read Léon Bloy, Claudel, Groussac, and Bernard Shaw. . . . At some point, I was moved up to the dizzying heights of Third Official. ("Essay," 1970, p. 242)

The irony of the last sentence cannot hide the pain of his situation. But reading, writing, and translating helped him. He put to good use his careful rereading of Gibbon. At least one tale ("The Story of the Warrior and the Captive," collected in *The Aleph*, 1949) and the background for another ("The Theologians") he owed to Gibbon. From López's *History* he undoubtedly took many details of his Argentine poems and tales. The debt to Bloy, Groussac, and Shaw is more diffuse: book reviews or essays show its mark. About the influence of Claudel on his writing nothing has yet been done. It is not at all apparent, and if Borges hadn't mentioned his name, it is doubtful that any critic would have thought of it. What is apparent is that three of the writers in that list are important if not great Catholic writers: Dante, Bloy, and Claudel. The fact that Bernárdez, the director of the Miguel Cané library, was a Catholic poet—then much in favor in Catholic Argentina—helps to explain the presence of those writers in the library. In 1962 Borges told James Irby that it seemed a bit incongruous to find such works in a library set in such a proletarian neighborhood, and attributed their presence to Bernárdez's beliefs. What he did not explain is why he, being an agnostic, felt tempted to read Bloy's works, "which I liked a lot," and Claudel's, "which I didn't like that much" (Irby, 1962, p. 8). Perhaps he sought some sort of consolation. But he found more. What he invariably quotes from Bloy is a sentence about self-knowledge: "No one knows who he is," which he extracted and condensed from a longer one in *L'âme de Napoléon* (1912). He has also written of the links between one of Bloy's stories and Kafka's use of infinite postponement. But only one of his many articles is entirely devoted to Bloy. "The Mirror of the Enigmas" shows Borges' familiarity with the French writer. What he likes in him is what clearly makes him a precursor of Borges: his view of the world as a language whose code we have lost or can hardly decipher. In summarizing Bloy, he stresses his own skepticism, but at the same time he praises his invention:

> It is doubtful that the world has a meaning: it is more doubtful still, the incredulous will observe, that it has a double and triple meaning. I agree; but I believed that the hieroglyphic world postulated by Bloy best befits the dignity of the intellectual God of the theologians. "No one knows who he is," said Léon Bloy. Who could have illustrated that intimate knowledge better than he? He believed himself to be a strict Catholic and he was a continuer of the cabalists, a secret brother of Swedenborg and Blake: heresiarchs. (*Inquisitions*, 1964, p. 128)

Borges' Bloy is, like Borges' Kafka, an enigmatic mirror.

His reading of Dante was to have an even more lasting influence on his work. He wrote several articles on the *Divine Comedy,* one of which ("The Meeting in a Dream") was included in *Other Inquisitions,* and in 1949 he wrote a long study, to date not included in his collected works, for an Argentine edition of the *Commedia.* Both the articles and the essay show how deeply Dante's poem had affected him. Its influence is clear in one of his strangest and most complex stories, "The Aleph."

Another writer he read while traveling in the tramcar that took him to and from the Miguel Cané library was Ariosto. The *Orlando Furioso* is not mentioned in the "Autobiographical Essay," but it is included in Alicia Jurado's biography (Jurado, 1964, p. 42). Ariosto's imagination—his power of escaping through poetic dreams from his native Ferrara into the colorful medieval world or to the moon, his gifts of showing "in the disorder of a kaleidoscope" the passions and marvels of a whole era—is celebrated by Borges in a beautiful poem, "Ariosto y los árabes" (Ariosto and the Arabs). There he stresses the supreme irony of the poet's fate: to have dominated the European imagination for two centuries and to have influenced both Cervantes and Milton, among others, only to be reduced in the eighteenth century to being the author of "a dream nobody dreams any longer." (When the tales of the *Arabian Nights* were first translated into French, they changed the shape of Western imagination so drastically that the *Orlando Furioso* was practically forgotten.) Borges observes:

> reduced to
> Mere scholarship, mere history
> [the poem] is alone, dreaming itself. (Glory
> Is one of the forms of oblivion.)
> *(Obra, 1964, p. 212)*

If readers had abandoned *Orlando* by the eighteenth century, Borges rediscovered it in the late 1930s. The poem became, next to the *Arabian Nights,* a challenge to his own capacity to invent dreams and to charm readers. Why, then, does he omit any reference to Ariosto in the pertinent passage of the "Autobiographical Essay"? The omission may be accidental, a lapse in recalling around 1969 what he had been reading thirty years before. But it may also be another sign of Borges' conscious resistance to acknowledging anything but his English and American sources. He invariably reports on the most obscure English-speaking writers he ever perused, but he rarely makes specific reference to Spanish and Spanish American writers or to Italian and even French books (in spite of Borges' schooling in Geneva). This is not because he is trying to hide his sources, as other writers often do. It is because his influences must be made to conform to the persona, the mask, he chose long ago: an eccentric Englishman lost in the cultural emptiness of the Spanish-speaking world. The persona is effective but, obviously, false.

Bloy, Ariosto, Dante: those were some of the writers who helped to make Borges' life at the library less miserable. They provided, in different ways, an escape into the world of imagination and dreams: dreams of carnal love and adventure; dreams of transcendence and metaphysical excursions.

Perhaps Borges needed that brutal sojourn in the library to finally emerge from his overprotected existence. If the library was, to begin with, a daily excursion into hell, it soon became a season in purgatory. Borges had still to pass through a last trial to discover the Paradiso of writing his own fiction.

11.
A Death in the Family

By the beginning of 1937 Father was too ill to leave any doubts about the coming end. He was only sixty-four, but he had been plagued all his life with weak eyesight and had been forced into retirement when he was barely forty. He was now totally blind and had developed a heart condition which forced him to rely more and more on Mother's care.

She had already become his eyes. As soon as it grew obvious that he was going blind, she made an effort to perfect her rather rudimentary English, so that by the time he could no longer read she knew the language well enough to help him.

Father was always a shy man. He was, in Borges' words, "such a modest man that he would have liked to be invisible" ("Essay," 1970, p. 206). Short of achieving that elusive goal, he used to keep quiet for hours on end. Even when there were visitors at home, he would hardly utter a word. His silence was extremely polite. On the rare occasions when he said something, it was generally to inquire about the visitor's comfort. In one of Borges' stories, "Tlön, Uqbar, Orbis Tertius," there is a minor character, Herbert Ashe, who was obviously modeled on Father:

> In life, he suffered from a sense of unreality, as so many Englishmen do; dead, he is not even the ghostly creature he was then. . . . I remember him in the corridor of the hotel, a mathematics textbook in his hand, gazing now and again at the passing colors of the sky. One afternoon, we discussed the duodecimal numerical system (in which twelve is written 10). . . . In September, 1937, . . . Herbert Ashe died of an aneurysmal rupture. (*Ficciones,* 1962, p. 21)

If one remembers that it was Father who taught Georgie both the general principles of mathematics and the fundamentals of metaphysical idealism, the reference to the character's "sense of unreality" is very telling. The image of Ashe, sitting quietly and looking at the sky, was also inspired by the many occasions in which Georgie had seen Father gazing and musing thus at the same hotel. Even the cause of Herbert Ashe's death duplicated Father's. It was his heart that finally failed him.

In one of the most reticent passages of his "Autobiographical Essay" Borges describes the event: "One morning, my mother rang me up [at the Miguel Cané library] and I asked for leave to go home, arriving just in time to see my father die. He had undergone a long agony and was very impatient for his death" ("Essay," 1970 p. 242). He died—as his mother, Fanny Haslam, had died two years before; as his own widow, Leonor Acevedo, would die almost forty years later—welcoming death as a relief, a way out from the pain of living. Borges, as usual, does not give the exact date. It was February 24, 1938. From that moment on, he became the head of the household. He was thirty-eight and had only recently begun to contribute regularly to the family budget.

On the surface, very little was changed with Father's death. Except for the relief of not having to witness his long agony, things went on as usual at home. Borges' literary and bureaucratic life continued unaltered. He went every day to the Miguel Cané library, wrote regularly for *El Hogar,* and continued to see Adolfo Bioy Casares and Silvina Ocampo in his spare time. The only external change was a subtle one. For five months he stopped contributing to *Sur.* He could not afford to stop working for *El Hogar,* which at least paid him something, but he was in no mood to write the more demanding reviews and articles *Sur* needed. His regular contributions to the journal resumed in the August 1938 issue with a review of *La amortajada* (The Shrouded Woman), a novel, by the Chilean writer María Luisa Bombal, about the dreams and hallucinations of a dead woman. The author was a friend of his, and Borges wanted to help to promote a book that had been published by *Sur.* The novel was important for him because it was the type of fantastic fiction he himself was exploring quietly at the time.

His last contribution to *Sur* had been, coincidentally, a note about Leopoldo Lugones' suicide. Lugones had been one of the major forces in shaping Georgie's poetry. At the time the young man began to publish his own poems, in the early 1920s, Lugones was undoubtedly the most important Argentine writer: a man whose work cast a long shadow over the ultraist generation. In an article written for *El Hogar* on February 26, 1937, exactly one year before Lugones' suicide, Borges discusses his influence on young poets. Entitled "The New Literary

Generations," the article attacks the then current notion that the young had stormed and conquered the Bastille of literary prejudices and forwarded the cause of new esthetic ideas. Borges laughs discreetly at the pomposity of that view and claims that it was based on a misconception or perhaps a lie. He affirms that the main preoccupation of the ultraists was the metaphor, which for them represented the whole of poetry. In discarding rhyme, the young believed they surpassed Lugones, who still believed in it. According to Borges, their independence was a delusion; they were "unwilling and fatal disciples" of Lugones' pioneering book, *Lunario sentimental* (Sentimental Moon Calendar). The book had been published in 1909; ten or twelve years later the young poets were still developing what was already contained in it. "We were," Borges concludes, "the tardy heirs of only one of Lugones' profiles."

One of Borges' companions in the ultraist crusade, Eduardo González Lanuza, wrote a rejoinder that was also published in *El Hogar* (March 12, 1937). The tone was friendly but the rebuttal firm. Borges did not reply; he was convinced that his was the right view and did not want to spend any more time arguing. But once Lugones died, he forgot his old arguments. In the article he wrote for *Sur* and later enlarged for a special issue on Lugones published by *Nosotros* in 1938, he summarizes his importance:

> To say that the first Argentine writer has died, to say that the first Spanish-speaking writer has died, is to say the mere truth and is to say very little. After Groussac's death, he is entitled to the first honor; after the death of Unamuno, to the second; but both proceed from a comparison and elimination; the two talk about Lugones and other people, not about the private Lugones; the two leave him very much alone. The two, finally (although not difficult to prove), are vague as any superlative. (*Lugones*, 1955, p. 81)

The ranking is Borges' way of beginning the discussion of Lugones' importance for Hispanic letters. The article does not attempt to hide Lugones' controversial attitudes. In registering his change from atheism to Catholicism, Borges observes curtly: "Only politicians do not change. For them, political fraud and democratic preaching are not incompatible." He also points out that Lugones' ideas were less attractive than his rhetoric and that his arguments rarely were convincing, although the words he used were. In mentioning some of his best pages, Borges also admits that Lugones had bad taste, but he finds an excuse in the fact that it is not so uncommon: for instance, Ortega y Gasset's style is also terrible. Borges points out: "In life, Lugones was judged by the most recent occasional article which his indifference had tolerated. Dead, he has the posthumous right to be judged for his best work" (ibid., p. 84).

The last paragraph of his article contains a subtle allusion to Lugones' suicide: "About the rest, about what we know . . . in the third of his *Hellenic Studies* one can find these words: 'Master of his own life, he is also of his death.' (The context deserves to be remembered. Ulysses refuses the immortality Calypso had offered him; Lugones argues that to refuse immortality is the equivalent of committing suicide, in the long run.)" (ibid., p. 84). Borges believes Lugones had the right to commit suicide and, very discreetly, approves it. In the context of the Argentine society of the time, such a statement was daring. The Catholic Lugones had committed a sin that would condemn his soul to eternal damnation. But Borges does not agree with that view. He prefers to place Lugones in a context the poet would have liked: that of a culture which respected the dignity of suicide. The suicide of Lugones, followed so closely by Father's death, must have affected Borges deeply. In a sense, Lugones was a father figure to him, but a figure he was not bound to respect. Remote, solitary, aloof, Lugones had represented a model against which Georgie could measure himself, a model which he could openly discuss and even defy—complementary, in more than one sense, to the model Father was.

If the surface of Borges' life was altered very little by Father's death, the full impact of his absence was enormous. An accident that Borges had on Christmas Eve 1938 reveals how deeply he had been affected. The episode has been described at least twice by him. In his "Autobiographical Essay" he has this to say:

It was on Christmas Eve of 1938—the same year my father died—that I had a severe accident. I was running up a stairway and suddenly felt something brush my scalp. I had grazed a freshly painted open casement window. In spite of first-aid treatment, the wound became poisoned, and for a period of a week or so I lay sleepless every night and had hallucinations and high fever. One evening, I lost the power of speech and had to be rushed to the hospital for an immediate operation. Septicemia had set in, and for a month I hovered, all unknowingly, between life and death. (Much later, I was to write about this in my story "The South.") ("Essay," 1970, pp. 242–243)

In "The South," after introducing the protagonist, Juan Dahlmann, in the first paragraph of the story, Borges describes what happened to Juan during "the last days of February 1939." There is a change of dates, perhaps to avoid Christmas' religious connotations and to mark (secretly) the exact time of Borges' own recuperation.

Dahlmann had succeeded in acquiring, on that very afternoon, an imperfect copy of Weil's edition of *The Thousand and One Nights*. Avid to examine this find, he did not wait for the elevator but hurried up the stairs. In the obscurity, something brushed by his forehead: a bat, a bird? On the face of the woman who opened the door to him he saw horror engraved, and the hand he wiped across his face came away red with blood. The edge of a recently painted window which someone had forgotten to close had caused his wound. (*Ficciones*, 1962, pp. 167–168)

If one compares this version with the one in the "Autobiographical Essay," it is possible to conclude that Borges invented some narrative details to make the story more concrete and believable: the finding of a copy of an obscure German translation of the *One Thousand and One Nights* (a translation he had reviewed in *History of Eternity*, 1936); the joy and greed that find brings to Dahlmann; his discovery of being wounded by the expression on the face of the woman who opens the door to him and the blood on his own hands. (These last two details are very cinematographic and show Borges' familiarity with both Hitchcock's and von Sternberg's imaginative style of editing.) But if one looks at another testimony of the real accident, it is easy to see that the fictional version presented in "The South" is perhaps closer to reality than the autobiographical summary. It comes from Mother:

He had another horrible accident. . . . He was for a time between life and death. It was Christmas Eve, and Georgie had gone to pick up a girl who was coming to lunch with us. But Georgie didn't come back! I was in anguish till we had a call from the police. . . . It seemed that, the elevator being out of service, he had climbed the stairs very quickly and did not see an open window; pieces of glass had gotten into his head. The scars are still visible. Because the wound had not been properly disinfected before it was sutured, he had a fever of 105 degrees the next day. The fever went on and it was finally necessary to operate, in the middle of the night. (Mother, 1964, p. 11)

By giving more details about the context of the real accident, Mother adds one significant element missing from Borges' accounts. The young woman he had gone to pick up is reduced to a horrified anonymous face in "The South" and is not mentioned at all in the "Essay." The anticipation of the Christmas Eve lunch is transferred in the story (very adequately, Freud would have said) to Dahlmann's greed upon discovering a copy of Weil's rare translation of the *One Thousand and One Nights*. Knowing Borges' reticence in romantic matters, it is understandable that he suppresses all reference to the girl in the "Essay" and alludes to her only briefly in the story.

The young woman has been identified by Borges' biographers as a Chilean friend. She was pretty and Borges apparently was fond of her, but he was fond of practically all pretty young women. She is important to the accident because in Borges' texts she is the repressed element that gives a clue to the story and to the real source of it. What one has to bear in mind is that Borges had gone to the girl's house to pick her up and take her to lunch with Mother. Being in a hurry, he made a fatal decision that led to the accident. The rush to get upstairs, and the emotionally charged context of the occasion, is what makes the accident revealing. Borges' reticence about the young woman makes it impossible to determine if the occasion had another meaning for him. Was he introducing the young woman to Mother for the first time? Was an engagement contemplated?

If he was really taking the young woman to see Mother for the first time, the whole accident takes on a different meaning. It can be seen as a way of escaping the responsibility of that type of situation, which symbolically implied taking another step toward maturity. Borges was not only the head of the household but was taking a young woman to meet Mother. The fact that, because of the accident, the meeting failed and, because of the accident, Borges temporarily became (like Father) an invalid totally dependent on Mother gives the whole episode another coloration. The accident can then be seen as a way of perpetuating his dependency, a refusal to enter fully into maturity.

But we do not know the exact circumstances of that frustrated lunch. And it would be wise not to speculate too much. What we know is that the accident made Borges more dependent than before on Mother's help. It also had another consequence: it freed him symbolically from Father's tutelage forever. To understand this we must look at the accident from a completely different point of view.

12.
Reading as
Writing

One of the immediate consequences of his accident on Christmas Eve 1938 was Borges' fear that he had lost his capacity to read and write. In his "Autobiographical Essay" he reports:

> When I began to recover, I feared for my mental integrity. I remember that my mother wanted to read to me from a book I had just ordered, C. S. Lewis' *Out of the Silent Planet,* but for two or three nights I kept putting her off. At last, she prevailed, and after hearing a page or two I fell to crying. My mother asked me why the tears. "I'm crying because I understand," I said. A bit later, I wondered whether I could ever write again. I had previously written quite a few poems and dozens of short reviews. I thought that if I tried to write a review now and failed I'd be all through intellectually, but that if I tried something I had never really done before and failed at that it wouldn't be so bad and might even prepare me for the final revelation. I decided I would try to write a story. The result was "Pierre Menard, Author of the *Quixote.*" ("Essay," 1970, p. 243)

As usual, Borges summarizes a longer and more complex process. In Mother's account of the accident there are added details:

> For two weeks, he was between life and death, with [a fever of] 105 or 106 degrees; at the end of the first week, the fever began to abate and he told me: "Read me a book, read me a page." He had had hallucinations, he had seen animals creeping in through the door, etc. I read him a page, and then he told me: "That's all right." —"What do you mean?" —"Yes, now I know I'm not going to be insane, I've understood everything." He began to write fantastic stories afterward, a thing that had never happened to him before. . . . As soon as he was back home again, he began to write a fantastic story, his first one. . . . And afterward, he wrote only fantastic stories, which scare

me a little because I don't understand them very well. I asked him once: "Why don't you write again the same things you used to write?" He answered: "Do not insist, do not insist." And he was right. (Mother, 1964, p. 11)

The difference between the two accounts is not only in the details but in the point of view. While Borges makes it very plain that it was Mother who insisted on reading him Lewis' book, she says that it was he who did it. Eyewitness accounts are bound to differ but not so drastically. Perhaps the difference corresponds only to the shifting of the narrative "I." In his version of the accident Borges is more concerned with communicating to the reader his fears for his "mental integrity," while Mother seems more interested in communicating both her concern for her son's health and her devotion to him. In her reminiscences she always presents herself as being totally at his service, while Borges generally underlines her independence and strength of character. This discrepancy is inevitable: mothers tend to believe they are slaves to their children while children know how dominant and insistent doting mothers can be.

The other major difference is one of tone. Mother is dramatic where Borges is detached and, apparently, devoid of any emotion. Even when he talks about how moved he was and admits to crying, he is distant. The emotional quality of his reaction when he discovered he was able to understand C. S. Lewis' book can be found in "The God's Script," collected in *The Aleph* (1949). Near the end, when the protagonist, an imprisoned Mayan priest, has a mystical vision of the Wheel (which is the universe, which is his god), he exclaims: "O bliss of understanding, greater than the bliss of imagining or feeling" (*Labyrinths*, 1962, p. 172). From that zone between life and death in which he had lingered, Borges (like the Mayan priest) slowly returned to the bliss of understanding.

His account of how he became a fiction writer is also foreshortened and contains a glaring anachronism. Borges had been writing fiction at least since 1933, when he published, in the multicolored pages of *Crítica's* Saturday supplement, a story called "Streetcorner Man," later collected in *A Universal History of Infamy* (1935). Many of the short biographies of that book were partly fictitious as well. And in his last book of essays, *History of Eternity* (1936), he had already planted a short story, under the guise of a book review of an imaginary detective novel published in Bombay. "The Approach to al-Mu'tasim" was actually the model of what was to be "Pierre Menard, Author of the *Quixote*." The links between that story and the new one are obvious: both are presented as literary essays that discuss the work of a writer who doesn't exist and give all kinds of bogus information (date and place of publication, name of publisher or journal, quotations from other critics) to make the hoax more believable. Both deal with a certain concept of what fiction is. Both use the trick of introducing a literary reality that is false.

There is, of course, a great difference between the two texts. The first story reviews a book that might have been written and published in Bombay (there is nothing fantastic in that kind of fiction); because of that, it was successful as a hoax. The second story gives the game away because it is based not only on an imaginary writer but on a writer who attempts an impossible task: to rewrite (not copy) *Don Quixote* literally. The fantastic is in Pierre Menard's behavior. It is difficult to see what this has to do with C. S. Lewis' novel. On the other hand, the links with Kafka seem obvious. In many of his novels and tales one finds examples of such "fantastic" conduct. But not in Lewis.

Borges deliberately misguides readers of his "Autobiographical Essay," leading them to believe that he came out of the accident transformed into a fiction writer directly influenced by C. S. Lewis' novel. Still, there is a grain of truth in what he says. If he is wrong in the chronology of events (he had already started his career as a fiction writer) and in the connection he establishes between "Pierre Menard" and *Out of the Silent Planet,* he is right in stressing the influence of Lewis' novel on his new fiction. (The story he ought to have mentioned is "Tlön, Uqbar, Orbis Tertius," in which an imaginary planet is superimposed on our planet.) He is also right about the importance of the accident in radically changing his writing. The accident did bring about a transformation: not as the original cause but as the end product of a complex metamorphosis Borges had undergone since Father's death.

In retelling the story of the accident, Borges makes an incidental remark: "It was on Christmas Eve of 1938—the same year my father died . . ." ("Essay," 1970, p. 242). Father's death had freed Borges, at thirty-eight, from a tutelage that had lasted too long. Since he was a child, and as long as he could remember, Father had led him to fulfill a literary destiny that his own lack of ambition and (perhaps) his rather modest resources had prevented him from accomplishing. Georgie was bound to become a writer because that was what Father had in mind for him. From that point of view, like many parents, Father had wanted Georgie to succeed where he had failed, to be his other self and even a better self than the one he had been. Father's failures as a poet, dramatist, and storyteller would be compensated for by Georgie's successes. This decision, which the child never questioned and the young man accepted and implemented, had placed an enormous responsibility on his shoulders. It is no wonder that Georgie had always been obsessed with the theme of the double and had found in Gustav

Meyrink's novel *The Golem* an adequate symbol for his own feelings of having been "made" by another. He was Father's Golem.

But there was another side to this situation. Father had been a reticent poet and a psychological novelist, while Georgie had attempted to fulfill his ambitions without following too closely the models Father respected. He had written poems, but his source was the cosmic Whitman, not the self-effacing Enrique Banchs; he had avoided psychological narrative and had worked hard at creating (almost surreptitiously) a different type of fiction: critical and even fantastic. With Father's death, the responsibility of fulfilling his destiny continued, but Borges was free to pursue the kind of writing he really liked.

The accident dramatized Borges' guilt over Father's death and his deep, totally unconscious need to be set free at last from Father's tutelage. From a symbolical point of view, the accident represented both a death (by suicide) and a rebirth. After the accident Borges emerged as a different writer, a writer this time engendered by himself. And that precisely is what he is trying to suggest when he says in the "Essay" that after the accident (and Father's death) he "tried something [he] had never really done before" (ibid., p. 243). That is, he tried to write openly a fantastic short story that was meant to be taken as a fantastic short story. He had, literarily, come out of the closet.

This new Borges would go further than Father had ever planned or even dreamed about. In attempting symbolically to kill himself, Borges was actually killing the self that was only Father's reflection. He assumed a new identity through the mythical experience of death and rebirth.

Borges did not dismiss the old self completely. The fantastic story he wrote after recuperating from blood poisoning was presented under the guise of a critical essay and was published in *Sur* (May 1939) with no indication that it was a piece of fiction. The new Borges did not mind being seen as the old one—"The other, the same," as the title of one of his volumes of poems puts it. The metamorphosis was not yet visible but it was final. "Pierre Menard, Author of the *Quixote*" was the first text written by the new Borges.

As soon as Borges was well enough, he resumed his contributions to *El Hogar*. There had been a lapse of more than a month between the last article he published before the accident (December 2, 1938, with the attack on Breton's manifesto) and the reappearance of the section "Foreign Books and Authors" on January 6, 1939. Although two of the pieces in that issue are unmistakably his (a review of Thomas Mann's book on Schopenhauer, another of a book of short stories), the rest of the section may have been put together by the staff of the magazine, using copy left over from previous issues. But the next issue, dated January 27, was obviously written by somebody else. It reveals some mistakes in translation Borges would never make ("El libro *es* terminado," instead of "El libro termina") and shows a Spanish, not Argentine, use of verbs ("no me dejar*íais* decir," instead of the simpler "no me dejar*ían* decir"). It also proliferates in clichés that reveal the hand of a wearied journalist. At the time the issue was put to bed, Borges was in the hospital and *El Hogar* probably had to rely on members of its staff. But by February 10 Borges was back in business. And the longest review of that issue was dedicated precisely to C. S. Lewis' *Out of the Silent Planet.*

The title of the review sets the tone: "A First Memorable Book." It begins by making a pointed reference to the fact that Wells now prefers "political or sociological divagation to the rigorous invention of imaginary events. . . . Luckily, two witty followers compensate for his abstractions." The first is Olaf Stapledon, a writer often reviewed in those pages. The other is C. S. Lewis. After summarizing the book, Borges observes: "It is a psychological book; the three strange 'mankinds' [that the visitor to the silent planet finds] and the vertiginous geography of Mars are less important to the reader than the reaction of the hero who begins by finding them atrocious and almost intolerable, and ends up by identifying with them." His enthusiasm for the novel does not blind Borges. He admits that "Lewis' imagination is limited. . . . What is admirable is the infinite honesty of that imagination, the coherent and thorough truth of that fantastic world."

From the review alone there is little to indicate that Lewis' novel had such an impact on Borges' work. To understand that impact it is necessary to place the novel and the review in the context of Borges' friendship and collaboration with Adolfo Bioy Casares and Silvina Ocampo. That is the context out of which "Pierre Menard" and "Tlön, Uqbar, Orbis Tertius" came to be written. The three friends used to meet at Victoria Ocampo's place in San Isidro to discuss literature and to plan works in collaboration. Some of these works were later published; others never reached that stage and remained fragments of vast enterprises. Among the planned works, Bioy Casares says in an article, "was a story about a young French provincial writer who is attracted to the work of an obscure master, deceased, whose fame has been limited to the select few. With patience and devotion, he collects the works of the master—a speech to praise the sword used by French academicians, written in an extremely correct style and full of clichés; a short pamphlet on the fragments of Varro's *Treatise of the Latin Language;* a collection of sonnets, as cold in their form as in their subject. Unable to reconcile the reputation of the master with these rather disappointing samples, the young man searches for and finally finds his unpublished manuscripts: they consist of rough drafts, "brilliant, hopelessly incomplete" (Bioy Casares, 1968, p. 145). Among the papers left by the master was a list of things a writer ought not to do, a list which Bioy transcribes. It is too long to be quoted here, but its substance is that the best thing is to avoid doing anything. One of the negative recommendations is to shun praise or censure in literary criticism. This wise precept is attributed to a certain Menard (ibid., p. 148).

Although the story was never written, Borges later decided to use it as the starting point for his "Pierre Menard, Author of the *Quixote.*" According to Bioy, the same day that they were jotting down the long list of prohibitions, Borges told them about his new story (ibid., p. 149). The real source of "Pierre Menard" is there. But Borges' imagination transformed an exercise in literary satire (modeled more or less on the artists' and writers' stories written by Henry James) into a truly fantastic story. In his version the original idea—the disillusionment of a young provincial writer upon realizing how frail fame is—is metamorphosed into the story of a writer who attempts the impossible: to rewrite in every detail, and without copying it, a famous text. By changing the focus from the young writer to the master and making the latter a sort of martyr to creative writing, Borges introduces the fantastic element that was lacking in the original plan. Now Menard's mad pursuit becomes the center of the story. Like Melville's Bartleby or Kafka's Hunger Artist, Menard sets himself an impossible task.

The actual story uses enough of the planned satire to be seen as a realization of it. In a sense, the never written work serves as a framework for the story. But instead of showing the young man's disappointing quest for the unpublished work of the master, Borges makes the young man the narrator of the tale and changes his point of view. Instead of being disillusioned by the actual work of Menard, he is enthusiastic. The story is presented as a parody of the kind of article written in defense of a misunderstood genius by one of his followers. By changing the perspective, Borges heightens the satirical aspects of the tale. It becomes a brilliant parody of French literary life, with its touches of bigotry, anti-Semitism, and adulation of the upper classes.

The first part of the story is dedicated to the petty disputes over Menard's work in which several characters are engaged: the anonymous narrator; Madame Henri Bachelier, a society lady too busy to write her own poems; and the Countess of Bagnoregio, another literary lady friend of Menard, married to an American philanthropist. The catalogue of Menard's work offered at the beginning of the story is a takeoff on Mallarmé's pursuit of the trivial and on Valéry's Monsieur Teste. The second part of the story is devoted to commenting on Menard's efforts to rewrite, literally, *Don Quixote.* Here Borges satirizes some of the Cervantists and Cervantophiles who are the plague of Spanish literature. The attempt to rewrite *Don Quixote* is not new. As early as 1614, one year before Cervantes' second part came out, a pseudonymous writer, Alonso Fernández de Avellaneda, published his own second part. Later Juan Montalvo of Ecuador and the Spaniards Miguel de Unamuno and Azorín wrote their own versions of the book and its characters. But none attempted to reproduce the work literally. It is that ambition which separates Menard's mad project from the rest.

As is well known, Menard succeeds in writing a few chapters. In comparing them, the narrator finds that they are literally the same but have a completely different meaning:

> Cervantes' text and Menard's are verbally identical, but the second is almost infinitely richer. (More ambiguous, his detractors will say, but ambiguity is richness.) It is a revelation to compare Menard's *Don Quixote* with Cervantes'. The latter, for example, wrote (part one, chapter nine):
>
> . . . truth, whose mother is history, rival of time, depository of deeds, witness of the past, exemplar and adviser to the present, and the future's counselor.
>
> Written in the seventeenth century, written by the "lay genius" Cervantes, this enumeration is a mere rhetorical praise of History. Menard, on the other hand, writes:
>
> . . . truth, whose mother is history, rival of time, depository of deeds, witness of the past, exemplar and adviser to the present, and the future's counselor.
>
> History, the *mother* of truth: the idea is astounding. Menard, a contemporary of William James, does not define history as an inquiry into reality but as its origin. Historical truth, for him, is not what had happened; it is what we judged to have happened. The final phrases—*exemplar and adviser to the present and the future's counselor*—are brazenly pragmatic. The contrast in style is also vivid. The archaic style of Menard—quite foreign, after all—suffers from a certain affectation. Not so that of his forerunner, who handles with ease the current Spanish of his time. (*Labyrinths,* 1962, pp. 42–43)

There is a joke within the joke: the phrase which Borges selected belongs to a passage in which Cervantes, introducing the "Arab historian" Cide Hamete Benengeli as the real author of *Don Quixote,* is laughing at the pretensions of the chivalric romances to tell the truth and nothing but the truth. The text that the narrator of "Pierre Menard" takes so literally was already satirical and contained a parody of the literary model Cervantes was attempting to discredit. But Borges does not mention this. His own joke points to a different goal. More unexpected than his dazzling exercise in critical jugglery over a fixed text is the story's conclusion:

Menard (perhaps without wanting it) has enriched, by means of a new technique, the halting and rudimentary art of reading: this technique is that of the deliberate anachronism and the erroneous attribution. This technique, whose applications are infinite, prompts us to go through the *Odyssey* as if it were posterior to the *Aeneid* and the book *Le jardin du Centaure* of Madame Henri Bachelier as if it were by Madame Henri Bachelier. This technique fills the most placed works with adventure. To attribute the *Imitatio Christi* to Louis Ferdinand Céline or to James Joyce, is this not a sufficient renovation of its tenuous spiritual indications? (ibid., p. 44)

Another of Borges' whims? That is what some readers believed, and the fact that "Pierre Menard" was first included in a collection of stories, *The Garden of Forking Paths* (1941), and reappeared in the more comprehensive collection *Ficciones* (1944), helped to heighten the impression of game playing and irresponsible invention that many readers had when they discovered the story in *Sur*. Nevertheless, some readers probably detected ideas that Borges had expressed in earlier essays. One of these, "La fruición literaria" (Literary Fruition), was originally published in *La Nación* (January 23, 1927) before it was included in *El idioma de los argentinos* (1928). Here Borges examines a metaphor about fire without revealing until the very end the name of the author. By discussing the metaphor as if it were coined by a contemporary poet, an ancient Chinese or Siamese poet, a witness to a fire, or the poet Aeschylus, Borges shows that we judge the metaphor differently according to its literary context. It is the context that fixes the reading and thus changes the text. In another article, "Elementos de preceptiva" (Elements of the Preceptive), published in *Sur* (April 1933), he comes to the conclusion that it is impossible to judge any work of some merit as a whole by simply "a marvelous emission of terrified praise, and without analyzing a single line." This essay, written only six years before "Pierre Menard," agrees on "the final impossibility of an esthetics."

Instead of taking the views of those skeptical articles literally, or merely laughing at the conclusion of "Pierre Menard," we can see in them the foundation of a new poetics, based not on the actual writing of a work but on its reading. This approach to Borges' texts has been favored by French critics since Gérard Genette's 1964 article "La littérature selon Borges." Taking as his starting point the final lines of "Pierre Menard," Genette stresses the importance of the Borgesian intuition that the most delicate and important operation of all those which contribute to the writing of a book is reading it. He concludes his analysis with these words:

> The genesis of a work in historic time and in the life of an author is the most contingent and most insignificant moment of its duration. . . . The time of a book is not the limited time of its writing, but the limitless time of reading and memory. The meaning of books is in front of them and not behind them; it is in us: a book is not a ready-made meaning, a revelation we have to suffer; it is a reserve of forms that are waiting to have some meaning; it is the "imminence of a revelation that is not yet produced" and that every one of us has to produce for himself. (Genette, 1964, p. 132)

Genette's last lines contain a reference to a key passage in Borges' essay "The Wall and the Books," first published in *La Nación* (October 22, 1950) and later collected in *Other Inquisitions* (1952): "That imminence of a revelation that is not yet produced is, perhaps, the esthetic reality" (*Inquisitions*, 1964, p. 5).

If "Pierre Menard" was meant to be a satire on French literary circles (which were, of course, the model for similar circles in Argentina), Borges soon changed the original project and took advantage of the occasion to create not only a fantastic story but also a critical essay on the poetics of reading. From that point of view, "Pierre Menard" is both a culmination of the many hoaxes he had played in two decades of writing and, above all, the beginning of his fully mature work. With his next story, "Tlön, Uqbar, Orbis Tertius," Borges would move even further.

13.
A Distorted Mirror to Reality

In May 1940, one year exactly after the publication of "Pierre Menard, Author of the *Quixote*" in *Sur,* the same journal published "Tlön, Uqbar, Orbis Tertius." This time, the story did not pretend to be an essay, although it had all the external characteristics of one. It began by reporting a conversation between Bioy Casares and the author about a puzzling quotation the first had found in an odd volume of a pirate encyclopedia; it told of the efforts made by both to locate that volume, which they finally did; it offered a summary of the article on "Uqbar," the unknown land which was the subject of the original conversation; it added more information about Uqbar that the author had gathered later under the most unusual circumstances; it revealed the existence of a whole encyclopedia devoted to describing Tlön, the planet to which Uqbar belonged; finally, it explained, calmly, that the whole affair was a hoax perpetrated by a group of eighteenth-century philosophers and carried to its completion in this century through the patronage of an American millionaire. In a postscript, which appears to put the hoax theory in question, the reader is informed, again calmly, that objects made in Uqbar have begun to be introduced on earth.

The postscript gives the game away because it is dated 1947 and reads: "I reproduce the preceding article just as it appeared in number 68 of *Sur*—jade green covers, May 1940." The fact that the reader of *Sur* had in his hands that jade green issue and that he was unmistakably reading it in May 1940 and not in 1947, created a curious perspective—a "mise en abîme," as André Gide used to say and the French critics now repeat. In the same way that the label of a tin of biscuits shows a picture of a tin of biscuits and so on, creating an infinite retrogression, Borges' text was *originally* published in the sixty-eighth

332

issue of *Sur* as a *reproduction* of a text already published in the sixty-eighth issue of *Sur*.

By dating the postscript 1947, Borges defined the "article" unmistakably as a piece of science fiction. From that point of view, it would be easy to establish the links between "Tlön, Uqbar, Orbis Tertius" and C. S. Lewis' novel *Out of the Silent Planet*. Both belong basically to the same genre: utopian science fiction. In both there is a great concern with imaginary languages: while Lewis describes in detail the efforts of the protagonist, a Cambridge linguist named Ransom, to learn the language of one of the three tribes of people in Malacandra, the narrator of "Tlön" describes in detail the language of that planet. There are even minor coincidences in the phonological value of words in both languages. They favor an almost Scandinavian grouping of consonants: one of the tribes' names in Lewis is "Hross," while in Borges some imaginary objects produced in Tlön are called "hrönir."

But what chiefly brings the two works together is their allegorical point of view. In describing Malacandra (which happens to be Mars, the red planet), Lewis is placing a mirror up to earth. In the best tradition of Thomas More and Swift, he describes an imaginary visit to that planet and the society he finds there, to best describe our world, the silent planet of the title. Borges, in a more oblique way, does the same: his Tlön is described as an inverted version of earth. It is a world in which matter is denied and imaginary objects become real. That is, it is a world made according to the theories about reality of the eighteenth-century British philosopher George Berkeley. The fact that the encyclopedic hoax was originated in the eighteenth century and that the American millionaire's surname is Buckley—which sounds almost like the British pronunciation of Berkeley—corroborates the identification proposed by James E. Irby (Irby, 1971, p. 420). Both Lewis and Borges are using one of the oldest methods of describing reality: through the distorted mirror of utopia.

Even the political allusions contained in Lewis' novel and Borges' tale function in a similar context (utopias, from Plato onward, were always political). While Lewis shows that red Mars is really a planet of peace (implying that silent earth is the planet of war), Borges shows that Tlön, being a rational version of earth, is a totalitarian world: the excess of reason leads to totalitarianism. And in the end, when objects made in Tlön begin to appear on this planet, Borges says:

> The dissemination of objects from Tlön over different countries would complement this plan. . . . The fact is that the international press infinitely proclaimed the "find." Manuals, anthologies, summaries, literal versions, authorized re-editions and pirated editions of the Greatest Works of Man

flooded and still flood the earth. Almost immediately, reality yielded on more than one account. The truth is that it longed to yield. Ten years ago any symmetry with a semblance of order—dialectical materialism, anti-Semitism, Nazism—was sufficient to entrance the minds of men. How could one do other than submit to Tlön, to the minute and vast evidence of an orderly planet? (*Labyrinths*, 1962, p. 17)

The reference to totalitarian regimes and ideologies is clear. One must remember that both *Out of the Silent Planet* and "Tlön, Uqbar, Orbis Tertius" were conceived and written at the time of the Spanish civil war, the time of the Munich and the Nazi-Soviet pacts, when Hitler had already begun to prepare his armies for the conquest of Europe. They are both works that belong to the prologue to World War II.

But it would be wrong to overstress the links between the two texts. The differences between them are more relevant. While Lewis writes in the tradition of utopian science fiction, concentrating on the protagonist's adventure in the No-place land, Borges changes the focus: instead of writing about the adventure of the discovery of utopia, he concentrates on the adventure of the discovery of texts about utopia. Lewis' Ransom "actually" travels to Malacandra, while Borges' narrator only reads about Tlön. At the end, by a switch that is typically Borgesian, the reality of Tlön is interpolated into the narrator's (the reader's) reality. To explain this switch it is necessary to study the other sources of the story.

There is no denying the impact that the reading of *Out of the Silent Planet* had on Borges while he lay in the hospital slowly recovering from the accident of Christmas Eve 1938. That reading was decisive because it happened at the right time. But Borges may already have found what he needed in the fictions of H. G. Wells and the other utopians. As a matter of fact, in a review written two years before, Borges advanced many of the points of view he later developed in "Tlön, Uqbar, Orbis Tertius." The review is of Adolfo Bioy Casares' collection of short stories, *La estatua casera* (The Domestic Statue), and was published in *Sur* in March 1936. The opening paragraph gives Borges' notion of utopian science fiction:

> I suspect that a general scrutiny of fantastic literature would reveal that it is not very fantastic. I have visited many utopias—from the eponymous one of More to *Brave New World*—and I have not yet found a single one that exceeds the cozy limits of satire or sermon and describes in detail an imaginary country, with its geography, its history, its religion, its language, its literature, its music, its government, its metaphysical and theological controversy . . . its encyclopaedia in short; all of it organically coherent, of course, and (I know I'm very demanding) with no reference whatsoever to the horrible

injustices suffered by the artillery captain Alfred Dreyfus. Of Wells' (and even Swift's) imaginary theories, we know that there is in each of them only one fantastic element; of the *One Thousand and One Nights,* that a good part of its marvel is involuntary because thirteenth-century Egyptians believed in talismans and in exorcisms. In short: I wouldn't be surprised if the Universal Library of Fantastic Literature did not contain more than a volume by Lewis Carroll, a couple of Disney films, a poem by Coleridge, and (because of the absent-mindedness of its author) Manuel Galvez's *Opera omnia. (Sur,* March 1936, pp. 85–86)

Borges is being facetious. The last phrase contains a dig at one of Argentina's most successful realistic narrators. His ironical reference implies that "realism" is a branch of fantastic literature. But what is really important in his statement is the notion that utopian literature is generally not very specific in describing the aspects that matter most in an imaginary world. His criticism is relevant not only as a general observation about utopias but, especially, because it already contains the germ of "Tlön, Uqbar, Orbis Tertius." When he presents that imaginary planet, Borges does not omit either its geography or its history, its religion or its poetry, its metaphysics or its music. A blueprint of the story can be seen here, as Irby has correctly pointed out. He also has indicated another source: one of Macedonio Fernández's most curious fantasies, that of becoming the president of Argentina by "very subtly insinuating his name among the populace." Macedonio began by inspiring a collective novel, *El hombre que será presidente* (The Man Who Will Become President), for which Borges and other friends served simultaneously as authors and characters. Only the first two chapters were completed. The novel had a secondary plot which concerned the attempt by a group of "neurotic and perhaps insane millionaires" to further the same campaign by undermining people's resistance through the gradual dissemination of "disturbing inventions." According to Irby's summary, these "were usually contradictory artifacts whose effects ran counter to their apparent form or function, including certain very small and disconcertingly heavy objects (like the cone found by Borges and Amorim toward the end of 'Tlön, Uqbar, Orbis Tertius'), scrambled passages in detective novels (somewhat like the interpolated entry on Uqbar, and dadaist creations like the 'transparent tigers' and 'towers of blood' in Tlön)." Irby concludes that "the novel's techniques and language were meant to enact as well as relate this whole process by introducing more and more such objects in a less and less casual way and by slowly gravitating toward a baroque style of utter delirium" (Irby, 1971, p. 417).

Another important piece in the puzzle that led to the writing of "Tlön, Uqbar, Orbis Tertius" is a literary discussion that Borges had with Adolfo Bioy Casares and Silvina Ocampo in the 1930s. The story itself begins by calling attention to it:

> I owe the discovery of Uqbar to the conjunction of a mirror and an encyclopaedia. The mirror troubled the depths of a corridor in a country house on Gaona Street in Ramos Mejía; the encyclopaedia is fallaciously called The Anglo-American Cyclopaedia (New York, 1917) and is a literal but delinquent reprint of the Encyclopaedia Britannica of 1902. The event took place some five years ago. Bioy Casares had had dinner with me that evening and we became lengthily engaged in a vast polemics concerning the composition of a novel in the first person, whose narrator would omit or disfigure the facts and indulge in various contradictions which would permit a few readers—very few readers—to perceive an atrocious or banal reality. (Labyrinths, 1962, p. 3)

The novel, as such, was never written, but both friends separately attempted versions of it: Bioy in 1945 with the novel A Plan for Escape, which presents just such a distorted reality; Borges in 1940 with "Tlön, Uqbar, Orbis Tertius," which ends by revealing a banal reality— Tlön is the real world. The conversation with Bioy is the seed of Borges' story in the same way that Borges' review of La estatua casera is the seed of Bioy's novel. The comic reference Borges makes in that review to the destiny of the artillery captain Alfred Dreyfus is taken literally, and parodied, by Bioy in A Plan for Escape, which is set on Devil's Island. One of the chief characters is a convict called Dreyfus whose real name is Bordenave.

There is still another text which sheds unexpected light on the writing of "Tlön, Uqbar, Orbis Tertius." It is an article Borges published in El Hogar on June 2, 1939, and it is titled "When Fiction Lives Inside Fiction." Its subject is the presence of a work of art inside another work of art. Borges makes explicit reference to well-known examples such as Velázquez's Las meninas, which he saw at the Museo del Prado, and Cervantes' Don Quixote, which includes a short novel of adultery in Part I. To this and other rather literal attempts to introduce fiction inside fiction, Borges opposes more elaborate versions, such as the Night 602 of the One Thousand and One Nights, when Scheherazade begins to tell the king his own story and thus almost creates a totally circular book. In Shakespeare's Hamlet the players in Act III present a fragment of a play which has some telling relation to the main story. Borges quotes De Quincey's opinion that the style of that fragmentary play makes Shakespeare's style more realistic; Borges argues that its essential purpose is to make the "reality" of the play more unreal. He gives other examples: Corneille's L'illusion comique, in which a magician shows the protagonist his son's life in a vision to reveal finally that what he has seen is not real—the son is a comedian, and his adventures are plays; and Gustav Meyrink's *The Golem,* which tells the story of a dream that contains dreams. But the most complex of these verbal labyrinths is the one Borges leaves for the end: a novel just published by Flann O'Brien, *At Swim Two Birds,* in which a Dublin student writes a novel about a Dublin innkeeper who writes a novel about his clients, one of whom is the student. After indicating the influence of Joyce on O'Brien, Borges concludes: "Arthur Schopenhauer wrote once that dreams and vigil were leaves of the same book and that to read them in order was to live, and to leaf through them was to dream. Paintings inside paintings, books that split into books, help us to intuit that identity" (*El Hogar,* June 2, 1939, p. 6).

The mention of Schopenhauer makes more explicit the general trend of the article. Borges is interested less in the poetic effect of including a work of art inside another work of art than in the metaphysical effect produced by works which erase the distinction between reality and dreams. If we apply this notion to the reading of "Tlön, Uqbar, Orbis Tertius," it is easy to see how Borges reaches the same conclusion. He begins by creating, inside the text of the story, the search for another text. When that text is found, it is described, analyzed, and finally declared a hoax. But precisely at that point, Tlön itself begins to proliferate: it creates objects which are introduced into the reality of Borges' text; it ends up by disseminating itself into that fictional reality, superimposing itself over it and probably obliterating it. At the end of the story, the narrator realizes that Tlön is taking over:

> The contact and habit of Tlön have disintegrated this world. Enchanted by its rigor, humanity forgets over and again that it is a rigor of chess masters, not of angels. . . . A scattered dynasty of solitary men has changed the face of the world. Their task continues. If our forecasts are not in error, a hundred years from now someone will discover the hundred volumes of the Second Encyclopaedia of Tlön. Then English and French and mere Spanish will disappear from the globe. The world will be Tlön. I pay no attention to all this and go on revising, in the still days at the Adrogué Hotel, an uncertain Quevedian translation (which I do not intend to publish) of Browne's *Urn Burial. (Labyrinths,* 1962, p. 18)

The search for an article in an encyclopedia has ended with the discovery that the world is being taken over by the encyclopedia. The limits between fiction and reality have been erased. In reaction, the narrator resigns himself to a remote corner of a remote country, devoting himself entirely to a useless occupation: the translation of a book, written by an English baroque writer, about funeral inscriptions. By relentless artifice, Borges has created in "Tlön, Uqbar, Orbis Tertius" more than a mirror to reality: he has created a mirror to the writing of fiction as well. The story finally reflects only itself.

The first seeds of "Tlön" were planted (as Irby has shown) in the early 1920s in conversations and literary projects Borges shared with Macedonio Fernández. They were brought to life again in the 1930s in conversations and literary projects Borges shared with Bioy Casares and Silvina Ocampo and in his own articles of the period. They came to fruition after the accident of Christmas Eve 1938 and the timely reading of Lewis' *Out of the Silent Planet*. With "Tlön, Uqbar, Orbis Tertius" Borges had become a new writer.

Part Four

1.
The Shape of Things
to Come

At the time of the accident on Christmas Eve 1938, Norah and Guillermo de Torre had been living for a while with the Borgeses. They had been forced to leave Spain and return to Argentina that same year because it was obvious that the civil war was taking a turn for the worse. After the accident, the family decided to move to a house at 1972 Anchorena Street. It was a two-story building in the Andalusian style, with a garden. They lived there until 1943, when the De Torres moved elsewhere and the Borgeses rented an apartment on Quintana Avenue.

In his conversations with De Milleret, Borges stresses the change that Father's death brought to the household: Mother was forced to become a career woman at sixty-three.

I must say that when my father died, she didn't even know how to draw a check; she was unfamiliar with what one does in a bank; she didn't know how to place her money, and now she is very good at it. And all that she learned after my father's death, in the same way she learned English correctly, because at the beginning she spoke a simple kind of English, an oral English to talk to my grandmother. Now she can even read and scan English verses. . . . And all this is very remarkable because in her family they had a cult of ignorance. (De Milleret, 1969, pp. 214–215)

Another less dramatic change brought about by 1939 was the format and location of Borges' literary section in *El Hogar*. The magazine's editors had already given signs that they were not totally satisfied with the section, which normally had appeared in the first part of the magazine, generally on page 28 or 29. Suddenly, on September 16,

1938, the section appeared on page 88. In the following issue (September 30) there was a change of a different nature: the capsule biography, one of its most important features, was excluded. It reappeared on February 10, 1939, but was again discontinued on March 24, this time for good. Other, more decisive alterations took place later. On May 5 the section was reduced to half a page of book reviews and continued to be published as such, squeezed among advertisements for Lux Soap, Ovaltine, Suchard chocolates, and other products an Argentine woman could not do without. The last time the section appeared was on July 7.

I once asked Borges, rather naïvely, why he had stopped contributing to El Hogar. In his usual self-mocking style, he told me that, probably because he had noticed that the magazine editors did not seem too enthusiastic, he had once forgotten to send in his copy. Realizing that nobody had called to ask for it, he came to the conclusion that they were relieved by his oversight. Probably El Hogar's editors had discovered at last that Borges' section was not entirely suited to the kind of woman whose chief objective in life was the purchase of luxury consumer items.

From Borges' point of view, the almost four years of work at El Hogar had been a formative experience, not only because it was his first important job in literary journalism but also because, by subtly enlarging and upgrading the rather anonymous section he had inherited from Anne Keen, he had practically created a new form: the book review page, which is a sort of literary microcosm, a magazine inside a magazine. Besides, the task of preparing the fortnightly section kept Borges busy reading new books and catalogues, wittily commenting on events of literary life, and led him into condensing and updating his views on many subjects. Some of the topics that appear constantly in the section—the detective novel, fantastic and science-fiction stories, the problems of narrative technique, the increasing possibility of a European war—are the themes and subjects of his most important writing in the next decade. In a sense, the section was a sort of open workshop, a place where Borges could present, once every two weeks, his views on literary matters and rehearse his many inventions. It was also a public performance that, somehow, taught him to write for a larger audience. Unfortunately, the experience had to stop precisely at a time when Borges had added responsibilities as the head of a household and needed to make more money.

By degrees, Borges had become involved in the actual editing of Sur. Victoria Ocampo had never had the patience or the editorial talent required to run a journal. She had the inspiration and the enthusiasm but was more than willing to let somebody do the dreary, boring, everyday work. Thus Sur had had a series of young promising writers as managing editors. The first was the son of Mexican humanist Alfonso Reyes; the second, the scholarly Raimundo Lida. But they did not last long in the job. Although careless about the actual details of editing, Victoria had very clear ideas about what she wanted and how the journal ought to look. The managing editor had to be somebody who was efficient and respectful of her views at the same time. Besides, she traveled a lot, spending practically every winter in Europe, so the managing editor for much of the year had to produce the journal almost on his own. Although Borges was not suited to the position, he was very helpful. And when finally Victoria persuaded José Bianco to become managing editor, Borges came to his rescue. He was always available to help with the correct wording of a quotation, the title of a book, or the spelling of a little-known author's name. He was a living encyclopedia.

During the twenty-three years Bianco was in charge of *Sur*, Borges paid regular visits to the journal's office in downtown Buenos Aires. In his reminiscences of Borges, Bianco describes these visits: " 'When do you expect the proofs to be ready?' Borges used to ask me while delivering his copy. And as soon as I told him that they were ready, he immediately came by. After publication, he never complained about a misprint. 'Bettered by misprints' was a phrase that he loved to repeat" (Bianco, 1964, p. 17). Bianco also contrasts the quality and wit of Borges' contributions to *Sur* with the other writers' contributions. For him, his copy "justified the publication, raised its content, and on some occasions made it uneven, producing in some issues frightful bottomless pits, such was the distance between Borges' metaphysical and esthetic preoccupations, the swiftness and daring of his style," and the rest of the journal's content (ibid., p. 18). The paradox was, according to Bianco, that because Borges was exceptional he could afford to be modest, while the other contributors were always more concerned about their own inflated egos than about the quality of their copy. Borges, on the contrary, was simplicity itself.

Bianco recalls meetings with Borges, Silvina Ocampo, and Bioy Casares in which they discussed literary matters and poked fun at everything and everybody. They all had excellent memories and loved to quote from unexpected sources. According to Bianco, they created "an atmosphere in which the real and the unreal got confused. Literature was, for the three, the most intoxicating of drugs: they were exalted by it, moved, became thoughtful. It also made them laugh" (ibid., p. 15). When Silvina and Bioy married in the summer of 1940, in Las Flores, a small suburban community, Borges was the best man. To inform Bianco of the event, which had been decided on rather suddenly, they sent him a telegram written in a language they invented, comprised of English, Italian, and Spanish words. It had been inspired by a certain article by De Quincey about a man named Pinkerton. The telegram, written in pure "Pinkertonio," said literally: "Mucho registro civil, mucha iglesia, dont tell anybodini whateverano." Roughly translated it would be: "Lots of civil marriage, lots of church, don't tell anybody [with an Italian ending] whatsoever [and also: what a summer]." The telegram showed the kind of humor Joyce had made famous in *Finnegans Wake*. It consisted of coining new words by unexpectedly combining two or more already existing ones. Borges had already discussed Joyce's last book in *El Hogar* (June 16, 1939) and in a *Sur* article, "Joyce and Neologisms," published in November 1939. Although his verdict was not totally favorable, he devoted some time in both pieces to discussing the portmanteau words. His contribution to "Pinkertonio" showed that he was not immune to that type of verbal wit.

By the summer of 1940 the European war (which later would be called World War II) was already some months old. In two weeks of September 1939, Hitler with some help from the Soviet Union had destroyed the Polish army and occupied the country. But the hostilities on the Western front, with the two armies separated by the Maginot line and the Siegfried line, had reached a sort of impasse. That period was to be called the "phony war" and would produce some satires, such as Evelyn Waugh's *Put Out More Flags,* which Hitler's subsequent destruction of Holland, Belgium, and France made obsolete. But still, in the summer of 1940, the war seemed at a stalemate, as if no country really wanted to fight seriously. In the River Plate area the war had been brought home unexpectedly by the naval battle fought late in 1939 between the German pocket battleship the *Graf Spee* and three British cruisers in the waters of the river near the Uruguayan resort of Punta del Este. The three cruisers were too light to sink the German ship, but in spite of heavy losses they forced her to seek refuge in Montevideo harbor. At the time, the Uruguayan government supported the Allies and did its best to send the battleship back into the open seas, where a British fleet was gathering. The Germans preferred to sink the ship themselves outside Montevideo and cross the river to seek asylum in Argentina, where the government was pro-Nazi. That was the only moment in which the European war came near the River Plate area.

Borges was clearly and outspokenly in favor of England. There was a small but very vocal contingent of British supporters in Argentina at the time, especially among the upper and upper middle classes, many of whom had British ancestors. Many young Argentines went to England to fight for the empire. Borges was, of course, too old and too nearsighted to contemplate such a move, but he took advantage of the occasion to write some articles on the war. Instead of defending En-

gland, he chose to attack Germany, especially the favor Germany enjoyed among Argentine nationalists. One of his best articles on the subject was published on the front page of *El Hogar* on December 13,
1940, at the time Hitler's armies had pushed England out of the Continent at Dunkirk, the Luftwaffe was mercilessly bombarding London,
and Germany had occupied France. The article is entitled "Definition
of the Germanophile." It begins with an apparent digression on the
mysteries of etymology:

> The implacable enemies of etymology argue that the origin of words does
> not teach what they now mean; the defenders may argue that it always teaches
> what they do not mean now. It teaches, for instance, that pontifices are not
> bridge builders; that miniatures are not painted with minium; that the mat-
> ter of crystal is not ice; that the leopard is not a hybrid of panther and lion;
> that a candidate may not have been whitened; that sarcophagi are not the
> contrary of vegetarians; that rubrics are not as red as blushing; that the dis-
> coverer of America was not Amerigo Vespucci; and that the Germanophiles
> are not devoted to Germany. (*El Hogar*, December 13, 1940, p. 1)

The surprise ending of that paragraph is typically Borgesian. It
introduces the subject in the most unexpected manner. The point
Borges is trying to make is that Germanophiles are not really interested
in Germany. To prove it, he argues that on the many occasions he has
had a chance to talk to Argentine Germanophiles, he has discovered
that they are not conversant with the names of Holderlin, Schopenhauer, and Leibnitz, and that their interest in Germany is only a sign of
their hostility to England, actually based on the fact that England ruled
the Falkland Islands, which the Argentines call Malvinas and claim to
this day as their legitimate possession.

Another characteristic of the Germanophiles, according to
Borges, is that they are saddened by the fact that British stockholders
own the Argentine railways and that the British had finally won the
1902 war against the Boers in South Africa; they also are anti-Semitic
and want to expel from Argentina "a Slavo-Germanic community in
which German surnames predominate (Rosenblatt, Gruenberg, Niere-
stein, Lilenthal) and which speaks a German dialect: Yiddish or Jue-
disch." All these signs indicate that the Germanophiles are really An-
glophobes. "They perfectly ignore Germany but resign themselves to
being enthusiastic about a country that fights against England."

To illustrate his point, Borges sketches a typical conversation
with a Germanophile. It begins with a discussion of the 1919 peace
treaty at Versailles, which was so unfair to Germany. When Borges
agrees with his speaker and observes that even then, the treaty was
strongly condemned by Wells and Bernard Shaw, the speaker assents

and maintains that a victorious country has to set aside oppression and revenge. But where Borges and the Germanophile part is in the conclusion the latter draws from this discussion: he sincerely believes that Germany has the right, now that it is victorious, "to destroy not only England and France (why not Italy?) but also Denmark, Holland, Norway: free of all guilt in that injustice. In 1919, Germany was badly treated by its enemies: this powerful reason allows it to burn, raze, and conquer all the nations of Europe and perhaps of the world. . . . The argument is monstrous, as you can see."

Very timidly, Borges points out this monstrosity, but the speaker laughs at his old-fashioned scruples and argues that ends justify means, and so on and so forth. "There is no other law than the will of the most powerful: the Reich is strong, the Reich's planes have destroyed Coventry, etc." Borges murmurs that if this is true, we cannot be sorry for what happened to Germany in 1919. But the speaker does not listen to the argument and starts a speech in praise of Hitler in which Borges finally discovers an irony: his opponent loves Hitler not in spite of his bombs and the blitzkrieg but because of them. "He is exhilarated by the evil, the atrocious in him. German victory matters less to him than the humiliation of England, the satisfactory burning of London." Borges comes to the conclusion that the Hitlerite is invariably "a spiteful person, a secret and sometimes public admirer of . . . cruelty." The article ends with these words: "It is not impossible that Adolf Hitler may have some justification; I know that the Germanophiles have none."

The fact that *El Hogar* printed the article on the first page showed that Borges' point of view had some backing in the magazine. Unfortunately, it was not equally popular in the rest of Argentina. In coming out openly not only against Nazi Germany but, especially, against the nationalists who in their hatred of England adored Germany and praised its destruction of Europe, Borges was taking a very unpopular stand. It was a stand that would become more and more unpopular with the development of the war and the increased leaning toward fascism of the Argentine army.

2.
A Theory of Fantastic Literature

Now that Silvina and Adolfito were married, a sort of routine was established. Borges visited them regularly and over dinner discussed literary projects or chatted endlessly. On Friday afternoons the Bioys held open house for their literary friends. Many were old acquaintances of Borges and even collaborators from the ultraist days, such as the painter and neolinguist Xul-Solar and the Dominican critic Pedro Henríquez Ureña. But the majority were younger writers who had come together under the *Sur* banner; among them were Eduardo Mallea, Ernesto Sábato (who was then beginning to publish very short, ironic essays in Borges' manner), Adolfo de Obieta (Macedonio Fernández's son), the Chilean novelist María Luisa Bombal, and the poet Ezequiel Martínez Estrada. In her biography Alicia Jurado observes that Borges was never too sociable on those occasions and that "Silvina remembers that . . . he always talked to one person at a time, as if the others were not there, as if his shyness would prevent him from ever giving up his privacy" (Jurado, 1964, p. 52).

But in the security of person-to-person talk Borges opened up a bit, and with some people he even became friendly. Among the visitors to the Bioys' apartment on Friday afternoons were a few who to this day are among Borges' most loyal friends. The poet Carlos Mastronardi was one; also the Dabove brothers, Santiago and César, and Manuel Peyrou, a journalist who worked for *La Prensa* and whose slightly fantastic detective stories Borges praised untiringly. They often met in the evenings in a downtown café, the favored place being the Florida's Richmond, not far from the offices of *La Prensa* and *La Nación*. There, echoes of English coffeehouses and American cocktail bars were discreetly blended with the Latin tastes of the customers. From the Richmond, Borges and his friends could command the busiest part of downtown Buenos Aires. The café was near both Corrientes Street, a main thoroughfare with large movie houses and legitimate theaters, cabarets, and restaurants, and Lavalle Street, where the twenty-odd smaller cinemas were packed with moviegoers all day long. Not too far away was the Southside, where Borges loved to roam and where old-style cafés with tango orchestras and billiard tables were not uncommon. Borges' evenings were thus taken up with the male ritual of going out after dinner to meet friends, to converse until the small hours about everything and nothing, or occasionally to even catch a late movie. Although he loved to maintain this ritual, his shyness prevented him from settling down in one particular café and having a regular *peña:* the sort of literary club he had attended while in Spain. He was not expected to pontificate the way Ramón Gómez de la Serna had done in the Pombo bar in the early 1920s or to subtly keep the conversation going, mastering it unobtrusively, the way Rafael Cansinos-Asséns had done in the Café Colonial during the same period. He despised the role of literary master and always preferred to carry on his endless questioning and probing in a smaller group. His notion of a literary café was more that of a place to meet informally and to use as a starting point for exploring the solitary and quiet streets of Buenos Aires' poorest suburbs.

In spite of the many excellent friends he had then, Borges led a terribly solitary life. He had always been haunted by the idea of suicide, and in writing about Lugones in 1938 he came as close as he would ever come to defending it. Since Father's death and the accident of Christmas Eve, suicide had become an obsession. In a piece he wrote in 1940, which he did not allow to be published until 1973, he described in the third person his own "suicide" at the Adrogué Hotel. An attached poem attempts to give some clue to it. As the poem was never finished, it is not easy to see from the published text how the different parts would have been finally connected. What is clear is that Borges was examining the paradox of attempting to use the same hand trained to write for putting a bullet in his head. To move from the pen to the revolver; from his life as an obscure municipal clerk to a rival of his heroic ancestors; from metaphysical speculation about death to the actual test of that speculation—in short, to move from inaction to action—that is what suicide promised him.

More striking than the argument itself are some details of the poem:

> Am I the municipal employee who brings home the kilo of
>   yerba given to him at the office, and one who knows the
>   habit of a key and a bus, the obese and epicene (terrible)

                      lurks
    face that   in (mirrors and windows + metals
                      floats
    and glass)?
                                        (Yates, 1973, p. 322)

In another stanza the poem also makes an explicit reference to two
decisive episodes in his life:

    Or perhaps I have died
    two years ago on a murky stairway on Ayacucho Street,
    twenty years ago in a venal bedroom in the heart of Europe.
                                        (Ibid., p. 323)

The first reference is to the 1938 accident; the second to the day he was
initiated into sex by a prostitute in Geneva—an episode he craftily introduces in the story "The Other," collected in *El libro de arena* (The
Book of Sand, 1975). Suicide, then, is not just the result of a metaphysical temptation or a deep *tedium vitae* (which he himself relates to Sen-
eca's stoic writings). It is deeply connected with experiences that had
shamed him: the symbolical suicide of 1938, after Father's death; the
overwhelming realization that orgasm was too close to real death for
him. His hatred of mirrors—which cruelly reflected his "obese" and
"epicene" face and multiplied men, as copulation did—can now be seen
in the context of an unconscious horror of his own body and of the activities it blindly, obsessively performs. In another, much earlier piece
which Borges wrote between 1924 and 1926 he describes in moving,
awkward words his disgust with his own naked flesh. "Boletín de una
noche" (Report on a Night) is the original title; one of its passsges
describes his return home very late at night and his undressing in darkness: "I am a palpable man (I tell myself) but with black skin, black
skeleton, black gums, black blood that flows through intimate black
flesh. . . . I undress, I am (an instant) that shameful, furtive beast, now
inhuman and somehow estranged from itself that is a naked being"
(ibid., p. 319). That naked being was carefully kept in the dark by
Borges. None of his close friends ever saw it.

    By 1940 Borges' literary life was beginning to settle into a pat-
tern that would not be significantly altered until 1956, when encroach-
ing blindness forced him to limit his outings. In this routine the visits to
the Bioys' comfortable apartment were the main event. They produced
not only the most stimulating conversation but some revolutionary
projects. At the time, Argentina's literary life had been deeply changed
by the outcome of the Spanish civil war. Even before its tragic ending,
some of the most important Spanish publishing houses had moved
their quarters to Argentina. It was in Buenos Aires that Espasa Calpe

launched its very popular Colección Austral, paperback editions of the classics and books of current interest. Soon thereafter one of the editors of that collection, Gonzalo Losada, founded a publishing house under his own name. He was a publisher with a sure literary instinct and a close friend of his authors, two of whom would later receive the Nobel Prize: the Guatemalan novelist Miguel Angel Asturias (1967) and the Chilean poet Pablo Neruda (1971). Don Gonzalo, as everybody called him, created a series of collections, edited by some of the leading Spanish and Spanish American intellectuals, that were to place Argentina in the forefront of the Hispanic publishing business. Borges' brother-in-law, Guillermo de Torre, became the principal literary editor. In 1938 Borges translated a collection of Kafka's stories for Losada's series of unusual contemporary works, La Pajarita de Papel (Paper Birds).

Following Espasa Calpe's and Losada's lead, other Spanish émigrés founded new publishing houses in Buenos Aires. One of the most important was Editorial Sudamericana, which made an agreement with *Sur* to use its imprint in one of its collections and which borrowed from the journal's vast reservoir of talent. Sudamericana published two anthologies, edited by Borges and the Bioys, that were instrumental in shaping the writers who were to become the avant-garde of the resurgence of Latin American literature. The first anthology, published on December 24, 1940, was entitled *Antología de la literatura fantástica* (Anthology of Fantastic Literature). To this day it is one of the most curious and unorthodox compilations on the subject. It includes texts from the East (Tsao Hsue-kin, the *One Thousand and One Nights,* Chuang Tzu) next to classics of Western literature (Petronius, Don Juan Manuel, Rabelais, Carlyle, Poe, Carroll, Maupassant, Kipling); famous modern masters (Wells, Chesterton, Kafka, Joyce) shared billing with local talent (María Luisa Bombal, Borges, Santiago Dabove, Macedonio Fernández, Arturo Cancela, Pilar de Luzarreta). The anthology was highly personal and (in the best sense of the word) arbitrary. The prologue, written and signed by Bioy, summarizes the trio's ideas about fantastic literature. It is divided into three parts. In the first, devoted to the history of the genre, Bioy observes that "old as fear, fantastic fictions are older than literature" (Bioy Casares, 1940, p. 7). He quotes stories with ghosts from the Zend-Avesta to the Chinese classics, mentioning in passing the Bible, Homer, and the *One Thousand and One Nights.* But as a genre, more or less defined, fantastic literature really belongs to the English literature of the nineteenth century. Bioy does not forget the precursors, and he quotes Don Juan Manuel, Rabelais, Quevedo, Defoe, Horace Walpole, and Hoffmann in nineteenth-century German literature.

In the second part, which discusses the technique of the fantastic story, Bioy observes that "literature is constantly changing its readers and, as a consequence, they demand a continuous changing in literature" (ibid., p. 8). Although he would like to accept a rigid set of rules, he is forced to admit that there is not one type of fantastic story but several; he believes that each writer has to follow the general rules while at the same time discovering his own. Then he makes some general observations on topics such as "atmosphere," "surprises," "the yellow peril," and "the yellow room." The last item contains a comic allusion to a well-known detective novel, *The Mystery of the Yellow Room*, by Maurice Leblanc, which discusses a murderous attack committed in a tightly closed room. By linking it with the famous scare slogan about the danger China represents to Western civilization ("the yellow peril"), Bioy pokes fun at both topics. He correctly observes that the earliest fantastic stories depended primarily on a certain type of atmosphere; later, writers discovered that it was more effective to introduce a single fantastic element into a rather banal reality. Wells is the master of what can be called the realistic tendency in fantastic literature. Writing about surprise, Bioy distinguishes between stylistic and thematic surprise. He does not seem to put too much value on that device but observes that it is almost inevitable in the genre. The last topic he discusses is somewhat frivolous. It applies a joke made by Chesterton about the detective story (the yellow peril is the danger of introducing too many suspicious characters) to fantastic literature. He praises Wells for having restrained himself in inventing a single invisible man and not a legion of invisible men.

In the same section Bioy lists the fantastic plots that writers seemed to prefer: they are based on the use of ghosts, travel in time, the realization of three wishes, travels into hell, dreams, metamorphoses, parallel actions which work analogically, immortality. In a closing paragraph Bioy describes very accurately the type of metaphysical story Borges was then inventing: it is "a new literary genre which is both essay and fiction; they are exercises of unceasing intelligence and fortunate imagination, they lack all languor, all *human elements*, pathetic or sentimental," and are aimed at "intellectual readers, interested in philosophy, and almost specialists in literature" (ibid., p. 13). Before ending his classification, Bioy includes two more items: Kafkaesque stories and stories that deal with vampires and castles. Although he likes the former, he finds the latter not very interesting and pointedly indicates that they have been excluded from the anthology. As an afterthought, he notes that fantastic stories can also be classified by their dénouements and establishes three categories: (1) those which need a supernatural explanation; (2) those which have a fantastic but not supernatural explanation; and (3) those which can be explained both super-naturally and naturally.

The last section is devoted to explaining the origin of the present anthology: "One evening in 1937 when we were talking about fantastic literature, we discussed the stories we preferred; one of us suggested that if we put them together and added fragments of the same nature we had collected in our notebooks, we would have a good book. We have done that book" (ibid., p. 13).

Bioy's prologue was, to say the least, disorganized. But if it was weak in theory and logic, it was effective in revealing the trio's literary intentions. The anthology appeared at a time when nineteenth-century realism was still the prevalent mode in Latin American letters. In calling attention to an alternate tradition in literature, the anthology helped both writers and readers to discover a new dimension for Latin American literature.

On November 14, 1940, a few weeks before publication of the anthology, Bioy Casares' novel *La invención de Morel* (The Invention of Morel) had been published by Losada. It carried a prologue by Jorge Luis Borges which amounted to a manifesto for literature of the fantastic. The prologue begins by discussing the ideas (then widely accepted in the Hispanic world) of José Ortega y Gasset about the contemporary novel. In 1925 Ortega had published a short essay called "The Dehumanization of Art" in which he claimed that modern readers were too sophisticated to be interested in adventure stories, that the invention of interesting plots was no longer possible, that the novel of the future was to be "psychological." Borges strongly disagrees, attacking the psychological novel on several counts. The first is poetic: "The typical psychological novel is formless. The Russians and their disciples have demonstrated, tediously, that nobody is impossible. A person may kill himself because he is so happy, for example, or commit murder as an act of benevolence. And one man can inform on another out of fervor or humility. In the end, such complete freedom is tantamount to chaos" (*Morel*, 1964, p. 6). But the psychological novel also pretended to be realistic; that is, "to have us forget that it is a verbal artifice, for it uses each vain precision (or each languid obscurity) as a new proof of verisimilitude." Disagreeing with Ortega, Borges finds Proust boring and claims there are pages (and even chapters) in his novels that are unacceptable as inventions. "We unwittingly resign ourselves to them as we resign ourselves to the insipidity and the emptiness of each day."

The adventure story, on the other hand, does not attempt to be "a transcription of reality." According to Borges, "it must have a rigid plot if it is not to succumb to the mere sequential variety of *The Golden Ass*, the *Seven Voyages of Sinbad*, or the *Quixote*." This criticism of the linear adventure story did not imply an absolute dismissal of the *Quixote;* if he objected to this aspect of the book, he admired the whole concept. He had already written extensively on Cervantes' craft as a novelist, and in 1949, in one of his most important articles, he would explain the "Partial Enchantments of the *Quixote.*" The essay was published in *La Nación* (November 6) and was later included in *Other Inquisitions* (1952). But in the prologue to *The Invention of Morel* he is chiefly concerned with criticizing Ortega's theories.

In the second paragraph he attempts to prove that Ortega was wrong in believing this century "lacks the ability to devise interesting plots." Borges compares Stevenson's inventions with Chesterton's, De Quincey's with Kafka's: all writers he admires. In both cases he finds the twentieth-century author superior, as a creator of plots, to his nineteenth-century counterpart. The sentence ending the paragraph is strong: "I believe I am free from every superstition of modernity, or any illusion that yesterday differs intimately from today or will differ from tomorrow; but I maintain that during no other era have there been novels with such admirable plots as *The Turn of the Screw, Der Prozess, Le voyageur sur la terre,* and the one you are about to read, which was written in Buenos Aires by Adolfo Bioy Casares" (ibid., p. 6).

In the next paragraph Borges takes still another shot at Ortega. He points out that "another popular genre in this so-called plotless century is the detective story, which tells of mysterious events that are later explained and justified by a reasonable occurrence." Then he observes that in his novel Bioy "easily solves a problem perhaps more difficult. The odyssey of marvels he unfolds seems to have no possible explanation other than hallucination or symbolism, and he uses a single fantastic but not supernatural postulate to decipher it" (ibid., p. 7).

What Borges does not explain in his prologue is that Bioy's novel belongs to the science-fiction variety of the adventure story and is modeled after Wells' famous *Island of Dr. Moreau,* published in 1896. In his novel Bioy has the protagonist shipwrecked on a deserted island. To his (and the reader's) surprise, he finds that at some hours of the day the island is the meeting place for a very elegant group of people; among them is a woman, Faustine, with whom he falls in love. The solution to the mystery of the deserted but populated island involves a movie machine which projects three-dimensional images and the protagonist's decision to become part of the film, at the risk of his own life, in order to share the same "reality" with Faustine.

In his prologue to Bioy's novel Borges, besides attempting to discredit Ortega's theories, is revising and expanding his own views on magic or fantastic literature. These views had been previously sketched in his article "Narrative Art and Magic" (*Discusión,* 1932) and would later be repeated in essays and lectures given during the 1940s as well as in stories written at the time and collected first in *The Garden of Forking Paths* (1941), later included in *Ficciones* (1944), and completed in the new stories collected in *The Aleph* (1949). Against mimetic realism, against the psychological novel, Borges defends a fiction that follows the order and the logic of magic, not of the chaotic "real" world of science and nature.

Although Borges never makes any explicit reference to surrealism, it is obvious that in his rejection of realistic and mimetic literature he is closer to Breton's approach as stated in the first *Manifesto of Surrealism* (1924) than to the Spanish American theoreticians of the time. Borges and Breton coincide in criticizing, although for different motives, both Dostoevski and Proust. A connection could be established between Borges' concept of the "magical" and the "fantastic" and Breton's own attempt to reach a "surrealité" through fiction. Their major point of disagreement lies in the question of plot. Breton seems not to be interested in plot at all, preferring what he calls "le hasard"—the chance meeting of his characters, illustrated in his 1928 novel *Nadja*— and rejecting any excessively rigorous concatenation of events. Borges, on the other hand, shows an almost Aristotelian concern with plot, both as a structural device in narrative and as a teleological key to the world. The fact that Borges developed his theories without any explicit reference to surrealism does not alter the importance of the connections between what he was then saying and what Breton had advanced in his *Manifesto*. At the critical level, Borges and Breton are linked not because Borges owed any allegiance to the surrealist movement but because both he and Breton believed that the chief concern of fiction was the creation of purely verbal objects.

Such a view was not popular in Latin America at the time. The literary establishment was still interested in realism of the nineteenth-century variety, while some of the new novelists were trying to apply social realism to the presentation of Latin America's grim realities. Borges' concept of fiction clashed with both those who had accepted Ortega's ideas about the psychological novel and the practitioners of social realism. In addition, by expressing admiration for popular genres such as the adventure story, the detective novel, and science fiction, Borges offended both groups. The social realists considered those genres escapist because they presented reality in a distorted way; the establishment rejected them as frivolous.

Bioy's novel as well as Borges' prologue found few supporters. The former remained largely unread, and the latter was ignored by many of Borges' critics. But the effect of the novel and the prologue would be lasting. They were carefully read by a small group of writers who would come to dominate Latin American fiction and criticism in the next two decades—people such as Octavio Paz, Juan José Arreola, Julio Cortázar, and Alejo Carpentier. In less than fifteen years those few readers would become a large audience.

3.
A New Type of
Fiction

One year exactly after the *Anthology of Fantastic Literature* came out, the same publisher launched the *Antología poética argentina* (Anthology of Argentine Poetry). The scope of the anthology was clearly defined by the jacket: it covered the 1900–1941 period in Argentine poetry and was "objective," not reflecting "a school or personal taste." It was "a truthful and vast panorama of the recent history" of Argentine literature. The jacket ended by assuring readers (the "researcher, the curious, the lover of pure esthetic enjoyment") that they would find in the book "the most admirable Argentine poems of the twentieth century."

Perhaps it is unfair to quote from a book's jacket, but it is necessary in this case because a vast, unbridgeable gap existed between the claims made by the publisher and those made by Borges in his prologue to the book. He begins by frankly admitting that nothing is more vulnerable to criticism than an anthology of contemporary local writings. Every piece can expect to be discussed by the reader (he emphasizes that he considers himself a reader of the anthology), who will find it too well known, weak in comparison with other poems not included, or superfluous because it is the work of a second-rate poet. Borges proceeds to describe the two basic types of anthology: the encyclopedic, which includes everything and for which the prototype is the mythical one-thousand-and-one-hundred-volume Chinese encyclopedia Borges loves to mention; and the hedonistic, which includes only those pieces the compilers really cherish. In the present anthology, he asserts, the editors decided to exclude their personal preferences: "The index registers all the names that a reasonable curiosity may look for" (*Poesía argentina*, 1941, p. 7). But their personal preferences were not totally

356

excluded. In selecting the poems, they have not followed "the romantic methods of our time"—instead of including those poems which are "more personal, characteristic" of each author, they have chosen "those we believe are better" (ibid., p. 8).

The rest of the prologue is dedicated to explaining the anthology's scope. Borges lists the most important poets included, beginning with Almafuerte, a poet unjustly forgotten, then Lugones, whose work anticipates everything done later by younger poets, and Martínez Estrada, "our best contemporary poet." Three other important writers are mentioned: Enrique Banchs, Evaristo Carriego, and Fernández Moreno. They do not belong to the mainstream (represented by the other three) but are instrumental in defining the new poetry. Borges mocks the old distinctions between rhyme and rhythm, pointing out that today political and religious distinctions are considered more important:

> Endlessly I hear people talk about Marxist, neothomist, nationalist poets. In 1831 Macaulay observed: "To talk about essentially Protestant or essentially Christian governments is like talking about essentially Protestant pastry shops or essentially Christian riding schools." No less demeaning is it to talk about poets of such a sect or party. More important than the subjects the poets treat or their opinions and convictions is the structure of the poem or its prosodic and syntactic effects. (Ibid., pp. 9–10)

The rest of the prologue discusses various ways of classifying poets. Borges prefers a purely literary method of linking writers (for instance, he links Lugones and Güiraldes because they were influenced by the same poet, Jules Laforgue, who also influenced T. S. Eliot). Borges also discusses why he has excluded the popular poetry represented by tango lyrics, which he believes to be inferior to poems in which national feelings are less obvious but are characteristically Argentine. To illustrate, he quotes the sonnets written by Enrique Banchs in a very Spanish style. The last two paragraphs comment on the wealth of Argentine poetry. He affirms that today "no other literary genre practiced by Argentines has attained the merit and diversity of their lyrical poetry" (ibid., p. 11). In concluding, he states his belief that if Argentina has not yet produced a writer of the international magnitude of Emerson, Whitman, Poe, James, or Melville, products of the "barbarous" North Americans, it has produced poets that are in no way inferior to those of other Hispanic countries. As proof he again mentions Lugones, Martínez Estrada, and Banchs.

The anthology was the least successful venture attempted by Borges and the Bioys. Both the anthology and the prologue were criticized for being too personal. Even their most faithful readers rejected it. In her reminiscences for *L'Herne*'s special issue on Borges Victoria Ocampo called the editors (her sister Silvina was one of them) the "accomplices" and justified the expression because "I found them slightly arbitrary. And they think the same of me" (Ocampo, 1964, p. 23).

Today the anthology looks tame and indecisive. It includes too many poets who have not traveled well, too many second-rate writers, too many good friends whose poems the editors loved and could not dismiss. But perhaps the main weakness is the omission of one of Argentina's most important contemporary poets: Jorge Luis Borges. At the time, Borges may have thought that being both one of the compilers and the prologuist barred him from the anthology. He once wrote an acid review of *The Oxford Book of Modern Verse*, edited by W. B. Yeats, in which the "complaisant compiler" had reserved for himself the lion's share: no less than fourteen poems (see *El Hogar*, May 28, 1937, p. 26).

Perhaps Borges' decision to omit his own poems was inspired not by modesty but by a conviction that he was no longer a poet. At the time, he was passing through a crisis. He had come to believe that he would never be a really good poet and had practically ceased to write verses. Perhaps he sincerely believed his poetry was of no consequence.

If Borges seemed unsure about the value of his poetry, he was more confident about his prose writings, and in spite of his show of modesty he knew perfectly well what he was after. At the end of the prologue to the *Anthology of Argentine Poetry,* after praising the quality of contemporary verse, he flatly states:

> The nineteenth century produced an excellent prose, a writing only slightly different from oral language; the twentieth century seems to have forgotten that art, which is still alive in many pages of Sarmiento, López, Mansilla, Eduardo Wilde. Lugones is the first to use a written language, and he cannot always resist the temptations of an oratorical syntax and an excessive vocabulary. . . . An anthology of our contemporary prose would be less diverse than this volume and would include fewer indisputable writers. (Ibid., p. 11)

If the *Anthology of Fantastic Literature* were used as a guide, "Tlön, Uqbar, Orbis Tertius" would have been included among the texts in Borges' hypothetical *Anthology of Argentine Prose*.

One can recognize his confidence in the next volume of his to appear: *The Garden of Forking Paths*, published by *Sur* in 1941 and included later in *Ficciones* (1944). A slim, elegant blue volume of exactly eight short stories, it is perhaps the single most important book of prose fiction written in Spanish in this century. A prologue helps the reader to place the stories. Borges classifies the eight pieces into two categories: the last story, which gives the book its title, is a detective story; the other seven are fantastic. In commenting on each story, Borges (as usual) gives some very perceptive views but leaves many things unsaid. About the title piece he observes only that readers would witness "the execution and all the preliminaries of a crime, a crime whose purpose will not be unknown to them but which they would not understand--it seems to me—until the last paragraph" (*Ficciones*, 1962, p. 15). Borges is right about that. The reader knows, from the very beginning, that the protagonist, a Chinese spy working for the Germans during World War I, has to transmit a message; they know that he has the police on his tracks; they also know that in his flight the spy visits an old Sinologist, leisurely discusses with him the work of one of his ancestors, and finally kills him. What they do not know until the last paragraph is that the message consisted of one word, Albert: both the name of the Sinologist and the name of the Belgian city the Germans had to attack. To communicate the message, the spy had to kill somebody (anybody) with that name. The neat little solution is too neat, of course. Any other writer would have avoided the coincidence of making the spy Chinese and making the victim a Sinologist. For Borges, on the contrary, it is precisely the coincidence that is interesting. To him, in a detective story plots have to be both very neat and mysterious. But if the story is more than an entertainment—to be placed next to Chesterton's, Hitchcock's, and Graham Greene's—it is because Borges (without warning his reader) has woven into it another story.

The title gives the second story away: any garden of forking paths is a labyrinth, and the labyrinth is both the subject and the structure of the story. When the protagonist, Yu Tsun, reaches the house of his future victim, he discovers that its garden is shaped like a labyrinth. In meeting Albert, he learns that he is a Sinologist and has been working on the manuscripts of Ts'ui Pên, one of Yu Tsun's ancestors. Yu Tsun knew that his ancestor was supposed to have attempted two different enterprises: the making of a labyrinth and the writing of an immense novel. At his death (by the hand of an unknown assassin), nobody could find the labyrinth and the unfinished novel seemed absurd. Albert tells Yu Tsun that he has found the solution to the enigma: the novel was the labyrinth his ancestor was building. In the same way, the solution to the enigma postulated by Borges' story is also a labyrinth; it keeps forking (its plot) until the reader is totally lost. There is, as in any labyrinth, one path that leads to the center, and that is the path the first story tells: the detective-story path. But all the other ramifications of the labyrinth are there to provide extra dimensions to the fictional reality. The text proliferates like a labyrinth; the detective-story path proliferates in a multitude of paths that lead to other genres. In the multiple image of the labyrinth (the two labyrinths built by Ts'ui Pên, the labyrinth built by Yu Tsun to trap Albert, the labyrinth built by Borges to trap his reader) one finds the symbol of a new type of narrative. The so-called detective story is much more than that.

In discussing the other stories, those of the fantastic variety, Borges is also tantalizingly elusive. About "The Babylon Lottery" he states only that it is not "innocent of symbolism." A humorous tale about a lottery which begins by distributing prizes and ends up by providing favors and punishments to all the citizens of Babylon, even if they do not possess a ticket, the story is meant to symbolize destiny: the lottery to which all of us are unwitting subscribers. But the story again contains a wealth of hidden allusion and jokes. The lottery system described at the beginning is modeled on the Argentine lottery; there is a reference to "a secret privy called Qaphqa" where "malign or benevolent people deposited accusations" to warn the lottery officers about some delinquencies that ought to be punished or some secret desire that ought to be granted. The name of the privy seems exotic enough, until it is read aloud: then it becomes Kafka. The story is symbolical in the same way Kafka's are. About another Kafkaesque story, "The Library of Babel," Borges notes in the prologue that it was inspired by the writings of Leucipus, Lasswitz, Lewis Carroll, and Aristotle. Not a word, of course, is said about the fact that Borges' own painful experience at the Miguel Cané library is at the root of it.

In commenting on another story, "The Circular Ruins," Borges emphasizes the fact that everything is unreal in that tale of an Indian priest, a worshipper of fire, who decides to dream a son and finally manages to translate his dream into reality. In the prologue Borges does not say a word about the story's epigraph, taken from Carroll's *Through the Looking Glass*—"And if he left off dreaming about you . . ."—which in a sense gives away the plot. But again, the story carries other meanings. The subject of the man created by another the way God has created man and the horror of the final discovery that we are all mere creations of dreams are very closely connected with Borges' (and Georgie's) most primeval fears. In spite of its beautiful prose style, the story is one of the most horrifying of Borges' works. The end is particularly memorable: "He walked toward the sheets of flame. They did not bite his flesh; they caressed him and flooded him without heat or combustion. With relief, with humiliation, with terror, he understood that he also was an illusion, that someone else was dreaming him" (*Ficciones*, 1962, p. 63).

Many years later Borges returned to the subject, this time using a different setting and a different medium. In the poem "The Golem," the Holy Rabbi Löw of Prague creates an artificial man, fit only to sweep the synagogue; this creation is used to explore the mystery of paternity:

> At the anguished hour when the light gets vague
> Upon his Golem his eyes would come to rest.
> Who can tell us the feelings in His breast
> As God gazed on His rabbi there in Prague?
> (*Poems*, 1972, translated by John Hollander, p. 115)

If everything was unreal in "The Circular Ruins," Borges observes that in "Pierre Menard, Author of the *Quixote*" what "is unreal is the destiny imposed upon himself by the protagonist" (*Ficciones*, 1962, p. 15). The observation is correct. In attempting to rewrite *Don Quixote* literally and in its entirety, Menard is embarking on a useless task: the book already exists. But the story, one of Borges' most labyrinthine, is about many other things, especially about the art of reading. Borges says nothing of this in the prologue because the story is explicit enough; the only thing he comments on is Menard's other imaginary productions: "The list of writings I attribute to him is not too amusing but neither is it arbitrary; it constitutes a diagram of his mental history" (ibid., p. 15). Again, the seemingly casual observation contains a valuable hint. There is an anticipation of the insane project in Menard's published work, which consists of essays and poems on subjects such as language, translation, permutations, symbolic logic, metaphysics, and metrical laws. All these activities reveal an obsession with the text as a place where language and the individual mind come together to produce a totally artificial object, be it a poem, a metaphysical treatise on reality, a metrical system, or a new way of playing chess. Literature as a game of permutations would lead Menard to discover reading as another game of permutations.

In the second paragraph of his prologue Borges elucidates one of the basic principles of his narrative work and offers a key to his own peculiar brand of fiction: a mixture of the essay and the tale.

The composition of vast books is a laborious and impoverishing extravagance. To go on for five hundred pages developing an idea whose perfect oral exposition is possible in a few minutes! A better course of procedure is to pretend that these books already exist, and then to offer a résumé, a commentary. Thus proceeded Carlyle in *Sartor Resartus*. Thus Butler in *The Fair Haven*. These are works which suffer the imperfection of being themselves books, and of being no less tautological than the others. More reasonable, more inept, more indolent, I have preferred to write notes upon imaginary books. (Ibid., pp. 15–16)

He then lists the three remaining stories: "Tlön, Uqbar, Orbis Tertius," "An Examination of the Work of Herbert Quain," and "The Approach to al-Mu'tasim." He gives the exact date on which "The Approach to al-Mu'tasim" was written but says nothing about the fact that it had already been included, as an essay, in his book *History of Eternity* (1936). He also compares it to Henry James' novel *The Sacred Fount* (1901), which he read quite recently and whose "general argument is perhaps analogous. The narrator . . . investigates whether or not B is influenced by A or C; in 'The Approach to al-Mu'tasim' the narrator feels a presentiment or divines through B the extremely remote existence of Z, whom B does not know" (ibid., p. 16). Although the connection is interesting, it sheds no light on what makes Borges' story unique: its deliberate use of the format of the book review to tell a tale about a mystical ascension to divinity.

Even more telling is the omission of any specific commentary on "Tlön, Uqbar, Orbis Tertius" and "An Examination of the Work of Herbert Quain," both labyrinths of the most subtle fabrication. "Tlön" is, as has already been shown, a key to Borges' fictions. "Herbert Quain" may seem only a variant of "Pierre Menard" in the sense that it deals with the work of an imaginary writer, but in the discussion of Quain's works Borges anticipates some of the themes and procedures he would use in the near future. Up to a point, Quain is a better mask for Borges than Menard. The first paragraph of the story hints about Borges' attitude toward his own work:

> Quain . . . was not a man who ever considered himself a genius, not even on those extravagant nights of literary conversation in which a man who has already worn out the printing presses inevitably plays at being Monsieur Teste or Doctor Samuel Johnson. . . . He was very clear-headed about the experimental nature of his books; he thought them admirable, perhaps, for their novelty and a certain laconic probity, but not for their passion. "I am like Cowley's Odes," he wrote me from Longford on March 6, 1939. "I do not belong to art, but merely to the history of art." In his mind, there was no discipline inferior to history. (Ibid., p. 73)

Quain's books abound in the kind of games Borges liked to play. One, a detective novel entitled *The God of the Labyrinth,* offers a solution which is accepted by the detective but which is actually false. Borges comments:

> Once the enigma is cleared up, there is a long and retrospective paragraph which contains the following phrase: "Everyone thought that the encounter of the two chess players was accidental." This phrase allows one to understand that the solution is erroneous. The unquiet reader rereads the perti-

nent chapter and discovers *another* solution, the true one. The reader of this singular book is thus forcibly more discerning than the detective. (Ibid., p. 74)

Like Borges, Quain always suggests a second reading which unveils a second plot.

Another of Quain's novels, *April, March,* anticipates some of Borges' inventions. Borges comments: "In judging this novel, no one would fail to discover that it is a game; it is only fair to remember that the author never considered it anything else" (ibid., p. 75). The novel is written in a "retrograde" fashion, in the same retrograde pattern as its title, which goes from April to March instead of the other way around. Borges even includes a diagram to explain the novel's structure, which is, of course, that of a labyrinth, a garden of forking paths. Quain also wrote a heroic comedy in two acts, *The Secret Mirror,* which again uses a "retrograde" device: the events in the first act are an imaginary transposition of the sordid realities in the life of the protagonist, a poor playwright. At the end of the story Borges tersely admits that he has borrowed from one of Quain's stories "my story 'The Circular Ruins' " (ibid., p. 78).

The real author borrows from his own characters a play that contains both the imaginary and the real life of the protagonists: Borges' Quain is a very Borgesian author. There is also in Quain a touch of the madness shown in Flann O'Brien's *At Swim Two Birds.* In reviewing that novel for *El Hogar* in one of his last long articles for that magazine (June 2, 1939, p. 6), Borges points out the unsettling effect of receding perspective created by a work in which "fiction lives inside fiction." Now he attributes to Quain the same games he himself plays. The importance of the story in making explicit his techniques cannot be overstressed.

The Garden of Forking Paths is a puzzling book, as its first readers discovered. Very few were able to follow its plots or recognize, under the different layers of irony and parody, its truly revolutionary nature. The majority may have reacted as Mother did, asking Borges why he insisted on writing that kind of scary story. One of those who understood what the book had to offer was, of course, Adolfo Bioy Casares. In a review published in *Sur* (May 1942) Bioy stresses the novelty of Borges' fiction: "Like the philosophers of Tlön, he has discovered the literary possibilities of metaphysics. . . . *The Garden of Forking Paths* creates and satisfies the need for a literature about literature and thought" (Bioy Casares, 1942, p. 60). He indicates that Borges' stories are not in the tradition of metaphysical poetry (*De Rerum Natura, Prometheus Unbound,* for instance) but in the best traditions of philosophy and the detective story. In defining the latter, he observes that its chief merit is that it produced not a book but an ideal, "an ideal of invention, rigor, elegance (in the sense used in mathematics) in plots. To underline the importance of structure: that is, perhaps, the meaning of the genre in the history of literature" (ibid., p. 61). He also stresses the fact that Borges' stories are exciting, and he uses the word in English to indicate its exact shade of meaning. Bioy is on less sure ground when he attempts to classify the stories. In his prologue Borges uses a simple distinction, as we have seen. In a footnote to his review Bioy unnecessarily argues that "Tlön" and "al-Mu'tasim" are fantastic stories: that is exactly what Borges has already said.

The rest of the long review evaluates the stories and discusses their importance in the context of Latin American literature. Bioy defends Borges' notion of fiction as a game. Borges has created a new genre, critical fiction, which refuses to indulge in local color and the exaltation of geography or the denunciation of international capitalism. Speaking especially about Argentine literature, Bioy concludes:

> We are on the periphery of the big forests and America's archeological past. I believe, without vanity, that we may be disappointed by our folklore. Our best tradition is that of being a country in the making. Rivadavia, Sarmiento, and all those who organized the Republic believed in that country. . . . For an Argentine, it is normal to think that his literature is the world's best literature. . . . Of that culture . . . and of a possible and perhaps future Argentina that will correspond to it, this book is representative. (Ibid., pp. 64–65)

The review was a landmark in Borges criticism. But the fact that it was written by Borges' closest associate and appeared in a journal owned by the same publishing firm that had published the book made the review suspect. For yet a while the number of Borges readers and admirers did not seem destined to increase.

4.
The Invention of
Biorges

The literary collaboration of Borges and Bioy Casares dates back to 1937 when they spent a week in El Pardo, where Bioy's father had a ranch. Speaking about that week in a chronology of his own life and work, Bioy writes: "We plan a story we will never write, which is the germ of *Seis problemas para don Isidro Parodi* [Six Problems for Don Isidro Parodi], about a German philanthropist, Dr. Praetorius, who by hedonistic methods—music, ceaseless games—murders children" (Bioy Casares, 1975, p. 37). Elsewhere, Bioy defines his debt to Borges: "Any collaboration with Borges is the equivalent of one year's work" (Bioy Casares, 1968, p. 140).

Borges has also written about their joint undertakings in his "Autobiographical Essay":

> It is always taken for granted in these cases that the elder man is the master and the younger his disciple. This may have been true at the outset, but several years later, when we began to work together, Bioy was really and secretly the master. He and I attempted many different ventures. We compiled anthologies of Argentine poetry, tales of the fantastic, and detective stories; we wrote articles and forewords; we annotated Sir Thomas Browne and Gracián; we translated short stories by writers like Beerbohm, Kipling, Wells, and Lord Dunsany; we founded a magazine, *Destiempo*, which lasted three issues; we wrote film scripts, which were invariably rejected. Opposing my taste for the pathetic, the sentadous, and the baroque, Bioy made me feel that quietness and restraint are more desirable. If I may be allowed a sweeping statement, Bioy led me gradually to classicism. ("Essay," 1970, pp. 245–246)

Borges is probably right, at least in part, about the influence of Bioy Casares' writing on his own. About the invention of Bustos Domecq,

the pseudonym under which Bioy and Borges began writing in collaboration, he has more specific things to say:

It was at some point in the early forties that we began writing in collaboration—a feat that up to that time I had thought impossible. I had invented
what we thought was a quite good plot for a detective story. One rainy
morning, he told me we ought to give it a try. I reluctantly agreed, and a
little later that same morning the thing happened. A third man, Honorio
Bustos Domecq, emerged and took over. (Ibid., p. 246)

In his conversation with Ronald Christ, Borges gives more details. To a question about the method they used, he replies:

BORGES: Well, it's rather queer. When we write together, when we collaborate,
we call ourselves H. Bustos Domecq. Bustos was a great-grandfather of mine
and Domecq was a great-grandfather of his. Now the queer thing is that
when we write, and we write mostly humorous stuff—even if the stories are
tragic, they are told in a humorous way or they are told as if the teller hardly
understood what he was saying—when we write together what comes of the
writing, if we are successful, and sometimes we are—why not? after all I'm
speaking in the plural, no?—when our writing is successful, then what comes
out is something quite different from Bioy Casares' stuff and my stuff; even
the jokes are different. So we have created between us a kind of third person; we have somehow begotten a third person that is quite unlike us.
[CHRIST:] A fantastic author?
BORGES: Yes, a fantastic author with his likes, his dislikes, and a personal style
that is meant to be ridiculous; but still, it is a style of his own, quite different
from the kind of style I write when I try to create a ridiculous character. I
think that's the only way of collaborating. Generally speaking, we go over the
plot together before we set pen to paper—rather I should talk about typewriters, because he has a typewriter. Before we begin writing, we discuss the
whole story; then we go over the details, we change them, of course, we
think of a beginning and then we think the beginning might be the end or
that it might be more striking if somebody said nothing at all or said something quite outside the mark. Once the story is written, if you ask us whether
this adjective or this particular sentence came from Bioy or from me, we
can't tell. . . . I think that's the only way of collaborating, because I have
tried collaborating with other people. Sometimes it works out all right, but
sometimes one feels that the collaborator is a kind of rival. Or, if not—as in
the case of [Manuel] Peyrou—we began collaborating but he is timid and a
very courteous, a very polite kind of person, and consequently if he says anything and you make any objections, he feels hurt and he takes it back. He
says: "Oh, yes, of course, of course, yes, I was quite wrong. It was a blunder."
Or if you propose anything, he says: "Oh, that's wonderful!" Now that kind
of thing can't be done. In the case of me and [Bioy] Casares, we don't feel as
if we are two rivals or even as if we were two men who play chess. There's no

case of winning or losing. What we're thinking of is the story itself, the stuff itself. (Christ, 1967, pp. 145–146)

There is more about Bustos Domecq in the "Autobiographical Essay." Borges seems chiefly interested there in defining Bustos' grip on the collaborators:

> In the long run, he ruled us with a rod of iron and to our amusement, and later to our dismay, he became utterly unlike ourselves, with his own whims, his own puns, and his own very elaborate style of writing. . . . Bustos Domecq's first book was *Six Problems for Don Isidro Parodi* [1942], and during the writing of that volume he never got out of hand. Max Carrados had attempted a blind detective; Bioy and I went one step further and confined our detective to a jail cell. The book was at the same time a satire on the Argentines. For many years, the dual identity of Bustos Domecq was never revealed. When it finally was, people thought that, as Bustos was a joke, his writing could hardly be taken seriously. ("Essay," 1970, p. 246)

Bioy is even blunter. According to his reminiscences, when the first Bustos Domecq book was published, "our friends and the critics [were] not amused" (Bioy Casares, 1975, p. 38). Apparently, the first not to be amused was Victoria Ocampo, whose journal *Sur* published two of the stories and the book as well. The two stories published in *Sur*—"The Twelve Figures of the World" (January 1942) and "The Nights of Goliadkin" (March 1942)—may have puzzled readers. In the first, Parodi has to solve the murder unwillingly committed by the very confused young man who comes to visit him and asks for his help. Full of apocryphal folklore (it takes place in a community of Armenians devoted to astrology), the story follows the Chestertonian pattern of a paradoxical beginning and a series of almost incredible if not miraculous coincidences. A parody of a parody (Chesterton is already a parody of both Poe and Conan Doyle), the story is more memorable for its writing than for its rather cluttered plot. But the real invention occurs in the dialogue. Each character uses colloquial Argentine speech in a way that reveals both his views and his psychology.

The second story is somewhat better. It uses one of the classical loci of detective and spy stories: the express train that runs nonstop from one remote corner of the world to the metropolis. Again, language is master. One of the characters, Gervasio Montenegro, is a successful caricature of the mediocre writer, full of clichés and French bon mots.

The book opens with these two stories, followed by four more. Two items deserve special attention. One is a short biography of H. Bustos Domecq, written in a delightful style, by one Adelia Puglione, a dedicated teacher in a provincial school. Her "silhouette" of Bustos Domecq is almost as comic as the one of Pierre Menard in the story of the same name—the difference being that Menard comes from a French province while Bustos Domecq comes from Santa Fe, Argentina. Even more outrageous is the foreword by Gervasio Montenegro, one of the book's characters. In a sense, Montenegro preempts all criticism because, despite his insufferable pretentiousness, he scores a few good points. After hailing Bustos Domecq, rather excessively, as the first Argentine writer of detective stories (he forgets, among others, Borges himself), he very ably condenses the author's method: to stick to the basic elements of the problem (the enigmatic presentation of facts, the clarifying solution). In commenting on the stories, he selects the three best, in decreasing order of importance: "The victim of Tadeo Limardo," in which the murdered man prepares his own sacrifice, thus disguising what is essentially a suicide; "The Long Search of Tai An," in which the author adds a variation on the problem of the hidden object that Poe and other precursors had postulated; and "San Giácomo's Foresight," in which a cuckold takes the most elaborate and invisible revenge on the bastard offspring his wife had borne. Montenegro also praises, perhaps excessively, the author's ability to draw characters and, in particular, the character of Don Isidro Parodi. He has a few reservations which reveal him to be a true bigot and anti-Semite, much like the obsequious narrator of "Pierre Menard."

What Montenegro does not talk about is what matters most today: the creation of language. Through Bustos Domecq, Borges and Bioy liberated their power of parody. The solemnity of spoken Argentine in all its variations (lower-class slang, the Frenchified speech of pseudo-intellectuals, the thick and obsolete Spanish of Spaniards. Italianate jargon) was exploded through characters who were less narrative figures than figures of speech. For the first time in Argentina a deliberate attempt to create narrative through the parody of narrative form and speech was successful. Although the initial reader reaction was poor, the book's effect on contemporaries was lasting. Both Leopoldo Marechal in his *Adán Buenosayres* and Julio Cortázar in *The Winners* and *Hopscotch* show that they were influenced by Bustos Domecq.

Few people realized that under the outrageous puns and the convoluted plots there were very serious intentions. At one level, the book anticipates some of Borges' most constant preoccupations. "San Giácomo's Foresight," for example, can be read as a draft of "The Dead Man," a tale he would include in his second important book of fantastic fictions, *The Aleph* (1949). Both stories are about a man who, led to believe he is lucky and omnipotent, ends in tragedy. The book is also important at a second level: that of describing Argentine reality. Through parody, the authors hold up a distorted and critical mirror. References to the ineptitude and/or corruption of the Argentine government, to the army and to the European war that was about to engulf the whole world, indicate that both authors were aware that their parodical enterprise had an extra dimension. And as a corrective against the self-satisfied literature of the Argentine establishment, this anarchistic parody was extremely effective. The fact that the detective was himself in jail (convicted of a murder committed by somebody who had very good connections both with the local authorities and the police) added to the satirical nature of the book.

In general, readers were puzzled, outraged, or bored with the book. Talking to Napoléon Murat, Borges recalls:

When the readers discovered that Bustos Domecq did not exist, they believed all the stories to be jokes and that it was not necessary to read them, that we were poking fun at the reader, which was not the case. I don't know why the idea of a pseudonym made them furious. They said: "Those writers do not exist; there is a name but there is not a writer." Then a general contempt took over, but it was a false reasoning. (Murat, 1964, p. 378)

The readers did not realize that a joke could be serious, and that irony and parody are among the deadliest forms of criticism. The gap between readers and authors was unbridgeable. Not until Bustos Domecq's first book was reissued a quarter of a century later would it be read by readers who could see its point.

One of the first to realize that in Bustos Domecq there was more than met the eye was the Mexican humanist Alfonso Reyes, who reviewed the book in the Mexican magazine *Tiempo* (July 30, 1943), extolling not only its humor and wit but its value as social criticism. Reyes, who had been ambassador to Argentina in the late 1920s and had then formed a long-lasting literary friendship with Borges, observed in his review:

Social testimony. In the meantime, we are transported to strange and baroque places, we visit the most secret corners of Buenos Aires life and in front of our eyes passes a gallery of types of all categories and races in a cauldron of imagination, each one speaking the language that best suits him. To the point that, if one puts aside the interest of the plot, the book has the value of a social testimony, strongly illuminated by poetical lights. Let's make it clear: poetical but not sentimental. There is not the least trace of sentimentality here, which would be contrary to the firm esthetics of Borges. (Reyes, 1943, p. 104)

But Reyes' prophetic reading of the book went unheard. That did not deter the co-authors, who continued to collaborate in the same vein. Two more books written or inspired by Bustos Domecq were published in the 1940s. One was *Dos fantasías memorables* (Two Memorable Fantasies), signed Bustos Domecq. The first story in the book, "El testigo" (The Witness), tells about a young girl who has a vision of the Holy Trinity and dies from the shock; the second, "El signo" (The Sign), offers the vision of an interminable procession of food, a glutton's paradise.

The other book, *Un modelo para la muerte* (A Model for Death), was signed by B. Suárez Lynch, a disciple of Bustos Domecq, and pretended to be a detective novel. Borges recalls that the book "was so personal and so full of private jokes that we published it only in an edition that was not for sale. The author of this book we named B. Suárez Lynch. The 'B' stood, I think, for Bioy and Borges, Suárez for another great-grandfather of mine, and Lynch for another great-grandfather of Bioy's" ("Essay," 1970, p. 247). What Borges does not say is that the parody goes further in these two books than in *Six Problems*. Even the publisher's imprint they invented was parodical: Oportet & Haereses alludes in Spanish to port and sherry wines (*oporto* and *jerez*).

The plot of *A Model for Death* is so buried under digressions and puns that it is almost impossible to remember, even after repeated readings. Following the format of *Six Problems,* the book has a preface, by Bustos Domecq, which offers a short literary biography of Suárez Lynch. As a detective novel, the book was a disaster. Even a friendly reviewer such as Carlos Mastronardi in *Sur* (December 1946) pointed out that "the charming and light plot, whose tracing is not easy at all, gets lost and reappears behind the long dialogues and the attractive incidental episodes." Borges and Bioy realized they had gone too far and for a while decided to stop writing as Bustos Domecq or Suárez Lynch. In his conversations with Napoléon Murat, Borges explains how they reached that conclusion:

> . . . We wrote a bit for us, and because this happened in an atmosphere of jokes, the stories became so impossible to unravel and so baroque that it was very difficult to understand them. At the beginning, we made jokes, and then jokes on jokes, it was like in algebra: jokes squared, jokes cubed. . . . Then, we decided to stop writing, because we had come to realize that it was difficult and even impossible to write in another way and that this way was painful, at least for the reader. (Murat, 1964, p. 378)

Bustos Domecq and Suárez Lynch had finally taken over. Borges and Bioy had been replaced by their own creations. A new writer had been born, a writer who ought to be called "Biorges" because he was neither Borges nor Bioy, and because he did not stick to one pseudonym. The only way to cope with his proliferation was to silence him. And that is what Borges and Bioy did in 1946. But they hadn't heard the last of Biorges.

5.
Two Forms of
Reparation

The same year that *Six Problems for Don Isidro Parodi* came out, the Borgeses moved again, to an apartment at 275 Quintana Avenue, near Rodríguez Peña Street, in the same neighborhood where the family had resided since returning from their last trip to Europe in 1924. They stayed there for a few years only, moving in 1944 to a two-bedroom downtown apartment at 994 Maipú Street, which Borges occupies today.

Their everyday life had begun to settle into a routine: Mother stayed at home, busy with household responsibilities (they had only one servant, who functioned as cook and maid) and with her own literary work; Borges went to the Miguel Cané library or also remained at home, writing in a painstaking, minuscule handwriting his articles and reviews, his stories and essays. Mother helped him with his readings and translations. Her English had improved to the point where she began to do some work on her own. Probably her best translation was of a collection of Katherine Mansfield's tales, published by Losada in the same series as Kafka's *The Metamorphosis* and under the title of one of the stories, *The Garden Party*. Borges himself translated William Faulkner's *The Wild Palms* for Sudamericana in 1940 and Henri Michaux's *A Barbarian in Asia* for *Sur* in 1941.

The translation of the Faulkner was significant. Earlier, in *El Hogar,* he had discussed or given favorable mention to Faulkner's novels. Although he never wrote a full-length article about him, he was consistently enthusiastic. He praised Faulkner for being as concerned with the verbal artifices of narrative as with the "passions and works of men" (January 22, 1937, p. 30); he discussed Faulkner's ability to play with time and also to write a straightforward novel, such as *The Un-vanquished,* and he noted that Faulkner's world was "so physical and fleshy" that in comparison Dostoevski's seemed too light (June 24, 1938, p. 30); he came to the conclusion that Faulkner was "the first novelist of our time" (May 5, 1939, p. 62). Of his books, he considered *Light in August* to be "perhaps his most intense work and one of the most memorable of our time" (January 21, 1938, p. 26), but he also had words of praise for *Absalom, Absalom!* and *The Sound and the Fury* (January 22, 1937, p. 30) and for *Sanctuary* (May 5, 1939, p. 62).

He was not so enthusiastic about *The Wild Palms.* In his review of that book for *El Hogar* on May 5, 1939 he observes that while in Faulkner's most important novels new techniques seem necessary and inevitable, in this one they seem "less attractive than inconvenient, less justifiable than exasperating." Discussing the two stories that form the book ("The Wild Palms," about a man "destroyed by the flesh," and "The Old Man," about a man who is given a "useless and atrocious free-dom" by a Mississippi flood), Borges observes that the second is superior. His conclusion—that *The Wild Palms* is not the best introduction to Faulkner—seems paradoxical in view of the fact that this is the Faulkner book he elected to translate.

His translation of *The Wild Palms* has been considered as good as or even better than the original. The style is perhaps tighter than Faulkner's, and the hardness and intensity of the novel's best passages (praised by Borges in his review as "notoriously exceeding the possibil-ities of any other author") indicate how much he put into the transla-tion—in spite of his claims that it was Mother who really did it ("Essay," 1970, p. 207). For the book jacket, Borges wrote a summary of Faulk-ner's work and life which condensed what he had already written in *El Hogar.* Describing *The Wild Palms,* he observes that "there are two dif-ferent plots, which never coincide, but that somehow correspond to each other. The style is passionate, meticulous, hallucinatory."

The importance of this translation for the new Latin American novel was considerable. Although Faulkner's novel *Sanctuary* had al-ready been translated into Spanish by the Cuban novelist Lino Novás Calvo and had been published in Spain in 1934, the translation was mediocre and had been tampered with by the publisher, who was afraid to be too specific about the way Popeye manages to rape Temple Drake. Borges' translation was not only faithful to the original but created in Spanish a writing style that was the equivalent of the origi-nal's English. For many young Latin American novelists who did not know enough English to read the dense original, Borges' tight version meant the discovery of a new kind of narrative writing. They had, in Borges, the best possible guide to Faulkner's dark and intense world.

In spite of so much activity, Borges was still largely unknown in Argentina, and his name was not recognized by the literary establishment. In 1942 his collection of short stories, *The Garden of Forking Paths*, received the second prize in the annual literary competition organized by the city of Buenos Aires. The first prize went to *Ramón Hazaña*, a gaucho novel by Eduardo Acevedo Díaz, Jr., son of one of Uruguay's leading historical novelists. Borges took the matter in stride. A comic reference to the prize appears in his story "The Aleph." There, the pompous poet, Carlos Argentino Daneri, gets second prize in the annual national literary competition. (The first prize is given to a real if second-rate writer, Antonio Aita, who was the secretary of the Argentine PEN Club; the third went to Mario Bonfanti, one of Bustos Domecq's most pitiful characters, borrowed by Borges to underline the inanity of the occasion.)

Although Borges made light of his disappointment, his friends reacted strongly. In July 1942 José Bianco of *Sur* organized a "Reparation to Borges," in which twenty-one writers joined together to praise his work. These included old and new friends—Eduardo Mallea, Patricio Canto, Pedro Henríquez Ureña, Gloria Alcorta, Adolfo Bioy Casares, Carlos Mastronardi, Eduardo González Lanuza, Enrique Amorim, Ernesto Sábato, Manuel Peyrou—as well as people whose points of view were not exactly those of Borges but who nevertheless respected and admired him for his work—Francisco Romero, Luis Emilio Soto, Amado Alonso, Aníbal Sánchez Reulet, Angel Rosenblat, Enrique Anderson Imbert, Bernardo Canal Feijoo. Borges reacted to the homage with amusement. According to Bianco in his reminiscences:

> I even selected (because I know he does not like green) a bull's blood red cover. As soon as the first copies were out, I sent a couple to his place. The following afternoon, when I went to visit him, he only had jokes about that friendly homage. He seemed happy, of course, but especially astonished that so many writers had taken the trouble to raise their more or less shocked voices because the [city's] Cultural Committee had not paid attention to his extraordinary book. (Bianco, 1964, p. 18)

In spite of the disappointment, Borges continued to write and publish. For Losada he collected his *Poemas* (1922–1943), in a rather slim volume. The cover illustration, by the Italian painter Attilio Rossi, depicted a white angel cutting a brown diamond which was inside a cobweb. Perhaps the illustration was a bit too fanciful for Borges' modest claims as a poet. The book contained his first three books of poems—*Fervor de Buenos Aires* (Adoration of Buenos Aires, 1923), *Luna de enfrente* (Moon Across the Way, 1925), and *Cuaderno San Martín* (San

Martín Copybook, 1929)—plus a section called "Other Poems," which included six new pieces, the only ones he had written in the last fourteen years. The old poems were revised, in some cases drastically. Some pieces were dropped; some added. The sprawling prologue to the first book was condensed into one sentence. If Borges' aim as a young man had been to emulate Whitman, by the 1940s he aspired to be a part-time poet only. A quotation, taken from an English author, helped him to define his attitude. It had already been used in *San Martín Copybook* and belonged to Edward FitzGerald, the urbane translator of Omar Khayyam's *Rubaiyat*. It read: "As to an occasional copy of verses, there are few men who have leisure to read, and are possessed of any music in their souls, who are not capable of versifying on some ten or twelve occasions during their natural lives: at a proper conjunction of the stars. There is no harm in taking advantage of such occasions" (*Poemas,* 1943, p. 119).

If the quotation seemed premature for a book that originally contained twelve poems written in four years, it admirably suited the collected poems of 1943. Three of the more recent poems helped Borges to define some of his metaphysical preoccupations. The second, "Del cielo y del infierno" (On Heaven and Hell), is not memorable in spite of the quasi-Quevedian intonation. The first, on the other hand, is one of his best. Under the title of "La noche cíclica" (The Cyclical Night), it develops a subject that he had already discussed in his essays: the eternal return of man and things. But in the poem it is the anguish of his own flesh, his fears and even terrors, that matter most. One passage is strongly confessional:

> Night after night sets me down in the world
>
> On the outskirts of this city. A remote street
> Which might be either north or west or south,
> But always with a blue-washed wall, the shade
> Of a fig tree, and a sidewalk of broken concrete.
>
> This, here, is Buenos Aires. Time, which brings
> Either love or money to men, hands on to me
> Only this withered rose, this empty tracery
> Of streets with names recurring from the past
>
> In my blood: Laprida, Cabrera, Soler, Suárez . . .
> (*Poems,* 1972, translated by Alastair Reid, p. 79)

The elegiac mood of the last verse is also visible in the book's last piece, "Poema conjetural" (Conjectural Poem), dedicated to his ancestor Francisco Narciso de Laprida, who was killed in a civil war battle. It is a dramatic monologue, in the style made famous by Browning. In recalling his ancestor's fate (to have his throat cut by the gauchos of Aldao), Borges suggests a subtle contrast with his own fate as an intellectual, living in a country that is slowly reverting to anarchy and barbarism. At the time the poem was published, the signs of the army's increased participation in Argentine political life were all too evident. Colonel Perón was being discussed as a future leader. Borges, who had always hated all forms of government and especially totalitarianism, here comes very close to writing a political poem. Although it is obviously a historical elegy, which may have fooled contemporary readers, if it is placed in the context of its time, the allusions become obvious. It will be sufficient to quote the first strophe:

> Bullets whip the air this last afternoon.
> A wind is up, blowing full of cinders
> as the day and this chaotic battle
> straggle to a close. The gauchos have won:
> victory is theirs, the barbarians'.
> I, Francisco Narciso Laprida,
> who studied both canon law and civil
> and whose voice declared the independence
> of this untamed territory,
> in defeat, my face marked by blood and sweat,
> holding neither hope nor fear, the way lost,
> strike out for the South through the back country.
> (Ibid., translated by Norman Thomas di Giovanni, p. 83)

The paradox is that Laprida is also able to recognize with joy that he has just come face to face with his South American fate: not the fate of a man of letters but the fate of a man brutally sacrificed for his country. The poem ends vividly, almost erotically:

> My feet tread the shadows of the lances
> that spar for the kill. The taunts of my death,
> the horses, the horsemen, the horses' manes,
> tighten the ring around me. Now the first
> blow, the lance's hard steel ripping my chest,
> and across my throat the intimate knife.
> (Ibid., p. 85)

In an article on the famous verses that the fifteenth-century Spanish poet Jorge Manrique devoted to the death of his father, Borges observes that they are too rhetorical and do not convey the poet's emotion (the article appears in *El idioma de los argentinos,* published in 1928). In his "Conjectural Poem," in spite of the historical distance, Borges manages to be moving. He himself underlined the political content of the poem by including it at the end of a lecture on gaucho literature that he gave in Montevideo in 1945. Making a pointed reference to the Argentine political situation of the time, he observed that he had come to the realization that "for a second time we had to face darkness and adventure. I thought that the tragic 1820s were back, that the men who had measured themselves against its barbarianism also felt amazement before the face of an unexpected destiny which, nevertheless, they did not flee from" (*Aspectos*, 1950, p. 34). For him, the "Conjectural Poem" was much more than an elegy; it was, in cipher, an image of his own fate. He would later write a story, "The South," which also deals with the destiny of a man torn apart by his double allegiance to European culture and life and to native barbarianism.

In 1943 Borges began his long association with a small publishing house, Emecé Editores, which had recently begun to expand its program by appointing some leading intellectuals (the Spaniard Ricardo Baeza, Eduardo Mallea) as literary editors. Pamphlets of the Chimera was the name given to a series of selected short stories, published singly in elegant little volumes and edited by Mallea; Borges wrote several prologues for it. One prefaced his own translation of Herman Melville's *Bartleby, the Scrivener* (Buenos Aires, 1943). Half of the prologue is devoted to discussing *Moby Dick;* the rest contains a short biography of Melville and a general evaluation of his work. Borges has this to say about *Bartleby:* "Kafka's work projects a curious retrospective light over *Bartleby.* [The story] defines a genre which Kafka would reinvent and deepen toward 1919: one that deals with the fantasies of behavior and feeling that now are wrongly called psychological" (*Prólogos*, 1975, p. 117). He also observes that the beginning of the story is reminiscent of Dickens. After a short bibliography, he concludes: "The vast populations, the high cities, the mistaken and clamorous publicity have conspired to make the great secret man one of America's traditions. Edgar Allan Poe was one of them; Melville, also" (ibid., p. 118).

His second contribution to the Chimera series was a prologue to a translation of Henry James' "The Abasement of the Northmores." In introducing James, Borges stresses his strangeness:

> I have perused part of Eastern literature and several Western literatures; I have compiled an anthology of fantastic literature; I have translated Kafka and Melville, Swedenborg and Bloy; I do not know of a work as strange as that of James. The writers I have just mentioned are, from the very beginning, surprising; the world they present in their works is almost professionally unreal; James, before showing what he is, a resigned and polite inhabitant of hell, risks seeming a mundane novelist, more nondescript than

others. As soon as we begin reading, we are upset by a certain ambiguity, a certain superficiality; after a few pages, we understand that these deliberate neglects have the effect of enhancing the book. (Ibid., p. 101)

After analyzing a few of his favorites among James' stories, Borges concludes with the customary bibliography and a quotation from Graham Greene in which the latter observes that James is as solitary in the history of the novel as Shakespeare is in the history of poetry.

Borges wrote other prologues to volumes edited by Mallea (one on the memoirs of Sarmiento) and to Ricardo Baeza's collection of classics. But his first important contribution to the Emecé list was an anthology called *The Best Detective Stories,* which he compiled in 1943 with Adolfo Bioy Casares. Some of the sixteen stories in the anthology are by obvious names such as Edgar Allan Poe ("The Purloined Letter"), Robert Louis Stevenson (a fragment from *The Master of Ballantrae*), Arthur Conan Doyle (*The Red-Headed League*), Gilbert Keith Chesterton ("The Honor of Israel Gow"), Ellery Queen ("Philately"), and Georges Simenon ("Les sept minutes"); others are by authors not generally associated with the detective genre: Nathaniel Hawthorne ("Mr. Higginbotham's Catastrophe"), Jack London (from *Moon Face*), Guillaume Apollinaire (from *L'Hérésiarque et Cie*), Eden Phillpotts (from *Peacock House*). The anthology also includes stories by Argentine writers such as Carlos Pérez Ruiz, Manuel Peyrou, and Jorge Luis Borges. Although there is no introduction to the volume, the jacket makes some sweeping statements: "Invented in 1841 by the famous poet Edgar Allan Poe, the detective story is the newest of literary genres. It can also be said that it is the literary genre of our time." To validate the statement, the jacket mentions several distinguished readers who favor the genre: André Gide, Keyserling, Victoria Ocampo, Jung, Alfonso Reyes, Aldous Huxley. The aim of the collection is, according to the blurb, to offer a panorama of a significant segment of contemporary literature. To accomplish that purpose, the compilers did not rely exclusively on former anthologies by Dorothy Sayers, Lee Wright, Rhode, Douglas Thompson, and Wrong, or on the studies of Fosca, Haycraft, and Roger Caillois; they used their long and pleasurable association with the original texts, not excluding, of course, the ones produced by Argentines. The blurb also indicates that the chronological order followed in the anthology is designed to help the studious reader to trace the evolution of the genre.

In spite of the jacket's words, the anthology is less the result of scholarship than of love. It reveals the extent to which both Borges and Bioy Casares valued the detective story, the vast knowledge they had of its practitioners, and the independence of their evaluations. In a sense, the anthology complements the one on fantastic literature they compiled in 1940 for Sudamericana. The new anthology had an enormous success and was the foundation of a series of detective novels that Borges and Bioy began to edit for Emecé Editores under the title— suggested by Dante's Inferno—of The Seventh Circle. The first volume to be published was Nicholas Blake's *The Beast Must Die*. On the jacket, unmistakably written by the compilers, the reader is informed that Blake is the pseudonym of the English poet Cecil Day Lewis. The collection later included some masterpieces of the genre (Dickens' *The Mystery of Edwin Drood,* Collins' *The Moonstone* and *The Woman in White*), as well as more contemporary writers such as Eden Phillpotts, Michael Innes, Anthony Berkeley, Vera Caspary, James M. Cain, and Graham Greene, whose *The Ministry of Fear* was hailed by Borges as one of the best novels to come out of the war. The success of The Seventh Circle created a new audience for Borges. It was a toally different audience from the one he had had earlier. Younger, less concerned with high literary standards, slightly iconoclastic, this audience soon moved from the detective stories and novels Borges and Bioy Casares recommended to the ones they themselves wrote. Through a genre generally snubbed by literary intellectuals, Borges came to find a devoted readership. It was a form of reparation.

6.
A New Volume of Stories

World War II was coming to an end. On August 23, 1944, Paris was liberated. Borges, who had always explicitly supported the Allies in an Argentina whose rulers favored the Axis, wrote a short piece for *Sur* (September 1944) that he later collected in *Other Inquisitions* ("A Comment on August 23, 1944," 1952). The article can be seen as a sequel, and perhaps a fit conclusion, to the series of notes and articles about Nazism that he wrote for *Sur* and *El Hogar*. For him, the liberation of Paris was less important than the total defeat of Nazism that he could now foresee. The article begins with a personal statement about August 23:

> That crowded day gave me three heterogeneous surprises: the *physical* happiness I experienced when they told me Paris had been liberated; the discovery that a collective emotion can be noble; the enigmatic and obvious enthusiasm of many who were supporters of Hitler. I know that if I question that enthusiasm I may easily resemble those futile hydrographers who asked why a single ruby was enough to arrest the course of a river; many will accuse me of trying to explain a chimerical occurrence. Still, that was what happened, and thousands of persons in Buenos Aires can bear witness to it. (*Inquisitions*, 1964, p. 134)

The article then tries to unravel the mystery. How was it possible to be on the side of Nazism and at the same time accept, joyously, its defeat? In a roundabout way, after summarizing some of the arguments he had used in previous articles, Borges comes to the conclusion that even Nazi sympathizers did not believe in a Nazi triumph. He quotes a passage from Shaw's *Man and Superman,* "where it is stated that the horror of hell is its unreality," and then tells an anecdote about the day Paris fell into German hands:

A certain Germanophile, whose name I do not wish to remember, came to my house that day. Standing in the doorway, he announced the dreadful news: the Nazi armies had occupied Paris. I felt a mixture of sadness, disgust, malaise. And then it occurred to me that his insolent joy did not explain the stentorian voice or the abrupt proclamation. He added that the German troops would soon be in London. Any opposition was useless, nothing could prevent their victory. That was when I knew that he too was terrified. (Ibid., p. 135)

The conclusion Borges extracts from his analysis of these two symmetrical episodes is clear:

Nazism suffers from unreality, like Erigena's hells. It is uninhabitable; men can only die for it, lie for it, kill and wound for it. No one, in the intimate depths of his being, can wish it to triumph. I shall hazard this conjecture: *Hitler wants to be defeated.* Hitler is collaborating blindly with the inevitable armies that will annihilate him, as the metal vultures and the dragon (which must not have been unaware that they were monsters) collaborated, mysteriously, with Hercules. (Ibid., pp. 135–136)

The accuracy of Borges' prophecy was plainly seen a few months later when Hitler died among the ruins of his bunker and of the Third Reich.

In spite of being neglected by the Argentine establishment, Borges continued to receive recognition from a perceptive few. One of the most important was the French critic and sociologist Roger Caillois. Invited by Victoria Ocampo on the eve of the war to come to Argentina to give a few lectures, Caillois remained there for the duration. An extremely imaginative and active man, Caillois could not remain idle while French culture was being destroyed by the German occupation. With the help of Victoria Ocampo, he launched a journal, *Lettres Françaises,* which was printed in Buenos Aires and had on its cover *Sur*'s downward arrow to call attention to the patronage. Some of the best French writers of the time contributed to the journal. In its fourteenth issue, published in October 1944, two of Borges' short stories (under the collective title of "Assyriennes") were translated into French for the first time. The pieces—"The Babylon Lottery" and "The Library of Babel"—were among Borges' most curious. Although the circulation of the journal in metropolitan France was rather limited, the issue came out at the exact moment, after liberation, when France was avidly renewing its contacts with the rest of the world. It would be tempting to date from that moment the beginning of French recognition of Borges, but in fact, Borges (and his promoter Caillois) would have to wait almost sixteen more years for international recognition—until the day in 1961 when the Formentor Prize, given by a group of international publishers, was divided between Samuel Beckett and the unknown Argentine writer.

Caillois' promotion of Borges was not based on a close friendship. As a matter of fact, Borges was ungenerous enough to write a rather catty article in *Sur* (April 1942) reviewing one of Caillois' pamphlets, on the detective novel. Against Caillois' statement that the detective story was born when Joseph Fouché created a well-trained police force in Paris, Borges observes that a literary genre invariably begins with a literary text and points out that the text in question is one of Edgar Allan Poe's stories. An exchange of notes ensued, and the relationship between Borges and Caillois cooled considerably. That did not affect Caillois' admiration for Borges' writings. He continued to promote Borges unflinchingly until he secured for him the Formentor Prize.

Before the end of 1944, *Sur* came out with a new collection of Borges' short stories. Under the title of *Ficciones,* the book included eight stories already collected in *The Garden of Forking Paths* (1941) and added six new ones, under the heading "Artifices." The title of the book and of its second part proved that Borges was adamant: he refused to compromise and follow the realistic line the establishment applauded, or the even staler one of social realism fostered by the Stalinist left. By his very titles, he was proclaiming his belief in a literature that was just that: literature—a fiction that did not pretend to be anything else. A literary text was an artifice, a verbal object; that is, just a text. To introduce the six new pieces, he wrote a short prologue in which he attempted to give clues to three of the stories. He begins with an apologetic statement: "Though less torpidly executed, the pieces in this section are similar to those which form the first part of the book" (*Ficciones,* 1962, p. 105). He proceeds to discuss at some length only two of the stories: "Death and the Compass" and "Funes, the Memorious." He points out that the second is "a long metaphor of insomnia," then moves to elucidate some aspects of the first, which, in spite of

the German or Scandinavian names, occurs in a Buenos Aires of dreams: the twisted Rue de Toulon is the Paseo de Julio; Triste-le-Roy is the hotel where Herbert Ashe received, and probably did not read, the eleventh volume of an illusory encyclopedia. After composing this narrative, I have come to consider the soundness of amplifying the time and space in which it occurs: vengeance could be inherited; the periods of time might be computed in years, perhaps in centuries; the first letter of the Name might be spoken in Iceland; the second, in Mexico; the third, in Hindustan. (Ibid., p. 105)

As a key to understanding both stories, Borges' comments are perhaps too selective. It is true that "Funes" can be seen as a metaphor of insomnia, but that curious tale—in which Borges invented a fantastic being: a man with total recall—contains more than that. In a sense, it is a self-portrait, a view of himself as a man immobilized by memory and insomnia, living in a world that is atrociously lucid, passive, marginal. As a persona, Irineo Funes is another of those characters through whom Borges reveals tantalizing fragments of himself.

The other story, "Death and the Compass," is Borges' second detective story—or perhaps the third, if one also counts "The Approach to al-Mu'tasim." It was written after the invention of Bustos Domecq and the Six Problems for Don Isidro Parodi. If the first two detective stories are basically Chestertonian, "Death and the Compass" has some touches of the parodical humor freed by the Bustos stories. It is neatly built around an ingenious, if not original, idea: that the victim the murderer is really trying to trap is the detective. (A similar inversion, the narrator who is the assassin, was used by Agatha Christie in The Murder of Roger Ackroyd.) The geometrical plot, which is highly ingenious, and the cool style reveal Borges' handiwork. But some of the atmospheric details (anti-Semitism is the subject of a witty digression) and some peripheral episodes bear the signature of Bustos Domecq—as does the fact emphasized in the prologue to "Artifices," that the geometrical city of the story is really a "Buenos Aires of dreams." Instead of using parody, as in the Bustos Domecq stories, Borges here uses the displacement of nightmares.

There are other levels to the story, which Borges does not attempt to explain. The end contains a double surprise. The obvious one is linked to the plot: the discovery that the fourth intended victim is the detective. But there is another surprise, as elegant as a geometrical problem. When Eric Lönnrot, the detective, realizes that he is going to be shot by Red Scharlach, he understands for the first time the real meaning of the geometrical figure (a rhomb) that the three previous murders in three different parts of the city suggested. He compares the assassin's scheme to a labyrinth:

"In your labyrinth there are three lines too many," he said at last. "I know of a Greek labyrinth which is a single straight line. Along this line so many philosophers have lost themselves that a mere detective might well do so too. Scharlach, when, in some other incarnation, you hunt me, feign to commit (or do commit) a crime at A, then a second crime at B, eight kilometers from

A, then a third crime at C, four kilometers from A and B, halfway en route between the two. Wait for me later at D, two kilometers from A and C, halfway, once again, between both. Kill me at D, as you are now going to kill me at Triste-le-Roy."
"The next time I kill you," said Scharlach, "I promise you the labyrinth made of the single straight line which is invisible and everlasting."
He stepped back a few paces. Then, very carefully, he fired. (*Ficciones*, 1962, p. 141)

The second ending doubly alters the meaning of the story. In the first place, a reversal makes Lönnrot the intellectual victor. He is killed, but first he points out the major flaw in Scharlach's plot: it has too many lines; therefore, it is unnecessarily prolix. In the second place, by referring to the ritual aspect of the killing, Lönnrot introduces the notion of circular time: there will be another time and another meeting and another killing. The concept of eternal return, which Borges had already explored in poems and essays, adds an extra dimension to the story. It changes Scharlach and Lönnrot into characters in a myth: Abel and Cain endlessly pursuing each other and endlessly performing the killing. The story becomes a cosmic charade in which circumstances may vary but the ritual is always the same. Even the fact that the word *red* (for blood) is contained in both protagonists' names adds to the mythical pattern. Borges, of course, gives no clue about that aspect of the tale. In the second edition of *Ficciones* (originally published in 1956), he provides information about the supposed cabalistic background: "Should I add that the Hasidim included saints and that the sacrifice of four lives in order to obtain the four letters imposed by the Name is a fantasy dictated by the form of my story?" (ibid., p. 105). It is a polite way of indicating that the cabala was used only in the story as a diversion.

The second paragraph of the prologue to the new stories in *Ficciones* is terse: "The heterogeneous census of the authors whom I continually reread is made up of Schopenhauer, De Quincey, Stevenson, Mauthner, Shaw, Chesterton, Leon Bloy. I believe I perceive the remote influence of the last-mentioned in the Christological fantasy entitled 'Three Versions of Judas' " (ibid., p. 129). The story postulates the existence of one Nils Runenberg, who devotes part of his existence to obsessively interpreting the real nature of Christ's sacrifice. His final conclusion (the third and most unorthodox of his theories) is that God did not become incarnate in Jesus when He assumed in full the human condition. Rather, "God became a man completely, a man to the point of infamy, a man to the point of being reprehensible—all the way to the abyss. In order to save us, He could have chosen *any* of the destinies which together weave the uncertain web of history; He could have been Alexander, or Pythagoras, or Rurik, or Jesus; He chose an infamous destiny: He was Judas" (ibid., pp. 155–156).

What Borges' prologue does not say is that the same device— the inversion of the functions of martyr and traitor, hero and villain— is also used in two other stories in the book. In "The Shape of the Sword" the protagonist tells the story of a betrayal as if he were the victim, not the betrayer. In "Theme of the Traitor and the Hero" the first becomes the second in a highly dramatic inversion of roles. In both stories, as in "Three Versions of Judas," the mythical and ritualistic view of the world, presented through the pair Abel and Cain, reinforces the double vision of reality. Borges suggests that the hero is as much a villain as the villain is a hero. They are two sides of the same character: man.

Ficciones contains another story that is not dealt with, even by implication, in the prologue. It is entitled "The Secret Miracle" and presents a Jewish playwright who is going to be executed by the Nazis. At the very last second he is saved by a miracle: God gives him a whole year to complete his play. Time is stopped: the executioners freeze while the playwright completes his task; as soon as it is finished, "a quadruple blast" brings him down (ibid., p. 150). This artifice, the playing with time, links the story with some of the experiments attributed to Herbert Quain in the story already included in *The Garden of Forking Paths*. The same interplay between objective, chronological, and subjective time is present here. Borges' love for Berkeleyan idealism is put to use in a fashion that produces an effective narrative. The story is not one of Borges' best and is perhaps a bit too mechanical, but it is one that readers favor. In a sense, it is easier to identify with its protagonist's plight than with Funes' or Nils Runenberg's hallucinatory destinies.

Ficciones was better received than *The Garden of Forking Paths*. A special prize was created to honor the book. At the behest of Enrique Amorim, the Argentine Society of Writers (SADE) awarded the book its first Great Prize of Honor, obviously intended as reparation for the offhand way the city of Buenos Aires had treated *The Garden* in 1942.

For another of Emecé's collections, Borges edited at the beginning of 1945 an anthology called *El compadrito* (The Buenos Aires Hoodlum); this time, the co-editor was not Bioy Casares but a young woman, Silvina Bullrich Palenque, who was beautiful and talented. The subtitle indicated the scope of the small anthology; it attempted to cover the hoodlum's destiny, his neighborhoods, his music. Borges begins the terse prologue by linking the city's hoodlums with the gauchos. He observes that "people believe they admire the gaucho, but essentially they admire the hoodlum" that some gauchos really are. After explaining the scope of the anthology and why the editors have not included either the plays that deal with hoodlums or the tango lyrics that praise them, Borges points out that they have preferred instead descriptions, dialogues, poems, and reports by historians and sociologists. The conclusion expresses the hope that sometime in the future somebody will write a poem that will do for hoodlums what *Martín Fierro* did for gauchos. That was one of Borges' long-cherished projects, of which only the *Evaristo Carriego* biography remains. Yet in 1945, fifteen years after the Carriego book came out, Borges was still dreaming of it.

If the publication of that anthology was, in a sense, a first for Borges—the first time his sole collaborator was a woman—his visit to Montevideo in October of the same year was also a first. He had been invited by the cultural service of the Ministry of Education to give a lecture on gaucho literature at the university. Shy and self-conscious, Borges had never trusted his own voice in public. He generally refused to lecture, and on the rare occasions on which he had been forced to do it he wrote a carefully rehearsed text, then asked a friend to read it for him. That is precisely what he did in Montevideo. While José Pedro Díaz, a young professor of literature, read the long lecture with impeccable diction and a beautiful, sonorous voice, Borges sat behind the podium prompting him, invisibly and inaudibly. It was an uncanny performance, as if he were a ventriloquist controlling his dummy from a distance.

It was there that I met Borges for the first time. I was in charge of the literary pages of *Marcha* (March), a left-wing weekly that was beginning to be known outside Uruguay. Very respectfully, I approached Borges after the lecture and asked him to let me print the complete text of the lecture in *Marcha*'s next issue. Perhaps because I had been introduced to him by two of his favorite cousins, who belonged to the Uruguayan branch of his family and were friends of mine, or perhaps because he was so generous and even careless about what he wrote, he gave me the original of his lecture and authorized me to print it in *Marcha*. I will not attempt to describe my enthusiasm. For years, since I had first discovered his articles and reviews in *El Hogar* in 1936, I had been his fan, collecting all his books, subscribing to the magazines to which he contributed, and imitating him in my own, hopelessly modest, reviews and articles. I was already convinced that he was the best writer the Spanish language had ever produced and was determined to fight to the death anyone who dared to challenge that conviction. In short, I was young and fanatic.

For Borges, that lecture at Montevideo had a different meaning. It was his first attempt to enlarge his audience using a new medium and exploring a new country. His name was known in Uruguay only in the most specialized circles. The lecture, which attracted one of the largest audiences I had ever seen in Montevideo, was a success precisely because it was about a safe subject and Borges handled it with his usual originality. But the lecture had another meaning. It clearly pointed out to him the way to keep contact with a public that was growing and that he had so far neglected. At the time, he did not need to enlarge his audience. He had a regular income from his position as third assistant at the Miguel Cané library and received some extra income from his contributions to journals and magazines. But if he could overcome his shyness and start lecturing, another source of income would be available to him. He was in no hurry. The tortures of having to face an audience were as yet too much for him. Unfortunately (or perhaps, fortunately) in 1946 Argentina would experience a radical political change that would force Borges, in less than a year, to become a lecturer and a teacher. The lecture hall was to be his arena for the rest of his life.

7.
The General and the Chicken Inspector

At the time Borges was lecturing in Montevideo, Argentina was already in the hands of a new leader, Colonel Juan Domingo Perón. His ascent to power was slow but unswerving. Born in 1896, he was a young captain when General Uriburu deposed President Irigoyen in 1930. In spite of joining the senior officers in the coup that overthrew the populist leader, Perón continued to show his independence. He was against Irigoyen, and especially against the palace guard that had isolated the aging leader from his constituency, but he did not subscribe to all the repressive measures the army took to destroy Irigoyen's social and political reforms. Many years later he would speak about the Mole (as Irigoyen was called) as the "first Argentine president to defend the people, the first to challenge the foreign and national interests of the oligarchy to defend his people" (Sanguinetti, 1975, p. 63). But army discipline prevented the young captain from making his criticism public. He accepted a position as private secretary at the Ministry of War (1930–1935) while also teaching at the ministry's high school during the same period. In 1937 he was sent to Chile as a military attaché, and later to Italy during the war. From 1939 to 1940 he joined the Italian army at the Alps and the Abruzzi. He also visited Franco's Spain and was impressed by the devastation that civil war had brought to the country. To some intimate friends he confided that he would always oppose armed conflict in Argentina.

Although practically unknown outside army circles, Perón was already an influential man. The Argentine army was then controlled by men who hated England and admired Italy and were sympathetic to Hitler's crusade for a new world order. Their position is hard to explain in an international context but easy to understand in the River

Plate context. Internationally, England in the early 1940s represented the last bulwark against fascism. It was the hope of democracy, the country of the free. But in Argentina, and to a lesser extent in Uruguay, England was seen merely as the center of imperialism. The economy of the River Plate area was then ruled from London; the chief investors were British: railroads, powerhouses, and even waterworks were in British hands. Only nominally were Argentina and Uruguay independent. To Argentines, British imperialism was intolerable. The army therefore favored fascism and viewed Hitler with sympathetic eyes because it sincerely believed he would help the world to get rid of the British.

Perón shared these views. While in Italy, he was favorably impressed with the way Mussolini had handled the corporate state; he would later borrow freely from his methods. He was not so keen on Hitler, although he admired him as Britain's most powerful enemy. But Perón was also an intuitive politician, a man who had a truly imaginative way of recognizing the popular mood and possessed an uncanny ability to cater to it. He knew he was still too young and unknown to come into the open and lead a coup d'état. Instead, he began by organizing a movement of Young Turks which put pressure on the senior officers and led them into action. The Argentine government of the time was ripe for a fall. Led since 1938 by the totally incompetent President Castillo, it was toppled on June 4, 1943, by a bloodless coup. The army took over openly. The new president was General Farrell, but the real power behind the scenes was Colonel Perón, who had modestly chosen to be appointed vice-president. He was also named minister of war and secretary of work and social protection (actually minister of labor and welfare). As minister of war, he controlled the army; as secretary of work, he was in a position to control the workers and build a power base. Perón realized that there were a large number of workers in Argentina whom the traditional parties had neglected and whom the left-wing parties appealed to only marginally. He began by expanding the Secretariat and increasing its budget. By a series of decrees, he first organized the men who worked in the fields, then began making inroads into the left-wing unions, which controlled local industries. By promoting competing unions (organized directly by the Secretariat) or by bribing the officials of the older unions, he gained in less than two years' time almost complete control over a mass of workers that had so far received no protection from the government and had been poorly represented by their own unions. Perón also learned how to use the state radio station to bring his plans for social reform and his union policy to the attention of all workers, both in the cities and in the fields. His speeches were plain and direct and effectively attuned to the language of his listeners. He was a colonel, but he spoke as one of "us." He also inaugurated a campaign to popularize his image. Very soon, the obscure colonel was recognized—his warm voice, his immense smile, his large, pale face and pomaded black hair—by thousands of people who had up till then felt no interest in the promises of the old-style politicians.

Perón was far less popular with the wealthy ranchers and the political bureaucrats. He was also dangerous to left-wing reformers and entrenched union leaders. They joined together in denouncing his demagoguery, his abuse of power, his bribing and/or terrorizing of his enemies. They called him a Fascist (which he was) and a Nazi (which he was not), a bully (which he was) and a satyr (which he probably was not). His liaison with a young, blonde radio actress, Eva Duarte, was a favorite subject of dirty jokes. The laws that regulated workers' salaries, new pensions, and an improved system of welfare were opposed by the ruling classes. For the first time somebody had dared to challenge their right to pay workers what they pleased. The left-wing parties were in turn furious with a man who was instituting the social reforms they had tried unsuccessfully to achieve for three or four decades. The Church also felt offended by the way he carried on with Evita, as everybody called his mistress. But Perón continued to smile and increase his popularity. Against his enemies, he resorted to torture. It was about this time that the Argentine police imported from Germany and perfected the *picana eléctrica,* a primitive system of electrodes that were generally applied to the genital area to coerce "confessions."

By October 9, 1945, everybody apparently had had enough of Perón. General Farrell was persuaded to ask him to resign all his official positions and retire. Perón agreed and was immediately sent to the Martín García, a small island, close to the Uruguayan coastline, where President Irigoyen had been confined after being deposed. Everybody was convinced that that was the end of Perón. He himself told his friends that he wanted only to marry Evita and retire to a quiet place to write his memoirs. He was then fifty and at the peak of his vitality. Eight days later he was back in Buenos Aires, addressing the biggest crowd so far assembled in that city and reassuring the masses that in next February's election he would be the official candidate for the presidency.

What exactly had happened in those eight days? Legends and myths have grown steadily to the point that it is hard to know exactly what went on behind the scenes. What is known is that hundreds of thousands of Argentines were not only transported to the capital but also fed; they camped in downtown Buenos Aires and refused to move until Perón had been produced and had addressed them, and a "collective orgasm" (to quote one of the most passionate accounts) between the Macho and his people was achieved.

Following these events, the government had to declare a holiday, which the people immediately baptized St. Perón's Day. President Farrell promoted Perón to general. The elections that took place on February 24, 1946, only certified what St. Perón's Day had proclaimed: that he was Argentina's first king.

Before the elections, Perón had married Evita in a discreet civil ceremony, and now she was Señora María Eva Duarte de Perón, Argentina's first lady. For the next ten years, and until her sudden death in 1952, Argentina had a royal couple.

Borges' reaction to the ascent of Perón was not mild. He sincerely believed Perón was a Nazi. Being of British extraction and having followed in detail the transformation of German culture under Hitler, Borges had no love for the new world order the Führer had so brutally attempted to impose on Europe. During the 1930s he used his section in *El Hogar* to discuss political matters, writing with deadly irony about totalitarianism of every kind. He concentrated his fire on Nazism and communism, devoting particular attention to the debasement of German culture by Hitler's propaganda machine and the follies of anti-Semitism. His standing on international matters mirrored his standing on national affairs. He viewed the Argentine situation from the larger perspective of the international fight against fascism.

A statement he made for a Uruguayan newspaper at the time of his lecture on gaucho literature appeared in print exactly fifteen days after Perón's triumphant return to Buenos Aires:

> The [political] situation in Argentina is very serious, so serious that a great number of Argentines are becoming Nazis without being aware of it. Tempted by promises of social reform—in a society that undoubtedly needs a better organization than the one it now has—many people are letting themselves be seduced by an outsized wave of hatred that is sweeping the country. It is a terrible thing, similar to what happened at the beginning of fascism and Nazism [in Europe]. But I must add that Argentine intellectuals are against it and fight it. I believe that the only possible solution is to delegate power to the Supreme Court. Nevertheless, I am pessimistic about a more or less speedy return of the Argentine government to democracy. (*El Plata*, Montevideo, October 31, 1945)

The suggestion that the army ought to delegate power to the Supreme Court before the elections had been one of the demands of the Popular Democratic Union, which opposed Perón's candidacy; but, obviously, Perón refused to relinquish the power he needed to be elected president. In that respect, Borges' skepticism was well justified. Perón used the power and the money of the Secretariat of Work to buy votes, to organize his forces, and to win the election by a bare 51 percent.

If Borges was right about the small chance of a return to democracy, he was wrong in his view that Perón was a Nazi. Perón was a Fascist and a nationalist. By identifying him and his party with the Nazis, Borges and his friends missed precisely what made Perón so attractive to the masses.

Perón's victory made clear to everybody that democracy in Argentina was shelved for the foreseeable future. Borges must have realized how frail his own position was. Although he was already acclaimed locally as one of the leading contemporary writers, he was only a third assistant at the Miguel Cané municipal library; that is, he depended entirely (or almost entirely) for his subsistence on a political appointment. In spite of that, and because he was a proud and free man, he continued to sign the anti-Peronist manifestos that still circulated freely in Buenos Aires. At the beginning, Perón paid little attention to the intellectuals. He was chiefly interested in consolidating his power among the unions, the army, and the industrialists. But after he felt secure, he turned to them and reduced them to silence.

For Borges he invented a truly Macho humiliation. In August 1946 Borges was officially informed that, by decision of city hall, he had been promoted out of the Miguel Cané library to the inspectorship of poultry and rabbits in the public market of Córdoba Street. This is the end of the story in his "Autobiographical Essay": "I went to the City Hall to find out what it was all about. 'Look here,' I said. 'It's rather strange that among so many others at the library I should be singled out as worthy of this new position.' 'Well,' the clerk answered, 'you were on the side of the Allies—what do you expect?' His statement was unanswerable; the next day, I sent in my resignation" ("Essay," 1970, p. 244).

In his account Borges makes no reference to the meaning of that "promotion," but it is obvious that he had been chosen to be the victim of a form of humiliation typical of the River Plate area. Perón and his friends were masters of the art of the *cachada* (to grab, to take somebody unawares). To promote one of the leading Argentine intellectuals to inspector of chickens and rabbits implied a linguistic pun. Chickens and rabbits are in Spanish, as in English, synonymous with cowardice. But Borges decided to ignore the affront and take the promotion as a sign of the regime's vast ignorance of the uses of language. He dutifully resigned but made a public statement in which he recounted the episode with deadpan accuracy. The last paragraph reads:

I don't know if the episode I have just told is a parable. I suspect, nevertheless, that memory and forgetfulness are gods that know perfectly well what they do. If they have forgotten the rest and if they only preserve this absurd legend, they probably have some justification. I formulate it in these words: dictatorships foment oppression, dictatorships foment subservience, dictatorships foment cruelty; even more abominable is the fact that they foment stupidity. Buttons which babble slogans, images of leaders, predesignated "hails" and "down withs," walls decorated with names, unanimous ceremonies, mere discipline taking the place of lucidity. . . . To fight against those sad monotonies is one of the many duties of writers. Would it be necessary to remind the readers of *Martín Fierro* and *Don Segundo Sombra* that individualism is an old Argentine virtue? ("Dele-Dele," 1946)

Using the same title *Sur* had used at the time *The Garden of Forking Paths* was passed over for the city prize, a group of intellectuals of all persuasions decided to organize a "Reparation to Borges." In the course of the banquet they held, the statement quoted above was read. Among the speeches, the most significant was by the president of the Argentine Society of Writers, Leonidas Barletta, a dedicated Communist and one of the participants in the old Boedo group. Barletta hailed Borges' courage in standing up for his convictions and refusing to be silenced by dictatorship. He recognized in him the true spirit of the resistance each Argentine intellectual ought to show in those "magnificent and terrible" days. His speech, printed with Borges' text in a page of the left-wing journal *Argentina Libre* (Free Argentina, August 15, 1946), was a political manifesto. Borges—the exquisite, apolitical Borges—had suddenly become, and would remain for the next decade, the symbol of Argentina's resistance to totalitarianism. It was an unexpected role for that shy, ironic man, but he performed it with simplicity and without once flinching. Somehow, Perón had chosen the wrong kind of inspector for his chickens and rabbits.

8.
Living in an
Occupied Town

The humiliation Perón and his associates had devised for Borges not only turned him into a popular figure of resistance to the regime; it also forced him to make a momentous literary decision. To resign his modest position as third assistant at the Miguel Cané library threatened to leave him with no regular income at the age of forty-seven. It is true that he had a few literary jobs: regular contributions to *Sur* and *La Nación,* anthologies compiled with friends, prologues and notes to books he edited. But all this activity was marginal and did not constitute a sufficient income. He had to look elsewhere.

The only thing left for him was to lecture. His shyness and a mild stammer that became really uncomfortable when he had to speak in public had prevented him from accepting a regular job as a lecturer or even teacher. But Perón, by promoting him to inspector of chickens and rabbits, had left him with no alternative. It was either starvation or the lecture hall. In anguish, Borges chose the latter.

At first he did not trust his own voice. He had always relied on close friends to read his speeches for him. Even the short text he wrote for the banquet offered by the Argentine Society of Writers was read by the critic Pedro Hendríquez Ureña. But it was unrealistic to believe that he could go on forever asking friends to read his lectures. Little by little he pushed himself into doing it. The account Borges gives of these events in his "Autobiographical Essay" is, as usual, too simplified. After summarizing his dismissal from the Miguel Cané library, he writes:

> I was now out of a job. Several months before, an old English lady had read my tea leaves and foretold that I was soon to travel, to speak, and to take

vast sums of money thereby. On telling my mother about it, we both laughed, for public speaking was far beyond me. At this juncture, a friend came to the rescue, and I was made teacher of English literature at the Asociación Argentina de Cultura Inglesa. I was also asked at the same time to lecture on classic American literature at the Colegio Libre de Estudios Superiores. Since this pair of offers was made three months before classes opened, I accepted, feeling quite safe. As the time grew near, however, I grew sicker and sicker. My series of lectures was to be on Hawthorne, Poe, Thoreau, Emerson, Melville, Whitman, Twain, Henry James, and Veblen. I wrote the first one down. But I had no time to write out the second one. Besides, thinking of the first lecture as Doomsday, I felt that only eternity could come after. The first one went off well enough—miraculously. Two nights before the second lecture, I took my mother for a long walk around Adrogué and had her time me as I rehearsed my talk. She said that she thought it was overlong. "In that case," I said, "I'm safe." My fear had been of running dry. So, at forty-seven, I found a new and exciting life opening up for me. ("Essay," 1970, pp. 244–245)

In spite of Borges' retrospective cheerfulness, things did not go so smoothly. In the first place, the preparation of each lecture took an inordinate amount of time. The first, on Hawthorne (which he later included in his collection *Other Inquisitions,* 1952), was too long and too erudite. It must have taken him the better part of several months to put all the information together and write out the dense text. When he realized that such a method was not suited to a regular course of lectures, he switched to making very precise notes on small pieces of paper. He then memorized these notes so thoroughly that he rarely needed to consult them in the lecture room. To overcome his insecurity, he rehearsed with a friend or with his mother; he also devised an elaborate ritual before each lecture—one that I was able to witness more than once when he came to speak in Montevideo.

The ritual consisted of two parts. The first part was a long walk toward the place where the lecture was to be given. Walking and talking with one or two friends about the subject of the lecture, Borges practiced the sort of peripatetic dialogue that had its roots in ancient Greece, when Aristotle took his disciples for long, learned walks in his garden. The second part of the ritual was perhaps less Aristotelian. When he approached the place where he had to lecture, Borges would go into a café to have a strong drink—generally a *caña* or a *grappa*—which he downed in one gulp and which helped to exorcise his fears.

The lecture had its own ritual. Borges sat very quietly, never looking directly at the audience and focusing his half-blind eyes on a distant spot. While lecturing, he would join his hands in small, precise movements of prayer or discreetly move them around; he would deliver his speech in a rather monotonous, low voice as if he were a priest or a rabbi. His style contrasted radically with the one favored in the River Plate area, where the traditions of Latin oratory were still very much alive. But Borges succeeded precisely because he was so different. His stillness, his precise gestures, the monotone of his voice created an almost incantatory space: a space in which what really mattered was the text, carefully meditated, carefully put together, and always unexpected. The immobility, the low tone, the almost fanatical concentration on the spoken words—all that was the lecture and not the usual histrionics of the orator. Borges had managed to create a spoken style that suited the written style of his work. Audiences, at first puzzled and perhaps slightly alarmed, began to recognize its effectiveness. In less than a few years Borges had become one of the most successful lecturers in the River Plate area.

In his "Autobiographical Essay" he has this to say about his success:

> I traveled up and down Argentina and Uruguay, lecturing on Swedenborg, Blake, the Persian and Chinese mystics, Buddhism, gauchesco poetry, Martin Buber, the Kabbalah, the *Arabian Nights*, T. E. Lawrence, medieval Germanic poetry, the Icelandic sagas, Heine, Dante, expressionism, and Cervantes. I went from town to town, staying overnight in hotels I'd never see again. Sometimes my mother or a friend accompanied me. Not only did I end up making far more money than at the library, but I enjoyed the work and felt that it justified me. ("Essay," 1970, p. 245)

What he fails to convey in his "Essay" is the exact context in which these lectures were given: it is the context of Perón's Argentina. I used to visit him in Buenos Aires during those years. As he came at least once a year to Montevideo, to lecture and see friends and relatives, we repaid his visits as often as we could. Buenos Aires was then literally wallpapered with enormous posters of Perón and his blonde wife, and each poster was covered with aggressive slogans. The city had the look of an occupied town. In that insulted Buenos Aires, Borges walked endlessly. He was then in his late forties, and he still had partial eyesight. He didn't use a cane. His step was nervous, almost brusque. Only when crossing a street would a natural prudence make him hold his companion by the sleeve, rather than the arm, with an imperious gesture that requested but did not beg help. With the same sudden brusqueness, he'd let go on the other side. But verbal communication never stopped.

Borges dimly saw (or guessed) the slogans of the regime, the infinite repetition of Perón's and Evita's names, the calculated humiliation of patrician Buenos Aires. He'd point to each enormous letter, underline each slogan, talk and talk furiously. Gone was the Buenos Aires of his poems and dreams, the suburban neighborhood with its general store and pink corners and local hoodlums wearing white, soft-brimmed hats, its twilight streets open to the invading pampas. Nothing was left of that mythical Buenos Aires of his tales. Now the city was ruled by a regime that proposed to break the back of a powerful oligarchy whose tastes had been formed in London and Paris. Borges was not excessively sorry about the humiliation of a class whose failures and weaknesses he had always satirized, but he hated the demagoguery of this leader who aired social grudges, petty fascist lessons, in a colossal display of mediocrity.

While he walked, Borges' pain was visible in the bitterness of his speech and the brusqueness of his gestures, rather than in the actual words he used. He was like a man skinned alive. Here and there the real Buenos Aires was visible to him. But from his talk a different, more ominous city emerged. It was a city of unrelieved horror, the one that was transcribed phantasmagorically and under European names in "Death and the Compass." Only a thin disguise of chessboard geometry and Chestertonian paradox separated that city where Good and Evil fought, from the real one. The same gray, nightmarish Buenos Aires reappeared in "The Wait," where a man waits in a rented room for his enemies to come to kill him. The ugliness, physical as well as moral, of the Perón capital was the background for some of the more dismal tales of this period.

Listening to Borges, I found it impossible not to feel a sense of rejection mixed with quiet impatience. I did not care if somebody heard us. It is true that the regime set out to persecute the intellectuals, but it did so in a casual, inconsistent manner. These petty persecutions were designed more to humiliate and harass than to frighten. I knew all this, and that is why I felt a sense of rejection: it was not that Borges' words seemed wrong to me; it was that I felt the shame of a person who spies on someone else's nightmares, who involuntarily listens to the cries and private words of a sleeper. Brutally, the passion with which Borges denounced Perón's Buenos Aires brought me into his own labyrinth. Listening to him, sympathizing with him, I wanted nevertheless to say no, to argue that Perón was more than a mediocre tyrant, that he represented something completely different for the workers and the poor, that he had introduced new and necessary social laws, that he was trying (perhaps unsuccessfully) to liberate Argentina from foreign powers. I wanted to tell him that the sinister Buenos Aires of his tales and nightmares hardly existed in reality, that it had another, more bureaucratic mask of informers, petty dealers, and arbitrary policemen. But how can one establish a dialogue with a dreamer?

Borges imposed his nightmare upon me, and I ended up feeling the viscosity of the air, the menace of the walls, the obsessive presence of the endlessly repeated names. His vision had created a labyrinth in this mediocre reality, and I too was lost in it.

As soon as we left the downtown streets and reached Buenos Aires' Southside, Borges' mood would change. The Southside seems (or seemed in the years between 1946 and 1949) like the setting of a Borges tale. He would drag me to see some surviving pink streetcorner; we would step onto patios whose stone pavements recalled another tyrant's times: the Juan Manuel Rosas who reappeared obsessively in his verses. We would cross squares which still held the dampness that had chilled his grandparents. Sometimes, in the evening, we would land in some café such as the Richmond del Sur, where a small band played old-time tangos above the incessant clacking of billiard balls at the back. Then, for a while, Borges would forget Perón and would even laugh. He would tap the table with his hand (somewhat short, with fat fingers) to the rhythms of the tango. I used to think then that Borges was providing me with local color, that he wanted to show the tourist (a Uruguayan is always considered a bit provincial in Buenos Aires) the remains, or perhaps the debris, of a mythical city that still lived in his poems and his biography of Evaristo Carriego. But there was more than that in his mind. Through that tango ritual, Borges managed to escape for a moment from Perón's moral prison, from the loud walls of his own nightmare. The Buenos Aires he loved was still alive in the music of the tango.

We often walked the streets of the Southside and also some quarters of the poorer Northside, which had nothing in common with the fashionable boutiques of Florida Street. I still remember one night when we walked through half of Buenos Aires (he walked to enjoy the quietness of suburban nights) to see a friend who lived in a Jewish neighborhood of sad and dusty streets. On that occasion Perón disappeared from the conversation, which branched off into the labyrinths of English literature that Borges loved so much. Stevenson, Kipling, Chesterton, and James filled the solitary streets with their inventions, brought to life by Borges' words. "Don't you agree?" he never tired of asking with his flawless courtesy. Quoting texts and commenting on them, developing precious hints and pursuing allusions, Borges managed to create, on the borders of the Peronist-made reality, an entire world. From those heady conversations we returned, half dazed, to sinister reality.

It was in March 1946 that he began a new literary venture, as editor of the literary journal *Los Anales de Buenos Aires,* launched by an institution modeled on the Parisian Société des Annales. Like its French counterpart, the Argentine association yearly invited internationally famous intellectuals to come to lecture in Buenos Aires; it also tapped the most brilliant local talent. The first two issues of the journal, which had been edited by the association, presented in a rather arbitrary way lectures given at the institution, pieces by more or less distinguished writers, and assorted texts. Only after Borges began to edit it did it take the shape of a literary magazine. The leading Argentine journal at the time was still *Sur,* although its position had been challenged by *Realidad* (Reality), a magazine whose subtitle, "Review of Ideas," attempted to subtly underline not only its main characteristic but one of *Sur*'s weaknesses. Borges had contributed some articles to *Realidad*—in particular one to the Cervantes issue (September–October 1947)—but he remained loyal to *Sur.* When he agreed to edit *Los Anales,* he continued to contribute to *Sur.* It was obvious to him that Buenos Aires had room for another, and different, monthly.

In a sense, *Los Anales* can be seen as two journals in one. Some of the articles reflected the institution's point of view, sedate and academic. But what gave the journal its distinction was Borges' taste and imagination. He not only included some of his friends' poems, short stories, and articles but went out of his way to find new writers who also favored imagination and had a sophisticated taste. Among the new writers he discovered for the Argentine public was a rather neglected Uruguayan surrealist, Felisberto Hernández, whose story "The Usher" was printed in the June 1946 issue. Another of his finds was Julio Cortázar. At the time, the Argentine novelist was a totally unknown shortstory writer. Borges printed several of his stories and a fragment of a rather elaborate version of the myth of Theseus and the Minotaur, a piece called "The Kings" (October–December 1947).

But perhaps the most successful contributions Borges made to *Los Anales* were his own. Under his own name or under several pseudonyms, Borges enhanced the quality of the magazine. Some of his best stories, later collected in *The Aleph* (1949), were originally published in *Los Anales:* "The Immortal" (February 1947); "The Theologians" (April 1947); "The House of Asterion" (May–June 1947); "The Zahir" (July 1947). He also published there some important essays: "Apollinaire's Paradox" (August 1946); "The First Wells" (September 1946); "On Oscar Wilde" (December 1946); "Note on Walt Whitman" (March 1947); "Note on Chesterton" (October–December 1947). The last four were collected in *Other Inquisitions* (1952); the first has never been included in his books.

With the help of Adolfo Bioy Casares and under the pseudonym of B. Lynch Davis (another composite of family names), he edited a section called "Museum." Among many pieces correctly attributed to real authors and works, Borges introduced at least six that were his alone. Not until he published a volume of miscellaneous prose and verse under the title of *El hacedor* (*Dreamtigers*, 1960)—and included in it a section called "Museum"—did he acknowledge the paternity of some of the most brilliant and ironic pieces. Now the map that was so faithful that it had the dimensions and topographical characteristics of the actual country was no longer attributed to the nonexistent Suárez Miranda; the poem about what gets lost in life, and about the limitations and limits of one's own experience, no longer belonged to the 1923 Uruguayan poet Julio Platero Haedo (another combination of family and friends' names). But the most telling admission regarded a piece which had been attributed to Gaspar Camerarius and which consisted of two terse lines:

> I, who have been so many men, have never been
> The one in whose embrace Matilde Urbach swooned.
> (*Dreamtigers*, 1964, p. 92)

Lost among the witty and strange pieces of *Los Anales'* "Museum," those two lines mean little; included at the end of a book that contained some of Borges' most personal writings, the verses have a completely different meaning. The title of the piece, in French, is "Le regret d'Heraclite" (Heraclitus' Regret). Under the double disguise of a German poet and a poetic persona (Heraclitus), Borges advertises very delicately that he will never have the woman he loves swooning in his arms. A sad, curious way of admitting his erotic powerlessness.

   Los Anales de Buenos Aires came to an end at the beginning of 1948. The last issue was devoted to the Spanish poet Juan Ramón Jiménez, who was then visiting Buenos Aires, invited by the association to lecture and read his poetry. It is obvious that Borges had nothing to do with that issue. Although he had been nominally the editor from the third issue onward, the head of the association had retained some power over the journal. She was a rather formidable woman whose literary tastes did not entirely coincide with Borges'. As I was also one of the regular contributors to the journal, I had a chance to meet her. It seemed obvious to me then that she wanted to have Borges' name in the journal but that she was not terribly impressed with the way he edited it. By the end of 1947 she also seemed disappointed with the reception the magazine had. Borges and she parted company without regrets.

   By the time Borges was preparing the next to last issue of *Los Anales*, Perón had discovered a new way to humiliate those Argentines who had opposed his regime from the very beginning. This time he (or perhaps Evita) chose a suitable target. On September 8, 1948, a group of ladies gathered together in the afternoon to sing the national anthem on Florida Street and pass around some pamphlets. They attracted the attention of passersby, and in no time a larger group—including two Uruguayan ladies who were buying shoes in one of Florida's boutiques—was formed. As they had no permit to demonstrate in such a way, they were arrested by the police. Among the ladies were Mother and Norah. The magistrate condemned them to one month's imprisonment, but because Mother was an old woman she was confined to her own apartment, with a permanent police guard at the door. In his conversations with Richard Burgin, Borges gives his version of the story:

BORGES: She was in prison in Perón's time. My sister also.
BURGIN: Perón put them in prison?
BORGES: Yes, My sister, well, of course; the case of my mother was different because she was already an old lady—she's ninety-one now—and so her prison was her own home, no? But my sister was sent with some friends of hers to a jail for prostitutes in order to insult her. Then, she somehow smuggled a letter or two to us, I don't know how she managed it, saying that the prison was such a lovely place, that everybody was so kind, that being in prison was so restful, that it had a beautiful patio, black and white like a chessboard. In fact, she worded it so that we thought she was in some awful dungeon, no? Of course, what she really wanted us to feel—well, not to worry so much about her. She kept on saying what nice people there were, and how being in jail was much better than having to go out to cocktails or parties and so on. She was in prison with other ladies, and the other ladies told me that they felt awful about it. But my sister just said the Lord's Prayer. There were eleven in the same room, and my sister said her prayers, then she went to sleep immediately. All the time she was in jail, she didn't know how long a time might pass before she would see her husband, her children, and her mother. And afterward she told me—but this was when she was out of jail—she said that, after all, my grandfather died for this country, my great-grandfather fought the Spaniards. They did all that they could for the country. And I, by the mere fact of being in prison, I was doing something also. So this is as it should be. (Burgin, 1969, pp. 118–119)

In *El grito sagrado* (The Sacred Cry), a book published almost ten years after the event by Adela Grondona, who was imprisoned with Norah, there is a description of Norah making drawings of the inmates and transforming them into angels. She kept finding beautiful objects in prison—a colonnade here, a face there—and kept up her spirits by singing, drawing, and praying. Her letters reflected her own magic vision of life.

The women were kept in prison for a month, but the sentence

might have been reduced if they had appealed directly to Mrs. Perón. Borges recalls the incident in his conversations with Burgin:

BORGES: They said, "If you write a letter to the Señora, you'll get out."—"What señora are you talking about?"—"This señora is Señora Perón."—"Well, as we don't know her, and she doesn't know us, it's quite meaningless for us to write to her." But what they really wanted was that those ladies would write a letter, and then they would publish it, no? And the people would say how merciful Perón was, and how we were free now. The whole thing was a kind of trick, it *was* a trick. But they saw through it. That was the kind of thing they had to undergo at the time.

BURGIN: It was a horrible time.

BORGES: Oh, it was. For example, when you have a toothache, when you have to go to the dentist, the first thing that you think about when you wake up is the whole ordeal; but during some ten years, of course, I had my personal grievances too, but in those ten years the first thing I thought about when I was awake was, well, "Perón is in power." (Burgin, 1969, p. 120)

To endure Perón: that was the main problem for Borges during those dark days. Buenos Aires was, to him, an occupied city.

9.
The Writer at Fifty

At the very time when Perón's government seemed more determined than ever to humiliate Borges and his family, his work was reaching full maturity. During those years he produced some of his best fiction and essays, paving the way for the publication of two of his most important books: *The Aleph* (1949) and *Other Inquisitions* (1952). Harassed or ignored by the official and corrupt Argentine press, forced to lecture to make a living, Borges was just then beginning to be acknowledged as Argentina's most distinguished writer and the best prose stylist in the Spanish language. The contrast between his public ignominy and his private distinction helps to explain the new dimension his work acquired. At the time, Borges represented not only an emergent culture; he also represented the dignity of the Latin American writer. He performed the role of writer in the public consciousness. This is what Perón, and his cultural advisers, could not destroy. Undaunted, Borges pursued his quest. It was a specifically literary quest, but in the context of the Argentina of those years it also had the dimensions of a moral quest.

One of the key texts was a slim pamphlet Borges published in 1947 under the title, "A New Refutation of Time." It was printed privately by the apocryphal publishing house Oportet & Haereses, which had also published two Biorges books in 1946. The essay was later included in *Other Inquisitions* (1952). It incorporated ideas about time which had appeared in pieces Borges wrote over the last twenty years. The earliest piece, a sort of autobiographical fantasy, was published in *El idioma de los argentinos* (The Language of the Argentines, 1928). Other treatments of the subject appeared in *Discusión* (1932) and *Historia de la eternidad* (History of Eternity, 1936). The point of departure for this new exploration of time was the writings of the British philosophical idealists. Borges observes: "Berkeley denied that there was an object behind some impressions. David Hume denied that there was a subject behind the perception of changes. Berkeley denied matter; Hume denied the spirit. Berkeley did not wish us to add the metaphysical notion of matter to the succession of impressions, while Hume did not wish us to add the metaphysical notion of a self to the succession of mental states" (*Inquisitions,* 1964, p. 180).

Following these philosophers to their ultimate conclusions, Borges also denies the existence of time: "Nevertheless, having denied matter and spirit, which are continuities, and having denied space also, I do not know with what right we shall retain the continuity that is time. Outside of each perception (actual or conjectural) matter does not exist; outside of each mental state the spirit does not exist; nor will time exist outside of each present instant" (ibid., pp. 183–184). To reinforce his arguments, Borges quotes from Schopenhauer. The German philosopher had observed: "No one has lived in the past, no one will live in the future; the present is the form of all life, it is a possession that no misfortune can take away" (ibid., p. 186). This conviction, which Borges reasons through and finally accepts, was not just the end product of his readings or the final step in an intellectual argument. It had its roots in an experience which might aptly be termed an illumination, if the word could be divorced from its occult connotations—an idea that Borges would flatly reject.

The experience is described in a piece written in 1928, "Sentirse en muerte" (Feeling in Death), later included in *Other Inquisitions.* It happened in the poverty-stricken outskirts of Buenos Aires. One evening, contemplating a simple rose-colored streetcorner, Borges felt that time had come to a halt and that past and present were the same thing. "This is the same as it was thirty years ago," he thought. Out of this uncanny experience, Borges concluded that

> that pure representation of homogeneous facts—clear night, limpid wall, rural scent of honeysuckle, elemental clay—is not merely identical to the scene on that corner so many years ago; it is, without similarities or repetitions, the same. If we can perceive that identity, time is a delusion; the indifference and inseparability of one moment of time's apparent yesterday and another of its apparent today are enough to disintegrate it. (Ibid., pp. 179–180)

The hallucinatory experience of time standing still, of a visible and palpable eternity, which Borges had that night, helped him not only to dispose of time but also to negate his personal identity. Faced with destructible time, Borges felt his identity annihilated: he felt transformed into an "abstract perceiver of the world." What he discovered was the impersonal identity of the perceiver and the object perceived. Time was abolished for him not because he felt eternal or because he believed his art capable of preserving him forever in the eternity of his work—all the feelings romantic poets had exalted—but because he, Borges, was nobody.

Nevertheless—and in spite of that conclusion—the essay on time does not end there. In a somersault that is characteristic of all his work, Borges denies in the last paragraph all that the long essay has tried vainly to prove:

> And yet, and yet—To deny temporal succession, to deny the ego, to deny the astronomical universe, are apparent desperations and secret assuagements. Our destiny (unlike the hell of Swedenborg and the hell of Tibetan mythology) is not horrible because of its unreality; it is horrible because it is irreversible and ironbound. Time is the substance I am made of. Time is a river that carries me away, but I am the river; it is a tiger that mangles me, but I am the tiger; it is a fire that consumes me, but I am the fire. The world, alas, is real; I, alas, am Borges. (Ibid., pp. 186–187)

That is not his only denial. The whole essay lies under the sign of contradiction. In a preface to it Borges emphasizes the pun implicit in its title:

> A word about the title. I am not unaware that it is an example of the monster which logicians have called *contradictio in adjecto,* because to say that a refutation of time is new (or old) is to attribute to it a predicate of a temporal nature, which restores the notion that the subject attempts to destroy. But I shall let it stand, so that this very subtle joke may prove that I do not exaggerate the importance of these word games. Apart from that, our language is so saturated and animated with time that it is very possible that not one line in this book does not somehow demand or invoke it. (Ibid., p. 172)

Neither the irony of the title nor the final rectification succeeds in obliterating his basic intuition of the world's lack of reality, of one man's lack of personal identity. Against the arguments of metaphysics, or logic, or language (the world is real, time exists; Borges, alas, is Borges), the inner vision, the hallucinatory experience, and the literary fiction continue to struggle, offering opposing theses.

The pamphlet was printed in May 1947 and circulated privately among Borges' friends. Even more secret was a piece he wrote with Bioy Casares in November of the same year. It is one of Biorges' stories. Called "La fiesta del monstruo" (The Monster's Celebration), it circulated only in typed copies, among the trusted few. In a grotesque

405

language which is a baroque exaggeration of *lunfardo* (Buenos Aires slang), the protagonist, a Peronist worker from a lower-class district, describes his participation in one of the party's greatest rallies. The story is told in all its comic or sordid details by a witness who is unaware of his own baseness. A satirical description of a type and a class, the story also lampoons the demogoguery of Perón and his friends. The humor is savage and the parody grotesque. But what makes the story unique is its central episode, in which a young intellectual Jew is murdered by the mob for refusing to shout Peronist slogans. The anecdote may seem farfetched today, but episodes of this kind were not uncommon in Buenos Aires at the time Perón was consolidating his power. Among his allies then was a vociferous Nazi group called the Alliance, which made the harassment and beating of Jews one of its specialties. Perón once condemned these practices, but he never ordered the police to interfere with the Alliance.

To publish "The Monster's Celebration" was impossible while Perón was in power. Even the circulation of typed copies was dangerous enough. Perón had made clear that he would not tolerate public opposition. In 1955, after his overthrow, the story was published in the Uruguayan weekly *Marcha,* whose literary section I then edited.

Among the many lectures Borges gave in Montevideo during the Peronist years, one was outstanding. It was dedicated to fantastic literature and was delivered on September 2, 1949. Some of the points of view he presented in that lecture had already been advanced in articles collected in *Discusión,* as far back as 1932, or published in *El Hogar* or *Sur* and *La Nación* during the 1930s and 1940s, especially in the 1940 prologue to *The Invention of Morel,* Bioy Casares' science-fiction novel. Two of the articles published in *La Nación*—"The Flower of Coleridge" (September 23, 1945) and "Partial Enchantments of the *Quixote"* (November 6, 1949)—were instrumental in shaping his views of the genre. They were collected in *Other Inquisitions,* thus preserving the substance of what Borges said so brilliantly in Montevideo.

After stating in his lecture that the literature of fantasy was older than that of realism, Borges outlined four procedures which allow the writer to destroy not only the conventions of realistic fiction but also those of reality. According to Borges, these procedures are the work of art inside the work of art, the contamination of reality by dream, travel through time, and the double. One observation which immediately comes to mind is that, with the exception of the first, these so-called procedures can be seen as subjects more than as technical devices. A work may show thematically how reality is contaminated by a dream; it can include travel in time or present doubles. But Borges was talking specifically about procedures. His implicit perspective was that of a critic who is discussing how to structure a plot. From that point of view (which he did not elucidate but assumed his listeners understood), the contamination of reality by dream, time travel, and the double are not just subjects but procedures used in the structuring of a plot. They belong to the formal and not to the thematic fabric of the story.

With this caveat, it is possible to follow his arguments. He found examples of the first procedure—the work of art inside the work of art—in many famous books: in the second part of the *Quixote* some of the characters have read, and do discuss, the first part; in *Hamlet* the players who visit Elsinore perform, in Act III, a tragedy that bears some similarity to the main one; in the *Aeneid,* the protagonist examines in Carthage a bas relief that depicts the destruction of Troy, and he sees himself among the figures there represented; in the *Iliad* Helen embroiders a double purple gown which represents the story of the poem. The procedure can be recognized in Borges' own stories. In "The Garden of Forking Paths" the labyrinth and the novel described by the Sinologist mirror the story's structure. But Borges has also inverted the procedure: instead of certifying the reality of his stories by introducing one part of them inside their own narrative structure, he has inserted contemporary reality into his strangest fictions. Thus, to avoid any suspicion about the existence of the apocryphal encyclopedia of Tlön, in the story of the same name, he has padded its pages with the names of real persons, from Adolfo Bioy Casares, who starts the quest by a seemingly innocent quotation of a text from Uqbar, to Enrique Amorim, who is with "Borges" at the time one of the magical objects from Tlön is produced. Another variant of the same procedure leads Borges to imagine that the text he is supposed to write has already been written by somebody else, and that his story is a review, or an article, about that book. "The Approach to al-Mu'tasim," "An Examination of the Work of Herbert Quain," and the famous "Pierre Menard" are examples of that procedure.

The second procedure, that of introducing images of a dream which alter reality, is one of the oldest. Borges mentions the folklore of many countries and finds in Coleridge a tantalizing quotation: "If a man could pass through Paradise in a dream, and have a flower presented to him as a pledge that his soul had really been there, and if he found that flower in his hand when he awoke—Ay!—and what then?" In one of his most famous stories, "The Circular Ruins," which has as an epigraph a quotation from another weaver of dreams, Lewis Carroll, Borges plays with the blurred limits between reality and dream: a man who has dreamed another discovers at the end that he is somebody else's dream.

In discussing the third procedure, time travel, Borges notes that it can be combined with Coleridge's flower. As an example, he cites H. G. Wells' novel *The Time Machine,* in which the protagonist, on returning from a trip to the future, brings back a faded flower. In another variation, Henry James once projected and half completed a novel, *The Sense of the Past,* in which the protagonist discovers an eighteenth-century portrait of himself and travels back in time to allow the painter to portray him. Borges observes: "James thus creates an incomparable *regressus in infinitum,* when his hero Ralph Pendrel returns to the eighteenth century because he is fascinated by an old painting, but Pendrel's return to this century is a condition for the existence of the painting. The cause follows the effect, the reason for the journey is one of the consequences of the journey" (*Inquisitions,* 1964, p. 12).

In submitting James' novel to that analysis, Borges clearly shows that he is thinking of travel in time not as a theme but as a procedure, a device to construct a plot in which the consequences engender the cause, and the narrative sequence is completely inverted. This is precisely what he attempted in the story "The Other Death," in which a man who behaved cowardly in a battle when he was very young corrects that cowardice on his deathbed and forces God into performing a miracle: in the memory of those who attended the battle he dies heroically and young. Again, what matters to Borges is not just the subject of the inversion of time but the procedure of inverting the sequence inside the plot: the consequence influences the cause, not the other way around.

The last procedure discussed in Borges' lecture, that of the double, had been used by Poe in "William Wilson" and by James in "The Jolly Corner." Borges' stories are full of doubles. In "Three Versions of Judas" a theologian advances the theory that God is incarnate in the betrayer and not the betrayed; in "Theme of the Traitor and the Hero" one man is successively both; in "The Theologians," in the divinity's eyes, the two antagonists engaged in an endless religious dispute are the same person. But in presenting the theme of the double, Borges has always shown a greater interest in the effects of the theme on the structure of the story than in its value as a subject. The first two stories mentioned are written in such a way that each successive unfolding of the plot implies a new "doubling" of its matter and a new articulation of the whole sequence. In the last example, what really matters to God is the fact that each theological argument used can be inverted to prove its contrary. It is not the opposed and symmetrical destinies of the theologians that make the texture of the story but this constant inversion of the theological arguments: the inversion, in this case, matches the inverted structure of the plot.

At the end of the lecture Borges explicitly states that against the common belief that fantastic literature is an evasion of reality he postulates that fantastic literature helps us to understand reality in a deeper and more complex way. That type of literature is a metaphorical version of reality. The two examples he quotes (Wells' *The Invisible Man* and Kafka's *The Trial*) help him to prove that in both cases the central subject is man's alienation. The same can be said about his own fictions. Under the guise of describing a remote planet, Borges presents a nihilistic view of our planet, the Orbis Tertius of the title; the lottery in Babylon and the library of Babel are metaphors of the labyrinthine fate that governs man and shapes his enigmatic existence. The real world permeates Borges' fantastic fiction to the point where it is almost impossible to draw the line between what is reality and what is fantasy.

10.
The Meeting in a Dream

On June 26, 1949, a new book of short stories by Borges was published by Losada in Buenos Aires. Its title, *The Aleph,* was also the title of the last story. As Borges himself observes in a short epilogue to the book, all the stories except two belong to the "fantastic genre." The two exceptions are "Emma Zunz" and "The Story of the Warrior and the Captive." When "Emma Zunz" was announced in *Sur,* before its publication, it was advertised as "a realistic story." In a sense, it is. The plot (according to the epilogue) had been suggested to Borges by a friend, Cecilia Ingenieros. With his usual modesty, he claims that the plot is "superior to its execution." Perhaps. What is clear is that the plot itself is not terribly realistic. A young woman wants to avenge the death of her father, who committed suicide after being cheated by a business associate. Her revenge takes an odd form: she will accuse the culprit of rape and then murder him for it. To achieve this end, she allows herself to be raped by an unknown sailor; then she goes to visit her father's business associate on a pretext and kills him. When the police come, she can prove that she has been raped.

Borges' terse commentary at the end of the story reveals the mechanism of the revenge: "Actually, the story [she told to the police] *was* incredible, but it impressed everyone because substantially it was true. True was Emma Zunz's tone, true was her shame, true was her hate. True was also the outrage she had suffered: only the circumstances were false, the time, and one or two proper names" (*Labyrinths,* 1962, p. 137). Borges' conclusion underlines the basic "unreality" of the story. Although everything in "Emma Zunz" is realistic, in the sense that it conforms to the principle of verisimilitude, the situation itself is "incredible." From the standpoint of believability, the plot is a failure: a good detective could have proved, by a careful examination of the man's body, that he could not have raped her. But what makes the story basically "unrealistic" is the fact that the whole plot is based on the fantastic behavior of the protagonist. "Emma Zunz" belongs, with Melville's Bartleby and Kafka's characters, to that fictional race of beings whose behavior is strange, "unbelievable."

In his prologue to the Spanish version of *Bartleby, the Scrivener,* Borges discusses this type of fantastic story. The end of his own story is typically Borgesian. It tells us that although Emma Zunz was lying, she was essentially telling the truth. She had been raped; the identity of the rapist (and the fact that she consented willingly) was irrelevant. What matters is the fact that an action committed by one man can be atoned for by another. It is the identity between men, not the differences in their personalities and individual acts, that is the real subject of the story. The so-called realistic story has been deprived of a basic element of realism: a compact between reader and writer, a system of conventions that allows the perfect communication of an accepted, and coded, reading of reality. By altering this compact, by introducing some small details that contradict it, and by finally brazenly declaring that Emma's fictional story "was substantially true," Borges violates the compact and creates a type of fantastic behavior that justifies a fantastic reading of "reality."

The other story which, in Borges' view, interprets reality faithfully is another example of strange and even fantastic behavior. Both the warrior and the captive of the title behave in a way that contradicts the expectations of their societies. The warrior is Droctfult, a barbarian who switches sides and dies defending the cause of Ravenna; the captive is an Englishwoman who is kidnapped by an Indian chieftain and becomes a savage. (The story was told to Georgie by Grandmother Haslam, who actually met the woman.) Their opposite destinies are underlined by Borges:

> A thousand three hundred years and the ocean lie between the destiny of the captive and the destiny of Droctfult. Both of these, now, are equally irrecoverable. The figure of the barbarian who embraced the cause of Ravenna, the figure of the European woman who chose the wasteland, may seem antagonistic. And yet, both were swept away by a secret impulse, an impulse more profound than reason, and both heeded this impulse, which they would not have known how to justify. Perhaps the stories I have related are one single story. The obverse and the reverse of this coin are, for God, the same. (*Labyrinths,* 1962, pp. 130–131)

Again, the characters' individual destinies are telescoped into a single, somehow impersonal destiny. The point of view of God is introduced at the end to abolish personal identity.

411

The same mechanism is used by Borges in another of *The Aleph*'s stories, "The Theologians," in which two men fight each other to prove the validity of their opposed theories only to discover, when both are dead and are facing God, that to the divine mind they are the same person. Borges' commentary on this story in the epilogue to the book is symptomatic: he calls it "a dream, a rather melancholic dream, about personal identity." But the only thing that separates that "dream" from "The Story of the Warrior and the Captive" is the fact that what is presented as a part of the story in "The Theologians" (both men face God in the kingdom of heaven) is presented only as a theoretical argument at the end of "The Story of the Warrior and The Captive." The viewpoint, and the concept of reality it implies, is the same.

The other ten stories in *The Aleph* belong to different levels of the fantastic. The first story, "The Immortal," is about a man who at one time may have been Homer and who is now a twentieth-century antiquary interested in Homer's texts and translations. In his epilogue Borges describes the story as "a draft of an ethics for immortals," but a better description might be that it allegorizes the fate of classical texts, which begin by being read as poetry and end up by being the pasture of scholars. In the narrative Borges parodies the conversion of a poem into a pretext for copious footnotes. The story begins with an almost symbolist reconstruction of the discovery of the City of Immortals by a Roman soldier; after a number of chapters which become more and more clustered with bibiliographic information, Borges concludes with a mere postscript in which the quotations have taken over. The story can thus be read as an allegory of reading.

The next story, "The Dead Man," presents the fate of a young man who joins a group of Uruguayan smugglers and very easily deposes its old chief—taking away his power, his favorite horse, and even his woman—only to discover that he has been allowed to do all that because the old man had, from the very beginning, condemned him to death. The story, set in Uruguay in the 1890s, could be considered realistic except that the old man's behavior is too eccentric and conforms too well to Borges' notion of an irrational fate. In the epilogue to the first edition he observes that the old man is "a rough divinity, a mulatto and barbaric version of Chesterton's incomparable Sunday" (*El Aleph,* 1949, p. 145).

Of the other stories, at least two are variations on existing works. "The Biography of Tadeo Isidoro Cruz (1829–1874)" is a development of a character in Hernández's *Martín Fierro,* but taken from an angle that makes it almost unrecognizable until the very end. Again, it is the story of a man who (like Droctfult and the captive) switches his allegiances at a crucial moment in life to become the opposite of what he was: a police officer ordered to capture the deserter Martín Fierro, he is so impressed by Fierro's courage that he sides with him and becomes an outlaw too.

The other variation on a famous work is more subtle. In "The House of Asterion" Borges retells the myth of the Minotaur from the point of view of the monster, a perspective suggested to him by a Watts painting which showed the Minotaur on a balcony sadly viewing the open country. Borges explains in the epilogue that he owes the story "and the character of its poor protagonist" to Watts' painting. The key word here is the adjective "poor."

A story remotely connected with a famous text is "The Other Death." Borges obviously was inspired by the character of Pier Damiani, whom he discovered in Dante's *Divine Comedy*. But the story itself (about a man who dies twice, first as a coward in bed, then as a valiant soldier in battle) is set in one of the gaucho provinces of Uruguay at the beginning of this century. (Perhaps because the story is located in my home state, Borges gives me a very minor role in the tale: I am supposed to be the person who writes a letter of introduction to one of the main characters.)

Another story, "Deutsches Requiem," was written to interpret the suicidal destiny of Germany. In the epilogue Borges observes: "In the last war, nobody could have wanted more than I that Germany should be defeated; nobody could have felt more than I the tragedy of German destiny; 'Deutsches Requiem' attempts to understand that destiny, which our 'Germanophiles' (who know nothing about Germany) were not able to lament, or to understand" (*ibid.*, p. 146). He also indicates the sources of the last three stories. One, "The God's Script," attributes to a Mayan priest "arguments of a cabalist or a theologian." So much for Borges' respect for accurate scholarship. Both "The Zahir" and "The Aleph" (which deal with a magic object and a magic place respectively) show the influence of one Wells story, "The Crystal Egg."

As usual with Borges, his comments on *The Aleph*'s stories are modest, giving little indication of their real value. This is especially true of "The Zahir" and "The Aleph." Both stories are deceptively simple. In both the protagonist is Borges, or really "Borges": a character who has the same name as the author but is not the author; he is a persona. In "The Zahir" Borges uses the cabalistic superstition of a magical coin to weave the story of a man who becomes obsessed with a twenty-cent Argentine coin he received at a bar. He gets rid of the coin but cannot stop thinking about it and eventually becomes haunted by its image. The fact that he received the coin after coming from the wake of Clementina Villar helps us to understand the erotic meaning of that obsession: the coin is a symbol of Clementina. To be obsessed by it is a way

of saying he is obsessed by her—by her beauty, her disdainful character, the unforgettable memory of her. But Borges being Borges, he has
to disguise the erotic fixation with his erudite, cabalistic narrative.
A similar situation is explored in "The Aleph." This time the
woman's name is Beatriz Viterbo; like Clementina, she is a brilliant society woman who utterly despises the narrator. But "The Aleph" is a
much more elaborate story. Beatriz Viterbo's portrait is paralleled by
the portrait of her cousin Carlos Argentino Daneri, a pompous poet
whose ambition to describe the whole world in a poem is mercilessly
satirized by the narrator. And the magical object here is not a coin but
a point in Daneri's cellar where the whole world can be seen at once. If
in "The Zahir" the erudite allusions distract the reader from the story's
secret center ("Borges'" obsession with Clementina Villar), in "The
Aleph" the obsession is plainly presented; what is displaced is the
model the story is based on. "The Aleph" is really a parodic reduction
of the *Divine Comedy*. From that point of view, "Borges" is Dante, Beatriz Viterbo is Beatrice Portinari (as disdainful of the Florentine poet as
the Argentine Beatriz is of the author), and Carlos Argentino Daneri is
both Dante and Virgil. His name, Daneri, telescopes the Florentine's
complete name (*Dante Alighieri*); like Virgil, he is a didactic poet and a
guide to the vision of the other world. And the Aleph Borges so beautifully describes in the crucial episode of the story can be seen as a
reduction of Dante's vision of the world. There is one major difference: Borges attempts in the short space of two pages to convey
what Dante (very wisely) refused to do in the conclusion to his *Comedy:*
to describe the ineffable. Using the Whitmanesque device of the ana-
phora, Borges, in order to describe a point in space which simultaneously contains all points in space and in time, resorts to a dazzling
and chaotic enumeration.

The parody is so subtly achieved that many readers of Borges
who also are devoted readers of Dante fail to recognize it. But it is
plainly there, especially in the comical and ironic allusions to each char-
acter's foibles and obsessions. As with all parodical reductions, "The
Aleph" is both irreverent and admiring. Even the person to whom
Borges dedicates the story, a young Argentine writer named Estela
Canto, has the right Dantesque name: Estela (Stella) was the word
Dante chose to end each of the three Cantiche of the *Divine Comedy;*
Canto was the name of each division in each Cantica. But the name
"Estela Canto" also means, in Spanish, "I sing to Estela." At the time
Borges wrote the story, he was more than ready to sing to that particu-
lar Estela. As homage, he gave her the manuscript, in his own minus-
cule handwriting, of "The Aleph."

Some critics have attempted to identify Beatriz Viterbo; it is a pointless task. She belongs, with Clementina Villar, to the category of the temptress, the femme fatale, la Belle Dame Sans Merci. She is less a woman than a prototype, and the fact that Borges used the same prototype in two stories that are so basically different proves the pointlessness of any identification. What really mattered to him was that Beatriz Viterbo, or Clementina Villar, belonged to the same category as Dante's Beatrice. Thus the best way to try to find out more about them is to read what Borges has to say about Dante, and Beatrice, in his introduction to a Spanish translation of the *Divine Comedy*, included in a collection of classics (Buenos Aires, Clásicos Jackson, vol. 31) the same year *The Aleph* was published.

In the introduction Borges provides the necessary information for the casual reader: a discussion of the date of composition of the poem and the meaning of its title; a description of the poem's topography, chronology, and symbolic meaning; and a commentary on the best editions, with a strong recommendation to read the text in the original. But the best part of the introduction is the specific analysis of a few episodes: the meetings with Ulysses (*Inferno*, XXVI), Ugolino (*Inferno*, XXXIV), and Beatrice (*Purgatorio*, XXXI). To the centuries of discussion of these famous episodes Borges brings a new and unconventional critical mind. Borges later published his comments on the meeting with Beatrice as a separate essay in *Other Inquisitions* under the title of "The Meeting in a Dream." After describing the episode, and insisting on the way Beatrice scolded and humiliated Dante, he quotes an observation made in 1946 by the German critic Theophil Spoerri: "Undoubtedly Dante himself had imagined that meeting differently. Nothing in the previous pages indicates that the greatest humiliation of his life awaited him there." In an attempt to explain Beatrice's severity, Borges comments:

> To fall in love is to create a religion that has a fallible god. That Dante professed an idolatrous adoration for Beatrice is a truth that does not bear contradicting; that she once ridiculed him and another time rebuffed him are facts recorded by the *Vita nuova*. . . . Dante, when Beatrice was dead, when Beatrice was lost forever, played with the idea of finding her, to mitigate his sorrow. I believe that he erected the triple architecture of his poem simply to insert that encounter. Then what usually happens in dreams happened to him. In adversity we dream of good fortune, and the intimate awareness that we cannot attain it is enough to corrupt our dream, clouding it with sad restraints. That was the case with Dante. Refused forever by Beatrice, he dreamed of Beatrice, but he dreamed her very austere, but he dreamed her inaccessible, but he dreamed her in a chariot drawn by a lion that was a bird and was all bird or all lion when it was reflected in her eyes (*Purgatorio*, XXXI, 121). Those facts can be the prefiguration of a night-

mare, which is set forth and described at length in the following canto. . . .
Infinitely Beatrice existed for Dante; Dante existed very little, perhaps not at
all, for Beatrice. Our piety, our veneration cause us to forget that pitiful
inharmony, which was unforgettable for Dante. I read and reread about the
vicissitudes of their illusory encounter, and I think of two lovers who were
dreamed by Alighieri in the hurricane of the Second Circle and who are
dark emblems, although he perhaps neither knew that nor intended it, of
the happiness he did not attain. I think of Francesca and of Paolo, united
forever in their Hell. *Questi, che mai da me non fia diviso.* With frightening
love, with anxiety, with admiration, with envy, Dante must have formed that
line. (*Inquisitions,* 1964, pp. 99–100)

At the beginning of his introduction to the *Divine Comedy*
Borges describes an imaginary engraving—Arabic or Chinese—in
which everything that ever was or would ever be is represented. Dante's
poem (observes Borges) is that engraving. Or, to use a different symbol, Dante's poem is an Aleph. Which brings us back to the story. To
read "The Aleph" after reading Borges' introduction to the poem is to
realize how much of his interpretation of that meeting between Beatrice and Dante went into the fabric of his story. "Borges" (the character) has his Beatriz Viterbo. Like Dante's, although in a crueler more
degrading way, she does not care very much for her devoted lover; like
Beatrice, she dies leaving him with no hope of meeting her again except in a dream (a poem or the story); as in Dante, the dream turns
into a nightmare. "Borges" comes out of his vision as humiliated as the
Florentine. The story is also a microcosm (an Aleph) in the same sense
that Dante's poem is. But, of course, in reducing the theological sublim-
ities of the model to the grotesque level of his story, Borges is practicing one of his favorite tricks: the parodic miniaturization of a vast work
of art. He had already attempted it with his "Pierre Menard, Author of
the *Quixote*" and with "Tlön, Uqbar, Orbis Tertius" (the model here was
Thomas More's *Utopia*). But he has never been more successful
than in "The Aleph," because the process of miniaturization and the
outrageous level on which the parody works are so radical that many
readers miss the obvious clues contained in Beatriz Viterbo's name, in
Carlos Argentino Daneri's insane poem, and in "Borges" ' quest, which
leads him to the vision of the Aleph (Dante's microcosm) in the cellar of
an old Buenos Aires house.

In a note Borges wrote for the American edition of *The Aleph*
he ambiguously disclaims any parodic intention: "Critics . . . have detected Beatrice Portinari in Beatriz Viterbo, Dante in Daneri, and the
descent into hell in the descent into the cellar. I am, of course, duly
grateful for these unlooked-for gifts" (*The Aleph,* 1970, p. 264). Borges'
modesty is really too much. The coincidences between the two texts are

not exclusively the ones he indicates; they are more complex and proliferate even further, as we have seen. But Borges always prefers to
keep one side of his texts (the best, generally) out of public scrutiny.
Nevertheless, in a conclusion to this note he acknowledges that "Beatriz
Viterbo really existed and I was very much and hopelessly in love with
her. I wrote my story after her death" (ibid., p. 264). The statement,
needless to say, enriches the parodical reading of the story.

He also comments in that note that Carlos Argentino Daneri
also exists and that he is a good friend of his "who to this day has never
suspected he is in the story. The verses are a parody of his verse.
Daneri's speech on the other hand is not an exaggeration but a fair
rendering. The Argentine Academy of Letters is the habitat of such
specimens" (ibid., p. 264). This last observation not only reinforces the
assumption of a parodical transposition but shows very clearly another
dimension of the story. In satirizing the habits of his compatriots, the
vanity of their literary prizes and academic associations, Borges vents
his feelings about the humiliation he was subjected to at the time his
first collection of fantastic stories, *The Garden of Forking Paths,* came out.
"The Aleph" was written and originally published in *Sur* in September
1945, when Borges was still smarting from that snub. But when the
story came out in the 1949 volume, Perón's regime had given him a different and more grotesque motive for feeling humiliated. Sordid reality had taken over from grotesque literary life.

11.
A Useless Debate

At fifty, Borges was on his way to becoming "Borges." He was not the young man who had signed those early poems in Europe or the man whose many volumes of essays, poems, and short stories had been published in Argentina during the 1930s and 1940s. He was beginning to be a persona: a mask behind which the young man and the mature man could hide; a mask which was immediately recognizable because it was a simplified and exalted version of the man. *The Aleph* (1949) and *Other Inquisitions* (1952) helped to define that persona. But it was not until the end of the 1950s that the persona took over, and Borges irrevocably became "Borges."

The "Borges" persona attracted a court of beautiful young women who functioned as erotic (not sexual) companions and/or as secretaries and even collaborators in his many-sided literary output. In the 1930s and early 1940s Borges had been at pains to gather around him a group of faithful young men who were ready to die for him (metaphorically speaking, of course). In the late 1940s and throughout the rest of his literary career Borges was surrounded by a group of young women who were eager to devote their intelligence and sensitivity to help, protect, and thoroughly spoil him.

One of the first of these young women was the beautiful Silvina Bullrich, with whom Borges compiled, in 1945, an anthology on Argentine hoodlums. Deeper and more complex was his relationship with Estela Canto, the young novelist to whom he dedicated "The Aleph." They saw each other regularly, spent some holidays together, and exchanged literary views. When *The Aleph* came out, Estela wrote a perceptive review for *Sur* (October 1949). The following month, to celebrate the twenty-fifth anniversary of the publication of the periodical

Martín Fierro, she published in *Nueva Gaceta* (November 7, 1949) a long interview with Borges. It soon became obvious that they had more than a literary relationship, but apparently Borges could not let himself go emotionally. Their friendship was complicated by his reticence and eventually ended.

Other young women took over. Borges began to be seen as a sort of Argentine Professor Higgins who mesmerized women into becoming, for a while at least, full-scale intellectuals. Like the Shavian Pygmalion, he fell in love with his creations but was too inconstant to pursue the matter to its utmost consequences. This legend was, as usual, based on some reality, but it was a legend nevertheless. In Borges' everyday life, what really mattered was the friendly company, the erotic stimuli produced by the young women; the series of books he produced with their help was less important.

One of the most successful of these books was a manual called *Ancient Germanic Literatures,* which he published in 1951 (Mexico, Fondo de Cultura Económica) with the collaboration of Delia Ingenieros, a sister to that Cecilia who had given him the plot of "Emma Zunz." The book was a restatement of the questions Borges had raised, in 1933, in his article on the metaphors of the ancient Icelandic poets. Borges' knowledge of the subject was insufficient to produce a truly scholarly manual, so in 1966 he published a revised version, *Medieval Germanic Literatures* (Buenos Aires, Falbro Editor), compiled this time with the help of a new Galatea, María Esther Vázquez. Even this second version proved to be faulty. He is still working on a new version of the same book.

In the meantime, between 1951 and 1955, he published four works with the help of various young women: *El "Martín Fierro,"* a rewriting of his essays on gaucho literature, done with Margarita Guerrero (Buenos Aires, Columba, 1953); "The Lost Image," a scenario for a ballet, signed in 1953 with Bettina Edelberg; *Leopoldo Lugones,* a collection of old and new pieces on the Argentine poet, compiled also with the help of Bettina Edelberg (Buenos Aires, Troquel, 1955); and *La hermana de Eloísa,* a collection of short stories by Borges and María Luisa Levinson, one of which was written in collaboration (Buenos Aires, Ene, 1955). None of these ventures was really important or new, and the titles could be omitted from Borges' bibliography without any visible damage; but they expanded Borges' literary empire, adding small, quaint provinces.

Those were years of great productivity. Borges continued his collaboration with Adolfo Bioy Casares. No less than four books came out as a result before the end of 1955: *The Best Detective Stories,* a companion to the 1946 anthology (Buenos Aires, Emecé, 1951); *The Hood-*

lums and *The Paradise of the Believers,* two film scripts which the authors claimed had failed to interest Argentine movie producers (Buenos Aires, Losada, 1955); *Short and Extraordinary Tales,* an idiosyncratic anthology (Buenos Aires, Raigal, 1955); and *Gaucho Poetry,* which in two volumes collected the masterpieces of a genre both compilers adored (Mexico, Fondo de Cultura Económica, 1955).

On his own, Borges published in 1951 a selection of his most popular stories under the title of one of the stories, *Death and the Compass* (Buenos Aires, Emecé). In Paris the same year Roger Caillois published a translation of *Ficciones,* which included as a prologue Néstor Ibarra's essay on Borges. It was the beginning of Borges' following in France. Two years later another collection of stories, *Labyrinths,* was included by Caillois in La Croix du Sud (The Southern Cross), a series on Latin American literature he was then editing. As if to celebrate Borges' new status, Emecé decided to begin printing his complete works in a series of slim gray volumes edited by José Edmundo Clemente. The first volume came out in 1953. It was a reissue of a 1936 book, *History of Eternity.* An expanded edition of Borges' 1943 book of poems and of the 1935 *Universal History of Infamy* were added to the series in 1954. Borges himself was not terribly impressed. The only comment that the publication of his complete works elicits from him in his "Autobiographical Essay" is deprecatory. In talking about his first books of essays, written and published in the 1920s, he says:

> Three of the four essay collections—whose names are best forgotten—I have never allowed to be reprinted. In fact, when in 1953 my present publisher— Emecé—proposed to bring out my "complete writings," the only reason I accepted was that it would allow me to keep those preposterous volumes suppressed. This reminds me of Mark Twain's suggestion that a fine library could be started by leaving out the works of Jane Austen, and that even if that library contained no other books it would still be a fine library, since her books were left out. ("Essay," 1970, pp. 230–231)

Despite his facetiousness, in 1953 the publication of his complete works must have meant something to him. Perón's disdainful and even humiliating treatment had not kept Borges from being recognized as a major Argentine writer. The slim gray volumes reached a new generation of readers, avid young university students or recent graduates who had had till then little opportunity to read Borges' earlier works. They became the avant-garde of a new readership—devoted but also polemical—that turned Borges into Argentina's most controversial and influential writer.

The most important of all the books Borges published during this phase of his career was *Other Inquisitions* (1952). It is a collection of thirty-nine essays which he had selected from among the many he wrote in the late 1930s and 1940s. The title of the volume alludes to Borges' first book of essays, *Inquisitions*, published in 1925. It is as if the writer wants to underline both the continuity of his quest (his inquiring spirit) and the difference in the style of the quest (it was another). In commenting on the collection in an epilogue, Borges makes no attempt to play down its miscellaneous character: "As I corrected the proofs of this volume, I discovered two tendencies in these miscellaneous essays" (*Inquisitions*, 1964, p. 189). At the same time, he subtly indicates the unity behind the plurality of views:

> The first tendency is to evaluate religious or philosophical ideas on the basis of their esthetic worth and even for what is singular and marvelous about them. Perhaps this is an indication of a basic skepticism. The other tendency is to presuppose (and to verify) that the number of fables or metaphors of which men's imagination is capable is limited, but that these few inventions can be all things for all men, like the Apostle. (Ibid., p. 189)

Many of the essays illustrate the first tendency—"Pascal's Sphere," "Time and J. W. Dunne," "The Creation and P. H. Goose," "The Biathanatos," "Pascal," "Avatars of the Tortoise"—but the best example is "A New Refutation of Time," the essay he had anticipated in a 1947 pamphlet. An exposition of his view of reality, the essay also testifies to Borges' skepticism regarding scientific or philosophical explanations of the world.

The second tendency—to recognize behind the variety of fables or metaphors a common unity—is evident in many of the best essays in this book: "The Wall and the Books," "The Flower of Coleridge," "The Dream of Coleridge," "Partial Enchantments of the *Quixote*," "Kafka and His Precursors," "On the Cult of Books," "Forms of a Legend," "From Allegories to Novels." Relying on a vast library and an even vaster memory, Borges finds the most unexpected connections, showing common points of view in authors whom critics have never put together. Following one idea, one image, one procedure through diverse languages and centuries, Borges can begin with Kafka and end up with Zeno, or start with Coleridge and arrive at Henry James; Benedetto Croce leads him to Chaucer, Buddha to Oscar Wilde, Pope to the Chinese emperor Shih Huang Ti, who ordered the building of the Great Wall. Relentless in his pursuit of the invisible mechanism which controlled the world and writing, Borges is also relentless in his ability to relate and connect, to combine and condense.

What he leaves out in his appraisal of the essays included in *Other Inquisitions* is a third tendency: that of metaphorically condensing the writer's style or approach. The essays on Quevedo, Hawthorne, Whitman, Valéry, Edward FitzGerald, Oscar Wilde, Chesterton, the "first" Wells, and Bernard Shaw, all attempt to discover the actual writer under the mask, or persona, each of these writers had created. In doing so, Borges is not concerned with ferreting out biographical truths. On the contrary, he is interested in discovering the type of literary destiny each particular writer managed to fulfill. In the case of Whitman, he shows the difference between the rather withdrawn and modest Walter Whitman and the emphatic persona Walt Whitman, the Son of Manhattan; in the case of Chesterton, he underlines the contradiction between the ardent believer who joyously proclaimed his Catholic faith and the nightmares in which this same faith is coded. What Borges is after in these literary portraits is the same kind of effect produced by his biographies in *A Universal History of Infamy:* the awareness of the paradoxical nature of all lives, the realization that to portray a man is to reduce the multiplicity of his traits to a composite (and unfaithful) sum of the traits we favor. But in moving from the infamous characters of his early book to the complex characters of these writers, Borges adds a new dimension. Each one of the writers began by creating not only a work but also a persona. And what truly concerned Borges was the creation of that persona.

In compiling the articles for *Other Inquisitions*, Borges was assisted by José Bianco. They worked in Bianco's private library and selected pieces from *Sur, La Nación,* and other well-known sources. According to Bianco, there was no attempt to produce a well-organized volume or to select the "best" essays. On the contrary, they left out (inadvertently or on purpose) some important pieces: the prologue to Bioy Casares' *The Invention of Morel* (1940), in which Borges advances a theory about fantastic literature; the prologue to Herman Melville's *Bartleby, the Scrivener* (1943) and to Henry James' "The Abasement of the Northmores" (1945), which contain important views on both writers; and the prologue to Dante's *Divine Comedy* (1949), of which only one section, on the meeting with Beatrice, is included in the book. Borges being Borges, he was unlikely to take the trouble to put all his most important essays together. Not until 1975 would he consent to the inclusion of these and other important pieces in *Prólogos,* a book of prologues which naturally included a "Prologue of Prologues." But even here, the long essay on Dante is omitted. Probably Borges did not own the copyright on that prologue; or perhaps he was too busy to attempt to save it from the solemn fate its publication in a collection of classics implied.

Following the publication of *Other Inquisitions* in July 1952, María Rosa Lida de Malkiel wrote a learned and witty study for *Sur*

(July–August 1952) entitled "Contribution to the Study of Jorge Luis Borges' Literary Sources." It was the first time that his work was approached with all the armature of serious scholarship. The same year, Enrique Pezzoni published in *Sur* (November–December 1952) a long review of *Other Inquisitions*. Entitled "Approximations to Borges' Latest Book," it is one of the best studies of the book, but it also has a wider intention: to place Borges' work and personality in the larger context of contemporary Argentine literature.

At that time, Borges had become the center of a controversy about the political and cultural role of the Argentine writer. Many of his new readers refused to accept the position that literature was best left to writers, and politics to politicians. In line with Sartre, they were beginning to demand that writers become engaged with their times. They wanted social and political debate to enter academia and assault Parnassus. Borges was, for them, the best example of a writer who could be viewed both as alienated (did he not write about fantastic worlds?) and engaged (was he not one of the most notorious of Perón's opponents?). The debate began in 1948 and continues to the present. But it reached its peak after Borges published *Other Inquisitions*. In a sense, that book, and Pezzoni's article, helped to focus the issues in the debate.

The debate began with a seemingly innocuous piece by one of Argentina's young essayists, H. A. Murena. In an article published in *Sur* (June–July 1948) Murena attacks Borges' poetry on the ground that he uses the symbols of Argentine nationalism but does not share the national feeling these symbols imply. It is obvious that Murena misses Borges' point. Instead of using the symbols of Argentina to emphasize what is unique (and thus parochial) in them, Borges uses them to show what is universal about them. In his poem about the *truco,* what Borges wants to show is not the quaint peculiarities of the popular cardgame but the fact that any game makes us unreal: in following the rules, we repeat the games other men have played before us; for a while, we are these men. In a second and later article, also published in *Sur* (October 1951), Murena advances his argument. This time what he objects to is that Borges represents a culmination of the eclecticism that makes Argentine writers heirs of all cultures. In a sense, Murena seems to resent the fact that Borges is truly cosmopolitan.

In his article Pezzoni reacted strongly to this type of reading. He points out Murena's fallacy in judging Borges' poems not by their texts but in their ethical context within Argentine reality (as Murena saw it). He underlines Borges' right to create his poems out of his own particular vision and craftsmanship. In criticizing the type of analysis Murena attempts, Pezzoni moves toward a more balanced literary and critical approach.

Unfortunately, few people read him. The general trend of the new critics was toward a sociological and political view of literature. Even more unbalanced than Murena's are Jorge Abelardo Ramos' views in his *Crisis and Resurrection of Argentine Literature* (1954). He sees Borges as a representative of the ranchowners' oligarchy and accuses him of writing an alienated, aristocratic, gratuitous kind of literature. The fact that Borges never owned a ranch in his life, and that his point of view (nihilistic if not anarchistic, to say the least) did not at all coincide with the pious, conservative, bourgeois philosophy of the ranchowners, did not bother Ramos at all. A pseudo-Marxist, Ramos believed that Perón was a genuine leader of the workers. For him, Borges, an anti-Peronist, had to represent the enemy.

In a similar vein, younger writers attempted to apply to Borges notions they had scarcely understood in Sartre, Merleau-Ponty, and perhaps even in Lukacs. An example is Adolfo Prieto's small book *Borges and the New Generation* (1954), which had some success. Equally critical of Borges, but less partisan, was a special issue of a new journal, *Ciudad* (no. 2–3, 1955), which was dedicated entirely to Borges. As friends and sympathizers of Prieto, the contributors attempted a balanced view of Borges but generally failed. One of the reasons was that (like Prieto) they lacked complete familiarity with Borges' work. Their ignorance about some of his key writings was embarrassing.

From a certain point of view, the debate was as disorganized and erratic as the colloquium that had been held at *Megáfono* in 1933, when the first edition of *Discusión* was published. Although the vocabulary and the so-called ideology had changed, the objections were pretty much the same: Borges was alienated from national reality; Borges was a foreigner who relished writing about Germans and Arabs, Scandinavians and Jews; Borges was a Byzantine writer, a European. The arguments were repeated, the level of critical inquiry constantly lowered.

Borges himself had answered many of his critics even before they put their ideas to paper. In a lecture he gave in 1951 called "The Argentine Writer and Tradition," later published in *Sur* (January–February 1955), he attacks the kind of literary nationalism which demands that a writer demonstrate he is Argentine or Zulu. He correctly points out that the discussion would be unintelligible to Shakespeare or Racine, who never doubted they had the right to present in their plays a Danish Hamlet or a Greek Andromache, an Egyptian Cleopatra or a Roman Nero. Borges comes to the conclusion that Argentines ought not to be afraid of not being Argentine enough: "Our patrimony is the universe." He adds:

> We should essay all themes. . . . We cannot limit ourselves to purely Argentine subjects in order to be Argentine; for either being Argentine is an inescapable act of fate—and in that case we shall be so in all events—or being Argentine is a mere affectation, a mask. I believe that if we surrender ourselves to that voluntary dream which is artistic creation, we shall be Argentine and we shall also be good or tolerable writers. (*Labyrinths*, 1964, p. 185)

The piece was later included in a new edition of *Discusión,* published as the fourth volume of his complete works in 1956. In a sense, it is a final statement about a subject that had misled and would continue to mislead Argentine criticism for decades.

12.
The End of a Nightmare

The Peronist years were coming to a close. After Evita's death in 1952, the regime seemed to wane in popularity. Opposing forces gathered strength; the Church and a coalition of foreign interests led by England fanned internal divisions in the army and supported the navy's traditional rivalry with Perón. By 1955 it was obvious that only through force could the regime continue. Although Perón threatened to arm the workers and turn them loose on the streets, he was secretly determined not to resort to violence. He was a politician and tried to survive as politicians do: by endlessly playing one force against another. But his room for maneuvering was being reduced by the hour. In September 1955, after the army started an uprising in Córdoba (the fortress of Argentine Catholicism) and the navy supported it, tightly blockading Buenos Aires, Perón accepted defeat and resigned. He was quickly spirited out of the country.

For Borges it was a day of joy. In his "Autobiographical Essay" he has this to say about the great event:

> The long-hoped-for revolution came in September 1955. After a sleepless, anxious night, nearly the whole population came out into the streets, cheering the revolution and shouting the name of Córdoba, where most of the fighting had taken place. We were so carried away that for some time we were quite unaware of the rain that was soaking us to the bone. We were so happy that not a single word was even uttered against the fallen dictator. Perón went into hiding and was later allowed to leave the country. No one knows how much money he got away with. ("Essay," 1970, pp. 248–249)

For Borges it was the end of a nightmare. Despite his increasing recognition as a writer, the Peronist decade had been for him a period of pain and humiliation. Two stories he wrote then echo the feelings of those years. "The South"—originally published in *La Nación* (February 8, 1953) and later included in the second edition of *Ficciones* (1956)—presents an Argentine who, like Borges, is of Nordic ascent. He is challenged to a knife fight by a hoodlum. The protagonist, Juan Dahlmann, accepts the challenge in spite of his lack of skill and goes into the open sure that he is going to be killed. During the Peronist years Borges must have felt like Dahlmann and probably dreamed of a similarly savage ending. The second story, "The Wait," also appeared in *La Nación* (August 27, 1950) and was later included in the second edition of *The Aleph* (1952). In the story a man waits for some hoodlums to come and kill him. Perhaps Borges also waited, or dreamed about waiting, for the police to come and get him.

If the allusions and nightmares in those stories are ambiguous, some poems Borges published during that decade explicitly reveal his hatred and fears. One is called "A Page to Commemorate Colonel Suárez, Victor at Junín" and was originally published in *Sur* (January–February 1945) at the precise time Perón came to power. Superficially it seems to be another of those poems Borges loved to write to celebrate his ancestors' unflinching courage in battle. But the last lines give the game away:

> His great-grandson is writing these lines,
> and a silent voice comes to him out of the past,
> out of the blood:
> "What does my battle at Junín matter if it is only
> a glorious memory, or a date learned by rote
> for an examination, or a place in the atlas?
> The battle is everlasting and can do without
> the pomp of actual armies and of trumpets.
> Junín is two civilians cursing a tyrant
> on a street corner,
> or an unknown man somewhere, dying in prison."
> *(Poems*, 1972, translated by Alastair Reid, p. 91)

By linking his ancestor's epic fight for freedom with civilian resistance to a tyrant, Borges was clearly indicating where the battlefield was located now: in the streets of Buenos Aires.

Another poem is even more explicit, and because of it, more dangerous. It is called "The Dagger" and was rejected by *La Nación*. I published it in *Marcha* (June 25, 1954).

A dagger rests in a drawer.
It was forged in Toledo at the end of the last century. Luis Melián Lafinur gave

427

it to my father, who brought it from Uruguay. Evaristo Carriego once held it in his hand.

Whoever lays eyes on it has to pick up the dagger and toy with it, as if he had always been on the lookout for it. The hand is quick to grip the waiting hilt, and the powerful obeying blade slides in and out of the sheath with a click.

This is not what the dagger wants.

It is more than a structure of metal; men conceived it and shaped it with a single end in mind. It is, in some eternal way, the dagger that last night knifed a man in Tacuarembó and the daggers that rained on Caesar. It wants to kill, it wants to shed sudden blood.

In a drawer of my writing table, among draft pages and old letters, the dagger dreams over and over its simple tiger's dream. On wielding it, the hand comes alive, sensing itself, each time handled, in touch with the killer for whom it was forged.

At times, I am sorry for it. Such power and single-mindedness, so impassive or innocent its pride, and the years slip by, unheeding.

(Ibid., translated by Norman Thomas di Giovanni, p. 95)

The dagger's obsession was Borges' obsession. It is obvious why *La Nación* was reluctant to print a poem that could have been easily construed as defending the assassination of tyrants. But the fact that not many of his countrymen were ready to follow Borges in his resistance to the regime did not discourage him at all. He went on with his solitary fight. In his "Autobiographical Essay," in recalling the dark days of the Perón regime, he comments on his colleagues' militancy. He had been elected president of the Argentine Society of Writers in 1950, a position he held until 1953. According to Borges, the society "was one of the few strongholds against the dictatorship. This was so evident that many distinguished men of letters did not dare to set foot inside its doors until after the revolution." The society was eventually closed by the regime.

> I remember the last lecture I was allowed to give there. The audience, quite a small one, included a very puzzled policeman who did his clumsy best to set down a few of my remarks on Persian Sufism. During this drab and hopeless period, my mother—then in her seventies—was under house arrest. My sister and one of my nephews spent a month in jail. I myself had a detective on my heels, whom I first took on long, aimless walks and at last made friends with. He admitted that he too hated Perón, but that he was obeying orders. Ernesto Palacio once offered to introduce me to the Unspeakable, but I did not want to meet him. How could I be introduced to a man whose hand I would not shake? ("Essay," 1970, p. 248)

Borges' resistance to Perón was to be recognized publicly by the new military regime. Through the initiative of two of Borges' friends,

428

Esther Zemborain de Torres and Victoria Ocampo, and the public support of the Argentine Society of Writers, he was appointed director of the National Library by the acting president of Argentina, General Eduardo Leonardi. In his "Autobiographical Essay" Borges records the event with pride and subtle self-mockery: "I thought the scheme a wild one, and hoped at most to be given the directorship of some small-town library, preferably to the south of the city." A few days before the appointment was made official,

> my mother and I had walked to the Library . . . to take a look at the building, but, feeling superstitious, I refused to go in. "Not until I get the job," I said. That same week, I was called to come to the Library to take over. My family was present, and I made a speech to the employees, telling them I was actually the Director—the incredible Director. At the same time, José Edmundo Clemente, who a few years before had managed to convince Emecé to bring out an edition of my works, became the Assistant Director. Of course, I felt very important, but we got no pay for the next three months. I don't think my predecessor, who was a Peronista, was ever officially fired. He just never came around to the Library again. They named me to the job but did not take the trouble to unseat him. (Ibid., p. 249)

For Borges, to become director of the National Library was, in a sense, to achieve one of his unacknowledged dreams. It meant reparation not only for the humiliation devised by the Perón regime when he was promoted to inspector of chickens but for the years he had been confined to a modest position in the Miguel Cané municipal library—and perhaps, even further back, for the years when, having returned from Europe, Georgie used to visit the National Library's reference room to read the *Encyclopaedia Britannica*. Too shy to go to the desk and ask for the books he wanted, Georgie kept consulting the only volumes he could borrow without having to ask for them. Now, he could command all the volumes he wanted. The library of Babel was finally his. But there was an even subtler symbolism in his promotion to director of the National Library. The building on Mexico Street where the library was situated had been originally designed to house the national lottery. The symbols of chance which decorated the building did not seem so incongruous after all to a man who had written "The Babylon Lottery." Finally, Borges had found a place where books and chance came harmoniously together.

One of his first decisions as director was to restore the National Library to the position it had had under the directorship of Paul Groussac. He made plans to reissue the journal *La Biblioteca*, which had been founded by Groussac, and asked Clemente to organize a series of lectures at the old building. I was invited in 1956 to lecture on the

Uruguayan short-story writer, Horacio Quiroga, who had lived and worked in Buenos Aires. After the lecture Borges took me to dinner, with some mutual friends, at a restaurant in an old restored warehouse of the Rosas era. The entranceway was through one of the carriage porches which appear in some of his poems. The somber stone-paved patio, the moist plants branching against the dirty whitewashed walls, an old mail coach which perhaps carried Facundo Quiroga to his death in Barranca Yaco (as in Borges' famous poem), comprised the entrance to an enormous room of thin, wooden columns which suggested a stable rather than a restaurant. There we continued to talk about literature, contemporary and old. But Borges was more interested in something else. He never tired of making me see, of looking through my eyes at this relic of Rosas' time. In his memory the ancient hatred for the old tyrant, inherited from grandfathers and great-grandfathers, blended almost perfectly with his hatred for Perón. It was easy to see that Perón and Rosas were one, that both served as a metaphor for Borges' attraction to those cynical men, with their jagged knives or electric-shock treatment, those smiling traitors of Argentine history, whom Borges despises and yet cannot help but admire. Obsessed by the consciousness of not having lived enough, he saw in these men of action the exact counterpart of his meditative self: he was the man of books, they were the men with knives. He denounced them in poems and stories and, at the same time, felt a horrible fascination for them. They were the "other," the dark side of the self. Now that Perón was gone, Borges could go back to Rosas and his times.

Borges was euphoric. He could again breathe in a city freed of demons. He endlessly repeated his loyalty to the new regime which had made him director of the National Library. Once again, I walked with him through the Southside. We visited a Greek church; inside, the still air seemed solid and the light was barely more than a dusky shade. The pale gold ornaments were alive in an atmosphere devoid of human presence. In that setting, like that of so many of his precisely crafted stories, Borges seemed to be in his natural habitat. The darkness of the church was his light.

Yet the complete reality of Borges, of the concrete person Borges is, escaped me until he invited me to tour the National Library the next day. The building over which Groussac had presided was going to seed but still had a certain grandeur. At the time, I didn't know that it had been built to house the national lottery and did not recognize the obvious symbols. Borges took me in hand and led me around, seeing only enough to know where each book he wanted was. He can open a book to the desired page and, without bothering to read—through a feat of memory comparable only to that of his fictional Irineo Funes—quote complete passages. He roams along corridors lined with books; he quickly turns corners and gets into passages which are truly invisible, mere cracks in the walls of books; he rushes down winding staircases which abruptly end in the dark. There is almost no light in the library's corridors and staircases. I try to follow him, tripping, blinder and more handicapped than Borges because my only guides are my eyes. In the dark of the library Borges finds his way with the precarious precision of a tightrope walker. Finally, I come to understand that the space in which we are momentarily inserted is not real: it is a space made of words, signs, symbols. It is another labyrinth. Borges drags me, makes me quickly descend the long, winding staircase, fall exhausted into the center of darkness. Suddenly, there is light at the end of another corridor. Prosaic reality awaits me there. Next to Borges, who smiles like a child who has played a joke on a friend, I recover my eyesight, the real world of light and shadow, the conventions I am trained to recognize. But I come out of the experience like one who emerges from deep water or from a dream, shattered by the (other) reality of that labyrinth of paper.

At that time, Borges was becoming increasingly blind. The doctors had already warned him that unless he stopped reading and writing, he would become totally blind. To save what little eyesight he had, he was forced to renounce one of his greatest pleasures.

He took the news with the usual stoicism. In his "Autobiographical Essay," he bravely attempts to understate it:

> My blindness had been coming on gradually since childhood. There was nothing particularly pathetic or dramatic about it. Beginning in 1927, I had undergone eight eye operations; but since the late 1950s, when I wrote my "Poem of the Gifts," for reading and writing purposes I have been blind. Blindness ran in my family. . . . Blindness also seems to run among the directors of the National Library. Two of my eminent forerunners, José Mármol and Paul Groussac, suffered the same fate. In my poem, I speak of God's splendid irony in granting me at one time 800,000 books and darkness. ("Essay," 1970, p. 250)

The ending of the poem underlines more than fate's irony. It makes visible the tragic condition of that man who, like Groussac, had been denied access to what he most longed for.

> Painfully probing the dark, I grope toward
> The void of the twilight with the point of my faltering
> Cane—I for whom Paradise was always a metaphor,
> An image of libraries.

Something—no need to prattle of chance
Or contingency—presides over these matters;
Long before me, some other man took these books and the dark
In a fading of dusk for his lot.

Astray in meandering galleries,
It comes to me now with a holy, impalable
Dread, that I am that other, the dead man, and walk
With identical steps and identical days to the end.

Which of us two is writing this poem
In the I of the first-person plural, in identical darkness?
What good is the word that speaks for me now in my name,
If the curse of the dark is implacably one and the same?

Groussac or Borges, I watch the delectable
World first disfigure then extinguish itself
In a pallor of ashes, until all that is gone
Seems at one with sleep and at one with oblivion.

> (*Poems,* 1972, translated by Ben Belitt, pp. 117–119)

But the blind, groping man was not destined to sleep or oblivion. More gifts were to be bestowed on him till his name would become known to the whole world. At fifty-six, Borges may have felt he had reached a zenith. He was still far from his real goal.

13.
The Birth of
"Borges"

Life changed drastically for Borges because of his blindness. From 1955 onward he became more and more dependent on others for even the simplest task. Unable to read or write, he had to rely on Mother or other members of the family, and even close friends, to help him with a new book or look for a particular quotation from an old one, to take dictation and type his manuscripts. Mother became his secretary and nurse. Others took turns helping him. One of his nephews learned to pronounce German in order to read aloud to him from German texts; Alicia Jurado, a young woman interested in Buddhism, read Oriental literature to him and under his dictation produced a small essay on the subject which would not be published until 1976. With Margarita Guerrero, Borges compiled a *Manual of Fantastic Zoology* (Mexico, 1957), which was later expanded into *The Book of Imaginary Beings* (Buenos Aires, 1967). Its final version appeared in the 1969 English translation done by the author in collaboration with Norman Thomas di Giovanni. Many of the chapters in these books were based on articles from encyclopedias and other sources, but some were solely the fruit of Borges' imagination. Another book he produced in those years of his increasing blindness was an anthology called *The Book of Heaven and Hell* (Buenos Aires, 1960), which he compiled with Bioy Casares.

He was able to write new books with the help of his friends and secretaries, but it became almost impossible for him to compose short stories or elaborate articles. Because he had trained himself to write in such a condensed form, adding pieces bit by bit to a highly complex structure of sentences and paragraphs, the composition of any long prose text was now out of his reach. For more than a decade he stopped writing stories and long articles. His first volume of new stories, *Dr. Brodie's Report,* would not come out until 1970. In compensation, he returned to poetry. Borges recalls:

> One salient consequence of my blindness was my gradual abandonment of free verse in favor of classical metrics. In fact, blindness made me take up the writing of poetry again. Since rough drafts were denied me, I had to fall back on memory. It is obviously easier to remember verse than prose, and to remember regular verse forms rather than free ones. Regular verse is, so to speak, portable. One can walk down the street or be riding the subway while composing and polishing a sonnet, for rhyme and meter have mnemonic virtues. ("Essay," 1970, p. 250)

But he was in no hurry to collect his poems. Not until the middle 1960s would he reissue in a new format his volume of *Poemas* (originally published in 1943 and enlarged in 1954). Called *Obra Poética* (Poetical Works), it came out in 1964 both as a large illustrated volume and as part of the complete works. Poetry written after 1943 makes up two thirds of the book. Borges himself has commented on these new poems:

> I wrote dozens of sonnets and longer poems consisting of eleven-syllable quatrains. I thought I had taken Lugones as my master, but when the verses were written my friends told me that, regrettably, they were quite unlike him. In my later poetry, a narrative thread is always to be found. As a matter of fact, I even think of plots for poems. Perhaps the main difference between Lugones and me is that he held French literature as his model and lived intellectually in a French world, whereas I look to English literature. In this new poetic activity, I never thought of building a sequence of poems, as I always formerly did, but was chiefly interested in each piece for its own sake. In this way, I wrote poems on such different subjects as Emerson and wine, Snorri Sturluson and the hourglass, my grandfather's death, and the beheading of Charles I. I also went in for summing up my literary heroes: Poe, Swedenborg, Whitman, Heine, Camões, Jonathan Edwards, and Cervantes. Due tribute, of course, was also paid to mirrors, the Minotaur, and knives. (Ibid., pp. 250–251)

This double switch, from prose to poetry, and from free verse to regular verse, radically altered Borges' work. He became, in the literal sense of the word, an oral writer; that is, a writer who was forced by blindness to compose his writings orally. He also had to learn how to dictate. Instead of going through endless drafts to refine his sentences and paragraphs, he learned how to compose from memory and how to rely on meter to achieve the effects he had earlier searched for in his minute, spidery handwriting. It was a momentous change. A new

Borges came out of it. No longer was he the master of a complex and subtle style of writing; he was a poet, a bard.

The fact that he was actually blind made him fall easily into another prototype. Instead of an Erasmus, holding a pen and an inkpot in his hands, the new Borges was easily associated with the blind bards—with Milton and with Homer. The blind poet ceased to be a writer and became a seer.

How did blindness affect his everyday life? On many occasions Borges has attempted to debunk the pathetic image of the blind writer. Talking to Richard Burgin, he explains in detail how blindness has changed his habits. To a question about his reading, he answers:

BORGES: I've always been a greater reader than a writer. But, of course, I began to lose my eyesight definitely in 1954, and since then I've done my reading by proxy, no? Well, of course, when one cannot read, then one's mind works in a different way. In fact, it might be said that there is a certain benefit in being unable to read, because you think that time flows in a different way. When I had my eyesight, then if I had to spend say half an hour without doing anything, I would go mad. Because I had to be reading. But now, I can be alone for quite a long time, I don't mind long railroad journeys, I don't mind being alone in a hotel or walking down the street, because, well, I won't say that I am thinking all the time because that would be bragging.

I think I am able to live with a lack of occupation. I don't have to be talking to people or doing things. If somebody had gone out, and I had come here and found the house empty, then I would have been quite content to sit down and let two or three hours pass and go out for a short walk, but I wouldn't feel especially unhappy or lonely. That happens to all people who go blind. (Burgin, 1969, pp. 4–5)

Borges' resignation must have come by degrees. His comments to Burgin in 1967 were the end result of years of preparation, of slowly accepting blindness and settling down to old age. Even in that interview there is a moment in which the pain of adjusting to blindness pierces through the elegant retelling of his experiences. When Burgin asks him specifically what he thinks about when he is alone, he replies very frankly:

BORGES: I could or I might not be thinking about anything, I'd just be living on, no? Letting time flow or perhaps looking back on memories or walking across a bridge and trying to remember favorite passages, but maybe I wouldn't be doing anything, I'd just be living. I never understand why people say they're bored because they have nothing to do. Because sometimes I have nothing whatever to do, and I don't feel bored. Because I'm not doing things all the time, I'm content.

BURGIN: You've never felt bored in your life?
BORGES: I don't think so. Of course, when I had to be ten days lying on my back after an operation, I felt anguish but not boredom. (Ibid., p. 5)

In spite of his brave statement, it was only through a hard and long period of training that Borges came to relish the solitude and emptiness that blindness brought to his life.

The early years of his blindness were crowded with honors. On April 29, 1956, he was given a doctorate honoris causa by the University of Cuyo, one of the oldest in Argentina. It was the first of such doctorates he gathered from universities all over the world. The following year, on June 14, he was appointed professor of English and American literature at the Faculty of Philosophy and Letters at the University of Buenos Aires. He taught there until 1968, when he retired at the age of sixty-eight. But the most important distinction he received came in 1956, when he was awarded the biannual National Prize of Literature. As usual, Borges took the distinction with a grain of salt. Talking to Jean de Milleret ten years later, he commented that it was a bit of a political prize (De Milleret, 1967, p. 82). He was probably right. At the time, the military government wanted to stress the fact that its attitude toward culture was the opposite of Perón's and that it had restored the dignity of Argentine culture. Borges was the most suitable writer to make this restoration visible.

New volumes of his complete works appeared; the fifth was a new edition of *Ficciones* (1956), with three new stories. In a postscript to the prologue to the second section of the book, Borges comments on the additions. He points out that one of the stories, "The End," develops a situation that is implicit in a famous book; his only invention is the character of Recabarren, through whom the story is seen. Although Borges does not reveal which book he is talking about, it is obvious that the model is *Martín Fierro* and that he had ventured to imagine what would have happened if the protagonist had a fight with the brother of one of his victims. In the second story, "The Sect of the Phoenix," Borges attempted the problem of presenting a very common fact in a "vacillating and gradual way which, at the end, became unequivocal." He isn't sure that he has succeeded, he adds. The truth is that many of the readers of that story fail to understand that the Secret of the Sect is the sexual act, which perpetuates and immortalizes men. The third story is one of Borges' most successful and personal. In "The South" Borges allegorizes the fate of a man who, like him, has a double allegiance: to his European roots and to the barbarous country in which he was born. In commenting on the story in the prologue, Borges points out only that it can be "read as a direct narration of novelesque facts and also in a different way." He doesn't say what that "different way" is, but the hint is enough to suggest that the second part of the story is a hallucination and didn't really happen. Juan Dahlmann never fought a knife duel in the pampas; he died under the surgeon's scalpel in a Buenos Aires hospital.

For the sixth volume of his complete works, Borges reissued *Discusión* (1957). It contains six new pieces, among which are two perceptive essays on Flaubert and *Bouvard et Pécuchet* and the lecture on "The Argentine Writer and Tradition," which contains an important statement on the pseudo-literary nationalists. He also took advantage of the new edition to eliminate a 1931 article, "Our Impossibilities," which bitterly satirizes some negative aspects of the national character. At the time it was originally published, Borges was openly critical of the national character, but in 1957, in the context of the so-called Liberating Revolution which had ended Perón's regime, he did not want to sound too harsh a note. The seventh volume was a new edition of *The Aleph* (1957), with four new stories. In a postscript to the epilogue he comments briefly on them. The tone is curiously apologetic, as if he himself is not convinced of the value of some of the stories. But at least one, "The Wait," is very characteristic of that period. In the postscript Borges informs the reader that the story is based on a police report a friend read to him in 1942, at the time he was working in the Miguel Cané library. The real protagonist was a Turk; Borges preferred an Italian in order "to be able to intuit him more easily." What he doesn't say in his comment is that there is an echo of Ernest Hemingway's "The Killers" in the situation of a man who waits for his former associates to come and kill him. Borges also forgets to mention that the waiting is, in a sense, a transposition of his own waiting, during the Perón years, for something terrible to happen to him.

In the 1950s fame began taking different shapes for Borges. Studies and books about him were proliferating. Beginning in 1955, with a monograph by José Luis Ríos Patrón of limited interest, four more books appeared: Marcial Tamayo and Adolfo Ruíz Díaz's *Borges: The Enigma and the Key to It* (1955); César Fernández Moreno's brilliant summary, *A Borges Outline* (1957); Ana María Barrenechea's stylistic examination, *The Expression of Unreality in the Work of Jorge Luis Borges* (1957); and Rafael Gutiérrez Girardot's *Essay of Interpretation* (1959). At the same time, his work was reaching a wider audience. Even before the fall of Perón, the film director Leopoldo Torre Nilsson had made a movie version of "Emma Zunz," under a title borrowed from Carl Theodore Dreyer: *Days of Wrath* (1954). Three years later René Mugica adapted to film the successful "Streetcorner Man." In 1966, in an interview with Jean de Milleret, Borges seemed pleased with the latter film, saying it was better than the original story. But two years later he told Richard Burgin that he found both films wrong and criticized them because they had padded the stories with local color. Yet even if his reactions were contradictory and on the whole negative, the fact was that he had become popular enough to be adapted to the movies.

Borges was sixty when the ninth volume of his complete works came out. (The eighth volume was a 1960 reprint of *Other Inquisitions*.) For the new book, he had thought up the title in English, *The Maker*, and had translated it into Spanish as *El hacedor;* but when the book came out in the United States the American translator preferred to avoid the theological implications and used instead the title of one of the pieces, *Dreamtigers*. According to Borges, the volume was put together almost by accident:

> Around 1954, I began writing short prose pieces—sketches and parables. One day, my friend Carlos Frías, of Emecé, told me he needed a new book for the series of my so-called complete works. I said I had none to give him, but Frías persisted, saying, "Every writer has a book if he only looks for it." Going through drawers at home one idle Sunday, I began ferreting out uncollected poems and prose pieces, some of the latter going back to my days on *Crítica*. These odds and ends, sorted out and ordered and published in 1960, became *El hacedor*. . . . ("Essay," 1970, p. 253)

The pieces that went back to the mid-1930s, when Borges was a regular contributor to *Crítica's Saturday Multicolored Review,* are "Toenails," "Dreamtigers," "Argumentum Ornithologicum," and "The Draped Mirrors." "Dialogue on a Dialogue" was published in *Destiempo* about the same time. But the most interesting pieces were relatively new. As a sort of prologue, Borges wrote a prose poem, "To Leopoldo Lugones," in which he relates a dream he had of visiting Lugones (who had preceded him as director of the National Library) to give him a copy of *El hacedor*. The dream attempts to persuade Borges that Lugones would read the book favorably: "If I am not mistaken, you were not disinclined to me, Lugones, and you would have liked to like some piece of my work. That never happened; but this time you turn the pages and read approvingly a verse here and there—perhaps because you have recognized your own voice in it, perhaps because deficient practice concerns you less than solid theory" (*Dreamtigers,* 1965, p. 21).

The end of the piece is characteristic: Borges realizes that the whole thing is a dream and that Lugones has been dead since 1938:

"My vanity and nostalgia have set up an impossible scene. Perhaps so (I tell myself), but tomorrow I too will have died, and our times will intermingle and chronology will be lost in a sphere of symbols. And then in some way it will be right to claim that I have brought you this book, and that you have accepted it" (ibid., p. 21). As usual, Borges comes to the conclusion that the differences between Lugones and himself are less important than the similarities. By a sleight-of-hand of which he is a master, he and Lugones finally become one.

The "Autobiographical Essay" also insists that in spite of the miscellaneous nature of the pieces collected in *El hacedor* the book has a unique quality:

> Remarkably, this book, which I accumulated rather than wrote, seems to me my most personal work, and to my taste, maybe my best. The explanation is only too easy: the pages of *El hacedor* contain no padding. Each piece was written for its own sake and out of an inner necessity. By the time it was undertaken, I had come to realize that fine writing is a mistake, and a mistake born out of vanity. Good writing, I firmly believe, should be done in an unobtrusive way. ("Essay," 1970, p. 253)

Borges is right about the personal character of the book. He had never been freer to write exclusively about what he liked or what caught his fancy at a given moment. Also, he had never been freer to talk about himself—his foibles and preferences, his manias and dreams—as in the miscellaneous pieces in this book. Two are memorable literary portraits of Borges, as persona and as he really is. One he himself singles out in the "Autobiographical Essay":

> On the closing page of that book, I told of a man who sets out to make a picture of the universe. After many years, he has covered a blank wall with images of ships, towers, horses, weapons, and men, only to find out at the moment of his death that he has drawn a likeness of his own face. This may be the case of all books; it is certainly the case of this particular book. (Ibid., pp. 253–254)

Even more explicitly autobiographical is the other piece, called "Borges and Myself," which became in a sense his final statement on his literary persona. In it, the theme of the double is presented through the opposition between Borges, the private man, and "Borges," the literary character created by the former who, little by little, usurps all of Borges' functions and privileges. The text begins: "It's to the other man, to Borges, that things happen." Everything that Borges now does, or likes, becomes the other's possession, "but in a showy way that turns them into stagy mannerisms." Although Borges admits that he is on

439

good terms with his other self, "I live, I let myself live, so that Borges can weave his tales and poems, and those tales and poems are my justification." The realization does not bring peace to him because he knows that "what is good no longer belongs to anyone—not even the other man—but rather to speech or tradition." He then comes to the sad conclusion that "I am fated to become lost once and for all, and only some moment of myself will survive in the other man." He is bound to leave no trace of himself other than what now belongs to "Borges." The conclusion is masterful:

> Little by little, I have been surrendering everything to him, even though I have evidence of his stubborn habit of falsification and exaggerating. Spinoza held that all things try to keep on being themselves; a stone wants to be a stone and the tiger, a tiger. I shall remain in Borges, not in myself (if it is so that I am someone), but I recognize myself less in his books than in those of others or than in the laborious tuning of a guitar. Years ago, I tried ridding myself of him and I went from myths of the outlying slums of the city to games with time and infinity, but those games are now part of Borges and I will have to turn to other things. And so, my life is a running away, and I lose everything and everything is left to oblivion or to the other man.
> Which of us is writing this page I don't know. (*The Aleph*, 1970, pp. 151–152)

By becoming "Borges," Borges had finally obliterated himself. In a sense, he had finally ceased to matter.

A few months after the publication of *El hacedor* a group of international publishers met on Majorca—the same island Georgie had visited as a teenager—and awarded him, jointly with Samuel Beckett, the first Formentor Prize. That prize marked the beginning of his international fame. It was also the beginning of "Borges" ' life and (consequently) the end of Borges' private life. From then on, "Borges" ruled completely. What belonged to Borges were the crumbs, the leftovers, the dregs. From that point on, "Borges" expanded his territory more and more while Borges was reduced to the periphery. It was "Borges" who visited American universities, got literary prize after literary prize, was written about and universally feted, and became a guru for thousands of young people on at least three continents. The other Borges (that is, Borges) slowly receded into nothingness.

Part Five

1.
A Modern Master

Borges was in his early sixties when the Formentor Prize made him internationally famous. The prize had been established in 1960 by avant-garde publishers from six different Western countries: Librairie Gallimard (France), Giulio Einaudi (Italy), Ernst Rowohlt Verlag (West Germany), Weidenfeld & Nicolson (England), Editorial Seix-Barral (Spain), and Grove Press (United States). It was designed as an "award of $10,000 to an author of any nationality whose existing body of work will, in the view of the jury, have a lasting influence on the development of modern literature." The aim of the prize, "in addition to recognition of exceptional merit," was to "bring the author's work to the attention of the largest possible international audience." The 1961 award was the first to be made, and Borges shared the $10,000 prize with Samuel Beckett. But the loss of half the prize money was worth it. For an obscure Argentine writer to be cited as one of the indisputable masters of twentieth-century literature was distinction enough. At long last, after a career that covered almost four decades, Borges had the fame he deserved.

It took him some time to get used to it. He was dining with Bioy, as he usually did on Sundays, when he heard about the award. His first reaction (he later told Jean de Milleret) was that it had to be a joke. The name Formentor didn't mean a thing to him (De Milleret, 1967, p. 83). In a 1964 interview he claimed that in the citation he had been identified as the "Mexican" writer Jorge Luis Borges. Perhaps some secretary goofed. But it was obvious that the jury knew perfectly well who he was. Recalling the occasion in his "Autobiographical Essay," he generously attributes the award to the efforts of his French translators.

Fame, like my blindness, had been coming gradually to me. I had never expected it, I had never sought it. Néstor Ibarra and Roger Caillois, who in the
early 1950s daringly translated me into French, were my first benefactors. I
suspect that their pioneer work paved the way for . . . the Formentor Prize
. . . , for until I appeared in French I was practically invisible—not only
abroad but at home in Buenos Aires. As a consequence of that prize, my
books mushroomed overnight throughout the Western world. ("Essay,"
1970, p. 254)

Borges' memory is faulty regarding the date of Ibarra's translations of his work into French ("The Babylon Lottery" and "The Library
of Babel" came out in *Lettres Françaises* on October 1, 1944), but he is
right about the importance of that pioneering effort. Furthermore,
Roger Caillois was a member of the jury that awarded him the prize.
The immediate consequence of the award was the simultaneous publication of *Ficciones* in six different countries. The Spanish title was kept
in the English and American editions, to indicate both the original language in which the book was written and the fact that its meaning was
internationally accessible.

The reception of *Ficciones* was extraordinary, and from then on
Borges was acknowledged as a modern master. In no time his name
began to be linked to those of Kafka and Joyce, Proust and Nabokov.
Another windfall from the prize was that Borges was discovered by
academia. The first to move was the University of Texas (Austin).
Using funds provided by the Edward Laroque Tinker Foundation, the
university invited him, in September 1961, to spend a semester as visiting professor. He enthusiastically accepted. For the first time since his
last trip to Europe in 1923–1924, he left the River Plate area. He was
sixty-two and practically blind, but he was delighted with his new status
as the first Latin American writer to be recognized worldwide. In spite
of his shyness and his British upbringing, Borges took to fame with an
almost childish glee. His time had finally come, and he was not one to
let the opportunity pass.

For Mother, Borges' newly acquired status was the fulfillment
of her deepest wishes. She had always known that her son was a genius
(to use the old-fashioned but, for her, accurate expression), and now it
was time to reap the labor of so many years. Since Father's death,
Mother had devoted herself completely to Borges, making it her task in
life to promote his career. She did not see eye to eye with him in many
literary matters, was mistrustful of some of his literary acquaintances,
and hated many of the subjects he preferred (hoodlums and slum
dwellers, the tango and *Martín Fierro*) as well as those terrifying fantastic stories; but she was entirely loyal to him and fulfilled her duties with
the utmost devotion. In a sense, she was more than a mother: she was

his eyes and his hands. Borges related to the external world through her; it was as if he had not left the maternal womb. Or, to be more precise, it was as if, by becoming blind, he had returned to it, for good.

It was Mother who accompanied him on his first triumphant visit to the United States. Everywhere people believed her to be his wife, not his mother. At the ripe age of eighty-five, Mother looked sixty. That is, she looked her son's age. And she was proud of it. He was also proud of having such a good-looking mother. The enthusiasm and even childish delight of that first visit can be recognized in the account he gives in the "Autobiographical Essay":

> It was my first physical encounter with America. In a sense, because of my reading, I had always been there, and yet how strange it seemed when in Austin I heard ditch diggers who worked on campus speaking English, a language I had until then always thought of as being denied that class of people. America, in fact, had taken on such mythic proportions in my mind that I was sincerely amazed to find there such commonplace things as weeds, mud, puddles, dirt roads, flies, and stray dogs. Though at times we fell into homesickness, I know now that my mother . . . and I grew to love Texas. She, who always loathed football, even rejoiced over *our* victory when the Longhorns defeated the neighboring Bears. ("Essay," 1970, p. 254)

I saw Borges in Buenos Aires on his return from the United States. In recounting his experiences, he told me an anecdote which, somehow, encapsulated his feeling of nostalgia. One of the members of the Spanish department at the university, a Paraguayan by birth, had once asked him to dinner and, to please him, had put on some tango records, sung by the popular singer Carlos Gardel. Little did he know that Borges hated Gardel's sentimental and (to him) Italianate vocal style. Borges told me that he tried to brace himself for the ordeal and even smiled. But after a few minutes, when Gardel's whining voice had begun to melt the audience, Borges heard, close at hand, sobbing and crying. It took him several seconds to discover that it was he who was so moved by that nostalgic voice.

His seminars on Argentine literature and Leopoldo Lugones' poetry were well attended, but he soon found that his twenty-five to thirty students were more interested in discussing his work than that of his predecessors. He was pleased that North American students, "unlike the run-of-the-mill students in the Argentine," were "far more interested in their subjects than in their grades" (ibid., p. 255). He also took advantage of the long visit (September 1961 to February 1962) to attend seminars on Anglo-Saxon literature, taught by Dr. Rudolph Willard, which helped him to correct some errors in his book *Ancient German Literatures* (1951). From Texas, on his way back to Buenos

Aires, he traveled extensively, lecturing in New Mexico and California, Washington, D.C., New York, Connecticut, and Massachusetts. He visited Columbia, Yale, and Harvard, gave lectures at the Library of Congress and at the Organization of American States in Washington, and was feted everywhere. In the "Essay" he summarizes his visit:

> I found America the friendliest, most forgiving, and most generous nation I have ever visited. We South Americans tend to think in terms of convenience, whereas people in the United States approach things ethically. This—amateur Protestant that I am—I admired above all. It even helped me overlook skyscrapers, paper bags, televisions, plastics, and the unholy jungle of gadgets. (Ibid. p. 255)

He was so enthusiastic about the United States that he even loved the Alamo, which he saw as an example of North American heroism. His views did not go down too well in Mexico, where Texas (and New Mexico and California) are still seen as lost Mexican territory. In spite of that, while Borges was in Texas some Mexican intellectuals broached the idea of inviting him for a visit. But they found strong opposition to him among left-wing intellectuals and others who wanted to pass as such. The cold war was then at its peak, and Castro's triumph in Cuba and his subsequent siding with the Soviets had polarized the Latin American intelligentsia into two irreconcilable factions. From the very beginning, Borges had been outspoken about Castro. He did not like his totalitarian methods—and Castro's association with the Soviet Union did not help at all. In this context, it is easy to understand why Borges' visit to Mexico was canceled even before it was announced.

One of the men behind the cancellation was then editor of the influential *Revista de la Universidad de Mexico;* in its June 1962 issue he published a statement that denounced Borges for "McCarthyism" while praising his literary achievements. In the same issue, the *Revista* included a long interview with Borges by James E. Irby and a short article on Borges' place in Latin American letters by the young Mexican poet José Emilio Pacheco. In a sense, the publication of these two pieces was an apology for the editor's tacit participation in the campaign to deny Borges access to Mexico.

Borges himself seems not to have realized what was going on in Mexico. He continued to praise the Alamo and sing of Texas, apparently unaware of the way his words sounded on the other side of the Rio Grande. His opposition to communism had never been McCarthyite and could not be compared in virulence to the anti-North Americanism so common among Latin American intellectuals. Basically an agnostic and an ideological anarchist, Borges had always criticized any regime, no matter what its ideology, that controlled the individual from womb to tomb. A follower of Spencer's more than of Bakunin's theories, Borges believed in the individual and maintained that the best state was the least visible. But if he was outspoken against communism (as he was then also outspoken against fascism), he was extremely tolerant of his friends' beliefs and politics. In the same way that he had refrained from criticizing Macedonio Fernández's and Leopoldo Lugones' sympathy for fascism, or Leopoldo Marechal's and Xul-Solar's support of Peronism, he abstained from criticizing, for instance, José Bianco's 1961 visit to Cuba. The episode is significant. Bianco was then the editor-in-chief of *Sur,* and when it was announced publicly that he had decided to visit Havana as a member of the Casa de las Américas' literary jury, Victoria Ocampo published a statement in the March–April issue disassociating the magazine from its editor's political allegiances. Bianco immediately resigned. Although Borges was closer politically to Victoria Ocampo than to Bianco, he decided to ignore the incident. In his memoirs, Bianco has this to say:

> We had dinner together a few days after my return. We did not talk about Cuba (he has stated his opposition to Castro's revolution) but he was as friendly as usual. Or even more: as he knew I had to resign my position, he offered me two jobs which later I did not accept. I was deeply hurt and he had the tact to drive away my sadness by leading the conversation toward light, impersonal subjects. . . . His attitude moved me more than he could have foreseen. (Bianco, 1964, p. 17)

The 1961 visit to the United States became the first of many trips Borges took to the principal countries of the Western world—to lecture or read his poems, to receive honors and prizes, to be interviewed and feted. In 1963 he returned to Europe, after an absence of nearly forty years. From January 30 to March 12 he visited Madrid, Paris, Geneva, London, Oxford, Cambridge, and Edinburgh. In all these places he lectured on gaucho poetry and the future of the Spanish language. In his "Autobiographical Essay" he partially summarizes this journey:

> Looking back on this past decade, I seem to have been quite a wanderer. In 1963, thanks to Neil MacKay of the British Council in Buenos Aires, I was able to visit England and Scotland. There, too, again in my mother's company, I made my pilgrimages: to London, so teeming with literary memories; to Lichfield and Dr. Johnson; to Manchester and De Quincey; to Rye and Henry James; to the Lake Country; to Edinburgh. I visited my grandmother's birthplace in Hanley, one of the Five Towns—Arnold Bennett country. Scotland and Yorkshire I think of as among the loveliest places on earth. Sometimes in the Scottish hills and glens I recaptured a strange sense

of loneliness and bleakness that I had known before; it took me some time to trace this feeling back to the far-flung wastes of Patagonia. ("Essay," 1970, p. 256)

Borges' memory, as usual, is highly selective. He forgets Madrid, Paris, and even Geneva, concentrating on the land where some of his ancestors were born.

In Madrid he paid a visit to his old master, Rafael Cansinos-Asséns, and for two days he reminisced in Geneva with his old schoolmates Maurice Abramowicz and Simon Jichlinski. In a sense, it was a return to the past, to the unique cultural experience he had during World War I. Six years later, while sitting on a bench along the Charles River in Cambridge, Massachusetts, Borges would dream a story involving an encounter between his young Genevan self (Georgie) and the old visiting professor (Borges). The story, "The Other," was later included in *El libro de arena* (The Book of Sand, 1975).

The following year an immense volume, the size of a telephone book, entirely dedicated to him, was published in France by *L'Herne*. It contained documents and reminiscences, articles and studies, interviews, a bibliography, and some illustrations. It was homage of a kind seldom given a living writer. Former titles in the same collection had concerned Céline, Ezra Pound, and Joyce. The volume included pieces by the new French critics—Gérard Genette, Jean Ricardou, Claude Ollier—as well as by a handful of specialists in Latin American literature. The importance of the book can be measured by the fact that it established Borges firmly as a writer to be read and studied. More books and special issues of learned journals would follow. The Borges industry was beginning to develop at a truly international level and with relentless speed. "Borges" was anointed a modern master.

2.
The Old Guru

In the spring of 1964 Borges returned to Europe, invited by the Congress for Cultural Freedom to participate in an international congress of writers in West Germany. This time, Mother stayed at home. She was finding these journeys a bit too exhausting for her eighty-eight years. A former student of Borges and a very good friend, María Esther Vázquez, accompanied him. The congress was one of the first to give Latin American literature a place of honor. It was attended by the Brazilian João Guimarães Rosa, author of the novel *The Devil to Pay in the Backlands* (1956), the Guatemalan novelist Miguel Angel Asturias (who received the Nobel Prize in 1967), the Argentine Eduardo Mallea, and the Paraguayan Augusto Roa Bastos. But it was Borges who received the lion's share of publicity. Visiting Paris on his way home, he was invited by UNESCO to participate with Giuseppe Ungaretti in a celebration of Shakespeare's quarter-centenary. Borges delivered in French a short piece, "Shakespeare and Us," which impressed the audience as being one of his most successful improvisations but which (according to María Esther Vázquez) took him the better part of two days to compose. He first dictated it in Spanish, then translated it into French, and finally had María Esther tape the text so he could play it over until he knew it by heart. The "Autobiographical Essay" makes no reference to the West German literary congress or to the UNESCO celebration, but concentrates on personal memories of England and Stockholm.

In England, we stayed with the late Herbert Read in his fine rambling house out on the moors. He took us to Yorkminster, where he showed us some ancient Danish swords in the Viking Yorkshire room of the museum. I later

449

wrote a sonnet to one of the swords, and just before his death Sir Herbert corrected and bettered my original title, suggesting, instead of "To a Sword in York," "To a Sword in Yorkminster." ("Essay," 1970, pp. 256–257)

Again, one can recognize here the return to his British ancestors, to the Anglo-Saxons and the Vikings. The visit to Copenhagen and Stockholm—which he counts "among the most unforgettable cities I have seen, like San Francisco, New York, Edinburgh, Santiago de Compostela, and Geneva" (ibid., p. 257)—at the invitation of his Swedish publisher, Bonnier, must have reinforced his feeling for his Nordic ancestors.

Short trips to different countries in Latin America (Peru, Colombia, and Chile in 1965) helped to increase Borges' popularity across the continent. But he was less impressed by the native cultures of America than he had been by the old cultures of Europe. A visit to the Inca fortress of Machu Picchu—which had inspired one of Pablo Neruda's most extraordinary poems—left Borges curiously unmoved. According to María Esther Vázquez, who was again his companion on that journey, "I have never seen him so politely bored than in his visit to Machu Picchu; the (for him) invisible terraces of the pre-Columbian past failed to move his esthetic passion" (Vázquez, 1977, p. 28).

Borges' second journey to the United States took place in 1967. He was invited by Harvard University to hold the Charles Eliot Norton Chair of Poetry. He gave a lecture ("to well-wishing audiences," as he put it in the "Autobiographical Essay") called "This Craft of Verse"; he also taught a seminar on Argentine writers for the department of Romance languages. It was his first opportunity to live for a while in New England, and he accepted it enthusiastically. As he facetiously remarks in the "Essay," he had a chance to travel all over New England, "where most things American, including the West, seem to have been invented"; he adds that he "made numerous literary pilgrimages—to Hawthorne's haunts in Salem, to Emerson's in Concord, to Melville's in New Bedford, to Emily Dickinson's in Amherst, and to Longfellow's around the corner from where I lived" (ibid., p. 255).

The seven months spent in Cambridge were important for the number of friendships he made, especially with the members of the Spanish department at Harvard (Raimundo Lida, an Argentine scholar, he had met in Buenos Aires in the 1940s, and Juan Marichal, a Spaniard and head of the Latin American studies program). He also became friends with the Spanish poet Jorge Guillén; he lived with his daughter Teresa, who was married to Professor Stephen Gilman of the Spanish department at Harvard. Lastly, at Harvard Borges met two young men to whom he became attached: the Anglo-Argentine John Murchison, who was his secretary during that visit, and Norman Thomas di Giovanni, who for the next eight years served as his secretary, translator, and literary agent.

As on his first visit to the United States, Borges traveled extensively, crisscrossing the American continent from Massachusetts to Iowa ("where I found my native pampas awaiting me"), from Chicago ("recalling Carl Sandburg") to Missouri, Maryland, and Virginia. In his "Essay" he reports that "at the end of my stay, I was greatly honored to have my poems read at the YM-YWHA Poetry Center in New York, with several of my translators reading and a number of poets in the audience" (ibid., p. 256). Borges' pride may be justified on the grounds that his success was so extraordinary he could afford to boast a little. Besides, being professionally skeptical about everything (even reality had always seemed unreal to him), Borges was in the best possible position to be a little vain. If nothing really matters, then fame and success and adulation can be accepted eagerly, as the fictions they actually are. There is no doubt that he enjoyed them and that he took every opportunity to go where he would find applause.

At the beginning of 1969 he visited Israel for the first time, to lecture at the government's invitation. In his "Autobiographical Essay" he gives an enthusiastic account of that visit:

> I spent ten very exciting days in Tel Aviv and Jerusalem. I brought home with me the conviction of having been in the oldest and the youngest of nations, of having come from a very living, vigilant land back to a half-asleep nook of the world. Since my Genevan days, I had always been interested in Jewish culture, thinking of it as an integral element of our so-called Western civilization, and during the Israeli-Arab war of a few years back I found myself taking immediate sides. While the outcome was still uncertain, I wrote a poem on the battle. A week later, I wrote another on the victory. Israel was, of course, still an armed camp at the time of my visit. There, along the shores of Galilee, I kept recalling these lines from Shakespeare:
>
> > Over whose acres walk'd those blessed feet,
> > Which, fourteen hundred years ago, were nail'd,
> > For our advantage, on the bitter cross.
> > (Ibid., p. 257)

Borges' deep sympathy for Israel was not shared by Latin America's left-wing intellectuals, who viewed the Palestinians as a dispossessed people and the Israelis as capitalist colonizers. For Borges, the right of the Jewish people to their native land was unquestionable. The poems and the statements he made in those years widened the gap between his view of the Middle East and that favored by the socialist Third World. Once more, Borges (without perhaps being fully aware of it) placed himself on the less popular side of the fence.

That same year, he returned to the United States to attend a "Borges Conference" held at the University of Oklahoma (Norman) on December 5 and 6. He gave some lectures and dutifully attended the elaborate discussion of his texts produced by a handful of specialists. Later, a volume entitled *The Cardinal Points of Borges* was edited by Lowell Dunham and Ivar Ivask with the papers and memorabilia produced by the conference. In his "Autobiographical Essay" Borges calls the editors "my two benefactors," has a nice word to say about his critics, and recalls an anecdote: "Ivask made me a gift of a fish-shaped Finnish dagger—rather alien to the tradition of the old Palermo of my boyhood" (ibid., p. 256). On his return to Argentina, he stopped at Georgetown University in Washington, D.C., to read his poems.

I saw him at the Borges Conference in Oklahoma. It was the first time we had met outside the River Plate area—the first time I had the experience of seeing him not as the almost closet genius who passed unnoticed among the inattentive crowd but as the guru of a new generation of readers (or shall I say listeners?). They were literally spaced out by his words, by the incantatory way in which he delivered them, by his blindness and his almost uncanny face. It was difficult for me to reconcile my many images of Borges—all based on an intimacy with his texts and a friendly, relaxed relationship with the man—with this new Borges. That is, with "Borges." Because by that time "Borges" had taken over almost completely. In spite of all that, I had no trouble finding the old Borges behind the formidable façade of the guru. Sitting with him in the university's cafeteria, I recalled the good old days when he was young and unknown and said something to the effect that we could never have foreseen our meeting in Oklahoma of all places, and on such a solemn occasion. He laughed heartily and observed that we were not that far from doing what we used to do: sitting in a café talking about literature in the middle of nowhere. Oklahoma was to him, mutatis mutandis, another version of the vast expanse of the pampas. I had to agree, especially when I realized that he hadn't lost any of that provocative skepticism and that he took all the tributes and homages in stride, as part of the movable happening his life had become. There was no question that Borges was still very much alive inside "Borges."

On August 22 of the same year he traveled to Brazil to receive the Inter-American Literary Prize awarded by the governor of the state of São Paulo. It consisted of $25,000. He was feted, interviewed, and generally lionized by one of the most sophisticated intellectual communities in Latin America. President Castelo Branco indicated that he would welcome his visit to Brasilia. On the day appointed, with everything set for the highly complex operation that would take Borges to the remote capital, he excused himself with the explanation that he had to return to Buenos Aires. Mother was having a ninety-third birthday party, and (president or no president) he could not miss it. The Brazilian intellectuals relished that involuntary snub to their president, but Borges was not trying to make a political point. He was deeply concerned with Mother. He knew she was getting terribly old and he wanted to be as close to her as possible on that particular occasion.

In 1971 he returned to the United States to receive an honorary doctorate from Columbia University and to participate in a conference attended by Latin American writers and artists, politicians, and critics of all persuasions. As usual, he became the focus of attention and was selected as a target of attack by a representative of a group of Puerto Rican students who wanted to protest the way Columbia was handling its responsibilities as slum landlord. Instead of criticizing the university, the student attacked the visitors for associating themselves with Columbia. In the heat of the discussion the student insulted Borges, making a remark about his mother's supposed profession and concluding that Borges had nothing to say about Latin America because he was already dead. Borges' skepticism failed him on that occasion. Instead of realizing that the student, Columbia University, and the whole world were only part of a larger state of unrest, he became furious and, banging on the table, challenged the student to settle matters outside. The student must have been barely twenty. Borges (at seventy-two) was frail, holding his cane in trembling hands. But he meant every word of his chivalrous invitation. Somehow things quieted down. At lunchtime I took Borges to the dining room. Awkwardly, I tried to explain the political situation that had prompted the attack. He stopped me dead and said that of course he knew the student did not intend to attack Mother, because if he had thought so, he would have taken his cane and smashed it over the student's head. He was trembling while he said it and his cane moved uncontrollably.

On that same occasion, he accepted an invitation to go to Yale University for "An Evening with Jorge Luis Borges." I was then chairman of Yale's Spanish and Portuguese department and of the council on Latin American studies. We had invited a handful of writers and critics to talk informally with Borges in front of an audience. We reserved a room for some two hundred people. When we reached the room, it was overflowing. Somehow, five hundred people had managed to squeeze inside, but there was no place for Borges. We decided to search for a larger room. Headed by Borges, a procession formed slowly and traversed the Yale campus. In no time a police car closed in on us (it was the days of student unrest and we had no permission to demonstrate). But we were so obviously men of peace that the police let us continue our search. At last we discovered that one of the largest halls was free. When we reached it, it was already jammed: the audience had filled every inch. The janitor (a very firm person when it came to regulations) began to complain loudly that he had not been properly warned and that, besides, the campus police would never allow more than five hundred people in that particular hall. We cajoled and pleaded with him, and finally managed to persuade the police and the janitor to give us the hall. But it took some extra persuasion to convince the audience that it had to clear the podium and the corridors. Finally, after a delay of an hour, the planned intimate conversation on literary matters took place. It was intimate only in the sense that everyone who participated felt very close to Borges. In spite of the crowd and the cavernous size of the hall, intimacy somehow resulted. The members of the audience had invested too much to secure a place, and they were determined to make the evening a success.

Borges began by answering, with his subtlest irony, questions politely put forth by writers and critics. That won them completely. He is one of us, they felt. When the floor was opened to questions, people rushed to ask him about everything that passed through their minds. Borges answered with humor and simplicity, never talking down to them, always comic and gentle. The last question ("Have you ever been in love?") elicited the shortest possible answer: "Yes." It was said with deep feeling, and the final *s* kept sounding for a while. At that the audience roared, and the happening ended.

Earlier, while we were sitting in a small room behind the podium waiting for permission to use the hall, I had asked Borges if he was afraid the audience would become unruly. He said no; besides, he added, he couldn't care less: reality always seemed a bit out of hand to him. Being blind, he was used to not controlling events, to letting reality invade him. At the end of his astonishing performance I understood better what he meant. That shy and extremely sensitive man I had met in Montevideo in 1945—a man who had not dared to read the text of a lecture he knew by heart—had become the grand old man of Latin American letters, the guru to a new generation that came to him not as we used to, to get some crumbs of his literary dinners, but just to see and listen and laugh and be moved by an experience that was not purely literary but belonged to another dimension. Borges could not see his listeners, but he sensed that a rapport existed between him and them; and because he knew it, because he sensed it, he was serene while all of us, who could see, were afraid. He trusted his audience, and it in turn loved him.

During the 1970s, Borges continued to visit the United States regularly: in 1972 he inaugurated a chair of Spanish American literature at the University of New Hampshire (Durham), visited Houston, Texas, and received another honorary doctorate, this time from the University of Michigan (East Lansing); in 1975 he returned to the Michigan campus for a short visit; in 1976 he visited the university for a third time, to lecture on Argentine literature. He traveled around, lecturing and reading his poems, and attended a symposium on his work sponsored by the University of Maine (Orono). On that occasion, in a last meeting with a panel of critics and professors, Borges spoke out against a type of criticism that he believed was going too far. He objected to having his stories and poems analyzed to extinction and stated that they were meant to be read simply as entertainment. He also stated firmly that in spite of all his debts to English literature his models were not British or American writers but the Franco-Argentine Paul Groussac and the Mexican Alfonso Reyes. He was right, of course, on the second count; as for the first, since his critics seldom read anything but his own works (as he complained to me later, in an epigram: "Poor things, they only read Borges!"), his comment was ironic.

On his return to Buenos Aires he stopped briefly in New York and, for the second time, had his poetry read at the YM-YWHA Poetry Center. It was again a triumph of the guru. Borges sat on one side of the podium, while Richard Howard and W. S. Merwin, two of his most distinguished translators, and I sat on the opposite side. The poems were read first in Spanish, by me, and then in English, by one of the translators. Borges said a few words on each text. The procedure could have been deadly boring. If it was not, it was because the audience was electrified by that fragile man, whose English sometimes got bogged down by a rather archaic North Country slur or by some mechanical frailties of old age. In spite of that, or perhaps because of that, the old man managed to create an incantatory space. The brusque gestures of his hand, the voice that perversely missed the microphone or plainly stammered, the blind eyes that traveled wildly, were not seen separately but as a single unit: the unit of a magic performance in which it was not what was said or done but what was subliminally communicated that mattered. Borges, like the Cuman sibyl, could never be wrong, or cease to haunt his listeners.

Some of these journeys to the United States included a European extension. In 1971, instead of returning directly to Buenos Aires, Borges flew for the second time to Israel—to receive, on April 19, the Jerusalem Prize of $2,000, an award that had previously been given to Max Frisch, Bertrand Russell, and Ignazio Silone. On his return he stopped in Scotland, went down to Oxford to receive another honorary doctorate, and visited London to lecture at the Institute of Contemporary Arts. In 1973, he made a second trip to Spain, at the invitation of the Franco-sponsored Institute of Hispanic Culture and the Argentine embassy. In December of that year he went to Mexico to receive the Alfonso Reyes Prize. A second trip to Mexico took place in 1976. That same year, he returned to Spain. Everywhere, he was interviewed to distraction, feted and lionized, crowded and almost mobbed with adulation. Everywhere, he lent himself meekly to public worship, stoically suffered bores and illiterate interviewers, polished off one cocktail party after another. Thin, frail, so white that from a distance it was hard to say whether he was standing or floating, Borges seemed to be made of invisible steel: untiring, unbored, undefeatable. He has long accepted the public persona and has resigned himself to being "Borges." What really happens inside that persona is (he firmly believes) nobody's business.

3.
The Art of
Dictating

With blindness, Borges learned how to compose a poem in his mind, polish it, and finally dictate it to Mother or to one of his scores of friends. Short stories and essays presented a greater problem, and for a while he hesitated, looking for the perfect amanuensis. Apart from Bioy Casares (with whom he had a rather symbiotic relationship before his blindness), his collaborators ranged from the merely mechanic—students who had followed his lectures and put them into writing—to the highly creative. Some were too subservient and did not dare to raise their voices, happy to sit at his feet and take down whatever he said. Others were too independent and Borges, after being extremely polite, finally tired of them. One of his regular collaborators, María Esther Vázquez, has described his methods in some detail:

> Borges has a strange way of working. He dictates five or six words, which are the opening of a prose piece or the first verse of a poem, and immediately he has them read back to him. The index finger of his right hand follows the reading on the back of his left hand, as if it were crossing an invisible page. Each phrase is read one, two, three, four, many times until he discovers how to continue and he dictates another five or six words. Then he has all that has been already written read. Since he dictates indicating the signs of punctuation, it is necessary to read all the signs as well. The fragment is read once more, and again he follows it with the movement of his hands until he finds the next phrase. I have read some dozen times a fragment of five lines. Each one of these repetitions is preceded by Borges' apologies, for he somehow torments himself quite a lot over the supposed inconvenience to which he submits his amanuensis. The result is that, after two or three hours of work, one has half a page which no longer needs correction. (Vázquez, 1977, pp. 28–29)

457

In spite of the exquisite slowness of the method, Borges never lacked for an amanuensis, or even distinguished collaborators. For several decades the first and most important was Mother. To her he dictated some of his most significant writings. He told Richard Burgin that while transcribing one of his darkest short stories, "The Intruder," Mother protested. "She thought that the story was a very unpleasant one. She thought it awful" (Burgin, 1969, p. 48). The story tells of two brothers who share the same woman and end up by murdering her. Brotherly love triumphs over heterosexual attachment. In spite of Mother's objections, she not only copied it but contributed a memorable line, which is spoken by the older brother when he invites the younger one to bury the woman. Borges could not find the exact tone, and after a while Mother (who knew how simple old-fashioned Argentines spoke) volunteered: "Let's get busy, brother. In a while the buzzards will take over" (*The Aleph*, 1970, p. 166).

Because Mother was beginning to show her age, Borges had to turn more and more to other people. His literary output was enormous. In 1961 he dictated the prologue to a selection of works by his old master Macedonio Fernández (*Prose and Verse*); compiled an anthology of his own texts, *Personal Anthology;* and wrote the introduction to a selection in Spanish of Gibbon's *Pages of History and Autobiography.* In 1962 it was the turn of another of his favorite Argentine poets, Almafuerte, whose *Prose and Poetry* he prefaced. In 1965 he published two books: a second version of his *Ancient German Literatures,* prepared with the help of María Esther Vázquez, and a collection of poems he wrote to be sung with the guitar, *For the Six Strings.* In 1966 he dictated "The Intruder" to Mother and included it in that year's new edition of *The Aleph;* he also published an enlarged edition of his *Poetic Works* (1923–1966), which came out both in an illustrated edition and as a new edition of the second volume of his complete works. In 1967 he and Bioy Casares published (this time under their own names) the *Chronicles of Bustos Domecq,* a collection of outrageous parodies of Argentine literary and artistic life. The same year, a slim volume based on his lectures came out; called *Introduction to American Literature,* it had been put together with the help of Esther Zemborain de Torres, an old friend. Two more books were added to the canon in 1968: the first was the *New Personal Anthology,* which complemented the one already published in 1961; the second was a new version of his *Manual of Fantastic Zoology,* under the better title of *The Book of Imaginary Beings* and with thirty-four new articles. A completely new volume of poems came out in 1969, *In Praise of Darkness,* as well as the first volume edited by Norman Thomas di Giovanni of the English translation of his work. It was *The Book of Imaginary Beings.*

The original Spanish had been entirely reworded and the result was a new book which contained 120 pieces compared with 82 in the first Spanish edition. Since he had first met Borges at Harvard, in the fall of 1967, Di Giovanni had been spellbound. He had already started publishing translations from the Spanish and had produced a book of Jorge Guillén's poems. But after meeting Borges, he decided to devote all his efforts to translating his writings into English. The task may have seemed easier than it is. The fact that Borges is bilingual and that he has a vast and minute knowledge of both the English language and English literature had undoubtedly influenced his writings in Spanish. But in spite of it, he is a Spanish writer, and very specifically a Spanish American writer, of the River Plate area. He may sound exotic to Spanish readers used to the stiff syntax and vocabulary of Spanish provinces or to the solemn horrors promoted by academies and universities all over the Hispanic world. But to readers of the best prose written in Latin America in the last century (Sarmiento, Groussac, Martí, Alfonso Reyes, Pedro Henríquez Ureña), Borges' writing seems, and is, very Spanish American. Some of his English translators had been too literal and thus had come across insoluble problems. The best example (provided by Borges himself) of the pitfalls of any literal translation can be found in a simple Spanish expression such as "Entró en una habitación oscura." The literal translation would be "He entered into an obscure habitation," which sounds a bit like Sir Thomas Browne. What the phrase means is "He came into a dark room."

Norman Thomas di Giovanni was unhappy with the stiffness and inaccuracies of the existing English versions of Borges, and he decided that the only effective way to translate Borges was to move to Argentina and work in close association with the writer. He managed to get help from the Ingram Merrill Foundation. Borges was delighted. For close to three years Di Giovanni lived in Buenos Aires, working regularly with Borges, doubling as his secretary on some of his journeys (Oklahoma, 1969; Columbia and Yale, 1971), and in general taking care of his rights in England and the United States, helping Borges to earn a substantial income for the first time in his life. In the process, several volumes of stories and poems were translated by Di Giovanni and the author, or by other writers under Di Giovanni's supervision and editorship. An official Borges canon was thus produced in English. Apart from the already mentioned *Book of Imaginary Beings,* the following titles came out of Di Giovanni's industry: *The Aleph and Other Stories: 1933–1969* (1970), a collection of stories not covered by the copyrighted American editions of *Ficciones* and *Labyrinths; A Universal History of Infamy* (1972); *Selected Poems: 1923–1967* (1972), with valuable information in the back of the book; *Borges on Writing* (1973), a transcript of Borges' conversations with students enrolled in Columbia University's graduate writing program, edited by Di Giovanni, with the assistance of Daniel Halpern and Frank MacShane; *In Praise of Darkness* (1974), in a bilingual edition; *Chronicles of Bustos Domecq* (1976); and *The Book of Sand* (1977).

Their unique method of translating Borges into English was described in the preface to *The Aleph and Other Stories:*

> Perhaps the chief justification of this book is the translation itself, which we have undertaken in what may be a new way. Working closely together in daily sessions, we have tried to make these stories read as though they had been written in English. We do not consider English and Spanish as compounded of sets of easily interchangeable synonyms; they are two quite different ways of looking at the world, each with a nature of its own. English, for example, is far more physical than Spanish. We have therefore shunned the dictionary as much as possible and done our best to rethink every sentence in English words. This venture does not necessarily mean that we have willfully tampered with the original, though in certain cases we have supplied the American reader with those things—geographical, topographical, and historical—taken for granted by an Argentine. (*The Aleph*, 1970, pp. 9–10)

Di Giovanni helped Borges to write and put together the original Spanish editions as well as English translations of several texts: *In Praise of Darkness* (1969); *Dr. Brodie's Report* (1970); "The Congress" (1971), a short story in which Borges returns to the subject of the secret society he had already explored in "Tlön, Uqbar, Orbis Tertius"; and *The Gold of the Tigers* (1972), a collection of prose and verse. In a foreword to his translation of *Dr. Brodie's Report,* Di Giovanni reiterates what Borges and he had already said in introducing *The Aleph* but adds a significant sentence: "One difference between this volume and the last lies in the fact that the writing and the translation were, except in one case, more or less simultaneous. In this way, our work was easier for us, since, as we were always under the spell of the originals, we stood in no need of trying to recapture past moods. This seems to us the best possible condition under which to practice the craft of translation." (*Brodie*, 1970, p. 7)

This close collaboration between author and translator raised a question neither Borges nor Di Giovanni seems to have faced: by becoming co-author of the translation, Borges had assumed the status of writer in English, a role he had so far avoided. Borges' knowledge of English is indisputable: he uses it as a native, perhaps even better, because he has also studied it as a foreign language. His knowledge of English and American literature is also vast. But all that does not make him an English writer, and especially it does not make him an English writer capable of writing with the freedom, inventiveness, and feeling for words that Borges, the Spanish writer, has. To put it differently, as a translator of his own texts, Borges seems old-fashioned, awkward. His Victorian, bookish handling of the English language does a disservice to the original's truly creative Spanish. On the other hand, Di Giovanni, being a North American and much younger, has a totally different concept of English, both written and spoken. The result, from a literary point of view, is sometimes strange. If their translations cannot be objected to from the point of view of accuracy and scholarship (they are the best one can ask for), they are less than unique from a purely creative point of view.

Borges and Di Giovanni parted company around 1972. But Di Giovanni is still committed to translating some of his older works and continues to receive 50 percent of the income from Borges' English rights. Borges, for his part, has continued to produce new books: his *Obras Completas* (Complete Works), in a bound volume printed on thin paper, was published in 1974. It was immediately sold out. The popularity of the book (extremely expensive by Argentine standards) is such that it is sold at newspaper and magazine stands in Buenos Aires. Borges was not aware of this fact until quite recently—the Argentine writer Ernesto Sábato called it to his attention. Three more titles came out in 1975: *El libro de arena* (The Book of Sand), a collection of thirteen short stories in which he returns to the fantastic genre; *La rosa profunda* (The Unending Rose), thirty-six new poems; and *Prólogos* (Prologues, with a Prologue of Prologues), an important collection of thirty prefaces he had written since 1923, which unfortunately does not include his prologue to the *Divine Comedy*. Three more books came out in 1976: *Libro de sueños* (The Book of Dreams), in which he retells his own and other people's dreams; *La moneda de hierro* (The Iron Coin), a collection of thirty-eight new poems; and *¿Qué es el budismo?* (What Is Buddhism?) a primer compiled with Alicia Jurado.

Of the fifteen-odd new or revised books Borges has published in Spanish in the last fifteen years, only half are truly original. In one of them (*Chronicles of Bustos Domecq*) he had the advantage of collaborating with a close friend and gifted writer. In another, *The Book of Imaginary Beings,* collaboration was less important at the beginning but became decisive as the book took final shape. There, the wit and imagination are totally his, but the painstaking scholarship, the tracing of all the sources half remembered, half invented by Borges, is Di Giovanni's main contribution.

Blindness also brought Borges back to poetry. In the last decade especially, poems seem to flow naturally from him. The old guru is a traditional poet who wisely sticks to the sonnet because it is easy to compose in the mind, who preserves rhyme because it keeps ringing, and who celebrates his discoveries (new places and new readings of old books and authors) but keeps coming back to a handful of trusted subjects: old age, blindness, emptiness (metaphysical and personal), and longing for a reality that has always eluded him. It is conventional in form, but it is made poignant by the intensity with which the poet handles each subject and the underlying pain that tradition and politeness cannot efface. As an old guru, Borges is shamelessly autobiographical. At the same time, decorum never leaves him, and the reader (although offered the chance for an intimate revelation) is finally denied any real exposure.

The short stories have been handled differently by Borges. The battle between the realistic and magic conventions of storytelling has not ceased. In 1966 Borges told César Fernández Moreno that he was tired of labyrinths, tigers, and mirrors, that he had decided to stop making stories about them and was leaving them to his followers: "Now, let them try it and get screwed" (Fernández Moreno, 1967b, p. 25). In the 1969 collection published under the title of *Dr. Brodie's Report,* he aimed at realism. The preface can be read as a manifesto of the old guru against the middle-aged Borges of *Ficciones:*

> I have done my best—I don't know with what success—to write straightforward stories. I do not dare state that they are simple; there isn't anywhere on earth a single page or single word that is, since each thing implies the universe, whose most obvious trait is complexity. . . . Apart from the text that gives this book its title and that obviously derives from Lemuel Gulliver's last voyage, my stories are—to use the term in vogue today—realistic. They follow, I believe, all the conventions of that school, which is as conventional as any other and of which we shall grow tired if we have not already done so. They are rich in the required invention of circumstances. (*Brodie,* 1969, pp. 9–10)

He also insists on the same page that he is not a "committed writer," and that he does not "aspire to be Aesop. My stories, like those of the *One Thousand and One Nights,* try to be entertaining or moving but not persuasive." As an afterthought, he adds that he has always been very open in expressing his political convictions:

> I am a member of the Conservative Party—this in itself is a form of skepticism—and no one has ever branded me a Communist, a nationalist, an anti-Semite, a follower of Billy the Kid or of the dictator Rosas. I believe that someday we will deserve not to have governments. I have never kept my opinions hidden, not even in trying times, but neither have I ever allowed

them to find their way into my literary work, except once when I was buoyed up in exultation over the Six-Day War. (Ibid., p. 10)

Borges' political allusions and his refusal to write "committed" literature have to be read in the context of the Argentine literary situation of the time. The inevitable return of Perón to power had made it virtually impossible for any man of letters to remain uncommitted. Borges seized the occasion offered by the preface to state his belief in a noncommitted literature, thus emphasizing one of the old guru's most provocative traits: to go against the grain, to avoid consensus, to maintain unpopular and even outrageous opinions. But if he was infuriating, he was right about refusing to use his work as a soapbox. He well knew that the author's ideology and the text's ideology rarely coincide. Balzac (whom Marx admired so much) believed in the monarchy, the Catholic Church, and the moral superiority of French women, but his novels presented France as a country run by a pack of capitalistic, greedy, and debauched characters. Dostoevski believed in the czar and the Russian Orthodox Church, was a rabid nationalist, and scorned revolutionaries: his novels tear to pieces the fabric of deceptions and crimes that the institutions he loved had created; his work paved the way for the revolution to come. D'Annunzio in Italy, Pound in the United States, and Céline in France were all in favor of different kinds of fascism, but their writings were not conservative or supportive of the status quo; rather, they dwelled on decadence, madness, and the final absurdity of the human condition.

The man Borges may vote conservative, reject socialism of any kind, and love strong regimes. The text we call Borges does not stoop to that kind of compromise: it is plainly in favor of skepticism, doubts reality has any meaning, and accepts the cruel paradoxes and ironies of the human condition without fear or remorse. Besides, the text is not subject to the infirmities of the flesh and the extravagances of old age. In his preface to *Dr. Brodie's Report,* Borges delivers a final statement: "The art of writing is mysterious, the opinions we hold are ephemeral, and I prefer the Platonic idea of the Muse to that of Poe, who reasoned, or feigned to reason, that the writing of a poem is an act of the intelligence" (ibid., p. 10). Thus it cannot come as a surprise to the reader that these so-called realistic stories are, essentially, similar to the "magic" ones Borges has been writing since he published the original edition of *A Universal History of Infamy* (1935). If the writing seems more terse, less baroque, and the use of circumstantial detail more frequent, the point of view has not changed that much. Not only does the title story, "Dr. Brodie's Report," deal with the uncanny; the other stories also provide examples of strange behavior or offer paradoxical viewpoints. "Pedro Salvadores," for instance, is in a sense a rewriting of Hawthorne's haunting "Wakefield," a story Borges loves. At least two of the remaining stories are frankly fantastic. In "The Meeting" two men fight a duel with knives they do not know how to handle; but because the knives know their job, they fight well. In "The Gospel According to Mark" a rather naïve student reads the Bible to a family of degenerate and illiterate Calvinists only to discover, at the last possible minute, that they take the story of Jesus' crucifixion too literally.

Borges' most recent book of original short stories, *The Book of Sand,* is unabashedly fantastic. Instead of a preface, in the Argentine edition it has an epilogue and a signed statement on the back cover. After declaring that it is wrong to discuss in a preface stories the reader has not yet read (but who reads prefaces anyhow?), Borges comments on each story, identifying its nature (fantastic, erotic, autobiographical, historical, and so forth) and insisting on the dreamlike quality throughout. The back cover reiterates, in a slightly different way, some of these arguments, calls the stories "blindman's exercises," and mentions Wells, Poe, and Swift as his models both for style and plot.

The stories (thirteen, a number Borges refuses to view as "magic") repeat some of his literary obsessions: the double ("The Other"), the infinite ("The Book of Sand"), the secret society ("The Congress"), the vagaries of behavior ("Avelino Arredondo"). Only one new topic is added: the splendor of carnal love, which Borges had earlier refused to treat explicitly in his work. Sexual allusions could be found, of course, in poems and even in some stories and essays, but they were always derogatory. Now, the old guru publishes a story about a Norwegian girl who sweetly gives herself to a puzzled and thankful Argentine; and in the labyrinthine narrative "The Congress" he introduces a rather Hemingwayesque version of carnal bliss.

Eroticism was never totally absent in Borges' work. It has always been hidden or disguised, masked or displaced. In his late seventies he has allowed himself finally to admit in print the validity of erotic dreams. Of course, the fact that in "The Congress" (a pun which alludes to copulation) the girl's name is the rather forbidding one of Beatriz Frost may have warned the careful reader about Borges' intentions. The original Beatrice, as is well known, did *not* love Dante and never condescended to anything more intimate than a formal greeting on the streets of Florence. Frost (needless to say) is not easily associated with the heat that love generates. In calling the girl Beatriz Frost, Borges alludes to the tantalizing nature, both warm and chilly, of that dream of carnal ecstasy.

Apart from the books he authored, alone or with the help of friends, Borges has authorized the publication in book form of some long and sometimes repetitive interviews. Three were published in 1967: by Georges Charbonnier, Jean de Milleret, and César Fernández Moreno (included in his book *Reality and Papers* and later condensed in my book *Borges par lui même,* 1970). In 1968 Rita Guibert conducted an extensive interview for *Life en Español* which was later included in her book *Seven Voices* (1973). In 1969 Richard Burgin came out with a volume called *Conversations with Jorge Luis Borges.* Victoria Ocampo's *Dialogues with Borges* came out the same year. In 1977 two more books of conversations were added to the ever increasing canon. The first reproduces a series of meetings between Borges and Ernesto Sábato, the well-known Argentine novelist; the second is the work of María Esther Vázquez and includes not only dialogues with Borges but also the author's own recollections of a long friendship and collaboration.

The number of interviews, of special issues of magazines, of books on any and every aspect of Borges' life and work keeps increasing. Today the Borges industry is at its peak. For better or for worse, Borges has reached a stage in which he no longer belongs to himself: he is public property. Perhaps the extent of his popularity can be measured by the way movies have treated him. Before he became "Borges," a few enthusiastic readers had attempted to translate some of his stories for the Argentine cinema: Leopoldo Torre Nilsson did "Emma Zunz" under the rather Dreyerian title *Days of Wrath* (1953–1954); René Mugica did a rather folkloric version of "Streetcorner Man" (1961–1962). But by the late 1960s and into the 1970s Argentine and European filmmakers began to compete for Borges' themes or subjects: Hugo Santiago made two films from scripts that were partially authored by Borges and Bioy Casares—*Invasion* (Argentina, 1968–1969) and *The Others* (France, 1973–1974); Alain Magrou had a second look at "Emma Zunz" (France, 1969); Bernardo Bertolucci based his *The Spider's Stratagem* (Italy, 1969–1970) on "Theme of the Traitor and the Hero"; Ricardo Luna filmed *The Hoodlums* (Argentina, 1975) from a script Borges had authored with Bioy Casares in 1955; Héctor Olivera adapted "The Dead One" for the screen (Argentina, 1975) with some help from the Uruguayan novelist, Juan Carlos Onetti.

Even more revealing than the existence of these adaptations is the fact that Borges is constantly "quoted" by some of the most sophisticated filmmakers. Jacques Rivette had one of the characters of *Paris Belongs to Us* (1958) read Borges' *Other Inquisitions.* In Jean-Luc Godard's *Alphaville* (1965) the computer which runs that futuristic world quotes some passages from Borges' "A New Refutation of Time." In Nicholas Roeg's *Performance* (1972) one of the characters, a gangster, is seen reading Borges' *Personal Anthology;* even more surprising is the fact that Mick Jagger seems also to have read it: in one scene he quotes lines from it, and in the climax of that movie the photograph of Borges which appears on the cover of the *Personal Anthology* is seen escaping from his head, brutally opened by a shot from James Fox's gun.

Borges, or rather "Borges," has become chic. The old guru has fallen in with fast company. But behind that mask, Borges (the sad, old-fashioned, shy, very Argentine old gentleman) is still very much himself.

4.
A Magic Space

For the last three decades of their life together, Borges and Mother lived in the same two-bedroom apartment on the sixth floor of a house on Maipú Street, in downtown Buenos Aires. From the balcony that runs along the bedrooms, a terrace filled with pots of flowers, one can see the tops of the trees of beautiful San Martín Square. The Borgeses moved to that apartment in 1944, after a rather unsuccessful attempt at sharing lodgings with Norah and her family and a transitional stay at an apartment on Quintana Avenue. The Maipú apartment was to become the final residence for this strangely matched couple.

The first time I went to visit them, in 1946, the apartment was still new (it was probably built in the late 1930s or early 1940s): the entrance hall, the corridors, and the small elevator had the smell of carefully maintained premises. They suggested a relatively affluent middle-class status. The door to their apartment had a small bronze plaque with the surname Borges. Inside, the rather large living room was cluttered with nineteenth-century furniture: in the dining area, a solid table and chairs, a cupboard with some old silver pieces; against the only large window, a small sofa and two chairs. An elegant marquetry cabinet with a marble top and Mother's small writing desk (a present she got on her First Communion) completed the living room area. All the items were good and solid, the mahogany gleamed, the upholstered chairs and sofa looked new in spite of their old-fashioned shape and colors. These pieces were family heirlooms which, in spite of the Borgeses' rather modest financial situation, certified their links with more spacious times. On the walls a few daguerreotypes illustrated the family museum; paintings or drawings by Norah, photographs of Father and Mother when young, of Georgie and his sister, completed the private iconography. A sword, a silver maté gourd, a book beautifully bound: those were the few treasures which they had managed to salvage. In one of the corners of the dining area open shelves contained half of Borges' rather small but select library, carefully put together by Mother's devotion to the books that both Father and Georgie had loved so much. Framing the opposite window, two more shelves contained less elegantly bound books and assorted paperbacks. That day I was not asked to venture any further into the apartment.

I had lunch with Borges and Mother. It was a very simple affair; the table was attended by a middle-aged maid who had been with the Borgeses for quite a long time. I cannot remember what we talked about, but it must have concerned, chiefly, our mutual friends and relations on both sides of the River Plate. Mother had been born in Uruguay, and as I came from there, the subject seemed inevitable. One thing I do remember to this day: when wine was offered (a simple but good Argentine wine), the maid asked Mother, not Borges, if he would also have some wine. Almost at once, Borges and Mother replied in the negative. But what struck me was Mother's way of phrasing her answer. She literally said, "El niño no toma vino," which could be translated as "Master Borges does not drink wine." Master, here, was used in the Victorian sense: male children were always called "Master" by the servants. Borges was then forty-seven, but as he was living in his mother's house and was still unmarried he continued to be addressed as "Master." Although I was then only twenty-five, I was already married. So I was "Mister" and drank wine with Mother.

In a sense, while Mother lived (and she lived to be ninety-nine), Borges never ceased to be a child. Since Father's death in 1938, Borges had, nominally at least, been the head of the house and the principal breadwinner. But at home, in the privileged space of the Maipú apartment, she was Mother and Borges was Georgie. Even the fact that, because of his increasing blindness, Mother doubled as secretary and nurse, and soon had to take on the functions of literary agent and ambassador-at-large, did not alter the basic relationship. She helped him with his literary work, took dictation from him, and read aloud to him in English and French, but it all was done the way a mother helps her child with his homework.

During the next thirty years I visited that apartment many times. To me it seemed like a unique place: a space where Borges and Mother continued to live as if the umbilical cord that once attached them had never been severed. Time passed; they grew old together. New nations emerged in Africa. The Vietnam war—at first a

French colonial enterprise—began to contaminate every corner of the globe. Perón fell, Cuba became socialist, Allende was murdered in Chile, the Uruguayan people were kept in prison by their own army, Perón returned. But the Maipú apartment (and its two incredibly delicate inhabitants) continued there, basically unchanged. Borges' fame did not alter things much. The apartment seemed made of a substance immune to time. It was a magic space, an *omphalós*, the navel or center of a mystical private world. On one of the living room walls a Piranesi engraving which depicts a circular space (an arena or a Roman orchestra) could be seen as an emblem of that apartment.

In due time I was to be casually asked to enter the bedrooms. Mother's was large and sunny: it had a French window which opened onto the balcony. She had kept the furniture she received when she was married at the turn of the century. The room was dominated by a double bed and a big solid chest of drawers, the top literally covered with family photographs. Mother's was the master bedroom. Georgie had the smaller one, reserved for children. It contained a very narrow iron bed with a minuscule night table, a small glass bookcase where he kept the book he was currently working on, a chair, and a narrow chest of drawers with some knick-knacks on top. Everything was very neat and sterile. Over the bed Mother had placed a crucifix. Georgie was indifferent to that symbol of a faith he did not share, but he was careful not to offend Mother.

When it became obvious that Mother was getting too old to take proper care of Georgie, they had to find someone willing to take Mother's place. They used to discuss the matter openly with friends. Both Georgie and Mother were unafraid of their personal deaths and made no bones about the fact that they knew their days were numbered. But the problem was to find somebody to replace Mother. Norah was unsuitable. She could hardly cope with her own family; besides, Borges and she had drifted apart since the fateful day in 1928 when she married Guillermo de Torre. For a while it seemed as if Adolfo Bioy Casares and Silvina could act as surrogate parents. But they traveled a lot and led very leisurely and in a sense separate lives. In spite of their friendship (Borges used to dine with them on Sundays), a certain British formality prevented them from discussing seriously his moving in with them in the event of Mother's death. So the idea of a marriage of convenience for Georgie began to take shape. Unfortunately, Georgie and Mother did not have the same notions about what kind of wife he needed.

In the early 1960s the conflict came into the open. The last trip Mother and Georgie took together (to Europe in 1963) put an enormous strain on her. When, the following year, Borges was invited to go to Germany, Mother decided to stay at home. Borges asked María Esther Vázquez to accompany him. According to her reminiscences, she was seventeen the first time she went to visit Borges at home, in the company of a group of students from the Faculty of Philosophy and Letters of the University of Buenos Aires. Later she began to collaborate regularly with him and became a close friend. Although Mother did not object to their friendship, she objected to Georgie becoming too dependent on her. She was afraid he might decide to ask María Esther to be his wife. Mother wanted Georgie to marry somebody closer to his own age, a mature woman who could also be a nurse. And she believed, rightly, that María Esther—in spite of her friendly attachment to Georgie—was not seriously interested in sharing her whole life with him. But apparently he could not be persuaded, was terribly stubborn and resented what he saw as Mother's interference. Some traces of his irritation can be found in his conversations with Jean de Milleret, taped in 1966, after he had to abandon his plan of marrying María Esther. He was outspoken then and obviously bitter in stressing the ignorance of Mother's branch of the family (De Milleret, 1967, p. 39); in a footnote De Milleret reports how displeased Mother was on seeing Georgie's name coupled with María Esther's on the cover of the book *Ancient German Literatures* (1965), which he authored with her help (ibid., p. 231n). In an even more tantalizing parenthesis De Milleret talks about Borges' despair at not being able to overcome a recent setback in love (ibid., p. 168). It is obvious that he is alluding to Georgie's disappointment at not marrying María Esther. Borges eventually overcame it, and to this day his friendship with her continues.

It is against this background that Georgie's decision to marry Elsa Astete Millán, barely one year after these events, can be better understood. Elsa had been an old if brief flame. They had met around 1927, when he was twenty-seven and she was seventeen. She lived with her family in La Plata, the capital of the province of Buenos Aires and a city whose main claim to distinction is its university. Through Pedro Henríquez Ureña, who was a professor at the university, Georgie met the Astete sisters. One eventually married, and later divorced, one of Georgie's first disciples, Néstor Ibarra; the second, Elsa, attracted Georgie's attention. But she did not seem to be terribly impressed by the young, bashful poet. Their romance (if there ever was one) did not last long. She married Ricardo Albarracín, a young man who was a descendant of Sarmiento, the great nineteenth-century Argentine man of letters. In 1964 Elsa's husband died; three years later, she met Georgie again. If time had changed him for the better (he was now Borges), blindness prevented him from modifying his image of Elsa. They soon decided to marry. Thirty years was a long enough wait. Mother did not like the idea at all. She openly expressed her reservations about the prospective bride. Once she observed, for instance, that Elsa was unsuitable because she did not speak English. From that point of view, Mother was prophetic. Elsa's and Georgie's enjoyment of their journeys to the United States and England were marred by Elsa's unfamiliarity with the English language. But Georgie did not want a repetition of the previous frustration and stubbornly went along with the engagement. On September 21, 1967, they were married. Mother was, of course, present. In a photograph of the occasion published in one of Buenos Aires' largest newspapers, one can see her hand resting on Georgie's. By that time, everything Borges did was public and the press extracted every inch of gossip from the ceremony.

In poems as well as in some documentary movies (such as the one Harold Mantell did in 1969), Georgie records the happiness of his married life. Elsa and he moved to an elegant apartment at 1377 Belgrano Street, not too far from the National Library. Borges soon settled into a routine which included working at the National Library and visiting Mother at her apartment on Maipú Street. In spite of her reservations about his marriage, Mother attempted to present a good face and even shared with Elsa some of Georgie's limelight. On numerous occasions he was photographed between the two women. He seemed to have achieved a long-sought goal.

In 1967 he visited Harvard with Elsa and in 1969 went with her to Israel. At the end of that same year, they returned to the United States to attend the Borges Conference held at the University of Oklahoma. I met Elsa then and she impressed me as a very sociable and energetic person, extremely interested in all the gadgets and amenities that North American technology offered. But she was obviously uncomfortable about the obstacle her unfamiliarity with English represented and was forced to remain aloof when the conversation was not in Spanish. Nevertheless, she tried to put her best foot forward. Borges seemed pleased with her. Less than one year later I found that they had taken the first steps toward divorce. Georgie returned to Mother.

The marriage had lasted some three years. Elsa kept the apartment on Belgrano Street and Georgie, his 1,500-volume library. The Argentine press covered the affair with obvious relish. Georgie managed to avoid being too explicit although he admitted (*Así*, Buenos Aires, September 1970) that the marriage had been a failure. Elsa was more confessional and seemed glad to explain in some detail the causes of that failure (*Confirmado*, Buenos Aires, November 11, 1970, p. 43). She made the obvious observation that Georgie, a confirmed bachelor, had no experience of married life at sixty-seven, while she had been married for some twenty-seven years. Her outspokenness did not endear her to Mother. Many years later, Borges broke his rule of silence and confided to María Esther Vázquez that one of the things he found strange in Elsa was that she did not dream. Being a great dreamer himself, he must have discovered that Elsa's incapacity to dream kept them hopelessly apart.

I visited the Borgeses again the following year, in August 1971. This time I meant to have a good look at the apartment. Everything seemed subtly dilapidated. It was obvious that Mother had long ceased to care for the furniture, the curtains, or the rugs. At ninety-five, she was still going out every afternoon to a nearby church to attend mass. But she was so frail and thin that she seemed more an animated cartoon than a real woman. Georgie was his usual self. He talked endlessly without paying too much attention to people's replies. Since he was becoming increasingly deaf, he tried to cover up that added curse by almost nonstop monologue. But politeness was ingrained in him. Every four or six sentences he would stop to ask his listener, with some hesitation and even urgency, "Don't you think so?"

At the time, the Argentine political situation was very tense. Perón was taking advantage of the general confusion to engineer his return. But literary matters finally had the day. Georgie told me the plot of a story he was then planning to write. It was based on a real event: the birth of a black daughter to a wealthy Argentine family of the last century. It was a practical joke the family genes had played on the proud patricians. To avoid exposure, the parents decided to keep the child upstairs, forever, attended by black servants. Their aim was to create for her a sort of magical world in which the question of color could never be raised. Georgie was very concerned with the ethics of the story (was the girl really happy in her confinement?) and also with the technical problem of how to tell the story. From her point of view? From an ironical observer's? From a member of the family's? I knew that he was less interested in my contribution to the solution of the problem than in the opportunity to rehearse aloud and with a receptive audience the intricacies of the plot. Nevertheless, I volunteered a few suggestions and even recalled a real story, told by André Gide in one of his books, of the woman whose family kept her sequestered in Poitiers for some twenty years. Georgie seemed to have forgotten that incident. The conversation drifted. When Suzanne Jill Levine, who had accompanied me, asked for permission to take a few color photographs to record the visit, Mother suddenly came to life and rushed to her bedroom to get a comb to smooth back Georgie's hair. In his usual manner, he was oblivious to Jill's camera and kept talking, brushing aside Mother's hand as if it were a fly. Later, Georgie invited both of us to take a stroll along Florida Street, one of his familiar hunting grounds. We walked a bit among busy people who suddenly stood still, as if transfixed, when they recognized him. "It's Borges," they would say, pointing their fingers in his direction. Unaware of his own popularity, Georgie went on walking and talking. We ended up in a nearby café, the very British St. James', at the corner of Maipú and Córdoba. A mirror was on the wall next to our table, and Jill could not resist the temptation of having our double images recorded forever.

The following day I returned alone to have a long chat with Mother. Knowing my preferences, she offered me tea, and we talked about her and Georgie's ancestors, about Georgie's schooldays in Geneva, and about many other episodes in their long, fruitful life together. She knew perfectly well that I was engaged in some research for this biography and wanted to help me. I had sent her a copy of an illustrated book on Borges I had published in 1970 in Paris, and she told me that she had liked it very much and had even read it aloud to Georgie. She was pleased with it because I had been thoughtful enough to place at the very end of the book a beautiful photograph of the two of them in New York. I did not tell her that I had put that photograph there because I wanted to make a point.

While we were discussing the family tree, she volunteered to show me one she once had made. She went to the marquetry cabinet, bending down to reach the bottom drawer; when she tried to get up, her legs did not obey her. I rushed to her and helped her to stand. She was so thin and weighed so little, her bones seemed so brittle and her skin so cold, that I shuddered. A few days later, I returned to New Haven. That was the last time I saw her.

Four years later, on July 8, 1975, she died. It had taken her almost two years to do it. The Argentine newspapers recorded the death in great detail and even published some horrid photographs of her lying in bed like a corpse, with Georgie stiffly standing next to her, on the occasion of her ninety-ninth birthday, forty-seven days before her death. The photographs of her funeral did not spare a closeup of Georgie's tears. Two months after she died I visited Buenos Aires again. I went to see Borges at his apartment. There was no point in talking about Mother's death, so I tried to avoid the subject completely, but somehow it came up naturally in the middle of our conversation. Without any warning, he began telling me about her agony, how she pleaded for months with God to be spared the pain; how she addressed her long-deceased mother and father, begging them to ease her out of life; how she also called on Father; how finally she begged the maid to come and throw her into the garbage can. For the last two years her moaning and her cries could be overheard even over the phone. When the end came, she was reduced almost to the bare bones, held together by only a film of parched skin, like a mummified image of herself.

Borges told me all these details, very quietly, in a neutral voice. He went on and on, in the halting, almost asthmatic monotone he generally uses when telling a story. At the end he switched abruptly to a general reflection about the strange things people say when dying, and he illustrated the point with an anecdote about his maternal grandmother. She was a lady of impeccable Victorian decorum. But on dying, she said the first four-letter word in her life: "Carajo, basta de sufrir." ("Fuck, enough of this suffering.") We couldn't stop laughing. It was a hysterical laughter in which repressed emotions found an outlet. The final loss, the cutting of the umbilical cord, was eased by an absurd anecdote.

I was to see him on other occasions, both in Buenos Aires and in the United States. By then he had adjusted to life without Mother. In Buenos Aires he was kept very busy with lectures, interviews, and participation in all kinds of literary events. He also worked regularly on a seminar that was (and still is) held at his home. The project began in the early 1960s. One day a small group of students from his course on English literature came to see him at the National Library, and on his suggestion they started a study of the origins of that literature. According to what Borges later told María Esther Vázquez, he was astonished by their enthusiasm. He tried to warn them that he knew as little as they did about the subject. Nevertheless, the following Saturday they began reading an Anglo-Saxon chronicle. A phrase they found—"Four hundred summers after Troy, the city of the Greek, was devastated"—somehow inspired them. "I don't know why we were so impressed by that phrase; perhaps it was the fact of finding the ancient fable of Troy washed up on the shores of the North Sea. This, and the discovery that Rome was called Romeburg, and the Mediterranean Sea, the Sea of Vandals, made me fall in love with that language" (Vázquez, 1977, p. 151).

After ten years of reading those ancient texts every Saturday and Sunday, Borges has an easy familiarity with the Anglo-Saxon language. To trace its roots, he has studied old Scandinavian writings, especially those of Iceland. He is proud of his small collection of Icelandic literature. On one of my recent visits to Buenos Aires he took me to his bedroom to show me the privileged place they occupy in the glass bookcase. To María Esther Vázquez he once confided that part of his fascination with the study of Scandinavian languages resides in the discovery of words.

BORGES: When one studies a language, one sees words closer. If I am reading Spanish or English, I hear the whole phrase; on the other hand, in a new language—

VÁZQUEZ: One hears word by word.

BORGES: Yes, it's like reading with a magnifying glass. I feel each word more than the native speakers do. This is why there is some prestige in learning foreign languages; there is, also, the prestige of things ancient; that is, to belong to a secret society. . . . (Ibid., p. 61)

Borges has kept the study group small—no more than six students—but he does a certain amount of promoting, even recruiting. I remember once, in January 1962, while we were having lunch in an Italian restaurant in Buenos Aires, he attempted to convince me to drop all my literary and scholarly work (I was then engaged in teaching English and American literature in Montevideo) and move to Buenos Aires to study with him. The invitation was only half-serious. He knew perfectly well that I was totally dependent on my teaching for an income. But I preferred to say no on different grounds. With mock seriousness, I explained to him that to the study of Anglo-Saxon or Scandinavian texts, I preferred the study of Borges' texts. He smiled a Cheshire-cat smile and abruptly changed the subject. Not everybody treated him so firmly. Among the young students who were attracted to the seminar was María Kodama, a young Argentine woman with Japanese ancestors. She became one of his most devoted students and also his part-time secretary. With a special talent for smiling reticence and self-effacement, María is always there when Borges needs her, patiently waits for her cue, and performs all the duties of a sensitive, intelligent, and erudite nurse to a man who is more and more dependent on external aid. In his last trips to the United States, María has been his constant companion.

While in Buenos Aires, she shares her responsibilities with other friends, among whom María Esther Vázquez is one of the most faithful. Now that Borges and Di Giovanni have parted company, María Esther takes care of his daily finances; one of his nephews, Luis de Torre, a lawyer, is responsible for long-range ventures. But the list of people who help Borges and care for him is immense. Not the least of them is Fanny, a solid Argentine woman who acts as housekeeper, cook, and nanny and treats him with the no-nonsense attitude grown-ups have toward children.

Despite all these friends and relatives, Borges is terribly alone. Although he has achieved in Buenos Aires the status of a folk hero (his popularity is second only to that of Carlos Gardel, the tango singer), Borges is totally cut off from the real world by his blindness. In a recent interview in the French magazine L'Express (reproduced in

Buenos Aires by *La Opinión*), he confided: "Now that I am blind—and blindness is a form of loneliness—I spend the greatest part of the day alone. Then, not to be bored, I invent stories, and make poems. Later, when somebody comes to see me, I dictate them. I do not have a secretary, and thus my visitors have to put up with my dictation" (*Opinión*, May 15, 1977, p. 28).

Blindness and the absence of Mother have practically abolished time. Borges lives forever inside a magic space, totally empty and gray, in which time does not count or (when it does) is brought about by the sudden invasion of people from the outside, people who still live in time. Protected and isolated by his blindness, in the labyrinth built so solidly by Mother, Borges sits immobile. He doesn't bother to turn on a light. Everything around him is quiet except his imagination. Inside his mind, the empty spaces are filled with stories of murder and wonder, with poems that encompass the whole world of culture, with essays that subtly catalogue the terrors and the painful delights of men. Old, blind, frail, Borges sits finally in the center of the labyrinth.

A Note on
This Book

On many occasions during the last five or six years I had the opportunity to discuss with Borges the project of writing a literary biography of him. Generally, he dislikes discussing his own work, and in this particular case things were made even more difficult because he is very reticent about his private life and finds biography an impossible genre. It is true that in 1930 he had attempted to sketch the life of a popular Argentine poet, Evaristo Carriego, but his book was short and very apologetic. The biographical chapter begins: "That a man would like to arouse in another man memories that only belong to a third is an evident paradox. To carelessly achieve that paradox is the innocent decision behind any biography" (*Carriego*, 1930, p. 31). In spite of this caveat, he *did* write a biographical chapter for that book, and even later wrote many biographical articles (on Hawthorne and Whitman, on Wilde and Edward FitzGerald, on José Hernández and Almafuerte). From 1936 to 1939 he also edited a literary page in *El Hogar,* one of whose features was a capsule biography of a contemporary writer. He has been an avid reader of biographies and, especially, autobiographies.

But in writing biographies, or in praising autobiographies, Borges has always drawn the line at the confessional. On several occasions, he has had good words to say about both Gibbon's and Kipling's autobiographies, never about Rousseau's *Confessions* or Amiel's *Intimate Journal.* What he likes in the former two is their reticence, what they manage to omit or barely suggest. He likes their refusal to surrender to the reader's morbid curiosity. In talking to María Esther Vázquez, he makes that point at least twice (Vázquez, 1977, pp. 155 and 166). In his own "Autobiographical Essay" he has practiced the same restraint. His marriage, for instance, is never explicitly mentioned, although there is one tantalizing reference to it when he discusses a story he hadn't yet made up his mind to write ("The Congress," announced as a work in progress as far back as 1945): "Finally, as I was telling it to my wife, she made me see that no further elaboration was needed" ("Essay," 1970, p. 259). About the happiness and pain of married life, there is not a word.

Because I had read his strictures against biographies and knew his praise of reticence in autobiographies, I was reluctant to discuss my project with him. Finally, one day in 1975 I summoned up enough courage and told him about the kind of biography I wanted to write. It was mainly to be the biography of the literary oeuvre called Borges: how it came to happen, how the experiences of the man (Georgie, Borges, Biorges, and, of course, "Borges") had shaped it, how it had developed inside and outside him, and even in opposition to him. I explained that my main sources would not just be the usual biographical data but the texts themselves: texts authored by Borges alone as well as texts Borges authored with the help of relatives, friends, collaborators, interviewers, critics, and even enemies. I also stressed the fact that I saw my biography of him, my text, as a commentary on and an extension of his "Autobiographical Essay." That is, I aspired to write on the interstices and margins left by his own account. While he had to split into two different personae while writing about himself (the narrator and the protagonist), my task was simpler: I had only to create the perspective of a third literary persona (the reader). My biography, in short, was to be equally concerned with the life of Borges (the *bio* in biography) and with the writing of the life (the *graphy*, of course).

He seemed to like the idea, or at least he was polite enough to let me believe so. From then on, every time we met in Buenos Aires or elsewhere, he was ready to answer my questions and even to offer (voluntarily) here and there, in a very unsystematic way, some nuggets of the unwritten text of his autobiography: personal anecdotes, literary evaluations, short descriptive pieces. There was nothing intimate or confessional in them. He assumed, and I also assumed, that I was to respect the reticence that was so common in old Argentine society and that now, with the growing popularity of psychoanalysis there, is almost unheard of.

By accepting that tacit pact, I did not feel restrained to mention in my book only the public facts of his life. On the contrary, in his own texts and even in some interviews, Borges had communicated tantalizing views of his private life. I felt free to use these texts as well as to read in them as much as I could with the proviso that my readings were exclusively mine and that I, in doing so, was not betraying his confidence. Because our relationship had always avoided the confessional, because I never asked him any intimate questions (as some other critics and interviewers did), I knew I was in no position to betray his confidence. My readings of Borges, as well as of Georgie, were based on what the texts, his or others', said to me.

To be totally free, I did not even ask him to authorize my biography. It was tacitly understood that I would be the only one responsible for it. He himself had trouble understanding what an "authorized biography" was. Discussing another biographical book on him that was in the making, I had to spell out what the author's claims of legitimate biography meant. He was astonished. Believing the reconstruction of a man's life by another practically impossible, he laughed at the idea of an official life. Besides, he was skeptical about some of the claims of scholarship. Once, in writing about Beckford's *Vathek,* he made this remark: "One biography of Poe consists of seven hundred octavo pages. The biographer, fascinated by Poe's changes of residence, barely managed to salvage one parenthesis for the 'Maelstrom' and the cosmogony of 'Eureka'" (*Inquisitions,* 1964, pp. 137–138). Borges' article was originally published in Buenos Aires in 1943. Thirty-three years later he made me promise not to concentrate on his changes of residence and forget all about his books. I solemnly promised to remember them. But in seeing me to the door of his apartment, and while lightly pressing my hand, he went back to one of the anecdotes he had told me about his summer vacations in Uruguay when he was a child, and insisted: "Emir, do not forget to put in that little stream in Paso Molino." He was alluding to a moment in his life when he was extremely happy, swimming in the shaded, cool, and heavy waters of that stream. I promised I would not forget. And I didn't.

E.R.M.

Yale University

Bibliography

This bibliography includes only the works quoted in the text. The books are first identified by the short titles used in the text references.

I. WORKS BY BORGES

El Aleph, 1949
First Spanish edition: Buenos Aires, Editorial Losada, 1949.
The Aleph, 1970
Complete title: *The Aleph and Other Stories, 1933–1969.* Edited and translated by Norman Thomas di Giovanni in collaboration with the author. New York, Dutton, 1970.
American Literature, 1971
Complete title: *An Introduction to American Literature.* Written in collaboration with Esther Zemborain de Torres. Translated and edited by L. Clark Keating and Robert O. Evans. Lexington, University of Kentucky Press, 1971. First Spanish edition: *Introducción a la literatura norteamericana.* Buenos Aires, Editorial Columba, 1967.
Aspectos, 1950
Spanish edition: *Aspectos de la literatura gauchesca.* Montevideo, Número, 1950.
Brodie, 1971
Doctor Brodie's Report. Translated by Norman Thomas di Giovanni in collaboration with the author. New York, Dutton, 1971. First Spanish edition: *El informe de Brodie.* Buenos Aires, Emecé Editores, 1970.
Carriego, 1930
First Spanish edition: *Evaristo Carriego.* Buenos Aires, Gleizer Editor, 1930.
Carriego, 1955
Second Spanish edition: *Evaristo Carriego.* Buenos Aires, Emecé Editores, 1955.
Dele-dele, 1946
"Dele-dele," in *Argentina Libre,* Buenos Aires, August 15, 1946, p. 5.
Discusión, 1932

480

First Spanish edition: Buenos Aires, Gleizer Editor, 1932.

Dreamtigers, 1964

Translated by Mildred Boyer and Harold Morland. Austin, University of Texas Press, 1964. First Spanish edition: *El hacedor*. Buenos Aires, Emecé Editores, 1960.

Essay, 1970

"An Autobiographical Essay," in *The Aleph and Other Stories, 1933–1969*. New York, Dutton, 1970, pp. 203–260.

Eternidad, 1936

First Spanish edition: *Historia de la eternidad*. Buenos Aires, Viau y Zona, 1936.

Fervor, 1923

First Spanish edition: *Fervor de Buenos Aires*. Buenos Aires, 1923. Privately printed.

Fervor, 1969

A new Spanish edition, thoroughly revised: *Fervor de Buenos Aires*. Buenos Aires, Emecé Editores, 1969.

Ficciones, 1962

Edited and with an introduction by Anthony Kerrigan. New York, Grove Press, 1962. First Spanish edition: Buenos Aires, Editorial Sur, 1944.

Figari, 1930

Spanish edition: Buenos Aires, 1930. Privately printed.

Héroes, 1956

"Estudio preliminar" to his translation of Carlyle's *On Heroes and Hero Worship* and Emerson's *Representative Men*. Buenos Aires, W. M. Jackson, 1956.

Idioma, 1928

Spanish edition: *El idioma de los argentinos*. Buenos Aires, Gleizer Editor, 1928.

Imaginary, 1969

Complete title: *The Book of Imaginary Beings*. Written in collaboration with Margarita Guerrero. Revised, enlarged, and translated by Norman Thomas di Giovanni in collaboration with the author. New York, Dutton, 1969. First Spanish edition: *El libro de los seres imaginarios*. Buenos Aires, Editorial Kier, 1967.

Infamia, 1935

First Spanish edition: *Historia universal de la infamia*. Buenos Aires, Megáfono (Tor), 1935.

Infamy, 1972

Complete title: *A Universal History of Infamy*. Translated by Norman Thomas di Giovanni. New York, Dutton, 1972.

Inquisiciones, 1925

Spanish edition: Buenos Aires, Editorial Proa, 1925.

Inquisitions, 1964

Complete title: *Other Inquisitions, 1937–1952*. Translated by Ruth L. C. Simms. Austin, University of Texas Press, 1964. First Spanish edition: *Otras inquisiciones*. Buenos Aires, Editorial Sur, 1952. (This book should not be confused with *Inquisiciones*, published in 1925, which has never been reprinted.)

Labyrinths, 1964

Complete title: *Labyrinths: Selected Stories and Other Writings*. Edited by Donald A. Yates and James E. Irby. New York, New Directions, 1964.

BIBLIOGRAPHY

Lugones, 1955
First Spanish edition: *Leopoldo Lugones.* Written in collaboration with Betina Edelberg. Buenos Aires, Editorial Troquel, 1955.

Luna, 1926
First Spanish edition: *Luna de enfrente.* Buenos Aires, Editorial Proa, 1926.

Modelo, 1946
First Spanish edition: *Un modelo para la muerte.* Written in collaboration with Adolfo Bioy Casares. Buenos Aires, "Oportet & Haereses," 1946. Privately printed.

Morel, 1940
"Prólogo" to Adolfo Bioy Casares' *La invención de Morel.* Buenos Aires, Editorial Losada, 1940. American translation: *The Invention of Morel and Other Stories* (from *La trama celeste*). Translated by Ruth L. C. Simms. Austin, University of Texas Press, 1964.

Obra, 1964
First Spanish edition: *Obra poética, 1923–1964.* Buenos Aires, Emecé Editores, 1964.

Pereda, 1927
"Palabras finales" to Ildefonso Pereda Valdés' *Antología de la moderna poesía uruguaya.* Buenos Aires, El Ateneo, 1927.

Poemas, 1943
First Spanish edition: *Poemas, 1923–1943.* Buenos Aires, Editorial Losada, 1943.

Poems, 1972
Complete title: *Selected Poems, 1923–1967.* Edited, with an introduction and notes, by Norman Thomas di Giovanni. New York, Delacorte Press, 1972.

Poesía argentina, 1941
"Prólogo" to *Antología poética argentina.* Edited by Borges in collaboration with Adolfo Bioy Casares and Silvina Ocampo. Buenos Aires, Editorial Sudamericana, 1941.

Prólogos, 1975
Spanish edition: Buenos Aires, Torres Agüero Editor, 1975.

San Martín, 1929
First Spanish edition: *Cuaderno San Martín.* Buenos Aires, Editorial Proa, 1929.

Sand, 1977
Complete title: *The Book of Sand.* Translated by Norman Thomas di Giovanni. New York, Dutton, 1977. First Spanish edition: *El libro de arena.* Buenos Aires, Emecé Editores, 1975.

Tamaño, 1926
Spanish edition: *El tamaño de mi esperanza.* Buenos Aires, Editorial Proa, 1926.

Tigers, 1977
Complete title: *The Gold of the Tigers: Selected Later Poems.* Translated by Alastair Reid. New York, Dutton, 1977. First Spanish editions: *El oro de los tigres* (Buenos Aires, Emecé Editores, 1972) and *La rosa profunda* (Buenos Aires, Emecé Editores, 1975).

BIBLIOGRAPHY

II. INTERVIEWS WITH BORGES

Alcorta, 1964
Alcorta, Gloria: "Entretiens avec Gloria Alcorta," in *L'Herne,* Paris, 1964, pp. 404–408.
Arias, 1971
Arias Usandívaras, Raquel: "Encuentro con Borges," in *Imagen* (no. 90), Caracas, February 1–15, 1971, pp. 2–5.
Burgin, 1969
Burgin, Richard: *Conversations with Jorge Luis Borges.* New York, Holt, Rinehart and Winston, 1969.
Christ, 1967
Christ, Ronald: "The Art of Fiction XXXIX," in *Paris Review* (no. 40), Paris, Winter–Spring 1967, pp. 116–164.
Correa, 1966
Correa, María Angélica: An unpublished interview with Borges. Buenos Aires, September–October 1966.
De Milleret, 1967
De Milleret, Jean: *Entretiens avec Jorge Luis Borges.* Paris, Pierre Belfond, 1967.
Fernández, 1967
Fernández Moreno, César: "Harto de los laberintos," in *Mundo Nuevo* (no. 18), Paris, December 1967, pp. 8–29.
Guibert, 1968
Guibert, Rita: "Jorge Luis Borges," in *Life en Español* (vol. 31, no. 5), New York, March 11, 1968, pp. 48–60.
Guibert, 1973
Guibert, Rita: "Jorge Luis Borges," in *Seven Voices.* New York, Knopf, 1973, pp. 77–117.
Irby, 1962
Irby, James E.: "Entrevista con Borges," in *Revista de la Universidad de México* (vol. 16, no. 10), Mexico City, June 1962, pp. 4–10.
Latitud, 1945
"De la alta ambición en el arte," in *Latitud* (no. 1), Buenos Aires, February 1945, p. 4.
Marx and Simon, 1968
Marx, Patricia, and Simon, John: "An Interview," in *Commonweal* (vol. 84, no. 4), New York, October 25, 1968, pp. 107–110.
Murat, 1964
Murat, Napoléon: "Entretiens avec Napoléon Murat," in *L'Herne,* Paris, 1964, pp. 371–387.
Opinión, 1977
"Las paradojas de Borges contra el castellano y contra sí mismo," in *La Opinión,* Buenos Aires, May 15, 1977, p. 28.
Peralta, 1964
Peralta, Carlos: "L'électricité des mots," in *L'Herne,* Paris, 1964, pp. 409–413.
Plata, 1945

BIBLIOGRAPHY

"De novelas y novelistas habló Jorge L. Borges," in *El Plata,* Montevideo, October 31, 1945.

Ribeiro, 1970

Ribeiro, Leo Gilson: "Sou premiado, existo," in *Veja* (no. 103), Rio de Janeiro, August 26, 1970, pp. 3–6.

Simon, 1971

Simon, Herbert: *"Primera Plana* va más lejos con Herbert Simon y Jorge Luis Borges," in *Primera Plana* (no. 414), Buenos Aires, January 5, 1971, pp. 42–45.

Triunfo, 1969

"Habla Jorge Luis Borges," in *Triunfo* (vol. 24, no. 389), Madrid, November 15, 1969, pp. 35–36.

Vázquez, 1977

Vázquez, María Esther: *Borges: Imágenes, Memorias, Diálogos.* Caracas, Monte Avila, 1977.

III. CRITICAL AND BIOGRAPHICAL WORKS

Alén, 1975

Alén Lescano, Luis C.: *La Argentina ilusionada, 1922–1930.* Buenos Aires, Editorial Astrea, 1975.

Anzieu, 1971

Anzieu, Didier: "Le corps et le code dans les contes de J. L. Borges," in *Nouvelle Revue de Psychanalyse,* Paris, July–August 1971, pp. 177–210.

Baudelaire, 1951

Baudelaire, Charles: *Oeuvres complètes.* Paris, Gallimard, 1951.

Bianco, 1964

Bianco, José: "Des souvenirs," in *L'Herne,* Paris, 1964, pp. 33–43.

Bioy, 1940

Bioy Casares, Adolfo: "Prólogo" to *Antología de la literatura fantástica.* Edited in collaboration with Jorge Luis Borges and Silvina Ocampo. Buenos Aires, Editorial Sudamericana, 1940.

Bioy, 1942

Bioy Casares, Adolfo: "Los libros," a review of Borges' *El jardín de senderos que se bifurcan,* in *Sur* (no. 92), Buenos Aires, May 1942, pp. 60–65.

Bioy, 1964

Bioy Casares, Adolfo: *La otra aventura.* Buenos Aires, Editorial Galerna, 1964.

Bioy, 1975

Bioy Casares, Adolfo: "Chronology," in *Review 75* (no. 15), New York, Fall 1975, pp. 35–39.

Borges, 1921

Borges, Jorge (Guillermo): *El caudillo.* Palma (Majorca), 1921. Privately printed.

Britannica, 1911

"The Tichborne Claimant," in *The Encyclopaedia Britannica.* Eleventh edition. New York, Encyclopaedia Britannica Company, 1911. Vol. 26, pp. 932–933.

Chesterton, 1940

Chesterton, G. K.: *The End of the Armistice.* London, Sheed & Ward, 1940.

BIBLIOGRAPHY

Christ, 1969

Christ, Ronald: *The Narrow Act: Borges' Art of Allusion.* New York, New York University Press, 1969.

Clouard, 1947

Clouard, Henri: *Histoire de la littérature française: du symbolisme à nos jours (de 1885 à 1914).* Paris, Albin Michel, 1947.

Corominas, 1967

Corominas, Joan: *Breve diccionario etimológico de la lengua castellana.* Madrid, Gredos, 1967.

Cozarinsky, 1974

Cozarinsky, Edgardo: *Borges y el cine.* Buenos Aires, Editorial Sur, 1974.

De Gourmont, 1912

De Gourmont, Rémy: *Promenades littéraires.* Quatrième série. Paris, Mercure de France, 1912.

De Quincey, 1897

De Quincey, Thomas: *Collected Writings.* Edited by David Masson. London, A. C. Black, 1897. Vol. 3.

De Torre, 1925

De Torre, Guillermo: *Literaturas europeas de vanguardia.* Madrid, Caro Raggio, 1925.

De Torre, 1965

De Torre, Guillermo: *Historia de las literaturas europeas de vanguardia.* Madrid, Guadarrama, 1965.

Fernández, 1967

Fernández Moreno, César: *La realidad y los papeles.* Madrid, Aguilar, 1967.

Genette, 1964

Genette, Gérard: "La littérature selon Borges," in *L'Herne,* Paris, 1964, pp. 323–327.

Gobello, 1953

Gobello, José: *Lunfardía.* Buenos Aires, Argos, 1953.

Grondona, 1957

Grondona, Adela: *El grito sagrado (30 días en la cárcel).* Buenos Aires, 1957. Privately printed.

Ibarra, 1964

Ibarra, Néstor: "Borges et Borges," in *L'Herne,* Paris, 1964, pp. 417–465.

Ibarra, 1969

Ibarra, Néstor: *Borges et Borges.* Paris, L'Herne éditeur, 1969. A revised and enlarged version of the 1964 article.

Irby, 1971

Irby, James E.: "Borges and the Idea of Utopia," in *Books Abroad* (vol. 45, no. 3), Norman (Oklahoma), Summer 1971, pp. 411–419.

Jurado, 1964

Jurado, Alicia: *Genio y figura de Jorge Luis Borges.* Buenos Aires, Editorial Universitaria, 1964.

Klein, 1975

Klein, Melanie: *Love, Guilt, and Reparation and Other Works.* New York, Delta, 1975.

485

BIBLIOGRAPHY

Lacan, 1966
Lacan, Jacques: "Le stade du miroir comme formateur de la fonction du Je," in *Ecrits*. Paris, Editions du Seuil, 1966, pp. 93–100.

Levine, 1973
Levine, Suzanne Jill: "A Universal Tradition: The Fictional Biography," in *Review 73* (no. 8), New York, Spring 1973, pp. 24–28.

Lucio and Revello, 1961
Lucio, Nodier, and Revello, Lydia: "Contribución a la bibliografía de Jorge Luis Borges," in *Bibliografía Argentina de Artes y Letras* (nos. 10–11), Buenos Aires, April–September 1961, pp. 43–112.

Marechal, 1948
Marechal, Leopoldo: *Adán Buenosayres*. Buenos Aires, Editorial Sudamericana, 1948.

Marechal, 1968
Marechal, Leopoldo: "Claves de Adán Buenosayres," in *Cuaderno de navegación*. Buenos Aires, Editorial Sudamericana, 1968, p. 133.

Megáfono, 1933
"Discusión sobre Jorge Luis Borges," in *Megáfono* (no. 11), Buenos Aires, August 1933, pp. 13–33.

Moore, 1929
Moore, Thomas: *The Poetical Works*. Edited by A. D. Godley. Oxford, Clarendon Press, 1929.

Mother, 1964
Acevedo de Borges, Leonor: "Propos," in *L'Herne*, Paris, 1964, pp. 9–11.

Neruda, 1974
Rodríguez-Monegal, Emir: "[Neruda:] The Biographical Background," in *Review 74* (no. 11), New York, Spring 1974, pp. 6–14.

Ocampo, 1961
Ocampo, Victoria: "Saludo a Borges," in *Sur* (no. 272), Buenos Aires, September–October 1961, pp. 76–79.

Ocampo, 1964
Ocampo, Victoria: "Vision de Jorge Luis Borges," in *L'Herne*, Paris, 1964, pp. 19–25.

Ocampo, Silvina, 1964
Ocampo, Silvina: "Image de Borges," in *L'Herne*, Paris, 1964, pp. 26–30.

PEN, 1937
PEN Club de Buenos Aires: *XIV Congreso Internacional de los PEN Clubs*. Buenos Aires, 1937.

Petit de Murat, 1944
Petit de Murat, Ulyses: "Jorge Luis Borges y la revolución literaria de *Martín Fierro*," in *Correo Literario*, Buenos Aires, January 15, 1944, p. 6.

Pezzoni, 1952
Pezzoni, Enrique: "Aproximación al último libro de Borges," in *Sur* (nos. 217–218), Buenos Aires, November–December 1952, pp. 101–103.

Prose, 1972
Kinzie, Mary, ed.: "Prose for Borges," in *Tri-Quarterly* (no. 25), Evanston (Illinois), Fall 1972.

Reyes, 1943

Reyes, Alfonso: "El argentino Jorge Luis Borges," in *Tiempo,* Mexico City, July 30, 1943, p. 104.

Rivera, 1976

Rivera, Jorge B.: "Los juegos de un tímido," in *Crisis* (no. 38), Buenos Aires, May–June 1976, p. 23.

Rodríguez-Monegal, 1970

Rodríguez-Monegal, Emir: *Borges par lui même.* Paris, Editions du Seuil, 1970.

Sanguinetti, 1975

Sanguinetti, Horacio S.: *La democracia ficta, 1930–1938.* Buenos Aires, Editorial Astrea, 1975.

Videla, 1963

Videla, Gloria: *El ultraísmo.* Madrid, Gredos, 1963.

Vignale, 1927

Vignale, Pedro Juan and Tiempo, César, eds.: *Exposición de la actual poesía argentina, 1922–1927.* Buenos Aires, Editorial Minerva, 1927.

Yates, 1973

Yates, Donald A.: *"Behind 'Borges and I,' "* in *Modern Fiction Studies* (vol. 19, no. 3), West Lafayette (Indiana), Autumn 1973, pp. 317–324.

Zigrosser, 1957

Zigrosser, Carl: *The Expressionists.* London, Thames and Hudson, 1957.

Index

489

INDEX

Borges, Norah (*continued*)
  as an artist, 27, 36, 63, 164, 168–69, 172,
    175, 183, 218–19, 401, 467
  childhood, 27–36, 37, 40, 46, 47, 56, 70,
    128
  marriage, 35, 219, 341, 469
  in Switzerland, 134–35
Borges, Señora (mother), 16, 19, 20, 61, 78,
  128, 226, 233, 254, 363, 449
  arrested, 401
  Borges' accident and, 321–24
  Borges' childhood and, 27, 28–29, 30,
    37–38, 79, 80, 81, 87, 96, 99, 100–101
  Borges' dependency on, 433, 444–45,
    458, 468, 476
  Borges' lectures and, 395
  Borges' romances and, 184, 470–71
  Borges' translations and, 293, 372, 373
  death, 473–74
  family ancestry, 3–7, 10, 13, 255, 473
  her husband's death and, 317, 318, 321,
    322, 341
  influence on Borges, 21–26, 285
  in old age, 453, 467–73
"Borges, The," 11
"Borges and Myself," 439–40
Borges and the New Generation (Prieto), 424
Borges et Borges (Ibarra), 239
Borges on Writing (Borges), 459–60
Borges Outline, A (Moreno), 437
Borgès par lui même (Monegal), 63, 465
Borges: The Enigma and the Key to It (Tamayo
  and Díaz), 437
Botana, Natalio, 251–52
Bouvard and Pecuchet (Flaubert), 118, 437
Bradley, Edward, 75
Branco, Castelo, 452–53
Breton, André, 301–302, 354
Brothers, The (Wells), 300, 301
Brothers Karamazov, The (Dostoevski), 287,
  292
Browne, Sir Thomas, 175, 191
Browning, Robert, 181, 375–76
Buenos Aires, Argentina, 7, 11, 18, 28, 37,
  40, 63, 84, 91, 100, 115, 125, 164, 243,
  348, 404
  Borges' return to, in 1921, 167–78,
    196–202
  in 1930s, 279–82, 291, 296, 297
  in 1940s, 349–50, 374, 390–91, 392,
    396–98, 401, 402
  in 1950s, 430
  see also Palermo, Argentina
Bullrich, Beatriz Bibiloni Webster de, 273
Bullrich, Eduardo, 237
Burgin, Richard, interviews with Borges,
  22, 36, 70, 81, 95–96, 99–103, 133,

  140–41, 142, 279–81, 283, 401, 402,
  435–36, 438, 458, 465
Burton, Richard, 23, 68, 71, 72, 74, 119,
  263, 264, 268, 274, 277
Byrnhild (Wells), 292, 300

Callois, Roger, 378, 381–82, 420
Cain, James M., 379
Calcomanias (Girondo), 208
Caldwell, Erskine, 289
Calle de la tarde, La (Lange), 215
"Calles," 176
Call of the Wild, The (London), 76
Calpe, Espasa, 349–50
Calvo, Lino Novás, 373
Camerarius, Gasper, 97, 184, 400
Campadrito, El, 385–86
"Campos atardecidos," 176
Cancela, Arturo, 350
Cano, Baldomero Sanin, 297
Cansinos-Asséns, Rafael, 129, 158, 159–61,
  162–63, 171, 182, 188, 193, 207, 218,
  348, 448
Canto, Estela, 190, 418
Canto, Patricio, 374
Canto general, 282
Caraffa, Brandán, 188, 191
Carátula, 193
Cardinal Points of Borges, The, 452
Carlyle, Thomas, 123, 125, 129–31, 135–36,
  148, 350
Carpentier, Alejo, 355
Carriego, Evaristo, 49, 50, 52–53, 55, 70, 85,
  90–92, 196, 206, 207, 226–28, 254, 357,
  398
Carril, Adelina del, 191
Carroll, Lewis, 74, 75, 311, 350, 360, 407
Cartaphilus, Joseph, 97
Casal, Julio J., 181
Casares, Marta, 290
Caspary, Vera, 379
Castillo, Ramón S., 389
Castle, The (Kafka), 68
Castro, Américo, 159
Caudillo, El (Borges), 7, 80, 81–83, 84, 101,
  153–54
Céline, Louis-Ferdinand, 119, 448, 463
Cendrars, Blaise, 158
Cervantes, Miguel de, 52, 74, 77–78, 79, 85,
  166, 181, 212, 247, 315, 329, 336, 353
Chambers' Encyclopaedia, 87–88
Chaplin, Charles, 249, 292
Charbonnier, Georges, 465
Chesterton, Gilbert Keith, 76, 125, 130–33,
  248, 252, 254, 292, 350, 351, 353, 367,
  378, 396, 422

INDEX